Beert C. Verstraete
Vernon Provencal
Editors

Same-Sex Desire and Love in Greco-Roman Antiquity and in the Classical Tradition of the West

Same-Sex Desire and Love in Greco-Roman Antiquity and in the Classical Tradition of the West has been co-published simultaneously as *Journal of Homosexuality*, Volume 49, Numbers 3/4 2005.

*Pre-publication
REVIEWS,
COMMENTARIES,
EVALUATIONS . . .*

"This wide-ranging collection engages with the existing scholarship in the history of sexuality and the uses of the classical tradition and opens up exciting new areas of study. The book is an important addition to queer theory."

Stephen Guy-Bray, PhD
*Associate Professor
University of British Columbia*

D0143872

Same-Sex Desire and Love in Greco-Roman Antiquity and in the Classical Tradition of the West

Same-Sex Desire and Love in Greco-Roman Antiquity and in the Classical Tradition of the West has been co-published simultaneously as *Journal of Homosexuality*, Volume 49, Numbers 3/4 2005.

Same-Sex Desire and Love in Greco-Roman Antiquity and in the Classical Tradition of the West, edited by Beert C. Verstraete and Vernon Provencal (Vol. 49, No. 3/4, 2005).*"This wide-ranging collection engages with the existing scholarship in the history of sexuality and the uses of the classical tradition and opens up exciting new areas of study. The book is an important addition to queer theory." (Stephen Guy-Bray, PhD, Associate Professor, University of British Columbia)*

Sexuality and Human Rights: A Global Overview, edited by Helmut Graupner and Philip Tahmindjis (Vol. 48, No. 3/4, 2005). *"An important resource for anybody concerned about the status of legal protection for the human rights of sexual minorities, especially for those concerned with attaining a comparative perspective. The chapters are all of high quality and are written in a straightforward manner that will be accessible to the non-specialist while containing much detail of interest to specialists in the area." (Arthur S. Leonard, JD, Professor of Law, New York Law School)*

Eclectic Views on Gay Male Pornography: Pornucopia, edited by Todd G. Morrison, PhD (Vol. 47, No. 3/4, 2004). "An instant classic. . . . Lively and readable." *(Jerry Zientara, EdD, Librarian, Institute for Advanced Study of Human Sexuality)*

The Drag Queen Anthology: The Absolutely Fabulous but Flawlessly Customary World of Female Impersonators, edited by Steven P. Schacht, PhD, with Lisa Underwood (Vol. 46, No. 3/4, 2004). "Indispensable. . . . For more than a decade, Steven P. Schacht has been one of the social sciences' most reliable guides to the world of drag queens and female impersonators. . . . This book assembles an impressive cast of scholars who are as theoretically astute, methodologically careful, and conceptually playful as the drag queens themselves." *(Michael Kimmel, author of* The Gendered Society; *Professor of Sociology, SUNY Stony Brook)*

Queer Theory and Communication: From Disciplining Queers to Queering the Discipline(s), edited by Gust A. Yep, PhD, Karen E. Lovaas, PhD, and John P. Elia, PhD (Vol. 45, Nov. 2/3/4, 2003). *"Sheds light on how sexual orientation and identity are socially produced–and how they can be challenged and changed–through everyday practices and institutional activities, as well as academic research and teaching. . . . Illuminates the theoretical and practical significance of queer theory–not only as a specific area of inquiry, but also as a productive challenge to the heteronormativity of mainstream communication theory, research, and pedagogy." (Julia T. Wood, PhD, Lineberger Professor of Humanities, Professor of Communication Studies, The University of North Carolina at Chapel Hill)*

Gay Bathhouses and Public Health Policy, edited by William J. Woods, PhD, and Diane Binson, PhD (Vol. 44, No. 3/4, 2003). *"Important. . . . Long overdue. . . . A unique and valuable contribution to the social science and public health literature. The inclusion of detailed historical descriptions of public policy debates about the place of bathhouses in urban gay communities, together with summaries of the legal controversies about bathhouses, insightful examinations of patrons' behaviors and reviews of successful programs for HIV/STD education and testing programs in bathhouses provides. A well rounded and informative overview." (Richard Tewksbury, PhD, Professor of Justice Administration, University of Louisville)*

Icelandic Lives: The Queer Experience, edited by Voon Chin Phua (Vol. 44, No. 2, 2002). *"The first of its kind, this book shows the emergence of gay and lesbian visibility through the biographical narratives of a dozen Icelanders. Through their lives can be seen a small nation's transition, in just a few decades, from a pervasive silence concealing its queer citizens to widespread acknowledgment characterized by some of the most progressive laws in the world." (Barry D. Adam, PhD, University Professor, Department of Sociology & Anthropology, University of Windsor, Ontario, Canada)*

The Drag King Anthology, edited by Donna Jean Troka, PhD (cand.), Kathleen LeBesco, PhD, and Jean Bobby Noble, PhD (Vol. 43, No. 3/4, 2002). *"All university courses on masculinity should use this book . . . challenges preconceptions through the empirical richness of direct experience. The contributors and editors have worked together to produce cultural analysis that enhances our perception of the dynamic uncertainty of gendered experience." (Sally R. Munt, DPhil, Subject Chair, Media Studies, University of Sussex)*

Homosexuality in French History and Culture, edited by Jeffrey Merrick and Michael Sibalis (Vol. 41, No. 3/4, 2001). *"Fascinating. . . . Merrick and Sibalis bring together historians, literary scholars, and political activists from both sides of the Atlantic to examine same-sex sexuality in the past and present." (Bryant T. Ragan, PhD, Associate Professor of History, Fordham University, New York City)*

Gay and Lesbian Asia: Culture, Identity, Community, edited by Gerard Sullivan, PhD, and Peter A. Jackson, PhD (Vol. 40, No. 3/4, 2001). *"Superb. . . . Covers a happily wide range of styles . . . will appeal to both students and educated fans." (Gary Morris, Editor/Publisher, Bright Lights Film Journal)*

Queer Asian Cinema: Shadows in the Shade, edited by Andrew Grossman, MA (Vol. 39, No. 3/4, 2000). *"An extremely rich tapestry of detailed ethnographies and state-of-the-art theorizing. . . . Not only is this a landmark record of queer Asia, but it will certainly also be a seminal, contributive challenge to gender and sexuality studies in general." (Dédé Oetomo, PhD, Coordinator of the Indonesian organization GAYa NUSANTARA: Adjunct Reader in Linguistics and Anthropology, School of Social Sciences, Universitas Airlangga, Surabaya, Indonesia)*

Gay Community Survival in the New Millennium, edited by Michael R. Botnick, PhD (cand.) (Vol. 38, No. 4, 2000). *Examines the notion of community from several different perspectives focusing on the imagined, the structural, and the emotive. You will explore a theoretical overview and you will peek into the moral discourses that frame "gay community," the rift between HIV-positive and HIV-negative gay men, and how Israeli gays seek their place in the public sphere.*

The Ideal Gay Man: The Story of Der Kreis, by Hubert Kennedy, PhD (Vol. 38, No. 1/2, 1999). *"Very profound. . . . Excellent insight into the problems of the early fight for homosexual emancipation in Europe and in the USA. . . . The ideal gay man (high-mindedness, purity, cleanness), as he was imagined by the editor of 'Der Kreis,' is delineated by the fascinating quotations out of the published erotic stories." (Wolfgang Breidert, PhD, Academic Director, Institute of Philosophy, University Karlsruhe, Germany)*

Multicultural Queer: Australian Narratives, edited by Peter A. Jackson, PhD, and Gerard Sullivan, PhD (Vol. 36, No. 3/4, 1999). *Shares the way that people from ethnic minorities in Australia (those who are not of Anglo-Celtic background) view homosexuality, their experiences as homosexual men and women, and their feelings about the lesbian and gay community.*

Scandinavian Homosexualities: Essays on Gay and Lesbian Studies, edited by Jan Löfström, PhD (Vol. 35, No. 3/4, 1998). *"Everybody interested in the formation of lesbian and gay identities and their interaction with the sociopolitical can find something to suit their taste in this volume." (Judith Schuyf, PhD, Assistant Professor of Lesbian and Gay Studies, Center for Gay and Lesbian Studies, Utrecht University, The Netherlands)*

Gay and Lesbian Literature Since World War II: History and Memory, edited by Sonya L. Jones, PhD (Vol. 34, No. 3/4, 1998). *"The authors of these essays manage to gracefully incorporate the latest insights of feminist, postmodernist, and queer theory into solidly grounded readings . . . challenging and moving, informed by the passion that prompts both readers and critics into deeper inquiry." (Diane Griffin Growder, PhD, Professor of French and Women's Studies, Cornell College, Mt. Vernon, Iowa)*

Reclaiming the Sacred: The Bible in Gay and Lesbian Culture, edited by Raymond-Jean Frontain, PhD (Vol. 33, No. 3/4, 1997). *"Finely wrought, sharply focused, daring, and always dignified. . . . In chapter after chapter, the Bible is shown to be a more sympathetic and humane book in its attitudes toward homosexuality than usually thought and a challenge equally to the straight and gay moral imagination." (Joseph Wittreich, PhD, Distinguished Professor of English, The Graduate School, The City University of New York)*

Activism and Marginalization in the AIDS Crisis, edited by Michael A. Hallett, PhD (Vol. 32, No. 3/4, 1997). *Shows readers how the advent of HIV-disease has brought into question the utility of certain forms of "activism" as they relate to understanding and fighting the social impacts of disease.*

Gays, Lesbians, and Consumer Behavior: Theory, Practice, and Research Issues in Marketing, edited by Daniel L. Wardlow, PhD (Vol. 31, No. 1/2, 1996). *"For those scholars, market researchers, and marketing managers who are considering marketing to the gay and lesbian community, this book should be on their required reading list." (Mississippi Voice)*

Gay Men and the Sexual History of the Political Left, edited by Gert Hekma, PhD, Harry Oosterhuis, PhD, and James Steakley, PhD (Vol. 29, No. 2/3/4, 1995). *"Contributors delve into the contours of a long-forgotten history, bringing to light new historical data and fresh insight. . . . An excellent account of the tense historical relationship between the political left and gay liberation." (People's Voice)*

Sex, Cells, and Same-Sex Desire: The Biology of Sexual Preference, edited by John P. De Cecco, PhD, and David Allen Parker, MA (Vol. 28, No. 1/2/3/4, 1995). *"A stellar compilation of chapters examining the most important evidence underlying theories on the biological basis of human sexual orientation." (MGW)*

Same-Sex Desire and Love in Greco-Roman Antiquity and in the Classical Tradition of the West

Beert C. Verstraete
Vernon Provencal
Editors

Same-Sex Desire and Love in Greco-Roman Antiquity and in the Classical Tradition of the West has been co-published simultaneously as *Journal of Homosexuality*, Volume 49, Numbers 3/4 2005.

HPP

Harrington Park Press®
An Imprint of The Haworth Press, Inc.

New York • London • Victoria (AU)
www.HaworthPress.com

Published by

Harrington Park Press®, 10 Alice Street, Binghamton, NY 13904-1580 USA

Harrington Park Press® is an imprint of The Haworth Press, Inc., 10 Alice Street, Binghamton, NY 13904-1580 USA.

Same-Sex Desire and Love in Greco-Roman Antiquity and in the Classical Tradition of the West has been co-published simultaneously as *Journal of Homosexuality*, Volume 49, Numbers 3/4 2005.

The development, preparation, and publication of this work has been undertaken with great care. However, the publisher, employees, editors, and agents of The Haworth Press and all imprints of The Haworth Press, Inc., including The Haworth Medical Press® and Pharmaceutical Products Press®, are not responsible for any errors contained herein or for consequences that may ensue from use of materials or information contained in this work. Opinions expressed by the author(s) are not necessarily those of The Haworth Press, Inc. With regard to case studies, identities and circumstances of individuals discussed herein have been changed to protect confidentiality. Any resemblance to actual persons, living or dead, is entirely coincidental.

Cover design by Jennifer M. Gaska

Library of Congress Cataloging-in-Publication Data

Same-sex desire and love in Greco-Roman antiquity and in the classical tradition of the West / Beert C. Verstraete, Vernon Provencal, editors.
      p. cm.
    "Co-published simultaneously as Journal of Homosexuality, Volume 49, Numbers 3/4 2005."
    Includes bibliographical references and index.
    ISBN-13: 978-1-56023-603-0 (hard cover : alk. paper)
    ISBN-10: 1-56023-603-5 (hard cover : alk. paper)
    ISBN-13: 978-1-56023-604-7 (soft cover : alk. paper)
    ISBN-10: 1-56023-604-3 (soft cover : alk. paper)
    1. Homosexuality–Greece–History. 2. Homosexuality–Rome–History. 3. Homosexuality–History. I. Verstraete, Beert C. II. Provencal, Vernon. III. Journal of homosexuality.
HQ76.3.G8S35 2006
306.76′60937–dc22
                                    2005030848

Indexing, Abstracting & Website/Internet Coverage

This section provides you with a list of major indexing & abstracting services and other tools for bibliographic access. That is to say, each service began covering this periodical during the year noted in the right column. Most Websites which are listed below have indicated that they will either post, disseminate, compile, archive, cite or alert their own Website users with research-based content from this work. (This list is as current as the copyright date of this publication.)

Abstracting, Website/Indexing Coverage . . . . Year When Coverage Began

- *Abstracts in Anthropology*
  <http://www.baywood.com/Journals/PreviewJournals.asp?id=0001-3455> 1982
- *Academic Abstracts/CD-ROM* 1989
- *Academic ASAP <http://www.galegroup.com>* 2000
- *Academic Search: database of 2,000 selected academic serials, updated monthly: EBSCO Publishing* 1995
- *Applied Social Sciences Index & Abstracts (ASSIA) (Online: ASSI via Data-Star) (CD-Rom: ASSIA Plus) <http://www.csa.com>* 1987
- *ATLA Religion Database. This periodical is indexed in ATLA Religion Database, published by the American Theological Library Association <http://www.atla.com>* 1983
- *ATLA Religion Database with ATLASerials. This periodical is indexed in ATLA Religion Database with ATLASerials, published by the American Theological Library Association <http://www.atla.com>* 1983
- *Book Review Index.* 1996
- *Business Source Corporate: coverage of nearly 3,350 quality magazines and journals; designed to meet the diverse information needs of corporations; EBSCO Publishing <http://www.epnet.com/corporate/bsource.asp>* 1974

(continued)

(continued)

(continued)

(continued)

Special Bibliographic Notes related to special journal issues (separates) and indexing/abstracting:

- indexing/abstracting services in this list will also cover material in any "separate" that is co-published simultaneously with Haworth's special thematic journal issue or DocuSerial. Indexing/abstracting usually covers material at the article/chapter level.
- monographic co-editions are intended for either non-subscribers or libraries which intend to purchase a second copy for their circulating collections.
- monographic co-editions are reported to all jobbers/wholesalers/approval plans. The source journal is listed as the "series" to assist the prevention of duplicate purchasing in the same manner utilized for books-in-series.
- to facilitate user/access services all indexing/abstracting services are encouraged to utilize the co-indexing entry note indicated at the bottom of the first page of each article/chapter/contribution.
- this is intended to assist a library user of any reference tool (whether print, electronic, online, or CD-ROM) to locate the monographic version if the library has purchased this version but not a subscription to the source journal.
- individual articles/chapters in any Haworth publication are also available through the Haworth Document Delivery Service (HDDS).

ABOUT THE EDITORS

Beert C. Verstraete, PhD, is Professor of Classics in the Department of History and Classics at Acadia University in Wolfville, Nova Scotia. He has contributed as a translator and annotator to the *Collected Works of Erasmus* and the *Index Emblematicus*, is co-author, with Arnold Lelis and William Percy, of *The Age of Marriage in Ancient Rome*, and has published several articles on homosexuality in the Greco-Roman world, Roman literature, including the Roman love elegists, and the Classical tradition in Western literature.

Vernon Provencal, PhD, is Associate Professor of Classics in the Department of History and Classics at Acadia University in Wolfville, Nova Scotia. He has published papers on Greek philosophy, literature and historiography including studies of the family in Plato and Aristotle, and the Classical tradition in English Canadian literature.

Same-Sex Desire and Love in Greco-Roman Antiquity and in the Classical Tradition of the West

CONTENTS

Preface

To the best of our knowledge, *Same-Sex Desire and Love in Greco-Roman Antiquity and in the Classical Tradition of the West* is the first published collection devoted to same-sex desire and love in the ancient Greco-Roman world. For more than a quarter of a century now, since the landmark publication of Kenneth Dover's *Greek Homosexuality* in 1978, there has been a steady stream of books, monographs, articles, and conference papers, many of these looking at the phenomena of homoeroticism and homosexuality within the context of sexuality in the ancient world as a whole. The time seems ripe, therefore, for a wide-ranging collection of papers that will demonstrate to classicists and non-classicists alike how much the study of same-sex desire and love in Greco-Roman antiquity has advanced in the past quarter-century. The papers of this volume reflect not only an ever-expanding range of specialized literary, socio-historical, and art-historical scholarship that has been brought to bear on the subject, but also the often heated debates on theoretical and foundational perspectives, such as those emanating from feminism or social constructionist thinking.

Same-Sex Desire and Love in Greco-Roman Antiquity and in the Classical Tradition of the West presents the work of scholars from Canada, the United States and Europe, including such distinguished scholars in the field of sexuality in classical antiquity as John Clarke, Thomas Hubbard, William Percy, Amy Richlin, and Thomas Scanlon, and introduces to an English-reading audience the work of Dutch scholar Charles Hupperts. Significant contributions are made by classicists James Butrica, Anne Klinck, Vernon Provencal and Beert Verstraete, and also by non-classicists Wayne Dynes, Donald Mader and John Lauritsen, as

[Haworth co-indexing entry note]: "Preface." Verstraete, Beert C., and Vernon Provencal. Co-published simultaneously in *Journal of Homosexuality* (Harrington Park Press, an imprint of The Haworth Press, Inc.) Vol. 49, No. 3/4, 2005, pp. xxvii-xxix; and: *Same-Sex Desire and Love in Greco-Roman Antiquity and in the Classical Tradition of the West* (ed: Beert C. Verstraete, and Vernon Provencal) Harrington Park Press, an imprint of The Haworth Press, Inc., 2005, pp. xv-xvii. Single or multiple copies of this article are available for a fee from The Haworth Document Delivery Service [1-800-HAWORTH, 9:00 a.m. - 5:00 p.m. (EST). E-mail address: docdelivery@ haworthpress.com].

well as the distinguished Renaissance scholar Armando Maggi. While it is unfortunate that *Same-Sex Desire and Love in Greco-Roman Antiquity and in the Classical Tradition of the West* contains the work of only two female scholars, several papers make important contributions to the study of female homoeroticism in the Greco-Roman world, an area recently enriched by the publication in 2002 of a pioneering and splendid collection of papers, *Among Women: From the Homosocial to the Homoerotic in the Ancient World*, edited by Nancy Rabinowitz and Lisa Auanger.

As many of our readers are probably aware, the paper originally chosen to conclude this volume on same-sex desire and love in the Greco-Roman world and the classical tradition had been that of psychologist Bruce Rind, for the purpose of connecting the historically based scholarship in this collection with the contemporary debate on attitudes toward intergenerational sexuality. Unfortunately, one statement in the abstract of his paper was misconstrued by certain sectors as advocating pedophilia, which made it the subject of media controversy, in light of which we (ourselves, our contributors and Dr. Rind) agreed with The Haworth Press that it would be in the best interest of scholarly debate that the article should appear in a supplementary volume of the *Journal of Homosexuality*, possibly in early 2007. We agree with Bill Palmer, Vice President of Haworth Press, that "the debate on issues surrounding intergenerational sexuality is a heated one" best met by a separate publication that will "provide a nonpartisan forum to examine these issues from as many perspectives as possible."

Same-Sex Desire and Love in Greco-Roman Antiquity and in the Classical Tradition of the West began as a proposal in 2002 by Beert Verstraete to John De Cecco, the editor of the *Journal of Homosexuality*, to publish a special issue on same-sex desire and love in classical antiquity that would appeal to classicist and non-classicist readers and scholars alike. In the eyes of many, the world of Greco-Roman antiquity still constitutes a distinct paradigm (or counterparadigm!) of human behavior and achievement, not least so in the area of sexuality. After a number of papers were received, Beert Verstraete invited his colleague, Vernon Provencal, a Hellenist, to join him as co-editor and take on responsibility for the Greek papers, while he would remain responsible for the Roman papers and those on the classical tradition, although each would be intensively involved in all aspects of the editorial work.

It is the pleasant task now of the editors to thank all those persons whose contributions made the successful completion of this project possible. First, we owe a great deal of gratitude to John De Cecco, the editor of the *Journal of Homosexuality*, for his enthusiastic and unflagging support from the very beginning. The strength of the collection, of course, rests squarely upon the labors of all of our contributors, who gave generously of their time, energy and expertise to produce the fine, eye-opening scholarship exhibited in their papers; we thank them from the bottom of our hearts in making this exciting collection possible. William Percy is to be thanked also for his encouragement to include papers on the classical tradition and for his suggestion that Beert Verstraete offer to translate Charles Hupperts' paper for this collection. We also owe many thanks to Katherine Liong, a 2004 graduate from our university, with a BA with Honors in Latin, who worked with us as an editorial assistant during the summer of the same year; she fulfilled her wide-ranging responsibilities in the preparation of the final manuscript with meticulous care, her knowledge of Latin and Greek proving especially useful in the completion of certain tasks. Finally, we render our cordial thanks to the outside readers at our university and other locations who read the manuscripts submitted to us and provided us with us with helpful comments and suggestions: Peter Booth, Rachel Cooper, Denise Hudson, Jim Jope, Leona MacLeod, Anna Migliarisi, Robert Morrison, Anne Quema, Patricia Rigg, and Thomas Voss.

We hope that this collection of papers will be a source of new insights on same-sex desire and love to a wide range of readers, classicists and non-classicists alike. *Same-Sex Desire and Love in Greco-Roman Antiquity and in the Classical Tradition of the West* should serve well not only the interests of a philological and historical scholarship focused on a vanished civilization and its legacy, but also those devoted to re-energizing a nuanced, non-dogmatic, humanistic perspective on the wondrously complex phenomenon that *eros* will always be.

Beert C. Verstraete
Vernon Provencal

REFERENCE

Rabinowitz, Nancy Sorkin, & Auanger, Lisa. (Ed.). (2002). *Among Women: From the Homosocial to the Homoerotic in the Ancient World.* Austin: U of Texas P.

Introduction

Beert C. Verstraete, PhD
Vernon Provencal, PhD

PRELIMINARY HEURISTIC CONSIDERATIONS

It is appropriate that at the beginning of the Introduction we should discuss the vastly expanded range of evidence from our ancient Greek and Roman sources that has been brought to bear on the study of homoeroticism and homosexuality in the classical world.

Dover's landmark *Greek Homosexuality* was the first major study that drew extensively on iconographic evidence provided by Greek vase-painting of the sixth and fifth centuries BC. The papers of Thomas Hubbard and Charles Hupperts, which are illustrated with photographs, exemplify how necessary this type of evidence is for our understanding of male same-sex desire and sexual relations in Greece of the later Archaic and the Classical periods. The articles of William Percy and Thomas Scanlon also take this evidence into account, although the former rightly reminds us that for the most idealized and sublime expressions of male homoeroticism we must turn to sculpture, starting with the *kouroi* of the sixth century BC.

The study of Roman male constructions of sexuality, including homosexuality, on the basis of the visual evidence provided by Roman fresco painting (surviving best from Pompeii) and iconography (e.g., vase decoration and carved gemstones) is more recent, and is well-exemplified by John Clarke's paper, which is amply illustrated by photographs. However, James Butrica's lengthy paper, based largely on the

[Haworth co-indexing entry note]: "Introduction." Verstraete, Beert C., and Vernon Provencal. Co-published simultaneously in *Journal of Homosexuality* (Harrington Park Press, an imprint of The Haworth Press, Inc.) Vol. 49, No. 3/4, 2005, pp. 1-11; and: *Same-Sex Desire and Love in Greco-Roman Antiquity and in the Classical Tradition of the West* (ed: Beert C. Verstraete, and Vernon Provencal) Harrington Park Press, an imprint of The Haworth Press, Inc., 2005, pp. 1-11. Single or multiple copies of this article are available for a fee from The Haworth Document Delivery Service [1-800-HAWORTH, 9:00 a.m. - 5:00 p.m. (EST). E-mail address: docdelivery@haworthpress.com].

study of literary sources, also makes good use of the famous Warren Cup and the Leiden gemstone. The reader will be struck by the fact that Butrica's reading of the Warren Cup diverges somewhat from that of Clarke but in such a way that Butrica's reading supplements Clarke's; in addition, it offers a radically alternative, lesbian interpretation of the Leiden gemstone. Such a divergence in interpretation on individual points (often inevitable because of the damaged or deteriorated condition of the material remains) should not, however, reduce the reader to heuristic despair since the 'big' picture informing our understanding most often remains unaffected by it. Thus, Butrica and Clarke reach the same basic conclusions regarding the construction of male homosexuality and male-male sexual relationships in Roman society; for example, regarding the typology of the *cinaedus* and the existence of adult male homosexual relations.

The basis of literary texts selected by Dover for detailed analysis in *Greek Homosexuality* was narrow, consisting mainly of pseudo-Demosthenes' fourth century BC courtroom speech, *Against Timarchus*, and the fifth century BC comedies of Aristophanes. Dover's selection of texts was perhaps justified by his focus on the construction of male homosexuality in Greece of the Classical period, so that, in his judgment, a heavy reliance on post-Classical literary texts of the Hellenistic or Roman imperial periods, with their retrospective biases, would lead to a distorted picture. However, as is confirmed by the articles dealing with the Greek world in this collection, post-Classical Greek prose literature (e.g., Plutarch and Athenaeus) in particular, if used critically, provides us with a wealth of information for the construction of plausible hypotheses about the rise of institutionalized pederasty in the seventh century BC and its subsequent mutations during the late Archaic and the Classical periods, and indeed about Greek homosexuality in general. Finally, much of the relevant literature surviving from the Archaic and Classical periods, whether it has survived in its entirety or in fragmented form, has been subjected to fresh scrutiny and analysis by our contributors, so that, to give one example, Anne Klinck, *contra* some recently expressed views, is able to demonstrate decisively that Sappho's eroticism was directed not to women who were her coevals but to adolescent girls.

The use of the abundant inscriptional remains from both the Greek and the Roman world will also enhance our understanding of the societies and cultures of the classical world, as is shown by Percy with his reference to the Thera inscriptions of the Archaic period and Butrica with his use of the Pompeii graffiti. The Roman world is especially rich in epigraphic material that can be utilized to this end. The most extensive use thus far of the Pompeiian graffiti and other Roman-Italian inscriptions in the study of Roman homosexuality is found in Craig Williams' major 1999 book, *Roman Homosexuality*, but their use for this purpose has not been exhausted.

GREEK PEDERASTY AND ROMAN PEDOPHILIA

A large number of papers in this collection discuss the ancient sexual practice of pederasty, that is, of intergenerational homoerotic relationships between adults and adolescents. It is important, in light of the stigmatization and criminalization of pedophilia in our society, to note that pederasty was not perceived by the Greeks to involve prepubescent sexual relations. As pointed out in Vernon Provencal's paper,

> pederasty (both ancient and modern) should not be confused with our meaning of pedophilia to designate the sexual exploitation—whether heterosexual or homosexual—of a child's immaturity. The distinction between the two is observed socially by recognizing an appropriate age for erotic interest on the part of the adult and for sexual consent on the part of the adolescent. The ideal age of the *eromenos* depicted on vase-paintings and described graphically as the age of a first beard is that of a 14 to 17-year old. (pp. 128-129, n. 1)

Butrica, however, in his paper on Roman perceptions of homosexuality, uses the term pedophilia to emphasize the coercive and exploitative nature of sexual relationships between masters and their adolescent (sometimes preadolescent) slaves. The sexual exploitation of slaves also took place in Greece, especially in such slave-owning societies as Athens; however, it was institutionalized pederastic relationships between free-born male adults and adolescents that represented the societal norm. This was clearly not the case in Rome where, as Butrica points out, the law prohibited sexual relations between free-born males.

All the papers in this collection accept from Dover and Percy that institutionalized pederasty was indigenous to the Greeks and cannot be traced back to distant Indo-European origins in initiatory rituals, as hypothesized by Patzer and Sergent. The evidence favors the view that institutionalized pederasty had its earliest origins in Crete in the post-Homeric phase of the Archaic age in the seventh-century BC. By the end of the sixth-century BC, institutionalized pederasty had spread throughout most of the Greek world. Scanlon demonstrates that Sparta played a crucial role in the "dispersion" of Greek pederasty, for having transformed it into a social institution devoted to the attainment of military and athletic prowess for the young male courted and mentored by his older lover. Our understanding of Greek pederasty is advanced considerably by Scanlon's and Hubbard's studies of how nudity, athleticism and eroticism formed an essential matrix that gave rise to what was most peculiar and definitive about institutionalized pederasty in ancient Greece.

It is commonly assumed that Greek pederasty is strictly a male phenomenon. There is some evidence, however, to suggest that the pederastic model served female same-sex relationships as well, especially in Sparta (Scanlon, p. 9). As already noted earlier, Klinck demonstrates convincingly that Sappho was erotically involved in intergenerational rather than coeval relationships. It is likely that these relationships contained the aspect of mentoring that that was essential to the male pederastic model.

Distortions in our understanding of Greek homosexuality, especially pederasty, that arise from Dover's psychoanalytical description of it as "quasi-sexual" (Preface to *Greek Homosexuality*) are fortunately absent in all the papers of this collection. Absent also are distortions which result from Halperin's use of social constructionism, wherein the male pederastic relationship is assimilated to the typical heterosexual relationship, in such a way that the *eromenos* is represented as dominated by his *erastes* on the quasi-feminist model of domination and victimization. Although Halperin has modified his view considerably in his recent book, *How to Do the History of Homosexuality*, by bringing in the Platonic concept of *anteros*, the quasi-feminist model remains. As a corrective to these distortions, Vernon Provencal reasserts the importance of Foucault's contribution to our understanding of Greek pederasty in *The Use of Pleasure*, especially for emphasizing the esthetic and moral dimensions of pederasty.

While Dover's publication of *Greek Homosexuality* provided a new foundation for study in this field, it had, as Percy points out, the severe drawback of a narrow focus on evidence that lay undue emphasis on the pure physical aspects of homosexuality. As mentioned earlier, a more comprehensive use of evidence is employed by the authors in this collection, with the result that the physical aspect is more carefully balanced against the esthetic, moral, and even spiritual aspects of pederasty. This more balanced approach is epitomized by Charles Hupperts' paper on the duality of Theban homosexuality, which was widely misconstrued in other Greek city-states as crudely physical and lustful. Hupperts' study of the iconographic evidence certainly brings out this licentious aspect of what he calls Thebes' "Dionysian" homosexuality; however, the literary evidence pointing to the coexistence of the ideal model of institutionalized pederasty in Thebes is also given its due weight.

ROMAN SEXUALITY

The sexuality of the Romans has never had good press in the West ever since the rise of Christianity. In the popular imagination and culture, it is synonymous with sexual license and abuse. Hollywood depictions of the most debauched Roman emperors, most notoriously *Caligula* (1979), have thrived on this cliché. The ancient Romans and Greeks sometimes did not see it much differently: for the private life of many a Roman emperor, witness Suetonius' *Lives of the Twelve Caesars*, and for the subject of sexual delinquency and depravity in the lives of (mostly) upper class Roman men and women, witness the epigrams and satires of Catullus, Martial, and Juvenal. The nadir of these outrages to (Christian) morality and decency was, of course, represented by homosexuality. Until well into the twentieth century, nearly all of the scanty scholarship that was expended on this unsavory subject did not go beyond these clichés. Only within the past few decades has the social construction of sexuality in ancient Roman culture and society become the focus for sustained, analytical, non-moralizing scholarship. It is within this context that the study of Roman homosexuality has also come into its own, although it was not until 1999 that there appeared a truly comprehensive book by the American scholar Craig Williams, *Roman Homosexuality: Ideologies of Masculinity in Classical Antiquity*.

Williams' approach is generally social constructionist, but not extremely so, constantly underlining how differently from the later Christian West Roman men, with their dominant-masculinist and phallocentric outlook, constructed their sexuality, how this outlook is governed heavily by considerations of civic and social status, and how these facts also color the Roman perception and, in certain cases, stigmatization of homosexual behavior. In a Roman society that by the time of the late Republic was far more stratified than any Greek city-state during the Classical period these considerations were of paramount importance. The prevalence of slavery was a key factor in either valorizing or stigmatizing sexual behavior. Thus Roman custom and law prohibited homosexual relationships between *ingenui*, freeborn male Roman citizens, but if between *ingenui* and slaves, did not see these at all problematic, provided that the *ingenuus* did not surrender the dominant role of sexual penetrator which was expected of him. In Roman society, where, in contrast to Classical Greece, pederasty was almost invariably associated with sexual attraction to, and sexual acts perpetrated on, adolescent (and even prepubescent) slaves, the institutionalized pederasty that was so characteristic of Greece in the late Archaic and the Classical periods could not take any real hold. With the exception, therefore, of Catullus' Juventius poems and possibly Horace's *Odes* 4.1 and 4.10, pederastic sentiments in Roman love poetry are directed to adolescent slaves (or former slaves).

James Butrica's article is one of the most detailed and far-ranging studies to be published on Roman homosexuality, both male and female, emending, as the title indicates, a number of misperceptions and misunderstandings commonly held by scholars. As such it is an essential supplement to Craig Williams' book, which it corrects on several points. Most radical and, in our judgment, quite persuasive is his rereading and reinterpretation of the literary texts (mainly Martial and Seneca the Elder), which virtually all previous scholars have judged to be severely condemnatory of female homosexuality. Carefully placing these texts in their full context (absolutely necessary, as he well demonstrates) and under the microscope of philological scrutiny, Butrica arrives at the conclusion that Roman men found lesbianism very odd, perhaps even bizarre, but certainly not repulsive or depraved and thus worthy of the most severe moral strictures. In this connection, he usefully points out that Roman law is much preoccupied with heterosexual female adultery, but does not address female homosexuality at all. He also, among others, clarifies who were the *exoleti* (not necessarily male prostitutes, but former *pueri delicati,* who as adult men were no longer fitting objects of pederastic desire but fulfilled other sexual roles to please their masters or former masters), as well as the transgressive social deportment and sexual behavior that were associated with the *cinaedus*, the nonconformist Roman male who was the counterpart of the Greek *kinaidos*. Butrica's discussion of the Warren Cup and the Leiden gemstone and the light they (especially the former, in his judgment) shed on the existence of homosexual relationships between adult males has already been mentioned.

We have also already pointed earlier to the importance of John Clarke's studies of the iconography of Roman society. In his study of Roman *cinaedi*, Clarke identifies, on the basis of certain visual signs (hairstyle, clothes, posture) in Pompeiian fresco painting, the depiction of *cinaedi* as recognizable social types, and, as Butrica also does, readdresses the interesting questions, already raised by Amy Richlin in 1993 and Rabun Taylor in 1997, of whether we can compare the stigmatized *cinaedi* to homosexual men in the modern West (as Richlin does) or whether the *cinaedi* constituted, in Taylor's term, a "pathic subculture." As already mentioned, his discussion of the Warren Cup and the Leiden gemstone, which should be compared to Butrica's, is equally insightful on the reality of non-pederastic male same sex-relations in ancient Roman society. What is so striking about the depiction of the sexual act of anal intercourse between two adult males on the Warren Cup is that the sexuality of the act is clearly presented in a romantic fashion as an esthetically pleasing sight, far removed in spirit from how such acts would usually be portrayed in Greek and Roman sources (literary and artistic) as physically ugly and therefore worthy of ridicule, if not outright moral stricture. The idealization of the physicality of this sexual encounter on the Warren Cup and also on the Leiden gemstone, according to Clarke's analysis, is quite different from the crude physicality of the sexual acts perpetrated in the Archaic Greek vase-paintings discussed by Hupperts, as well as in much Roman sexual iconography. It seems paradoxical that the Romans, notorious for their brutalized portrayals of sex, should also romanticize it, perceiving in sex dimensions of meaningfulness that were nearly alien to the Greek mentality. This valorization of adult homosexuality is an uniquely Roman contribution to the classical legacy of erotic love in the West.

We are truly indebted to Clarke and Butrica for introducing this radical new perspective on adult male love in Roman society as possibly romantic. It seriously challenges the prevailing stereotype of Roman sexuality as predicated exclusively on power and domination. Beert Verstraete's article on the originality of the Marathus poems of Tibullus also challenges this stereotype, though from a different perspective, given that the relationship between Tibullus and Marathus is pederastic. Although the social status of Marathus is deliberately left ambiguous (possibly Tibullus' favorite slave?), he is invested with an individuality that is almost without exception lacking in the centuries-long tradition of pederastic poetry in Greek and Roman literature. These relatively lengthy poems are full of dramatic verve and playful irony, and one of them, 1.8, presents a mis-en-scene which is indeed unique. The Marathus elegies, together with Catullus 99, Vergil, *Eclogues* 2, and Horace's *Odes* 4.1, represent a new departure, which unfortunately was not continued in the later verse of classical pederastic poetry. We trust that the Roman papers will correct the stereotype of

Roman sexual decadence. Beyond the ignominy of slavery and ridiculed *cinaedi*, we also have glimpses of more positive possibilities in same-sex adult male love.

PLATONIC INFLUENCE AND THE CLASSICAL TRADITION

As in other areas of Greek culture, such as religion and philosophy, the legacy of Greek pederasty was mediated largely by Plato, who, like Xenophon, clearly sublimated the physical aspect of pederasty to its moral and spiritual aspect. This was not entirely a Platonic innovation. All papers in this volume share the view that pederasty, though sexual in origin and practice, was, as institutionalized in the aristocracies of the Greek city-states, primarily pedagogical in character. Both physical and spiritual aspects of institutionalized pederasty appear in the *Symposium* and *Phaedrus*. What most interested Plato was how institutionalized pederasty sublimated the physicality of erotic attraction to its pedagogical purpose. It is the spiritual aspect of pedagogical pederasty which Socrates idealizes most beautifully in the climactic discourses on love in *Symposium* and *Phaedrus*, and it is this Platonic idealization of pederasty that most influenced later Greek culture and eventually the Christian West, where it came to be known simply as "Platonic love."

In his *Laws*, Plato makes the physical expression of same-sex love problematic and his Athenian Stranger condemns it as "contrary to nature." In his article "Pederasty and democracy: the marginalization of a social practice," in *Greek Love Reconsidered* (2000), Hubbard severely criticizes Plato for capitulating to the democratic prejudice against pederasty as an aristocratic institution in the fourth century. Vernon Provencal, however, argues that Plato would be the last person to make concessions to democratic sentiments. He finds that a closer study of the *Laws* reveals that Plato's attitude toward pederasty remains largely unchanged: pederasty, as a pedagogical institution, is still recommended as the ideal form of love, provided that it is divested as much as possible of its sexual physicality.

Together with the theory of the Ideas or Forms, the concept of Platonic love has been Plato's most important legacy to the West. However, because of the harsh condemnation of homosexual desire and behavior in the Jewish and Christian traditions, the notion of Platonic love could be entertained only if it was completely stripped of its erotic and physical associations. Only thus could the spiritualization of homoerotic love expounded by Socrates in Plato's *Phaedrus* and *Symposium* be carried to even loftier heights, so that the Platonic soul's ascent on the Ladder of Love to the vision of Absolute Beauty could be refashioned as the Christian soul's progress towards union with God. Provencal's paper shows how Dante was able to assign such an anagogical meaning to the myth of Ganymede as it had been reinterpreted by Plato.

However, the problem of the physicality of Platonic *eros* remained. The paper by Armando Maggi shows how the Italian humanists of the fifteenth and sixteenth centuries such as Ficino and Trevisano, who, through their translations of the original Greek texts, commentaries, and treatises, reintroduced Platonic love into the high-level scholarly and intellectual discourse of the West, were unable to valorize the physical eroticism of Platonic love, let alone outright homosexual behavior. Wayne Dynes' paper makes it clear that the earliest German scholarship on Greek love that started in the eighteenth century preferred to see a Platonic love that was entirely 'chaste'; only thus could Socrates be hailed as a saintly pederast. In John Lauritsen's paper we see a homoerotically inclined Percy Bysshe Shelley–a Platonist if there ever was one–who, in both his prose and his poetic writings, has to remain guarded about the physical expression of male same sex-desire.

In his lengthy and detailed paper, Donald Mader shows that an important advance in reconciling the physical-sexual and supra-physical (moral, ethical, spiritual) dimensions of male homoerotic love was made by the Anglo-American "Uranian" poets of the late nineteenth and early twentieth centuries (see below); in this respect, they followed in the footsteps of John Addington Symonds, perhaps the greatest apologist of the nineteenth century for same-sex erotic love. Plato's authority as classical antiquity's supreme exponent of ideal homoerotic love continued into twentieth century. Thus Herbert Marcuse drew upon Plato for key aspects–most notably the concept of non-repressive sublimation–of the otherwise largely Marxist, Freudian, and Reichian melange of ideas in his *Eros and Civilization*, the paradigmatic text of the sexual revolution of the sixties and seventies. In Amy Richlin's paper, however, we catch a glimpse of the impatience in the emerging gay and lesbian subcultures of the fifties and sixties with what is perceived to be Plato's elitism and sexual repression–in short his increasing irrelevance to the progressively more vocal and audacious liberation movements that were not hesitant to assert the rightfulness also of the physicality of homoerotic love.

THE CONTRIBUTION OF THE CLASSICAL LEGACY
TO THE BIRTH OF GAY CONSCIOUSNESS

As documented by Wayne Dynes, a new interest in the Greek legacy began to manifest itself in the European culture of the eighteenth century, above all in German literature and scholarship, which led to a fresh scholarly interest in Greek pederasty that was recognized and even eulogized as an integral and positive aspect of Classical Greek civilization. Percy, Dynes and Mader draw our attention to the importance of Winckelmann, the great German art historian of the eighteenth century, who created a new appreciation of the homoerotic significance of the idealized nude male figure in Greek sculpture. Although initially reluctant to highlight the sexual physicality of same-sex love, by the nineteenth century German classical scholarship had created an aura of cultural legitimacy which fostered an emergent gay consciousness.

Hellenism also contributed to the emergence of gay consciousness in England and America, as documented by John Lauritsen and Donald Mader. Lauritsen's study of the life, writings, and friendships of Shelley, fervent hellenophile, Platonist, and ardent admirer of German romanticism which was so receptive to Greek homoeroticism, finds sufficient evidence to warrant the view that Shelley possessed a gay consciousness, that is, that he knew himself to prefer homoerotic relations within his close circle of male friends to heterosexual relations with either of his two wives, or other women. Mader offers a very detailed study of a large number of male British and American poets of the late nineteenth and early twentieth centuries, sometimes referred to as the "Uranian" poets. The Uranian poets drew especially on classical models which mirrored their own erotic sensibilities in order to valorize same-sex love. The Uranians derived their classical models not only from Plato but also from a wide range of Greek and Latin poetry, and from their knowledge of Greek and Roman history. Favorite models drawn from classical history were the relationships between Alexander and Hephaestion, and Hadrian and Antinous. These historical examples were used to fashion a new homosexual ethos for themselves and their contemporaries, an ethos which brought together the Greek ideal of *arēte* ("human excellence"), often regarded as an aristocratic concept of virtue, with the egalitarian principle of Greek democracy through the mediation of male homoerotic friendship. This idealization of male homoeroticism based on classical models found more systematic expression in the prose writings of John Addington Symonds and Edward Carpenter.

Amy Richlin's study of the archival holdings of the institute and magazine *ONE* documents in great detail how the nascent gay and lesbian liberation movements of the United States in the 1950s and '60s used classical models on which to base claims for gay rights. By this time sufficient in-depth studies had been made of human (homo)sexuality, notably the Kinsey reports, to provide a justification for more liberal attitudes toward male and female same-sex relations. One gets the impression from some of the correspondence received by the magazine, however, that gays did not always find classical models relevant to their own experience. The liberal sentiments of the contemporary Western world, especially gays, were offended by the entrenchment of social and cultural elitism, and the practice of slavery in the ancient world. Plato, once the Hellenic high priest of male love, was now pilloried as the totalitarian enemy of Karl Popper's "open society." Richlin also documents how the bugbear of Roman sexual depravity inherited from earlier generations persisted in the minds of many gays.

REFERENCES

Dover, Kenneth J. (1978). *Greek Homosexuality. Updated and with a New Postscript.* Cambridge: Harvard UP.

Foucault, Michel. (1985). *The Use of Pleasure. The History of Sexuality: Volume II.* (R. Hurley, Trans.). New York: Vintage Books.

Halperin, David M. (2002). *How to Do the History of Homosexuality.* Chicago: U of Chicago P.

Hubbard, Thomas K. (2000). Pederasty and Democracy: the marginalization of a social practice. In T. Hubbard (Ed.), *Greek Love Reconsidered* (pp. 1-11). New York: Wallace-New Hampton.

Marcuse, Herbert. (1955). *Eros and Civilization: A Philosophical Inquiry into Freud.* Boston: Beacon Press.

Patzer, Harald. (1982). *Die Griechische Knabenliebe.* Wiesbaden: Franz Stiener.

Percy, William Armstrong. (1996). *Pedagogy and Pederasty in Archaic Greece.* Urbana: U of Illinois P.

Richlin, Amy. (1993). Not Before Homosexuality: The Materiality of the *Cinaedus* and the Roman Law against Love between Men. *Journal of the History of Sexuality, 3,* 523-573.

Sergent, Bernard. (1986). *Homosexuality in Greek Myth.* (A. Goldhammer, Trans., with a preface by Georges Dumézil). London: Athlone.

Taylor, Rabun. (1997). Two Pathic Subcultures in Ancient Rome. *Journal of the History of Sexuality, 7,* 319-371.

Williams, Craig A. (1999). *Roman Homosexuality: Ideologies of Masculinity in Classical Antiquity.* New York and Oxford: Oxford UP.

Reconsiderations About Greek Homosexualities

William Armstrong Percy, III, PhD

University of Massachusetts, Boston

SUMMARY. Focusing his analysis on (mostly Athenian) vase paintings of the sixth- and early fifth-century and on a handful of texts from the late fifth- and early fourth-century (again Athenian), Dover depicted the pederastic relationship of *erastes* (age 20 to 30) and *eromenos* (age 12-18) as defined by sexual roles, active and passive, respectively. This dichotomy he connected to other sexual and social phenomena, in which the active/penetrating role was considered proper for a male adult Athenian

William A. Percy, III is Senior Professor of History at the University of Massachusetts, Boston Campus. He obtained his doctorate in history at Princeton University. A medievalist by virtue of his graduate training, Dr. Percy has also written extensively on society and sexuality in ancient Greece and Rome and in the Western world. His major publications include *The Age of Recovery: The Fifteenth Century* (co-author with Jerah Johnson), the two-volume *Encyclopedia of Homosexuality* (as co-editor with Warren Johannsen and Wayne Dynes), *Pederasty and Pedagogy in Archaic Greece*, and *The Age of Marriage in Ancient Rome* (as co-author with Arnold Lelis and Beert Verstraete). The reader might be interested to know that he is related as first cousin once removed to William Alexander Percy, one of the 'Uranian' poets discussed by D. H. Mader in his paper; as a young boy he personally knew William Alexander as "Uncle Will." The late Walker Percy, the well-known American novelist and a second cousin of Professor Percy, is similarly related to "Uncle Will." Correspondence may be addressed: Department of History, University of Massachusetts at Boston, Boston, MA 02125.

[Haworth co-indexing entry note]: "Reconsiderations About Greek Homosexualities." Percy, William Armstrong. Co-published simultaneously in *Journal of Homosexuality* (Harrington Park Press, an imprint of The Haworth Press, Inc.) Vol. 49, No. 3/4, 2005, pp. 13-61; and: *Same-Sex Desire and Love in Greco-Roman Antiquity and in the Classical Tradition of the West* (ed: Beert C. Verstraete, and Vernon Provencal) Harrington Park Press, an imprint of The Haworth Press, Inc., 2005, pp. 13-61. Single or multiple copies of this article are available for a fee from The Haworth Document Delivery Service [1-800-HAWORTH, 9:00 a.m. - 5:00 p.m. (EST). E-mail address: docdelivery@haworthpress.com].

citizen, while the passive/penetrated role was denigrated, ridiculed, and even punished. Constructing various social and psychological theories, Foucault and Halperin, along with a host of others, have extended his analysis, but at the core has remained the Dover dogma of sexual-role dichotomization. Penetration has become such a focal point in the scholarship that anything unable to be analyzed in terms of domination is downplayed or ignored.

To reduce homosexuality or same-sex behaviors to the purely physical or sexual does an injustice to the complex phenomena of the Greek male experience. From Sparta to Athens to Thebes and beyond, the Greek world incorporated pederasty into their educational systems. Pederasty became a way to lead a boy into manhood and full participation in the *polis*, which meant not just participation in politics but primarily the ability to benefit the city in a wide range of potential ways. Thus the education, training, and even inspiration provided in the pederastic relationship released creative forces that led to what has been called the Greek 'miracle.' From around 630 BCE we find the institution of Greek pederasty informing the art and literature to a degree yet to be fully appreciated. Moreover, this influence not only extends to the 'higher' realms of culture, but also can be seen stimulating society at all levels, from the military to athletic games, from philosophy to historiography. An understanding of sexual practices–useful, even essential, to an appreciation of Greek pederasty–cannot fully explicate its relationship to these other phenomena; pederasty is found in many societies, and certainly existed before the Greeks. It is time that we move beyond Dover and recover the constructive dynamics of Greek pederasty. *[Article copies available for a fee from The Haworth Document Delivery Service: 1-800-HAWORTH. E-mail address: <docdelivery@ haworthpress.com> Website: <http://www.HaworthPress.com>* © *2005 by The Haworth Press, Inc. All rights reserved.]*

KEYWORDS. Homosexualities, lustful, male beauty, pederasty, pedagogy, Cretan revolution, warfare, political institutions. literature, art, learning, Greek "miracle"

It seems to me that something must also be said about the love of boys; for this too has a bearing on education.

–Xenophon[1]

PROLOGUE

Certain inconvenient facts have plagued classicists ever since the development of *Altertumswissenschaft* in the late 18th century.[2] Their heroes and models, the ancient Greek elites, unlike other highly cultured peoples, exercised nude together in gymnasia and dined and drank without ladies in symposia from the 7th century BCE until the triumph of Christianity in the 4th century CE. Throughout that millennium, the art that was funded and produced by Greek males–and was later to be so greatly admired by the classically educated western elites–was dominated by the male nude, usually idealized, and not infrequently sensualized, as testimony to which stands the surviving sculpture (mostly Roman copies), described so lovingly in the 18th century by Winckelmann in his three-volume masterpiece.[3]

In addition, from the Renaissance on, Greek literature became the cornerstone of classical education. This was the case even more so in England and Germany, where Romantics, such as Byron, Shelley, and Goethe, embraced homosexuality, than in the Latin lands of France and Italy, where cultural pride, as well as linguistic inheritance, naturally gave rise to a greater admiration for Rome.[4] Yet, however one construes the love between Achilles and Patroclus in Homer[5]–"[m]ost ancient writers and commentators assumed Achilles and Patroclus were lovers in every sense of the word" (Clarke, 1978, p. 381) and quite possibly "Homer" conceived them that way as well[6]–explicit homoeroticism gushed from the poets of the seventh and sixth centuries BCE until at least the time of Hadrian, when Strato collected pederastic epigrams, including his own, into what now has become Book 12 of the *Greek Anthology.*[7]

Classicists long refused to acknowledge this fundamental aspect of Greek life.[8] Just as the private parts of statues were 'modestly' covered over by curators–often for clerical collectors–offensive texts were routinely bowdlerized–often by professors trying to "protect" youths;[9] translators either simply omitted the objectionable passages altogether, or translated them from Greek into Latin or from Latin into Italian rather than English. Monographs claimed that Greek love was pure, 'platonic,' except among a few degenerates.[10]

Boldly tackling the issue in 1873, John Addington Symonds concisely summarized *Altertumswissenschaft*'s findings about Greek pederasty in *A Problem in Greek Ethics*, which he privately published in ten copies (1883).[11] A century later, K. J. Dover (now Sir Kenneth), while hypercritically disregarding late sources, demolished Symonds' heroic interpretation, substituting in its place a denigration of Greek homosexuality, and concentrating on the physical and purely sexual aspects.[12] Yet both sides of this debate ignore crucial and well-documented aspects of Greek pederasty, thereby oversimplifying an enormously complex phenomenon.

An entire constellation of causes gave rise to Archaic Greek culture and, at the same time, to the intertwining of pederasty and pedagogy, which in turn augmented that flourishing. With all the other early civilizations, the Greeks shared slavery, the seclusion and oppression of women (although, unlike the Egyptian, and Hebraic and other Asiatic cultures, they were not polygamous), and the poverty of the masses. However, athletic nudity, all-male symposia, and delayed marriage for men were unique to Greek civilization.[13] These unique elements, along with the absence of religious taboos so prominent in the Abrahamic religions, may go some way to explaining why, in general, Greek men formed pederastic relationships. With very little religious intolerance and an ever growing reliance on reason, only the Greeks supported constitutions, freedom, rights, and even at times democracy–all of these features significantly influenced by the special form that their pederasty took. Although several of the factors contributing to liberty and progress, such as the development of the city-state, a non-obtrusive religion, the absence of caste, and the perfected alphabet, appeared before pederastic pedagogy, the Greek 'miracle' only occurred after pederasty was institutionalized.

In this article, I attempt a nuanced compromise. I recognize both the reality of the raw lust illustrated on Dover's vases and in the seamy lawsuits he privileges, as well as the inspirational pedagogy that Symonds admired in this unique institution. The pederastic pedagogy that Symonds traced in Plutarch, Lucian, Athenaeus and in the Greek historians, as well as in the Archaic and Classical authors that Dover restricted himself to, began around 630 BCE and was essential for the Greek 'miracle,' but lustful homosexualities coexisted with it, indeed preexisted and postdated it.[14] My goal is not only to demonstrate the centrality of institutionalized pederasty existing alongside other forms of homosexuality, or rather homosexualities,[15] through three key centuries from the late seventh century to the death of Alexander in 323 BCE, but also to trace the changes in their literary, artistic, and historical aspects from generation to generation, as far as the admittedly skimpy evidence allows.[16] Just as styles in art and literature changed along with fashions, carried in part by interactions with other peoples and greater understanding of the world in the general, so too did views about pederasty.[17] What follows is not meant to be in any sense comprehensive, but rather tentative, suggestive, and selective; texts and issues have been chosen to suggest some new perspectives for discussion.

PART I:
BEFORE 630–THE AGE OF HOMER

While certain pre-Archaic artifacts have been interpreted as evidence for specific kinds of homosexual behavior, these interpretations are not beyond refutation. Items like the Minoan Chieftain Cup depicting a youth and a boy facing each other in military garb, or the Cretan bronze Kato Syme figurine consisting of a pair of age-differentiated ithyphallic warriors holding hands (7th or 8th century BCE), have been interpreted as providing early proof of pederasty, or of initiation rites in which pederasty was prominent (Koehl). However, they are not at all obviously androphilic or pederastic in the way later vase paintings are. Some authors, such as Sergent, Patzer, and Bremmer, conjecture, by stretching these meager hints found in the scarce remains from this earliest period, that those remote societies 'constructed' some form of homosexuality, specifically intergenerational or pederastic. Certainly there were homosexual practices to be found among the Minoans, Mycenaeans and Dark Age Greeks since, in general, practices of this sort are found to some degree among all peoples, as well as among many other species, and most especially among the higher mammals.[18] However, explicit evidence of *paiderastia* first appears only after 630.[19]

We do find implicit evidence about kinds of homosexualities in the *Iliad*, but there are several reasons why that evidence must be treated with some caution. Through Milman Perry and Albert Lord's pioneering work we now feel reasonably confident that the stories Homer tells were handed down orally (possibly for centuries) before ever being written down, and even afterwards they did not achieve a finalized or authoritative edition until the Hellenistic period. The *Iliad* and the *Odyssey* notoriously contain material from the Mycenaean through the Archaic eras, perhaps even later. Furthermore, many myths (and not just ones contained in the Homeric works) were later 'homosexualized' after the institutionalization of pederasty and athletic nudity c. 630.[20] Given all this it may seem strange that, as Symonds and others have observed, there is no explicit *paiderastia* in Homer.[21] However, Symonds' error (and one widely shared) was his failure to realize that there does exist evidence for other types of homosexuality in Homer.

In book 20 of the *Iliad*, four verses appear about Ganymede, "hand-somest of mortals, whom the gods caught up to pour out drink for Zeus and live amid mortals for his beauty's sake" (*Il.* 20.232-35; cf. 5.265f.). Traditional elements, like the rape by an eagle, are missing, but the story is only mentioned in passing so one cannot say what version(s) Homer knows. Dover (1989) argues that "if the original form of the Ganymede legend represented him as eromenos of Zeus, Homer has suppressed this important fact" (p. 196). Doubtless any professional storyteller 'suppresses' many stories and many details he knows perfectly well, but that are not germane to the current tale unfolding. Certainly the erotic aspects of the story appear in the seventh-century *Hymn to Aphrodite* (ll. 202-6) and in a sixth-century fragment of the lyric poet Ibycus (fr. 289). Dover ponders the question why Zeus would want a boy based solely on his beauty, but fatuously quips that perhaps the gods "simply rejoiced in the beauty of their servants," like Muslim men in paradise (Dover, 1989, p. 196), impishly implying that these servants were not (necessarily) bedmates. By such non-argument, the intergenerational sex presumed by virtually all later Greeks in the myth of Ganymede is summarily dismissed from the Homeric world.

Yet the Ganymede story, whatever the interpretation, does not fit the mold of the later pederastic relationship. Zeus did not teach Ganymede the *arete* (virtue, courage, excellence) of a man, for he would never grow up to fight heroically or to become a good citizen. Thus there was no *pedagogy* involved, though there was pederasty. Whatever boudoir tricks the god may have taught the immortal boy, Ganymede would re-main forever in the bloom of youth, lingering unchanged in the world of pederastic fantasy as his adolescent beauty has captured the imagina-tions of poets and artists for millennia.[22] The *puer aeternus*–the boy who remains eternally at the peak of his adolescent beauty–finds its re-flex in the preoccupation of the modern pederast with photographing his *eromenos*,[23] as a Greek lover could not do, but sculptors of *kouroi* and painters could and did, so as to catch and preserve that evanescent qual-ity for all time. Afterwards, the homoerotic potential of the *harpagmos*–the abduction of the youth–only latent in the *epos*, was anachronisti-cally pressed into the mold of institutional pederasty in its ritualized Cretan form (whereby the Homeric version can be deemed an etiologi-cal myth that sacralized the rite) and the later aristocratic Spartan and Athenian variants, but of these Homer had as little inkling as the Semitic and Hamitic 'Orientals' did.[24]

The late date for the institutionalization of pederasty may account for the long passages describing the passionate comradely love of Patroclus and Achilles. That form of male love, paralleled in the stories of Gilgamesh and Enkidu or David and Jonathan, was not identical with classical Greek pederasty. It was instead love between approximately coeval foster brothers, comrades-in-arms, not that between a god and a slave-like cupbearer in the setting of a Near Eastern banquet of the gods. (How often such bonding goes over into sexual action of any sort is anybody's guess, and has occurred among soldiers of all ages.)[25]

Suffice it to say that from the Classical period on, most Greeks (and Romans) assumed that Achilles and Patroclus were lovers of the very sincere, everlasting, and heroic type that every honorable pair of upper-class *erastai* and *eromenoi* would have aspired to be. The problem for later authors was that in the idealized form the lover should be distinctly older than the beloved, while Homer made Patroclus the slightly older foster brother of Achilles (*Il.* 11.78f.; 23.84ff.). In Plato's *Symposium* (179e-180b), Phaedrus takes Aeschylus to task for making Achilles the *erastes*. Thus even the ancients had trouble fitting the love of Achilles and Patroclus into the pederastic model because Achilles was both the more beautiful and youthful of the two, features of the *eromenos*, as well as the more noble and excellent in warfare, ideal attributes of the *erastes*. Phaedrus questions how the pederastic model could be applied in any straightforward manner to the Achilles-Patroclus romance.

Already present in Homer, and impossible to deny, is an uninhibited appreciation of male beauty together with an acute sense of male bonding darkened by no religious guilt, and with no condemnation of intimacy between males.[26] The Homeric ideal of male beauty, however, tends to be ephebophilic (focused on young men), not pederastic, that is, directed towards teenagers, Ganymede being the exception. For instance, Odysseus says that Hermes met him, on the island of Circe, "in the likeness of a young man with the first down upon his lip, in whom the charm of youth is fairest" (*Od.* 10.276ff., Trans. A. T. Murray). The Greek vocabulary indicates a young man who has just become an *ephebe*. Later poets indicate that, when a boy grows facial or body hair, he is considered past the age of pederastic attractiveness.[27] Patroclus and Achilles, called the most beautiful of the Greeks, as well as Paris, famous for his beauty, and even Hector, whom Homer says was still in his youth (*hebe*) at his death (*Il.* 22.363), are all described as of the *ephebic* age in the *Iliad*. In general, there seems to be little reticence in Homer for a man to comment upon another man's beauty; Priam viewing the battle from the wall of Troy calls Agamemnon handsome (*kalos*) (*Il.* 3.69).

Of course, virtually all of Homer's heroes, including Achilles and Patroclus, enjoyed sex with women and indeed most upper class Greek males seem after 630 to have married at about 30. They also had access even when younger to flute girls, slaves, prostitutes, captives, and *hetairai*. The great majority of Greek males, like the majority everywhere else, preferred to have sex with females most of the time. Some Homeric heroes like Hector, who loved Andromache, and certain 'effeminates' like Paris, who probably also loved only women (Kinsey's 0's), seem to have lacked the Greek penchant for bisexuality as reflected in myths developed after 630 about almost all the gods and heroes—only Ares, of the major gods, seems to lack a pederastic affair. No exclusive homosexuals appear in any Greek epic or myth. Myths, however, continued to be homosexualized not only into the Hellenistic but even into the Roman period.

Inscriptions from the late eighth and seventh centuries in various Greek alphabets attest the establishment of colonies from Spain to the Black Sea, as do shards of vases and other artifacts. Unlike Mycenaean Linear B, which contain only archival and religious material, a very few of these record verses.[28] None, however, attest with certainty to any pan-Hellenic games, or to wrestling schools or gymnasia that sprang up to provide the athletes for these games. Shrines there were for sure, at Olympia and at some other places where games later took place, but the Olympic victor list compiled by Hippias of Elis, the late fifth-century polymath and sophist, seems to me to be an act of *campanilismo*, an attempt to make these games associated with the *poleis* near his birthplace more venerable and prestigious than rival pan-Hellenic contests, such as the Pythian, Nemean, and Isthmian games, which were founded after 600. In connection with this, I believe it is no coincidence that the "earliest evidence that the Greeks recognized themselves as a distinctive [and pan-Hellenic] culture comes from an inscription at Olympia dating from 600 BC which talks of the judges of the games as *hellanodikai* ('Greek judges')" (Freeman, 1999, p. 24).

The spread of literacy and the increase of population, trade and prosperity marked the earlier phase (800-630) of the Archaic age (800-500). In the new *poleis*, tyrants and hoplites appeared and multiplied to the horror and disgust of aristocratic families. The evolution of the hoplites is so shrouded in mystery as to defy description. If Pheidon, king of Argos (early 7th c.), did not develop coinage to pay his hoplites he may nevertheless have used hoplites. Cartledge argues persuasively that

Spartans became hoplites in the first half of the seventh century (perhaps in response to the threat from Pheidon and other Argives).[29] About tyrants and poets before 630, however, such as Archilochus, literally 'leader of the troop,' with a peg date based on the solar eclipse of 648, and Pheidon, who supposedly ejected the Elean controllers of the Olympic games in 668, we know little for certain.[30]

PART II:
630-600–THE CRETAN 'REVOLUTION'

A revolution within the social system began around 630 on Crete. Because of the dearth of good land on that island to support the horses and other luxuries of a rapidly multiplying upper-class and even of estates large enough to support hoplites, marriages for males were postponed to 30 and pederasty institutionalized. Aristotle believed that this practice, aimed at limiting childbirth, began on Crete (*Pol.* 1272a):

> The [Cretan] lawgiver has devised many wise measures to secure the benefit of moderation at table, and the segregation of the women in order that they may not bear many children, for which purpose he instituted association with the male sex. (Trans. Rackham) [Fewer males survived to 30 to become husbands than if they had married at 18 or 20.]

Institutional pederasty thus emerged along with delayed marriages for males, seclusion of upper class women and crude messes in Crete. These innovations created a radically new society without interrupting colonization, itself in part the result of overpopulation, and the process of *synoikisis*, the joining together of separate villages to form a unitary *polis*.

These practices spread north, probably first to Sparta, the nearest large Dorian area, where some ancients (e.g., Plato, *Laws* 636a, 836b) and many moderns have thought that these practices originated.[31] It is likely in Sparta that pederasty became associated with gymnasia and athletic nudity; Spartans early on established a festival called the *gymnopaidiai*, when young boys would dance naked (*gymnos*). Spartans certainly developed its usefulness in the military training of adolescent boys. The coupling of young unmarried adult males with teenage youths had to stimulate homosexuality, whatever "Lycurgus" decreed and Xenophon believed.[32] Not only did males benefit from a prolonged adolescence encouraging self-development and creativity, but each young upper-class male had a teenager to educate and in this relation-ship of *paideia* he himself also learned. The fathers, relatively older than their sons compared to other societies that sanctioned marriage of males in their teens, were more distant from their sons in age and in interests and thus "big brothers" were more needed by their children.[33]

Cartledge (2001) sees the *agoge* (educational system), gymnasia, ado-lescent beloveds, *syssitia* (common messes), and various other elements as part of what he calls the Spartan contest-system, which in many ways defined the citizen in what was a "quintessentially agonal society" (p. 103). All these elements, which had the goal of creating the ultimate fighting machine, came together and solidified, one might almost say os-sified, in the second half of the seventh century and by the end of the sixth century. Cartledge states that it would be "remarkable, to say the least, if institutionalized pederasty had not been somehow linked to and expres-sive of the Spartan contest-system" (2001, p. 103). Other Greeks adopted gymnasia and pederastic pedagogy, but preferred the more elegant, vol-untary dining clubs known as symposia–consisting mostly of the elite,[34] usually adults or at least those over 16 (with serving boys and/or flute-girls attending)–to the common mess hall (*syssitia*), which in Sparta bound together all ranks and ages of *homoioi* (equals).

In the late 7th century the first *kouroi*, idealized sculptures of nude young men, appear.[35] The artistic portrayal of nude male youths cer-tainly does not begin with this development and thus cannot be com-pletely a response to institutionalized pederasty, but the fact that these *kouroi* come into popularity at the same time as the emergence of the Olympic games as a pan-Hellenic phenomenon (linked with nudity in early gymnasia) and at the same time as these Cretan and Spartan re-forms, cannot be mere coincidence. The stiff early *kouroi* are nude, but not yet very realistic, or to most straights very homoerotic. They form first attempts at an idealizing of the male form. Though exemplifying the nude adolescent or young man, their attitude is at odds with the raw lust depicted on the early black figure vases and with the languid homo-sexuality of the later red figure ones. None of the very few surviving large scale Greek sculptures are lewd and surely they deserve as much attention as the vases, certainly more than Dover gives them.

PART III:
600-560–THE AGE OF SAPPHO AND SOLON

During the generation from 600 to 560 these new institutions spread from Crete and Sparta to the other advanced parts of the Hellenic world, perhaps even earlier to such places as Thera which like them was Dorian.[36] During this same period creativity surged and innovations proliferated. Henceforth we have more secure knowledge about real people and events; historical individuals emerge from the mists, although no sculptures of identifiable mortals were yet made. It was the age of Thales and the first attempts to describe the world rationally and without recourse to the divine. This same attitude can be seen in attempts to set the laws and constitutions of the various *poleis* on a more rational and civic basis, where previously regional or aristocratic interests had prevented greater unity within the state.

Along with the increase in symposia, crude gymnasia multiplied. Various pan-Hellenic and athletic festivals, so dependent on gymnasia, arose and began to assume a greater importance; three of the four major pan-Hellenic games, namely the Pythian, Isthmian, and Nemean games, were founded between 586 and 573 BCE. Even the games at Olympia, which probably antedate 600 as a small local religious festival, only take their classical form of nine key events, including running, wrestling, and chariot racing, in the late 7th or early 6th century. These major athletic events connected to religious festivals led to the spread of "an agonistic element in the major local festivals of pre-established cults" throughout Greece (Scanlon, 2002, p. 29). Thus these pan-Hellenic games initiated and accelerated the spread and/or development throughout Greece of gymnasia, nude athletics, idealization of the youthful male body, and institutionalized pederasty, all of which became mutually reinforcing, and to this new set of institutions, intellectual and moral instruction were often added to the physical and martial elements taught by *erastai* to *eromenoi*.

At private symposia, lyric poets sang of love and hate, and other personal feelings, creating for themselves poetic identities. Many of the archaic elegies, lyrics, and, iambics, like vase paintings from the same period, did indeed express lust for young males, concentrating on the physical attributes (notably the eyes, hair and smooth skin), with seemingly less concern for non-physical aspects such as character.[37] According to tradition, even Solon, the great Athenian politician and lawmaker, took time out from his political poetry to write of pederastic love: "while one loves boys among the lovely flowers of youth, desiring their thighs and sweet mouth" (fr. 25 West).[38]

Among the melic poets the tradition surrounding Sappho is the most confusing. We can say with some certainty that she lived for a while in Mytilene on Lesbos (probably early 6th century) and that she composed love poetry that was greatly admired in antiquity. In fact, we cannot be certain that even a single line now attributed to Sappho—we have only one such complete poem—was actually sung, much less written by her. Given that so little remains of her corpus, and that what remains is so fragmentary, and given that the surviving *testimonia* are so various, late, and contradictory, the reconstruction of her sexual orientation is problematic, to say the least.[39]

Some ancients ranked Sappho with the greatest of poets. "The Parians glory in Archilochus, the Chians in Homer, and the Mytileneans in Sappho" (Aristotle *Rhetoric* 1398b). Plato called her the "tenth Muse" (*Anth. Pal.* 9.506), as did Antipater of Sidon (*Anth. Pal.* 9.66), who in another elegy said that just as Homer's songs surpass those of other men, so too do those of Sappho surpass those of other women (*Anth. Pal.* 7.15). To Strabo she was a "marvellous woman; for in all the time of which we have record I do not know of the appearance of any woman who could rival Sappho, even in a slight degree, in the matter of poetry" (13.2.3; Trans. H. L. Jones).

About her sexual orientation and practice, however, they arrived at no consensus. Most ancients portrayed her as passionately heterosexual;[40] a few, notably Ovid, considered her bisexual (*Tr.* 2.365f.; *Her.* 15). In our times, the attention paid to her poetry as such pales in comparison with the vehement debates about her character and sexual activity. She has even been invoked in highly conjectural and improbable arguments that female homosexuality preceded male.[41] She has been portrayed as a decorous schoolmistress, a chaste priestess, a proper matron, a lascivious tribade, a courtesan, a prostitute, and even a nymphomaniac, even though—or perhaps because—we possess so little and such contradictory information about her life, and so little and such ambiguous bits of poetry attributed to them. We must remember, also, that until recently almost all of the speculation about her life, sexual tastes, and place in society had been done by men. It is perhaps unsurprising that Sappho's poems have often been interpreted along the model of Greek *male* pederasty.

Except for fifth-century Pindar, who clearly wrote his works, the only one of these lyric *corpora* which has come down to us in a complete manuscript is that of Theognis the elegist. This divan is allegedly the result of the scholarship of a 'pious' Byzantine scholar who reorganized the corpus into two books, with the not fully successful intent of relegating all of the homoerotic verses to Book II. "Theognis" lived sometime within the century from 650 to 550, but scholars are today virtually unanimous in seeing the poems collected under his name as a potpourri of writings by various poets gathered together under the name of a single "author." He is particularly important for us because he does reveal explicit concern in his beloved's character and over his beloved's choice of friends, not merely lusting after physical beauty: "boy, you were born good-looking, but your head is crowned with stupidity. In your brain is lodged the character of a kite, always veering, bending to the words of other men" (2.1259-62; *HGR* 1.53). But then again "he" was realistic enough to know that "pretty boys get away with doing wrong" (2.1282; *HGR* 1.59).

Artistic progress accelerated after 600. Sculpture confirms that the appreciation of the youthful male body clearly advanced in this generation among both Dorians and Athenians. The *kouros* at the New York Metropolitan Museum of Art, dated 610-590 by Gisela Richter, is perhaps the earliest life-size *kouros*, and was probably Attic. The *kouroi* become less stiff and show greater diversity as sculptors work with the possibilities of that form. The stocky Argive nudes, for example, such as the heroic brothers Kleobolis and Biton dedicated at Delphi (c. 580), may be typical of the Peloponnese; they have on their rigid, muscled bodies large scrotums, the penises now missing. They seem more masculine than, for example, the delicate and smaller-penised, but fetchingly-buttocked, *kouros* from Sounion (590-580).

PART IV:
560-527–THE AGE OF PEISISTRATUS AND POLYCRATES

From 560 to 522 the wealthy tyrants Polycrates of Samos (d. 522) and Peisistratus of Athens (d. 527), both given to pederasty,[42] subsidized intellectuals and poets, such as Ibycus and Anacreon. They also employed sculptors and architects with extensive building programs, which included civil engineering projects. It is even possible that they established libraries.[43] The Peisistratid editions of the Homeric works were preserved in Athens, at the very time that the Persians were overrunning the older centers of culture in Ionia, precipitating a flight of refugees westward, especially to Athens and to Magna Graecia.

Around 550 our most incontestable proof of sensual homosexuality, particularly pederasty, among the ancient Greeks began to appear and proliferate: the erotic vase-paintings that emphasized lust even more than their poetry did. The most important part of Dover's *Greek Homosexuality* was his use of Sir John Beazley's[44] incomparable archive of erotic vases (housed in the basement of the Ashmolean museum), and of the work of Beazley's chief disciple, Sir John Boardman. Their various representations of pederastic courtship and other homoerotic scenes cannot, unlike the epics, the myths, and the lyric poetry, have been contaminated by later interpolations whether of rhapsodes, choruses, or editors.

One can certainly argue that these vases show no signs of pedagogical motivation on the part of the lover, nor any concern for the beloved's soul, as Dover does.[45] They do, without question, depict various levels of sexual desire. Most but by no means all of such erotic scenes, stretching from the early sixth to the early fifth centuries, portray bearded adults in their twenties courting beardless youths, positions described by Beazley. The earlier ones tend to be more lascivious. After 530, red figure vases from Athens tend to show younger beloveds in less crude lovemaking.

Martha Nussbaum (2002) has well described the tension that can be found on many of these vases. She believes that the vases sometimes do show (*contra* Dover) the two desires that may motivate the lover: the impulse to improve the beautiful youth and cultivate his character, and more carnal urges:

> An older man stands close to a younger man, who looks up (or, as the case may be, down) at him, often with fond affection. The older man beams beneficently at the young man's beardless face, and with one hand cups the younger man's chin, in a gesture of tender personal affection. His other hand, however, has other ideas: it fondles the young man's genitals, which are usually exposed. The older man's penis is often erect, the younger man's almost never. The young man sometimes repels the groping hand, but often, too, contentedly allows it. In this highly conventional and popular ancient Greek image of sexual courtship–named by Sir John Beazley the "up and down position" and found on dozens on vases from the classical period–we see a tension in the Greek concept of *eros*. (p. 55)

Nussbaum then goes on to discuss the ways Platonic, Epicurean, and Stoic philosophy subsequently attempted to deal with this tension. Whether or not Nussbaum is correct in her understanding of the tension depicted on the vases is debatable; it could also be understood as just two levels of physical desire. But her essay does illustrate how the Greeks, in their philosophy, acknowledged and struggled to come to terms with two major, often opposing, drives involved in the pederastic relationship.

In general, however, these homoerotic vases seem to have been passing fashions. They have been both overpriced in modern times, and their importance for ancient times scholars have exaggerated. They represent a relatively minor art form, and a private one intended to please the tastes of the aristocratic few, those who could afford or get invited to very exclusive dinner parties.[46] So while these vases are an important piece in our understanding of Greek pederastic practices, they show us a small portion of the full picture.

PART V:
530-500–THE AGE OF THE TYRANNICIDES AND CLEISTHENES

Athens developed remarkably in the decades before and after it became democratic in 507. Thereafter we know so much about her (whence come most written sources, as well as our vases) that our perspective necessarily becomes one-sided. Her poets as well as her tyrants were enthusiastic lovers of youths. Hippias and his younger brother Hipparchus continued to patronize poets and the arts, and to undertake building projects, most especially temples. The pseudo-Platonic dialogue the *Hipparchus* lauds Hipparchus (228d-229d), whom it, however, denotes as the elder son, saying that he was the first to bring the poems of Homer to Athens and that he compelled the rhapsodes at the Panathenaea to recite these poems one after another in succession, a practice the author says is still current. Hipparchus surrounded himself with poets such as Anacreon and Simonides, and inscribed the herms (pillars about 5 feet high with bearded head and erect phalluses, to Attica as boundary markers) that he and his brother, insouciant, fun-loving, pederastic tyrants, set up with his own elegiac couplets.[47] All this, the author of the *Hipparchus* exclaims, he did in order to educate the citizens. Depictions on vases of the Ionic dress for males that became popular in Athens in the last decades of the 6th century led scholars in an earlier day to presume that the men were in drag, but we now understand that this was merely a passing fad (like the unisex styles of the 1970s).[48]

Tyrants, however, came to fear the courage of pederastic couples. The Persians may have not learned pederasty from the Greeks as Herodotus claimed (1.135), but they banned it in Ionia because of its reputation for creating heroes and tyrannicides, if we can believe

Phaedrus in Plato's *Symposium* (182c). Certainly many pederastic couples can be found in stories of resistance to tyrants or assassinations of them. Hieronymus the Aristotelian writes that "love with boys was fashionable because several tyrannies had been overturned by young men in their prime, joined together as comrades in mutual sympathy." Athenaeus, who provides the preceding quote, goes on to mention several famous pederastic tyrannicides (13.602; *HGR* 2.21).

The aristocratic leaders of the revolution in Athens attributed the overthrow of the tyrants to a pederastic couple. Herodotus (5.62-65) and Thucydides (6.54-59) tell of how Hipparchus insulted Harmodius and his family after Harmodius, Aristogeiton's beloved, spurned his amorous advances. The plot to kill both Hipparchus and Hippias resulted only in Hipparchus' death and their own (514 BCE). A mythology quickly grew up around them, a sign of which is that soon after the fall of the tyranny bronze statues of the pederastic couple were erected in the agora, the first "political monument in Greek history. The Tyrannicides are the first historical figures so honored, and remained the only such figures for over 100 years" (Monoson, 2000, p. 43). Conversely, the fact that the couple did not actually end the tyranny, which became more oppressive during Hippias' remaining four years in power, faded from the public consciousness.[49] After Cleisthenes established Athens on a more democratic basis in 507, the heroes, receiving almost cultlike status, began to be toasted routinely at symposia, where drinking songs praising them were sung, and their descendants fed at the Prytaneum.[50] Thucydides, a century later, criticized the Athenians for getting important facts of the story wrong (1.20.2-3): "so little pains do the vulgar take in the investigation of truth, accepting readily the first story that comes to hand" (Trans. Crawley).

Athenian sculptors continued to present the male figure in very alluring ways. The Anavysos *kouros* (530-520) has a large scrotum and penis, and is rather voluptuously shaped; Stewart (1990, p. 122) believes that the unusually fleshy nature of the sculpture (especially noticeable in the hips, thighs, and buttocks) shows possible eastern influence. A beautifully erotic marble Theseus torso (520-510) from the Athenian Acropolis, in a semi-*kouros* pose, is shown in competition or combat, the paired opponent statue lost. This statue compares in sensuality with the homoerotic bronze Piraeus Apollo (530-520) excavated in 1959. These presage "the Kritias boy" (490-480), which is so named because its head so resembles that of Harmodius in the tyrannicide statues done by Kritias and Nesiotes about 479 to replace the original carried away by Xerxes in 480.

PART VI:
500-460–THE AGE OF PINDAR AND AESCHYLUS

After the triumphs over the Persians at Marathon in 490, and again in 480-479, when the Athenians and their allies liberated their compatriots in the north and began to free those on the Aegean islands and the Anatolian coast, the Greeks, and especially the Athenians, triumphantly reaffirmed their own culture, society, and liberties with a self-confident creativity, as the Florentines had when they defeated the tyrant of Milan just after 1400, precipitating the Italian Renaissance, and as the English did after the defeat of the Armada in 1588, enriching their literature and beginning their empire and rise to preeminence. Thus began the golden age of classical Greece, which saw an unparalleled burst of creativity in the arts, literature, and thought, together with untold wealth especially in Athens through trade and empire.

Between 480 and 460 Cimon expanded the Delian League, for which Themistocles (ostracized in 479) had laid the foundations, and on which the first assessments of tribute were established by Aristides the Just, said to have been Themistocles' rival for a boy's love as well as for political leadership according to Plutarch (*Life of Themistocles* 3). Declining to participate in the annual naval attacks that liberated the Greeks of Asia Minor, the Spartans, resting on their laurels, returned home to oversee their ever restive Helots, *perioikoi*, and league. Athenians gained not only in booty but also in trading partners and new members, who often chose to pay dues rather than contributing ships to the Delian fleet.

Cimon's favorite sculptor Myron (fl. 470-440) perfected the Severe style, excelling in bronze male nudes that he carefully proportioned (Pliny *N.H.*, 34, 58). His *Discobolos* (Discus Thrower), one of the finest statues of any age, incomparably captured arrested motion, muscles taut like a loaded spring. Copies of his *Marsyas* and some of his other athletes show his admiration for the male body. In sculpture, symbolism decreased and the male nude shown in naturalistic action expressed grace and gravity as well as a greater sensuality than in the earlier 5th century depiction of the tyrannicides or the Critias boy.[51] *Sophrosyne* (self-restraint) characterized sculpture, whether in bronze as in the Zeus from Artemesium (460-50 BCE) and the Riace Statues (450 BCE), or the marble sculptures on the pediments of Zeus's temple at Olympia (470-456 BCE), which exemplify the Severe style, and combine elements of idealism and realism, a realism that "was to disappear in the second half of the century under the influence of Phidian sculpture" (Biers, 1996, p. 219).

Both Pindar and Aeschylus developed homosexual themes. Aeschylus makes explicit the sexual nature of the relationship between Achilles and Patroclus in his *Myrmidons*: "You abjured the holy sacrament of the thighs! You spurned a profusion of kisses!"[52] Pindar pointed to his own innovations preferring to substitute a pederastic for a cannibalistic theme in *Olympian Ode* 1, wherein Poseidon falls in love with Pelops, explicitly paralleling the love of Zeus for Ganymede.[53]

Dover, who relied so heavily on pederastic vase scenes for his thesis, never ventured to explain why such scenes suddenly began to appear on vases around 550 and virtually stopped after 470. Hubbard, in a 1998 article, suggested that the gradual democratization of Athens during the early and mid-fifth century forced the aristocrats to stop so publicly advertising their "vice," presuming that the good old boys in those days were as homophobic as today's plebeians. But I would like to suggest a more material cause for this mysterious disappearance.

Michael Vickers and David Gill claim that the aristocratic Greeks always supped and ate from silver and that ceramics were considered as bourgeois commodities made for common people with little taste by artisans with little talent; the homoerotic painted vases (so prized since the eighteenth century for *connoisseurs* who were 'that way' from Lord Hamilton to Ned Warren and beyond to Beazley and others), like all pottery, were merely "saleable ballast" (Vickers & Gill, 1994, p. 90) exported to such places as Etruria, where most of the unbroken ones were found in graves, unpilfered by robbers because until the late 18th century they were of little value. No specimens of such silver service survive before the Hellenistic period, and then only one is explicitly homoerotic, the famous cup for which Warren had so long and diligently searched that he dubbed it the 'Holy Grail' when he found it. Boardman, on the other hand, contends that upper class Greeks only began to use silver and gold service beginning toward the end of the 4th century with the vast riches that Alexander brought to Greece.

I believe that the elite in Athens, who set the style there and in many other cities, became rich enough after 470 to begin the transition to the use of silver vessels for their symposia, and that these silver dishes may well have continued to have the explicit homosexual and pederastic scenes that were hardly ever thereafter found on pottery. Plutarch (*Alc.* 4.5) indicates that Alcibiades and his hosts were using silver at their symposia; bad-boy Alcibiades, as the story goes, stole half of the silver and gold cups from the tables of Anytus, one of his lovers. Athenians opened their lucrative silver mines at Laurium in the late 490s and became much richer in the decades after the defeat of the Persians by raiding and liberating wealthy Ionian cities in the Aegean and along the coasts of Ionia (which also granted them trade concessions). Thus, having a natural supply of silver and an influx of wealth, Athenian aristocrats probably switched more and more away from earthen to silver tableware. Like most of the large-scale bronze statues, and all of the chryselephantine ones, from the Archaic or Classical periods, such silverware would have been melted down long ago. The lack of silver vases or cups from the latter two-thirds of the 5th century (when explicit homosexual scenes disappeared from pots), does not prove that they did not exist.

PART VII:
460-429–THE AGE OF PERICLES

Influential already after the ostracism of Cimon (462), Pericles dominated Athens from the 440s until his death in 429. During his last two decades he was elected general (*strategos*) every year in succession and brought Athens to its zenith. He surrounded himself with the stars of the intellectual and artistic worlds. In fact he and his close associate Phidias were tried for embezzlement together. They were acquitted, but another of Pericles' associates, Anaxagoras, didn't fare as well when he was tried for atheism, a charge similar to one that Socrates would later face. Even Pericles' mistress, Aspasia, was famous for her learning and cultivation; the comic poets joked that she, in fact, was the ruler of Athens and not Pericles (Aristophanes, *Acharnians* 515ff). Pericles, who moved the League's treasury from Delos to Athens, began dipping into it to ornament the Acropolis with the Parthenon. His extensive building program, as a lasting monument to him, brought him criticism from such as Thucydides.

Pericles, who may have been a Kinsey "0" since we do not hear of even a single *erastes* or an *eromenos* (and ancient authors were never reluctant to discuss such affairs), seems to have had a favorable view of the value of pederasty. In the funeral speech ascribed to him by Thucydides, he urges the citizens of Athens "to gaze, day after day, upon the power of the city and become her lovers (*erastai*)" (2.43.1).[54] Monoson, in a 1994 article, analyzes the implications of denoting the citizens as pederastic lovers of their *polis*. The metaphor "suggests a way of thinking about the relationship between citizen and city" (p. 253). To understand how Pericles wanted the Athenians to picture that relationship we must "realize that the metaphor alludes to the highly formalized and valorized erotic relations between adult, citizen males (*erastai*) and adolescent, free-born boys (*eromenoi*) that were common among Athenians" (Monoson, 1994, p. 253). In conclusion, Monoson stated that the speech urged "them actively to guide the city in the exercise of its own powers and to help frame its conception of its best interests and aspiration. The metaphor also suggests that democratic citizenship demands that obviously unequal parties–the city and each individual citizen–struggle to forge a relationship of mutuality and reciprocity" (p. 271). If she is correct in her analysis, then Pericles' speech provides tremendous proof that the ordinary Athenian male citizen would construe a pederastic relationship, at least at its best, as one of mutual exchange wherein the *eromenos* benefited from the *erastes* and in ways that spurred the development of an honorable character. Even if we deny the authenticity of the speech, we are still left with the fact that Thucydides believed that the reader, both the Athenian and posterity, would be able to decode the metaphor in the appropriate way.

In these years Sophocles perfected tragedy. His *Niobe* and *The Colchian Women* incorporated pederastic themes. In the former play, for instance, he says that Ganymede "lit the fire of tyrant Zeus with his thighs" (Athenaeus 13.602).[55] In addition, we have several amusing anecdotes about Sophocles' own passion for boys (Athenaeus 13.603f.; *HGR* 2.21). Seemingly he knew a thing or two about the fire a boy's thighs could arouse. Even his own may have aroused a few men in his youth; "the sixteen-year old Sophocles, his naked body gleaming with oil, led the victory parade in Athens after the battle of Marathon" (Crompton, 2003, p. 10).

The perfection of sculpture came in these years, as well. The aging Myron and his slightly later contemporaries, Phidias and Polyclitus, breathed life and grandeur into their sculpture, the beautiful male body always predominating. With his bronze spearbearer (the *Doryphorus*), the Argive Polyclitus developed a new canon for the muscular male youth, describing in a treatise the precise proportions that a statue of the male form should have to be most beautiful (Pliny *N.H.*, 34, 55). Lithe and poised for motion, this statue proved the standard for the future. Phidias, on the other hand, was more famous for his treatment of gods than of youths. His chryselephantine masterpieces of Zeus at Olympia and Athena in the Parthenon depicted their majestic power. Paid for by Pericles, his patron, the friezes and metopes that he had sculpted or directed by assistants on the Parthenon (447-432) narrated the exaltation of Athens and ordinary Athenians, who find their place on the friezes where normally only gods, heroes, or other mythological beings stood. Here, in these most expensive and most public of adorations of the male nude body, there was never a hint of lasciviousness.

PART VIII:
429-399–THE AGE OF SOCRATES
AND THE 'LOST GENERATION'

Pericles died in 429. In devastated Athens, without Pericles' leadership, blockaded by the Spartans and ravaged by war and plague, Athenians began to question their system. This was the perfect atmosphere for the Sophists, who found a ready audience among the disillusioned youth. Just two short years after Pericles' death, they were mesmerized by the speeches and performances of Gorgias. Traveling throughout Hellas, but concentrating in Athens, the Sophists lectured for a fee to the public. They specialized in rhetoric foremost, but thought, taught and talked on nearly every subject imaginable. Hippias and Protagoras claimed grammar, semantics, and literary criticism as their specialties. Conservatives criticized them for subverting morals and religion with their relativism, but elite youths flocked to them for help in their legal and political careers and possibly *because* of the subversive element as well. (Concerning what the Sophists may or may not have said about pederasty and other forms of homosexuality we are not informed.)

Despite the distinctions that Plato later drew, it is likely that the average Athenian did not find the teachings and activities of Socrates that different from those of the Sophists. In his *Clouds* Aristophanes satirized Socrates in his work by making him the embodiment of Sophistic thought with parodies of some Ionian physics thrown in for good measure.[56] At one point in the play (889-1104) two characters–one might rather say two personifications–come on stage to praise the old, conservative method of education against the new style, and vice versa. These characters, 'Better/Stronger Speech (*logos*)'[57] and 'Worse/Weaker Speech,' personify arguments going on in Athens that were provoked by the teachings of the Sophists, most especially those dealing with nature (*phusis*) versus culture (*nomos*). These two Speeches each attempt to persuade the youth Pheidippides to accept the type of education he's peddling.

Dover (1989) mentions this passage in his *Greek Homosexuality* only to discuss lines dealing with Better Speech's obvious fascination with boys' genitals (p. 124f.).[58] He completely misses, or ignores, the implications that this passage has for our understanding of pedagogical pederasty; the debate or competition (*agon*) here in the *Clouds* is, after all, about educating the young: "everything is now at stake for higher education's sake" (953f.).[59] The Better Speech, "who crowned the men of old with solid traits of character" (959f.), represents the old school, where pederasty instilled virtue and manliness into the boy by very Spartan-like activities. Through all his bluster about how he raised the men of Marathon and how well-behaved the youth used to be, Better Speech keeps letting slip (Freudian perhaps?) mentions of boys' thighs and genitals, and these slips become more pronounced as he proceeds:

> When in gym-class, all the boys would cross their legs when sitting down, so they'd not expose to the grownups anything provocative. When they rose again, they'd have to smooth the sand they'd sat upon, careful not to leave behind the marks of their manhood for lovers to see. No boy then would dare anoint himself below the belly-button: thus their genitals were dewy and downy, like a succulent peach. (983-994)

He ends his speech with a peroration on how the effect of his training will make the young boy look:

> Follow up on my suggestions,
> give them serious consideration,
> then you'll be in proud possession
> of a chest that ripples, skin that gleams,
> shoulders humongous, tongue petite,
> buttocks of iron, prick discreet. (1009-14)[60]

Worse Speech, in turn, makes his case for an education that will teach the boy how to do whatever he naturally desires and how to argue his way out of any consequences that may result:[61]

> Just look, young man, at all the toil the virtuous life consists of, and look at all the fun you stand to lose, if you pursue it: young boys, young women, games of chance, good eating, drink and laughter. Why live a life at all if you're deprived of all these pleasures? OK, then, let's proceed to look at the necessities of nature. Let's say you've messed up, fallen in love, been taken in adultery. You're screwed if you can't talk your way out of trouble. Come

with me, though, you'll indulge your instincts, leap and laugh, consider nothing shameful. (1076-91)

In the end, Worst Speech persuades even his opponent that he's right; Better Speech agrees that there's nothing wrong with having a "gaping asshole" (1086ff.). Deserting to the other side, Better Speech takes off and hands over his cloak, signifying, as it were, the dropping of the pretence that his pederasty has the virtue of the boy at heart and not the creamy young thighs.

Aristophanes, in a highly subtle and yet not-so-subtle way, is calling into question the true motives of Socrates and others who claim to be pedagogically motivated pederasts.[62] Regardless of whether we think him right in his final analysis, it remains that Aristophanes is highlighting a tension in Athenian society between those who see pederasty as beneficial to youths and those who see it as purely sexual, the same types of pederasty this paper is attempting to explore. It is worth noting that the gross reference to pederastic and other forms of homosexual sex appear in the Old Comedy only a generation after such scenes disappear on the vases which are replaced with decorous and comely nude youths who can be gazed at admiringly by the viewer but with no explicit or vulgar sex display.

Leaving behind Aristophanes now, but not Socrates, a word should be said about the 'love affair' between Socrates, considered one of the ugliest men of his time, and Alcibiades, by all accounts the most beautiful youth. The most famous account of this is given at the end of the *Symposium* (212c-223b), and one can easily imagine that Plato, for dramatic and philosophical purposes, made up what must have seemed like a bizarre coupling to the Greeks. However, Plato is not the first to write of this affair. In fact, the relationship of Socrates and Alcibiades became quite a common topic within the genre of Socratic dialogues.[63] The *Alcibiades* of Aeschines of Sphettus is likely prior to Plato's dialogue, and so can be said to have been the first to tell of their love:

[Socrates]: And I, through the love I had for Alcibiades, felt just as the Bacchants do. For whenever they are inspired they draw honey and milk where others cannot even draw water. And I, knowing no lesson through which I could benefit a man by teaching, nevertheless believed that by being together with this man I could make him better through love.[64]

At least three other Socratics wrote dialogues on the same topic (Phaedo of Elis, Euclides of Megara, and Antisthenes, the founder of Cynicism), none of which survives however. Xenophon, on the other hand, distances Socrates from Alcibiades in his *Memorabilia*, which actually may lend credence to the more intimate portrayal found in Plato and others since Xenophon was at pains to show how unjust the Athenians were for condemning Socrates–possibly with Alcibiades in mind–on the count of corrupting the youth of the city, and thus has motives for diminishing the extent of their involvement with each other.

The rigid prohibition of new music in Sparta came, I think, by 500. Plato's condemnation of the wrong sort of new music as pernicious, morally and politically (The *Laws* 397-424), seems to imply that it was lewd. Aristophanes has the music as well as other tastes of the younger generations shock their elders as has been the case in the 20th century in the Western countries with wild, sensual, sexy song and dance. Singing as well as dancing often became lewd and homoerotically so, not just in choruses and satyrs or in extemporaneous performances at symposia, but even in mimes and other less organized and even amateur revels of the common people. Youths normally express their rebellion in song and dance as well as dress and hairstyle and the homosexually inclined and/or effeminate of all ages and societies are likely by nature to take the lead in shocking their elders, with histrionics and bizarre costumes. This "new music" was routinely chastised by moralists ever since Aristophanes. By the time of Menander music like drama became saccharine.

PART IX:
399-359–THE AGE OF PLATO, XENOPHON, AND THE 'SACRED BAND'

With the defeat of Athens by Sparta in 404, the status of power seemed to shift to Sparta, but, as Sealey (1976, p. 378) points out, this was "illusory," for Sparta now had to fear her former allies, Corinth and Thebes, and for this reason decided against the destruction of Athens, although Sparta did insist that Athens destroy the long walls and renounce her empire. Athens, though diminished, remained a major player in the Greek world, and even allied with Thebes against Sparta in 395. In addition, Conon began reconstructing parts of the Delian League and restored some prosperity to Athens after his victory at Cnidus in 394. With the surprisingly quick recovery of Athens, and threats from Thebes and Corinth, Sparta was unable to solidify the ascendancy she had briefly enjoyed.

In 371 the Spartans fell before the Theban Sacred Band at Leuctra and again at Mantinea in 362 and never fully recovered their losses of territory, slaves, or influence.[65] Thus effectively ended the 'mystique' of the Spartan military as invincible in the Peloponnese, and with it came a decrease in the admiration other states held, even if often begrudgingly and critically, for the Spartan system. That system–reliant as it was on the Helots' ability to provide surplus food for Spartiates so that they could devote all their time to the art of war–had been founded both on the servitude of the Helots and on Spartan fear of them. Consequently, with the loss of land and slaves, the Spartans had to undergo drastic changes and much of what has been called the Spartan 'mirage' began in this period as the Spartans reinterpreted and exalted their gloried past.

Thebes, on the other hand, reached its zenith with these triumphs, and mainly as a result of the effectiveness of their elite infantry unit comprised of 150 pairs of lovers.[66] It has long been debated whether this 'Sacred Band' was created (probably in 379 by Gorgidas) before Plato wrote the *Symposium*, in which he has Phaedrus theorize an army of lovers. In any case, these men were rightly considered the finest fighting force in Greece, and Philip of Macedon, as we shall soon see, was much impressed with this formation and Theban tactics in general; he would use a modified Theban model for his own forces when he became king.

Recently, however, the existence of such a band of heroic lovers has come into question. Citing Xenophon's surprising failure to mention it in his work the *Hellenica*–a political and military history of the first part of the 4th century–as one damning piece of evidence, Leitao (2002) argues that "the historicity of an erotic Sacred Band rests on the most precarious of foundations" (p. 143).[67] Although he believes there wasn't any such Band of Lovers, he states that his "goal in problematizing the truthfulness of this tradition is not ultimately to offer decisive proof that Thebes never had an erotically constituted fighting force . . . but rather to redirect our attention to the discursive conditions that made it possible for an erotic Sacred Band, based on however small a kernel of historical truth, to take its first steps onto the scene of history" (p. 143). While skepticism is a good thing in the pursuit of truth in history, it must be admitted that the Sacred Band rests on authority less shaky than many things accepted from ancient historiography. Furthermore, it should be noted that Leitao's project is not to dismiss the historicity altogether of an elite Band in Thebes at this time, but rather to put into doubt that it consisted of couples who were current *erastai* and *eromenoi*. He admits that many armies, not just at Thebes, involved beloveds or former beloveds in the battle in some form, even if only standing by to provide inspiration: "occasionally *paidika* are described as being present during battle itself, but when our sources are specific about what they are doing there it often turns out that they are not actively engaged in fighting" (Leitao, 2002, p. 144).

Xenophon, a well-seasoned soldier himself, gives us some insight into 'gays' in the military of his time.[68] Brawls and bragging over desirable boys seem to have been not at all uncommon. When Agesilaus, one of the two kings of Sparta, hears of the death of his co-ruler, Agesipolis, he weeps, mourning his companion, and reminiscing over the fun they had in their shared tent talking about "youthful days, hunting exploits, horses, and love affairs [*paidika*]" (*Hell.* 5.3.20). *Paidika*, which the Loeb translator so delicately phrases as "love affairs," refers specifically to boy beloveds. Soldiers fighting over a boy cannot have been unknown since Xenophon, when accused of hitting another soldier, in denying the charge, lists coming to blows over a beloved boy (*paidika*) as one of several possible, but rejected, motives he could have had (*Anabasis* 5.8.4). Later, on the same expedition (*Anabasis* 7.4.7-11), Xenophon intercedes on behalf of a fellow soldier by the name of Episthenes–a boy-lover (*paiderastes*) as Xenophon tells us–who wants the life of a beautiful lad spared by Seuthes II, a local Thracian ruler who had captured the boy in battle. Xenophon, to win the release of the boy, tells Seuthes about how Episthenes had previously put together a company of soldiers with their beauty as the sole criterion, and that, when they fought side by side, Episthenes had proved himself a very brave man. The story ends happily with the boy and Episthenes embracing and Seuthes II laughing at them both.

Xenophon, of course, is one of our main sources for Socrates and his circle of friends. As in Plato, they are shown to have an intense interest in youths. Socrates, in Xenophon, however, takes a rather harsh view of sexual activity, even kissing, between lover and beloved: "Socrates advised that one abstain resolutely from sex with beautiful boys; for he said it was not easy for a man who engaged in such things to behave moderately." Xenophon, by way of illustration, proceeds to tell about a conversation he had with Socrates wherein Socrates tries to warn him away from boys by likening the kiss from a beautiful boy to the bite of a tarantula, both poisonous, but the kiss actually more dangerous (*Memorabilia* 1.3.8-14; *HGR* 5.2). Yet, Xenophon records his own disagreement with Socrates over the matter, since in this same passage Xenophon replies that he would happily be considered a fool if that meant being able to kiss Alcibiades' son, "a boy with a beautiful face and right in the bloom of boyhood." Perhaps Xenophon, on one hand, admired the noble sentiments and almost inhuman self-control Socrates taught and practiced, but he was, on the other hand, enough of a practical man to see that such idealism was not always either practicable nor even constructive. Self-control (*enkrateia*) was certainly important to Xenophon, and understandable given his military background, but it was only part of larger context.[69] As Clifford Hindley (1994) argues,

> opportunities for homoerotic pleasure available to Greek armies and their commanders in the field must have been many, and the resulting relationships complex. . . . Xenophon recognised that such relationships might well be honourable, and motivate men to valour in battle. But experience also taught him that situations could well arise where to indulge in *eros* was fraught with military or political danger. In such situations, he had no doubt that the welfare of the city should take precedence over individual impulse, and for him the ability to resist erotic desire *where necessary* ranked high among the qualities required by a military leader. (356f; italics added)

Plato's Socrates, although certainly no hedonistic pursuer of boys, takes a more constructive view of boy-love. Volumes have been written about *eros* in Plato's philosophy, and so it is unnecessary here to go into all that has been said. However, I do want to point out a couple of features that highlight matters at issue in this article by focusing on three speeches in the first half of the *Phaedrus*.

In the *Phaedrus*, Socrates follows Phaedrus outside the city walls, drawn by what the young beauty is holding in his left hand under his cloak (228d), which turns out to be the scroll of a speech by Lysias, the most famous orator of the day. This mixture of eroticism and learning that Plato playfully joins together here will be important throughout the dialogue, which in many ways is about the erotic pull of philosophy. Lysias' speech purports to be that of a man who, though not in love with the youth, attempts to persuade him to give him his favors. Against the common scholarly view of this speech, Martha Nussbaum (2002) argues, I think correctly, that Lysias' speech is to be taken seriously within the dialogue, and for the reason that it raises important issues about the institution of pederasty: the speech "is indeed a brilliantly clever response to a young man's dilemma" (p. 66). The 'dilemma' Nussbaum refers to is how does a boy choose the man that will actually benefit him, and not simply one who wants sex.

Lysias' argument is that the non-lover will benefit the boy more for several reasons. Most importantly, the lover is more interested in the physical aspects of the boy; as the non-lover points out, "lovers generally start to desire your body before they know your character. . . . Non-lovers, on the other hand, are friends with you even before they achieve their goal . . . you can expect to become a better person if you are won over by me [the non-lover], rather than by a lover" (232e-233a). At the end of Phaedrus' recitation of Lysias' speech Socrates says that he is in ecstasy from having watched Phaedrus' face while he read. Socrates, however, says that he could do better than Lysias and proceeds to give his own version of a plea by a non-lover for the favors of a boy. In his speech, Socrates says that we are all led by two principles: "one is our inborn desire for pleasures, the other is our acquired judgment that pursues what is best. Sometimes these two are in agreement; but there are times when they quarrel inside us" (237d-e). The lover, according to Socrates, will act to maximize his own pleasure, which will result in the boy remaining ignorant and becoming inferior in body and soul.

However, no sooner has Socrates finished his own speech than he feels that he has been impious by speaking ill of *Eros*, a god and the son of Aphrodite. So he then launches into a third and final speech, but this time in defense of the lover. The speech is a *tour de force*, containing vivid imagery and lyrical language as well as philosophical argument. In the final part of the speech, the soul is likened to a charioteer with two horses, one horse a lover of honor and self-control and modesty, the other without modesty, full of boasts and indecency. If the lover-beloved couple is able to master the bad horse and

> the victory goes to the better elements in their minds, which lead them to follow the assigned regimen of philosophy, their life here below is one of bliss and shared understanding. They are modest and fully in control of themselves now that they have enslaved the part that brought trouble into the soul and set free the part that gave it virtue. After death, when they have grown wings and become weightless, they have won the first of three rounds in these, the true Olympic Contests. There is no greater good than this that either human self-control or divine madness can offer a man. If, on the other hand, they adopt a lower way of living, with ambition in

place of philosophy, then pretty soon when they are careless because they have been drinking or for some other reason, the pair's undisciplined horses will catch their souls off guard and together bring them to commit that act which ordinary people would take to be the happiest choice of all; and when they have consummated it once, they go on doing this for the rest of their lives, but sparingly, since they have not approved of what they are doing with their whole minds. So these two also live in mutual friendship (though weaker than that of the philosophical pair). . . . In death they are wingless when they leave the body, but their wings are bursting to sprout, so the prize they have won from the madness of love is considerable . . . their lives are bright and happy as they travel together, and thanks to their love they will grow wings when the time comes. (256a-e)[70]

In all three speeches, the tension between sexual love and a more character-driven love becomes a central focus. Despite the differences among the speeches, a common theme is that love that has only the (sexual) interests of the lover at heart is to be shunned, while more mutual loves that strive for the enrichment of both sides, but especially the beloved, have great value. Hupperts (2000, 2002) has recently argued that Plato and Xenophon virtually invented the idea of pederastic pedagogy. In doing so he ignores evidence against his contention, including Aristophanes' attacks on those pederasts who claim to have pedagogical intentions, the corpus of Theognis, and what we know about the role of pederasty in the Spartan educational system, among other things. Without a doubt we find, in Plato, the first systematic investigation into pederasty's role in the state and its claim to character formation, but that is different from originating that claim. Plato builds on the ideas common in the Athenian discourse of his day, using them as a foundation to lead the reader towards a greater and deeper sense of true reality, as he sees it; this is the essence of the dialectical form he gives to his philosophy.

A good illustration of this method comes from Diotima in Socrates' speech in the *Symposium* as she erects a stairway to the ultimate vision of true Beauty starting from the erotic impulse felt by a man in the presence of an individual youth's beauty.[71] This impulse would be the one most familiar and most immediate to the Athenian reader, and from familiarity he would be led by the dialectical process to new experiences that could not have been achieved in any other manner. This method we saw as well in the three speeches from the *Phaedrus*; the third speech, while moving beyond the previous two speeches, does so only by incorporating their truths into it.

Returning from the ethereal realms of Platonic thought, a few words should be said here about sculpture. Sculptors tended to imitate Polyclitus rather than Phidias, although the Parthenon frieze did influence other such works. Many *poleis* were too poor to finance great buildings and ornamental sculpture in this period. Paeonius, at work in the late 5th century and early 4th, was one of Phidias' successors in Athens. He is famous for his Nike, which made creative use of drapery and was the first partially nude female divinity in Classical Greek art. This statue introduced the flamboyant or 'Rich' style, which presaged the Hellenistic in its ornate decoration and outward-flowing focus. His greatest effort seems to have been spent on female figures. They all lessened the emphasis on the ideal male body to portray the "subjective and the theoretical" under the influence of the Sophists.[72] The frieze from Apollo's temple at Bassai in Arcadia, now in the British Museum, is dated a little after 400. Although smaller and less perfect than the slightly earlier Parthenon frieze, it still emphasizes the rugged large-headed but squat male nude, now in more strenuous, even twisted and contorted, action.

Although flourishing into the next generation, two sculptors introduced important innovation. The Athenian Praxiteles revolutionized Greek sculpture, creating the first life-sized fully nude female: the famous Aphrodite of Cnidus. His male nudes, such as his Hermes, were softer than those of his predecessors, and though magnificent, they did not outdo those of Polyclitus. They were more coy, sometimes almost effeminate, and for the tastes of some, more sensual. His contemporary Scopas (fl. 370-330) concentrated on young gods, male as well as female, and depicted passion and suffering (*pathos*) as seen in the male nude from the Mausoleum frieze. One can see the same mixture of the erotic and pathetic in the Pergamon statues of the Dying Gaul and the Gaul Killing Himself. Scopas greatly influenced the so-called 'baroque-style' of Hellenistic sculpture.

The Middle Comedy had far fewer ribald references to scat, farting, and other anal preoccupations than did the Old Comedy. Grotesque phalluses along with the foul language disappeared from it. This was a trend away from the old gay aristocratic unconcern with propriety and to what we might call bourgeois taste. This was an age of anxiety—one that lacked exuberance and with less wealth and self-confidence.

PART X:
359-323–THE AGE OF ARISTOTLE AND ALEXANDER

The 5th century was really the century of Athens, and of Sparta to a lesser degree. The first part of the 4th century saw a dispersal of power to include Thebes and Corinth, in addition to those traditional powers. This outward shift in focus continued as Thessaly and then Macedonia became important players in the political fortunes of Greece. The defeat of the Theban Sacred Band in 338 by Philip of Macedon at Chaeronea, where his son Alexander played a crucial role, effectively ended the era of the independent city-states of Greece. Symonds ended his *A Problem in Greek Ethics* with the loss of freedom which he thought also ended that heroism that pederastic love had inspired.

Philip, as mentioned before, had taken and applied Theban formations and tactics to his own army. As a youth Phillip had been given to Epaminondas, whose *eromenos* he may have become, as hostage to Thebes, during which time he acquired intimate knowledge of the Theban phalanx. At Chaeronea, it is said that Philip, looking out over some of the dead on the battlefield, "when he learned that this was the band of lovers and beloveds, he wept and exclaimed, 'May utter destruction fall upon those who suppose these men did or suffered anything disgraceful'" (Plutarch, *Life of Pelopidas*, 18.7; *HGR* 2.14). Now that he had Greece under his control he could set out to conquer Persia, to which goal the mastery of Greece was only a necessary step. His assassination two years later, quite possibly by one of his former *eromenoi*,[73] left him little time to enjoy his success or carry out his plans for Persia.

Those plans would fall to his successor Alexander. His conquests would further open up Greece to increased interactions with other cultures, a development that would have as much influence on Greece as on the rest of the Hellenistic world from Afghanistan to Egypt. Alexander, like his father, certainly had homosexual relationships. It is, however, difficult to categorize any of them as pederastic in the usual sense. The closest to a traditional pederastic relationship we hear of is his love for Bagoas, "a eunuch of remarkable beauty and in the very flower of boyhood, who had been loved by Darius" (Quintus Curtius Rufus, 6.5.23; quoted in Green, 1991, p. 333). A closer parallel would be with the Ganymede myth, where a king, albeit Zeus, takes a foreign boy, who will never become a man, to be his lover. It is hard to imagine this as a pedagogical relationship.

Like Achilles and Patroclus, coevals, Alexander's friendship from boyhood with Hephaestion is even more problematic. They seem to have viewed themselves as modern-day versions of the Homeric lovers, for we hear of them paying homage at Troy to those two fallen heroic comrades. According to Aelian, an early third-century CE writer, "Alexander laid a wreath on Achilles' tomb and Hephaestion on Patroclus', hinting that he was the object of Alexander's love [*eromenos*], as Patroclus was of Achilles" (12.7, Trans. N. G. Wilson). Like his role model Achilles, Alexander wished never to lose his youthful beauty, so he introduced shaving. In the opening sections of her recent article Jeanne Reames-Zimmerman (1999) argued that the relationship of Alexander and Hephaestion was homosexual. She showed that the 'Dover model,' based as it was on mostly Athenian sources and Athenian vase paintings, cannot account for many of the practices found in other places, such as Sparta, Thebes, or Macedonia. She noted, for instance, that "Theopompus (*FGrH* 115 F225) reports that Macedonians not only engaged in homoerotic affairs, but took a passive role even after their beards were grown" (p. 86). Her article surveyed the evidence for homosexual affairs in Macedonia up to the time of Alexander. She concluded about the nineteen-year association that, "in terms of affectional attachment, *Hephaistion*–not any of Alexander's three wives–was the king's life partner. Whatever the truth of any sexual involvement, their emotional attachment has never been seriously questioned" (p. 92f.).

One important consequence of Alexander's conquests is the spread of many Greek institutions to newly founded cities and to Greek colonies set up in preexisting non-Greek cities and even to some Hellenized Jews in Jerusalem itself: gymnasia, symposia, athletic contests, even language. Most of these institutions would continue to have a vigorous life down to the breakup and then collapse of the Roman Empire and the domination of the Christian religion.

A marker of this cultural influence can be seen in the *ephebeia*, an institution in existence in Athens from at least the 330s, but likely in some form prior to that. From the beginning associated with the city gymnasium, it demarcated the passage from adolescence to manhood (ages 18-20) and consisted in military training at first, but later became much more educationally oriented. This institution spread throughout the Hellenistic world to become virtually universal. It is last attested at Oxyrhynchus, Egypt, in 323 CE. Its "final disappearance in the 4th cent. reflects the depleted finances of the late Roman city and the eventual devaluation of physical education."[74] This devaluation was part and parcel of the devaluation of the body and the stigmatization of sexuality by the Christian church.

Another development that was to have long-term effects, both on Western society in general and on the conception of same-sex relationships, was the rise of the scientific enterprise. Already evident in the Ionian physicists and Hippocratic theorists, it got tremendous impetus from Plato's student and Alexander's tutor, Aristotle. Although he provides us with historical information on pederasty in Greece and Macedonia, pederasty is almost completely absent from his philosophy.[75] He does discuss sexual relations between men, but in several of these places it is clear that it is not pederasty that is at question.

For Aristotle an understanding of the causation of homosexuality, or more precisely male-male sexual pleasure, is more important than evaluating it morally. His approach is actually rather modern-looking in that he looks for its biological and psychological causes; men that enjoy intercourse with other men do so because they are born that way or have become that way through some sort of childhood habituation. Those that are that way naturally have a kind of natural deformity or natural disease. This belief of Aristotle's is quite possibly the ultimate source for the notion of homosexuality as a disease. It should be noted, however, that there is no opprobrium connected with it, in fact the opposite: "no one would label men who are subject to this condition because of nature 'unrestrained'" (*Nic. Ethics* 7.5.3-5; *HGR* 5.13). A passage in *Problems* (4.26; *HGR* 5.16), which may or may not be by Aristotle, gives a very detailed biological/physiological explanation, based on misdirected flow or blockage of secretions, to account for why certain men enjoy being penetrated. Even if not by Aristotle it is certainly Aristotelian.

Overall Aristotle's remarks dovetail with other features of his biology and philosophy; the human male is the highest of animals, a deviation from that is the human female, which Aristotle also calls a natural deformity (*Generation of Animals* 4.3 767b8ff.), and he gives reduced amount of heat as the physiological cause for this deviation.[76] So too are natural slaves deformities in that they lack full deliberative power. Although Aristotle is not explicit about this, his use of the term natural deformity for men who achieve pleasure through intercourse with other men may indicate a similar view to that of women and natural slaves. However reprehensible we might find this terminology, we should remember that in all these cases Aristotle sees the condition as natural and not a reason for any sort of condemnation.

In their own different ways, Alexander and Aristotle changed the worldview of the Greeks forever. Whole new vistas were opened up for culture and thought, and Greek art kept pace with these other dynamic transformations. From Sicyon, the most prolific of Hellenistic sculptors, Lysippus (fl. 370-310), who was Alexander's favorite portraitist, altered the standard for the male nude. In distinction to Polyclitus, his new slimmer canon, with a proportionately smaller head and a different slant for the body, created a new style (Pliny *N.H.* 34, 65). The saccharine flavor of the heterosexual themes in the New Comedy coincide with the introduction of the female nude and the more effeminized male nude by the followers of Praxiteles.

Though the Greek world had never been a fully homogeneous culture, there had been some commonalities reflected in language and literature and worldview. As many of these elements flowed out into the broader Hellenistic realms of the 4th and 3rd centuries, the original Greek lands imported various new elements, such as Eastern and middle-Eastern cults and religions. Society and institutions became more complex. However, many of the original Greek institutions retained their influence until Christianity shut down gymnasia and Plato's academy along with the other Athenian schools and philosophies: the Peripatetic, the Stoic, and the Epicurean.

PART XI:
POST-323–GREECE UNDER ROME

Alexander had so transformed Hellenism Johann Gustav Droysen coined the word Hellenistic (Greek-like) to describe the new culture a blend of Greek and "Oriental."[77] This hybrid culture included so many strange lands and peoples that it could no longer be called Hellenic–even in the homeland. But among Greek speakers of whatever descent common institutions and culture persisted: gymnasia, symposia, seclusion of ladies, late marriage for gentlemen, and pederastic pedagogy. Almost all Romans and other Latin speakers, however Hellenophilic, continued quite different and to each other shocking social customs. On this subject, Cornelius Nepos eloquently wrote:

> Many things that among the Greeks are considered improper and unfitting . . . are permitted by our customs. Is there by chance a Roman who is ashamed to take his wife to a dinner away from home? Does it happen that the mistress of the house in any family does not

enter the anterooms frequented by strangers and show herself among them? Not so in Greece: there the woman accepts invitations only among families to which she is related, and she remains withdrawn in that inner part of the house which is called the gynaeceum, where only the nearest relatives are admitted.[78] . . . For it was not shameful for Cimon, the best man of the Athenians, to marry his sister, given that his fellow citizens did the same thing. But by our standards, this is considered an abomination. Quite young men in Crete are praised for having had as many lovers as they could. No widow in Sparta is very celebrated if she does not come to dinner hired for a wage. Olympic victors generally received great praise in all of Greece, and to enter the stage for public entertainment was not shameful among those same peoples, when for us all of those things are held in some cases as causes of disgrace, in others as base and lacking in dignity. (in Hubbard, 2003a, p. 336)

Thus the unheard-of destruction and devastation in the wars of Alexander's successors, so many of which were fought in and over Greece itself, and in the Roman conquests of the Hellenistic states and as well as in the Roman civil wars, which were mainly decided in the Greek-speaking East, the Hellenes continued their basic social and sexual lifestyles. Fashions continued to change from generation to generation but with widely different speed and style in the vast areas of the Hellenistic and Roman world, both of which had several centers to be emulated. The fundamental structure, however, of gymnasia and symposia endured to flourish again under the Pax Romana with an intellectual flowering that Philostratus dubbed the Second Sophistic. At this time Plutarch, Lucian, and Athenaeus and the continued rivalry and debates as to whether the love of women excelled that of boys flourished attesting to pedagogical pederasty. Nepos succinctly captured the basis of Greek society and culture and its enduring difference from the Romans.

EPILOGUE

In my earlier work, *Pederasty and Pedagogy*, I established that a major revolution occurred in Greek society around 630 BCE–the institutionalization of pedagogical pederasty and its closely associated customs, such as nudity in athletics and at gymnasia (both connected to the rise of the pan-Hellenic games), symposia, seclusion of ladies, and delayed marriage for upper-class males. That these institutions preceded and coincided with breakthroughs in art, philosophy, and political institutions, I claim not to be altogether unrelated causally.[79]

Herein I have argued that the portrayal of pederasty and other forms of male homosexual acts and sentiments in ancient Greece changed from generation to generation with close parallels in literature and art, and that throughout this period lustful pederasty coexisted with pedagogical pederasty, not necessarily as two separate phenomena, but as two ways in which the Greeks understood the desire and the relationship involved in boy-love. In so doing, the Greeks channeled the (private) energy of the libido into paths that benefited the *polis* as a whole. As Hubbard (2000) aptly puts it when describing the simplistic bifurcation that has tended to dominate studies of Greek pederasty: "Oscar Wilde's and J. A. Symonds' idealistic version of Greek love was just as much an over-simplification of the complex historical phenomenon as Halperin's ghastly nightmare vision of a society where the penetrating phallus was the universal wrench of subordination" (p. 11).

Dover, who confined himself to sources from the Archaic and Classical periods (thus disdaining Plutarch as well as Lucian and Athenaeus) and to vases (which indeed, as he says, emphasize lust over pedagogy) as opposed to sculpture (the most important aspect of Greek art), completely ignored the idealized male nude, the importance of which Andrew Stewart has so incisively demonstrated. Dover, along with Foucault and Halperin, has been justly criticized by James Davidson in a recent article. Though proclaiming, and perhaps imagining, himself to be unprejudiced, Dover's myopic view of the institution of pederasty shows that he suffers from a lack of understanding of homosexuality verging on homophobia.[80] His conception of homosexuality, and of same-sex behavior among the Greeks, relies heavily on the psychoanalytic work of his friend Devereux, whom Dover himself quotes as telling him, "I hate queers."[81] However, Dover does deserve credit for reopening the debate suppressed by Hitler, and that had not been seriously broached in England either since Symonds.[82]

Believing that enough of what I argue will stand scrutiny, I hope we can begin the process of restoring Greek pederasty to the great central role that it played in Greek history and warfare, politics, art, literature and learning, in short to the Greek miracle, in which changes in homosexual representations and practices both reacted to and contributed to transformations in the political, economic, and cultural realms. Much that is beautiful and good in Western civilization was passed to it from the glorious flame of Greece, a flame ignited by the erotic spark between man and boy.

NOTES

1. Xen. *Constitution of the Lacedaemonians*, 2.12 (passage 2.10 in Hubbard, 2003a, *Homosexuality in Greece and Rome: A Sourcebook of Basic Documents*, henceforth = *HGR*).

2. *Altertumswissenschaft* ('scientific knowledge of antiquity') was an attempt by German scholars, such as Humboldt and Wolff, to put Classical philology, and study of the ancient world in general, on a more professional and institutional basis. The movement, which inaugurated the modern study of Classics, saw Classical literature and values as means to both the education and the character-formation of young students. See the collection of articles in Most, 2002.

3. Winckelmann's (1849) groundbreaking work led to a renewed obsession with the ancient world and its esthetics. His own (homosexually based) response to the art of the Greeks is quite interesting, especially given its influence on subsequent European thought (e.g., the Romantics). Winckelmann was often moved to spiritual, esthetic, and erotic ecstasy by the male nudes of the classical period in a way reminiscent of the erotically charged rapture of medieval mystics. In describing the Apollo Belvedere he states, "from admiration I pass to ecstasy, I feel my breast dilate and rise as if I were filled with the spirit of prophecy; I am transported to Delos and the sacred groves of Lycia–places Apollo honoured with his presence–and the statue seems to come alive like the beautiful creation of Pygmalion." For Winckelmann's homosexuality and esthetics see Aldrich (1993, chap. 2), from which the preceding quotation is taken (p. 51). See also Potts, 1994.

4. Crompton's *Byron and Greek Love* (1985) and *Homosexuality and Civilization* (2003); see also John Lauritsen's and Wayne Dynes' articles in this book.

5. One problem with defining homosexuality in purely physical terms, as Dover does, is that there can be no homosexuality unless there is clear proof of a sexual act or the explicit statement of the desire for such an act. The term homosocial, a term currently in vogue, does not quite catch the erotic tenor of certain relationships *even* where sexual acts do not occur.

6. In Homer it is hard not to view Patroclus as a spouse-figure to Achilles. Certainly the desire by Patroclus and Achilles to be buried in the same urn could be viewed in terms of a married couple ("may the same urn hide our bones" *Il.* 23.91), and when Achilles tries to throw his arms around the ghost of Patroclus we are reminded of other similar scenes in ancient literature usually reserved for fathers, mothers, or spouses. Furthermore, there may be an indication, in Homer, that the other Achaeans recognized this quasi-spousal relationship. In the embassy scene in book 9, Achilles' former mentor Phoenix tells the story of Meleager and his unabating anger, meant to provide a parallel, a tale of warning, to Achilles. Meleager, in the story, is a stand-in for Achilles, and Patroklos is subtly likened to Meleager's wife, Kleopatra. The parallel even runs to the similar roots in their names ('patr' and 'kl' meaning something like 'glory of the father,' as Herakles means 'glory of Hera'). Through this story Phoenix attempts to persuade not only Achilles, but Patroclus as well, who is meant to catch his parallel to Kleopatra. So too, later on, his mother, Thetis, tells Achilles–who, while mourning Patroclus, is abstaining from food, drink and sex–that he should eat and drink, and that it is good to sleep with a *woman also* (*Il.* 24.130f.), the language used emphasizing 'woman' (*gunaiki per*).

7. Within the *Greek Anthology* are epigrams from as late as the reign of Justinian (AD 527-65) or Justin II (AD 565-78), when Agathius collected poems of his contem-

poraries. However, none that have come down to us from this late period have pederastic themes, a fact that does not preclude their existence, since pederastic poetry was certainly a common epigrammatic *topos.*

8. I wonder why, in the often precious debates about Black Athena (Bernal, 1985-1991; Lefkowitz & Rogers, 1996), neither side refers to pederasty. Bernal told me on the phone several years ago that, though he hadn't yet done so, he intended to in a future volume. Meanwhile Lefkowitz and her husband, Lloyd-Jones, and most other Hellenophiles, in this no-holds-barred debate, conveniently ignore it. Black Athena and its critics fail, in my opinion, to emphasize the importance of pederasty and athletic nudity amongst the ancient Greeks. Bernal does not wish to attribute these to Egyptians or Semites, and the classicists generally avoid these distasteful habits of their heroes, except for Dover, and Halperin, and their countless followers who marginalize their importance.

9. This article owes much of its accuracy to the contributions of Thomas K. Hubbard and a PhD candidate in Classics who has worked with him at the University of Texas, Mark R. Warren. I would also like to thank Beert Verstraete for his unflagging help over the years and Gregory Nagy for his inspiration to be bold in questioning the dogma of classicists. We have used various translations with the result that "youth" and "boy" are used herein interchangeably. If a prepubescent male is meant, I use the word "young boy" or "child." I would also like here to acknowledge my indebtedness to Andrew Porter of the University of Missouri at Columbia for his various felicitous contributions and insights.

10. For a scathing attack on pederasty in Plato and its insidious, perverting influence on western culture, one should browse John Jay Chapman's appalling *Lucian, Plato and Greek Morals* (1931).

11. On the history of the publication of *A Problem in Greek Ethics*, see John Lauritsen (Ed.), *Male Love* [which includes Symond's *A Problem in Greek Ethics*], (New York: Pagan Press, 1983), pp. iii-iv. Already his earlier work, *Studies of the Greek Poets* (1873) had prejudiced Oxford against giving him a professorship; see Phyllis Grosskurth, *The Woeful Victorian: A Biography of John Addington Symonds*, (New York, Chicago, San Francisco: Holt Rinehart & Winston, 1964), p. 271.

12. In general he states that he is inclined to treat homosexuality "as a subdivision of the 'quasi-sexual' (or 'pseudo-sexual'; not 'parasexual')" and to retain the word 'sexual' for heterosexual relations, an inclination he defends in his 1989 Postscript (pp. vii-viii and 206); compare the use of the term 'pseudo-homosexuality' by Devereux, a psychoanalyst and anthropologist who was originally intended to co-author *Greek Homosexuality* with Dover. The civilization of ancient Greece is neither unique, nor first, in exhibiting homosexual behavior and desire, but rather it is the first that western culture was forced to deal with in a systematic way. Dover is correct, of course, in the fact that many of the Greeks felt desire for those of the same sex, and were not in the least ashamed to incorporate it into its high literature, discuss it philosophically, or depict it artistically. What is unique to the Greeks, and which Dover does not quite see as the unique element, is how the Greeks molded those behaviors and desires, transforming them into a creative social institution that released much of the erotic energy in ways that elevated not only literature, philosophy, and art, but even the military and *polis* as a whole.

13. Certainly there were those who had homoerotic experiences in these other cultures, but this must be kept distinct from what I want to examine here, that is, pederastic pedagogy. That homosexual relations were known in other cultures can be seen from

the polemic against homosexuality found in the Pentateuch, which suggests that it was practiced without rebuke by the Hebrews' neighbors.

14. Since most Greek males, even those who were pederastic in early adulthood, married and had sexual relations with their wives, we would consider few of them to be exclusively homosexual or gay in the modern sense, but among those who had the time and money to indulge their proclivities more may have had homosexual experiences than Kinsey's 37%. Kinsey's number is based upon American males who climaxed with another male at least once after age 16 and more. Although desire as well as experience figured in the Kinsey scale–from 0's (those who never had a homosexual experience to climax after age 16) to 6's (those who had only homosexual experiences and/or desires after age 16)–the ancient Greeks, like all other peoples, can fit into his classification, whatever one thinks about the essentialism versus constructionism debate. I presume that very few upper class Greeks were either 0's or 6's.

15. The more the complexities of human psychosexuality come to light, the less valid it is to talk about homosexuality in the singular: "while homosexual desires and activities are probably ubiquitous, the specific forms that they assume are intimately shaped by particular sociohistorical contexts. Instead of talking about homosexuality, we should really speak in terms of *homosexualities*, plural, for there are many variations on the theme of same-sex relations" (Bagemihl, 1999, p. 44). So too Lingiardi (2002), an Italian psychoanalyst of the Jungian stripe: "now that psychoanalysis is no longer so intent on establishing a link between homosexuality and perversion, it has become clearer and clearer that the range and variation in psychosexual structures is such that the plural is called for when making statements about heterosexuali*ties* or homosexuali*ties*" (p. 15).

16. Greek homosexual practices and representations of them certainly varied synchronically as well as diachronically. There were not only class differences, such as between those who had the leisure to spend their time at gymnasia or symposia and those who could not afford to do so, but also geographical differences between *polis* and *polis* or the sundry regions (which I sketched in *Pederasty and Pedagogy*), and also between rustics who could rarely, if ever, go to gymnasia and symposia, which were mostly phenomena of the cities, and the urban elites who could. The article by Charles Hupperts in this collection underlines this variability: Greek homosexuality was not uniformly intergenerational and pederastic. While not ignoring these other distinctions and tensions, I will focus in this article on the generational differences, which tended to affect styles and attitudes but did not necessarily increase or decrease the number of males engaging in homosexual activities or the frequency of the acts themselves.

17. Dates concerning the ancients in this article are all BCE, unless otherwise indicated. On the earlier periods, namely the pre-Archaic and Archaic, the reader should consult my book, *Pederasty and Pedagogy in Archaic Greece*, where I establish these points in more detail.

18. Bagemihl (1999), in his thorough and quite fascinating book on animal homosexuality, provides scientifically documented data on some 300 species, and these are restricted, for reasons of space, to bird and mammals. "Homosexual behavior occurs in more than 450 different kinds of animals worldwide, and is found in every major geographical region and every major animal group. It should come as not surprise, then, that animal homosexuality is not a single, uniform phenomenon. Whether one is discussing the forms it takes, its frequency, or its relationship to heterosexual activity, same-sex behavior in animals exhibits every conceivable variation" (p. 12). Studies

show that "nearly every type of same-sex activity found among humans has its counterpart in the animal kingdom" (p. 44).

19. See Dover (1988) for a critique of these attempts to argue for pederastic initiation rites in pre-historic Greece.

20. See Percy, 1996, chap. 5.

21. "There seems to be no pederasty in Homer: Ganymede is Zeus's cup-bearer, not his favourite; between Achilles and Patroclus there is simply a boyish friendship and a comradeship in arms" (Marrou, 1964, p. 480).

22. See Lingiardi (2002) for an exploration of the Ganymede story as Jungian archetype-motif. See, of course, also Vernon Provencal's article in this collection for a detailed study of how the Ganymede myth evolved from Homer onwards.

23. The highly artistic and Hellenic-inspired photographs of Baron Wilhelm von Gloeden provide superb examples.

24. This paragraph was largely conceived by Warren Johannsen.

25. See Burg (2002) for a selective history of 'gays' in the military from Homer to the Clinton era.

26. The fascination with male beauty will inform the art, especially the sculpture, of the Greek world. See Hawley's article (1998) for the existence of male beauty contests at Athens, Sparta, and Elis, among other places.

27. This is true from the time of Theognis to Hellenistic times and beyond. "Boy, as long as your cheek is smooth, I'll never stop praising you, not even if I have to die" (Theognis 1327-34; *HGR* 1.67). "Nicander's light is out, all his body's bloom is gone, and not even the name of his charm is left, whom before we thought among the immortals. But think, young men, only mortal thoughts, for hairs do exist" (Anonymous Hellenistic poet, *Anth. Pal.* 12.39; *HGR* 6.55).

28. On the earliest Greek alphabetic inscriptions, see Pomeroy et al., 73-75.

29. See Cartledge's article "The Birth of the Hoplite," in his collection *Spartan Reflections*, pp. 153-166.

30. Archilochus is said, by a 2nd c. CE source (Oenomaus), to have written poetry about *kinaidoi* ('perverts,' often passive homosexuals; the word is used by Oenomaus and not likely by Archilochus), but we have no fragments to such effect. See *HGR* 1.3.

31. "The most widely accepted generalisation about Greek homosexuality at the present time is that it originated in the military organisation of Dorian states" (Dover, 1989, p.185). Dover considers the theory of a Cretan or Spartan origin for institutionalized pederasty a non-answer. Even so, he does admit that the "earliest representation of homosexual 'courting' is from Crete: a bronze plaque of the period 650-625 BC, in which a man carrying a bow faces a youth who has a wild goat over his shoulders, and the man grasps the forearm of the youth (Boardman [1973] fig. 49)" (p. 205). On the crucial role played by Sparta in the "dispersion" of institutionalized pederasty, see Thomas Scanlon's article in this collection.

32. Xen. *Constitution of the Lacedaemonians* 2.12-14 (*HGR* 2.10). Lycurgus allowed for boy-lovers to spend time with and educate his beloved based on admiration for the boy's soul, but not to lust after the boy or lay hands on him. Even Xenophon, who seems to have believed that sexual acts did not occur in the Spartan system, admits that "it does not, however, surprise [him] that certain people do not believe this."

33. See Lelis, Percy, and Verstraete, 2003, pp. 4-8 for a recent discussion of the late age of marriage for males in the ancient Greek world (by way of comparison with ancient Roman society).

34. Socrates, born into the artisan class, was certainly welcome at the *symposia* of his rich friends.

35. The nude male figure would dominate sculpture for the next two and half centuries (and beyond), during which time sculptures of female figures were all clothed. Boardman (1986) draws similar connections to the ones I am making in this article: "The images were of man, the male body, and generally naked. In classical Greece athletes exercised naked, warriors could fight nearly naked, and in everyday life the bared young male must have been a fairly common sight. Artists did not need to look for naked models of their idealized athlete figures; they had grown up in a society in which male nudity was commonplace and a well developed body was admired" (p. 276).

36. See Brongersma, 1990. Inscriptions dating from either the 7th or 6th centuries attest to same-sex relations on Thera, an island geographically close to Crete, and known to have been influenced by both the Cretan and the Spartan cultures. "The Spartans brought to Thera their 'gymnopaideia' in honour of Apollo Karneios. Athenaios writes in his fourteenth book that all boys ('paides') participating in the gymnopaideia danced completely naked ('gymnos')–hence the name–and that the boys made graceful leaps with their bodies, interrupting their motions with soft gesticulations of their hands and enchanting movements of their feet in imitation of fighting and wrestling" (p. 38). Brongersma defends (*contra* Dover, 1989, p. 122f.) the theory originated by Hiller von Gärtringen, who discovered the inscriptions and published them in 1897, that these writings were "a testimony to ritual sacred acts" (Brongersma, 1990, p. 31), specifically to the god Apollo, whose temple is nearby. One inscription reads "by Delphinius Apollo, here Cimon penetrated the son of Bathycles, brother of . . ." (*HGR* 2.22). An association with Apollo, the eternal ephebe, would be quite appropriate, especially in consideration of his own pederastic loves (Hyacinthus, Cyparissus).

37. However, the poet always tends to be concerned about the faithfulness of the boy, and there are certainly issues concerning the boy's character in Theognis and others. With that said, lyric and epigrammatic poetry of the pederastic kind is very aware of physical beauty, as well as its ephemeral nature.

38. = *HGR* 1.28.

39. See Parker (1996), who humorously debunks the tradition that Sappho ran a 'finishing school' for girls, or for that matter any other kind of educational institution. He, curiously ignoring his earlier proper skepticism of various attempts to reconstruct her *milieu*, concludes with the suggestion that Sappho belonged to a sympotic circle of age-equal women. In her article in this collection, Anne Klinck convincingly reaffirms the intergenerational nature of Sappho's relationships.

40. See the various *testimonia* in Edmonds (1928, pp. 141-181). Halperin, in his 2002 article, says that it "took six centuries for Sappho's same-sex erotic attachments to attract recorded comment. . . . Sappho was represented in classical Athenian comedies of the fifth and fourth centuries B.C. as the lover of various men, sometimes even as a prostitute . . . the first writers to touch on the question of Sappho's erotic deviance, so far as we know, were the Roman poets of the late first century B.C. and early first century A.D. [Horace and Ovid]" (p. 231f.).

41. Halperin (2002): it is the "constant and inescapable relation to a social structure that varies relatively little, both historically and culturally, which endows female same-sex relations with a greater degree of continuity, of thematic consistency, over time and space, making each historical instance both different and the same, both old and new. It is also the threat that love between women can pose to monopolies of male authority that lends plausibility to the hypothesis that a notion of female-female eroti-

cism may have been consolidated relatively early in Europe, even before similar notions emerged that could apply to all forms of male homoeroticism. Perhaps lesbianism was the first homoeroticism to be conceptualized categorically as such" (p. 260).

42. Peisistratus was said to have been the *eromenos* of Solon, and in turn had Charmus as his *eromenos* (Plut. *Solon* I). Athenaeus records the rivalry of Polycrates of Samos and Anacreon, the poet, over the same *eromenos* (12.540e-f).

43. Platthy (1968, pp. 97-110) collects the *testimonia* for the establishment of a library by Peisistratus. Many of the *testimonia* deal more specifically with the Homeric texts. On a library in general, see Gellius *NA* 17.1-2 and Isidorus *Etym*. 6.3.3-5.

44. Boardman clearly indicates his great mentor Beazley had a homosexual side like so many other earlier admirers and collectors of these erotic vases. In his *magnum opus* he twice opines that the younger partners on all of these Greek vases tended to be between 12 and 14, when any connoisseur of the male body would know that they tended to range from 14 to 18, and given that the onset of puberty occurred later in the ancient world at an average age of about 16-18 for males, 14-16 for females.

45. One is left wondering exactly how an artist would depict, on a scene of courtship, one person's interest in the other's soul, or even why the artist would want to depict it on a vessel intended for a drinking party.

46. See Vickers and Gill (1994, chap. 1), who demolish the notion that Greek pottery, in general, was an especially valuable commodity in the ancient world.

47. What evidence does Emily Wilson, in a *Times Literary Supplement* review (2004), have that a phallus "was used . . . as a protective image at the doorway of most ordinary houses [even in Attica]"? This reviewer totally misunderstands that these were boundary markers originally set up by the tyrants later and placed in front of a few of the fanciest houses. She went on to state that "in antiquity, the phallus was primarily a religious symbol" and that "in modern times, it is [primarily] an obscenity." By whatever name the phallus, membrum virile, penis, prick, dick, it is always been the same, a very versatile organ and useful in many ways if often abused.

48. For the view that these vases depicted men in drag, see W. J. Slater, Artemon and Anacreon: No Text Without Context. *Phoenix, 32* (1978), 185-194.

49. In his 1966 article, Podlecki, developing ideas of Jacoby (*Atthis*, 1949, chap. 2), examines the political reasons for the rise of the legend, seeing it as part of aristocratic intra-class rivalry wherein the anti-Alcmeonid nobles had reason to elevate the status of the tyrannicides. Hubbard (2003a) locates it instead in an inter-class tension: "one can perhaps see an attempt by mainly upper-class enthusiasts of pederasty (whose sympathies might otherwise be suspected of being undemocratic) to contextualize their practices as integral with Athens' developing democratic constitution by granting pederasty a prominent place in the democracy's foundational mythology" (p. 55f.). Monoson (2000) argues instead that a "number of factors combined to make the tale particularly attractive to various classes of people" (p. 45).

50. "Some time after the middle of the [5th] century a decree [*IG* I^2 77] confirming the right of the oldest living descendant of each to public maintenance in the Prytaneion was passed, almost certainly on the motion of Pericles himself" (Podlecki, 1966, p.129).

51. However we are to understand the nudity of the earlier *kouroi*, Osborne (1997) maintains that, with the more individualized sculpture of the 5th century, these nude male figures "can no longer make a pretence at sexual innocence: the viewer stands to the statue in a relationship of desire" (p. 512).

52. Achilles is here addressing the dead body of his beloved Patroclus (*fr.* 228). Athenaeus (13.601; *HGR* 2.21) reports that "love affairs were such an open and every-day matter that the great poet Aeschylus, and Sophocles too, put sexual themes on the stage in their tragedies, Aeschylus showing Achilles' love for Patroclus, Sophocles love of the boys in *Niobe* (which is why some people call this play *Paiderastria*)–and their audiences enjoyed such themes." See Crompton, 2003, p. 51.

53. See Hubbard, 1987 for an analysis of this theme in *Ol.* 1. Hubbard, 2002 examines the pederastic theme in another Pindaric poem (fr. 123) through comparisons with homoerotic pottery of the period and a Lacanian analysis of the 'gaze.'

54. Quotation in Monoson, 1994, p. 253; Trans. Hornblower.

55. = *HGR* 2.21. See Crompton, 2003, p. 51f., for a good summary description of pederasty in tragedy.

56. When Aristophanes chooses to ridicule an historical individual, it is almost invariably an Athenian. Socrates likely becomes 'the Sophist' for him because the other major Sophists were all non-Athenian.

57. *Logos* is a notoriously difficult word to translate, having a wide range of meanings. The appropriate meanings here are speech, word, argument, or thought, all of which are at play in this passage.

58. Considering that he is a well-respected scholar of Aristophanes (and deservedly so), Dover, in his *Greek Homosexuality*, has a surprisingly superficial analysis of homosexuality in Aristophanes.

59. All quotations from the *Clouds* are from Jeffrey Henderson's excellent Loeb translation.

60. Notice here how close this description corresponds to the *kouroi* statues, which have grown more erotic over the two centuries leading up to Aristophanes' time.

61. The claims of Worse Speech echo in many ways those of the character Callicles in Plato's *Gorgias*.

62. It is often conjectured that the same actor who plays the role of Socrates, who is offstage at this point, also plays the character of Better Speech. If so, then this highlights Aristophanes' contentions about Socrates and his ilk, almost as though he were bringing on Socrates' subconscious in the figure of Better Speech.

63. No less an authority on literary theory than Aristotle classified the Socratic dialogue as its own genre (*Poetics* 1447b10f.). Alexamenus of Teos, a disciple of Socrates, seems to have been the first to use this form.

64. Fragment from Aelius Aristides, *In Defense of Oratory* 74, quoted in and translated by Johnson (2003, p. 97), who collects all the fragments of Aeschines' *Alcibiades*. Johnson's work also includes the texts of the (possibly pseudo-) Platonic *Alcibiades* I, pseudo-Platonic *Alcibiades* II, and the Alcibiades scene from the end of the *Symposium*.

65. "The loss of the Messenian Helots was the greatest blow the Spartans had ever suffered. It meant the definitive end of their status as a first-rate power. . . . [They lost] territory which was as populous as Lakonia and which they had exploited for some three and a half centuries" (Cartledge, 2002, p. 255).

66. The fullest account of the Sacred Band comes in Plutarch, *Life of Pelopidas*, 18-19.

67. Beert Verstraete, in a soon-to-be-published review in *Phoenix* of *The Sleep of Reason* (Nussbaum and Sihvola, Eds.), suggests that the story of the sacred band, however much it is dubious, reflects powerful and durable Greek ideas vis-à-vis male homoeroticism.

68. See Hindley's two articles for Xenophon's view on male love.

69. Foucault's excessive focus on the Greek notion of *enkrateia* in Xenophon and Plato (1985, Pt. 1, chap. 2 of *The Use of Pleasure*) leads to his extrapolation of the ideals of Socrates and Plato to Greek society in general. Even Xenophon, as we've seen, doesn't fully subscribe to this ideal, although he may find it admirable and appealing, and even applicable where appropriate.

70. It is interesting to note that Plato depicts a mutual love (*eros* and *anteros*) between the lover and the boy, and a love that remains beyond usual age boundaries of *erastes* and *eromenos*; they are seen as life partners in some sense, even into the afterlife. Furthermore, although lovers that consummate their love form a relationship inferior to one built purely on philosophical love, they are still accorded happiness by Plato, and there is not the condemnation found in the *Laws*, a late work of Plato.

71. Perhaps the best illustration of the dialectical method is the *Symposium* itself, where each speech builds on the previous ones to certain degrees, and ideas conceived and elucidated in one part of the dialogue are enriched, altered, and brought to fruition in latter parts.

72. On Paeonius' initiation of the "subjective approach" in Greek sculpture, see Stewart, vol. I, 81, and on the influence of "sophistic relativism" on his work, Stewart I, 91.

73. For the story of his assassination by Pausanias, one of his former *eromenoi*, who had been disgraced (reminiscent of, but not exactly parallel to, the story of Harmodius and Aristogeiton since Harmodius had never been the beloved of Hipparchus), see Green, 1991, pp. 105-110. The original story can be found in Diodorus (16.93-4; 17.2.1) and Justin (9.6.4-8). Aristotle (*Pol.* 1311b2) mentions it, but without reference to Pausanias' status as a beloved.

74. S. Hornblower and A. J. S. Spawforth (1996). Epheboi. In Hornblower and Spawforth, (Eds.), *Oxford Classical Dictionary* (3rd ed., p. 527). Oxford.

75. For what Aristotle does have to say about pederasty, and about love and sex in general, see Sihvola, 2002. Overall, his comments seem fairly non-prejudiced, even positive.

76. The teleological cause is a separate issue, and one that Aristotle does not discuss in relation to homosexuality.

77. See Droysen's *Geschichte des Hellenismus*, first published in 1836.

78. Ferrero, *The Women of the Cæsars* (1911), p. 3.

79. Some reviewers opined incorrectly that I agreed with Dover, others with Sergent, and still others that I was hopelessly ignorant and tendentious. In a review, Paul Cartledge (1997), on the other hand, perceived that I was "the first to try to move beyond Dover." In a review in *Gnomon* (1999) the most distinguished, and waspish, of my critics, Sir Kenneth Dover, only quibbled: while correcting me on minor points and disdaining me as a medievalist, he did not address my principal thesis as to the origin and influence Greek pederasty.

80. Davidson (2001), while attempting to remain diplomatic, states, "I have no wish either to impress Dover or to accuse him of homophobia, but it is clear that *Greek Homosexuality* shares Devereux's goal of shielding the Greeks from attacks that homophobia might inspire. . . . What happened in Greece [according to Devereux and Dover] was not homosexuality, just sex, part of the marginalia of any normal person's sexuality–superficial, episodic or gestural, but always quasi-sexual" (p. 34).

81. "According to Dover, Devereux did not like homosexuals, announcing 'I hate queers' shortly after agreeing to collaborate with him on his book, and Devereux's concept of pseudo-homosexuality is a clear attempt to distance the Greeks from perverts."

The account of Devereux's statement comes from K. J. Dover, 1994, *Marginal Comment: A Memoir*, London, p. 123.

82. The notable exception being *Greek Love* (1965) authored by J. Z. Eglinton (pseudonym for Walter Breen). See the article on Breen and mine on Johansson in Bullough, 2002.

REFERENCES

Aldrich, R. (1993). *The Seduction of the Mediterranean: Writing, Art, and Homosexual Fantasy*. London: Routledge.

Bagemihl, B. (1999). *Biological Exuberance: Animal Homosexuality and Natural Diversity*. New York: St. Martin's Press.

Bernal, M. (1985-1991). *Black Athena: the Afroasiatic Roots of Classical Civilization*. (2 vols.). New Brunswick, NJ: Rutgers UP.

Biers, W. R. (1996). *The Archaeology of Greece*. (2nd ed.). Ithaca, NY: Cornell UP.

Boardman, John. (1964). *The Greeks Overseas*. Baltimore: Penguin Books.

_____. (1973). *Greek Art*. (2nd ed.). London: Thames and Hudson.

_____. (1978). *Greek Sculpture, the Archaic Period: A Handbook*. Oxford: Oxford UP.

_____. (1985). *Greek Sculpture, the Classical Period: A Handbook*. London: Thames and Hudson.

_____. (1986). Greek Art and Architecture. In J. Boardman, J. Griffin, and O. Murray, (Eds.), *The Oxford History of the Classical World* (pp. 275-310). Oxford: Oxford UP.

_____. (1995). *Greek Sculpture: the Late Classical Period and Sculpture in Colonies and Overseas*. London: Thames and Hudson.

_____. (2001). *The History of Greek Vases*. London: Thames and Hudson.

Bremmer, J. (1980). An Enigmatic Indo-European Rite: Paederastry. *Arethusa, 13,* 279-98.

Brongersma, E. (1990). The Thera Inscriptions Ritual or Slander? *Journal of Homosexuality, 20*(4), 31-40

Bullough, V. (1980). *Sexual Variance in Society and History*. Chicago: U of Chicago P.

_____. (Ed.). (2002). *Before Stonewall: Activists for Gay and Lesbian Rights in Historical Context*. New York: Harrington Park Press.

Burg, B. R. (Ed.). (2002). *Gay Warriors: A Documentary History from the Ancient World to the Present*. New York: New York UP.

Cartledge, P. (1981). The Politics of Spartan Pederasty. *Proceedings of the Cambridge Philological Society*, n.s., *27*, 17-36. Repr. 2001 in *Spartan Reflections* (pp. 91-105). London: Duckworth.

_____. (1997). Review of the book *Pederasty and Pedagogy in Archaic Greece*, by William A. Percy. *International History Review, 19*, 887.

_____. (2002). *Sparta and Lakonia: A Regional History 1300-362 B.C.* (2nd ed.). London: Routledge. [1st ed. 1979].

Clarke, W. M. (1978). Achilles and Patroclus in Love. *Hermes, 106*, 381-396.

Crompton, Louis. (1985). *Byron and Greek Love: Homophobia in 19th Century England*. Berkeley: U of California P.

_____. (2003). *Homosexuality and Civilization*. Cambridge, MA: Belknap Press of Harvard University.

Davidson, J. (1997). *Courtesans and Fishcakes: The Consuming Passions of Classical Athens*. New York: St. Martin's Press.

_____. (2001). Dover, Foucault and Greek Homosexuality: Penetration and the Truth of Sex. *Past and Present, 170*, 3-51

Devereux, G. (1967). Greek Pseudo-homosexuality and the 'Greek Miracle.' *Symbolae Osloenses, 42*, 69-72.

Dover, K. J. (1978). *Greek Homosexuality*. Cambridge, MA: Harvard UP. Rev. Ed. 1989.

_____. (1988). Greek Homosexuality and Initiation. In K. J. Dover, (Ed.), *The Greeks and their Legacy: Collected Papers. Vol. II: Prose Literature, History, Society, Transmission, Influence* (115-134). Oxford: Blackwell.

_____. (1994). *Marginal Comment: A Memoir*. London: Duckworth.

_____. (1999). Review of the book *Pederasty and Pedagogy in Archaic Greece*, by William A. Percy, *Gnomon, 71*, 472-473.

Duberman, M. (1997). *Queer Representations: Reading Lives, Reading Cultures*. New York: New York UP.

Edmonds, J. M., (1928). *Lyrica Graeca. Vol. 1*. (Loeb Library, 2nd ed.). Cambridge, MA: Harvard UP. [1st ed. 1922].

Ferraro, Guglielmo. (1911). *The Women of the Cæsars*. New York: The Century Co.

Foucault, M. (1985). *The History of Sexuality: Volume 2. The Use of Pleasure*. (R. Hurley, Trans.). New York: Random House.

Freeman, C. F. (1999). *The Greek Achievement: The Foundation of the Western World*. New York: Penguin.

Golden, M. (1990). *Children and Childhood in Classical Athens*. Baltimore: Johns Hopkins UP.

Goldhill, S. (2002). The Erotic Experience of Looking. In Nussbaum and Sihvola (pp. 374-399).

Green, P. (1991). *Alexander of Macedon, 356-323 B.C.: A Historical Biography*. Berkeley: University of California Press. [Repr. of 1974 edition].

Greene, E., ed. (1996a). *Reading Sappho: Contemporary Approaches*. Berkeley: U of California P.

_____. (1996b). *Re-reading Sappho: Reception and Transmission*. Berkeley: U of California P.

Greenberg, D. (1988). *The Construction of Homosexuality*. Chicago: U of Chicago P.

Halperin, D. (1990). *One Hundred Years of Homosexuality and Other Essays on Greek Love*. New York: Routledge.

_____. (2002). The First Homosexuality. In Nussbaum and Sihvola (pp. 229-268).

Hawley, R. (1998). The Dynamics of Beauty in Classical Greece. In D. Montserrat, (Ed.), *Changing Bodies, Changing Meanings: Studies on the Human Body in Antiquity* (pp. 37-54). London: Routledge.

Hindley, C. (1994). *Eros* and Military Command in Xenophon. *Classical Quarterly*, n.s., *44*, 347-66.

_____. (1999). Xenophon on Male Love. *Classical Quarterly*, n.s., *49*, 74-99.

Hirschfeld M. (2000). *The Homosexuality of Men and Women*. (M. A. Lombardi-Nash, Trans.). Amherst, New York: Prometheus Books.

_____. (1997). Questions of Evidence. In Duberman (pp. 39-54).

Hornblower, S. and A. J. S. Spawforth. (Eds.). (1996). Epheboi. Entry in Hornblower and Spawforth (Eds.). *Oxford Classical Dictionary* (p. 527). Oxford: Oxford UP.

Hubbard, T. K. (1987). The 'Cooking' of Pelops: Pindar and the Process of Mythological Revisionism. *Helios, 14*, 3-21.

_____. (1998). Popular Perceptions of Elite Homosexuality in Classical Athens. *Arion*, ser. 3(6.1), 48-78.

_____. (Ed.). (2000a). *Greek Love Reconsidered*. New York: Wallace Hamilton Press.

_____. (2000b). "Pederasty and Democracy: The Marginalization of a Social Practice." In Hubbard 2000a (pp. 1-11).

_____. (2002). Pindar, Theoxenus, and the Homoerotic Eye. *Arethusa, 35*, 255-96.

_____. (Ed.). (2003a). *Homosexuality in Greece and Rome: A Sourcebook of Basic Documents*. Berkeley: U of California P.

_____. (2003b). Sex in the Gym: Athletic Trainers and Pedagogical Pederasty. *Intertexts, 7*(1), 1-26.

Hupperts, C. (2000). *Eros Dikaios: Vol. 1*. Dissertation, University of Amsterdam.

_____. (2002). *De macht van Eros: Lust liefde en moraal in Athene, met een nieuwe vertaling van Plato's* Symposion. Amsterdam.

Johnson, D. M. (2003). *Socrates and Alcibiades: Four Texts*. Newburyport, MA: Focus Publishing.

Keuls, E. C. (1985). *The Reign of the Phallus: Sexual Politics in Ancient Athens*. New York: Harper & Row.

Koehl, R. B. (1986). The Chieftain Cup and a Minoan Rite of Passage. *Journal of Hellenic Studies, 106*, 99-110.

Konstan, D. (2002). Women, Boys, and the Paradigm of Athenian Pederasty. *Differences, 13*(2), 35-56.

Kyle, D. G. (1984). Solon and Athletics. *Ancient World, 9*, 91-105.

Lefkowitz, M. (1981). *The Lives of the Greek Poets*. London: Duckworth.

Lefkowitz, M, and Rogers, G. (1996). *Black Athena Revisited*. Chapel Hill: U of North Carolina P.

Lauritsen, J. and Symonds, J. A. (Eds.). (1983). *Male Love: A Problem in Greek Ethics and Other Writings*. New York.

Leitao, D. (2002). The Legend of the Sacred Band. In Nussbaum and Sihvola (pp. 143-169).

Lelis, Arnold A., Percy, William A. and Verstraete, Beert C. (2003). *The Age of Marriage in Ancient Rome*. Lewiston, New York.

Licht, H. (2000). *Sexual Life in Ancient Greece*. London. [1st ed. 1931].

Lingiardi, V. (2002). *Men in Love: Male Homosexualities from Ganymede to Batman*. (R. H. Hopcke and P. A. Schwartz, Trans.). Chicago: Open Court.

Lord, A. B. (1960). *The Singer of Tales*. Cambridge, MA: Harvard UP.

Marrou, H. I. (1964). *A History of Education in Antiquity*. (G. Lamb, Trans.). New York: New American Library. [Repr. of 1956 edition].

McDonnell, M. (1991). The Introduction of Athletic Nudity: Thucydides, Plato, and the Vases. *Journal of Hellenic Studies, 111*, 182-193.

Meier, M. H. E. (1930). *Histoire de l'amour grec dans l'antiquité par M.-H.-E. Meier; augmenté d'un choix de documents origineaux et de plusieur dissertations complémentaires.* (L.-R. de Pogey-Castries, Ed.). Paris: Stendhal.

Monoson, S. S. (1994). Citizen as *Erastes*: Erotic Imagery and the Idea of Reciprocity in the Periclean Funeral Oration. *Political Theory, 22*, 253-76.

_____. (2000). The Allure of Harmodius and Aristogeiton. In Hubbard 2000a (pp. 42-51).

Most, G. W. (Ed.). (2002). *Disciplining Classics–Altertumswissenschaft als Beruf.* Göttingen: Vandenhoeck & Ruprecht.

Nussbaum, M. C. (2002). *Erōs* and Ethical Norms: Philosophers Respond to a Cultural Dilemma. In Nussbaum and Sihvola (pp. 55-94).

Nussbaum, M. C. and Sihvola, J. (Eds.). (2002). *The Sleep of Reason: Erotic Experience and Sexual Ethics in Ancient Greece and Rome.* Chicago: U of Chicago P.

Osborne, R. (1997). Men without Clothes: Heroic Nakedness and Greek Art. *Gender & History, 9*, 504-28.

Parker, H. N. (1996). Sappho Schoolmistress. In Greene 1996b (pp. 146-183).

Parry, M. (1971). *The Making of Homeric Verse: The Collected Papers of Milman Parry.* (A. Parry, Ed.). Oxford: Clarendon Press.

Patzer, H. (1982). *Die griechische Knabenliebe.* Wiesbaden: F. Steiner.

Percy, W. A., III. (1996). *Pederasty and Pedagogy in Archaic Greece.* Urbana: U of Illinois P.

Platthy, J. (1968). *Sources on the Earliest Greek Libraries with the Testimonia.* Amsterdam: Hakkert.

Podlecki, A. J. (1966). The Political Significance of the Athenian 'Tyrannicide'-Cult. *Historia, 15*, 129-41.

Pollini, J. (1998). The Warren Cup: Homoerotic Love and Symposial Rhetoric in Silver. *Art Bulletin, 81*, 21-52.

Pollitt, J. J. (1965). *The Art of Greece: 1400-31 B.C.* Englewood Cliffs, NJ: Prentice-Hall.

Pomeroy, Sarah. B., Stanley M. Burstein, Walter Donlan, and Jennifer Tolbert Roberts. (1999). *Ancient Greece: A Political, Social, and Cultural History.* New York and Oxford: Oxford UP.

Potts, A. (1994). *Flesh and the Ideal: Winckelmann and the Origins of Art History.* New Haven: Yale UP.

Powell, A. (2002). Dining Groups, Marriage, Homosexuality. In M. Whitby (Ed.), *Sparta* (90-103). Edinburgh: Edinburgh UP.

Puterbaugh, G. (2000). *The Crucifixion of Hyacinth: Jews, Christians, and Homosexuals from Classical Greece to Late Antiquity.* San Jose, CA: Authors Choice Press.

Reames-Zimmerman, J. (1999). An Atypical Affair? Alexander the Great, Hepaistion Amyntoros and the Nature of their Relationship. *Ancient History Bulletin, 13*, 81-96.

Richter, G. M. A. (1970). *Kouroi.* (3rd ed.). London: Phaidon.

Robinson, D. M. and Fluck, E. J. (1937). *A Study of Greek Love Names, Including a Discussion of Paederasty and Prosopographia.* Baltimore: Johns Hopkins Press.

Ridgeway, B. S. (1999). *Prayers in Stone: Greek Architectural Sculpture ca. 600-100 B.C.E.* Berkeley: U of California P.

Rind, B. (2001). Gay and Bisexual Adolescent Boys' Sexual Experiences with Men: An Empirical Examination of Psychological Correlates in a Non-clinical Sample. *Archives of Sexual Behavior, 30,* 345-368.

Scanlon, T. F. (2002). *Eros and Greek Athletics.* Oxford: Oxford UP.

Sealey, R. (1976). *A History of the Greek City States: 770-338 B.C.* Berkeley: U of California P.

Sergent, Bernard. (1986). *Homosexuality in Greek Myth.* (A. Goldhammer, Trans.). Boston: Beacon Press.

_____. (1987a). *L'homsexualité initiatique dans l'Europe ancienne.* Paris: Payot.

_____. (1987b). To the Origins of the Expansion of Homosexuality in Ancient Greek Society. *Homosexuality, Which Homosexuality? International Scientific Conference on Gay and Lesbian Studies. History, 2,* 89-93. Amsterdam: Free University of Amsterdam.

Shapiro, H. A. (1989). *Art and Cult under the Tyrants in Athens.* Mainz am Rhein: P. von Zabern.

_____. (2000). Laegros and Euphronios: Painting Pederasty in Athens. In Hubbard 2000a (pp. 12-32).

Sihvola, J. (2002). Aristotle on Sex and Love. In Nussbaum and Sihvola (pp. 200-221).

Stewart, A. F. (1990). *Greek Sculpture: An Exploration.* (2 vols.). New Haven: Yale UP.

_____. (1997). *Art, Desire, and the Body in Ancient Greece.* Cambridge: Cambridge UP.

Symonds, J. A. (1873). *A Problem in Greek Ethics.* Privately published, expanded and included as an appendix in H. Ellis & J. A. Symonds, (1897) *Sexual Inversion.* Repr. 1975. New York: Arno Press.

_____. (1928). *Studies in Sexual Inversion: Embodying: A study in Greek Ethics and A study in Modern Ethics.* Privately printed.

_____. (1971). *A Problem in Modern Ethics.* New York: B. Blom. [Repr. of 1896 edition].

Thornton, B. S. (1997). *Eros: The Myth of Ancient Greek Sexuality.* Boulder, Colo.: Westview Press.

Tripp, C. A. (1975). *The Homosexual Matrix.* New York: McGraw-Hill.

Verstraete, Beert. (in press). Review of the book *The Sleep of Reason*, by Nussbaum and Sihvola (Eds.). To be published in *Phoenix.*

Vickers, M. and D. Gill. (1994). *Artful Crafts: Ancient Greek Silverware and Pottery.* Oxford: Clarendon Press.

Whitley, J. (2001). *The Archaeology of Ancient Greece.* Cambridge: Cambridge UP.

Wilson, Emily. (2004, June 25). Why exactly do we look back? Review in *The Times Literary Supplement, 5282,* p. 6.

Winckelmann, J. J. (1849). *The History of Ancient Art.* (3 vols.). Boston.

The Dispersion of Pederasty
and the Athletic Revolution
in Sixth-Century BC Greece

Thomas F. Scanlon, PhD

University of California, Riverside

SUMMARY. Dorian Crete and Thebes are conventionally seen by ancient sources as the originators of pederasty; modern historians see support for this view in Dorian male-centered militarism and sexual segregation in upbringing. Here athletic culture, including training, nudism, and competition, is argued to be a chief 'trigger' for the emergence of pederasty in Sparta and its relatively rapid spread to other Greek states in the seventh to sixth centuries BC. Athletic nudity, in particular, was not a device to enforce civic egalitarianism, as some have argued, but is a persistently erotic incentive that reinforces hegemonic maleness and advertises the individual's virtuous exercise of restraint. In particular, Sparta is found to be the likely source of generalized athletic nudity combined with open pederasty in the early seventh century BC. Nudism in Greek art is erotically charged and not, as others argue, simply a gen-

Thomas F. Scanlon is Professor of Classics at the University of California, Riverside, and author of *Eros and Greek Athletics* (New York: Oxford University Press, 2002). Correspondence may be addressed: Department of Comparative Literature and Foreign Languages, 900 University Avenue, University of California, Riverside, CA 92521.

[Haworth co-indexing entry note]: "The Dispersion of Pederasty and the Athletic Revolution in Sixth-Century BC Greece." Scanlon, Thomas F. Co-published simultaneously in *Journal of Homosexuality* (Harrington Park Press, an imprint of The Haworth Press, Inc.) Vol. 49, No. 3/4, 2005, pp. 63-85; and: *Same-Sex Desire and Love in Greco-Roman Antiquity and in the Classical Tradition of the West* (ed: Beert C. Verstraete, and Vernon Provencal) Harrington Park Press, an imprint of The Haworth Press, Inc., 2005, pp. 63-85. Single or multiple copies of this article are available for a fee from The Haworth Document Delivery Service [1-800-HAWORTH, 9:00 a.m. - 5:00 p.m. (EST). E-mail address: docdelivery@haworthpress.com].

der marker in the seventh century. Generalized athletic nudity spread to other Greek states emulating the successful Spartan model by the 'athletic revolution' of the early sixth century. With athletic nudity, open pederasty, again following Sparta, was fostered. *[Article copies available for a fee from The Haworth Document Delivery Service: 1-800-HAWORTH. E-mail address: <docdelivery@haworthpress.com> Website: <http://www.HaworthPress. com> © 2005 by The Haworth Press, Inc. All rights reserved.]*

KEYWORDS. Athletics, Homer, initiation, nudity, Olympics, pederasty, Sparta, Thucydides

THE PEDERASTIC TRIGGER

I have recently discussed the question of the relation of pederasty to initiation and to athletics in early Greek culture (Scanlon, 2002, chap. 3). There I followed Dover in postulating that Greek overt homosexuality was not the remnant of an Indo-European ritual, but began in the seventh century BC and spread rapidly among Greek states (Dover, 1988, pp. 116-119). Dover argued that there is no literary evidence for overt homosexuality prior to the seventh century BC and its absence in Homer and elsewhere is unexplained by theories that are based mainly on myth or very ambiguous archeological testimony.

The "rapid spread" of pederasty gives rise to other questions: Was the practice simultaneously and broadly adopted, or was it diffused from one or more centers? Did pederasty adopt similar forms in different cities, suggesting a single cultural source? Can likely catalysts for the public generalization and/or dispersion of the custom be identified? To these complex questions, the limitations of the sources will not allow absolute certainty in the answers. Art, literature, and archeological sources all have their limits. This essay, however, seeks to establish the strong likelihood that Greek athletic contests and training centers were among the most crucial catalysts for a remarkable phenomenon in human sexual history.

In Greece prior to the eighth century BC there is no clear evidence that same-sex relations among men and boys were openly practiced. That these relations were not yet 'out of the closet' is suggested by their absence in art and literature or their euphemistic treatment as with Achilles and Patroclus, in Homeric texts (Scanlon, 2002, pp. 67-72; Dover, 1988, pp. 116-119; Percy, 1996, pp. 38-40). The Achilles and

Patroclus story is more easily understood as a legend that paved the way for generalized pederasty in the seventh century than a reflection of its open practice in the eighth.

At some point between the eighth century and the mid-seventh, by general scholarly consensus, openly pederastic institutions appear among the Dorian regions, notably Crete and Sparta, but also in non-Dorian Thebes, then by the late seventh century and into the sixth century they are copied by other states (Dover, 1989, pp. 185-196; Percy, 1996, pp. 58-92). Dorian origins are conventionally ascribed to the militaristic orientation of those states, the leveling of citizen status in subordination to the state, and the disestablishment of conventional nuclear family structures in favor of communal groups (*agelai* or "herds") (Dover, 1989, pp. 192-193). In Thebes, though the social structures of the eighth century seem to have been less generally regimented than those in Sparta and Crete, there did emerge the strong tradition of a city friendly to male homoeroticism. Thebes was the home of the legendary King Laius, who introduced homosexuality to that city, the place where the 'lawgivers' after Laius fostered Eros as part of the education in the palaestra (according to Plutarch *Pelop.* 19.1-2 [287-288]), and the place where a "Sacred Battalion" of homosexual lovers was formed. Equally noteworthy for Thebes is the conjunction of pederasty, athletic *paideia*, and a hero's tomb all combined in the legend of Diocles and Philolaus, as explained by Aristotle:

> Philolaus of Corinth became a lawgiver for the Thebans. Philolaus was of the family of the Bacchidae, and became the lover of Diocles, the Olympic victor [in the stade race in 728]. When Diocles, disgusted at the lust of his mother Alcyone, left Corinth, he went to Thebes, and there both of them lived out their lives. Even now people point out their tombs, which are easily in view of one another, but one is open to view in the direction of Corinth, the other is not. (Aristotle, *Politics* 2.9.6 [1274a]; translations are by the author unless otherwise indicated)

There is likely a historical core to this story since Diocles is elsewhere attested as an Olympic victor and Philolaus is an honored lawgiver. The importance of Thebes is that it links athletics and open pederasty, at least for a restricted elite, in the eighth century, but we also note that it does not attest generalized pederasty in the city nor is there any tradition of athletic nudity beginning in Thebes. It appears that pederasty is starting to become an open practice, but the catalyst of common nudity has not yet appeared.

It is a cliché among authors of the Classical period that homosexuality was more acceptable in Sparta and Crete than elsewhere. This is essentially the Platonic model found most explicitly in *Laws*. There the Spartan and Cretan colleagues brag of the moderation afforded by their common messes and athletic training, and the Athenian responds:

> Gymnasia and *syssitia* on the one hand benefit states in many other ways, but are injurious in promoting civil strife (as shown by the cases of the youth of Miletus, Boeotia, and Thurii). Moreover this custom, which is long-standing, seems to have corrupted the lifestyle and pleasures of sex that are natural not only for humans but also animals. Someone might make these accusations first of your states and of whatever other states are particularly inclined to the gymnasium. (636ab; Dover, 1989, p. 186)

Not long after Plato, the historian Timaeus (F144) also posited that the Cretans invented pederasty. These lone testimonia of fourth century authors themselves critical of the practice are not compelling proof that this view was commonly shared. There is particularly strong evidence that pederasty was widely acceptable in Classical Greece beyond the Dorians. Plato's Athenian states an antihomosexual bias that is out of step with his fellow citizens. But the implication that pederasty spread from the Dorian states is worth closer examination. First, it is an *a priori* plausibility that sexually segregated camps of male citizens would seek same-sex relations, and secondly, the Dorian promulgation of athletic nudity, as argued below, fostered pederastic liaisons.

As Dover observed, "a very slight shift in one social variable can trigger major and lasting changes, and, once social approval has been given to an activity which is physically, emotionally and aesthetically gratifying *to the adult males* of a society, it is not easily suppressed" (Dover, 1988, pp. 131-132, original emphasis). Of course origins are complicated and notoriously difficult to discern for Greek social customs ascribed to the Archaic Period. Here our focus is on one likely "trigger" for the dispersion of pederasty, namely the simultaneous appearance of athletic nudity at Sparta, and its adoption widely by the rest of the Greeks soon after Sparta saw great success at the Olympic Games. This is not to say that there were not other cultural catalysts to bring about broad social approval in a short period of time. But athletic nudity is arguably a major factor in this social movement.

The question of how, when and why athletic nudity was adopted by the Greeks has recently provoked a great deal of scholarly interest (e.g., Ludwig, 2002, pp. 261-318; bibliography in Scanlon, 2002, p. 405 n. 27). The 'whys' have been inventive and ingenious. Some cite origins and motivation from rites of initiation, others from military practice, from hunting conventions, or from attempts to enforce civic egalitarianism. Most of these may have played some role in the process and some will be noted in passing, but central to the question why is, I believe, the use of nudity to manipulate erotic response generally (Ludwig, 2002, pp. 261-318), and homoerotic in particular. My erotic etiology seeks to locate the 'how' and 'when' of this move more precisely in seventh century Sparta, and seeks better to explain why this convention spread so rapidly and successfully because of its fortunate point of origin.

INITIATION AND ATHLETIC NUDITY

The most easily disputable motive for adopting athletic nudity is that of primitive Indo-European initiation rites. I have elsewhere argued at length against the attempts, mainly of Brelich and Jeanmaire to connect athletics and pederasty with primitive initiation (Scanlon, 2002, chap. 3; Jeanmaire, 1939; Brelich, 1962; 1969). For similar reasons I find the connection of nudity with such rites equally improbable. One reason is that formal resemblances like age grouping, separation from society, and special clothing are not in themselves cogent proof of the phenomena being related in prehistoric periods. Many salient aspects of athletics, nudity and age-groupings, for example, were in fact begun in historical periods. This argues against their arising out of initiation rites without some complicated theory of the practices being re-instituted for obscure reasons. Another reason to question the primitive origins of athletic nudity is that standard Greek gymnic (track and field and combat sports) and hippic contests did not figure in known rites of passage, for example as part of the tests of strength. Thirdly, no standard athletic event is typically incorporated into Greek intiatory ritual. Apart from occasional footraces, such rites are usually marked with special rules or paraphernalia such as items carried by runners. At Sparta, for instance, one finds the cheese-stealing or whipping contests, likely instituted first in the Hellenistic period, the Platanistas contest with its virtual battle (again Hellenistic in origin), and the choral performances of the Gymnopaidiai (early 7th c. BC). Finally, nudity is not characteristic of most or even many initiation contests, though it is in a few of them, including the Gymnopaidiai. Just as often initiation rites are marked by the wearing of special clothing. For these reasons, the connection of nudity and athletics to primitive initiation is, in my view, unlikely.

CIVIC OR MILITARY EGALITARIANISM AND NUDITY

One may argue, alternatively, that athletic nudity at Sparta and later in other states was a device to erase the status marker of clothing between elite and non-elite male warrior citizens (Miller, 2000, pp. 277-296). The elite warrior-athlete's wearing of the *perizōma, diazōma,* or loincloth, described by Homer in *Iliad* 23, or simply the hitched-up garments of servants boxing in Odyssey 18, preceded nudity. The *perizō*ma itself was not an elite marker; there is no evidence of plainer and fancier loin-cloths by which status could be claimed. So the very inclusion of non-elite with elite in actual contests of the eighth century, before gen-eralized nudity, was a measure to level status. Nudity need not be adopted to make that point.

Homers' athletics, to be examined more closely below, reflect the do-main of the elite in the eighth century. Like most cultural phenomena, athletics was co-opted by its practitioners and imbued with an inherent significance by the elite in power; in this case, athletic prowess was taken as evidence of a general "manly excellence" (*aretē*). With the rise of the polis and the advent of politically egalitarian institutions, the democratic aspects of sport were touted by the ruling citizenry, and dis-dained by critics of democracy such as 'Pseudo-Xenophon,' the anony-mous fifth century author of the so-called *Constitution of the Athenians,* and by Alcibiades, the famous fifth-century Athenian politician (Pseudo-Xenophon, *Constitution of the Athenians* 1.13; Isocrates, *On the Two-horse Chariot* 33). Nudity is, I maintain, politically epipheno-menal and can take on whatever political significance those holding po-litical power choose to give it.

One case requires closer attention. Sparta's system of upbringing, the *agōgē,* emerged at some point in the seventh century BC, by Cartledge's dating (Cartledge, 2001, pp. 21-38), perhaps within the first half of that century when the major political changes were also instituted. Sexual segregation was, by the fifth century at least, a fixed part of that institu-tion. The *agōgē* likely fostered both male and female pederasty and hence made athletic nudity an acceptable and attractive custom. Tyrtaeus' poem of mid-seventh century Sparta (fragment 9; Lattimore,

1960, pp. 14-15) praises martial prowess above the athletic, alluding to Sparta's significant athletic culture by that period. If Spartan athletic nudity and pederasty can be dated to the early seventh century, this would seem to be the earliest generalized appearance of both these practices in Greece. The arguments for the early dating of athletic nudity will be addressed below. But it is not clear that Sparta's main or only motive for the adoption of this custom was to promote homogeneity among civic factions.

Most telling against the warrior-homogeneity thesis is the fact that Spartan girls also adopted nudity. Was that also to erase elite/non-elite social barriers? The girls were certainly not part of the hoplite group, but erotic motivation was apparently there, Plutarch's *Lycurgus* 14.2-15.1 explains, and doubtless homosocial bonding too, as evident in Alcman's *Parthenion* (Scanlon, 2002, pp. 121-38, 220). The homoerotic imagery in Alcman's poem (second half of seventh century BC) describes choruses of Spartan girls and women whose social organization may have mirrored that of the boys and men. Also against this thesis is the fact that Sparta backed equestrian competition, and allowed charioteers to remain clothed in competition. Why not cease participation in the non-egalitarian hippic events if there was a sincere movement to homogenize through dress or athletics?

So the significance of athletic nudity at Sparta, as the most likely innovator of the custom, needs to be sought in other areas of social expression like the valuation of health, eroticism, and gender. Perhaps demonstration of machismo in line with the overall warrior culture, advertisement of fitness in the pervasive body culture, simplicity of lifestyle (as also in diet, etc.), avoidance of needless shame, and promotion of sexual attraction for eugenic aims played a role. Quite probably all such motives collectively led to the adoption of nudity in Spartan gymnic sports, and no single motive dominated.

Since the political egalitarianism argument is related to that of military cohesion of fighting units, we should here address also the conventional assumption that athletic contests and the gymnasia originated or blossomed at an early stage as a form of military training. Christian Mann has argued convincingly that athletics was not thought to constitute useful training in the Archaic of Classical Greek periods (Mann, 1998, pp. 7-21). Homeric contests are loosely organized and of an ad hoc nature. Tyrtaeus (fragment 9; Lattimore, 1960, pp. 14-15) and Herodotus (7.208-9), writing respectively in the mid-seventh and late fifth centuries BC, both see athletics as a sphere of activity separate from military training in Sparta. Literature and visual arts indicate that the practice of associating athletics with military training occurs in the fourth century BC. Hence it is unlikely that nudity was introduced to encourage toughness and uniformity among soldiers of the city-state.

THE GENEALOGY OF ATHLETIC NUDITY

Given the controversial genealogy, we must begin with a brief survey of the artistic and literary evidence on the origins of athletic nudity. Poliakoff (1987, p. 32) and Decker and Herb (1994) both chronicle a few nude wrestlers in the early Egyptian art of 3000 and 2400 BC, but most wrestlers and other Egyptian athletes wore belts or loincloths, as did, to my knowledge, almost all Near Eastern athletes in images from the Bronze Age (Rollinger, 1994). Mouratidis (1985) cites images of seemingly naked athletes on Bronze Age vases from Cyprus (Enkomi), ca. 1300 BC, yet one (fig. 6) may show a workman, not an athlete, with a pick; others (figs. 7 and 10) may shows boxing contests, but none shows genitalia and their schematic style does not allow a conclusion on the absence or presence of trunks.

In the eighth century, as mentioned earlier, athletes were clothed and sports was primarily the domain of the elite, notably as reflected in Homer's *Iliad* 23, the funeral games in honor of Patroclus, where the boxers and wrestlers wore loincloths (*diazōmata*). Here we acknowledge the problem of the historicity of the Homeric account, and indeed the Homeric question of when the athletic passages were composed in the form we now have them. For the present purposes, we accept that the depictions of Homeric athletics, in particular *Iliad* 23, are probably authentic descriptions of the norm with regards to costumes for competition in the eighth century BC, the earliest recension of the epics. Homer himself never mentions the nudity of any athlete. Hesiod's fragment 74 in scholia to Iliad 23.683 (West, 1966), composed about 700 BC, refers to Hippomenes as "naked" (*gumnos*), though the isolated reference to a very unusual bride-contest makes this a less reliable reflection of contemporary convention than Homer's testimony on the topic. The geometric figures on eighth-century vases do, in some instances, clearly depict silhouetted nude images of male athletes with genitals (Scanlon, 2002, pp. 302-303 fig. 9-2; Legakis, 1977, p. 33 no. 1, p. 127, nos. 1-7, p. 189 nos. 1-2; Fittschen, 1969, p. 28 nn. 99-103, pp. 29-30 nos. F1-F5). Scholars have argued that these are likely artistic shorthand for demarcating males from females in the sketchy figures (Stewart

1997, pp. 27-42; Osborne 1997; Osborne 1998). Though this may be generally true, we will see shortly how some ancient sources place the first naked Olympic athlete in the fourteenth or fifteenth Olympiads (724-720 BC). Thus the gender-marking convention in art may also reflect an actual incipient or occasional nudity not yet generalized in eighth century practice.

When we move from eighth to seventh century artistic evidence, we find an interesting blossoming of public images of nudity in statues and athletic vases beginning in the mid- to late-seventh century, with a real profusion in the early to mid-sixth century. The artistic 'shorthand' of the male nude ends, I believe, with the (late) geometric vases of about 700 BC. Here I depart from the views of Stewart and Osborne who see the gender marking of nudity in art as enduring into the sixth century. More realistic images of the seventh century more easily show and realistically portray clothing and nudity. In this period, the earliest unambiguous Greek representation of nude athletes is found on a bronze relief of two boxers and a tripod prize dated to ca. 650 BC, followed by nude wrestlers shown on the Protoattic Cynosarges amphora (ca. 640 BC) (Legakis, 1977, pp. 189, 449 fig. 55; McDonnell, 1991, p. 184). There are nude runners on some Corinthian vases of ca. 625-600 BC (McDonnell, 1991, p. 184). Wrestlers are shown on a bronze shield band from Olympia dated 600-575 (Legakis, 1977, p. 189; Laser, 1987, T 54 fig. 169). Late Corinthian vases (575-550 BC) and a Boeotian tripod-kothon (570-560 BC) show nude wrestlers (McDonnell, 1991, p. 184; Legakis, 1977, p. 189). Thereafter, nude male athletes are fairly commonly the subjects of vases from the mid-sixth century onwards (Goosens & Thielemans, 1996; Miller, 2000, p. 284).

In sculpture, the nudity of *kouroi*, muscular male youths, produced mainly from 650-600 and the nudity of small unclothed male bronzes and Geometric vase figures in the eighth to seventh centuries has been argued to stand merely for gender differentiation, without erotic significance. Leaving aside from the vexed question of whether the *kouroi* and early bronzes represent human or divine figures, we ask here whether the proliferation of representations of male nudity reflected a simultaneous spread of athletic nudity and/or pederasty. The vases cited above evidence the simultaneous first appearance of nude athletes in graphic art and the proliferation of *kouroi*. Might a few pioneers in naked competitive costume have inspired *kouroi*? Bonfante (1998) and others suggest that some *kouroi* may represent athletes in the seventh century. At the very least, we can posit a greater willingness by artists and patrons to present idealized male nude portraits and the growing acceptance of the convention argues for athletic nudity beginning to be more generally practiced in this era.

But is the athletic and artistic nudity also evidence of pederasty or eroticism at this time? Only in the sixth century, some say, did nudity become individualized and eroticized (Osborne, 1997; 1998a; 1998b; Stewart, 1997). Another scholar has recently argued the reverse, namely that generalized nudity was introduced in athletics, and importantly also at the symposia of the elite, as a device for dampening erotic desire. Nudity removes the covering that only heightens eroticism by leaving more to the imagination and removing the subject-object hierarchy between observer and observed (Ludwig, 2002, pp. 277-317). Hence Plato endorsed this ideal of leveling citizens by extending nudity even to women in the education of the ideal state (*Republic* 5). Plato's ideal is, of course, not the reality. Against both views, one saying that nudity only became erotic late and the other that nudity dampened the erotic, it is more likely that in practice eroticism is never wholly absent from the nude figure, whether in art or in athletics and whether wholly or only partly naked. And so the emergence of the nude male in art and athletics in the course of the seventh century to common adoption in the early sixth is marked throughout by erotic appeal and the fostering of pederastic eroticism among Greek citizen males.

Without digressing to a broader theoretical discussion on nudity and desire that space does not permit, I will only state my assumption here that erotic response to the naked body may be sublimated or repressed, and the degree of the erotic affect varies with each individual. But in general a naked figure presents a high potential for erotic response, and it simultaneously invokes gendered values such as machismo, potency or fertility. Erotic and gendered responses are frequently combined, and are not, I argue, absent from even the earliest Greek nude images prior to the sixth century. One early city notable in the history of athletic nudity is Megara, the polis between Athens and Corinth, home of the reputed eighth century originator of Olympic nudity, Orsippus, discussed further below. Also native to Megara was the poet Theognis to whom have been attributed the following verses (*Theognidea* 1335-36), possibly written in the early to mid-sixth or even the late seventh century BC, and, if so, the earliest explicit text associating eros with athletics:

Happy is the lover who after practicing naked athletic exercise goes home to sleep all day long with a beautiful young man.

The verb *gumnazetai*, "practice gymnic competition," evidences that those athletes were "naked" (*gumnos*) by the author's day. If authentic, the lines support seeing eroticization as simultaneous with the earliest nude athletes on vase. Apart from Theognis' lines and generally sensual poems, and the story of Orsippus, Megara disappears from our present story, but it is noteworthy that in the seventh century the city operated with good relations toward the Dorian communities of the Peloponnese and may have been culturally attracted to imitate Spartan athletic practices (Hammond, 1989,[3] p. 150). But it is impossible to pinpoint when and where the Greek male nude, athletic and otherwise, became eroticized, and safer to assume that it always was to some degree. The more important observation so far is that a critical mass of evidence indicates that athletic nudity and artistic male nudity were adopted at the same general time as the emergence of pederasty, namely in the first or possibly the second half of the seventh century.

THE INTRODUCTION OF ATHLETIC NUDITY AT OLYMPIA

As noted above, several ancient testimonies, mostly late, say that athletic nudity was first introduced at Olympia either in the late eighth century or mid-seventh century, variously as the fourteenth (724 BC), fifteenth (720 BC) or thirty-second (652 BC) Olympiad (McDonnell, 1991, p. 183 note 2; Sweet, 1987, pp. 124-127; Mouratidis, 1985; Crowther, 1982; Scanlon, 2002, pp. 77-83, 220, 325-326). Orsippus of Megara (or Sparta) was most frequently said to be "first of all the Greeks to be crowned victor naked" and won in the stade race in 720 BC. An inscription so attesting from the mid or late Roman Empire is written in a verse text possibly originally written by Semonides (seventh-sixth century BC) (Sweet, 1987, p. 125; Pausanias 1.44.1). Sextus Julius Africanus, in his *List of Olympic Victors*, under the entry for the fifteenth Olympiad, says

> In the Fifteenth Olympiad [720 BC] Orsippus of Megara won the stade. The long-distance footrace (*dolichos*) was added and they ran naked; Acanthus of Sparta won.

Acanthus of Sparta is also noted by Dionysius of Halicarnassus, *Roman Antiquities* (7.72.2), writing in the first century BC describing a religious procession with athletes in Rome:

. . . the competitors for the light and heavy events came naked for the rest of their bodies but with their genitals covered. This custom can be seen still in my time in Rome, just as it had been originally by the Greeks. It is now ended in Greece, and the Spartans ended it. The person who first removed his clothing and ran naked was Acanthus, a Spartan, in the fifteenth Olympics. Before that time all the Greeks considered it shameful to appear in games with their bodies entirely naked, as Homer testifies, the oldest and most trustworthy authority, when he presents his heroes wearing loin-cloths. (Trans. Sweet, 1987, p. 127).

It is not clear how the introduction of nudity to Olympic events relates to a more generalized athletic nudity throughout Greece. Did Olympic practice inspire Spartan? Or did athletic nudity become more common at Olympia in imitation of the broad institution of it at Sparta? A statement by the fifth-century historian Thucydides regarding the assumption of nudity "not many years" before his time (1.6.5) has puzzled modern scholars. In an attempt to reconcile conflicting literary and artistic evidence, modern theories have posited various complex and unconvincing scenarios wherein nudity had been begun in the eighth or seventh centuries, was then later dropped, and picked up again in the early fifth century, about the time of the Persian Wars (McDonnell, 1991, pp. 184-186). The only advantage to such hypothesizing is that it allows for Thucydides' statement to be reconciled with literary and artistic evidence of earlier athletic nudity.

If there was nudity at Olympia in 720 BC and there was not some prehistoric initiation behind it, as seems correct to me, then nudity must have been an option from 720 onward but not one followed widely until after Sparta had become identified with it. The Olympic introduction of the custom can be reconciled with the post-650 development of civic nudity in the Spartan *agōgē* by assuming that the late eighth century date marks the simple first examples of athletic nudity in competition, while the seventh century date marks its generalization at Sparta. The fact that all the traditions of Acanthus and some of those about Orsippus name the innovators as Spartan indicates that ancients would find a Spartan origin at least plausible. Nudity at Olympia, then, seems to have emerged as an option in athletic style from 720 BC. But it was an option not followed widely until after Sparta had developed it.

THUCYDIDES ON THE ORIGINS OF ATHLETIC NUDITY

The evidence of the historian Thucydides on the origin of athletic nudity, mentioned above, is particularly important since he is the earliest direct source on the question in a passage written in the last third of the fifth century BC (following the standard paragraph numbering of this text):

> 2. Those parts of Hellas that still live in this way are an indication of what was also the former way of life for all alike. 3. The Athenians were the first to put aside weapons and make their lives more sumptuous as well as more relaxed, and the elder of their rich men not long ago gave up the indulgence of wearing linen tunics and tying their hair up in a knot fastened with golden grasshoppers; by which custom this same fashion lasted for a long time among the Ionian elders. 4. By contrast it was the Lacedaemonians who first adopted a simple mode of dress in the present style, and in general their wealthier men began to live in a style very nearly on a par (*isodaitoi*) with most people. 5. They were the first both to strip naked, and undressing publicly to anoint themselves with oil while exercising. But formerly (*to palai*) even in the Olympic contest gathering athletes contested wearing loincloths (*diazōmata*) around their genitals and this ended not many years ago. Even now there are some barbarians, especially the Asians, who hold boxing and wrestling contests and do it wearing loincloths. 6. And there are many other ways in which someone might show that early Hellenic lifestyle was similar to that of contemporary barbarians. (Thucydides, *The Peloponnesian War* 1.6.2-6, adapted from Lattimore (1998) and Hornblower (1997))

Thucydides' statements are characteristically pithy and require exegesis. The main point is the juxtaposition of the luxurious lifestyle of early Athenians with Spartan simplicity. Paragraph 3 talks of earlier Athenian men's linen tunics, long hair, and fancy gold hairpins, all now abandoned. Paragraph 4 in contrast discusses the communalization of clothing and lifestyle among the wealthy and non-wealthy Spartans. Paragraph 5 adds the points about public nudity and application of oil during exercise. Certainly this emphasizes the additional communal elements of a non-luxurious lifestyle and overcoming the shame of the body by Spartans generally. But it focuses on Sparta, seen as the earliest model of a simplicity now common to all cities contrasted with Athens, indulging its luxurious habits at an earlier stage and in a way no longer common among Greeks. Paragraph 5 further says that some barbarians still do box and wrestle with loincloths, echoing the opening points of 6.1-2 which argue that isolated, contemporary habits can evidence what had been done in the past.

So to the luxury-simplicity contrast are added the ones of Athenian-Spartan and Greek-barbarian lifestyles. Nudity is central and common to these contrasts, but arguably makes points that can overlap and extend the contrasts. As said above, athletic nudity can have many motivations, notably pride in manliness and lack of the prudish shame to hide genitals that characterizes non-Greeks. Civic egalitarianism is a clearer motivation in daily dress, such as the lack of linens or jewelry of paragraph 4, but status is not evident in the wearing of a *diazōma*. So the removal of even a *diazōma* and the adoption of nudity are issues touching rather on shame, the encouragement of beauty, a positive assertion of male identity, and a conventional simplicity in lifestyle than on the erasure of civic status.

Thucydides is not primarily making a link between nudity and economics or anti-elitism. The sentence that begins section 1.6.5 comments on the Spartan origin of both nudity and anointing oneself with oil during exercise. Both practices are given equal weight in the sentence and the anointing with oil is not a measure to demonstrate frugality and absence of adornment. Indeed, the provision of oil for gymnasia was the major expense in gymnasia and required great public or private subsidies. The oil on a gleaming, tanned, healthy body was in itself a literally 'flashy' adornment. Thucydides' point is that the Spartans led the way in what had by his day become the widespread practices among all athletes, practices that incidentally reinforce the devotion to exercise and display of strength associated with that state.

It is also important to note the historian's distinction between nudity in exercise and in competition. The Spartan innovations of stripping naked and anointing occurred specifically "while exercising" (*meta tou gymnazesthai*) and not during festival competition. The Spartan tradition of systematic education of their youths in the *agōgē* provided the opportunity for the innovation of nudity. This *agōgē* system, as mentioned above, likely formed gradually during the first half of the seventh century (Cartledge, 2001, p. 101). The Gymnopaidiai festival, founded traditionally in 668 BC or possibly earlier, suggests that the Spartan cult of the naked male body was celebrated publicly at this early date (Cartledge, 2001, p. 102; Pettersson, 1992; Robertson, 1992, pp. 164-165). The festival origin corresponds to the period in which pederasty may have appeared openly as part of the *agōgē* system not long after 700. The marked presence of nudity (*gymno-*) in the name of the festival suggests that nudity was not the usual state of dress for dance in this period, and it may indicate that an athletic nudity, imitated in the dance, was part of the Spartan regimen by the early seventh century. Thus the Gymnopaidiai dating appears to support a seventh century chronology for the beginning of generalized nudity in athletics at Sparta at the same time as the beginnings of open pederasty.

Athletic nudity was from the start a style, not apparently a strict religious or initiatory ritual at Sparta. The style liberated and eroticized athletes, but we cannot claim that it was particularly a badge of citizen unity. Throughout Greece, the hoplite movement in the last part of the seventh century brought more citizens into the central activity of the state, and the opening up of pederasty in the same period lent further cohesion to the citizen nexus. Greek gymnic events, track, field, and combat sport athletics themselves, and not simply athletic nudity, were the primary media of social equalization that attracted participants in city states gradually all over Greece. Sparta, the dynasty of the Olympics during this period, innovated its naked style that became identified with their winning ways and was imitated by Spartan athletic rivals. Nudity was probably adopted in a manner analogous to other elements of athletic 'style,' for instance male "infibulation," *kunodesmē*, a tying up of the foreskin of the penis, evident in the images of athletes (and symposiasts) on vases from about 510 to 460 BC. The infibulation fad, presumably at its height during the period it appears on vases, occurs at the same period as the greatest production of vases with athletic themes, to be discussed shortly below. The visual display of eros in athletic images was at its peak in the first half of the fifth century. Infibulation was both an overt public display of modesty that simultaneously calls attention to the genitals as an erotic object and as an overt sign of masculine prowess (Osborne, 1998, p. 91). Infibulation was not, so far as we know, a Spartan innovation in athletic style, but it was a practice that took athletic nudity one step further toward heightened eroticism in the period after nudity had been widely adopted in Greece. Another element of athletic style adopted over time and highlighting the erotic body was oiling the skin, not found in Homeric sports but in use possibly simultaneously with the adoption of nudity. Athletes' oiling up may be derived from Spartan practice, but in any case was in general use at least by the time of Solon (early sixth century) (Jüthner & Brein, 1965, pp. 14-15; Aeschines, 1.138). The non-erotically motivated custom of jumping with weights seems to have sprung up after 570, if its absence on vases before then is any indication (Legakis, 1977, pp. 281-295). Like these and other non-political aspects of style that became fixed to athletic practice, at some point between the late seventh and early sixth centuries athletic nudity seems to have been widely and quickly adopted by cities throughout the Greek world, if we can deduce this mainly from its common appearance on vases after 570 BC.

Spartan nudity began and was fostered during physical training at first on an open-air "track" (*dromos*), and later in gymnasia (Delorme, 1960, pp. 72-74; Mann, 1998, pp. 8-9). It may well be that there was no actual gymnasium structure before the late sixth or early fifth centuries BC, and in the seventh and sixth centuries the open-filed track area served both as a training and competition ground (Glass, 2002). Competition in public festivals is not identifiably the place which gave rise to nudity in athletics; more probably the training ground is the logical source whence the nudity and oil-anointing was first established at Spartan and then spread to actual festival contests in other states. So Thucydides' passage 1.6.5 discusses the adoption of nudity outside of Sparta. The context shifts from Spartan training to Olympia and to the "gathering for a contest" (*agōn*) held there (Scanlon, 1983). The Spartan custom of nudity has spread from exercise and from the Spartan track. The word "even" is noteworthy in Thucydides' statement that "formerly even at the Olympic contest gathering athletes competed wearing loincloths." The Olympic festival was hugely famous in Thucydides' day for being the first great panhellenic festival, a model to other festivals and one which itself was reluctant to adopt innovations. The historian's readers might be surprised to hear that the custom of nudity had not been there from the start, or even originated there. Thucydides' ambiguous "formerly" (*to palai*) has frustrated modern scholars wanting to pin a date to the introduction of nudity at Olympia. Although the phrase "formerly" (*to palai*) is not precise, it is used in another passage of Thucydides describing a social practice in Athens before the tyrants, ca. 560 BC (2.15.5). It occurs elsewhere in his reference to the Bronze Age period in Minoan Greece (1.5.1) and in the Peloponnese (1.13.5). It alludes to a vague, distant antiquity in 1.45.3, and in a discussion of the holding of the Delian Games in legendary antiquity (3.104.3, 6). Finally *to palai* alludes to the period of the legendary Dorian Invasion in the eleventh century BC. Only once does the phrase refer to a contemporary person who had been maintaining something "for a long time" (8.94.1). So in the great majority of references, *to palai* refers to the distant past, centuries prior to the author's time, and it is entirely possible that in 1.6.5 it refers to the earliest days of the Olympic Games, perhaps in the eighth century and into the seventh century.

The real problem of chronology is the assertion in Thucydides 1.6.5 that the custom of wearing loincloths "ended not many years ago," and the apparent contradiction between that statement and the proliferation of athletic nudity on almost all Greek vases from the mid-sixth century onwards. McDonnell has the most reasonable explanation of what Thucydides might be up to in this context, namely down-dating nudity to bolster his own schema of progress (McDonnell, 1991, p. 190). This is the only explanation that makes sense in the face of huge numbers of vases depicting nude athletes, and no likely Greek images of athletes with loincloths. The historian has digressed to make a point about cultural progress, luxury and simplicity paralleling Athenian and Sparta or barbarian and Greek habits in dress as they do in other, larger issues of state character. His readers, he may have reasoned, will not hold him to precise dating on clothing styles since these are peripheral to the bigger picture, and Thucydides himself blurs the issue by not giving any precise time referent like "since the Persian Wars" or similar. He therefore can deny strict inaccuracy. Finally it may be that the phrase "even at Olympia" alludes to the notorious conservatism of that site, where contests were added or subtracted more slowly than elsewhere and where rules seem to have been stricter, for example, prohibiting women from attending the Olympics on penalty of death. Might it be that Olympia welcomed competitors still in loincloths long after they had been abandoned at other contests? Perhaps a few conservative athletes kept to the old style into the fifth century and it was only then that athletic nudity was universally and at last adopted. This is a possibility, but still less convincing than MacDonnell's claim of historical distortion to make a point. If some odd athletes have still clung to their loincloths into the early fifth century, we would expect to see scenes with mixed naked and non-naked athletes on the vases. In any case, we note that Thucydides restricts his claim of when nudity was used in competition to Olympia, which allows that nudity could have been proliferated earlier at the many festivals apart from Olympia, including the Panathenaia and the other three panhellenic festivals.

NUDITY, PEDERASTY, AND THE SIXTH CENTURY ATHLETIC REVOLUTION

We now turn to the questions of how and why athletic nudity spread from Sparta. How was it adopted at a time in the eighth and seventh centuries when it was not widespread at Olympia and presumably other Panhellenic festivals? And how was the dispersion of nudity conducive to generalized pederasty? Simple social egalitarianism is no more a convincing motive for the dispersion of civic nudity than for its origin. Of course the political reforms and egalitarian political forms gradually spread over Greek states from ca. 600 to 500 BC, notably in Athens from Solon to Cleisthenes, at the same time that vases first clearly show nude athletes. Yet, as said above, even loincloth-garbed athletes can be seen as egalitarian and nudity is not primarily a marker of equality, but of eroticism and of a "masculineness of restraint" (Ludwig, 2002, p. 294). Nudity in contests, in gymnasia, and at symposia accompanies the rise of the polis. Operating in the erotic sphere, civic nudity makes two contradictory or complementary statements. Eros can be controlled and moderated despite the public display of nudity by restraining oneself from arousal, by not ogling others, and of course by not indulging promiscuously in sex. In effect naked athletes proclaim "we are civilized beings, not satyrs." Simultaneously erotic desire and self-indulgence are in fact fostered by the public display of the naked male body in contests and gymnasia, as many ancient sources attest (Scanlon, 2002, pp. 198-273). But by both views of how civic nudity operated, such nakedness is an issue centered on attitudes to the erotic. Generalized athletic nudity was, then, a sexualized phenomenon and a necessary or essential condition for the generalization and long-term establishment of open pederasty in Greek states. Of course civic nudity was by itself not sufficient. It was doubtless one part, arguably the major source of public opportunities to encourage male same-sex desire, in a complex nexus of social conditions that fostered pederasty.

If Sparta was the probable innovator of athletic nudity, the question remains how and why emulation of the Spartan custom took root in other Greek states. By the eighth and seventh centuries BC, Olympia had succeeded in becoming a leading political and religious center for all Greeks. Sparta was the preeminent athletic powerhouse in the late eighth to early sixth centuries, and Olympia was its showcase. The early seventh century was Sparta's era of political and military reform, and presumably the period during which the *agōgē* system began. So

Sparta's internal renewal is mirrored by its success in the Olympic Games for the period 720-580 BC, for which are recorded 36 victories by Spartans in gymnic events, though none in the equestrian contests which first appeared in 680 BC (Moretti, 1957; Hodkinson, 1999, pp. 161-165). Most Olympiads in that period show at least one Spartan victory. From 576 to 372, by contrast, there are only six (or possibly seven) known Spartan victories in Olympic gymnic events, and eleven in equestrian events. The decline in gymnic victories by Spartans is too sharp to be attributed to an accident of preservation. If the extant victories reflect a true shift in participation, it is most likely due to a new cultural focus after the seventh century Spartan cultural 'revolution' in which the *agōgē* was established, with open pederasty as a likely by-product of the *agōgē*, as, for example, in Alcman's *Parthenion*. Perhaps the Spartan *paideia* system also placed greater emphasis on athletic training displayed only in local festivals, while the Spartan élite could enjoy greater Panhellenic visibility through equestrian victories. In any case, after the first quarter of the sixth century, Sparta's athletic fortunes waned as other states learned from its techniques of training in more formalized gymnasium-like institutions.

The success of the Olympics as a panhellenic festival, the model of Spartan athletic prowess, and the participation of contestants from ever more distant reaches of the Greek world led, by the sixth century BC, to an "athletic revolution" in Greece characterized by three significant events. First, some regions established their own Olympic-style panhellenic games at the prominent sanctuaries of Delphi (from 582 BC), Isthmia (from 581 BC), and Nemea (from 573 BC). This happened alongside the widespread establishment of regularly held local athletic festivals, most prominent among which was the quadrennial Great Panathenaia of Athens, organized in 566 BC. Secondly, cities generally fostered participation in athletic contests by establishing local training centers, gymnasia, wrestling schools, or specially designated "tracks" (*dromoi*), an early one being the original *Dromos* at Sparta (Pausanias 3.14.6). With facilities came special trainers or coaches and training programs, the model again being the Spartan training system, and the earliest of which outside Sparta may have been that of the philosopher Pythagoras in Croton in the last third of the sixth century. Finally, to judge mainly from vase paintings, the custom of athletic nudity seems to have been widely adopted by the early sixth century.

It is clear that gymnic athletics became much more widely popular in the early sixth century than it had ever been before that. Black figure and red figure vases begin depicting naked athletes with a few instances in the first and second quarters of the sixth century, then in significant numbers in the third quarter, with 200 examples by one count, increasing to 250 instances in the last quarter of the sixth century, then climbing sharply to 412 examples by the first quarter of the fifth century and 381 in the second quarter. Thereafter the instances dip to 240 in the third quarter of the fifth century, and strikingly drop to only 84 examples in the last quarter of the fifth century (Goosens & Thielemans, 1996, p. 68). Even if we allow for accidents of preservation, the quantitative evidence allows us to say that vase paintings of naked athletes reflect the enthusiasm for and novelty of the topic in the last half of the sixth century, and they evidence a significant boom in its popularity in first half of the fifth. The first significant quantity of such vase images about 550 BC lags slightly behind the start of the athletic revolution of new panhellenic festivals about 582-573 BC. By the mid-sixth century, most of Greece enthusiastically followed where Sparta had led in the athletic culture of nudity, training, and pederasty.

CONCLUSIONS

We have seen how the athletic culture of Sparta was particularly crucial to the dispersion of pederasty in Greece. The present thesis thus agrees with the fundamental ancient view, epitomized in Thucydides 1.6 and echoed in Plato, that Sparta began the custom of nudity in athletic training, though we differ with the historian on details about the period when the practice was introduced to Olympia. The other economy of the present hypothesis is that it allows for the eroticization of the naked male earlier than most other studies. Athletic nudity had already been present as an option since the late eighth century at Olympia, even if it was not broadly adopted until much later, and the erotic dimension should be allowed even for that early date. The *kouroi* sculpture of Greek art during the second half of the seventh century also carry an erotic force, since that genre appears after Spartan athletic nudity and, I argue, pederasty had already been generalized to its male citizens by the mid-seventh century. The *kouroi* appear simultaneously with the earliest naked athletes on vases, at the point when the Spartan version of an eroticized athletic nudity was spreading to other states.

The evidence for the origin of widespread pederasty in Greece points generally to a gradual process between the early seventh to mid-sixth centuries. The Spartan *agōgē* (and possibly but less likely the even more poorly attested Cretan system of *paideia*) appears to have been largely formally established in the early seventh century, and pederasty occupied a formal part of it. Sparta's athletic acme at Olympia accompanied the early *agōgē*, but ended by 580 BC, just as the rest of Greece was experiencing its "athletic revolution." Sparta is, therefore, the most likely source for the custom of public athletic nudity, and to this extent we can generally agree with Thucydides, Plato and other ancient sources.

Possibly the earliest use of the terminology of athletic nudity comes in the *Theognidea* and is notably tied to a lover who "returning home after exercise enjoys the whole day with a handsome youth." In the words of Plutarch cited earlier, pederastic eros came later than heterosexual eros, entered the gymnasium, slowly "grew wings," and grew bolder as a presence there (Plutarch *Amatorius* 751f-752a). Lactantius (*Divine Institutions* 1.20) quotes Cicero as saying that the fusion of Eros with the gymnasium was a "bold plan." More probably it was the natural and inexorable movement of complementary, seventh- to sixth-century practices. The "athletic revolution," whereby once disparate Greek cities felt a new unity with one another in their sharing of festivals and training practices, called for a new and visible expression of the spirit. Athletic nudity that appears to have been inspired by the Spartan model of undress seems also to have been adopted as a free expression of Greek self-confidence, esthetic inclination, and a movement of erotic liberation. Since the Bronze Age, the athletes of Greece and of other eastern Mediterranean cultures had worn little; by abandoning all vestiges of clothing, the "costume" of nudity now made Greek athletes resemble their statues of the gods. Athletic nudity attested at once to the self-sufficiency of individuals and the freedom of a civilization easily distinguished from "the barbarians." It simultaneously, and in a more mundane but no less crucial function, served the physical and social needs of homosocial desire in the city-state.

The growth of pederasty in this context was probably fundamentally fostered by erotic desire from the visual and tactile stimuli of the gymnasia and simultaneously shaped by cultural and political agendas of the day. Pederastic *erōs* was not literally "invented" in the gymnasium, but it was to some extent given a focus there and, under the restrictions of various formal and informal conventions, allowed to flourish there. The gymnasium became a locus of erotic affiliation, and of social and political ties that resulted from legitimate relationships formed therein. Desire itself, the "all-conquering," took on a life of its own and invaded the gymnasium through the emotions of the habitués of the gymnasium apart from the moral or political attitudes of any citizens. Solon, for one, seems to have implicitly endorsed pederasty in the gymnasium and even seen it as a phenomenon properly restricted to freeborn citizens (Kyle, 1984). As often, it may well have been a case of policy being written both to sanction a prevailing popular norm and to keep it under control.

REFERENCES

Bonfante, L. (1998). Nudity as a Costume in Classical Art. *American Journal of Archeology*, *93*(4), 543-570.

Brelich, A. (1962). *Le Iniziazioni: Parte seconda*. Rome: Edizione dell'Ateneo.

_____. (1969). *Paides e Parthenoi: Volume I. Incunabula Graeca*. (36 vols.). Rome: Edizioni dell' Anteneo.

Cartledge, P. (2001). *Spartan Reflections*. Berkeley and Los Angeles: U of California P.

Crowther, N. (1982). Athletic Dress and Nudity in Greek Athletics. *Eranos*, *80*, 163-168.

Decker, W. and Herb, M. (Eds.). (1994). *Bildatlas zum Sport im Alten Ägypten: Corpus der bildlichen Quellen zu Leibesübungen, Spiel, Jagd, Tanz und verwandten Themen: Volume I. Text, Volume II. Abbildungen*. Leiden, New York, and Cologne: Brill.

Delorme, J. (1960). *Gymnasion: Étude sur les Monuments consacrés a l'Éducation en Grèce (des origines à l'Empire romain)*. Paris: Editions E. De Boccard.

Glass, S. (2002). The Greek Gymnasium. Some Problems. In Raschke (2002), 155-173.

Goosens, E. and Thielemans, S. with a note by O. Thas. (1996). The Popularity of Painting Sport Scenes on Attic Black and Red Figure Vases: a C.V. A.-Based Research–Part A. *Bulletin Antike Beschaving*, *71*, 59-94.

Hammond, N. G. L. (1989). *A History of Greece to 322 BC* (3rd ed.). Oxford: Clarendon Press.

Hodkinson, S. (1999). An Agonistic Culture. In S. Hodkinson and A. Powell (Eds.), *Sparta: New Perspectives* (pp. 147-187). London: Duckworth.

Hornblower, S. (1997). *A Commentary on Thucydides. Volume I: Books I-III*. Oxford, U.K.: Clarendon Paperbacks.

Jeanmaire, H. (1939. Repr. 1974). *Couroi et Couretes. Essai sur l'education spartiate et sur les rites d'adolescence dans l'antiquité hellénique*. Lille: Bibliotheque universitaire, New York: Arno Press.

Jüthner, J., with F. Brein (Ed.). (1965). *Die Athletischen Leibesübungen der Griechen* (2 vols.). Graz, Vienna, and Cologne: Herman Böhlaus. Vol 1.

Kyle, D. G. (1984). Solon and Athletics. *Ancient World*, *9*, 99-102.

Lattimore, R. (1960). *Greek Lyrics*. Chicago: U of Chicago P.

Lattimore, S. (Trans.). (1998). *Thucydides. The Peloponnesian War*. Indianapolis and Cambridge: Hackett.

Legakis, B. (1977). *Athletic Contests in Archaic Greek Art*. Doctoral dissertation, University of Chicago, Chicago.

Ludwig, Paul W. (2002). *Eros and Polis. Desire and Community in Greek Political Theory.* Cambridge, U.K.: Cambridge UP.

Mann, Christian. (1998). Krieg, Sport und Adelskultur. Zur Entstehung des griechischen Gymnasions. *Klio, 80,* 7-21.

McDonnell, M. (1991). The Introduction of Athletic Nudity: Thucydides, Plato, and the Vases. *Journal of Hellenic Studies, 111,* 182-193.

Miller, S. (2000). Naked Democracy. In P. Flensted-Jensen, T. Heine Nielsen, and L. Rubinstein, (Eds.), *Polis and Politics: Studies in Ancient Greek History. Presented to Morgens Herman Hansen on his Sixtieth Birthday* (pp. 277-296). Copenhagen: Museum Tusculanum Press, University of Copenhagen.

Moretti, L. (1957). *Olympionikai, i Vincitori negli Antichi Agoni Olimpici, MemLincei* ser. 8.8.2. Rome: Accademia Nazionale dei Lincei.

Mouratidis, J. (1985). The Origin of Nudity in Greek Athletics. *Journal of Sport History, 12,* 213-232.

Osborne, R. (1997). Men without Clothes: Heroic Nakedness and Greek Art. *Gender and History, 9,* 504-28. Repr. In Wyke (1998), 80-104.

———. (1998). Sculpted Men of Athens: Masculinity and Power in the Field of Vision. In Lynn Foxhall and John Salmon, (Eds.), *Thinking Men: Masculinity and Self-Representation in the Classical Tradition* (pp. 23-42). London: Routledge.

Percy, W. Armstrong. (1996). *Pederasty and Pedagogy in Archaic Greece.* Urbana and Chicago: U of Illinois P.

Pettersson, M. (1992). *Cults of Apollo at Sparta: The Hyakinthia, the Gymnopaidiai and the Karneia.* Stockholm: Skrifter Utgivna av Svenska Insitutet i Athen.

Poliakoff, M. 1987. *Combat Sports in the Ancient World: Competition, Violence, and Culture.* New Haven: Yale UP.

Raschke, W. (Ed.). (2002). *The Archaeology of the Olympics. The Olympics and Other Festivals in Antiquity* (2nd ed.). Madison: U of Wisconsin P.

Robertson, N. (1992). *Festivals and Legends: the Formation of Greek Cities in the Light of Public Ritual.* Toronto, Buffalo, and London: U of Toronto P.

Rollinger, Robert. (1994). Aspekte des Sports im Alten Sumer. Sportliche Betätigung und Herrschaftsidiologie im Wechselspiel. *Nikephoros, 7,* 7-64.

Scanlon, T. F. (1983). The Vocabulary of Competition: *Agon* and *Aethlos,* Greek Terms for Contest. *Arete,* 1(l), 147-162.

———. (2002). *Eros and Greek Athletics.* New York and Oxford: Oxford UP.

Stewart, A. (1997). *Art, Desire, and the Body in Ancient Greece.* Cambridge: Cambridge UP.

Sweet, W. (1987). *Sport and Recreation in Ancient Greece. A Sourcebook with Translations.* New York and Oxford: Oxford UP.

West, M. L. (1966). *Hesiod. Theogony.* Oxford: Clarendon.

Wyke, Maria (Ed.). (1998). *Gender and the Body in the Ancient Mediterranean.* Oxford, U.K. and Malden, MA: Blackwell.

Glukus Himeros:
Pederastic Influence
on the Myth of Ganymede

Vernon Provencal, PhD

Acadia University

SUMMARY. Pederastic influence on the myth of Ganymede enables it to evolve, in a continuous line of development easily traced in the history of Greek literature from Homer to Plato, into a homoerotic emblem of the spiritual union of the human and divine. Continuity in this history is marked by the thematic use of the Homeric phrase γλυκὺς ἵμερος (*glukus himeros*, "sweet longing") to describe sexual desire in association with the Ganymede myth in the *Hymn to Aphrodite*, Pindar and Plato. *[Article copies available for a fee from The Haworth Document Delivery Service: 1-800-HAWORTH. E-mail address: <docdelivery@haworthpress.com> Website: <http://www.HaworthPress.com> © 2005 by The Haworth Press, Inc. All rights reserved.]*

KEYWORDS. Pederasty, homosexuality, Ganymede, Aphrodite, pedagogy, Pindar, Phaedrus, *Erōs*, homoerotic, *himeros*

Vernon Provencal, PhD, is Associate Professor of Classics at Acadia University. Correspondence may be addressed: UPO 223, Department of History & Classics, Acadia University, Wolfville, NS B4N 1L6 Canada (E-mail: Vernon.provencal@acadiau.ca).

[Haworth co-indexing entry note]: "*Glukus Himeros:* Pederastic Influence on the Myth of Ganymede." Provencal, Vernon. Co-published simultaneously in *Journal of Homosexuality* (Harrington Park Press, an imprint of The Haworth Press, Inc.) Vol. 49, No. 3/4, 2005, pp. 87-136; and: *Same-Sex Desire and Love in Greco-Roman Antiquity and in the Classical Tradition of the West* (ed: Beert C. Verstraete, and Vernon Provencal) Harrington Park Press, an imprint of The Haworth Press, Inc., 2005, pp. 87-136. Single or multiple copies of this article are available for a fee from The Haworth Document Delivery Service [1-800-HAWORTH, 9:00 a.m. - 5:00 p.m. (EST). E-mail address: docdelivery@haworthpress.com].

Available online at http://www.haworthpress.com/web/JH
© 2005 by The Haworth Press, Inc. All rights reserved.
doi:10.1300/J082v49n03_04

In its earliest appearance in ancient Greek culture, the relationship between Ganymede and Zeus is not an erotic one. The eroticization of the myth of Ganymede reflects the cultural influence of the rise of pederasty as a social institution in archaic Greece.[1] The pederastic evolution of the myth is marked by the thematic use of the Homeric phrase *glukus himeros* (γλυκὺς ἵμερος *Il.* 3.446, 14.328, "sweet longing") as a kind of motif in the post-Homeric narrative context of the Ganymede myth in the pseudo-Homeric *Hymn to Aphrodite* (*h. Aph.* 2, 53), Pindar's *Olympian* 1 (*O.* 38), and Plato's *Phaedrus* (*Phdr.* 255c1). The phrase as used originally in Homer and in the post-Homeric *Hymn to Aphrodite* refers only to heterosexual relations; it later takes on homoerotic meaning in the pederastic poetry of Pindar; finally, through Plato, pederastic *himeros* is converted into a homoerotic symbol for the spiritual longing of the soul for the divine.

HISTORICAL OUTLINE

> But, the fact is, we all accuse the Cretans of being the originators of the myth of Ganymede: since their laws were believed to have come from Zeus, they added this myth about Zeus so that they could be following the god as they continued to reap the enjoyments of this pleasure. (*Leg.* 636c7-d4; Pangle, 1980, p. 16)

In Plato's *Laws*, the Cretans are universally accused of fabricating the myth of Ganymede to justify their "unnatural" practice of pederasty. In his study of homosexuality in Greek myth, Bernard Sergent renews this ancient theory when he speculates that Ganymede was originally "a founding hero of initiatory homosexuality in Crete and, even earlier, in Greece," and avers that the pederastic origin of the myth is suppressed in Homer (Sergent, 1987, p. 213). Sergent's view is based on the Indo-European initiation theory of the origins of pederasty in Bronze Age Greece (Sergent, 1987, p. 212; Bremmer, 1980; Dowden, 1992, pp. 113-115). Kenneth Dover and William Percy have criticized the Indo-European theory as needlessly speculative ("Not a single ancient ever argued that the Greeks acquired the institution of pederasty from any other people," Percy, 1998, p. 48) and contrary to evidence that the Greek practice of pederasty was indigenous to archaic Crete (Dover, 1988, pp. 116-119; 1989, pp. 185-196; Percy 1990, p. 22 [in Dynes, p. 378]; 1996, pp. 15-26). One consequence of the spread of "overt homosexuality" throughout the Greek world in the seventh century BC is that "new (homosexual) variants of existing myths . . . were generated by poets, who in this as in other fields accommodated their material to the tastes, interests and beliefs of the society in which they worked" (Dover, 1988, p. 116).

Dover and Percy both argue that the original Ganymede myth was neither initiatory nor pederastic. In their view, the history of the myth in Greek art and literature evinces its pederastic modification, and reflects the indigenous rise of pederasty as a social institution in archaic Greece (Dover, 1988, pp. 130-131; 1989, pp. 196-197; Percy, 1996, pp. 38-39). One particularly compelling reason Dover gives for rejecting the initiatory thesis is that

> it would be hard to find any myth more inimical to the theme of initiation. The point of initiation is to effect the initiand's transition from one status to another, but Ganymede is denied that transition; he becomes an immortal boy who . . . never grows up. (Dover, 1988, p. 130)

(The perennial youth of Ganymede is first mentioned in the *Hymn to Aphrodite*; it does not appear in Homer.) Nonetheless, Barkan (1991) still prefers to follow Sergent in his speculation that "the pederastic dimension of the story may have been invented to domesticate a mysterious practice handed down from time immemorial" (pp. 30-31). Likewise, Claude Calame (1999) has reasserted the need to acknowledge the plausibility for the initiatory origins of pederasty, against the arguments of Dover, Foucault, Shapiro and Percy: "So-called 'Greek homosexuality' must be understood as a practice that was part and parcel of educational procedures that still stemmed largely from the rites of tribal initiation" (pp. 96-97). Thomas Scanlon, on the other hand, is persuaded that Dover's critique and alternative theory of an indigenous Greek versus Indo-European origin of Greek pederasty better fits the evidence (2002, pp. 64-97).

In fact, the origins of the myth of Ganymede are lost. The original myth in its entirety did not survive its translation into Homeric epic, where it is preserved by way of citation in Aeneas' account of his lineage in *Iliad* 20, along with mention of Zeus compensating Tros, Ganymede's father, for the loss of his son with horses, in *Iliad* 5. Later citations of the myth obviously draw on Homer, so it appears that no other account of the original myth was available after Homer. Homer's version is slightly altered and embellished by his successors. The *Little Iliad* introduced the variation that Ganymede was the son of Laomedon, rather than Tros (Gerber, 1982, p. 79). A more important and permanent modification of the Homeric myth occurs in the pseudo-Homeric *Hymn to Aphrodite*, where Ganymede is abducted by Zeus himself, rather than by the gods, and granted perennial youth. Another post-Homeric modification is that Zeus either becomes or is represented by an eagle (Robson, 1997, p. 66). Eventually, Ganymede's immortality is identified with the constellation Aquarius (Saslow, 1986, p. 5).

As in Homer, the myth exists in extant Greek literature *only* by way of citation. No complete or autonomous account of Ganymede's abduction to Olympus exists, nor is known to have existed, in Greek literature. The myth seems never to have inspired an epic hymn, lyric poem or drama of its own, at least none noteworthy enough to have obtained bare mention of its existence. Of course this is true of many myths cited in Homer, the judgment of Paris being a particularly apt example. Like the judgment of Paris, the abduction of Ganymede was enormously popular in the culture of Hellenic Greece, as attested by its frequent appearance in archaic and classical Attic painting and sculpture, and by a continuous history of citation in Greek literature. After its citation in the *Iliad* and *Hymn to Aphrodite*, the myth continues to be cited in archaic and classical Greek lyric (Ibycus, Theognis, Pindar), Greek drama (Sophocles, Euripides) and in the fourth century philosophic dialogues of Xenophon (*Symposium*) and Plato (*Phaedrus, Laws*). The Ganymede myth remains popular in later times as well, as evidenced (to cite a few milestones) by its appearance in the Hellenistic *Idylls* of Theocritus; in Virgil's *Aeneid* (where he is abducted by Zeus's emissary, an eagle 5.249-257); and Ovid's *Metamorphoses* (where Zeus becomes an eagle 10.155-61). Nor did its popularity diminish in the Middle Ages, where it is best known from Dante's dream of being abducted by an eagle on Mount Purgatory (*Purg.* 9.19-33). Two recent books testify to its enormous popularity in Renaissance art as well, especially in drawings by Michelangelo (Barkan, 1991; Saslow, 1986).

By the fifth century, Zeus' abduction of the handsome youth Ganymede was being cited as the origin of pederasty, which had become institutionalized among the Greek aristocracy. In Greek practice, pederasty was a homoerotic and overtly sexual (albeit one-sided) relationship between an adult male, called the *erastēs* (active lover), and an adolescent youth (*pais*), called the *erōmenos* (passive beloved). By 600 BC, pederasty was instituted socially as a pedagogical relationship, first on the island of Crete, then in Sparta, after which its institutionalization spread to the rest of Greece (Percy,

1996, p. 95). Its rise in social prominence is reflected in the art and literature of the late archaic age (Calame, 1999, pp. 95-97). "Vase painters and lyric and elegiac poets such as Alcaeus, Alcman, Stesichorus, Ibycus, and Anacreon made . . . the earliest unmistakable references to such pederastic activity" (Percy, 1996, p. 54). One sign of pederastic influence on the evolution of the Ganymede myth was that some accounts changed the place of abduction (*harpagion*) from its traditional location in Ganymede's native Troad to the island of Crete, where pederasty was generally assumed to have originated in Greece (Percy, 1996, pp. 56, citing Athenaeus XIII, 601 f.).

Artistic evidence of the rise of pederasty as a social institution among the Greek aristocracies of archaic Greece is particularly well documented in Shapiro's study of courtship scenes in Attic vase-painting c. 560-475 BC. Shapiro's inquiry into the historical, social and political circumstances that limited this genre to this period brings him to the conclusion that it belonged very much to the aristocratic tastes of the Greek tyrants. "In particular, close ties between Pesisistratid Athens and Ionian Greece, exemplified by the presence of the poet Anakreon at the court of Hippias, suggest the creation of a cultural milieu in which the *erastēs/erōmenos* relationship and its depictions in art might flourish" (Shapiro, 1981, p. 133; in Dynes, 1992, p. 401).

A fundamental transition in the archaic and classical artistic depiction of the relationship of Zeus and Ganymede reflects the rise of pederastic influence on the myth.[2] The Oltos painting of 510 BC (the only pre-500 BC painting of which Ganymede is certainly the subject) depicts Ganymede in a nonsexual context, in which "the cupbearer stands before Zeus on his throne in the middle of the assembled gods [in] . . . the timeless, archaic splendour of Olympos" (Schefold, 1992, p. 26). The static splendor of Oltos' archaic vase-painting depicts the non-pederastic relationship of Zeus and Ganymede in the *Iliad*, as is clear in Woodward's (2003) concise description of the vase: "Ganymede, still a young boy. . . . stands attentively before Zeus holding a jug, while the impressive god sits facing him, thunderbolt gripped in his left hand, the right holding out a libation bowl; other gods and goddesses flank the central group" (p. 119). Fifth-century paintings, on the other hand, frequently favor depictions of Zeus' amorous pursuit of Ganymede, which document the rising influence of institutionalized pederasty on Greek life and culture. An Attic red-figure vase by the Brygos Painter (c. 490-480 BC) is typical in depicting Zeus, "dignity thrown to the winds, in hot pursuit of the quarry, sceptre held in one outstretched hand, the other with fingers extended, ready to grasp the elusive boy" (Woodward, 2003, pp. 119-120).

In literary evidence, while pederastic influence on the myth of Ganymede is implied in the late seventh century *Hymn to Aphrodite* (Percy, 1996, p. 38), the "earliest surviving testimony to Zeus's homosexual desire for Ganymede is [the 6th century] Ibykos fr. 289, where the ravishing (*harpage*) of Ganymede is put into the same context as the rape of Tithonos by Dawn" (Dover, 1989, p. 197). The pederastic implications of the myth are made explicit in the verses attributed to the late sixth century elegist, Theognis (though these may be later, and even possibly influenced by Pindar):

> And there is some pleasure in loving a boy,
> Since once, in fact, even the son of Cronos, king of the immortals,
> Fell in love with Ganymede, seized him, carried him off to Olympus,
> And made him divine, keeping the lovely bloom of boyhood.
> (*Thgn.* 2.1345-1348; Trans. Gerber, 1999, pp. 378-379)

Fifth-century Greek drama clearly reflects the establishment of the pederastic version of the Ganymede myth in Greek culture. For example, Sophocles fr. 345, which Athenaeus tells us referred to Ganymede (*Deipnosophists* 3, 602E), has the youth "warming with his thighs the royal might of Zeus" (Trans. Lloyd-Jones, 1996, pp. 188-189); Euripides' *Orestes* (1.1392) describes Troy as the "riding place" of Ganymede, Zeus's bedmate" (Trans. Kovacs, 2002b, pp. 566-567), where "riding place" is a double entendre referring to a sexual situation (Eden, 1988, p. 561).

Artistic and literary evidence, then, shows that the pederastic version of the myth of Ganymede was well established in the fifth century. In the fourth century, however, the Socrates of both Xenophon and Plato championed nonsexual aspects of the pederastic relationship through dubious etymologies that would enable its translation via allegory into Christian culture.[3] Xenophon's Socrates explicitly denies the sexual aspect of the pederastic relationship between Zeus and Ganymede in favor of its intellectual aspect:

> in the case of Ganymede, it was not his person but his spiritual
> character [οὐ σώματος ἀλλὰ ψυχῆς ἕνεκα 8.30] that influenced
> Zeus to carry him up to Olympus. This is confirmed by his very
> name . . . Gany-mede, compounded of the two foregoing elements,

signifies not *physically* but *mentally* attractive; hence his honour among the gods. [Socrates takes the name Ganymede to be compounded of the two archaic words *ganytai* ("he joys," "exults") and *medea* ("devices," "thoughts") Todd's note.] (X. *Smp.* 8.28-31; Todd, 1923, pp. 622-625)

Xenophon's interpretation of Zeus' love of Ganymede as *intellectual* suggests the association of pederasty with pedagogy that is elaborated in Socrates' second speech on *erōs* in Plato's *Phaedrus*. The pedagogical aspect of pederastic *erōs* was allegorized even further in the Middle Ages and Renaissance. Ganymede was reinterpreted as "the incarnation of the innocent soul finding its joy in God. He prefigured St. John the Evangelist who was transported to heaven; he was human intellect beloved by Jupiter, to wit, the Supreme Being" (Mayerson, 1971, p. 386; see also Barkan, 1991 and Saslow, 1986). In Dante, Zeus' abduction of Ganymede symbolizes the act of divine grace required before embarking on the spiritual ascent of Mount Purgatory.

KALLOS *AND* TIMĒ: *GANYMEDE IN* THE ILIAD

ἀντίθεος Γανυμήδης,
ὃς δὴ κάλλιστος γένετο θνητῶν ἀνθρώπων·
τὸν καὶ ἀνηρείψαντο θεοὶ Διὶ οἰνοχοεύειν
κάλλεος ἕνεκα οἷο, ἵν' ἀθανάτοισι μετείη.
    godlike Ganymedes,
he who was the most beautiful ever born of mortal humans:
and whom the gods snatched up and carried off to pour out wine for Zeus
on account of his beauty, in order that he be with the immortals.
(*Il.* 20.232-35; Monro and Allen, 1920, my translation)

The allegedly homoerotic aspect of Ganymede's abduction on account of his beauty (*kallos*) is the basis of Sergent's speculation that Homer is suppressing a pederastic relationship between Zeus and Ganymede that belonged to the original myth. While Zeus and Ganymede fit the age-asymmetrical pattern of pederasty, there is no textual evidence of pederasty in Homer to support Sergent's hypothesis. Zeus himself does not take part in the abduction, which is carried out by the other gods, and shows no interest in Ganymede's youthful beauty

(Percy, 1996, p. 38). Furthermore, the myth as we have it in Homer is perfectly explanatory in its own terms, if we allow that the esthetic value of Ganymede's beauty could be as much of interest to the Olympians as the erotic aspect that is exploited in sixth century art and literature (Dover, 1989, p. 197).

The strongest evidence, then, that Homer is not suppressing a pederastic relationship in the original Ganymede myth is that Zeus is not the one who abducts Ganymede. (Also, Ganymede is conspicuously absent in Zeus' famous catalogue of his affairs that he recites to Hera in the *Iliad*.) As Aeneas tells the story in Homer, it is the other gods (excluding Zeus) who appear to be attracted by Ganymede's "godlike beauty" as "the most beautiful of human mortals" and desire to have the youth "be with the immortals." They accomplish their purpose by offering the youth to Zeus as his personal servant. Zeus apparently grants him this Olympian honor on account of his godlike beauty. Had they not made Ganymede a gift to Zeus, it is quite likely that there would have been a quarrel over honor (*timē*), not unlike the quarrel that broke out between Achilles and Agamemnon over their captive women. Like the Trojan captive women distributed among the heroes according to their *timē* (honor, prestige, social status, self-esteem), the gift of Ganymede's beauty acknowledges the supreme *timē* of Zeus as ruler of Olympus, father of gods and mortals.[4] In this way the gods avoid any quarrel over the loss of *timē*, such as motivates Zeus' deception of Aphrodite in the *Hymn to Aphrodite*.

This aspect of the abduction of Ganymede–his godlike beauty (*kallos*) that makes him a gift worthy of honoring Zeus' *timē*, which in turn, confers upon Ganymede the divine *timē* of Olympian citizenship conferred on few mortals–survives in the post-Homeric tradition. In this respect, the Ganymede myth becomes an emblem of divine *timē* conferred by grace. Thus we find Virgil using the myth in the *Aeneid* as a pederastic emblem of *honores* when he refers among the causes of Juno's wrath to *rapti Ganymedis honores*, the stolen honors of ravished Ganymede. "These *honores* are translated into a less ambiguous form later in the poem [5.249-57] when they become the *honores*, or first prize, that Aeneas hands out to the winner of the epic games, a purple and gold cloak on which is woven the story of Ganymede" (Barkan, 1991, pp. 19-20).

In Homer, where Zeus is not personally involved in Ganymede's abduction, there is little sense that he is sexually attracted to the youth, whose beauty appeals to all the gods. Nor does the verb used to describe his abduction, ἀνηρείψαντο, suggest an erotic interest on the part of the gods. ἀνερείπομαι ("snatch up and carry off," *Liddell & Scott Greek Lexicon* [*LSJ⁹*]) does not have the sexual overtones of ἁρπάζω used (by Paris) to describe the abduction of Helen (ἁρπάξας *Il*.3.444); the abduction of Ganymede in *H. Aph.* (ἥρπασεν 201), Ibycus fr. 289 (Dover, 1989, p. 197) and Theognis (ἥρατο 2.1346); of Pelops in *Olympian* 1 (ἁπράσαι 1.40); and of Io, Europa, Medea and Helen in Herodotus (1.1-5). ἁρπάζω is sometimes rendered 'rape,' but is often better translated as 'abduct' or 'ravish,' depending on context, where rape for us means sexual assault. Powell's lexicon (1966) gives "*ravish* women" for the Herodotean abductions cited above (p. 47). Zeus doesn't 'rape' Ganymede in that sense, no more than is Io or Helen raped. But they are abducted for sexual purposes, whether later they are willing partners or not; so that the verb has that connotation of abduction for sexual purposes. It may be that Homer's use of ἀνερείπομαι at *Il*. 20.234 to describe the gods' nonsexual abduction of Ganymede influenced Hesiod's use of ἀνερείπομαι in the *Theogony* to describe Aphrodite's nonsexual abduction of Phaethon, son of Eos (Dawn) and Cephalus, which bears striking similarities in detail to Ganymede's abduction:

ἴφθιμον Φαέθοντα, θεοῖς ἐπιείκελον ἄνδρα.
τόν ῥα νέον τέρεν ἄνθος ἔχοντ' ἐρικυδέος ἥβης
παῖδ' ἀταλὰ φρονέοντα φιλομμειδὴς Ἀφροδίτη
ὦρτ' ἀναρεψαμένη, καί μιν ζαθέοις ἐνὶ νηοῖς
νηοπόλον νύχιον ποιήσατο, δαίμονα δῖον.
strong Phaethon, a man like the gods,
whom, when he was a young boy in the tender flower of glorious youth
with childish thoughts, laughter-loving Aphrodite
seized and caught up and made a keeper of her shrine
by night, a divine spirit. (Hes. *Th.* 987-991; Evelyn-White, 1974, pp. 152-53)

Like Ganymede, Phaethon is abducted as a youth and immortalized in order to serve a god, in this case by and for Aphrodite, who is attracted to his immaturity. (Unlike Ganymede, Phaethon is allowed to mature into a 'strong' man, at which age he resembles the gods.) As with the abduction of Ganymede, there is no explicit suggestion of sexual interest on the part of Aphrodite–she doesn't abduct him to be her boy-toy, but her servant. It is highly doubtful that Phaethon is the heterosexual object of divine pederasty. Rather, the interest seems to be one of likeness in character–Phaethon's lack of serious-mindedness is what attracts 'laughter-loving' Aphrodite and appeals to the lighthearted side of her divinity. Phaethon doesn't turn Aphrodite on; he makes her laugh.

As with Phaethon, then, Ganymede's beauty appears to be the Olympian object of a nonsexual, and, in his case, explicitly esthetic interest. The *locus classicus* for the state of awe aroused by 'godlike beauty' is that of the Trojan elders when, standing upon the besieged wall of Troy, they are moved to wonder and praise the 'immortal' beauty of Helen with 'winged words' as worthy of such a terrible war:

> Surely there is no blame on Trojans and strong-greaved Achaeans
> if for long time they suffer hardship for a woman like this one.
> Terrible is the likeness of her face to immortal goddesses.
> (*Il.* 3.157-58; Lattimore, 1951, p. 104)

Ganymede, like Helen, possesses an earthly beauty in which one glimpses the divine and is moved to gaze and wonder.

By contrast with the *Iliad*, in which Ganymede's beauty arouses in the gods an esthetic interest in beauty (*kallos*), a sense of wonder (θαῦμα ἰδέσθαι) comparable to that aroused by Helen in the Trojan elders, the *Hymn to Aphrodite* places Zeus' attraction to Ganymede's beauty in a highly eroticized context that suggests a response reminiscent of Paris's response to Helen's reproach–no matter, the very sight of her arouses in him a sexual longing that sets all her abuse aside (cf. Calame, 1999, p. 40):

> Come, then, rather let us go to bed and turn to love-making.
> Never before as now has passion enmeshed my senses
> (οὐ γάρ πώ ποτέ μ' ὧδε γ' ἔρως φρένας ἀμφεκάλυψεν),
> not when I took you for the first time from Lakedaimon the lovely
> and caught you up (ἀπράξας) and carried you away in seafaring
> vessels,
> and lay with you in the bed of love on the island Kranae,
> *not even then, as now, did I love you and sweet desire seize me*
> (ὡς σεο νῦν ἔραμαι καί με γλυκὺς ἵμερος αἱρεῖ).
> (*Il.* 3.441-46; Lattimore, 1951, p. 112, emphasis and Greek added)

In Homer, the esthetic appreciation of Ganymede's beauty eclipses *erōs*. In the *Hymn to Aphrodite,* the erotic context of the Ganymede myth suggests that the esthetic appreciation of Ganymede's beauty arouses in Zeus the same sexual desire (*glukus himeros*) that Helen arouses in Paris.

ERŌS, KALLOS *AND* TIMĒ:
HYMN TO APHRODITE

Tell me, Muse, the works of richly golden Aphrodite,
the Cyprian, who both arouses sweet longing (γλυκὺν ἵμερον) in
gods,
and seduces the tribes of mortal humans,
and birds winging through the sky, and all the beasts,
  as many as the land nurtures, and as much as the sea:
all are concerned with the works of fair-crowned Cytherea.
(*H. Aph.* 1-6; West, 2003, p. 162, my translation)

The Homeric use of *glukus himeros* to describe the sexual desire inspired by Aphrodite and aroused by beauty (*kallos*) is taken up in the
seventh-century[5] *Hymn to Aphrodite*, where it becomes *contextually* associated with the Ganymede myth. Pindar later uses it to describe Poseidon's attraction to Pelops, which he parallels with Zeus' attraction to
Ganymede. In the *Phaedrus*, Plato alleges that *himeros* was the term
Zeus himself used of his love of Ganymede. In this way, *glukus himeros*
becomes a thematic marker of continuity in the post-Homeric history of
the myth. As an explicit term of sexual desire, it also serves as a bench-
mark for the degree of pederastic influence on the myth.

The *Hymn* begins by establishing the universality of Aphrodite's
power of *glukus himeros* to which all mortal creatures, and nearly all the
immortals, are subject. (Athena, Artemis and Hestia are capable of resistance.) *Glukus himeros* inspires sexual intercourse (συνέμειξε,
μιχθήμεναι) for the sake of pleasure, with the cosmic purpose of procreation. And while sexual desire is as mundane as fish spawning in the
sea, it is also sublime, beguiling gods to beget heroes. Ironically, the
work (*ergon*) which the Muse chooses to disclose is Aphrodite's seduction of Anchises, in which Aphrodite herself falls prey to *glukus
himeros*. This is more the *ergon* of Zeus than of Aphrodite herself. To
prevent Aphrodite from boasting how easily she had duped the most
wise and powerful father of the gods into coupling with mere mortal
women (ρηιδίως συνέμειξε καταθνητῆισι γυναιξίν, *H. Aph.* 39),
Zeus compels Aphrodite, the very goddess of love, to betray herself by
using her own power of *glukus himeros* against her:

τῆι δὲ καὶ αὐτῆι Ζεὺς γλυκὺς ἵμερον ἔμβαλε θυμῶι
ἀνδρὶ καταθνητῶ μιχθήμεναι ...
’ Αγχίσεω δ’ ἄρα οἱ γλυκὺν ἵμερον ἔμβαλεν θυμῶι

Into the heart of Aphrodite herself Zeus injected sweet longing
(*glukus himeros*)
for sex with a mortal man . . .
for sex with Anchises did he inject a sweet longing in her heart
(*H. Aph.* 45-46, 53; West, 2003, p. 162, my translation)

The first half of this tale of Aphrodite's *ergon* is devoted to Aphrodite's seduction of Anchises, in which there is considerable emphasis on the esthetic relationship between (physical) beauty and (sexual) passion, and its enhancement by youth, virginal innocence, and adornment. Sexual arousal in both goddess and mortal arises from gazing upon the beauty of the other; *erōs* is intimately connected with the pleasure of the visual reception (*aisthēsis*) of beauty.

Anchises is a young man ("at that time he tended cattle on the heights of Ida," *H. Aph.* 54; West, 2003, p. 162), "with a body like that of the gods" (δέμας ἀθανάτοισιν ἐοικώς, *H. Aph.* 55; West, 2003, p. 162, my translation). He stands before Aphrodite as "hero Anchises, possessing his beauty from the gods" (Ἀγχίσην ἥρωα θεῶν ἄπο κάλλος ἔχοντα, *H. Aph.* 77; West, 2003, p. 164, my translation). The sight of Anchises' beauty arouses Aphrodite's passion (ἰδοῦσα ... ἠράσατ', *H. Aph.* 56-57; West, 2003, p. 164) and "a terribly excessive sexual longing seized her mind" (ἐκπάγλως δὲ κατὰ φρένας ἵμερος εἷλεν., *H. Aph.* 56-57; West, 2003, p.164, my translation). Likewise, it is the sight of the goddess's beauty, in the guise of an elaborately adorned virginal maiden, that arouses passion in Anchises:

Ἀγχίσης δ' ὁρόων ἐφράζετο θαύμαινέν τε
εἶδός τε μέγεθός τε καὶ εἵματα σιγαλόεντα ...
θαῦμα ἰδέσθαι ... Ἀγχίσην δ' ἔρος εἷλεν
Anchises gazed and studied her appearance, amazed
at her form, her stature and her shining dress . . .
a wonder to behold . . . and *erōs* seized Anchises
(*H. Aph.* 84-91; West, 2003, p. 166, my translation)

In Anchises, sexual desire (ἔρως) is aroused by a sense of wonder inspired by the sight of Aphrodite's beauty (ὁρόων ... θαύμαινέν; θαῦμα ἰδέσθαι). The esthetic context elevates the erotic encounter of the divine and human above its mundane commonality with the animal world at large.

Aphrodite enhances her desirability by flaunting her (pretended) virginal innocence as an unmarried maiden. As part of her cover story designed to allay Anchises' fear of reprisal after intercourse with a possible deity, she assures him that Hermes had abducted her from a dance in celebration of Artemis (goddess of chastity) to be Anchises' bride. She then offers herself as "a virgin with no experience of love" (ἀδμήτην ... ἀπειρήτην φιλότητος, *H. Aph.* 133; West, 2003, pp. 168-169). The total effect of Aphrodite's seductive charm and deceptive reassurance is to inflame Anchises with sexual excitement that guarantees his seduction: "Neither, then, shall any god nor mortal man restrain me here, not before I make love to you, right now!" (*H. Aph.* 149-51; West, 2003, p. 170, my translation).

The last part of the *Hymn* deals with the aftermath of the seduction, which brings *erōs* in relation to *timē* (honor, esteem, prestige, status). When Anchises awakens to realize that he has slept with a goddess, he again fears divine retribution: "leave me not to dwell among men a mere shadow of a man, but have mercy, for the man who goes to bed with immortal goddesses loses his vitality" (*H. Aph.* 188-190; West, 2003, pp. 172-174, my translation). Aphrodite's response, "You have no need to fear that you will suffer any harm from me *or the other blessed ones*" (οὐ γάρ τοί τι δέος παθέειν κακὸν ἐξ ἐμέθεν γε, οὐδ' ἄλλων μακάρων, *H. Aph.* 194-95; West, 2003, p. 174, my translation), encompasses Anchises' fear of immediate reprisal within a wider possibility of divine retribution for having transgressed the boundary between god and mortal by making love with a goddess (a boundary of which Apollo reminds Diomedes [*Il.*5.440-442] after he has wounded Aphrodite and Ares with the help of Athena).

A clear emphasis on the inherent inferiority in *timē* of mortals to immortals in the *Hymn to Aphrodite* creates a zero-sum context for the citation of the Ganymede myth that we did not find in the Homeric citation of Ganymede. The zero-sum interpretation of *timē* based on a competitive view of the achievement, possession and loss of *timē* among the mortal heroes of the *Iliad* has been tempered among scholars by a co-operative view of *timē* based on mutual emulation among social equals (Cairns, 1993; Finkleberg, 1998). Indeed, Achilles' wrath is aroused precisely by Agamemnon's foolish appeal to a competitive sense of *timē* based on his superiority among the Achaeans as their sceptred king to Achilles as their greatest warrior, which makes Achilles' further cooperation in the siege of Troy seemingly impossible. Here, however, we are not concerned with the distribution or recognition of honor among equals, but between unequals, mortals and immortals. It should, then, appear puzzling that in Homer divine *timē* is conferred on Ganymede without cost to Zeus or other members of the Olympian family, especially Hera. (There is no evidence elsewhere in the *Iliad* of Hera suffering Juno's indignation at the *rapti Ganymedis honores.*) And while it may be true that Homer depicts the gods as intimately involved with their favorite heroes, we are constantly reminded that there is always a limit to their involvement, a limit imposed by the fated distinction between mortal and immortal. Thus, we are reminded by the closing banquet scene of *Iliad* 1 that it would be obscene for the gods so to involve themselves in human affairs as to disrupt profoundly their immortal familial harmony; and though Athena might inspire Diomedes to put Aphrodite and Ares to flight, the hero loses all courage in face of Apollo's warning that he remember that he is, after all, but mortal; and though Zeus might so grieve Sarpedon's death as to command the sky to rain blood in his honor, he does so in deference to Hera's reminder that Sarpedon, though he be Zeus' son, is (after his mother) still mortal. What seems more reasonable to expect in Homer is the zero-sum relation to *timē* which governs the sexual unions of gods and mortals in the *Hymn to Aphrodite*, and provides a general context to the citation of Ganymede. It is just this zero-sum situation in relation to the *timē* of gods and mortals that sets it apart from the Homeric citation of Ganymede.

That a zero-sum situation exists in the *Hymn to Aphrodite* is clearly evinced in Aphrodite's prophecy of the birth of Aeneas:

> You will have a beloved son, who shall rule among the Trojans . . .
> and his name shall be Aeneas (Αἰνείας), because *dread distress* (αἰνὸν ἄχος) possessed me, since I fell into the bed of a mortal man.
> (*H. Aph.* 196-199; West, 2003, p. 174, my translation)

Aphrodite's name for Aeneas acknowledges that Zeus has paid her back in kind for diminishing his *timē* among the gods. As Jenny Strauss Clay (1989) points out, "a situation in which the supreme god who possesses the greatest *timē* is at the mercy of a lesser divinity threatens to undermine the entire Olympian hierarchical system in which Zeus alone distributes and confirms divine *timai*" (p. 163). In effect, Aphrodite is confessing to her 'fall.' It reminds us of how deception has played a crucial role in the affair, as it did with the many affairs with mortals into which she had deceived Zeus. Aphrodite had deceived the mind of Zeus; Zeus deceived the mind of Aphrodite; Aphrodite deceived the mind of Anchises. The effect of succumbing to the power of Aphrodite is to take leave of one's senses so as to act contrary to one's own mind—and this seems to be a necessary prerequisite to overstepping the natural boundary between mortal and immortal.

> I shall have great reproach among the gods (μέγ᾽ ὄνειδος ἐν ἀθανάτοισι) evermore on your account. Formerly they used to be afraid of my whisperings and wiles, with which at one time or another I have coupled all the immortals with mortal women, for my will would overcome them all. But now my mouth will no longer open wide enough to mention this among the immortals, since I have been led very far astray [by my *infatuation* ἀάσθην], awfully and unutterably gone out of my mind and got a child under my girdle after going to bed with a mortal.
> (*H. Aph.* 247-255; West, 2003, pp. 178-179, Greek added)

The result of the union of god and mortal is a simultaneous decrease of *timē* for the god among their fellow immortals (by whom they are subject to ridicule), and an increase of *timē* for the mortal.[6] Anchises will gain renown as the father of Aeneas. Aeneas, as the son of Aphrodite, will exceed even the stature of his father in godlikeness. Greater still is the stature gained by Ganymede, whose story Aphrodite now relates to Anchises.

The apotheosis of Ganymede exemplifies the greatest *timē* to be won by a mortal. "Apotheosis is granted to very few mortals—a Heracles, for his heroic labours and sufferings, a Ganymede, for his superhuman beauty . . . Ganymede's fate, to become immortal and unaging . . . remains the highest and best imaginable" (Clay, 1989, pp. 186-187). Having been made the object of divine passion, Ganymede is taken up into heaven and granted the immortal life of the gods:

> ἤτοι μὲν ξανθὸν Γανυμήδεα μητίετα Ζεὺς
> ἥρπασεν ὃν διὰ κάλλος, ἵν᾽ ἀθανάτοισι μετείη
> καί τε Διὸς κατὰ δῶμα θεοῖς ἐπιοινοχοεύοι,
> θαῦμα ἰδεῖν, πάντεσσι τετιμένος ἀθανάτοισιν,
> χρυσέου ἐκ κρητῆρος ἀφύσσων νέκταρ ἐρυθρόν.
> Verily, wise Zeus *abducted* golden-haired Ganymede
> because of his beauty, so that he could be among the immortals
> and pour out wine for the gods in Zeus' house,
> *a wonder to see, honored by all the immortals*

as he draws the red nectar from the golden bowl.
(*H. Aph.*. 200-206; West, 2003, p. 174, my translation)

The *Hymn*'s debt to the *Iliad* for the Ganymede myth is obvious. In both citations, it is Ganymede's extraordinary godlike beauty that makes him desirable company among the gods (θαῦμα ἰδεῖν), and worthy of the divine honor (τετιμένος) of serving as Zeus' cupbearer. To be sure, there is a stark contrast in the general context of the Ganymede citations in the *Iliad* and the *Hymn*. In the *Iliad*, the context is war in which the principal concern is *timē*: Aeneas cites Ganymede as part of his genealogical boast that he is not Achilles' inferior in *timē*. In the *Hymn*, the context is love and the principal concern appears to be *erōs*, where Aphrodite cites Ganymede as a divine precedent to assuage her lover's fear of reprisal. However, the erotic context of the Ganymede myth in the *Hymn* never eclipses the heroic concern with *timē* that it shares with the *Iliad*.

The main differences between the two citations are (1) the use of ἁρπάζω (ravish) to describe Ganymede's abduction, which bears the sexual overtones of Paris' abduction of Helen and others and (2) that his abductor is specifically Zeus, rather than the gods in general.[7] These changes in vocabulary and agency indicate a change in motivation from a general esthetic interest to a specifically erotic interest in Ganymede's beauty. The indication of erotic interest is amplified by the *Hymn*'s addition to the Homeric account that Ganymede, in contrast to his less fortunate relative, Tithonos, is not only abducted to Olympus and made immortal, but also granted eternal youth. (In *Iliad* 5 we learn only of Tros' compensation for the loss of his son.) Zeus' desire to preserve the beauty of Ganymede's youth to which he is attracted makes permanent the age asymmetry of their relationship. Age asymmetry is the definitive characteristic of pederasty, and Zeus' desire to immortalize it in his relationship with Ganymede is the most specific indication of pederastic influence on the myth. Its permanence would make it an ideal pederastic relationship, for which reason it became the emblem of pederasty in late archaic Greek art and literature.

The erotic context of the citation, to which the erotic potential of Ganymede's abduction is most relevant, strengthens these indications of pederastic influence. It is precisely because Anchises has found himself in bed with a deity that the happy outcome of Ganymede's abduction is cited in contrast with the unfortunate fate of Tithonos. As in the Ibycus fragment, both the vocabulary of abduction and the parallel drawn between the homoerotic relationship of Zeus and Ganymede and the heterosexual relationship of Dawn and Tithonos suggests Zeus' relationship with Ganymede is not simply esthetic, but also sexual. As Dawn sleeps with Tithonos, and Aphrodite with Anchises, so, too, we infer, does Zeus take Ganymede to bed for his erotic pleasure.

The whole context of the *Hymn to Aphrodite*, then–the prologue describing Aphrodite's power of *glukus himeros* and the tale of Aphrodite's seduction of Anchises and its aftermath–places Zeus' attraction to Ganymede's beauty in a highly eroticized context that certainly *suggests* the sexual response of *glukus himeros* that Helen aroused in Paris. Perhaps more to the point, it implies that Ganymede's *kallos* arouses in Zeus the same *glukus himeros* that Hera arouses in him wearing Aphrodite's girdle in the famous seduction scene of *Iliad* 14, where Zeus repeats the *exact plea* which Paris offered to Helen: ὥς σεο νῦν ἔραμαι καί με γλυκὺς ἵμερος αἱρεῖ (*Il.*14.328; cf. 3.446). Indeed, this episode, in which Aphrodite enables Hera to seduce Zeus against his own better judgement and interest, stands together with Paris' seduction of Helen as the *loci classici* of the seductive power of Aphrodite's *glukus himeros*. No doubt these Homeric episodes of seduction are intended to form an immediate background to the whole *Hymn* in the listener's imagination.

Given the erotic context of the myth in the *Hymn*, one would expect a further alteration of the Homeric account to bring it in line with the universality of Aphrodite's power of *himeros*, sexual desire, over all creatures, including the gods. But *himeros* is conspicuously absent from Aphrodite's own account of the abduction of Ganymede, which, we should note, she does not claim to have inspired. The absence of *himeros* to describe Zeus' attraction to Ganymede reminds us that Aphrodite's *himeros* is said to be responsible specifically for Zeus' attraction to mortal *women*. Zeus' use of *glukus himeros* in his plea to the Aphrodite-girdled Hera in the *Iliad* is particularly instructive here, for it concludes his famous catalogue of affairs with mortal *women*, in which there is no mention of Ganymede (*Il.* 14.312-28). The repeated use of *himeros* in the *Hymn* to describe sexual longing, and its notable absence in Aphrodite's citation of the Ganymede myth, suggests that Zeus' abduction of Ganymede is outside Aphrodite's influence, that is, not inspired by *himeros*, sexual longing. The reason must be that *himeros* is explicitly tied in the *Hymn* to procreation, especially the procreation of heroes, and more especially to those sired by Zeus.[8]

The procreation of the hero Aeneas is the shameful result of the *glukus himeros* which a vengeful Zeus inspired in Aphrodite for

Anchises. It is not that Aphrodite desired to beget Aeneas; rather, as his name makes perfectly clear, his birth will be proof that she too has stooped to folly. This aspect of *himeros*, that it deceives the gods into generating a race of heroes against their better judgment and self-interest, is based on the zero-sum economy of relations between gods and mortals, by which increase of *timē* among mortals is at the expense of a loss of *timē* among the gods. The gods suffer the shame of being immortal parents to mortal children, while the mortals enjoy the honor of being mortal parents of semi-divine heroes:

> [lest Aphrodite] boast among the assembled gods with a merry laugh
> how she had coupled gods with mortal women,
> and how *they had borne mortal sons to immortal fathers*
> [καί τε καταθνητοὺς υἱεῖς τέκον ἀθανάτοισιν,]
> and how she had coupled goddesses with mortal men.
> (*H. Aph.* 49-52; West, 2003, pp. 162-163, emphasis and Greek
> added)

So, while at first it appears that Aphrodite cites the Ganymede myth as parallel to Anchises' situation, it turns out that this is not *exactly* the case–even, perhaps, exactly *not* the case. The situation of handsome Anchises falls between the extremes of his even more handsome forebears, Ganymede and Tithonos, and is marked off by contrast with them. The honoring of Ganymede is precisely a case in which the usual transference of *timē* from god to mortal does not occur. Ganymede does not gain honor at Zeus' expense, since Zeus does not 'fall' from his Olympian height into an earthly affair with a mortal. Rather, Zeus abducts Ganymede and brings him to Olympus where he enjoys honor among the immortal company of the gods: θαῦμα ἰδεῖν, πάντεσσι τετιμένος ἀθανάτοισιν, *a wonder to see, honored by all the immortals* (*H. Aph.* 205; West, 2003, p. 174, my translation). The Ganymede citation in the *Hymn* emphasises that Ganymede enjoys the honor of all the gods, which would only increase the prestige of his abductor, who brought him to Olympus.

Unfortunately for Anchises, Ganymede's reward will not be his:

> you will soon be enfolded by hostile, merciless old age, which attends men in the time to come, accursed, wearisome, abhorred by the gods;
> (*H. Aph.* 244-46; West, 2003, p. 179)

Aphrodite recognizes she is in no position to request for her mortal lover the honor of immortality Zeus granted to Ganymede. She knows that she has been paid back in kind by Zeus for having deceived his mind into coupling with mortal women, and subjecting him to the same shame and divine ridicule that she is now to suffer on account of Anchises. Such was Zeus' purpose from the beginning:

> But Zeus cast a sweet longing [*glukus himeros*] into Aphrodite's own heart to couple with a mortal man; he wanted to bring it about as soon as possible that not even she was set apart from a mortal bed (*H. Aph.* 45-48; West, 2003, pp. 162-163, Greek added in square brackets)

If Anchises were granted immortal status, Aphrodite would not suffer dishonor, and Zeus' purpose would not be accomplished. Anchises can only take heart that he will not suffer the horrible fate of Tithonos, whom Zeus granted immortality at Dawn's behest, while withholding the gift of youth, so that Tithonos ages forever. Anchises will suffer old age, but will receive what now appears as one of Zeus' mixed blessings, death. The glory of Ganymede remains beyond Anchises' mortal reach; it is a gift only Zeus can give, and which he gives seldom. Still, the birth of Aeneas will increase Anchises' *timē* among mortals and immortals, and that is another gift of divine love. For that is precisely what heroes are–the offspring of unions initiated by the gods (under Aphrodite's influence) with mortals, the children of divine *erōs*.

It is just this aspect of Anchises' heterosexual relationship with Aphrodite which stands in stark contrast with the homoerotic relationship of Zeus and Ganymede. Ganymede is the one and only instance in which Zeus shows erotic interest in a male. Thus, we might expect that the implied pederastic relationship would differ substantially from a heterosexual relationship, especially since, in the cosmic economy of the *Hymn*, heterosexual intercourse between gods and mortals is procreative of the race of heroes, whereas homosexual intercourse is not. The difference in cosmic result suggests a difference in cosmic purpose. The difference in cosmic result appears at first simply to be that there is no cosmic result: no hero will result from their relationship (as is also the case with Aphrodite's nonsexual relationship with Phaethon). Therefore, there is no cosmic purpose. But, in fact, there is a cosmic result: instead of a hero, the offspring of a god who has joined the mortal community of humans, we have a new divinity, a mortal human who has joined the immortal company of the gods. Surely that is the whole point of the Ganymede myth, in both the *Iliad* and the *Hymn to Aphrodite*.

Clearly Zeus abducts Ganymede because he is enamoured of his god-like beauty (διὰ κάλλος). As in Homer, Ganymede is brought to Olympus to become "a wonder to behold" in the eyes of the gods. As noted earlier, this is more like the esthetic awe Helen's beauty inspires in the Trojan elders than the sexual *glukus himeros* Helen arouses in Paris, and Hera in Zeus. The difference between the *Iliad* and the *Hymn*, however, is that the situation seems to be reversed. In the *Iliad*, the gods desire to enjoy Ganymede's beauty; therefore, they abduct him and (to avoid an Olympic quarrel) make him a gift to Zeus. In the *Hymn*, Zeus abducts Ganymede (with sexual overtones) for his own pleasure, which the other gods find acceptable on account of his beauty. The difference in situation points to the cosmic purpose of the abduction in the *Hymn*: the creation of a non-zero-sum situation in which mortals and immortals are brought together without the concomitant loss of divine *timē*. Although the *timē* of Ganymede is increased in his elevation to Olympus, that of Zeus is not thereby lessened; rather, it is mutually increased by the addition of Ganymede's beauty to the divine life of Olympian pleasures. Surely this is what is most peculiar about the myth of Ganymede. As would be pointed out in late Classical and Hellenistic times by Xenophon's *Symposium* (8.28-31, cited above) and Achilles Tatius' *Leucippe and Clitophon* (2.35-38), the myth of Ganymede is outstanding on two accounts: it the only myth in which Zeus takes a male lover, and in which a mortal lover of Zeus is elevated to a divine status (Barkan, 1991, pp. 34-36; Saslow, 1986, p. 5). Of course, this brings us back again to the relation of *timē* and *kallos* in the *Iliad*, only here a third term, *erōs*, mediates between the two: the divine *erōs* for *kallos* confers *timē* upon the human, and increases the *timē* of the gods.

Of the citation of the Ganymede myth in the *Hymn to Aphrodite*, then, we may say that the erotic context of the *Hymn* and the sexual overtones of the language describing Ganymede's abduction strongly imply an erotic relationship. This eroticization of the esthetic motive in Homer reflects the influence of institutional pederasty in the archaic period on the interpretation of the myth. We may even go so far as to say that in the *Hymn to Aphrodite* the homoerotic, asymmetrical relationship between Zeus and Ganymede is patently pederastic: Ganymede's godlike *kallos* wins for him a godlike *timē* as *erōmenos* of Zeus' *erastēs*, which is a boon for the gods, and, an honor among mortals. As such, the

Hymn to Aphrodite paves the way for Pindar to transform the myth of Ganymede into an emblem of institutional pederasty as an *ennobling love,* expressing a heroic *erōs* for *kallos* that confers *timē* upon *erastēs* and *erōmenos.*

PEDERASTY AND TIMĒ: *PINDAR*

At the end of the fifth century, Euripides cites the Ganymede myth in a choral ode celebrating the marriage of the mortal Peleus and divine Thetis that gave birth to Achilles, in which the erotic and explicitly pederastic takes precedence over the esthetic.

> What cry, in their wedding hymns, did they raise to the Libyan pipe and the cithara that loves the dance and to the strains of the reedy syrinx,
> when upon Pelion's ridges the fair-tressed Pierian Muses were coming,
> striking their gold-sandaled feet on the earth, to a feast of the gods, the marriage of Peleus? Upon the Centaurs' mountains on the wooded slopes
> of Pelion they hymned with songs melodius Thetis and the son of Aeacus.
> Dardanus' son, the luxurious darling of Zeus's bed
> [Διὸς, λέκτρων τρύφημα φίλου]
> the Phrygian Ganymede, poured the wine from the mixing bowl into golden cups.
> (*IA* 1036-53; Kovacs, 2002, pp. 280-281, Greek added)

In Euripides' citation, we see the integration of the pederastic version of the Ganymede myth with the Homeric theme of heroic honor, which is provided by the context of the birth of the greatest of all heroes, Achilles, born of the same passion between gods and mortals as Zeus felt for Ganymede. Like the *Iliad*, and unlike the *Hymn to Aphrodite*, the sexual union of god and mortal is celebrated on the human side as increasing the *timē* of mortal humans. Here, the Ganymede citation obviously helps to celebrate that honor, which implies that it is cited as an honorable example of erotic union of god and mortal, where the difference between heterosexual and homosexual affairs appears not to matter, as we might expect it would. Of course, it is not the future birth of Achilles the

Chorus celebrates (which would make the Ganymede citation incongruous), but the nuptial consummation of the marriage, with its concomitant elevation of Peleus to the same status as Anchises, as mortal *erastēs* of an immortal *erōmenos*, which is not incongruous with the elevation of Ganymede as the mortal *erōmenos* of his immortal *erastēs*, Zeus.

A different concern for the loss of *timē* was expressed much earlier in the late sixth or early fifth century pederastic verses attributed to Theognis:

> Alas, I am in love with a soft-skinned boy,
> Who shows me off to all my friends in spite of my unwillingness.
> I'll put up with the exposure–there are many things
> That one is forced to do against one's will–
> For it's by no unworthy boy that I was shown to be captivated.
> (*Thgn.* 2.1341-1345; Gerber, 1999, p. 379)

Although the poet appears to express social anxiety about public knowledge of his pederastic interests, it may be more playful than earnest. Given the author's self-publication of the affair, it appears rather to be a boast that plays against the expectation of social anxiety:

> And there is some pleasure in loving a boy,
> Since once, in fact, even the son of Cronos, king of the immortals,
> Fell in love with Ganymede, seized him, carried him off to Olympus,
> And made him divine, keeping the lovely bloom of boyhood.
> So, don't be astonished, Simonides, that I too have been revealed
> As captivated by love for a handsome boy.
> (*Thgn.* 2.1345-1350; Gerber, 1999, p. 379)

How is one to interpret the citation of Ganymede here? When we think of the accusation made against the Ganymede myth in Plato's *Laws*, it is tempting to suppose the myth became popular because it served to sanction pederasty, which it was able to do on account of its association with *timē* in Homer and the *Hymn to Aphrodite* (cf. Garrison, 2000, p. 162). Just as Zeus' love ennobled Ganymede, elevating him to immortal status, so does Zeus' pederastic example ennoble the practice of pederasty among mortals, elevating its status in society. But the playful context within which this appeal is made suggests that there is not, at least within the poet's aristocratic audience, any real need to defend pederasty.

According to Thomas Hubbard, Plato's apparent condemnation of pederasty in the *Laws* reflects the loss of status which institutional pederasty held in the sixth and early fifth centuries. As pederasty became "progressively deinstitutionalized and covert" in "the broader and more radicalized democracy of the late fifth- and fourth-centuries . . . [p]hilosophers took refuge in the fiction of a 'chaste' pederasty, which only contributed further to the marginalization of actual physical love" (Hubbard, 2000a, p. 10). David Dodd makes a similar case against Plato's Athenocentric view of pederasty, which he notes has made him a less reliable source of ethnographic information than the fourth century historian Ephorus, whose description of Cretan pederastic practices is generally taken by social historians as more historically accurate than the Platonic idealization of Athenian pederasty in *Lysis*, *Symposium* and *Phaedrus* (Dodd, 2000, pp. 33-34). Dodd finds Ephorus himself less reliable as a historian of ancient Crete than he is of the attitudes of the Athenian elite (2000, p. 41). Nevertheless, he argues that "Ephorus offers an account of pederasty in Crete in which the meaning of pederasty is clear: it is an institution in which the best men are clearly recognized as the best men" (p. 38). Above all, one learns that pederasty had no need of mythic ennoblement; as a social institution it was founded on the values of aristocratic *timē*: "participation in a pederastic relationship offered both *erastes* and *eromenos* opportunities to demonstrate a noble character that deserved the respect of other men" (p. 41).

If to Dover we are indebted for bringing Greek homosexuality out of its academic closet, it is Foucault's *The Use of Pleasure* that has provided the theoretical basis for its continued study. Whatever theoretical or ideological axes we have to grind against Foucault's social constructionist theory of sexuality in terms of knowledge and power, they can hardly be brought to bear on his "problematicizing" approach to Greek sexuality in *The Use of Pleasure*.[9] The fundamental axiom of Foucault's analysis of Greek sexuality in general, and Greek pederasty in particular, is the sexual hierarchy of penetrator/penetrated with which he would correct the anachronistic classification of Greek pederasty as a subgenre of (what we mean by) homosexuality as the antithesis of heterosexuality. Equally important, however, is the attention Foucault gives to the esthetic and ethical aspects of pederasty as a social institution in the final parts of *The Use of Pleasure*, "Erotics" and "True Love."

Foucault (1985) sets out the pederastic relationship between *erōs*, *kallos* and *timē* quite clearly from the standpoint of the *erōmenos* in the chapter, "A Boy's Honor," which studies Demosthenes' *Erotic Essay*:

> The young man–between the end of childhood and the age when he attained manly status–constituted a delicate and difficult factor for Greek ethics and Greek thought. His youth with its particular beauty [*kallos*] (to which every man was believed to be naturally sensitive [*erōs*]) and the status [*timē*] that would be his (and for which, with the help and protection of his entourage, he must prepare himself) formed a "strategic" point around which a complex game was required; his honor [*timē*]–which depended in part on the use he made of his body and which would also partly determine his future role and reputation–was an important stake in the game. (p. 213, corresponding Greek equivalents added in square brackets.)

While he may sometimes describe pederastic relationships in terms of mastery and power (p. 212), Foucault clearly recognizes that pederastic relationships are fundamentally concerned with the acquisition, possession and potential loss of *timē* (self-esteem and social status). He notes, for instance, that "it was especially in the sphere of amorous conduct that the distinction between what was honourable and what was shameful operated" (p. 207). So it is that we learn best from Foucault how *timē* was the very ground of the complex Greek practice of pederasty:

> Sexual relations thus demanded particular behaviours on the part of both partners. A consequence of the fact that the boy could not identify with the [passive/penetrated] part he had to play; he was supposed to refuse, resist, flee, escape. He was also supposed to make his consent, if he finally gave it, subject to conditions relating to the man to whom he yielded (his merit, his status, his virtue) and to the benefit he could expect to gain from him (a benefit that was rather shameful if it was only a question of money, but honourable if it involved training for manhood, social connections for the future, or a lasting friendship). And in fact it was benefits of this kind that the lover was supposed to be able to provide, in addition to the customary gifts, which depended more on status considerations (and whose importance and value varied with the condition of the partners . . . The love of boys could not be morally

honourable unless it comprised (as a result of the reasonable gifts and services of the lover and the reserved compliance of the beloved) the elements that would form the basis of a transformation of this love into a definitive and socially valuable tie, that of *philia*. (pp. 224-225, my addition in square brackets)

The grounding of pederasty in *timē* goes back to its archaic origins among the aristocracy, in what Daniel Garrison calls (in a simplified overstatement) "the ruling class cult of pederasty" (Garrison, 2000, p. 109). The distinctively Greek settings of the *gymnasia* and *symposia*, the sites of civic nudity in athletic training and intellectual discourse, were social prerequisites for the institutionalization of pederasty. The work of Percy, and now especially that of Thomas Scanlon, have focused our attention for the peculiar origins of Greek pederasty on its relationship with the gymnasium (Scanlon, 2002, pp. 64-97, 211-219; 2005; Percy, 1996, p. 95-121). Scanlon finds that "the earliest explicit literary evidence" associating pederasty with athletics is another of the pederastic verses attributed to the early to mid-sixth century elegist, Theognis of Megara (reproduced here as cited and translated in Scanlon, 2002, p. 211), in which we have what is possibly the earliest use of the verb *gumnazetai*:

Ὄλβιος ὅστις ἐρῶν γυμνάζεται οἴκαδε ἐλθών
εὕδειν σὺν καλῶι παιδὶ πανημέριος.
Happy is the lover who after spending time in the gymnasium goes home
to sleep all day long with a beautiful young man.
(Theog. *Elegiae* 2.1335-36)

Scanlon's study of circumstantial evidence suggests that athletic nudity and athletic pederasty "had become normative customs in Greek poleis by the mid sixth century" (2002, p. 211), and that the "high value placed on an athletic type of physical beauty and nudity contributed to the establishment of gymnasia and the sanctioning of homosexuality among athletes, at least from the sixth century onward" (p. 212).

The chief spokesman for the cult of pederasty at its height was Pindar, the revered early fifth century epinician poet who hailed from Boeotian Thebes, a city renowned for its aristocratic blend of militarism, athletics and pederasty, which even held an athletic festival to honor Iolaus as the *erōmenos* of Heracles (Percy, 1996, p. 134). Pindar used the pederastic myth of Ganymede *erōmenos* in two of his victory odes to confer honor and immortality upon victors at the Olympic games. The connection of these elements is most evident in the conclusion of *Olympian* 10, commissioned to commemorate the victory of the athletic youth, Hagesidamos of Western Lokroi, at the Olympiad of 476 BC in the boys' boxing, which opens with reference to Heracles as the Olympiad's founder. Just as the poets have preserved the memory of the heroic deeds of Heracles, so too will Hagesidamos' achievement win immortal renown in Pindar's victory ode.

> . . . so, when a man who has performed noble deeds,
> Hagesidamos, goes without song to Hades'
> dwelling, in vain has he striven and gained for this toil
>   but brief delight. Upon you, however, the sweetly
> speaking lyre and melodious pipe are shedding glory [χάριν],
> and the Pierian daughters of Zeus
> are fostering widespread fame [κλέος].
> (*O.*10.92-96; Race, 1997, pp. 172-173)

In this context, the basis of comparison between Hagesidamos and Ganymede *erōmenos* appears to be the same matrix of the heroic and esthetic that one has in the *Iliad* and the *Hymn to Aphrodite*. However, the homoerotic aspect of the myth as an emblem of pederasty is also central to the poet's design:

> παῖδ᾽ ἐρατὸν <δ᾽>᾽Αρχεστράτου
> αἴνησα, τὸν εἶδον κρατέοντα χερὸς ἀλκᾷ
> βωμὸν παρ᾽᾽Ολύμπιον
> κεῖνον κατὰ χρόνον
> ἰδέᾳ τε καλόν
> ὥρᾳ τε κεκραμένον, ἅ ποτε
> ἀναιδέα Γανυμήδε μόρον ἄ-
>   λακε σὺν Κυπρογενεῖ.
> I have praised the lovely son of Archestratos,
> whom I saw winning with the strength of his hand
> by the Olympic altar
> at that time,
> beautiful of form
> and imbued with the youthfulness that once averted
> ruthless death from Ganymede,
>   with the aid of the Cyprus-born goddess.
> (*O.* 10.99-106; Race, 1997, pp. 172-173)

The poet's flattering comparison of the youthful Olympian victor to the beautiful Ganymede "suggests that the poem (with the aid of the Muses) will also immortalize the young man as an act of love" (Race, 1983, p. 120). The youthful beauty of his subject inspires the poet to assume, by way of analogy, Zeus' role of *paiderastēs* in order to confer upon Hagesidamos, as his *erōmenos*, a poetic form of immortality analogous to what Zeus mythically conferred upon Ganymede.

It speaks volumes about the cultural status of Ganymede as an symbol of pederasty that Pindar should employ it so beautifully as a noble exemplar by which to fulfill his commission owed to the youth's father, Archestratos. Pindar may even be asking Archestratos' permission for Hagesidamos to become his *erōmenos*, since the poet's works show that he was a renowned pederast, with several *erōmenoi* over his lifetime, the last of which was Theoxenus. "Supposedly, while attending a contest at the theatre in Argos, he died with his head resting on the shoulders of his beloved youth Theoxenus (Valerius Maximus, 9, 2)" (Percy, 1996, p. 135). To Theoxenus he addressed a marvellous choral ode in praise of his beauty, which confesses the Sapphic intensity of the pederast's desire for his *erōmenos*: "But I, to grace the goddess [Aphrodite], like wax of the sacred bees when smitten by the sun, am melted when I look at the young limbs of boys (Athenaeus, XIII, 601c-d)" (Percy, 1996, p. 137). (Garrison suggests that the poem is "less autobiographical than protreptic," and encapsulates the values of the "Pederastic Code," according to which pederasty is "a litmus of 'true nobility,' which is above all a social category" (2000, p. 110).)

Olympian 1 is a victory ode commissioned by Hieron, King of the Dorian colony of Syracuse, as winner of the single-horse race in the same Olympiad of 476 BC in which Hagesidamos won the boys boxing. The poem takes for its subject Pelops, legendary founder of the Peloponnese, "with whom mighty Eartholder Poseidon fell in love" *Olympian* 1.25-26 (Race, 1997, pp. 48-49). Hieron's victory is celebrated by revising the traditional stories regarding Pelops and his father, Tantalos, which Pindar claims were lies. Tantalos had been accused of inviting the gods to a banquet at which he served up his own son, Pelops, in a stew to test the gods' omniscience (Powell, 2000, pp. 510-511). Pindar argues that, like Ganymede, Pelops was abducted by Poseidon at the banquet to receive the Olympian honor of becoming his *erōmenos*:

τοτ᾽ Ἀγλαοτρίαιναν ἀπράσαι,
δαμέντα φρένας ἱμέρῳ, χρυσέαισί τ᾽ ἀν᾽ ἵπποις
ὕπατον εὐρυτίμου ποτὶ δῶμα Διὸς μεταβᾶσαι·
ἔνθα δευτέρῳ χρόνῳ
ἦλθε καὶ Γανυμήδης
Ζηνὶ τωὔτ᾽ ἐπὶ χρέος.

then it was that the Lord of the Splendid Trident seized you,
his mind overcome by desire, and with golden steeds
conveyed you to the highest home of widely honored Zeus,
where at a later time
Ganymede came as well
for the same service to Zeus.
(*Olympian* 1.40-45; Race, 1997, pp. 50-51)

Pindar's reference to the mind (φρένη) of the god being overtaken by sexual longing (ἵμερος) draws on the eroticized account of the Ganymede myth in the *Hymn to Aphrodite*. According to Gerber (1982), Pindar's euphemistic use of χρέος, 'service,' strongly suggests the pederastic relationship between Zeus and Ganymede implied in the *Hymn to Aphrodite* (p. 81), a suggestion intensified by comparison with the relationship between Poseidon and Pelops. That the latter is pederastic is "obvious from vv 25 (ἐράσσατο), 41 (δαμέντα ... ἱμέρῳ), and 75 (φίλια δῶρα Κυπρίας)" (p. 81). The comparison between Pelops and Ganymedes "serves as a means of praising Pelops and therefore Hieron, his analogue" (p. 79). This works because of the honor and immortality conferred upon Ganymede *erōmenos* by the gods: "Part of the praise is implicit in the position of the honour enjoyed by Ganymedes, and hence by Pelops, but part is also implicit in the immortality which Ganymedes had acquired. This is clearly stated in *O*.10.105 (cf. *H. Aph.* 214) where he is said to have escaped ἀναιδέα ... θάνατον (ruthless death)" (p. 79).

The direct line of interpretation of the Ganymede myth which we have traced through Homer, the *Hymn to Aphrodite* and Pindar shows the evolution of the pederastic version of the Ganymede myth into an emblem of how human *erōs* may obtain *timē* of the highest order: divine immortality and a place in the company of the gods. To Pindar belongs the *explicit* association of human *erōs* with divine *timē* in the pederastic relationship of Zeus and Ganymede that is later idealized by Plato. Pindar also marks the culmination of a literary trend, simultaneously evidenced in contemporary artistic depictions of Zeus *erastēs* in pederastic pursuit of Ganymede *erōmenos*, of bringing the heroic aspect of the myth out of the realm of gods and heroes and into relation to actual human relationships. This trend is evident in the pederastic citations of the myth in Ibycus and the Theognid verses. In the latter case, however, the lustre of Ganymede's mythic *timē* among the gods seems slightly tarnished by the very comparison through which the poet seeks to polish his *timē* among his aristocratic peers. In Pindar, this is not the case. Nothing is lost by comparison of Pindar and Hagesidamos with Zeus and Ganymede, or Ganymede with Hieron: the association is noble on both sides, and the association of the two only serves to increase each other's *timē*. In other words, Pindar's use of the Ganymede myth accords with its meaning: here is a form of love in which the human is elevated in *timē* by its approximation to its divine exemplar.

In Plato's *Phaedrus*, the myth of Zeus' love of Ganymede is taken up into a transcendent vision of the *erōs* of the soul. Pindar's athletic *erōs* is brought together with a pederastic pedagogy in which the sexual is sublimated in the spiritual, and in which the heroic pursuit of godlike *timē* and immortality takes on the form of the philosophic pursuit of the immortal life of the ideal realm of being.

HIMERŌS *AND* PHILIA: *PEDERASTY AND PEDAGOGY IN PLATO'S* PHAEDRUS

The *Phaedrus*, like the *Symposium* and other of Plato's dialogues, presupposes the establishment of pederasty as a pedagogical institution among the Athenian aristocracy since at least the sixth century. In keeping with the distinction between public and private life in Athens, pederasty was not institutionalized as in Crete and Sparta, but was first introduced by Solon (himself a pederast; see Percy, 1996, pp. 177-179) as more of an aristocratic social custom and "freer practice associated, inter alia, with gymnasia and symposia" (Scanlon, 2002, p. 213).[10]

The pedagogical role of the *erastēs* was chiefly that of mentor to his protégé, the *erōmenos*. The *erōmenos* received the benefit of the *erastēs'* life-experience in civic affairs, social graces, and, by association, the prestige and favor attendant upon the *erastēs'* social standing, and influence in political, military and other civic spheres of power and responsibility. In exchange, the *erastēs'* erotic attraction was favorably received by the *erōmenos* and formally recognized in public activities, as well as by the granting of sexual favors, normally intercrually and privately. The pederastic relationship ended when the *erōmenos* reached the age of citizenship, and the bond established between the lovers would take the form of a nonsexual adult *philia* (friendship). In essence, then, pedagogical pederasty enabled a youth to make the social transition from adolescence to adulthood, and the civic transition from legal dependant to enfranchised citizen. (See relevant chapters in Dover, 1989; Foucault, 1985; Percy, 1996; Garrison, 2000; Scanlon, 2002; Ludwig, 2002.)

As Paul Ludwig (2002, drawing on the argument developed in Halperin from Dover and Foucault)[11] shows in relation to his analysis of Pausanias' speech in Plato's *Symposium*, the Athenian relationship of pedagogy and pederasty arises from the social expectation that the *erōmenos* should not share the erotic interest of his *erastēs*.[12]

> It was the boy's assumed lack of desire that gave rise to the need for some different 'coin' to attract the boy into a relationship, something extrinsic to a love relationship, that the older lover possessed but the boy did not. Doubtless what the lover had to offer was often athletic coaching and advice. Men who had the wherewithal to hold office, however, could also compete for the favors of boys of their own class by graduating from athletic mentorship, as the boy's intellect matured, to political mentorship and even political preferment. (pp. 30-31)

Socrates, however, uses the pederastic myth of Ganymede *erōmenos* at *Phaedrus* 255b7-c4 to illustrate the Platonic doctrine of erotic reciprocity or *anterōs*. This places the myth at the center of the Platonic relationship of pedagogy and pederasty, which is the subject of Socrates' second discourse on *erōs* in the *Phaedrus*, in which Socrates uses the allegory of a charioteer driving two horses to explain the relation of reason, spirit and desire in the soul.[13] Near the end of this allegory, he cites Zeus' *himeros* for Ganymede, the erotic term specifically used for sexual longing in the *Hymn to Aphrodite* and Pindar:

> When the lover has been doing this [courting the beloved] for some time, and there has been physical contact between them at meetings in the gymnasium and elsewhere, then at last the flowing stream (which Zeus called "desire" [ἵμερον] when he was in love with Ganymede) pours down on the lover in such great quantities

that while some of it sinks into him, the rest flows off outside as he fills up and brims over. (*Phdr.* 255b7-c4; Waterfield, 2002, p. 40, Greek added in square brackets)

We may need to recall that in the *Hymn to Aphrodite*, Aphrodite's *glukus himeros*, which deceived the mind of Zeus to beget heroes with mortal women and deceived Aphrodite to beget Aeneas by Anchises, was not explicitly used to account for Zeus' abduction of Ganymede. Nor was the patently pederastic relationship to be inferred from the erotic context of Aphrodite's narration of Ganymede's abduction made explicit either. Though its contextual narration in the *Hymn* shows pederastic influence, the Ganymede myth only becomes explicitly pederastic upon its translation into the pederastic tradition of archaic Greek lyric, beginning with Ibycus. *Himeros* is first used to describe Zeus' attraction to Ganymede in the pederastic verses attributed to Theognis and in the Olympian odes of Pindar. It is most directly the pederastic version of the myth (and especially that of Pindar for Plato) that is intellectualized in the philosophic discourses of Xenophon and Plato. Xenophon, we recall, had Socrates argue that Zeus's attraction was not to the physical beauty of Ganymede, but to his soul (καὶ Γανυμήδην οὐ σώματος ἀλλὰ ψυχῆς ἕνεκα ὑπὸ Διὸς εἰς Ὄλυμπον ἀνενεχθῆναι, *Symp.* 8.30). To support his argument, Xenophon's Socrates etymologized Ganymede's name. Likewise, Plato's Socrates etymologizes the sexually explicit *himeros* as part of his strategy to relate pederasty and pedagogy. *Himeros* is interpreted scientifically[14] at 251c as an ethereal flow of particles emanating from the visible beauty of an *erōmenos* through the eyes of the *erastēs* and into his soul:[15]

When it [the soul of the *erastēs*] gazes on the young man's beauty [which reflects the intelligible being of beauty], and receives the [hot and moist] particles emanating from it as they approach and flow in—which, of course, is why we call it desire [ἵμερος]–it is watered and heated, and it recovers from its pain [of growing wings] and is glad. (*Phdr.* 251c5-d1; Waterfield, 2002, p. 35, additions in square brackets)[16]

Whereas Zeus was inspired to abduct Ganymede and make him his immortal *erōmenos*, the soul of the *erastēs* is inspired by the beauty of the *erōmenos* to return to the eternal realm of being, the realm of beauty itself, wherein it recollects the knowledge of its own immortal nature. In the language of Plato's myth, the *erastēs'* soul is irrigated by the particles of beauty emanating from the *erōmenos*, and begins to grow the wings of reason that will carry it aloft to the realm of being. His *erōs* for the *erōmenos* awakens in the *erastēs* the soul's *erōs* for the form of beauty. The *erōmenos*, in turn, experiences the same effect by way of the reciprocal overflow of *anterōs*.

> Just as a gust of wind or an echo rebounds from smooth, hard objects and returns to where it came from, so the flow of beauty returns into the beautiful boy through his eyes, which is its natural route into the soul, and when it arrives and excites him, it irrigates his wings' channels and makes his plumage start to grow, and fills the soul of the beloved in his turn with love. So he is in love, but he has no idea what he is in love with. He does not know what has happened to him and he cannot explain it . . . he fails to appreciate that he is seeing himself in his lover as in a mirror . . . He has contracted counter-love [ἀντέρωτα] as a reflection of his lover's love, but he calls it and thinks of it as friendship (*philia*) rather than love (*erōs*). His desires are more or less the same as his lover's, though weaker–to see, touch, kiss, lie down together–and as you might expect before long this is exactly what he does. (*Phdr.* 255c4-e4; Waterfield, 2002, p. 40)

Anterōs is a pederastic innovation by Plato, as erotic interest traditionally resided only in the *erastēs* (Halperin, 1990b, pp. 268-269).[17] The *anterōs* of the *erōmenos* mirrors that of the *erastēs*, but the *erōs* of neither is ultimately directed toward or inspired by the other. Rather, they are being affected by Beauty itself, whose divine, inspirational effluence is described in Diotima's speech in the *Symposium*. In truth, both are simultaneously the *erastai* and *erōmenoi* of Beauty itself.[18] As Halperin (1990b) points out, it is the Platonic *anterōs* that has the liberating effect on the pederastic relationship of releasing its pedagogical potential: "Plato all but erases the distinction between the "active" and the "passive" partner . . . both members of the relationship become active, desiring lovers; neither remains a merely passive object of desire. By granting the beloved access to a direct, if reflected, erotic stimulus, . . . Plato . . . allows the beloved to grow philosophically in the contemplation of the Forms" (p. 269).

Plato translates the Homeric emphasis on *timē*, the heroic element of pederastic *erōs* employed by Pindar to confer honor and immortality on athletic victors, into the philosophic life. The sexual aspect of a pederastic relationship is allowed to the desiderative element of the soul (black horse in Socrates' chariot myth of the soul) in both *erastēs* and *erōmenos*, by the soul's rational element (charioteer). Eventually, however, the sexual aspect of the pederastic relationship is purged as a kind of 'necessary evil' that needs be tolerated no longer:

> When they lie together, the lover's undisciplined horse makes suggestions to the charioteer and demands a little pleasure to reward it for all its pains. The boy's undisciplined horse has nothing to say, but in its desire and confusion embraces the lover and kisses him ... lying down together it is inclined not to refuse to play its part in gratifying any request the lover might make. Its team-mate (white horse = spirited element), however, sides with the charioteer and resists this inclination by arguments designed to appeal to its sense of shame. If the better aspects of their minds win and steer them towards orderly conduct and philosophy, they live a wonderful, harmonious life here on earth, a life of self-control and restraint, since they have enslaved the part which allowed evil into the soul and freed the part which allowed goodness in. (*Phdr*.255e4-256a6; Waterfield, 2002, p. 41)

In both *erastēs* and *erōmenos*, the Platonic sublimation of the pederastic *erōs* prepares the soul's return to the immortal realm of being:

> And when they die, as winged and soaring beings they have won the first of the three truly Olympic bouts, which brings greater benefits than either human sanity or divine madness can supply. (*Phdr*.256a7-b7; Waterfield, 2002, p. 41)

Plato's transformation of the Ganymede myth in the *Phaedrus* into an symbol for the psyche's *erōs* for the divine *timē* of immortality articulates the fundamental meaning which the myth has for Homer, the *Hymn to Aphrodite* and Pindar. Plato's abstraction of the pedagogical aspect of pederastic influence on the myth from its sexual aspect does not actually contradict the earlier history of pederastic influence, nor the Greek institution of pederasty as a pedagogical institution. It does, however, tend toward the sublimation of the sexual in the spiritual in a way that is especially characteristic of the Platonic philosophy of the sensible realm as an image of the intelligible.

The effect of the Platonic abstraction of the intelligible meaning of the Ganymede myth from the myth itself is twofold. On the one hand, it makes possible the transition of the pederastic eroticization of the myth as a spiritual icon into orthodox Christian culture; on the other hand, it effectively isolates the strictly sexual longing of *glukus himeros*, and its overtly pederastic characterization, to the marginalized tradition of erotica. For Plato, the separation of the spiritual and carnal aspects of pederastic *erōs* paves the way also for the censorship of the Ganymede myth in the *Laws*, where it appears to be regarded no longer as the philosophic emblem of the soul's desire for the divine, but as an societal emblem of social degeneracy and decadence among Greek aristocracies of the fourth century.

ERŌS *AND* NOMOS:
PLATO'S LAWS

> Males coming together with males, and females with females, seems against nature; and the daring of those who first did it seems to have arisen from a lack of self-restraint with regard to pleasure. But, the fact is, we all accuse the Cretans of being the originators of the myth of Ganymede: since their laws were believed to have come from Zeus, they added this myth about Zeus so that they could be following the god as they continued to reap the enjoyments of this pleasure. (*Leg.* 636c7-d4; Pangle, 1980, p. 16)

The myth of Ganymede is censored in the *Laws* for justifying pederasty as a primarily (homo) sexual rather than pedagogical practice. Pedagogy was the basis on which pederasty rose to prominence in archaic Greece and was established as a social institution among the aristocracy of Crete, Sparta, Thebes, Athens, and other cities. According to Xenophon and Plutarch, civic harmony was the social and political good aimed for in sanctioning pederastic pedagogy. The Spartan system of *paideia* sought to inculcate that greatest of Spartan virtues, "obedience to the law." In *Laws* 1, Plato's Athenian ties the Greek origins of pederasty to that of the gymnasium and communal institutions of Sparta and Crete intended to promote political unity. But he then criticizes these communal institutions for their dangerous potential to fraction rather than unify the political community in times of civic strife:

So it is with these gymnastics and common meals [in Sparta and Crete]: in many other ways they now benefit cities, but in the event of civil strife they are harmful (as shown by the examples of the Miletian, Boeotian, and Thurian boys). (*Leg.* 636b1-4; Pangle, 1980, p. 15)

It is in support of the political good of unity that the Athenian Stranger criticizes pederasty as a subspecies of homosexuality for contradicting *nomos* (*law, custom tradition*), as well as the natural order (*phusis*), a law of nature to which human and animal are equally subject:

What's more, there is an ancient law (παιλαιὸν νόμου) concerning sexual pleasures (τὰ ἀφροδίσια) not only of humans but of beasts, a law laid down even in nature (καὶ κατὰ φύσιν), which this practice seems to have corrupted. For these offenses your cities might be the first to be accused by someone, along with other cities that zealously pursue gymnastics.[19] (*Leg.* 636b4-c1; Pangle, 1980, p. 15, Greek added)

It is worth noting that the grounds on which Plato's Athenian advances his argument are antithetical to those on which Socrates advocates the education of women in *Republic* 5 (451-457). Whereas the Athenian argues on the basis of the *commonality* of human and animal nature, Socrates argues on the basis of the *radical distinction* between our distinctively rational human nature (*anthropinē phusis* 453a1) and our common animal nature (*phusis*). Socrates proposes the coeducation of female guardians, which would require gymnastic training (452a). The Greek practice of exercising in the nude is said to have originated in Crete, spread to Sparta, and then the rest of Greece (452c6-d1). Indeed, by the fifth century, nude athletics had become emblematic of the Greek way of life. Yet, Socrates argues, this practice was at first abhorred by the Greeks as barbaric until they saw the good of it, whereupon it became an ethnic custom (*ethos*) distinctive of the Greek way of life (452d3-6). In the same way, Socrates reasons (452-457), Hellenes will ridicule their proposal that women exercise naked in the gymnasium as contrary to custom (*para to ethos* 452a-e3), contrary to reason (*antilogikon* 452e4-454e3), and contrary to nature (*para phusin* 454e6-456c3). But once they see the good of it according to reason, they will accept it as in accord to our (specifically human) nature (*phusis*), and will be adopted as a new custom (*nomos*) (456b12-c2).

Precisely the opposite argument is brought against homosexuality and pederasty in book eight of the *Laws*. The Athenian appeals to the pre-political state of nature as a guide to human conduct that Socrates aligns with primitivism and barbarism, and criticizes the progressive rationality of the pedagogical institutions of Sparta and Crete on which Socrates had modeled his ideal state:

> For although in quite a few other matters Crete as a whole and Lacedaimon have been decent enough to give us considerable aid as we establish laws that differ from the ways of the many, in regard to erotic things–speaking now among ourselves–they are totally opposed to us. If someone were to follow nature and lay down the law that prevailed before Laius, if he were to say that it was correct to avoid, with males and youths, sexual relations like those one has with females, bringing as a witness the nature of the beasts and demonstrating that males don't touch males with a view to such things because it is not according to nature to do so, his argument would probably be unpersuasive, and not at all in consonance with your cities. (*Leg.* 836b4-c7; Pangle, 1980, p. 227)

Ironically, the Athenian argues from a common animal nature *in cause of the same end* for which Socrates argues from a distinctively human nature, the attainment of the political good of unity by way of establishing a community of pleasure and pain among the citizenry (cf. *Rsp.* 462):

> About the myth no more need be said; but about human beings who inquire into laws almost their entire inquiry concerns pleasures and pains, in cities and in private dispositions. (*Leg.* 636d4-e7; Pangle, 1980, p. 16)

Pederasty as a sexual practice directed primarily to self-gratification, along with homosexuality, masturbation, incest and adultery, is criminalized by the sexual regulations of in book eight of the *Laws* (835-42) as depriving society of the procreation of desirable offspring, which result from heterosexual marriages. Plato's Athenian still seeks, however, to incorporate the pedagogical ideal of pederasty, based on the esthetic attraction of *kallos* and of the *erōs* for *timē* described in *Symposium* and *Phaedrus*, into the pedagogy of the *Laws*.

The description of the 'third' form of erotic attraction, in which is mixed the gentle attraction of similars and the violent attraction of opposites, at *Laws* 8.837b-c is remarkably similar to the description of the soul in terms of the charioteer and two horses in the *Phaedrus*. Here, as there, an idealized pederasty is described in terms of an *erastēs'* struggle to overcome his sexual attraction to the physical beauty of the *erōmenos* (the dark horse of the *Phaedrus*), on the one hand, so as to realize his intellectual attraction to the beauty of the *erōmenos'* soul (the white horse guided by the charioteer), on the other:

> because he is drawn in opposite directions by the two loves, he finds himself at a loss, with one bidding him to pick the bloom of youth and the other telling him not to. For the man who loves the body, hungering for the bloom as for the ripe fruit, bids himself take his fill without honouring the disposition of soul of the beloved. The other sort of lover holds the desire for the body to be secondary; looking at it rather than loving it, with his soul he really desires the soul of the other and considers the gratification of the body to be wantonness. He holds in awe and reverence what is moderate, courageous, magnificent, and prudent, and would wish to remain always chaste with a beloved who is chaste. (*Leg.* 837b6-d1; Pangle, 1980, p. 228)

Plato's Athenian, like Socrates in the *Symposium*, *Phaedrus* and *Republic*, would, if at all possible, salvage the nonsexual pederastic *erōs* for *kallos* and *timē* from the sexual impulse toward self-gratification, in the *philia* that arises between those of similar disposition toward the beautiful and good:

> should the law exclude all [three forms of love–between similars, opposites, and mixed] and prevent them from arising among us, or isn't it obvious that we would want to have in our city the type [love between similars] which belongs to virtue and desires that the youth become as excellent as possible, while we would forbid the other two, if we could? (*Leg.* 837d2-7; Pangle, 1980, p. 228, additions in square brackets)

As far as the myth of Ganymede goes, its non-procreative aspect had always made it outstanding in Greek mythology as a divine exemplar for the erotic union of the human and divine, as well as a divine exemplar for homoeroticism. Likewise, the non-procreative aspect of homo-erotic *erōs* allowed it to be institutionalized socially as a pedagogical institution, in which *erōs* was directed towards the inculcation of virtues necessary to obtain *timē*. Excessive ambition ruined the polis, and, in Plato's view, to some extent pederastic associations worked to provoke that sort of championing one's own (as in Pindar's victory odes). So long as the private citizen sought his good in the good of his polis, where his personal victory is celebrated as increasing the *timē* of his city, all is fine. But where private ambition became stronger than patriotism, where *timē* tore apart the polis into political factions such as Thucydides describes, private associations became unwelcome to the political thinking of Plato and he sought to eradicate them for what they had become: institutions of private ambition rather than public service.

The Platonic purgation of pederasty in *Phaedrus* and *Laws*, in which the aphrodisiacal element of *himeros,* sexual longing, is wholly sublimated into the spiritual longing of the soul, easily offends those who take the physically erotic element to be primary and essential to the Greek practice of pederasty. For this reason, Socrates' idealisation of pederasty in *Symposium* and *Phaedrus*, and the Athenian Stranger's criminalization of homosexuality in the *Laws* (the idealisation of pederasty is overlooked) are equally criticized by Thomas Hubbard (2000a) as acts of intellectual and moral hypocrisy, designed to appease a popular backlash of democratic prejudice against the practice of pederasty among aristocratic intellectuals in the fourth century:

> Indeed, Plato's latest work, the *Laws* (636B-E, 836B-841E), drops all pretence of defending pederasty as chaste love or as a metaphor for union with ideal Beauty; instead it is dismissed as an unnecessary and "unnatural" pleasure, best regulated out of existence . . . By creating such a sharp dichotomy between Uranian, intellectual love and sexual love, Plato and other fourth-century intellectuals unwittingly promoted a conceptual matrix in which all physical love of boys came to be only physical love. Robbed of cultural status and its civic mission of providing role models to future citizens, pederasty came to be identified more with male prostitution . . . (pp. 9-10)

In Hubbard's view, "Plato and others sold out the real pederasts by pretending that there could be a chaste, purely spiritual pederasty" (2000a, p. 11).[20] Hubbard's allegations of moral and intellectual hypocrisy are generally ill-founded. Neither Plato's most famous and influential work, the *Republic*, nor his least famous and influential, the *Laws*, can be accused of pandering to the *hoi polloi*–that much, at least, Karl Popper got right in his attack on Plato as an 'enemy of the open society.' Certainly, the *Laws* is no less vulnerable to charges of elitist, aristocratic prejudice against the *demos* and democracy than the *Republic*.[21] Democracy, which puts government in the hands of the *demos*, is consistently vilified as the worst condition next to tyranny on the one hand and anarchy on the other. If anything, the *Laws* appears even less trusting of the ability of the populace to live according to the dictates of reason than the *Republic*; the Athenian's theocracy of 'Magnesia' under the rule of the Nocturnal Council is even more open to charges of totalitarianism than is Socrates' 'Callipolis.' There is no obvious attempt in either work to appease a popular prejudice against the Athenian aristocracy (most of whom still ran the democratic government of Athens). Few persons in Plato are not of the aristocracy, either of Athens or abroad. There are no characters that could be said to represent a noble *demos*. If anything, it is not with the popular opinion of the largely illiterate *demos* with which Plato is principally concerned, especially in fourth-century Athens. Rather, it is with a badly demoralized and degenerate aristocracy that had always manipulated the *demos* in aristocratic struggles for power, and which championed the popular cause for personal gain.

Plato's idealization and criminalization of pederasty is comparable to, and most closely associated with, his representation and reform of the *oikos* (family, household; *oikoi* is the plural form) in the *Republic* and *Laws*. In both dialogues, Plato reforms the private *oikos* as an institution of selfishness detrimental to the political good of civic harmony, even as he reforms the polis in the accord with the *oikos* as an institution of unity conducive to the public good, by instituting communal *syssitia*, which makes the polis into a kind of *oikos*. In the *Republic*, there are essentially three representations of the *oikos*: the moderate arcadian *oikoi* of the city of pigs; the degenerate *oikoi* of extreme wealth and poverty of the artisans in the city of luxuries; and the ideal communal *oikoi* of the guardians in the city of the blessed, or Callipolis. It is the argument of the *Republic* that the original familial harmony of the moderate *oikoi* is corrupted by the political disease of pleonexia, and degenerates into the immoderate *oikoi* of wealth and poverty, which are restored to health in the communal *oikoi* of the guardians. It is easy to recognize that the *oikoi* of wealth and poverty are characteristic of the fifth and fourth century *oikos*, in which the family as an institution of membership has degenerated into the institution of ownership. The argument is precisely the same with respect to the idealization of pederasty in the *Phaedrus* as an institution of pedagogy, and its criminalization in *Laws* as an unlawful and unnatural sexual practice. What it reflects is not the prejudice of the *demos*, but the moral degeneracy of the aristocracy, and with it, of pederasty from a pedagogical institution concerned above all with *timē* in the sixth and early fifth centuries, into an ignoble practice concerned primarily with sexual gratification in the late fifth and fourth centuries. Plato's argument suggests not that he drove pederasty into prostitution, as Hubbard avers, but that it took that course as an aspect of political and social decline in Athens. With profound consistency, Plato idealized its original nobility as a pedagogical institution in the *Symposium* and *Phaedrus*, even as he described its degenerate tendency toward sexual abasement of which it was ultimately purged in the *Laws*.

CONCLUSION

By tracing the history of the Ganymede myth in Greek art and literature from Homer to Plato, we have been able to establish that pederastic influence on the Homeric myth of Ganymede enabled it to evolve (in a continuous line of development easily traced by the thematic use of the Homeric phrase, *glukus himeros*, in association with the myth) into a pederastic emblem of the erotic union of the human and divine. Perhaps it would be fitting, by way of conclusion, to reflect on the pederastic influence on the characterization of *glukus himeros* in this history.

In the *Iliad*, *glukus himeros* is used by Paris (3.446), and repeated by Zeus (14.328), to describe their respective sexual longings for Helen and Hera. Both situations are under the direct influence of Aphrodite, and in both sexual desire is aroused by the sight of immortal beauty, providing an esthetic context to the erotic situation. In the *Hymn to Aphrodite* we learn that *glukus himeros* is a power of sexual longing which Aphrodite yields over all mortal creatures, and all the gods, except Athena, Artemis and Hestia. Zeus, especially, falls prey to its capacity to deceive one's mind (φρενα) to engage in sexual affairs with mortals that lessen his *timē* among the gods. In the account of Aphrodite's seduction of Anchises, as in Hera's seduction of Zeus in *Iliad* 14, there is great emphasis upon the esthetic context of the erotic union of human and divine. In neither the *Iliad* nor in the *Hymn*, however, is the sexually explicit *glukus himeros* used to describe the attraction which Ganymede's "godlike beauty" inspires in the gods, and in Zeus. The reason for this would seem to be that in the *Hymn*, as in Zeus' catalogue of his affairs to Hera in *Iliad* 14, *glukus himeros* not only inspires sexual union, but also procreation as the result of heterosexual attraction. Indeed, we are told that is precisely what brings about public disgrace to the gods, as it does with Aphrodite.

On the one hand, then, it would seem that Aphrodite's esthetic-erotic power of *glukus himeros* is of a purely heterosexual nature in the *Iliad* and *Hymn to Aphrodite*. On the other hand, the contextual association of *glukus himeros* with the Ganymede myth in the *Hymn* is sufficient to suggest, in conjunction with the sexual connotation of ἁρπάζω, and the direct agency of Zeus as Ganymede's abductor, sexual longing in Zeus as the *erastēs* in a pederastic relationship with Ganymede as *erōmenos*. This is the first suggestion in Greek literature of pederastic influence on the Ganymede myth, reflecting the rise of pederasty in prominence as a social institution among the aristocracies of archaic Greece. It is also the first suggestion that *glukus himeros* might be oriented to another end than sexual union and, where this occurs between mortals and immortals, procreation of heroes. Indeed, Ganymede's apotheosis itself suggests another possibility for the erotic union of the divine and human, and a profound alteration in the characterization of *glukus himeros* as we have it in the *Iliad* and the *Hymn to Aphrodite*. For Zeus' affair with Ganymede did not fall within the zero-sum situation of *timē* that governed heterosexual unions of gods and mortals. Rather, the union increased the *timē* of both. Such a love as that which Ganymede's beauty inspired in Zeus would seem to have this extraordinary potential, not for the procreation of semi-divine heroes, but for the elevation of the human to the divine.

But we should also take into consideration that in the two most famous instances of the seductive power of *glukus himeros* we have mentioned–Hera's seduction of Zeus and Paris' seduction of Helen–the esthetic relationship of *erōs* and *kallos* is removed from its cosmic procreative function. It may be that the relationship of Zeus and Ganymede should be thought of as exploring the implications of an erotic desire which has for its end a divine enjoyment, and for which the cosmic purpose is not the procreation of heroes, but precisely the satisfaction of the longing in the immortal and divine for that which falls outside itself–the mortal and human–which is reciprocated on the human side by a mutual desire to become the object of that divine love.

Pindar brings *glukus himeros* into even closer proximity to the Ganymede myth by ascribing it to Poseidon's abduction of Pelops, as a parallel instance to Zeus' abduction of Ganymede. On the one hand,

Pindar is drawing on the pederastic tradition already established by Ibycus and possibly Theognis, in which the divine attraction of Zeus to Ganymede is brought down to earth, as an example pled by *erastai* embarrassed by their *erōmenoi*. On the other hand, it is more the case that Pindar is relating this earthly love back, via the *Hymn to Aphrodite*, to the heroic status of Ganymede in the *Iliad*. In Pindar, the potential of Aphrodite's *glukus himeros* to confer *timē* rather than to deprive one of it is realised in the explicitly pederastic paradigm of Zeus and Ganymede. Here Pindar reflects the aristocratic concern for *timē* that governed the institutionalization of pederasty as a pedagogical institution, that is, as an erotic relationship within which the adolescent *erōmenos* was educated by his *erastēs* and made the transition into adult society.

Ironically, it is Plato who applies Aphrodite's *glukus himeros* explicitly to the erotic relationship of *erastēs* and *erōmenos* as fundamentally pedagogical. Ironically, because in the act of doing so, he so alters its characterization that its sexual meaning is entirely subsumed by its esthetic-heroic aspect, and its potential to express the primal longing of the soul to regain its *timē* as a immortal being in its own right. Rather than describing the state of sexual arousal that results from gazing upon the sensuous beauty of a person's appearance, Plato uses *himeros* to describe an esthetic-erotic longing in the soul for the form of the beautiful that is aroused by the sensual aspect of physical beauty. The Platonic *himeros* expresses the deepest arousal in the soul of an erotic longing for its true immortal life. As such, Plato's citation of the Ganymede myth as an emblem of pederasty and pedagogy can be seen to articulate the deepest implication of its potential meaning for the erotic union of the human and divine.

NOTES

1. Current discussion of Greek homosexuality and pederasty start from Dover and Foucault. By pederasty we mean what the Greeks meant: a consensual, homoerotic relationship between adolescent and adult males, which *we* would categorize (somewhat anachronistically) as homosexual. Ped-erasty refers to the *erōs* of the *erastēs* for a *pais*, the adult love of an adolescent. In the pederastic verses attributed to Theognis, the cognate term, pedophilia, is used. Needless to say, pederasty (both ancient and modern) should not be confused with our meaning of pedophilia to designate the sexual exploitation–whether heterosexual or homosexual–of a child's immaturity. The distinction between the two is observed socially by recognizing an appropriate age for erotic interest on the part of the adult and for sexual consent on the part of the adolescent. The ideal

age of the *erōmenos* depicted on vase-paintings and described graphically as the age of a first beard is that of a 14- to 17-year-old. The Theognid verses which praise the erotic beauty of boys from ages twelve to seventeen does so within a spectrum of erotic interest which begins with the anticipation of the full bloom of beauty in late adolescence suggested at its earliest age. At any rate, there is no evidence of (socially acceptable) pederastic interest in prepubescent boys.

2. For a review of explicitly sexual depictions of the myth, see Dover, 1989, pp. 6, 71, 92; Calame, 1999, pp. 66, 71, 80; and Kilmer, 1997, pp. 128-129. To place in the larger context of Greek erotica, see Kilmer (1993). See also Shapiro's more recent study (2000) of pederastic courtship scenes, "Leagros and Euphronius: Painting Pederasty in Athens."

3. For an overview of fourth century erotics, see Garrison, 2000, chap. 6. See also Nussbaum, 2002, and Price, 2002.

4. For brief discussions of the distributive and other applications of *timē* in Homeric and post-Homeric literature, and the complexity of its private/public, personal/social, competitive/co-operative meanings, see Cairns (1993, esp. pp. 83-103) and Finkleberg (1998, esp. pp. 14-20). I am indebted to Leona McLeod, Department of Classics, Dalhousie University, for helping to clarify the Greek concept of *timē*.

5. There is consensus that the *Hymn to Aphrodite* is the earliest and most Homeric of the Homeric hymns, but it has proven difficult to date. "There are only general indications of date . . . the seventh century seems to be the latest date possible" (Evelyn-White, 1974, p. xxxviii). A new translation of the Homeric Hymns cites R. Janko's 1982 study of "diachronic development in epic diction" as providing a date of c. 675-600 BC (Crudden, 2001, p. 129).

6. Clay makes an highly instructive argument in support of her contention that the "final upshot of Zeus' intervention is to make Aphrodite cease and desist from bringing about these inappropriate unions between the gods and mortals, which, in turn, will mean the end of the age of heroes." However, the text does not actually confirm her thesis. Nor she is able to cite any ancient authority to support her argument; among modern scholars, she notes that "only van der Ben . . . has grasped this essential point" (Clay, 1989, p. 166 n. 46). Simply, why is Aeneas not recognized in the classical tradition as the last of the heroes?

7. "The *Hymn to Aphrodite* 202-206 draws heavily on *Il.* 5.265f. and 20.231-235 but makes Zeus himself the ravisher of Ganymede and goes on (218ff.) to speak of Dawn and Tithonos" (Dover, 1989, p. 197).

8. "To quote Flacelière, 'Eros presided primarily over the passionate devotion of a grown man to a boy; Aphrodite over the sexual relations between man and woman' [citing Robert Flacelière, *Love in Ancient Greece*. (J. Cleugh, Trans.). New York, 1962; p. 51]" (Percy, 1996, p. 112). In Plato's *Symposium*, Pausanias argues that the earthly and heavenly Aphrodites preside over pederastic relationships, while Agathon would attribute erotic attraction to a youthful Eros.

9. See the review articles by John Thorp and Beert Verstraete. Thorp (1992) makes a reasoned critique of Foucault's thesis (and Halperin's defence of it in *One Hundred Years of Homosexuality*) that "homosexuality is not a natural but a social category" (p. 54). Verstraete (2000) finds *The Use of Pleasure* "highly original and insightful in its unravelling of the complex ideational fabric—with its moral, dietetic, economic, and erotic strands—of the privileged male discourse in Classical Greece on sexuality" (p. 147). For a self-promotional and wildly unfocussed attack on Foucault, see Camille

Paglia (1992, pp. 187-188, 223-233). I am indebted to Anne Quéma, Department of English, Acadia University, for her helpful comments on Foucault.

10. As Halperin (2002) pointed out in his terse response to the reassertion of the initiatory thesis of pederasty, "Greek pederasty of the sort practiced by the Athenians of the classical period was often a highly conventional, elaborately formal, and socially stylized affair, involving lengthy courtship and conspicuous public display . . . But it was far removed from an initiation rite, as that term is understood by anthropologists" (p. 142).

11. "As K. J. Dover and Michel Foucault pointed out long ago, the protocols governing paederasty, especially in classical Athens, were elaborately crafted in such a way as to protect boys from any suggestion that they were motivated in their sexual relation with adult men by sexual desire or sexual pleasure, let alone that they took any pleasure in being sexually penetrated" (Halperin, 2002, 72).

12. Artistic and literary evidence demonstrating erotic reciprocity on the part of the *erōmenos* poses a challenge to this fundamental connection of Athenian pedagogy and pederasty. Ludwig (2002) takes from Dover that such evidence leaves one "to pick between two distortions: romantic or debunking" (p. 30, n. 8), even though vase depictions depicting erotic interest in the *erōmenos* (even of an *erōmenos* showing more interest than the *erastēs*) are not rendered any differently than those which depict the ideal or norm of the aroused *erastēs* and merely affectionate *erōmenos*. Keith DeVries (1997) challenged the assumption that "an unreceptive *eromenos* was grasping the erastes' wrist to ward off the opening sexual move of touching his genitals" with the view that, "With the expression of intimacy and affection being the overall meaning of the wrist-grasping and chin-touching in nonsexual scenes, surely that is the meaning the gestures are meant to convey in the heterosexual and homosexual scenes as well, but with the emotions no doubt escalated in the sexual atmosphere" (p. 20). Halperin, however, allowed to DeVries only that friendly affection (*philia*) was acceptable–never sexual desire (*erōs*): "expressions of reciprocal affection are one thing, and expressions of reciprocal eros–mutual desire and sexual passion–are quite another. What was absolutely inadmissible, and what our sources stop abruptly short of suggesting, was the possibility that a decent boy might feel for a man a passionate sexual desire, an eros or anteros, of the same sort that animated the older lover. No extant source from the classical period of Greek civilization assigns the junior partner in a paederastic relationship a share of eros or anteros–with the sole exception of Plato, in a highly tendentious philosophical passage [*Phaedrus* 255c-e]" (DeVries, 1997, p. 49; Halperin, 2002, p. 150).

13. The best comments on the charioteer myth, so far as the study of pederastic influence on the Ganymede is concerned, are those of Foucault, Halperin, Price and Ludwig. Price (2002) starts with an astute observation: "What concerns us here is how pederasty becomes pedagogy" (p. 177). Generally, classical scholars have not shown much interest in the Ganymede citation or in the significance of *himeros* at *Phaedrus* 251 and 257. Geier (2002) neglects it in his exploration of the esoteric meaning of the dialogue through the dynamic of speaker and listener; Ferrari mentions it (1987, p. 155), but it is not of much interest to his study of the relation of Platonic *erōs* to Freudian libido (the same applied to Gould, who was interested in Platonic and Freudian psychology). Nussbaum observes the importance of sight (2002, p. 70), but fails to relate it to the esthetic context given to *himeros* by association with Aphrodite, which we found in the *Iliad* and the *Hymn to Aphrodite*. (However, she does cite another reference to Ganymede in Euripides' *Trojan Women* [*Tro.* 821 ff.]: "Zeus, says Euripides'

chorus, fell in love with Ganymede when he saw him bathing after running a race," from which she infers that "so even here excellence, not just a pretty face, was the focus of desire," which helps to draw the moral: "Plato's suggestion . . . is that the real object of love's intensity is the divine" (p. 71).

14. Halperin (1986) lists some older literature dealing with "Plato's willingness . . . to combine mechanistic and metaphysical orders of reasoning to describe the operation of eros" (p. 63 n. 6).

15. As part of *The Phaedrus Kit*, a useful Website designed for a popular interest in the homosexual themes of the *Phaedrus*, the *LSJ* definitions for *himeros* are collected together with its uses in Plato as listed by *Perseus*, which are connected with the beginnings of an informal essay on "The lexica of desire in Plato's *Phaedrus*," by Earl Jackson Jr. Jackson rightly makes the connection with the tradition of the erotic gaze and of love as a disease going back in archaic Greek lyric. (Halperin (1986) notes that it is precisely in Socrates' use of *himeros* to describe erotic reciprocity in the *erōmenos*, that "Plato is actually making a startling point about love and counter-love" (p. 63).

16. As Waterfield (2002) notes, "Plato is hazarding a fanciful etymology, according to which ἵμερος ('desire') is derived from the *i* in the Greek word for 'approach,' *merē* ('particles'), and *rhein* ('flow')" (p. 93). (Editors suspect that *himeros* is an interpolation, on which see textual notes in G. J. De Vries, 1969 and Rowe, 1988.) The etymology of *himeros* is also given in the *Cratylus* (which belongs to the same "middle period" of the Platonic dialogues as the *Phaedrus*), where it is explained in relation to other terms in the Greek lexicon of desire:Nor is there any difficulty about (ἐπιθυμία) desire, for this name was evidently given to the power [δυνάμει] that goes (ἰοῦσα) into the soul (θυμός). And has its name from the raging (θύσις) and boiling of the soul. The name ἵμερος (longing) was given to the stream (ῥοῦς) which most draws [ἐπισπᾶ, *draw on, allure, persuade (LSJ)*] the soul; for because it flows with a rush (ἱέμενος) and with a desire for things and thus draws the soul on through the impulse of its flowing, all this power gives it the name of ἵμερος ... when its object is present . . . . And ἔρως (love) is so called because it flows in (ἐσρεῖ) from without, and this flowing is not inherent in him who has it, but is introduced through the eyes. . . . (*Cratylus* 419d8-420b1; Fowler, 1926, additions in square brackets)

Desire in both *Cratylus* and *Phaedrus* is generally thought of as an ethereal stream of energy which acts much like a magnet or the tractor beam of modern science fiction, especially in *Phaedrus*, where the stream is said to be composed of what appear to be Democritean particles. Generally in ἐπιθυμία, the soul's desire for an object, we experience an attraction toward the object of our desire which results, for instance, in our reaching for an apple. This motion toward the object is actually the effect which the stream flowing from the object has on us–the flowing in and flowing out is the same thing, differentiated only by the subjective standpoint of experiencing the effect and the objective standpoint of causing the effect. ἵμερος specifies that stream which has the most urgent effect (μάλιστα ἕλκοντι) on the soul. This would seem to denote the physicality of sexual desire, the nearly irresistible 'sweet longing' inspired by Aphrodite in the *Hymn to Aphrodite*. In light of the *Phaedrus*, which describes the stream of *himeros* in terms of the traditional erotic gaze familiar from archaic love poetry, *erōs* is best understood as a further specification of *himeros* as sexual longing. *Erōs* is that form of *himeros* which is specifically inspired or mediated by the erotic gaze, and which may well be that which is specific to humans as an aspect of their godlikeness.

The explanation of *himeros* in *Phaedrus* may help us to make sense of why the erotic stream is described in *Cratylus* as "not belonging to the one who has it, but is brought in from outside through the eyes" [οὐκ οἰκεία ἐστὶν ἡ ῥοὴ αὕτη τῷ ἔχοντι ἀλλ ἐπείσακτος διὰ τῶν ὀμμάτων]. It is unlikely that Socrates in the *Cratylus* wishes to emphasize that erotic longing stems not from the soul itself, since the etymology of *erōs* means that it is a flowing in from without. It may be, then, that Socrates wishes to highlight that the flow stems from the sight (visible beauty) of its object, and belongs to the explanation of the erotic gaze of love poetry. But what if "the one possessing the flow" refers not to the subject experiencing the effect, but to the source of the flow, the erotic object causing the effect–the *erōmenos* rather than the *erastēs*? If so, it points to a third party as the source of the flow, which is in fact precisely the meaning denoted by the use of ἐπείσακτος, a derivative of ἐπείσαγω, which means to "*bring in besides* or *over*, esp. of bringing in a second wife" (*LSJ⁹*). According to the *Phaedrus*, the source of erotic inspiration is to be found in the eternal form of beauty, which is imaged in or mediated by the beauty of the beloved.

17. "Plato makes a clean break with the conventional ethos of Athenian pederasty only in the *Phaidros*, when Socrates describes the dynamic of attraction obtaining in a proper relationship between lover and beloved" (Halperin, 1990b, p. 268). Halperin believes "Plato's remodelling of the homoerotic ethos of classical Athens has direct consequences for his program of philosophical inquiry" (p. 270).

18. A point eloquently articulated by Vernant (1990): "To say that love is a divine madness, an initiation, a state of possession, is to recognize that in the mirror of the beloved it is not our human face which appears, but that of the god by whom we are possessed . . . On the beloved face in which I see myself, what I perceive, what fascinates and transports me, is the figure of Beauty" (pp. 470-471). The significance of Plato's reinterpretation of the nature and potential of pederastic *erôs* for Medievals can be seen in Dante's vision of Love as the supreme principle of the universe, which operates in and through his love for Beatrice, and hers for him, to move toward itself as the true object of his soul.

19. Much attention has been directed to this and like passages as a result of the Colorado trial participated by Nussbaum in which the *Laws* was cited as evidence that homosexuality was contrary to nature. Randall Clark offers what he considers a "neutral" summary of the debate that spilled over in the trial's aftermath. (Clark's own assessment of the Athenian's argument dovetails with the familiar criticism that homosexuality is "by nature" narcissistic and thus detrimental to the social good (2000, p. 27).) This debate neglects the important point raised by Foucault (1985, pp. 222-223) that what is contrary to nature for Plato in pederasty is not the action of the pederast, but that of the *pathic*. The social danger of pederasty is that it might engender in the *erōmenos* the shameful desire to be penetrated that would result in the loss of that honor which the pederastic relationship was instituted to instill in the adolescent.

20. Plato's motivation in idealizing pederasty is better understood by Foucault as a new erotics emergent in the sublimation of sexual desire in the Platonic quest for truth. Garrison (2000, pp. 157-158) presents a clear picture of Plato's customary indifference to the *demos* and desire to improve the *aristoi*: "Plato's idealization of the love of males was not a mindless class reflex but an assimilation of his class to what he saw as its highest calling: the pursuit of wisdom via the one-on-one method of dialectic" (p. 158).

21. There is scant attention given to Plato's political bent in studies of the *Laws*, which tend to focus on the political theory advanced in the dialogue in its relation to the *Republic* and *Statesman*; there is also very little attention given to Plato's treatment of pederasty (Saunders, 1972; Pangle, 1980; Stalley, 1983; Laks, 2000; Diamond, 2002; Bobonich, 2002).

REFERENCES

Liddell & Scott Greek Lexicon. (1968⁹). Sir Henry Stuart Jones, Ed. Oxford: Clarendon.

Barkan, L. (1991). *Transuming Passion: Ganymede and the Erotics of Humanism.* Stanford: Stanford UP.

Bobonich, C. (2002). Plato on Utopia. In E. N. Zalta (Ed.), *The Stanford Encyclopedia of Philosophy* (Winter 2002 Edition). Retrieved December 1, 2003, from http://plato.stanford.edu/archives/win2002/entries/plato-utopia/

Bremmer, J. (1980). An enigmatic Indo-European rite: pederasty. *Arethusa, 13,* 279-298. Repr. in W. R. Dynes (Ed.), *Homosexuality in the Ancient World* (pp. 49-74). New York and London: Garland Publishing, 1992.

Burnet, I. (1902a). *Platonis Opera, Tomvs I, Tetralogias I-II, Cratylus.* Oxford: Clarendon.

_____. (1902b). *Platonis Opera, Tomvs II, Tetralogias III-IV, Phaedrus.* Oxford: Clarendon.

_____. (1902c). *Platonis Opera, Tomvs V, Tetralogias IX, Leges.* Oxford: Clarendon.

Cairns, D. L. (1993). Aidos*: the Psychology and Ethics of Honor and Shame in Ancient Greek Literature.* Oxford: Clarendon; New York: Oxford UP.

Calame, C. (1999). *The Poetics of Eros in Ancient Greece.* (J. Lloyd, Trans.). Princeton: Princeton UP.

Cartledge, P. (1981) The politics of Spartan pederasty. *Cambridge Philogical Society, Proceedings, 27,* 17-36. Repr. in W. R. Dynes (Ed.), *Homosexuality in the Ancient World* (pp. 75-94). New York and London: Garland Publishing, 1992.

Clark, R. B. (2000). Platonic love in a Colorado courtroom: Martha Nussbaum, John Finnis, and Plato's *Laws* in *Evans v. Romer. Yale Journal of Law & the Humanities, 12*(1), 1-38.

Clay, J. S. (1989). *The Politics of Olympus. Form and Meaning in the Major Homeric Hymns,* Princeton: Princeton UP.

Crudden, M. (2001). *The Homeric Hymns.* Oxford World Classics. Oxford: Oxford UP.

De Vries. G. J. (1969). *A Commentary on the Phaedrus of Plato.* Amsterdam: Hakkert.

DeVries, K. (1997). The 'frigid eromenoi' and their wooers revisited: a closer look at Greek homosexuality in vase painting. In M. Duberman (Ed.), *Queer Representations. Reading Lives, Reading Cultures* (pp. 14-24). A Center for Lesbian and Gay Studies Book. New York & London: New York UP.

Diamond, E. (2002). Understanding and individuality in the three cities: an interpretation of Plato's *Laws. Animus, 7.* Retrieved December 1, 2003, from http://www.swgc.mun.ca/animus.

Dodd, D. B. (2000). Athenian ideas about Cretan pederasty. In T. Hubbard (Ed.), *Greek Love Reconsidered* (pp. 33-41). New York: Wallace-New Hampton.

Dover, K. J. (Ed.). (1982). *Plato. The Symposium.* Cambridge: Cambridge UP.

_____. (1988) *The Greeks and their Legacy.* Oxford and New York: Basil Blackwell.

_____. (1989). *Greek Homosexuality. Updated and with a New Postscript.* Cambridge: Harvard UP.

Dowden, K. (1992). *The Uses of Greek Mythology.* London and New York: Routledge.

Eden, P. T. (1988). Two notes on Euripides. *The Classical Quarterly*, *38*(2) [New Series], 560-561. Retrieved December 1, 2003, from JSTOR http://links.jstor.org/sici?sici=00098388%281988%292%3A38%3A2%3C560%3ATNOE%3E2.0.CO%3B2-5.

Evelyn-White, H. G. (1974). *Hesiod, the Homeric Hymns and Homerica*. With a second appendix added by D. L. Page. Loeb Classical Library. Cambridge: Harvard UP; London: Heinemann.

Ferrari, G. R. F. (1987). *Listening to the Cicadas: A Study of Plato's* Phaedrus. Cambridge: Cambridge UP.

_____. (1992). Platonic love. In R. Kraut (Ed.), *The Cambridge Companion to Plato* (pp. 248-276). Cambridge: Cambridge UP.

Finkleberg, M. (1998). *Time* and *Arete* in Homer. *Classical Quarterly*, *48*(1), 14-28. Retrieved June 7, 2004 through *Research Library*.

Foucault, M. (1985). *The Use of Pleasure. The History of Sexuality: Volume II*. (R. Hurley, Trans.). New York: Vintage Books.

Fowler, H. N. (1926). *Plato with an English Translation: Volume VI. Cratylus, Parmenides, Greater Hippias, Lesser Hippias*. Loeb Classical Library. London: Heinmann.

Garrrison, D. H. (2000). *Sexual Culture in Ancient Greece*. Norman: U of Oklahoma P.

Geier, A. (2002). *Plato's Erotic Thought: the Tree of the Unknown*. U of Rochester P.

Gerber, D. E. (1982). *Pindar's* Olympian One: *A Commentary*. Phoenix supplementary volume xv. Toronto: U of Toronto P.

_____. (Ed. and Trans.). (1999). *Greek Elegiac Poetry from the Seventh to the Fifth Centuries BC*. Loeb Classical Library. Cambridge and London: Harvard UP.

Gould, T. (1963). *Platonic Love*. New York: The Free Press of Glencoe.

Halperin, D. M. (1986). Plato and Erotic Reciprocity. *Classical Antiquity*, *5*(1), 61-80.

_____. (1990a).*One Hundred Years of Homosexuality*. New York and London: Routledge.

_____. (1990b). Why is Diotima a woman? Repr. in D. M. Halperin, J. J. Winkler and F. I. Zeitlin (Eds.), *Before Sexuality: The Construction of Erotic Experience in the Ancient Greek World* (pp. 257-308). Princeton: Princeton UP.

_____. (2002) *How to Do the History of Homosexuality*. Chicago and London: U of Chicago P.

Harrison, T. (1997). Herodotus and the ancient Greek idea of rape. In S. Deacy and K. F. Pierce (Eds.), *Rape in Antiquity* (pp. 185-208). Wales: Duckworth in association with The Classical Press of Wales.

Hubbard, T. (2000a). Pederasty and democracy: the marginalization of a social practice. In T. Hubbard (Ed.), *Greek Love Reconsidered* (pp. 1-11). New York: Wallace-New Hampton.

_____. (2000b). A Medley of Greek Verse. In T. Hubbard (Ed.), *Greek Love Reconsidered* (pp. 52-56). New York: Wallace-New Hampton.

Jackson, Jr. E. (2003). The lexica of desire in Plato's *Phaedrus*. Retrieved December 1, 2003, from http://www.anotherscene.com/phaedrus/elexmain.html.

Kilmer, M. (1993). *Greek Erotica on Red-Figure Vases*. London: Duckworth.

_____. (1997). 'Rape' in early red-figure pottery. Violence and threat in homo-erotic and hetero-erotic contexts. In S. Deacy and K. F. Pierce (Eds.), *Rape in Antiquity* (pp. 123-141). Wales: Duckworth in association with The Classical Press of Wales.

Koehl, R. B. (1997). Ephoros and ritualized homosexuality in Bronze Age Crete. In M. Duberman (Ed.), *Queer Representations. Reading Lives, Reading Cultures* (pp. 7-13). A Center for Lesbian and Gay Studies Book. New York & London: New York UP.

Kovacs, D. (Ed. and Trans.). (2002a). *Euripides. Bacchae, Iphigenia at Aulis, Rhesus.* Loeb Classical Library. Cambridge and London: Harvard UP.

_____. (Ed. and Trans.). (2002b). *Euripides. Helen, Phoenecian Women, Orestes.* Loeb Classical Library. Cambridge and London: Harvard UP.

Laks, A. (2000). The *Laws.* In C. Rowe and M. Schofield in association with S. Harrison and M. Lane (Eds.), *The Cambridge History of Greek and Roman Political Thought* (pp. 258-292). Cambridge: Cambridge UP.

Lattimore, R. (1951). *The Iliad of Homer.* Translated with introduction. Chicago: U of Chicago P. Repr. 1980.

Lloyd-Jones, H. (Ed. and trans.). (1996). *Sophocles Fragments.* Loeb Classical Library. Cambridge and London: Harvard UP.

Ludwig, P. (2002). *Eros & Polis. Desire and Community in Greek Political Theory.* Cambridge: Cambridge UP.

Mayerson, P. (1971). *Classical Mythology in Literature, Art, and Music.* New York: John Wiley & Sons.

Monoson, S. S. (2000) The allure of Harmodius and Aristogeiton. In T. Hubbard (Ed.), *Greek Love Reconsidered* (pp. 42-51). New York: Wallace-New Hampton.

Monro, David B. and Allen, Thomas W. (Eds.). (1920). *Homeri Opera* 1 (*Iliad* 1-12) and 2 (*Iliad* 13-24). (3rd ed.). Oxford Classical Texts. Oxford: Clarendon. Repr. 1962.

Nussbaum, M. C. (2002). *Eros* and ethical norms: philosophers respond to a cultural dilemma. In M. C. Nussbaum and J. Sihvola (Eds.), *The Sleep of Reason: The Erotic Experience and Sexual Ethics in Ancient Greece and Rome* (pp. 55-94). Chicago and London: U of Chicago P.

Paglia, C. (1992). *Sex, Art, and American Culture.* New York: Vintage Books.

Pangle, T. L. (1980). *The Laws of Plato.* Translated with notes and interpretive essay. Chicago: U of Chicago P.

Percy, W. A. III, (1990). Sexual revolution 600 B.C.–400 A.D.: the origins of institutionalized pederasty in Greece. *Gay Review, 1,* 19-24. Repr. in W. R. Dynes (Ed.), *Homosexuality in the Ancient World* (pp. 375-380). New York and London: Garland Publishing, 1992.

_____. (1996). *Pedagogy and Pederasty in Archaic Greece.* Urbana: U of Illinois P.

Powell, B. B. (2000). *Classical Myth.* (3rd ed.). Upper Saddle River, NJ: Prentice-Hall.

Powell, J. E. (1966). *A Lexicon to Herodotus.* (2nd ed.). Hildesheim: Olms.

Price, A. W. (2002). Plato, Zeno, and the object of love. In M. C. Nussbaum and J. Sihvola (Eds.), *The Sleep of Reason: The Erotic Experience and Sexual Ethics in Ancient Greece and Rome* (pp. 170-199).Chicago and London: U of Chicago P.

Race, William H. (1986). *Pindar.* Boston: Twayne Publishers.

_____. (Ed. and trans.). (1997). *Pindar, Olympian Odes, Pythian Odes.* Loeb Classical Library. Cambridge and London: Harvard UP.

Robson, J. E. (1997). Beastiality and bestial rape in Greek myth. In S. Deacy and K.F. Pierce (Eds.), *Rape in Antiquity* (pp. 65-96). Wales: Duckworth in association with The Classical Press of Wales.

Rowe, C. J. (1988). *Plato:* Phaedrus *with translation and commentary*. Warminister: Aris & Phillips.

Saslow, James M. (1986). *Ganymede in the Renaissance: Homosexuality in Art and Society*. New Haven and London: Yale UP.

Saunders, Trevor J. (1972). *Plato. The Laws*. Translated with introduction. Harmondsworth: Penguin Books.

_____. (1992). Plato's later political thought. In R. Kraut (Ed.), *The Cambridge Companion to Plato* (pp. 464-492).Cambridge: Cambridge UP.

Scanlon, Thomas F. (2002). *Eros and Greek Athletics*. Oxford: Oxford UP.

_____. (2005). The dispersion of pederasty and the athletic revolution in sixth-century B.C. Greece. *Journal of Homosexuality, 49*(3/4), 63-85.

Schefold, Karl. (1992). *Gods and Heroes in Late Archaic Greek Art*. With the assistance of Luca Giuliani. (A. Griffths, Trans.). Cambridge: Cambridge UP.

Sergent, B. (1986). *Homosexuality in Greek Myth*. (A. Goldhammer, Trans., with a preface by Georges Dumézil). London: Athlone.

Shapiro, H. A. (1981). Courtship scenes in Attic vase-painting. *American Journal of Archaeology, 85*, 133-143. Repr. in W. R. Dynes (Ed.), *Homosexuality in the Ancient World* (pp. 401-416). New York and London: Garland Publishing, 1992.

_____. (2000). Leagros and Euphronius: painting pederasty in Athens. In T. Hubbard (Ed.), *Greek Love Reconsidered* (pp. 12-32). New York: Wallace-New Hampton.

Stalley, R. F. (1983). *An Introduction to Plato's Laws*. Indianapolis: Hackett Publishing Co.

Thorp, J. (1992). The social construction of homosexuality. *Phoenix, 46*(1), 54-65.

Todd, O. J. and Marchant, E. C. (1923). *Xenophon. Memorabilia, Oeconomicus* (E. C. Marchant, Trans.).; *Symposium, Apology* (O. J. Todd, Trans.). Loeb Classical Library. Cambridge and London: Harvard U P. Repr.1992.

Vernant, J-P. (1990). One . . . Two . . . Three: *Eros*. In D. M. Halperin, J. J. Winkler and F. I. Zeitlin (Eds.), *Before Sexuality: The Construction of Erotic Experience in the Ancient Greek World* (pp. 465-478). Princeton: Princeton UP.

Verstraete, B. (2000). Recent scholarship on homosexuality in the Greco-Roman world. *Journal of Homosexuality, 40*(1), 145-162.

Waterfield, R. (2002). *Plato Phaedrus*. Translated with an introduction and notes. Oxford: Oxford UP.

West, M. L. (Ed. and Trans.). (2003). *Homeric Hymns Homeric Apocrypha Lives of Homer*. Loeb Classical Library. Cambridge and London: Harvard UP.

Winkler, J. J. (1990). Laying down the law: the oversight of men's sexual behavior in Classical Athens. In D. M. Halperin, J. J. Winkler and F. I. Zeitlin (Eds.), *Before Sexuality: The Construction of Erotic Experience in the Ancient Greek World* (pp. 171-209). Princeton: Princeton UP.

Woodward, S. (2003). *Images of Myths in Classical Antiquity*. Cambridge: Cambridge UP.

Pindar's *Tenth Olympian* and Athlete-Trainer Pederasty

Thomas Hubbard, PhD

University of Texas at Austin

SUMMARY. The comparison of the adolescent boxer Hagesidamus and his trainer Ilas to Patroclus and Achilles in Pindar's *Olympian* 10.16-21 and the subsequent comparison of Hagesidamus to Ganymede in *Olympian* 10.99-105 suggest that the relationship was in some sense pederastic, particularly in the wake of Aeschylus' treatment of Achilles and Patroclus in these terms in *Myrmidons*. This possibility motivates a broader examination of the evidence for such relationships in fifth-century Greece. There is no doubt that the *palaestra* was a central locus for the formation of pederastic liaisons and that athletic nudity was integral to the esthetic construction of adolescent beauty. There is also no doubt that

Thomas Hubbard is Professor of Classics at the University of Texas, Austin. He received his PhD from Yale University in 1980, and has authored *The Pindaric Mind: A Study of Logical Structure in Early Greek Poetry* (1985), *The Mask of Comedy: Aristophanes and the Intertextual Parabasis* (1991), and *The Pipes of Pan: Intertextuality and Literary Filiation in the Pastoral Tradition from Theocritus to Milton* (1998). In addition, he has edited a collection of essays on ancient homosexuality, *Greek Love Reconsidered* (2000), and a sourcebook of primary texts, *Homosexuality in Greece and Rome* (2003). His current research focuses on epinician poetry and the ideology of athletic competition in classical Greece. A shorter version of this paper was published as "Sex in the Gym: Athletic Trainers and Pedagogical Pederasty," in *Intertexts*, 7 (2003), 1-26. Correspondence may be addressed: Dept. of Classics, University of Texas, 1 University Station (C3400), Austin, TX 78712.

[Haworth co-indexing entry note]: "Pindar's *Tenth Olympian* and Athlete-Trainer Pederasty." Hubbard, Thomas. Co-published simultaneously in *Journal of Homosexuality* (Harrington Park Press, an imprint of The Haworth Press, Inc.) Vol. 49, No. 3/4, 2005, pp. 137-171; and: *Same-Sex Desire and Love in Greco-Roman Antiquity and in the Classical Tradition of the West* (ed: Beert C. Verstraete, and Vernon Provencal) Harrington Park Press, an imprint of The Haworth Press, Inc., 2005, pp. 137-171. Single or multiple copies of this article are available for a fee from The Haworth Document Delivery Service [1-800-HAWORTH, 9:00 a.m. - 5:00 p.m. (EST). E-mail address: docdelivery@haworthpress.com].

the trainer's position afforded him regular intimacy and close physical contact with boys; several Hellenistic texts take for granted the erotic opportunities connected with the position. The "Solonian" law presuming to protect pupils from such relationships, attested in Aeschines, was probably a late fifth-century development in reaction to their common occurrence in earlier generations. Evidence also exists for lovers acting as financial backers to boy athletes or as informal trainers. Some of the most intriguing evidence for the conflation of the trainer's and lover's roles can be found in red-figure vase painting of the late sixth and fifth centuries.

[Article copies available for a fee from The Haworth Document Delivery Service: 1-800-HAWORTH. E-mail address: <docdelivery@haworthpress.com> Website: <http://www. HaworthPress.com> © 2005 by The Haworth Press, Inc. All rights reserved.]

KEYWORDS. Athletics, Pindar, pederasty, pedagogy, teaching, nudity, iconography, vase painting

After a lengthy prologue apologizing for the poet's delay in delivering his promised composition,[1] Pindar's *Olympian* 10 finally names the athlete who is to be celebrated, Hagesidamus of Epizephyrian Locris, an adolescent victor in boxing in 476 BCE:

πύκτας δ᾽ ἐν᾽ Ὀλυμπιάδι νικῶν
῝Ἴλᾳ φερέτω χάριν
῾Αγησίδαμος, ὡς
᾽Αχιλεῖ Πάτροκλος.
θάξαις δέ κε φύντ᾽ ἀρετᾷ ποτί
πελώριον ὁρμάσαι κλέος ἀνὴρ θεοῦ σὺν παλάμαις.

Victorious as a boxer in the Olympics, let Hagesidamus give thanks to Ilas, just as Patroclus did to Achilles. A man aided by the arts of a god would whet one who is born to excellence and spur him toward awesome fame. (*O*.10.16-21)

The ancient commentators on Pindar speculated that Ilas must have been the boy's athletic trainer, as suggested by the gnome in verses 20-21; most modern scholars have followed this view.[2] What most critics have not fully understood, however, is why Ilas receives so much emphasis as to be mentioned side-by-side with the first naming of the victor, and in particular why his relation to Hagesidamus should be likened to that of Achilles and Patroclus.[3] William Mullen (1982, p. 186) and Deborah Steiner (1998, p. 140) have both suspected that there might be an erotic dimension to their relationship, but neither has argued the point in detail. On the other side, Verdenius (1988) has explicitly rejected this possibility: "it would have been tasteless to suggest that there existed an erotic relation between the victor and his trainer" (p. 64). The present essay aims to contextualize consideration of this passage within the broader perspective of the evidence we can glean from a variety of sources about athletic trainers and their personal relationship to young athletes under their care.

No one can doubt Pindar's own interest in the attractiveness of boys and pederastic themes generally.[4] The central reason for interpreting the Ilas-Hagesidamus relationship as not merely didactic is the application of Achilles and Patroclus as a mythological analogy. Nothing in the *Iliad* or mythological tradition makes Achilles a teacher of Patroclus; the one admonition Achilles offers Patroclus in the *Iliad* Patroclus fatefully disobeys. However, it is well-known that the myth of Achilles and Patroclus had been interpreted in explicitly pederastic terms in Pindar's own time by Aeschylus' tragedy *Myrmidons*.[5] This would therefore be one of several cases where Pindar reacts to a myth Aeschylus had recently put on stage.[6] Achilles is a teacher to Patroclus inasmuch as he is Patroclus' *erastēs* and role model. This association of functions raises the obvious question whether Ilas, in addition to being Hagesidamus' athletic trainer, was also his lover or at least was presented as such. The term χάρις, which is used here to designate the thanks owed to the teacher, frequently bears erotic connotations in Greek, referring to the reciprocal favors a beloved grants his lover, whether physical or emotional (see, for instance, Theognis 956-57, 1263-66, 1299-1304, 1319-22, 1327-34, 1367-68). Verses 20-21 certainly suggest that Ilas' role involved building character as well as teaching the fine points of the pugilistic art.

The coupling of Hagesidamus' name with Ilas in the first actual naming of the victor in the poem stands as the climax of the entire first triad.[7] Interestingly, Pindar's last mention of the boy at the end of the poem links his name with the erotically charged epithet ἐρατόν and with an allusion to another pederastic myth, that of Zeus and Ganymede:

παῖδ᾽ ἐρατὸν δ Ἀρχεστράτου
αἴνησα, τὸν εἶδον κρατέοντα χερὸς ἀλκᾷ
βωμὸν παρ᾽ Ὀλύμπιον

κεῖνον κατὰ χρόνον
ἰδέᾳ τε καλόν
ὥρᾳ τε κεκραμένον, ἅ ποτε
ἀναιδέα Γανυμήδει θάνατον ἄλκε σὺν Κυπρογενεῖ.

I have praised the love-inspiring son of Archestratus, whom I saw triumphant in strength of hand beside the Olympian altar at that time, beautiful in physique and blessed with that youthful effloresence which, together with Cyprian born Aphrodite, once warded off from Ganymede death that knows no shame. (O.10.99-105)

Pindar specifically praises the boy's beauty and his ὥρα, that "perfect moment" of adolescent ripeness which became immortal for Ganymede and, by implication, will become immortal for Hagesidamus through Pindar's poetic celebration.[8]

Hagesidamus' relation to Ilas raises the question whether the prominence of trainers in Pindar's epinicia for boy victors may have been due to the trainer conventionally being an *erastēs*. As abhorrent as teacher-student relationships may be to some modern constructions of sexual morality, as institutionalized today in the ethical codes of virtually every school and university, we must recognize that the bugbears of sexual harassment and child molestation did not possess the same valence in antiquity; pederasty and pedagogy were intimately linked. The educational historian H. I. Marrou (1964), although no enthusiast for homosexual causes, was nevertheless forthright in acknowledging the pederastic basis of advanced education in all spheres:

> Pederasty was considered the most beautiful, the perfect, form of education–τὴν καλλίστην παιδείαν. Throughout Greek history the relationship between master and pupil was to remain that between a lover and his beloved: education remained in principle not so much a form of teaching, an instruction in techniques, as an expenditure of loving effort by an elder concerned to promote the growth of a younger man who was burning with the desire to respond to this love and show himself worthy of it. (p. 57)

This romantically engaged mentorship would be particularly characteristic of the most elite forms of aristocratic education, based on personal rather than group instruction. It might also be appropriate for some forms of technical apprenticeship. Marrou continues:

. . . it was still under the shadow of masculine erotic love that this high technical instruction flourished: no matter what branch was involved, it was carried on in the atmosphere of spiritual communion that was created by the disciple's fervent and often passionate attachment to the master to whom he had given himself, whom he took as his model, and who gradually initiated him into the secrets of his science or art. For a long time, the lack of proper educational institutions meant that only this one type of thoroughgoing education was possible–the type whereby a disciple was attached to a tutor who had honoured him by summoning him to his side, by electing him. Let us emphasize the *direction* of this vocation: it was a call from above, to one whom the tutor deemed worthy. For a long time the opinion of antiquity was to despise the teacher who made a business out of teaching and offered his learning to the first customer who came along. The communication of knowledge, it was believed, should be reserved for those worthy of it. (pp. 58-59)

Socrates' relationship with his pupils is often characterized in pederastic terms, even if he never actually sought physical consummation of the relationship.[9] Later biographical sources, although not always trustworthy, suggest numerous teacher-student relationships of a pederastic nature: the philosophers Parmenides and Zeno, Xenocrates and Polemon, Polemon and Crates, Crantor and Arcesilaus, the sculptors Pheidias and Agoracritus of Paros, the physicians Theomedon and Eudoxus of Cnidus.[10] Iconographic evidence confirms that teacher-student relationships could be eroticized even in musical and other non-athletic contexts.[11]

In a bold and challenging revaluation of ancient educational models, Yun Lee Too (2000) has questioned the concept of educational mentorship as merely a "call from above," as Marrou termed it, in favor of an economy of reciprocal, two-way desire on the part of both teacher and student: in her view, the eroticization of the relationship can serve a beneficial purpose precisely inasmuch as it equalizes or "peers" the teacher and student, deconstructing the traditional model of prescriptive, omniscient pedagogy in favor of a more open, conversational, and dialectical exchange in which the student becomes closer to an equal of the teacher, able to develop and contribute his own original ideas like an adult, rather than as an acolyte kneeling before a magisterial discourse of self-contained totality and impassionate wisdom (pp. 73-75). The teacher's desire for proximity to his student's beauty complements the student's desire to learn by proximity to his teacher's experience and wisdom; this mutual, if differentially determined, need makes each partner to the relationship of exchange equally vulnerable to the other's disapprobation. This conceptualization of a two-way relationship of mutual vulnerability and need is surely preferable to the reductive phallocratic formulation of Greek pederasty advanced by David Halperin (1990, p. 30) and others.[12] On the other hand, it is precisely by refusing to make love to the beautiful student, as Socrates does with Alcibiades, that the teacher retains his self-sufficient authority and mastery: as Leo Bersani (1985) has noted in explicating Foucault's articulation of Greek ascesis, "the elimination of sex has transformed a relation of problematic desire into a pure exercise of power" (p. 17).

The applicability of the pederastic model to athletic training is clear. Later sources distinguish between the *paidotribēs,* who would lead classes of group instruction, and the *gymnastēs,* a more accomplished professional who would train a competition-level athlete one-on-one and who would supplement his instruction in bodily maneuvers with a systematic dietary regimen and supervision over every aspect of the athlete's lifestyle.[13] Although the term *paidotribēs* probably encompassed both forms of instruction in the fifth century, the separation between the two types of training nevertheless probably existed, with the *gymnastēs* more likely to accommodate Marrou's pederastic model. The trainer would accompany an Olympic-level boy athlete on what could often be an extremely long and arduous journey (as in Hagesidamus' case, an overseas voyage from the toe of Italy) and would stay with him for the mandatory 30-day training period at Olympia, perhaps lodged together at close quarters in accommodations that probably consisted of little more than a tent.

The private wrestling school (*palaestra*) is certainly identified as the prime arena of pederastic courtship in a range of texts from a variety of genres in both the fifth and fourth centuries.[14] Numerous Greek vases depict scenes of clothed men or youths admiring, crowning, or presenting gifts to naked athletes; strigils and oil flasks hanging in the background are also common means of giving a gymnastic setting to courtship scenes.[15] Some would argue that the institution of athletic nudity and the addition of separate competitions for boys at the major festivals reflect the emergence of a homoerotic esthetic centered upon athletics during the archaic period.[16] Indeed, contests of *euandria* centered upon male beauty were a part of the Panathenaea and several other local festivals.[17] Is it legitimate to assume that pederasty entered the wrestling schools only from the influence of outside spectators and never among the participants themselves?

More than one Hellenistic epigram takes it for granted that a position as athletic trainer afforded almost unlimited potential for physical and even sexual intimacy with boys.[18] An early Hellenistic papyrus (*P. Lugd. Bat.* 20.51, datable to 257 BCE) contains a letter by a man worried that his supervision of a *palaestra* will give his enemies plausible grounds for accusing him of pederasty.[19] As the teacher responsible for a developing boy's physical formation and health, the trainer would closely inspect every inch of his anatomy; indeed, it was a trainer's role to massage sore muscles after a workout.[20] Touching and visual appreciation of the boy's physique would be daily activities. In the athletic, as in the military and sympotic realms, the boundaries between "homosocial" and "homosexual" were not always clearly demarcated.[21]

There were concerns in some parts of Greece that this pedagogical authority could be misappropriated or abused: Aeschines cites a "law of Solon" (*Tim.* 10-12, 138-39) regulating the hours at which gymnasia and schools could be open. This regulation, which probably dates much later than Solon, appears to reflect concern about after-hours contact between boy athletes and trainers under the cover of darkness. Kyle (1984) has argued that the one part of this law that is genuinely Solonian (based on other citations as such) is the prohibition against slaves "oiling themselves in the gymnasium (ξηραλοιφεῖν) or acting as lovers (ἐρᾶν)" (pp. 99-102). The fact that these two verbs are coupled together in all the citations of this law implies that athletics and pederasty were routinely coupled in Solon's time as the prerogatives of free men and that the social context for both activities was the same.[22] The more restrictive and sexually conservative environment of the late fifth century may have chosen to expand Solon's law into restricting relationships between boys and trainers, but the fact that such a regulation was felt to be necessary is itself evidence that such relationships were far from unknown.[23] It is commonly accepted that the institutionalization of public gymnasia in Athens evolved together with the state's growing democracy.[24] It may be that the eventual addition of publicly appointed or elected gymnasiarchs and *paidotribai*, of which there is some evidence in the fourth century,[25] reflected not only further democratization of athletic training, but also a desire to remove it from the realm of private patronage and pederastic influence, which was increasingly marginalized by Athenian democratic discourse as a social practice only of the elite.[26]

Not only did perceptions of what was appropriate and inappropriate vary over time, but they also depended on the local customs of each city state: Plato's Pausanias (*Symp.* 182A-C) tells us that the Boeotians (Pindar's native people) and the Eleans (the sponsors of the Olympics) were completely unashamed in their conduct of man/boy love, whereas the Athenians and Spartans were exceptions to the norm in their ambivalence. Other sources attest a strong Cretan identification with the practice.[27] In considering whether trainers might be lovers of some boys under their tutelage, we should remember that being an *erastēs* might also mean something very different in different parts of the Greek world. The Spartans practiced what was at least officially a chaste version of pederasty in which men and boys paired off as lover and beloved, but actual sexual contact was forbidden.[28] Acting as a boy's trainer might also be either a more or less formalized arrangement: Theognis 1335-36 implies that it was common for a lover to exercise naked together with his boy,[29] and the Spartan myth of Hyacinthus features the god Apollo doing gymnastics with his young companion.[30] Vase paintings frequently show youths of approximately the same age and stature acting as trainer,[31] suggesting that such activity was often more an offering of friendship than a certification of experience or professional standing, although this representational development may also imply the equalization of the teacher-student relationship that takes place once an erotic element dominates.

The forms of patronage a lover could offer a protegé were also variable. Xenophon's *Symposium* presents Callias as the lover of the young athlete Autolycus with the full knowledge and consent of the boy's father.[32] Callias was of course one of the wealthiest Athenians, a man known for his generosity and even extravagance.[33] What little is known of Autolycus' father Lycon suggests that he was comparatively poor,[34] which raises the possibility that it was Callias' role as *erastēs* to pay for the boy's trainer and defray the costs of his travel to various athletic venues. Nick Fisher (1998), drawing on the work of Young, Kyle, and others, has recently argued that quite a few young athletes would come from backgrounds that were less than wealthy and would rely on precisely such patronage, often erotically motivated (pp. 96-98). Graffiti from the stadium entrance at Nemea (fourth to third century BCE in date) attest that lovers would be present at the games to cheer on their young companions (*SEG* 29.349 [g] and [i]). Hence the nexus between the *palaestra* and pederastic courtship may be founded on a complex array of connected social interactions and needs.

Pindar's *Pythian* [*P.*] 10, written for the Thessalian boy victor Hippocleas, offers a likely parallel for precisely this situation, in that the ode itself was commissioned by Thorax, a member of the local ruling family, but not a relative of the boy.[35] It would therefore seem that Thorax was indeed a patron and financial backer who was in a significant way involved with the boy's athletic success. The scholia speculate that he was also the boy's *erastēs*,[36] a possibility that appears to be supported by the context in which he is mentioned. The ode concludes by commending to the boy Thorax's character and friendship (vv. 61-72), after a priamel (vv. 55-60) describing the new erotic opportunities which may now be available to him as a famous athlete: celebrated by Pindar's songs, he will be still more beautiful to look upon in the eyes of both "youths his own age" (ἅλιξι) and "older men" (παλαιτέροις), and he will be a care to "young maidens" (νέαισίν τε παρθένοισι).[37] Verse 60 (ἑτέροις ἑτέρων ἔρωτες), which one might loosely translate as "different strokes for different folks,"[38] encapsulates the sequence in a neat summary priamel. In contrast to this priamelistic foil, Pindar warns the boy not to look too far afield, but stick with the good which is at hand. Verse 64 and following make it clear that the boy's present good is Thorax, presumably his present *erastēs*, whose virtues Pindar warmly recommends in the lines that follow. Girls and marriage are among τὰ δ' εἰς ἐνιαυτόν ("the things a year in the future"), which the poet warns the boy not to try foreseeing right now. If my interpretation of this passage is correct, Pindar's ode and its public celebration could be viewed as an extravagant love gift from Thorax, even as Callias' feast (the setting of Xenophon's *Symposium*) was a public love gift celebrating the Panathenaic victory of his *erōmenos* Autolycus.

There is, however, a key difference between *O.*10 and *P.*10, which is the lack of any indication that Ilas is the one who commissioned Pindar's services, in contrast to the very specific announcement in *P.*10.64-66 that it is Thorax who has yoked Pindar's chariot of song.[39] The shorter *O.*11, which celebrates the same victory, makes no mention of Ilas at all, which would be strange if he were the one paying for it. Ilas' role in *O.*10.20-21 seems entirely involved with training and encouraging Hagesidamus. While his financial patronage cannot be excluded as a possibility, it does not appear to be the primary emphasis.

But Fisher (1998) notes that the roles of trainer and financial backer were in some cases conflated, in that it would not be unusual for a trainer to volunteer his services out of romantic attraction to a promising youth (pp. 96-97). One of the most frequently and enthusiastically praised trainers in Pindar is the Athenian Melesias (*O.*8.54-66, *N.*4.93-96, *N.*6.64-66), also noted as the father of the "other Thucydides," the conservative and aristocratic political rival of Pericles.[40] *O.*8.65-66 tells us that Alcimedon has brought this trainer his thirtieth victory. It is difficult to believe that someone of Melesias' prominence and high station would have undertaken to train so many young Aeginetan wrestlers purely out of a profit motive. More likely his motivations were love of the sport and his enjoyment of close contact with developing adolescent athletes. How "close" the contact was we cannot of course say, but Melesias clearly found his considerable investment of time worthwhile. That Melesias was not the only rich man who chose to pursue an avocation as a trainer is confirmed by the example of Timarchus' uncle Eupolemus (Aeschines, *Tim.* 102).

Some of the most suggestive fifth-century evidence concerning the relation of trainers and athletes is found in the iconography of Attic red-figure vase painting. There are dozens of representations of such scenes extant,[41] and this motif is arguably an even more common form of adult-youth interaction than the explicit courtship scenes so often discussed in treatments of Greek pederasty. What is often striking about these images is just how much they have in common with courtship representations; in many cases it is impossible to tell whether the clothed figure watching or crowning a nude athlete is a trainer or a lovestruck admirer. The one certain and distinctive attribute that identifies a character as a trainer is the cleft staff or branch, which would be used to prod or position an athlete's limbs; however, trainers are sometimes represented with an ordinary staff, so the absence of a cleft staff need not exclude a character as trainer.

A common and normative image is of a bearded trainer, sternly imperious and usually supervising more than one pupil, whose air of adult authority and command seems unquestionable (see Figure 1). What may be a bit surprising, however, is that it is just as common to find youths of an age apparently equal to the athlete(s) holding the cleft stick and acting as trainer, as if to deemphasize any concept of hierarchy and suggest that a friend or companion could just as well assume the role.[42] This is in fact the most frequent way of representing trainers on late fifth-century vases, such as those of the Eretria Painter, Calliope Painter, and Disney Painter, all of whom especially favored athletic scenes, but it is also common in the work of earlier red-figure artists such as the Andocides Painter, Euthymides, Epictetus, the Kleophrades Painter, Onesimus, the Antiphon Painter, the Brygos Painter, Douris, and even on at least one black-figure vase.[43] These youthful trainers are

FIGURE 1. Amphora signed by Euthymides. Munich 2308 = *ARV*² 26.2. Reproduced by courtesy of the Staatliche Antikensammlungen und Glyptothek München.

more likely to be paired off with athletes one-on-one and to show a closer degree of personal engagement.

The Calliope Painter produced a series of pelikai featuring a common compositional scheme, of which a dozen examples are extant (Lezzi-Hafter, nos. 163-74; see Figure 2) dated to the period 440-20 BCE: on one side of each pelike is a pair of figures (in two cases male-female [Lezzi-Hafter, nos. 165-66], in the others two age-equal male youths), and on the other side is a single male figure who appears to be watching the interaction of the pair on front. Six of the ten vessels with male-male couples show a trainer (identified as such by the forked stick) and athlete; the other four merely show two clothed youths in conversation, but one of those (Lezzi-Hafter, no. 174) features a young trainer as the solo figure on the reverse. The mutual engagement and eye contact of these four non-athletic couples suggest that the images could be construed as courtship scenes; the two heterosexual couples are unquestionably

FIGURE 2. Pelike attributed to the Calliope Painter. Tampa 1986.068 = *ARV*²
1262.69bis. Reproduced by courtesy of the Tampa Museum of Art, Joseph
Veach Noble Collection.

such, since the young man in both cases hands an alabastron to the woman as a gift. It is interesting that this painter would regard trainer-athlete pairs as a variation or substitute for courtship scenes. Even more significant, however, is what we find on some of the pelikai with trainers and athletes: three of the six (Lezzi-Hafter, nos. 163 = Figure 2, 168 [Verona 53 = *ARV*² 1262.67], 169 [New York 25.78.68 = *ARV*² 1262.69]) show the youth disrobing himself in front of the trainer, as if to open up his body for the trainer's inspection.[44] The trainer bends over slightly and fixes his gaze on the boy's midsection, as if the boy's penis were his real object of interest. From our position to the boy's side, we do not actually see the boy's penis, but it is clear that the boy's clothing is opened just enough that the trainer, who stands in front of him, can steal a peek at this visual prize, which seems to be reserved for him alone. In earlier red-figure vase painting (see, for example, Figure 3), a boy's opening up his clothing and showing his body to an interested suitor is a convention to express his consent to the suitor's gifts and advances.[45] That the Calliope Painter chose to model some of his

FIGURE 3. Kylix attributed to Makron. Munich 2655 = *ARV*² 471.196. Reproduced by courtesy of the Staatliche Antikensammlungen und Glyptothek München.

trainer-athlete pairs on the iconography of pederastic courtship suggests that he saw the relationships as parallel and perhaps even equivalent.

Another interesting case is Figure 4, a plate signed by Epictetus, active from about 520 to 490 BCE, in which two age-equal youths stand face-to-face at close quarters, with reciprocal eye contact. The youthful trainer at the right, holding a forked staff in one hand, reaches out with the other to his companion's hip to tie a fillet around him. This gesture recognizes an athletic triumph and could thus appropriately be a

FIGURE 4. Plate signed by Epictetus. Gymnasium scene: athlete and trainer. Red-figure plate c. 520-510 BCE. Inv. G7 = *ARV*[2] 78.97. Photo: H. Lewandowski. Louvre, Paris, France. Reproduced by courtesy of the Réunion des Musées Nationaux/Art Resource, NY.

trainer's way of honoring his pupil, but iconographic parallels also suggest that such ribbons are commonly offered by lovers or suitors. New York 1979.11.9 (= Kunisch no. 250), a kylix by Makron, shows bearded men (no staffs) wrapping elaborate, even excessive ribbons around nude athletes;[46] that this is meant as a courtship vase is indicated by the other side, which clearly shows lovers offering gifts. See also London E440 (ARV^2 289.1 = Koch-Harnack, Fig. 111), a stamnos by the Siren Painter showing Erotes carrying such a ribbon along with other love-gifts, and Paris G45 (ARV^2 31.4 = R59 in Kilmer), an amphora by the Dikaios Painter, where one clothed youth-naked boy pair kisses, and another shows the clothed youth crowning the naked boy discus-thrower.[47]

On some vases, one sees trainers and wooers explicitly parallelled. Figure 5, a kylix by Douris, who was active throughout the first half of the fifth-century BCE, provides an interesting example. One side depicts four naked youths and two bearded men: the two youths at the left

FIGURE 5. Kylix signed by Douris. Young man in robe holding the trainer's baton. Red figure cup. 490-480 BCE. Inv. G 118 = ARV^2 430.35. Photo: H. Lewandowski. Louvre, Paris, France. Reproduced by courtesy of the Réunion des Musées Nationaux/Art Resource, NY.

hold hand weights, emphasizing their athletic activity. A trainer, recognizable by his forked rod, reaches out with the palm of his hand to touch one of these youths, perhaps to position the young man's back or buttocks. On the right side we see another group of three, again with the youth on the outside margin watching. In this group, the bearded man holds in his right hand a typical walking staff rather than a trainer's rod and gesticulates with his left hand as if talking to the youth in front of him, who turns around to look at him, but walks away and raises his right hand in what appears to be a gesture of refusal.[48] This scene is evidently one of courtship, not athletic supervision. Its juxtaposition with the trainer reaching out to touch the youth in front of him prompts us to reconsider the dynamics and intention of that grouping. The parallelism in the composition and orientation of each pair is clear: in each case the man appears to pursue from the right, while the youth walks away to the left. Moreover the youth twists around to look back at the man, who advances his right arm in the youth's direction. Could the vase painter's intention be to show that the wooer and trainer are in some sense both pursuing the same thing, even if from the standpoint of different roles?[49] Or are we meant to contrast the ready availability of a boy's body for touching by a trainer with the non-availability of the other boy to the non-trainer?

There are many cases where one simply cannot tell whether the figure in question is a trainer or an engaged admirer. A good example is Figure 6, a neck amphora attributed to the Painter of Altenburg 273, from the second half of the fifth-century BCE. A naked youth holds a hand-weight as he stands to the right of a goalpost, while a well-clothed bearded man on the other side of the post bends over to talk with him, leaning on his walking staff, his right hand positioned on his hip. He lacks the forked staff characteristic of trainers, which is always held, never leaned upon. His hands are static and make no gesture indicating instruction or demonstration to the youth. But nothing prevents him from being a trainer either. On the other side of the amphora is a running Nike, perhaps suggesting that the man is admiring a youthful victor. The two figures, like those of Figure 4, stand in reciprocating eye contact, which often indicates emotional engagement.[50] Other equally ambiguous cases can be identified.[51] That the iconographical conventions are so undefined that we cannot distinguish between trainers and admirers in these cases raises the possibility that the ancients themselves did not sharply distinguish between the two: a trainer was an admirer, whose emotional orientation toward a favored trainee was in some sense that of a lover.

FIGURE 6. Neck amphora attributed to the Painter of Altenburg 273. Munich 2333 = *ARV*² 1194.1. Reproduced by courtesy of the Staatliche Antikensammlungen und Glyptothek München.

The work of one vase painter deserves particular mention. The Eretria Painter, active between 440 and 420 BCE and closely associated with the Calliope Painter, produced a series of kylixes with athletic (or in some cases musical or pedagogical) scenes: each cup features a pair of (usually age-equal) youths in the interior, and two pairs on each side.[52] Typically, one youth in each pair is clothed and the other a nude athlete; it is often uncertain whether the clothed figure is a trainer or a lovestruck admirer.[53] One vase where at least two or three of them are certainly trainers is Figure 7a-c: the clothed figure in the tondo (7a) is clearly recognizable as a trainer in virtue of his forked staff and distinctive wreath. Similarly, one of the youths on the side of the cup (7b) holds a forked staff. The comparable youth on the other side (7c) who

FIGURES 7a, b, c. Red-figure kylix, attributed to the Eretria Painter, c. 430-420 B.C., acc. #1980.38 = *ARV*^{2} 1254.73. Reproduced by courtesy of the Jack S. Blanton Museum of Art, The University of Texas at Austin, Archer M. Huntington Museum Fund and the James R. Dougherty, Jr. Foundation, 1980.

holds a staff is probably a trainer; although the staff is not forked, it is too long to be merely a walking stick.[54] The other pair on each side is distinguished by the giving of a sprig or crown; on one side (7c) the clothed admirer holds it out toward the athlete as a reward he is presenting,[55] whereas the other side (7b) shows a curious inversion of the usual pattern in that the naked athlete boldly strides forward and appears to present the gift to his admirer. Although this athlete's groin area is damaged by a large scratch, one can make out the tip of an obviously erect penis, something quite without parallel in athletic scenes, but perhaps intended to suggest the aphrodisiac power of athletic success as well as the complete deconstruction of all active-passive distinctions between lover and beloved. What is common to all these pairs, however, is the deeply engaged mutual eye contact in each case. While eye contact generally becomes more important as red-figure style develops in sophistication, such intense ocular interaction seems to be a special hallmark of this painter's style, particularly noticeable in the age-equal couples,[56] and cannot fail to imply a two-sided eroticization of the relationship. The trainer-figures in each case make no authoritative gestures and appear unconcerned with how the athletes hold the discus. Note particularly how close together the trainer and youth stand in 7a, as if their arms touch. The trainers here are, for all practical purposes, admirers, and their emotional engagement with the athletes puts them on a level of complete equality.

A curious and unique illustration is offered in Figure 8, a kylix attributed to Onesimus, active in the first quarter of the fifth century, where we see an adult trainer fully naked, like the two young athletes under his charge. Even more unusual is the fact that he is about to come to blows with one of the youths, who holds a measuring rod or a javelin above his head.[57] The trainer's weapon is, on the other hand, merely a sandal, which is never found elsewhere on athletic vases as an instrument of punishment or discipline.[58] Its most common function is as a stimulant to lovemaking on sexually explicit vases, usually of a heterosexual character; in most of these cases, it may be meant as a tool of intimidation allowing men to force their way on unfortunate slave girls, but on at least one kylix (Berlin 3251/Florence 1B49 = ARV^2 113.7 = R192I in Kilmer) a man appears to derive pleasure from being sandal-whipped by a woman.[59] The closest pederastic parallel is a pelike by Euphronius (Villa Giulia, unnumbered = ARV^2 15.11 = Keuls, Fig. 255), showing a seminude youth about to fall off his chair as he reaches out to grab hold of a naked boy and sandal-whip him; that something of an erotic character is involved is suggested by the boy's erection and the *kalos*-inscrip-

FIGURE 8. Kylix attributed to Onesimus. Munich 2637 = *ARV*^{2} 322.28. Reproduced by courtesy of the Staatliche Antikensammlungen und Glyptothek München.

tion between the two figures.[60] Given these associations of the sandal in the iconographic tradition, as well as the man's nakedness, one is entitled to wonder whether the clash in Figure 8 might represent a trainer who has made unappreciated physical advances on the youth and has been forcibly repelled. Compare the pelike by the Aegisthus Painter (Cambridge 37.26 = *ARV*² 506.21 = Dover R684) in which a youth violently wards off a pushy suitor by brandishing a lyre above his head.

Another anomalous, but intriguing, illustration appears in Figure 9, an amphora by the Andocides Painter, active in the last quarter of the sixth century and one of the earliest red-figure painters. Martin Kilmer, who includes an illustration, aptly captions "Wrestlers and effeminate trainer."[61] At the left-hand margin of the picture we see a long-haired, willowy youth dressed in a robe with an elaborate border and a flowery decoration, more typical of what one might expect a woman to wear.[62] In his right hand he holds a rod, but with his thin, delicate left hand he raises to his nose a flower, as if to imply that the delight he takes in watching naked athletes is a sensual pleasure like sniffing a rose.[63] A

FIGURE 9. Neck amphora signed by Andocides, Berlin. Andokides-Amphora F 2159 = *ARV*[2] 3.1. Reproduced by courtesy of the Antikensammlung, Staatliche Museen zu Berlin–Preussischer Kulturbesitz.

similar flower-sniffing youth appears on other works of the same painter as an aesthete appreciating musical entertainment.[64] Figure 9 is unusual in more than one respect: note also the bearded figure on the extreme right, who is lifted up by his larger and younger companion like a plaything, emphasizing that the usual categories of age superiority are inverted.[65] But in showing that youth and beauty captivate even those one might expect to exercise authority, the vase speaks to a more profound truth in erotic relations. While it cannot be ruled out that the flower-sniffer is an umpire rather than a trainer, either way he shows that supervision in the ring is not necessarily defined in terms of superior physical strength or masculinity, so much as a role assumed by those most appreciative of athletic beauty.

None of the evidence we have adduced, either textual or iconographic, is by itself definitive. But in its cumulative totality, the evidence does suggest that the *palaestra* was a sanctuary of pederastic culture and that it was not uncommon for the relationships between a trainer and young athlete to be intimate and eroticized. The iconographic evidence in particular suggests that there was sometimes very little difference in age between the two, and the trainer's position need not necessarily be based on long experience or even athletic skill. However, the better trainers–Melesias and the others whom Pindar praises in connection with their pupils' victories–were probably experienced professionals, which does not, however, in itself mean they offered their services for hire. Indeed, Pindar's allusive suggestion that Ilas was the lover as well as the trainer of the young Hagesidamus in *Olympian* 10 does not necessarily prove that he actually was the boy's lover, but that it would be received positively for Pindar to imply that he was, as if to affirm that he was motivated by genuine and authentic admiration of Hagesidamus' qualities rather than any mercenary motive.[66] Just as Socrates could pride himself on not being motivated by money, like other sophists, but by the pleasure afforded him in the company of young and open minds in search of moral excellence, a trainer might be excited by the opportunity to guide young and eager bodies in pursuit of an excellence that combined physical and moral self-control. We should not be unduly prejudiced by modern assumptions that may define erotic involvement with youth and moral guidance as mutually exclusive and antithetical spheres of activity.[67]

NOTES

1. For a more detailed interpretation of the context of these lines, see Hubbard (1989).
2. Σ *O*.10.19c, 21a (Drachmann). This view is accepted by most modern Pindaric commentators (e.g. Dissen (1830, II, p. 130); Mezger (1880, p. 429); Christ (1896, p. 82); Verdenius (1988, p. 64)). That training is at issue here is certainly suggested by the image of "whetting" (θάξαις) "one with natural ability" (φύντ' ἀρετᾷ) "by means of divine arts" (θεοῦ σὺν παλάμαις). The trainer is also characterized as a "whetstone" in *I*.6.73. Gildersleeve (1885, p. 216) cites additional parallels.
3. Fraccaroli (1894, pp. 294-295) and Viljoen (1955, pp. 72-85) note that Ilas is given special prominence in this poem beyond what one normally expects of a trainer (who is usually mentioned only in the last triad), but fall back on the speculation of the scholia (Σ *O*.10.19c, 21a [Drachmann]) that Ilas gave the boy special encouragement or advice during the match itself that turned a looming defeat into a victory. This explanation fails to motivate the Patroclus/Achilles allusion.
4. See especially frr. 123, 127-28 S-M, *N*.8.1-5. Köhnken (1974, pp. 200-204) has argued that Pindar is the one who introduced the pederastic dimension into the myth of Poseidon and Pelops in *O*.1; even if it was traditional, Pindar certainly emphasizes it. Athenaeus 13.601C, in quoting fr. 127, calls Pindar οὐ μετρίως ἐρωτικός. Pindar frequently uses erotic motifs in the epinicia as an extension of the symposiastic

relationship of *philotēs* between poet and victor. See von der Mühll (1964); Lasserre (1974, pp. 18-19); Crotty (1982, pp. 92-103); Instone (1990); Steiner (1998, pp. 136-142); Nicholson (1998, pp. 28-33). Kurke (1990, pp. 94-95) argues that the paideutic role of Cheiron in *P.*6 is inherently pederastic; if so, it would provide a parallel to what is here proposed for Ilas and Hagesidamus.

5. See Plato, *Symp.* 180A, and Aeschylus, frr. 135-37 *TGrF.* Clarke (1978) has argued that the Achilles-Patroclus relationship is already erotic in the *Iliad.* Against this view, see Barrett (1981) and Patzer (1982, pp. 94-98). Halperin (1990, pp. 75-87) is more cautious and views the relation in terms of warrior-partnerships in Near Eastern tradition that are not necessarily sexual. The Platonic passage suggests that Aeschylus' innovation was not only to interpret the relationship in pederastic terms, but also to invert the ages (Patroclus was usually imagined as the elder of the two) so that Achilles could be cast as the *erastēs.* Among Pindaric commentators, Lehnus (1981, p. 175) is the only one to perceive the erotic nature of this relationship, but he fails to recognize the influence of Aeschylus here or to draw the necessary inference about the analogous relationship of Hagesidamus and Ilas.

6. For the influence of the *Oresteia* on *P.*11, see Hubbard (1990, pp. 348-351), and the additional bibliography therein. For *O.*6 and *N.*9 as responses to Aeschylus' *Eleusinians,* see Hubbard (1992, pp. 97-100).

7. The climactic coupling of the trainer Orseas' name with the victor at the very end of *I.*4, together with the evocation of the erotically suggestive term χάρις, leads Nicholson (1998, pp. 31-32) to conclude that their relationship may also have been pederastic.

8. *N.*8.1-5 opens its praise of the young victor Deinias with an invocation to῾Ωρα, called "herald of the ambrosial love acts of Aphrodite, who sits on the cheeks of maidens and boys." The word unquestionably marks a love object for Pindar. Deinias' exact age is unclear, but the emphasis on῾Ωρα and the explicit reference to boys in verse 2 suggests that he was probably still a boy and in any event not much over 18. Hamilton (1974, p. 108, nn. 5-6) adduces formal grounds to support the information of Σ Pindar, *N.*8.inscr. a (Drachmann) that the ode commemorates a double victory of father and son, suggesting that Deinias must in fact be quite young, if his father is still an active athlete winning footraces.

9. See especially Plato, *Charm.* 154A-155D, *Lysis* 204A-206A, *Symp.* 216A-219E; Xenophon, *Symp.* 4.27-28.

10. See Meier and de Pogey-Castries (1930, pp. 84-85) for a catalogue of the sources, mainly in Diogenes Laertius. Even if we reject the historicity of all these relationships, the traditions demonstrate that by the Hellenistic period, such teacher-student pederasty was taken for granted.

11. While it is easy to understand why boys undergoing athletic instruction are depicted nude on vases, there was no necessary reason why students of music and literature should be so presented, unless to emphasize their role as beautiful objects of their teacher's gaze: see the interior of a kylix by the Eretria Painter (Paris G457 = *ARV²* 1254.80 = Lezzi-Hafter no. 21), pointedly paralleled to athletic scenes on the sides of the cup. For other examples of classroom nudity, see the interior of a kylix by a painter related to Apollodorus (Basel BS465 = *Beazley Addenda²* 398 = *CVA Switzerland* VI, pl. 19.1), a chous by the Berlin Painter (New York 22.139.32 = *ARV²* 210.186 = Beck, Fig. 104), a kylix of the Cage Painter (Paris G318 = *ARV²* 348.3 = Beck, Fig. 57), the interior of a kylix by the Akestorides Painter (Leiden PC91 = *ARV²* 781.3 = Beck, Fig. 121), a kylix by the Tarquinia Painter (Tarquinia RC1121 = *ARV²* 866.1), a chous by

the Shuvalov Painter (London E525 = *ARV²* 1208.38 = Beck, Fig. 80), an unattributed chous (Brussels A1911 = Beck, Fig. 69), and a South Italic marble grave relief datable to c. 400 BCE (Munich G481 = Beck, Fig. 122). Even in cases where the pupil is fully clothed, the erotic relation to his teacher can be clear: see a kylix by the Telephus Painter (Munich 2669 = *ARV²* 818.26 = Beck, Fig. 120), where a boy sings in front of his seated teacher, who plays the flute, while an Eros crowns the boy from the rear, or a kylix by Douris (Getty 86.AE.290 = *Para.* 375.51bis = Buitron-Oliver no.93), where suitors and love gifts enter the classroom. An interesting series of terra-cotta figurines show teacher-student couples huddled closely together, often with the teacher's arm or hand around the (typically naked) boy's shoulder: see Berlin TC8033 (= Beck, Fig. 67), Paris MYR287 (= Beck, Fig. 74), Athens 4899 (= Beck, Fig. 82), London, Life Coll. 31 (= Beck, Fig. 83). The most famous and flamboyant sculptural example is of course Heliodorus' late Hellenistic group of Pan teaching music to a naked Daphnis (the most famous example of which is in the Museo Nazionale, Naples). Red-figure scenes of Heracles and his music teacher Linus typically show the young hero naked (see *LIMC* IV, 833, especially nos. 1667-73), raising the possibility that his reason for attacking Linus may have been related to unwanted physical intimacies rather than punishment; see our discussion of Figure 8 below.

12. For a more detailed critique, see Hubbard (1998; 2002, pp. 273-290; 2003, pp. 10-14).

13. See Gardiner (1910, pp. 503-505); Schween (1911, pp. 16-20); Forbes (1929, pp. 64-69); Jüthner (1965, pp. 183-88).

14. This is clear from the setting of Plato's *Lysis* (206E-207B) and *Charmides* (153A-154C), as well as references in Attic comedy (Aristophanes, *Nub.* 973-76, *Vesp.* 1023-28, *Pax* 762-63, *Av.* 139-42). See the discussions of Delorme (1960, pp. 19-20, 35); Dover (1978, pp. 54-55); Buffière (1980, pp. 561-572); Reinsberg (1989, pp. 179-180); Steiner (1998, 126-129); Fisher (1998, pp. 94-104); Scanlon (2002, pp. 199-273).

15. See, for example, Gotha 48 (*ARV²* 20 = Koch-Harnack, Fig. 17), Berlin 2279 (*ARV²* 115.2 = Dover R196a), Florence 12 B 16 (*ARV²* 374.62 = Koch-Harnack, Fig. 10), Vatican H550 (*ARV²* 375.68 = Koch-Harnack, Fig. 9), Yale Univ. 1933.175 (*ARV²* 576.45 = Koch-Harnack, Fig. 5). See the survey of iconographical evidence by Scanlon (2002, pp. 236-249), including several examples where the god Eros is shown crowning or in other ways recognizing victorious athletes.

16. For the connection of athletic nudity and pederasty, see the remarks in Plutarch, *Amatorius* 751F, Papalas (1991, p. 172), and Scanlon (2002, p. 96). Bonfante (1989) emphasizes the evolution of athletic nudity in connection with ritual initiation of the young, a context in which pederasty also figured. Arieti (1975, pp. 434-436) argues that athletes' nudity was a means of displaying their sexual modesty. For a brief survey of other recent scholarship on the question, see Golden (1998, pp. 65-69). Pausanias 5.8.9 dates the addition of separate boys' contests at Olympia to 632 BCE. Evidence suggests that they became part of the other major festivals during the same general period; see Papalas (1991, pp. 166-67) and Golden (1998, pp. 104-112). Significantly, this is also the period to which we owe our earliest evidence of generalized male and female pederasty (Sappho, Alcaeus, Alcman, the Thera graffiti). On athletics generally as eroticized spectacle in this period, see the recent work of Larmour (1999, pp. 139-144) and Scanlon (2002, pp. 199-273).

17. These would include some kind of performance displaying bodily size, strength, and agility. Crowther (1985, pp. 285-291) collects the evidence. On their Athenian

version as represented on Attic vases, see Reed (1987, pp. 59-64) and Neils (1994, pp. 154-159). For their connection with homoeroticism, see Spivey (1996, pp. 36-39).

18. For example, Automedon, *AP* 12.34; Strato, *AP* 12.206, 12.222. Wrestling imagery is commonly applied to love-making in a variety of texts: see Aristophanes, *Pax* 894-905, *Eccl.* 962-65, and Lucian, *Asin.* 8-10. The association may be present in Pindar's description of Hippolyta's machinations in *N.*5.26-27. On the strong element of homoeroticism involved in naked bodies wrestling together and the possibility that infibulation of the penis was introduced specifically to avoid sexual arousal during the event, see Larmour (1999, pp. 140-141).

19. See Montserrat (1996, pp. 150-151) on the implications of this text.

20. See Galen's treatise Περὶ τρίψεως παρασκευαστικῆς (= 6.13 Oribasius) for the importance of this practice, and 11.476 Kühn for the trainer's role in it. This activity probably formed the basis for the etymology of the term *paidotribēs* (literally "boy rubber") and the synonomous *aleiptēs* (literally "anointer"). See Forbes (1929, pp. 63, 91); Jüthner (1965, pp. 161-162); Harris (1966, p. 171). For the most complete study of athletic massage in antiquity, see Jung (1930, pp. 8-23). The practice is certainly attested in vase painting as early as 480 BCE: see a kylix by the Antiphon Painter (Villa Giulia 50430 = *ARV*² 340.62 = Gardiner 1930, Fig. 46). Scanlon (2002, p. 212) notes that the term *tribein* is also used in explicitly erotic contexts, and thinks the erotic potential of massage is the reason it was limited to practice by a professional.

21. On the concept of "male homosocial desire," or the need for nonsexual male bonding which nevertheless forms a seamless continuum with actual homosexuality, see Sedgwick (1985, pp. 1-5). For an exploration of the issue with respect to modern athletics, see Pronger (1990).

22. See Scanlon (2002, pp. 212-213).

23. Kyle (1984, p. 100) suggests that this expansion of the law may date to the systematic reform of Athenian law in 403 BCE. See also Scanlon (2002, pp. 91, 213-214).

24. Delorme (1960, pp. 24-30) associates the foundation of public gymnasia with cities' needs to prepare the young for an expanded hoplite force. Kyle (1987, pp. 71-101) sees the major periods of building activity as the fifth century, under Cimon and Pericles, and the fourth century, under Lycurgus. On the connection of gymnasia with democratic developments, see Humphreys (1974, pp. 90-91); Golden (1998, p. 144); Fisher (1998, pp. 84-94); Ps.-Xenophon, *Const. Ath.* 2.10 provides key evidence for the association in the fifth century.

25. Although the first certain evidence for publicly elected or appointed gymnastic officials is in a third-century inscription from Teos (*SIG*³ 578), Plato at least conceives of such an institution (*Laws* 764C-766C, 813E) and Aristotle (*Const. Ath.* 42.2-3) attests such a system for electing supervisors of ephebic training, with an emphasis on choosing mature men over 40 who could be trusted with the care of youths. The third-century gymnastic law of Beroea (*SEG* 27.261, Side B, 13-15, 26-32) makes it clear that it was part of the gymnasiarch's job to protect boys from precisely those corrupting influences that were associated with the private *palaestra*. This seems to be confirmed for the late fifth century by the story of Prodicus' expulsion by the gymnasiarch of the Lyceum for being a bad influence on the young (Ps.-Plato, *Eryxias* 398E-399A). See also Aeschines, *Tim.* 12, although the text of the law is probably a later addition.

26. On the developing prejudice against pederasty in Athens as a radical democratic reaction against upper-class predilections during this period, see Hubbard (2000, pp. 7-11). See also Nicholson (1998, p. 39).

27. See Plato, *Laws* 636B-D; Aristotle, *Polit.* 2.10, 1272a22-26; Ephorus, fr. 149 *FGrH*; Athenaeus 13.601F, 602F.

28. See Xenophon, *Const. Lac.* 2.12-14, *Agesilaus* 5.4-6; Aelian, *VH* 3.12. Plutarch, *Lyc.* 17.1, emphasizes the athletic setting of such relationships in Sparta.

29. On this couplet, see Delorme (1960, pp. 19-20).

30. On this myth, see Sergent (1986, pp. 84-96). Euripides, *Helen* 1468-75, attests it as the basis of the Spartan ritual of the Hyacinthia (cf. Pausanias 3.19.3-5, Athenaeus IV, 138E-139F, citing earlier local historians, and the extensive note of Kannicht 1969.II, pp. 383-85, listing further sources and bibliography), which included a contest of discus-throwing and must have been a ritual of some antiquity. Tarentum had a tomb of Apollo Hyacinthus (cf. Polybius 8.28.2), suggesting that the association of the two must have predated the colony's foundation by Sparta in 706 BCE. Hesiod, fr. 171 MW, may also attest the myth, but the reading here is uncertain. For iconographic evidence connecting Hyacinthus with the cult of Apollo dating back to the last quarter of the sixth century, see *LIMC* V, 546-49, especially nos. 3-40. The eroticization of the relationship is clearly implied in an early Laconian inscription (*SEG* 28.404), as also in the visual representations of the boy astride an obviously phallic swan of Apollo; see especially the skyphos of the Zephyrus Painter, Vienna IV.191 (*ARV*^{2}976.2 = *LIMC* V, 379, no. 41), where the jealous Zephyrus pursues the boy on the other side of the cup.

31. See n. 43 and our discussion below. Schween (1911, pp. 78-80) and Forbes (1929, p. 72) suggest that these might be instances of older pupils who take over instruction in the master's stead, but often there is no indication of age difference at all. These may be analogous to the cases of age-equal courtship.

32. Xenophon, *Symp.* 1.2-4, 8.11.

33. See Eupolis, *Flatterers,* especially frr. 156, 160, 174-75 PCG; Σ Aristoph., *Aves* 283a, 284b (Holwerda); Philostratus, *Vit. Sophist.* 2.610; Libanius, fr. 50b.2 (Foerster).

34. See Cratinus, fr. 214 PCG; Xenophon, *Symp.* 3.13. This is also the conclusion of Fisher (1998, p. 99).

35. Thorax is nowhere identified as a relative, and Pindar is normally very careful in specifying familial relationships, when they exist.

36. Σ Pindar, *P.*10.99a (Drachmann) calls Thorax the ἑταῖρος of the boy, which is probably to be understood as a synonym for *erastēs*. Among modern commentators, only Schroeder (1922, p. 91) and Coppola (1931, p. 29) have explicitly acknowledged the likely nature of the relationship. The remarks on Thorax's *xenia* to the poet in verses 64-66 and his gold being put to the touchstone in verses 67-68 make it clear that he, not the boy's father Phrikias, was the one who commissioned the epinician. For a more detailed exposition of this passage and its significance, see my remarks in Hubbard (1995, pp. 41-45).

37. This passage is parallel to *P.*9.97-100, on the young victor's enhanced sex appeal to women, in an ode critics have long seen as pervaded by concerns with marriage. In *P.*10 females are the climactic term in a series, represented as the final goal (in the form of marriage) *after* a period of homoerotic and homosocial involvement. The Pelops myth in *O.*1 suggests that Pindar did in fact view pederasty as in some way an initiatory preparation for adult sexual responsibilities: after a pederastic interlude with Poseidon on Olympus, Pelops with Poseidon's help competes for and wins the hand of

Hippodameia, upon whom he fathers a race of heroes. For iconographic representations of a victorious athlete admired by women, see Scanlon (2002, pp. 246-249).

38. For the idea that men are differentiated by sexual preference, compare Archilochus, fr. 25.1-4 W., and Pindar, fr. 123.4-9 S-M.

39. The mention of *xenia* (πέποιθα ξενία προσανέι Θώπακος) confirms the patronage relationship here. See Kurke (1991, pp. 135-159) for an extended discussion of this institution's meaning in Pindar's work.

40. Wilamowitz (1922, pp. 397-398) doubts the identity of Pindar's Melesias with Thucydides' father, largely based on his assumption that the trainer's vocation must have been that of a lowly hireling. But Pindar would be unlikely to devote so much attention to the praise of trainers if such were the case. Σ Pindar, *N*.4.155a (Drachmann) identifies Melesias as Athenian, and the circumspection with which Pindar refers to possible envy against him in Aegina (*O*.8.55, *N*.4.93-96) fits with his being Athenian. The date also seems right. In favor of the identity of the two figures, see Wade-Gery (1958, pp. 243-247), who notes that Thucydides and his sons are referred to as wrestlers in several sources; Bowra (1964, pp. 150-151); Golden (1998, p. 109); and Fisher (1998, p. 89). Woloch (1963, p. 102) thinks the identification "plausible" and believes that Melesias was in any event an aristocrat. Other sources tell us that Thucydides was of aristocratic pedigree (Plutarch, *Pericles* 11.1) and married into Cimon's family (Aristotle, *Const. Ath.* 28.2), suggesting that his father was also wealthy and prominent.

41. In a well-catalogued and extensive collection, that of the British Museum, there are at least 14 scenes involving trainers with athletes out of 819 red-figure vases of the best period (the late-sixth and fifth centuries), compared to 12 scenes of men approaching or conversing with youths in non-athletic contexts. See the descriptive catalogue of Smith (1896).

42. See n. 31 above.

43. For the Andocides Painter, see Figure 9; for Euthymides, see Berlin 2180 = ARV^2 13.1; for Epictetus, see Figure 4; for the Kleophrades Painter, see Tarquinia RC4196 (ARV^2 185.35 = Plate 142 in Buitron-Oliver); for Onesimus, see Paris Bibl. Nat., Cab. Med. 523 (ARV^2 316.4 = Patrucco, Fig. 126) and Boston 01.8020 (ARV^2 321.22 = Schroeder 1927, Plate 54b); for the Antiphon Painter, see Villa Giulia 50430 (discussed in n. 23 above) and Oxford 1914.729 (ARV^2 340.73 = Patrucco, Fig. 81); for the Brygos Painter, see Boston 10.176 (ARV^2 381.173 = Schroeder 1927, Plate 53a); for Douris, see the interior of Paris G118 (same cup as Figure 5), and the interior and Side B of Basel Ka452 (ARV^2 430.31 = no. 51 in Buitron-Oliver). See also the Painter of the Paris Gigantomachy, London E288 (ARV^2 423.119 = *CVA Great Britain*, VII, Plate 47.3), the Aberdeen Painter (Boston 03.820 = ARV^2 919.3 = Beck, Figs. 181 & 184), the Penthesilea Painter (Boston 28.48 = ARV^2 882.36 = Beck, Figs. 143 & 150), and a kylix in the style of the Colmar Painter (Bologna 362 = ARV^2 357 = Beck, Fig. 196). Other possible examples include the work of Polygnotus (London E337 = ARV^2 1031.47 = *CVA Great Britain* VII, Plate 65.3a,b) and the Berlin Painter (Munich 2313 = ARV^2 198.12 = *CVA Germany*, XII, Plate 196).

44. In Lezzi-Hafter no. 173 (London E414 = ARV^2 1262.65), the seated trainer looks down at the midsection of a completely nude discus-thrower. In no. 164 (Copenhagen Thorvaldsen 108 = ARV^2 1262.66), the nude jumper holds weights and is about to leap over a hurdle as his trainer watches. In no. 170 (Vienna 814 = ARV^2 1262.68), the athlete is clothed, but holds a strigil, as if to emphasize that he has just finished bathing.

45. Makron clearly uses clothing to designate varying degrees of engagement or interest: in Figure 3, the man on the right offers a flower or crown to an unresponsive boy

who remains tightly wrapped in his mantle, whereas the youth in the center offers a hare to a boy who reaches out to accept it and throws back his garment enough to reveal his shoulder and breast, and the boy on the left opens up his clothing to reveal a view of his entire body to the youth who offers him a cock and visibly looks down to examine his penis. The more flesh is revealed, the more responsive a boy appears to be; interestingly, the boys reveal more corresponding to the value of the gifts offered, but it also bears noting that the least responsive boy is the one with the greatest age difference relative to his suitor. We see the same use of clothing in Vienna 3698 (ARV^2 471.193 = Hubbard 2003, Fig. 16), where the boy who has accepted a hare throws back his cloak, whereas the two boys on each side keep their arms tightly wrapped. A wine cooler by Smikros (Getty 82.AE.53) displays four pairs in a continuous wraparound sequence, ranging from clear rejection of the suitor by a fully clothed boy who walks away (Hubbard 2003, Fig. 12c) to a youth who places one hand on a boy's bare shoulder and reaches for his chin with the other (Hubbard 2003, Fig. 12d) to a youth who reaches out to touch another's penis (Hubbard 2003, Fig. 12b–the beloved here opens up his mantle to reveal his naked body to his wooer and reciprocates by touching the wooer's arm) to a pair who embrace and kiss as well as the lover fondling the boy's penis (Hubbard 2003, Fig. 12a–again the body is revealed by an opened cloak). Again, we note that the two pairs who are furthest advanced in their contact and reciprocation are the two who appear to be closest to each other in age and stature, as if to imply that boys are more likely to accept physical intimacy with youths who are closer in age to themselves.

46. See also the tondo of a kylix attributed to the Ashby Painter (Paris Bibl. Nat., Cab. Med. 532 = ARV^2 455.10 = Patrucco, Fig. 3). The inscription ὁ παῖς καλός emphasizes the erotic character of the man's admiration.

47. On the ambiguity of whether such figures offering crowns or ribbons are trainers, umpires, or private admirers, see Jüthner (1965, pp. 172-174). Scanlon (2002, pp. 243-245) lists some other vases showing Eros crowning or carrying a fillet to a victorious athlete. At least one of these (Frankfurt WM06 = *Para.* 501.12bis = Scanlon, Fig. 8-13) shows a fillet-bearing Eros on the interior of the cup, a trainer admiring the athlete on the exterior.

48. See another cup of Douris, New York 52.11.4 (ARV^2 437.114 = Buitron-Oliver, no. 152), Side B: a man offers a flower to a youth with a lyre: the youth does not look at the flower, but looks straight ahead into the man's eyes and holds up his hand in a similar gesture of refusal. Compare two cups of Makron: Boston 08.293 (ARV^2 475.265 = Kunisch no. 522) and Munich 2658 (ARV^2 476.275 = Kunisch no. 475). However, Frontisi-Ducroux (1996, pp. 83, 87-88) suggests that such returned looks could form an implicit consent despite the boy's pretense of flight, a typical rapist's fantasy (i.e. s/he says no, but means yes). In contexts of divine pursuit, this might be plausible, but seems less likely to me here. There can certainly be no implied consent in Cambridge 37.26 (ARV^2 506.21 = R684 in Dover), where a youth hits a man over the head with his lyre, while looking straight into his eye. Rejection, like reciprocated love, can be a form of emotional engagement with one's wooer and therefore appropriate for face-to-face interaction.

49. Another kylix of Douris that may show both a trainer and wooer/admirer is Basel Ka452 (ARV^2 430.31 = no. 51 in Buitron-Oliver), Side B, where the clothed youth on the extreme left holds a forked staff, whereas the clothed youth on the extreme right merely watches the three naked jumpers in the middle. Compare a kylix by the Aberdeen Painter (Boston 03.820, listed in n. 43 above), where both sides show the same compositional scheme: the trainer with a long rod on the right, another clothed

youth who merely watches from the left, the athlete in the middle. Another possible example is the Beugnot amphora, attributed to Phintias (Paris G42 = *ARV²* 23.1 = Hoppin 1917, Plate 31), where the naked man on the right holds a long staff, suggesting that he is a trainer, and the clothed man on the left holds a shorter, thicker staff, more like a walking stick. Hoppin (1917, p. 124) suggests that the bearded man on the right is an athlete rather than a trainer, but one rarely finds bearded men under a trainer's supervision or in direct competition with youths (but see the rather unusual Figure 9). Jüthner (1965, pp. 175-177) suggests two other examples: a cup signed by the Euergides Painter (London 1920.6-13.2 = *ARV²* 88.1, line sketch in Hoppin 1919, I, p. 367) showing a nude javelin-thrower in the center (ὁ παῖς καλός across the top), a trainer signalling to him on the left, another clothed youth offering him a flower on the right, and a Panathenaic amphora attributed to the Aegisthus Painter (Naples, SA693 = *ABV* 407 = *CVA Italy* XX, III.H.g, Plate 3), with two naked boys in the center, a bearded trainer with forked staff on the left, and another bearded and fully clothed man on the right, about to place a crown on the victorious boy's head (however, Smets (1936, p. 95) identifies this figure as another trainer or official).

50. For a more extensive treatment of this topic in relation to homoerotic vases, see Hubbard (2002, pp. 273-283).

51. On the conflation of these two roles in vase painting generally, see Osborne (1998, pp. 138-139). Kilmer (1993) captions one of the pairs on Paris G45 (discussed above) as a "trainer" watching a boy do the stretches. If so, then the other two youths (one crowning a boy, one kissing a boy) might also be seen as trainers. But all three could just as well be lovers or admirers. See also Munich 2313 (listed in n. 43 above), showing a discus-thrower on one side (inscribed *Sokrates kalos*) and on the other side a youth with a staff, holding out his hand in a demonstrative gesture. Or see London E337 (also listed in n. 43 above), showing a naked boy on horseback on one side, a clothed youth with a staff on the other. But the two sides of such amphoras are not always connected in theme or subject, so these two examples are uncertain.

52. This painter's work has been fully catalogued and analyzed by Lezzi-Hafter: see nos. 11, 13-14, 17-24, 32, 35, 39, 42, 48, 55 for cups of the type I describe. A gender-mixed variant form also exists, usually with one figure in the tondo and three on each side.

53. On Lezzi-Hafter, no. 32, Side B, located in a private collection, the tightly wrapped figure at the far left can hardly be a trainer: in fact, the naked athlete reaches out toward him as if the clothed figure is the modest *erōmenos*. This example does at least prove that the clothed figure in these pairs was not always a trainer.

54. On Side A and the tondo of Lezzi-Hafter no. 39 (Ferrara T11C = *ARV²* 1254.77) and on the tondo of no. 32, we see nude athletes holding long staffs, so these are not necessarily markers of a trainer.

55. The tondo of Lezzi-Hafter no. 17 (San Antonio 86.134.80) presents a clear parallel for a crown being offered as a reward in a musical, rather than athletic, context by an admirer, not a teacher. On the other hand, a trainer could be the figure to offer a crown, as we see with the figure holding the forked staff on Side A of Lezzi-Hafter no. 39.

56. See especially Lezzi-Hafter nos. 11, 17-20, 32, 42, 48.

57. Gardiner (1907, pp. 264-265) interprets the scene as non-conflictual and thinks the youth is merely throwing the javelin, although he admits that the position is unusual. That the youth is holding the rod/javelin in a threatening way is suggested by the parallel of London E78, a kylix by the Foundry Painter (*ARV²* 401.3 = Patrucco, Fig. 150), where an umpire holds the forked staff over his head in just this way as he is about

to intervene to prevent eye-gouging in the pancratium. See also Cambridge 37.26, discussed below.

58. Jüthner (1965, pp. 175-176) believes that London B596 may offer a parallel for a trainer holding a sandal, but the original publication of this vase (Smith, 1902, pp. 42-43) identifies the object as a hand weight. Jüthner believes that the trainer in Figure 8 is merely demonstrating a movement, but a sandal would seem an inappropriate object with which to show a pupil how to throw a javelin. Gardiner (1910, pp. 473-474) thinks the trainer is holding a hand weight, but the object's shape is different from the weights held by the youth to his left, and most commentators have therefore considered it a sandal.

59. For a full discussion of the erotic overtones of sandal-whipping, documented with many examples, see Kilmer (1993, pp. 104-124).

60. See the comments of Keuls (1985, pp. 284-285), who believes the boy has just been caught masturbating, and Kilmer (1993, pp. 104-105).

61. Simon (1981, p. 92) also considers him a trainer, but Frontisi-Ducroux (1995, p. 127) calls him a "judge." Knauer (1965, pp. 19-20) finds the figure too feminine in appearance for either vocation, and considers him merely a spectator who has taken up the trainer's staff in play.

62. Note how similar the robe and the position of the youth's hand are to those of Artemis, who stands as a spectator at the right edge on the other side of the amphora, watching Heracles and Apollo wrestle over the tripod. See Knauer, Plates 7-8 for good details.

63. Simon (1981, p. 92) suggests a more mundane interpretation: he holds the flower to his nostrils to avoid being overcome by the stench of oil and sweat in the ring. Even if true, this would still suggest a more delicate and sissified constitution than that of the athletes themselves. See the remarks of Friedrich Hauser in Furtwängler, Hauser, and Reichhold (1932, III, p. 74), echoed by Jüthner (1965) (my translation): "two wrestling pairs supervised by a *paidotribēs*. We can understand the youth at the left only as such because of his long staff, as little as his over-refined appearance seems suited for this profession. As he stands there shyly, with his flowery mantle pulled up over the back of his head to protect him from the sun, and as he brings a rose up to his nose with his long sewing fingers, he gives us the impression of a decadent aesthete rather than a trainer. An exceptional over-cultivation" (p. 176). His long hair certainly implies that he did not wrestle himself, since wrestlers of necessity kept their hair close-cropped: compare Simonides, fr. 507 PMG, Euripides, *Bacch.* 455 and *Electra* 527-29 (with Denniston's note *ad loc.*), and Golden (1998, pp. 78, 157).

64. See Paris G1 (*ARV*[2] 3.2 = Shapiro, Plate 20b) and perhaps Basel BS491 (*ARV*[2] 3.4 = Shapiro, Plate 20c).

65. Note that the bearded man looks straight at us, what Frontisi-Ducroux (1995, pp. 126-130; 1996, pp. 85-89) calls *apostrophē* or "interpellation of the spectator," summoning us (here assumed to be adult, male, and homoerotically inclined) into the scene as participants who may assume the position of the male figure turned frontally toward us like a mirror reflection. Knauer (1965, pp. 18-19) argues that the central pair of wrestlers also consists of a bearded and unbearded figure (although the face of the latter is partly obscured), with the younger wrestler gaining a superior hold over his rival.

66. See Too (2000, pp. 13-36) on the abiding suspicion of "teaching for hire." The kind of personal exchange involved in pederastic mentorship was perceived as an altogether different practice; Pindar himself emphatically distinguishes between merce-

nary and romantic motives in *I*.2.1-11, foregrounding the romantic as preferable. See Nigel Nicholson's (1998) acute analysis of the superior truth claims of pederastic commitment.

67. Nicholson (1998, pp. 33-36) points to Theognis, who mingles admonitory advice poetry to Cyrnus with amatory poetry addressed to the same youth. There is no reason to think that Pindar or most aristocrats of the archaic period would have viewed the matter differently.

REFERENCES

Alexander, Christine. (1925). *Greek Athletics.* Metropolitan Museum of Art. New York.

Arieti, James A. (1975). Nudity in Greek Athletics. *Classical World, 68*, 431-436.

Barrett, D. S. (1981). The Friendship of Achilles and Patroclus. *The Classical Bulletin, 57*, 87-93.

Beck, Frederick A. G. (1975). *Album of Greek Education.* Sydney: Cheiron Press.

Bersani, Leo. (1985). Pedagogy and Pederasty. *Raritan, 5*, 14-21.

Bonfante, Larissa. (1989). Nudity as Costume in Classical Art. *American Journal of Archaeology, 93*, 543-570.

Bowra, C. M. (1964). *Pindar.* Oxford: Clarendon Press.

Buffière, Félix. (1980). *Eros adolescent: la pédérastie dans la Grèce antique.* Paris: Belles Lettres.

Buitron-Oliver, Diana. (1995). *Douris: A Master-Painter of Athenian Red-figure Vases.* Mainz: Philipp von Zabern.

Christ, Wilhelm. (1896). *Pindari carmina prolegomenis et commentariis instructa.* Leipzig: BG Teubner.

Clarke, William M. (1978). Achilles and Patroclus in Love. *Hermes, 106*, 381-396.

Coppola, Goffredo. (1931). *Introduzione a Pindaro.* Rome: L'Universal tipografia poliglotta.

Crotty, Kevin. (1982). *Song and Action: The Victory Odes of Pindar.* Baltimore: Johns Hopkins UP.

Crowther, Nigel B. (1985). Male 'Beauty' Contests in Greece: The Euandria and Euexia. *L'antiquité Classique, 54*, 285-291.

Delorme, Jean. (1960). *Gymnasion: Étude sur les monuments consacrés à l' éducation en Grèce.* Paris: Éditions E. De Boccard.

Dissen, Ludolphus. (1830). *Pindari Carmina quae supersunt.* Gotha: Hennings.

Dover, Kenneth J. (1978). *Greek Homosexuality.* Cambridge, MA.: Harvard UP.

Fisher, Nick. (1998). Gymnasia and the Democratic Values of Leisure. In P. Cartledge, P. Millett, & S. von Reden (Eds.), *Kosmos: Essays in Order, Conflict, and Community in Classical Athens* (pp. 84-104). Cambridge: Cambridge UP.

Forbes, Clarence A. (1929). *Greek Physical Education.* New York: AMS (Repr. 1971); London: Century (Repr. 1978).

Fraccaroli, Giuseppe. (1894). *Le odi di Pindaro dichiarate e tradotte.* Verona: G. Franchini.

Frel, Jirí. (1983). Euphonios and His Fellows. In Warren G. Moon (Ed.), *Ancient Greek Art and Iconography* (pp. 147-158). Madison: U of Wisconsin P.

Frontisi-Ducroux, Françoise. (1995). *Du masque au visage: Aspects de l' identité en Grèce ancienne.* Paris: Flammarion.

_____. (1996). Eros, Desire, and the Gaze. In N. B. Kampen (Ed.), *Sexuality in Ancient Art* (pp. 81-100). Cambridge: Cambridge UP.

Furtwängler, A., Hauser, F., and Reichhold, K. (1932). *Griechische Vasenmalerei.* Bayerische Akademie der Wissenschaften. Munich: Bruckmann.

Gardiner, E. Norman. (1907). Throwing the Javelin. *Journal of Hellenic Studies, 27,* 249-273.

_____. (1910). *Greek Athletic Sports and Festivals.* London: Macmillan and Co.

_____. 1930. *Athletics of the Ancient World.* Oxford: Clarendon Press.

Gildersleeve, Basil L. (1885). *Pindar: The Olympian and Pythian Odes.* New York: Harper & Brothers.

Golden, Mark. (1998). *Sport and Society in Ancient Greece.* Cambridge: Cambridge UP.

Halperin, David M. (1990). *One Hundred Years of Homosexuality and Other Essays on Greek Love.* New York: Routledge.

Hamilton, R. (1974). *Epinikion: General Form in the Odes of Pindar.* The Hague: Mouton.

Harris, H. A. (1966). *Greek Athletes and Athletics.* Bloomington: Indiana UP.

Hoppin, Joseph Clark. (1917). *Euthymides and his Fellows.* Cambridge, MA.: Harvard UP.

_____. (1919). *A Handbook of Attic Red-Figured Vases.* Cambridge, MA.: Harvard UP.

Hubbard, Thomas K. (1989). Pindar's Κύκνεια μάχα: Subtext and Allusion in *Olympian* 10.15-16. *Materiali e discussioni per l'analisi dei testi classici, 23,* 137-143.

_____. (1990). Envy and the Invisible Roar: Pindar, *Pythian* 11.30. *Greek, Roman, and Byzantine Studies, 31,* 343-351.

_____. (1992). Remaking Myth and Rewriting History: Cult Tradition in Pindar's *Ninth Nemean. Harvard Studies in Classical Philology, 94,* 77-111.

_____. (1995). On Implied Wishes for Olympic Victory in Pindar. *Illinois Classical Studies, 20,* 35-56.

_____. (1998). Popular Perceptions of Elite Homosexuality in Classical Athens. *Arion* ser. *3*(6.1), 48-78.

_____. (2000). Pederasty and Democracy: The Marginalization of a Social Practice. In T. K. Hubbard (Ed.), *Greek Love Reconsidered* (pp. 1-11). New York: W. Hamilton Press.

_____. (2002). Pindar, Theoxenus, and the Homoerotic Eye. *Arethusa, 35,* 255-296.

_____. (2003). *Homosexuality in Greece and Rome: A Sourcebook of Basic Documents.* Berkeley: U of California P.

Humphreys, S. C. (1974). The Nothoi of Kynosarges. *Journal of Hellenic Studies, 94,* 88-95.

Instone, Stephen. (1990). Love and Sex in Pindar: Some Practical Thrusts. *Bulletin of the Institute for Classical Studies, 37,* 30-42.

Jung, Albert. (1930). *Massage und Sport in Altertum und Gegenwart.* Doctoral dissertation, Rheinische Friedrich-Wilhelms-Universität, Bonn.

Jüthner, Julius, and Brein, Friedrich. (1965). *Die athletischen Leibesübungen der Griechen.* Vienna: Böhlau.

Kannicht, Richard. (1969). *Euripides: Helena.* Heidelberg: C. Winter.

Keuls, Eva C. (1985). *The Reign of the Phallus.* New York: Harper & Row.

Kilmer, Martin F. (1993). *Greek Erotica on Attic Red-Figure Vases.* London: Duckworth.

Knauer, Elfriede R. (1965). *Die Berliner Andokides-Vase.* Stuttgart: Reclam.

Koch-Harnack, Gundel. (1983). *Knabenliebe und Tiergeschenke: Ihre Bedeutung im päderastischen Erziehungsystem Athens.* Berlin: Gebr. Mann.

Köhnken, Adolf. (1974). Pindar as Innovator: Poseidon Hippios and the Relevance of the Pelops Story in Olympian 1. *The Classical Quarterly,* NS *24,* 199-206.

Kunisch, Norbert. (1997). *Makron.* Mainz: P. von Zabern.

Kurke, Leslie. (1990). Pindar's Sixth *Pythian* and the Tradition of Advice Poetry. *Transactions of the American Philological Association, 120,* 85-107.

_____. (1991). *The Traffic in Praise: Pindar and the Poetics of Social Economy.* Ithaca: Cornell UP.

Kyle, Donald G. (1984). Solon and Athletics. *Ancient World, 9,* 91-105.

_____. (1987). *Athletics in Ancient Athens.* Leiden: E.J. Brill.

Larmour, David H. J. (1999). *Stage and Stadium: Drama and Athletics in Ancient Greece.* Hildesheim: Weidmann.

Lasserre, F. (1974). Ornements érotiques dan la poésie lyrique archaïque. In J. L. Heller and J. K. Newman (Eds.), *Serta Turyniana: Studies in Greek Literature and Palaeography in Honor of Alexander Turyn* (pp. 5-34). Urbana: U of Illinois P.

Lehnus, Luigi. (1981). *Pindaro: Olimpiche.* Milan: Garzanti.

Lezzi-Hafter, Adrienne. (1988). *Der Eretria-Maler.* Mainz: P. von Zabern.

Marrou, H. I. (1964). *A History of Education in Antiquity* (G. Lamb, Trans.). New York: Sheed & Ward.

Meier, M. H. E. & de Pogey-Castries, L. R. (1930). *Histoire de l' amour grec dans l' antiquité.* Paris: Stendhal et Compagnie.

Mezger, Friedrich. (1880). *Pindars Siegeslieder.* Leipzig: B.G. Teubner.

Montserrat, Dominic. (1996). *Sex and Society in Graeco-Roman Egypt.* London: Kegan Paul International.

Mullen, William. (1982). *Choreia: Pindar and Dance.* Princeton: Princeton UP.

Neils, Jennifer. (1994). The Panathenaia and Kleisthenic Ideology. In William D. E. Coulson (Ed.), *The Archaeology of Athens and Attica under the Democracy* (pp. 151-160), Oxford: Oxbow Books.

Nicholson, Nigel. (1998). The Truth of Pederasty: A Supplement to Foucault's Genealogy of the Relation Between Truth and Desire in Ancient Greece. *Intertexts, 2,* 26-45.

Osborne, Robin. (1998). *Archaic and Classical Greek Art.* Oxford: Oxford UP.

Papalas, A. J. (1991). Boy Athletes in Ancient Greece. *Stadion, 17,* 165-192.

Patrucco, Roberto. (1972). *Lo Sport nella Grecia antica.* Florence: L.S. Olschki.

Patzer, Harald. (1982). *Die griechische Knabenliebe.* Wiesbaden: F. Steiner.

Pronger, Brian. (1990). *The Arena of Masculinity: Sports, Homosexuality, and the Meaning of Sex.* New York: St. Martin's.

Reed, Nancy B. (1987). The *Euandria* Competition at the Panathenaia Reconsidered. *Ancient World*, *15*, 59-64.

Reinsberg, Carola. (1989). *Ehe, Hetärentum und Knabenliebe im antiken Griechenland*. Munich: C. H. Beck.

Scanlon, Thomas F. (2002). *Eros and Greek Athletics*. New York: Oxford UP.

Schroeder, Bruno. (1927). *Der Sport im Altertum*. Berlin: H. Schoetz & Co.

Schroeder, Otto. (1922). *Pindars Pythien*. Leipzig: B.G. Teubner.

Schween, P. G. Hermann. (1911). *Die Epistaten des Agons und der Palaestra in Literatur und Kunst*. Diss. Kiel: Graphische Kunstanstalt L. Handorff.

Sedgwick, Eve Kosofsky. (1985). *Between Men: English Literature and Male Homosocial Desire*. New York: Columbia UP.

Sergent, Bernard. (1986). *Homosexuality in Greek Myth*. (A. Goldhammer, Trans.). Boston: Beacon Press.

Shapiro, H. A. (1989). *Art and Cult under the Tyrants in Athens*. Mainz: P. von Zabern.

Simon, Erika. (1981). *Die griechische Vasen*. 2nd ed. Munich: Hirmer.

Smets, A. (1936). Groupes chronologiques des amphores panathénaïques inscrites. *L'antiquité Classique*, *5*, 87-104.

Smith, C. H. (1896). *Catalogue of the Greek and Etruscan Vases in the British Museum: Volume. III. Vases of the Finest Period*. British Museum. London.

_____. (1902). A Proto-Attic Vase. *Journal of Hellenic Studies*, *22*, 29-45.

Spivey, Nigel. (1996). *Understanding Greek Sculpture: Ancient Meanings, Modern Readings*. New York: Thames and Hudson.

Steiner, Deborah. (1998). Moving Images: Fifth-Century Victory Monuments and the Athlete's Allure. *Classical Antiquity*, *17*(1), 123-149.

Too, Yun Lee. (2000). *The Pedagogical Contract: The Economies of Teaching and Learning in the Ancient World*. Ann Arbor: U of Michigan P.

Verdenius, W. J. (1988). *Commentaries on Pindar: Volume II*. Leiden: E.J. Brill.

Viljoen, Gerrit van N. (1955). *Pindaros se tiende en elfde Olympiese odes*. Dissertation. Leiden: Drukkerij "Luctor et emergo."

von der Mühll, Peter. (1964). Weitere pindarische Notizen. *Museum Helveticum*, *21*, 168-172.

Wade-Gery, H. T. (1958). *Essays in Greek History*. Oxford: Blackwell.

Wilamowitz-Moellendorff, Ulrich von. (1922). *Pindaros*. Berlin: Weidmann.

Woloch, Michael. (1963). Athenian Trainers in the Aeginetan Odes of Pindar and Bacchylides. *Classical World*, *56*, 102-4, 121.

Boeotian Swine:
Homosexuality in Boeotia

Charles Hupperts, PhD

University of Amsterdam

SUMMARY. This article shows that the accounts in our ancient sources regarding Boeotian attitudes towards homosexuality, namely that the Boeotians were different from other Greeks in that they enjoyed great freedom in this respect and seemingly everything was permissible to them, present a distorted picture of the homosexual practices in this region. In fact, vase paintings with homosexual iconography dating from the sixth century BC reveal marked similarities with Attic and Corinthian pottery ware of the same period. The view that the Boeotians conducted themselves in an 'uncivilized' manner in their homosexual relations is therefore better understood as an attempt by other Greeks to

Charles Hupperts studied classical languages and philosophy at the University of Amsterdam, where he is currently an instructor of Greek. He successfully defended his two-volume doctoral dissertation, *Eros dikaios*, there in 2000; this contains the results of his research into the practices and ethics of homosexuality in classical Athens and offers a detailed study of Plato's *Symposium*. In addition, he has published a number of books on various topics related to ancient civilization and has translated ancient texts such as Aristotle's *Nichomachean Ethics*. The author would like to express sincere thanks to Beert Verstraete for preparing the translation of this paper and for his comments on the initial draft. Correspondence may be addressed: Willemsparkweg 125, 1071 GW Amsterdam, The Netherlands.

[Haworth co-indexing entry note]: "Boeotian Swine: Homosexuality in Boeotia." Hupperts, Charles. Co-published simultaneously in *Journal of Homosexuality* (Harrington Park Press, an imprint of The Haworth Press, Inc.) Vol. 49, No. 3/4, 2005, pp. 173-192; and: *Same-Sex Desire and Love in Greco-Roman Antiquity and in the Classical Tradition of the West* (ed: Beert C. Verstraete, and Vernon Provencal) Harrington Park Press, an imprint of The Haworth Press, Inc., 2005, pp. 173-192. Single or multiple copies of this article are available for a fee from The Haworth Document Delivery Service [1-800-HAWORTH, 9:00 a.m. - 5:00 p.m. (EST). E-mail address: docdelivery@haworthpress.com].

distinguish themselves from the 'boorish' Boeotians and to justify their own aversion to this form of erotic love. *[Article copies available for a fee from The Haworth Document Delivery Service: 1-800-HAWORTH. E-mail address: <docdelivery@haworthpress.com> Website: <http://www.HaworthPress.com>*

KEYWORDS. Greek male homosexuality, Boeotia, sixth century BC, Greek literature, Greek vase-painting

Boeotia is a part of Central Greece that borders on Attica, the district in which Athens is situated. It is a mountainous region with two famous mountains, Mt. Helicon, the dwelling place of the Muses, and desolate Mt. Cithaeron, where the god Dionysos was celebrated by his followers. Its most important city was Thebes, but other cities, too, were well known, such as Plataeae, Orchomenus, and Tanagra, where an important pottery ware industry was located. The population derived its livelihood mainly from agriculture and the raising of cattle, and so the Boeotians were thought of as peasants. In particular by their neighbors, the Athenians, they were depicted as coarse and uncultured. In his *Olympian Ode VI* Pindar, the great Boeotian poet of the fifth century BC, refers to this reproach: ". . . and next to know if we can put to flight with words of truth that ancient term of abuse, 'Boeotian swine'" (*O.* 6.89-90. Cf. Plutarch, *Moralia* 995 ff.).

Books on Greek homosexuality usually contain a chapter on Boeotia. Sergent (1986, pp. 42-52), for instance, devotes much attention to the Sacred Band, seeing many resemblances between Theban pederasty and the initiation rituals of Crete. Dover (1978, p. 190 ff.), Buffière (1980, pp. 95-101, 261-266), and Percy (1996, pp. 133-138) provide a more balanced treatment of Boeotia, letting the sources speak for themselves without forcing them into a specific straitjacket. Our knowledge of homosexuality in Boeotia is hampered not only by the problem that the sources available to us are very brief, but also by the fact that the majority of these are not of a primary nature, with non-Boeotian authors writing about the state of affairs in Boeotia, or writers who are indeed Boeotian reaching back to a period of many centuries earlier. For various reasons, therefore, these sources are biased. For instance, the level of culture in Boeotia may be looked down upon, as in Plato, or an author may not have much use for homosexuality, such as Xenophon or Plutarch. Plutarch, moreover, although himself a Boeotian, bases his knowledge of Boeotia on other literary sources and chronologically, too, stands at a far remove from the subject about which he gathers his information. There are only a few primary sources which furnish us with 'direct' insight into the homosexual practices of the city of Thebes: vase paintings stemming from the sixth century BC and the poetry of Pindar (518-c. 438 BC). I shall first set out in summary form the information supplied by the secondary sources and next discuss to what extent the poetry of Pindar and the Boeotian vase-paintings supplement and confirm this body of information.

SECONDARY SOURCES

1. There are two 'homoerotic' myths connected with Thebes.

a. Chrysippus, the son of Pelops, was abducted by Laius, the father of Oedipus and king of Thebes. The latter was hospitably received by Pelops after he had been exiled from Thebes. Laius, however, fell in love with Chrysippus and as soon as his exile had been lifted, he took the boy with him to Thebes, this in order to escape the oracle which had foretold that he would be murdered by his own son. The playwright Aeschylus is believed to have devoted a tragedy to Laius' story which was first staged in 467 BC, but it is not certain if it dealt with the abduction of Chrysippus. We do know for certain that this was the case in Euripides' drama written in 411-409 BC; here Laius was represented as the first man who fell in love with someone of his own sex. Plato, too, has this in mind in his *Laws* (836c) when he speaks of "the custom that prevailed before Laius."[1]

b. Iolaus, Heracles's comrade, who helped him in his Twelve Labours, received in Boeotia the status of *eromenos*. In Aristotle's lifetime Iolaus' tomb in Thebes was a sacred site where homosexual lovers pledged their faithfulness to each other (Aristotle, fr. 97).

2. There are also general observations on homosexual practices in Boeotia.

a. Our most ancient source is Plato's account in his *Symposium*, which was written between 384-379 BC. Here he makes Pausanias, the second speaker on the subject of Eros, present a comparative ethnographic description of attitudes to homosexual behavior in the different cities and regions of the Greek world. The situation in Athens and Sparta is compared to that in Elis and Boeotia:

Eros in Athens and Sparta is a complex matter. For in Elis and Boeotia, where skills in speaking are lacking, the straightforward rule is that it is good to gratify one's lover sexually. No one, young or old, would consider this shameful; because their skill in the use of language is not very good, they wish, I suppose, to save themselves the trouble of having to win over boys with persuasive speech. (*Symp.* 182b1-b6)

At the conclusion of this passage he says: "But where the rule is that this is straightforwardly right, it is on account of people's mental sluggishness" (182d2-4). It is obvious to Pausanias that homosexual behavior occurs everywhere in the Greek world. He just wants to make it clear that attitudes towards this state of affairs vary. These differences, according to him, have nothing to do with the either natural or unnatural character of such behavior. While sexual identity is, in his eyes, a question of someone's nature, he gives a constructionist explanation of the different positions on homosexuality. He regards it as a lack of culture that in Elis and Boeotia any form of homosexuality is approved. The lovers' linguistic capacities are not well developed and they are unable to talk their boys into having sex with them. The lovers do not want to exert themselves since they suffer from a mental laziness, for which reason no curtailment is imposed on the boys' going to bed with their lovers. This permissive attitude stems, therefore, according to Pausanias, from the primitive quality of the culture. Pausanias' observations wish to make it clear that not only does the Athenian moral code with respect to homosexual behavior occupy a higher plane than that of other Greek city-states, but also that, on account of this, Athens enjoys a higher level of civilization than Boeotia.

b. In the *Symposium* written by Xenophon (c. 430-354 BC), most probably after and in response to Plato's *Symposium,* the same Pausanias says, in the context of an army consisting of couples of lovers and their beloveds: "Both the Thebans and the citizens of Elis would station their beloveds next to themselves in combat, even if they were sleeping with them" (8.32-34. Cf. Hupperts, 2000, Vol. 2, pp. 30-31). To Xenophon, who suffered from a strongly antihomosexual attitude, it is remarkable that lovers should share their bed with their beloveds.

c. In his treatise on the Spartan constitution, Xenophon seems to go even a step further. Within the framework of his discussion of Spartan education, he states:

> I think I have to say something about boy-love, for this aspect, too, is related to education. In other Greek city-states, such as in Boeotia, a man and a boy may have a relationship with each other as if they were married. (*Lac.* 2.12)

It is worthy of notice that Xenophon uses here the verb *suzeugnusthai* ("to be joined to one another"), which is applied especially to marriage. He sets the homosexual practices of the Boeotians over against those of the Spartans in order to demonstrate all the better the superiority of the latter. He has to admit that homoeroticism is also present among the Spartans, but with them it is a love like that of a father for his son or between two brothers. Sexuality is excluded here. In this passage, too, therefore, the Boeotians are brought into the discussion in order to accentuate the superiority of other Greeks.

d. In the fourth book of his *De re publica*, Cicero (106-43 BC) deals with the education of young people and enters upon a discussion of athletic training. In this context he says: "How free and easy are their associations and love relationships. Not to mention the inhabitants of Elis and Thebes, who enjoy free rein in their lust in amorous relationships with free men" (4.4). Obviously, Cicero is very negative regarding homosexual behavior in Thebes; his choice of words–he speaks of *libido* being allowed free play–emphatically expresses his aversion.

e. There are three passages in which Plutarch (AD 46-120), himself a Boeotian, makes references to homosexual practices among the Boeotians. He himself was strongly opposed to open homosexual behavior and in his treatises where love is discussed he leans heavily on Plato and Xenophon. In his biography of Pelopidas, the renowned Theban leader and general of the fourth century BC, who, together with his friend Epaminondas, strove for the liberation of his native city, and in connection with the unexpected Theban victory over Sparta in the battle of Tegyra in 375 BC, Plutarch begins to speak of the Sacred Band and homosexuality among the Thebans. He explains the latter phenomenon as follows:

> Generally speaking, it was not Laius' lust which, according to the poets, provided the basis for the customary Theban attitude towards lovers; rather, it was their lawgivers who desired to pacify and moderate their men's passionate and impetuous character from youth onwards. They accomplished this by giving the flute a prominent place in work and in all forms of entertainment, taking care that this instrument should become popular and gain prefer-

ence; and furthermore, by granting love an important place in the athletic schools, thus keeping the temperament of youth in check. And rightly they gave to the goddess, of whom it is said she is the daughter of Ares and Aphrodite, a place in their city, thinking that wherever combative and warlike natures are firmly coupled to an age that possesses the powers of persuasion and charm, the state receives, thanks to Harmonia, its most balanced and orderly structure. (*Pelopidas* 18-19).

In his treatise on the education of boys, Plutarch takes up the subject of love and sexuality in connection with boys with a great deal of reluctance. He has to admit that individuals such as Socrates, Plato and Xenophon have shown which form of pederasty is acceptable, and he is inclined to follow them. Next he says:

> Therefore, we have to keep away from them those who lust after their physical beauty, but, in general, those who are 'lovers' of a boy's inner character may have our permission. To be avoided are both the form of eros encountered in Thebes and Elis as well as the so-called Cretan abduction; however, we should strive after the eros of Athens and Sparta. (*Moralia* 15)

Finally, in his *Dialogue on Love*, Plutarch makes the following remark:

> Not only do the most warlike peoples such as the Boeotians, Spartans, and Cretans have the strongest erotic nature, but also the heroes of antiquity such as Meleager, Achilles, Aristomenes, Cimon and Epaminondas. This last hero had two beloveds, namely Asopichus and Caphisodorus; the latter fell together with him in the battle of Mantinea and was buried next to him. Asopichus was such a fearsome and dangerous warrior that the first man who resisted and wounded him, namely Eucnamus of Amphissa, received a hero's status among the Phocians. (*Moralia* 761d)

The first passage from Plutarch's *Life of Pelopidas* offers an interesting observation. In order to guide the impetuous character of youth into the right channels, the Boeotians adopted two measures: young men were taught to handle the flute in all sorts of activities, perhaps with the effect of making these take place in an orderly, rhythmical pattern. We know of the same custom in Athens where athletic training, for instance, was accompanied by flute music. The second measure pertains even more to our subject. It was encouraged, or at least permitted, that athletic schools should be the places par excellence where amorous friendships were formed, where boys allowed themselves be seduced by lovers, and where, perhaps, the sexual act could even be consummated. However, we need to remind ourselves that this utilization of athletic schools was already customary in Athens from the sixth century onwards and that, in this respect, Thebes was no different from Athens (Hupperts, 2000, Vol. 1, p. 235). The fact that later generations in Athens no longer were aware of this custom or, in any case, wished to 'liberate' their city from it is another matter.

3. There are several sources which make mention of the Sacred Band, that part of the Theban party which was composed exclusively of lovers and their beloveds. The first source which mentions this army explicitly is Xenophon's *Symposium*, in the passage which I cited above. While in Plato's *Symposium* Phaedrus speaks of a possible army of amorous couples, there is no explicit reference to the Theban army. The passage in Plutarch's *Life of Pelopidas* is the most detailed, but there are several other sources.[2]

The most important pieces of information provided are:

a. The Sacred Band was established by Gorgidas in 378 BC; however, he still distributed the couples throughout the rest of the army's vanguard and in this way let them participate in the battle. After the battle of Tegyra in 375 BC, Pelopidas let them operate as a separate unit of the army.

b. The Sacred Band consisted of three hundred men in couples of an *erastes* and an *eromenos*. It is, however, striking that Plutarch formulates this piece of information with some hesitation, for he simply observes that this is said by some persons to have been the case. Xenophon, on the other hand, had expressed it as a fact.

c. The Sacred Band remained invincible until the battle of Chaeroneia in 338 BC, where the entire unit was slain by Philip II of Macedonia. Plutarch relates how Philip felt compelled to weep when he was confronted with their bodies and learned that these had been the men who formed the Sacred Band.

d. The reason often provided by our sources for the invincible character of the unit is that the close friendship between the lover and his beloved and the sense of shame of each before the other made sure that they would not abandon one another.

e. According to Plutarch, it was the custom in Thebes that the lover presented his beloved with all his weaponry as soon as the boy became eligible for military service.

Thus far the secondary sources. We can conclude that the various texts emphasize that the Theban attitude towards homosexuality was very free, or, rather, too free. Free rein was given to sexual desire; without any hesitation it was approved that the boys could yield themselves sexually to older men; they would sleep with one another, and their relationship showed characteristics comparable to those of marriage. In any case, it was a form of love which was not to be held up as a good example. Furthermore, there was a close relationship between athletics and homoeroticism, and perhaps within this framework we should also understand the link between warfare, eroticism, and friendship. The Thebans, in fact, were regarded as the inventors of homosexuality. This negative picture created by our secondary sources is used, on one hand, to distinguish oneself from the shameless and dull-witted Thebans, and, on the other, to justify one's own aversion to this form of love.

PINDAR

We can now turn to our primary sources: Pindar and vase-paintings, starting with Pindar (518-c. 438 BC). In his odes there are a number of allusions to pederasty in connection with certain myths: Ganymede (*Olympian Odes* 1.37 and 2.43) and Pelops (*Olympian Odes* 1). He also often praises the beauty of the young athletes for whom he composed his epinicia. His manner of doing so makes clear his sensitivity to the physical beauty of athletes. This impression is confirmed by the anecdotes about his love of boys.[3] Here we are confronted with the traditional image of pederasty and not with the picture drawn by authors such as Xenophon and Cicero of sexual behavior in Thebes. Even so, what is underscored is the close relationship between athletics and sexual desire. The young athletes' physical beauty awakens unmistakably erotic longings.[4]

However, to use the odes of Pindar as a direct, uncomplicated source for homosexual practices in Thebes poses a problem. We know that Pindar traveled a great deal and for long periods of time lived elsewhere, as, for instance, in Athens, Aegina, and Sicily. Moreover, Pindar composed his odes as commissions for wealthy, aristocratic families who paid him for his poems. In certain instances, therefore, the poet had to take into close account the tastes of his patron and the person to whom the ode was dedicated. However, there are two homoerotic poems which do not belong to the epinicia and possess a more personal character, presenting a different image from that in the odes. They are preserved and quoted by Athenaeus in his *Deipnosophistae* (601c). In the following fragment, the poet speaks of the roles in a homosexual relationship:

> May both loving and an obliging response to loving
> Take their turns at the right moment.
> Do not strive, my heart, for the deed
> which exceeds the right measure. (fr. 127, Snell & Mähler, 1975-1980)

Since the poet addresses himself, it appears that in this poem he is thinking of both roles in a homosexual relationship: loving as a characteristic of the role of the lover, and compliance, a customary euphemism for the boy's sexual surrender, as a decription of the role of the *eromenos*. It seems that in the poet's eyes there is a right time for the one role and a right time for the other. The Greek word for "deed" may be a euphemism for the sexual act. It is not good, then, to aim for a sexual activity that is not appropriate to a certain age. Perhaps the poet is thinking of the active penetrating and the passive role, but this is not entirely clear from these few lines.

Nearly all modern authors who write on Pindar and homosexuality quote the following poem, but without much commentary. It is cited by Athenaeus almost immediately after the previous piece. The following is a fairly literal translation. (For the Greek text and the problems it poses, see Hupperts, 2000, Vol. 1, pp. 68-71 and 344-345; my choice of text differs slightly from that of van Groningen.)

> You should pluck the fruits of love at the right time,
> My heart, while you are still young.
> The man who is not driven by desire when he sees the rays of light
> Shimmering from the eyes of Theoxenus
> His black heart has been forged of steel or iron
>
> In a cold flame, and he is dishonored by quick-glancing Aphrodite,
> Either slaving hard after riches
> Or with a woman's rash confidence
> Dragging himself along every road, offering his services.
>
> But I, stung by the flame at the doing of the goddess,
> Melt away like bees' wax

Whenever I behold boys in the prime of their youthful limbs.
So, too, in Tenedos dwell Persuasion
And Charm in the son of Agesilas. (*Encomia*, fr. 108)

Pindar here contrasts those who do not allow themselves to be enchanted by a sight such as Theoxenus and those who do let themselves be overwhelmed by the beauty of boys, in this case that of Theoxenus. Evidently, there are those in whom the rays beaming from Theoxenus' eye do not arouse a passionate desire; such persons are as insensate and hard as steel and iron. The goddess Aphrodite appears in this poem as the goddess of pederasty, which is not unusual. Men of the sort who are not susceptible to Theoxenus' charms are inexorably turned away by her. This type falls into two categories. First, there are those who feel compelled to make money. The Greek words which are used to characterize the second category offer a number of difficulties, which are dealt with in my book (2000, Vol. 1, pp. 69-71). These words are traditionally translated as follows: "Or he lets himself be led by woman's shamelessness along a road which offers only coldness, while he is serving her." This interpretation, defended and explained by van Groningen in his *Pindare au Banquet* (1960, p. 66) rests therefore on the assumption that heterosexual men form the second category, so that a contrast is established between the homosexual man who knows true desire and the heterosexual man whose desire is directed to an inferior being. I have demonstrated that major objections with regard to the poem's theme can be brought against this interpretation. For instance, Aphrodite is represented as a goddess who actually favors the homosexual man while turning away the heterosexual man. This would be most strange. Furthermore, the antithesis between exclusively homosexual and exclusively heterosexual makes a most un-Hellenic impression. Additionally, to regard the heterosexual man as a woman's slave seems dubious. However, the Greek also permits an alternative interpretation that the poet speaks here of a man who, in his sexuality, behaves like a woman, the *kinaidos* (Hupperts, 2000, Vol. 1, pp. 70-71). This was someone who, in Greek eyes, was unable to control himself. The poem suggests that this man offers in every way his sexual services. The pederast is the special protégé of Aphrodite, and in him true desire manifests itself, while the money-maniac does not enjoy Aphrodite's esteem because he represses his erotic passion, and the *kinaidos* because he is possessed by a perverse erotic drive.

THE VASE-PAINTINGS

Boeotian vase-paintings give occasion for surprise in their homosexual representations, which have received very little attention in modern discussions of Boeotian homosexuality. I am familiar with exclusively black-figure depictions of this subject dating from the period c. 570-500 BC. On the lid of bowl 3366 in Berlin (Figure 1),[5] three naked satyrs (or possibly, men disguised as satyrs) and four naked men, all wearing

FIGURE 1. Berlin vase. Reproduced courtesy of Antikensammlung, Staatliche Museen Zu Berlin-Preussicher Kulturbesitz, V. 1. 3366. Photo: Jutta Tietz-Glagow.

shoes, are shown dancing to the music of a double flute of a decorously clad female flute player. Two of the satyrs and the four men, who each are bearded and have long, wavy hair reaching down as far as their shoulders, form three pairs, in which the partners stand opposite one another. The third satyr is standing opposite the flute player, who, however, towers head and shoulders over him. The three satyrs are ithyphallic, while the two who form a pair are so sexually aroused that they masturbate. The gesture the satyr on the right makes with his right hand–he is stroking his hand along the other satyr's beard–looks like a courting sign. The men who stand right behind the satyrs are both aroused and show a phallus of more human dimensions which, however, leaves nothing to be guessed at. The man on the right appears to be offering to his friend his *kantharos*, a typical Dionysian symbol. The other is courting his partner by stroking his beard, as was also done by the satyr; in this way the vase-painter indicates that this man's sexual arousal is directed at his partner. In the third pair, too, who are dancing around a *krater*, the man on the right is ithyphallic. His partner's penis does not project forward as prominently. The latter holds his rather small *keras* against his buttocks, so that there is a suggestion that he wishes to use this as a kind of dildo or wishes to signal that he wants to be penetrated. Just as the satyrs, the men project their buttocks backwards. Evidently, we are invited to consider this posture as part of their dance, but also as an erotic motion. The men are intoxicated, make lascivious motions, and are passionately aroused by each other. The vase-painting depicts two worlds: the human world and the world of satyrs, who provide the right example: human activity, therefore, takes place in a Dionysian sphere. In the world of Dionysus males are permitted to let themselves go in every respect, also sexually. The men, in their excitement, do not lay hands on the female flute player, but are interested only in one another. Male homosexual behavior unfolds in the world of Dionysus.

There are some other depictions of a *komos* of dancing men where the participants show signs of sexual excitement while there are no women present. Dancing men are represented on both sides of a Berlin vase in the shape form of a boar (Figure 2),[6] a total of five. A few are completely naked, the others wear briefs. One is ithyphallic and is masturbating. Is he aroused by the naked buttocks which the man in front of him is projecting backwards as he dances? In any case, the painter wishes to indicate that the men exercise no restraint in relation to one another. On both sides of a *kantharos* in Heidelberg (Figure 3)[7] appear three komasts and a flute player. One of them holds a drinking horn in

FIGURE 2. Berlin vase. Reproduced courtesy of Antikensammlung, Staatliche Museen Zu Berlin-Preussicher Kulturbesitz, V. 1. 3391. Photo: Jutta Tietz-Glagow.

his hand, a sign that the dance is connected with the god Dionysus. There is wild dancing to the rhythm of the *aulos* music. On Side A, a man and a youth are standing opposite each other. The young man looks behind, perhaps at the man who is making passionate dancing movements behind the flute player. The young man is gripping with his left hand the penis of the man in front of him. The latter, however, has seized the youth by his hair and with his other hand is gripping his left wrist. How should this scene be interpreted? Kilinski thinks the youth is tugging at the man's penis "in retribution for having his hair pulled" (1990, p. 44). This does not seem correct to me. The man's penis is extraordinarily big in comparison to the other men's, and the painter appears to indicate that the man is being sexually aroused by the youth.

FIGURE 3. *Kantharos,* Heidelberg University 166, 6th century B.C. Used with permission.

Thus it is plausible that he is seizing the latter by his hair because he wants the youth to have eyes only for him and not to look at someone else.[8]

On one of the lower panels of the black-figure tripod *kothon* 1981.170 in Dallas (Figure 4)[9] of the period 570-560 BC, there are two adult men dancing opposite each other. While dancing, the left komast stretches an inviting hand to his friend's chin in the hope that the latter will respond to this gesture. This is the courting gesture which we have noted already in Figure 1. Both komasts are bearded. The only difference between the two is that the left one, who takes the initiative, is somewhat heavier than the other.

There is a striking depiction of courting on the lid of a *pyxis* in Bologna (Figure 5).[10] Among three bystanders, including a child, are two male persons wrapped in a mantle. Dover, I believe, is correct in his suggestion that we have to assume this couple is "copulating" (1978, on ill. B 538). The person on the right is a youth with curls running down his cheeks to his neck. With a few incisions the painter has indicated in

FIGURE 4. *Kothon*, Black-figure tripod. Greek, Boeotia, 6th century B.C. ceramic (1981.170). Reproduced courtesy of Dallas Museum of Art, an anonymous gift in memory of Edward Marcus.

the partner's cheek and chin the start of hair growth. None of them has a beard, as is shown on the face of the man on the right. Evidently, the left person in the couple is a youth showing the first growth of hair on his face. In any case, I would characterize him as a young man. The two figures are of equal size and, therefore, the only difference is their hair style. Can we determine on the basis of these details which of the two is the *erastes*? To all appearances, the painter allows the viewer to draw his own conclusion. The mantle covers and conceals from us what is ac-

FIGURE 5. *Pyxis*, vase-painting PU 239, CVA Bologna 2 taf. 44, 3. Copyright Bologna, Museo Civico Archeologico.

tually happening. There are homosexual mantle scenes also among the Attic representations, and I have demonstrated in my book (2000, Vol. 1, pp. 144-145), that this mantle is a kind of pictorial euphemism. Finally, a possible seduction scene involving two boys on a *skyphos* (Figure 6).[11] In Attic vase-paintings, too, occur seductions where one boy approaches the other from behind (Hupperts, 2000, Vol. 1, ill. Z30 and Z41). In the Boeotian *skyphos* the boys are dancing, but there is contact between the two and the boy on the left seems to be touching the other.

FIGURE 6. Black-figure *skyphos* c. 500 BC, Akraiphia inv. no. 19447. Thebes Nr. KOL/95. Reproduced courtesy of the Ministry of Culture, IX Ephorate of Prehistoric and Classical Antiquities, Archaeological Museum of Thebes, Thebes, Greece.

CONCLUSIONS

Taking a comprehensive view of the information provided by our primary sources, we reach the following conclusions. The material we have, although quite scanty, shows that different forms of homosexual behavior were possible in Thebes: there is the traditional pederasty in which the boy's physical beauty is central, but we also find examples of the *kinaidoi,* adult men who court one another, and of youths who have an erotic interest in each other. When we compare the Boeotian with Attic vase-painting, we notice that we do not find on the Boeotian vases the so-called up-and-down posture, no seduction scenes in which gifts are offered to the *eromenos*, no examples of intercrural penetration. However, before we reach our conclusions too quickly concerning the ways in which male homosexuality was practiced in Boeotia, we have to be cognizant of two facts. A great deal of Boeotian pottery ware has never been published and is now lost (see Kilinski II, 1990, p. 2). In addition, much pottery in Boeotia was imported from Attica and Corinth. It is difficult, therefore, to draw far-reaching conclusions concerning customs on the basis of differences with Attica. It makes good sense, rather, to observe that the material available to us which was unmistakably crafted by Boeotian painters shows, in fact, strong resemblances to the Attic and Corinthian vase-paintings, with expressions of homosexuality being represented in the context of *komoi*, groups of dancing men who, perhaps under the influence of wine, are letting themselves go sexually. Thus, in fact, we discover a general characteristic of homosexual practices in the sixth century BC in cities such as Corinth, Thebes, and Athens, namely that this behavior was perhaps linked in part with festivals in honor of the god Dionysus. However, the fact that we find in representations on Corinthian and Attic vases, among which the so-called Tyrrhenian amphoras are included, sexual acts between two men sometimes even more explicitly portrayed makes this other fact no less remarkable. It is incorrect, therefore, to suggest with Sergent (1986, p. 47) that homosexuality in Boeotia had already from the beginning a military character. The relationship between athletics and homosexuality, too, which is averred by Plutarch, is found for the first time in Pindar and not in the vases. The general impression left by many secondary sources, starting with Plato's *Symposium*, namely that, when it came to homosexuality, great freedom was enjoyed in Thebes, and that it was indeed noticeably far greater than in Athens, appears therefore incorrect. On the basis of the sources available to us, it was an image created by Athenians in order to distinguish themselves from their neighbors to such an extent that the latter might be caricatured as swine.

NOTES

1. Compare Dover, 1978, pp. 199-200; Sergent, 1984, pp. 84-87; Apollodorus, *Bibliotheca* 3.5.5; Pausanias 9.5, 6, and 9; Hyginus, *Fab.* 9; Athenaeus 13.602; Plutarch *Pel.* 19; scholiast on Euripides *Phoenissae* 1760.

2. See Xenophon, *Symp.* 8.32; Dinarchus, 1.72-73; Plutarch, *Alex.* 9; Plutarch, *Moralia* 761b; Athenaeus 602a; Dio Chrysostom 22; Phaidimos, *Anth. Pal.* 13.22.3-8. For a complete overview of our sources for the Sacred Band see DeVoto, 1992 and Leitao, 2002. I am not convinced, in the final analysis, by the arguments adduced by Leitao to cast doubt on the historicity of the Sacred Band.

3. For information on Pindar and his beloved boys, see Buffière (1980, pp. 261-266) and Percy (1996, pp. 136-138).

4. For an overview of the odes with homoerotic allusions, see Percy, 1996, p. 210 n. 27; he speaks, however, of *Pythian Odes* 14, which must be a printing error since it does not exist.

5. Berlin, Staatliche Museen 6. 1. 3366, c. 570 BC. See also *Corpus Vasorum Antiquorum* 4, p. 74; Kilinski II, Boeotian Trick Vases, *American Journal of Archaeology* 90 (1986), 153-158; 1990, plates 11, 3-4.

6. Berlin Staatliche Museen 3391, 2nd quarter of the sixth century BC. See also *Corpus Vasorum Antiquorum* 4, plate 203; Kilinski II, 1990, plate 11, 2; John Boardman, *Early Greek Vase Painting*, (London: Thames and Hudson, 1998), ill. 449.

7. Heidelberg Universität 166, 2nd quarter of the sixth century BC. See also J. D. Beazley, *Attic Black-Figure Vase-Painters*, (Oxford: Oxford University Press: 1956), 30, 10; *Corpus Vasorum Antiquorum* 1, plate 24, 3-4; Kilinski II, The Boeotian Dancers Group, *American Journal of Archaeology*, 92 (1978), 186; 1990, plate 9, 3.

8. Two other examples are: a *kantharos* of 580-570 BC, from a tomb near Rhitsona (86. 274), where, on one side, in the midst of non-ithyphallic dancers, a man with a gigantic pendulous phallus clearly shows himself to be aroused by his dancing with his friends. See Jean-Jacques Maffre, Collection Paul Canellopoulos (VIII), *Bulletin de correspondence hellénique*, 99 (1975), 449 ff. On Side A of a *kantharos* of 550 BC in the Stoddard Collection are depicted four ithyphallic men, of whom one is not bearded. The second from the right has a drinking horn. Their sexual excitement is clearly directed to one another. See Paul V. C. Bauer, *Catalogue of the Tebecca Darlington Stoddard Collection* (New York: AMS Press, 1922), figure 42, no. 184.

9. Dallas, Museum of Fine Arts, 1981.170 (from the Schimmel collection), 570-560 BC. See also O. W. Muscarella (Ed.), *Ancient Art: the Norbert Schimmel Collection* (Mainz: Philipp von Zabern, 1974) no. 53; Kilinski II, The Boeotian Dancers Group, *American Journal of Archaeology*, 92 (1978), 174; H. A. Shapiro (Ed.), *Art, myth and culture. Greek vases from Southern Collections*, (New Orleans Museum of Art: Tulane University, 1981), pp. 142-143; Kilinski II, 1990, plate 1, 1.

10. Bologna, *Musico Civico PU*, 239. See also *Corpus Vasorum Antiquorum*, Bologna 2, plate 44, 3; Dover, 1978, B 538; Gundel Koch-Harnack, *Erotische Symbole. Lotosblüte und gemeinsamer Mantel auf antiker Vasen*, (Berlin: Mann, 1989), figure 9; Kilinski II, 1990, plate 24, 3.

11. Black-figure *skyphos* of c. 500 BC, Akraiphia inv. no. 19447. See A. K. Adreiomenou, To Nekrotapheion Tēs Akraiphias, *Archaiologikē Ephēmeris*, 133 (1994), 212, ill. 76.

SELECT BIBLIOGRAPHY

Buffière, F. (1980). *Eros adolescent: la pédérastie dans la Grèce antique*. Paris: Les Belles Lettres.

DeVoto, J. (1992). The Theban Sacred Band. *Ancient World, 23*, 3-19.

Dover, K. J. (1978). *Greek Homosexuality*. Cambridge MA and London: Harvard UP.

Groningen, B. A. van (1960). *Pindar au banquet*. Leiden: A.W. Sythoff.

Hupperts, C. A. M. (2000). *Eros dikaios*. (3 vols.). Doctoral Dissertation, University of Amsterdam.

Kilinski II, K. (1990). *Boeotian Black Figure Vase Painting of the Archaic Period*. Mainz am Rhein: Philipp von Zabern.

Leitao, D. (2002). The legend of the Sacred Band. In M. C. Nussbaum and J. Sihvola (Eds.), *The Sleep of Reason: Erotic Experience and Sexual Ethics in Ancient Greece and Rome* (pp. 143-169). Chicago and London: U of Chicago P.

Meier, M. H. E. & de Pogey-Castries, L. R. (1980). *Histoire de L' Amour Grec*. Paris: Guy le Prat.

Percy, W. A. (1996). *Pederasty and Pedagogy in Archaic Greece*. Urbana and Chicago: U of Illinois P.

Sergent, B. (1984). *L'Homosexualité dans la mythologie grecque*. Paris: Payot.

_____. (1986). *L'Homosexualité initiatique dans L'Europe ancienne*. Paris: Payot.

Snell, B. & Mähler, H. (Eds.). (1975-1980). *Pindari Carmina cum fragmentis*. Leipzig: B. G. Teubner.

"Sleeping in the Bosom of a Tender Companion": Homoerotic Attachments in Sappho

Anne L. Klinck, PhD

University of New Brunswick

SUMMARY. This paper reexamines the ancient evidence to see what light it sheds on homoeroticism in Sappho. From the Hellenistic period on there are derogatory references to her homosexuality–and also denials that she was involved in same-sex relationships. From the late archaic period on there are hints that women from Lesbos had a reputation for being sexually adventurous. Yet there is a discontinuity between these quips about Sappho and/or "Lesbianism," and her own poetry, which is intense, sometimes voluptuous, but really not very carnal. Sappho's oeuvre is so fragmentary that the evidence it offers is tentative at best. Nevertheless, if her homoerotic poetry is at all autobiographical it reflects a circle of mainly adolescent girls or very young women around a somewhat older and more authoritative Sappho. Passionate at-

Anne L. Klinck is Professor of English at the University of New Brunswick. She writes on ancient and medieval poetry, especially woman's-voice lyric. Her publications include *The Old English Elegies* (McGill-Queen's UP, 1992, 2001), *Cursor Mundi* 5, co-edited with Laurence Eldredge (University of Ottawa Press, 2000), and *An Anthology of Ancient and Medieval Woman's Song* (Palgrave-Macmillan, 2004). Correspondence may be addressed: Department of English, University of New Brunswick, Fredericton, New Brunswick, Canada, E3B 5A3.

[Haworth co-indexing entry note]: "'Sleeping in the Bosom of a Tender Companion': Homoerotic Attachments in Sappho." Klinck, Anne L. Co-published simultaneously in *Journal of Homosexuality* (Harrington Park Press, an imprint of The Haworth Press, Inc.) Vol. 49, No. 3/4, 2005, pp. 193-208; and: *Same-Sex Desire and Love in Greco-Roman Antiquity and in the Classical Tradition of the West* (ed: Beert C. Verstraete, and Vernon Provencal) Harrington Park Press, an imprint of The Haworth Press, Inc., 2005, pp. 193-208. Single or multiple copies of this article are available for a fee from The Haworth Document Delivery Service [1-800-HAWORTH, 9:00 a.m. - 5:00 p.m. (EST). E-mail address: docdelivery@haworthpress.com].

tachments exist between members of this group as well as between individual girls and Sappho. Although many modern scholars believe Sappho's relationships were egalitarian and same-age, the collective evidence of her own poetry together with the ancient testimonia and commentaries does not support that inference. *[Article copies available for a fee from The Haworth Document Delivery Service: 1-800-HAWORTH. E-mail address: <docdelivery@haworthpress.com> Website: <http://www.HaworthPress.com> © 2005 by The Haworth Press, Inc. All rights reserved.]*

KEYWORDS. Sappho, lesbian, Lesbos, homoeroticism, same-sex, pederasty, ancient Greek lyric

What readers have found most characteristic of Sappho is her expression of intimate attachments: passionate desire ("You came, and I was wild for you; and you cooled my heart, burning with desire," ἦλθες, ἔγω δὲ σ' ἐμαιόμαν, / ὂν δ' ἔψυξας ἔμαν φρένα καιομέναν πόθῳ, Fr. 48); physical tenderness ("May you sleep in the bosom of a tender companion," δαύοις ἀπάλας ἐτα<ί>ρας ἐν στήθεσιν, Fr. 126); jealousy ("Atthis, you hate the thought of me now, and fly off to Andromeda," Ἄτθι, σοὶ δ' ἔμεθεν μὲν ἀπήχθετο / φροντίσδην, ἐπὶ δ' Ἀνδρομέδαν πότῃ, Fr. 131); and the dysfunction which overwhelms the lover's body in the presence of the beloved (Fr. 31).[1] Few would now deny that these feelings are homoerotic,[2] but we still wonder what that implies. This is the question I would like to raise again here, looking at external and internal evidence for the kinds of homoerotic relationships to be found in Sappho, relationships which may or may not be specifically lesbian (I will use the lower-case *l* to indicate the modern meaning of that word).[3]

It is not clear that Sappho had a reputation in contemporary Lesbos, or even in classical Greece, for having same-sex liaisons. There are plenty of references to her homosexuality in later antiquity, and that reputation is regarded as a slur on her character. The ancients, of course, thought in terms of homosexual behavior rather than homosexual identity.[4] And it seems there were those in ancient as in modern times who felt that so highly regarded a poet should not be besmirched in this way. The earliest evidence for Sappho as a lesbian[5] is a papyrus of the late second or early third century CE whose contents seem to be based on the lost treatise on Sappho by Chamaeleon (fourth century BCE): "She has been accused by some people of being licentious in her lifestyle and a woman-lover" (κ[α]τηγόρηται δ᾽ ὑπ᾽ ἐν[ί]ω[ν] ὡς ἄτακτος οὖ[σα] τὸν τρόπον καὶ γυναικε[ράσ]τρια).⁶ *Ataktos*, "not properly regulated," "out of line," is definitely an adverse criticism. The name Chamaeleon and the word *eplanēthē*, "went astray," appear a little later on. It is impossible to tell whether it was Chamaeleon, Sappho, or someone else who "went astray." The writer of the papyrus biography thus reports the rumor that Sappho was a woman-lover, but does not endorse it.

There are, however, some early suggestions that the women of Lesbos were supposed to be generally *ataktos* in sexual matters. In the late archaic period, Anacreon complains that an attractive girl with pretty sandals isn't interested in his grey head; she comes from Lesbos and is gaping after some other female: πρὸς δ᾽ ἄλλην τινὰ χάσκει (Anacreon 358.8).⁷ *Possibly* the feminine *allēn* refers to hair (*komēn*, line 6) rather than another girl. But the implication seems to be that Lesbian women have a certain reputation. At the end of Aristophanes' *Wasps*, Philocleon says he snatched the flute-girl away when she was just going to "lesbianize" the symposiasts (λεσβιεῖν τοὺς συμπότας, *Wasps* 1346), which looks as if he means she was going to perform oral sex on them. "The Muse didn't lesbianize" (ἡ Μοῦσ᾽ οὐκ ἐλεσβίαζεν, *Frogs* 1308) and "l- in the Lesbian way" (λάβδα κατὰ τοὺς Λεσβίους, *Ecclesiazusae* 920) are less clear, but undoubtedly off-colour.

It is hard to evaluate how these later allusions to the practices of Lesbian women bear on Sappho's situation around 600 BCE. Were female homoerotic liaisons characteristic of early Lesbian society? Were these liaisons looked down upon by men later on? Or, as the Aristophanes passages imply, were Lesbian women supposed to be given to fellatio? Again, was Sappho so famous that her own reputation, which came to be associated with sexual license, attached itself to her countrywomen? Whatever the connection, there is a discontinuity between Sappho's poetry, sometimes voluptuous but never prurient, and these later quips about Lesbian sexuality.

Whether because of Sappho herself or because of the customs on Lesbos, from classical Greece on two disparate strands appear in her reception: one celebrates the gifted poet, the Tenth Muse, as she is called in an epigram attributed to Plato in the Palatine Anthology; the other represents her as a woman of unmanageable sexual appetites, homo- or hetereosexual. In the comic poets she becomes the crazed lover of the beautiful youth Phaon. Menander, in the later fourth century BCE, tells

how she cast herself from the Leucadian Rock into the sea out of unrequited love for him.[8] Attitudes towards sexuality changed in the fifth
and fourth centuries BCE, and perhaps the poetry of female passion
came to be regarded as unseemly.[9] From the Hellenistic period and
later, some sources even speak of two Sapphos, the poet and a courtesan. This idea first appears in the third-century Nymphodorus, quoted
by Athenaeus (13.596e). Aelian, contemporary with Athenaeus, also
mentions this theory (*Varia Historia* 12.19). The tenth- or eleventh-cen-
tury *Suda*, a Byzantine lexicon, has two entries under Sappho: one, the
poet, who admittedly has a reputation for *aischras philias*, "disgraceful
friendship"–that is, lesbian relationships–and the other a lyre player.
Among Roman literati Sappho's homosexuality seems to have been
widely credited, though sometimes challenged. A scholion on Horace's
"mascula" Sappho (*Epistles* 1.19.28) explains that epithet as attribut-
able either to her excellence as a poet or to her reputation as a tribad
(*quia tribas diffamatur fuisse*), the derogatory term for a lesbian, "one
who rubs," from *tribein*. And another scholion on the same passage asserts that she was neither given over to voluptuousness nor unchaste
(*nec fracta voluptatibus nec impudica*).[10] Ovid's, or Pseudo-Ovid's,
fictionalized Sappho says she has loved girls *non sine crimine*
(*Heroides* 15.19). Sappho was well known as the author of poems expressing homoerotic affection, "lamenting the girls of her country on
Aeolian strings," as Horace put it (*Aeoliis fidibus querentem / Sappho
puellis de popularibus, Odes* 2.13.24-25). Then, as now, she was widely
regarded as a lesbian, but some people were uncomfortable with that
reputation.

Some light may be shed on Sappho's homoerotic friendships by similar relationships existing in other contexts in ancient Greece. The status
of this evidence is problematic, however, because we cannot be sure
that the cases are parallel, and the evidence itself may be suspect. The
most familiar model is that obtaining in upper-class male circles in classical Athens: the partnership between an older mentor, the "lover,"
erastēs, and a younger protégé, the "beloved," *erōmenos*, an adolescent
beardless boy. In their influential studies of Greek homosexuality, Sir
Kenneth Dover (1978) and David Halperin (1990) regard this relationship as very much one between an active dominant and a passive dominated partner, but this view has recently been questioned, notably by
Thomas Hubbard (2003).[11]

Erastēs-erōmenos love is discussed by the speakers in Plato's *Symposium*: it is an important socializing process, and, as Pausanias says, at

its best "when the former [the lover] has the power to contribute towards wisdom and distinction, and the latter [the beloved] needs to acquire education and accomplishment" (ὁ μὲν δυνάμενος εἰς φρόνησιν καὶ τὴν ἄλλην ἀρετὴν συμβάλλεσθαι, ὁ δὲ δεόμενος εἰς παίδευσιν καὶ τὴν ἄλλην σοφίαν κτᾶσθαι, *Symposium* 184e). Around 100 CE, Plutarch, in his account of customs in earlier Sparta, comments that "noble and good" Spartan women (καλαὶ καὶ ἀγαθαὶ γυναῖκες–that is, distinguished women from good families) took girls as lovers (*Lycurgus* 18). This phenomenon is explicitly linked by Plutarch with its male counterpart, about which he has much more to say. The passage, if it is not merely idealization of the past, testifies to the existence in early Sparta of a female version of the institutionalized male *paiderastia* well documented in accounts of Spartan and Cretan, as well as Athenian society.[12]

However, a rather different reflection of female homoeroticism emerges from a remark of Aristophanes in the *Symposium*. In connection with people's different sexual orientations, he specifically mentions lesbians, *hetairistriai*, but places them on a lower moral plane, along with heterosexually inclined men and women, than *men* who are capable of spiritual refinement through homoerotic love (*Symposium* 191e). This passage, in contrast to that from Plutarch, implies that the male and female situations were not parallel. It is probably significant too that in Plato's time *hetaira*, originally "female friend," means "prostitute." *Hetairistriai*, like *tribas*, sounds like a term of disapprobation.

It is somewhat doubtful, then, whether ancient references to male and female homoeroticism entitle us to regard Sappho as playing the role of an *erastēs* in relation to his *erōmenos*. This model is endorsed by Claude Calame, who sees Sappho's sexual relationship to her friends as an asymmetrical one, in which she assumes a pedagogical role and an initiatory function. Calame and others see a parallel between Sappho's role–both educative and erotic–in relation to her circle, and that of the chorus-leaders in Alcman's partheneia ("maiden songs") in relation to the girl-choruses.[13] Alcman 1, and more conspicuously Alcman 3, use the language of erotic love as the generic chorus-member praises her leader: "Hagesichora afflicts me with love" (Ἀγησιχόρα με τείρει, 1.77); "with limb-loosening desire, she looks at [me] more meltingly than sleep and death" (λυσιμελεῖ τε πόσω, τακερώτερα / δ' ὕπνω καὶ σανάτω ποτιδέρκεται, 3.61-62).[14] The existence of such a parallel has been questioned in recent scholarship. Eva Stehle claims that "neither of the poems [Alcman 1 and 3] is an expression of young women's real physical/emotional attachment to their leader," and points out that Sappho fulfils the roles of both Alcman and Hagesichora.[15] But the erotic feelings–whether "real" or not–expressed by the chorus are too potent to be regarded as mere compliment. They do resemble the sentiments found in Sappho's poetry, though as woman and lover Sappho composes from within the group, unlike Alcman who directs the chorus from outside it.

Many modern scholars are convinced that Sappho's relationship to the members of her circle was much more egalitarian than the *erastēs-erōmenos* association found in male bonding, and feminist analyses of Sappho's poetry often argue that the love-relationships she depicts represent two loving subjects, rather than a dominating active subject and a dominated passive object of affection.[16] This line of thinking was given an impetus by Dover's remarks about Poem 1, in which Aphrodite promises Sappho that her beloved will cease to flee and instead will pursue. Whom she will pursue is unstated, but Dover assumes it is Sappho, and comments on the "obliteration of the usual distinction between a dominant and a subordinate partner" (Dover, 1978, p. 177). However, not everyone has accepted this view of a reciprocal relationship between Sappho and her beloved in Poem 1.[17] As we shall see, the evidence from Sappho's poetry more generally is mixed, and cases can be made for different positions on this subject. There are passages that imply a role of some authority for Sappho, and there are others that suggest erotic attachments between members of her group, not just intimacies between the poet herself and particular girls or young women.

What, then, does Sappho herself say about her loves and friendships, and how much is explicitly homoerotic? Poem 1, the Hymn to Aphrodite, the only Sapphic composition preserved intact, has Aphrodite address the author by name when she responds to Sappho's petition for help in securing the affections of an unresponsive beloved. The latter person is generally taken to be female, but her gender is indicated by a single inflection in line 24, κωὐκ ἐθέλοισα, "even if she's unwilling," and the reading is rather tentative.[18] The poem gives us precious little information about this woman/girl. We assume that she is young and attractive. In fact, it is more about Sappho's gaining control of her own feelings than it is about her beloved. We learn nothing at all about her appearance, her nature, or her relationship to Sappho–except that she is hard to get and that Aphrodite will deal with this problem.

The expression of admiration for Anactoria in Fragment 16 is clearer: in her absence, something has reminded Sappho of her lovely step and shining face (lines 15-18). This poem pits a feminine set of values against the male values of epic poetry: armies splendid in their flashing metal. But Sappho prefers the sparkle of a young woman's face and the lightness of her movement. On the surface it is a purely physical contrast between two things that are bright and in nimble motion, the latter insignificant beside the former. And, of course, it is also about Helen, who, like Sappho herself, chooses what in cosmic terms is the lesser good, in this case the appeal of a lover over the claims of family. Again, all of this tells us little about Anactoria. But we may infer that Sappho's admiration for her is not merely predictable and conventional; there is an element of personal defiance in it.

Fragment 22 is *very* lacunose, but does seem to be about desire between females. It speaks of Gongyla (apparently–the first two letters of the name are missing), "desire for whom flies around you, the lovely one (ἆς σε δηὖτε πόθος... / ἀμφιπόταται, / τὰν κάλαν, 11-13), and whose dress "set you aflutter as you looked at her" (ἀ γὰρ κατάγωγις αὔτα[ς σ' / ἐπτόαισ' ἴδοισαν, 13-14). The sigma for σε, "you," is a restoration. *Eptoaise*, "terrified," "violently excited," is precisely the same word that Sappho uses for the effect of the beloved girl (or woman) on herself in Fragment 31 (line 6). In 22, Sappho–if the speaker *is* Sappho–seems to find both young women attractive, but to be more interested in the one she is addressing, Abanthis, if the restoration is correct. Sappho herself, then, and a girl or woman that she knows, have both experienced this agitated arousal in the presence of another attractive girl/woman.

Like the Hymn to Aphrodite, Fragment 31, "He seems to me just like the gods," tells us virtually nothing about the beloved; the focus is on Sappho herself and her feelings. This poem, preserved in the Pseudo-Longinus discourse *On the Sublime*, must be the one that prompted Byron's allusion to "burning Sappho"[19]: she is physically overwhelmed when she looks at a certain girl (or woman); happy the man who sits opposite that girl. One thing Fragment 31 does tell us, in conjunction with Fragment 22, is that, if these two are to be taken autobiographically, it was an expected thing in Sappho's circle for someone to perform erotic songs about another female. Sappho does it, and so does someone else.

Fragment 94 is also one of the clearer portrayals of intimate feeling between Sappho and a young woman. Another speaker, her gender established by a feminine ending, addresses the poet by name: "Really, Sappho, I'm leaving you unwillingly" ("Ψάπφ' ἦ μάν σ' ἀέκοισ' ἀπυλιμπάνω," line 5). Sappho responds to the other's rather extravagant grief at the separation by urging her to think of the joyful things they have done together, "because you know how much we cared for you" (οἶσθα γὰρ ὡς σε πεδήπομεν). It is not clear whether the plural "we" refers to a group or simply to Sappho. Some of the activities to be remembered must have been performed in a group: dancing (if ορος, line 27, is to be supplemented into χόρος), and participation in ritual–indicated by the words ἶρον, "shrine" (line 25), and ἄλσος, "grove" (line 27). The other woman, or girl, also beautified herself with perfume and flowery garlands, and satisfied her desire on soft beds (στρώμν[αν ἐ]πὶ μολθάκαν /. . . / ἐξίης πόθο[ν], 21-23). This could be erotic; the words explaining what the desire was for are missing. Campbell supposes they were in the intervening line: ἀπάλαν ... ων, "for tender–somethings"). A subtler inference that may be drawn from the tone of the poem is that Sappho assumes a dominant role with regard to the other speaker, who, essentially, is told to pull herself together. I am inclined to assign the first line, "No kidding, I want to die" (τεθνάκην δ᾽ ἀδόλως θέλω) to the "blubbering" (ψισδομένα, line 2) girl/young woman. But some attribute it to Sappho.[20]

Poem 96, which contains some of Sappho's most haunting poetry, describes love not between Sappho herself and another girl or woman, but between another person and Atthis, a name which recurs in the Sapphic fragments. This other woman is unmistakeably adult. She is in Lydia, where she stands out among the Lydian *women* (Λύδαισιν ἐμπρέπεται γυναί/κεσσιν, 6-7). There she grieves for gentle Atthis. The poem then modulates into an imagined moonlit scene in which the light is spread over dewy meadows of roses, chervil, and clover. The woman is compared to the moon outshining the stars, but her physical presence is embodied in the other elements of the scene, with their coolness, moisture, tenderness, and fragrance. Like Fragment 22, this poem suggests that erotic relationships existed not only between individual girls and Sappho, but also between the girls themselves. These feelings may have been collective, individualized, or very likely both.[21]

Several of the other fragments imply feelings of attraction towards young women. Fr. 62 implies this, although only a few scattered words are left: "to come . . . gentle . . . you (pl.) got in first . . . lovely" (ἵκεσθ᾽ ἀγανα ... / ἔφθατε κάλαν ... , 10-11). In Fragment 81, Sappho bids Dica, who also, it is implied, is beautiful, to put lovely garlands on her hair. Fragment 82 speaks of Mnasidica as more lovely than tender Gyrinno (εὐμορφωτέρα Μνασιδίκα τὰς ἀπάλας Γυρίννως). The very damaged 88 presents a *female* speaker loving (φίλα φαῖμ᾽ ἐχύρα, 17, "I have been a firm friend"; φιλήσω, 24, "I shall love"), but it is not clear from the surviving words whom she will love, or who is speaking. Similarly, Fragment 41, with plural, feminine, objects of affection or admiration: "towards you lovely ones my mind is unchanging" (ταὶς κάλαισ᾽ ὔμμιν <τὸ> νόημμα τὦμον οὐ διάμειπτον). These might be feelings of Sappho towards women or girls she knows–and they might not be. The speaker may not be Sappho. And the addressees might be, say, goddesses rather than humans. Fragment 99(a) contains the words ὀλισβ- δόκοισ<ι>, which may mean "receiving the dildo," but the poem may be scurrilous rather than erotic, and it may not be by Sappho.[22]

Sometimes, too, there is erotic content, but the genders involved are uncertain. I am excluding here the numerous fragments from the epithalamia, for example, which obviously refer to heterosexual love. Fragments 47 and 130 startlingly capture the power of Eros, blastingly violent in the former, serpent-sly in the latter: "like a mountain wind falling on oak-trees" (ὠς ἄνεμος κὰτ᾽ ὄρος δρύσιν ἐμπέτων), "irresistible, insidious, bitter, though sweet"–to shift around the three epithets (γλυκύπικρον, ἀμάχανον, ὄρπετον).[23] And 48 is pretty torrid: "You came, and I was wild for you; you cooled my heart, burning with desire." Someone in Fragment 65 says, "Sappho, I love you" (Ψάπφοι σεφίλ-, line 5). But the speaker may be Aphrodite, possibly mentioned in the next line. Fragment 126, "May you sleep in the bosom of a tender companion," does not reveal the gender of the addressee–unless δαύοις is δαύοισα, the Aeolic feminine participle, rather than the optative. Fragment 129(b) speaks of loving someone else more than me. τιν᾽ ἄλλον ἀνθρώπων is masculine, but this may not be significant.

One or two fragments seem to express sexual jealousy between women. 57 is cited by Athenaeus as addressed to Andromeda: "What country girl bewitches your mind, . . . too ignorant even to pull her dress up over her ankles" (†τίς δ᾽ ἀγροΐωτις θέλγει νόον ... †/... / οὐκ ἐπισταμένα τὰ βράκε᾽ ἔλκην ἐπὶ τῶν σφύρων;). It sounds as if Sappho wishes that she herself was the object of Andromeda's affections. But *if*, as Maximus of Tyre says (in the second century CE), Andromeda was the leader of another female circle, the jealousy is more complicated. Fragment 131 reproaches Atthis for tiring of the speaker and flying off to Andromeda. And in Fragment 133(a) "Andromeda has a nice exchange" (κάλαν ἀμοίβαν). Again, Fragment 144 refers to people who are "fed up with Gorgo" (κεκορημένοις), using the masculine participle, but not necessarily with specifically masculine reference. Fragment 213 comments on the use of the term "yoke-mate," σύνδυγος, for Archeanassa, a companion of Gorgo, another rival of

Sappho's. Whether or not Andromeda and Gorgo were other mentors, these snippets suggest a milieu of rivalries and shifting affections.

From this poetry emerges a world of becoming clothing, personal adornments, flowers, intimate feelings: a world that would be cloyingly lush–and, indeed, trivial–were it not for the economy, the control, the resonances–and occasionally the ironic bite–of Sappho's language. The poetry is peopled with names of girls or women with whom Sappho is associated and who are attractive, either to her or to other girls/women: Abanthis, Anactoria, Archeanassa, Atthis, Dica, Gongyla, Gorgo, Gyrinno, Mnasidica. There is much eroticism, but no individualizing, nothing that we can visualize, except in a general, rather symbolic, way. There *is* a strong physicality in constant references to touch, scent, and motion. But it is often very idealized, and, really, none of it is very carnal. Interpretations now tend to see this eroticism as conventional, and essentially fictive.[24] Still, we should note that it is neither untroubled nor wholly complimentary, and, if Sappho and her female companions have a basis in reality, it is not unreasonable to suppose that the interrelationships between them also do.

To turn, now, to the issue of whether Sappho's relationship to her friends was that of a mature woman to young girls. If Cleis, mentioned in Fragments 98 and 132, really is Sappho's daughter, an assumption supported by Papyrus Oxyrhynchus 1800, mentioned above, then Sappho cannot be very young. 98 complains of being unable to get a fancy headband from Lydia for Cleis, implying that she is a grown girl. 132 gives the impression that Cleis is decidedly young, but not an infant: "I have a beautiful girl, her form like golden flowers, my beloved Cleis" (Κλέις ἀγαπάτα). The *kala pais* could be a favourite, but *agapān* is not a word used of sexual feeling.[25] Fragment 49, to Atthis, seems to convey the love of an older for a younger person–*if* the two lines are consecutive, which is doubtful: "I loved you a long time ago, Atthis, ... / just a little girl you seemed to me, and ungainly" (ἠράμαν μὲν ἐγω σέθεν Ἄτθι πάλαι ποτά ... / σμίκρα μοι πάις ἔμμεν ἐφαίνεο κἄχαρις). The second line is quoted by Plutarch (and attributed to Sappho); the name Atthis is an editorial emendation.

There may, too, be some slight evidence about Sappho's age in references to the putting on of garlands, an activity regarded as proper for the young and attractive. Fragment 125, a few words quoted in a scholion on Aristophanes, may imply that Sappho is older–*if* the speaker is Sappho: "I myself in my youth used to weave garlands" (†αυταόρα† ἐστεφαναπλόκην), suggesting that she is no longer young. Sappho speaks of others putting on garlands, but not herself: Dica in Fragment 81, the young woman who is leaving in 94. In this latter poem we are told that she put on many garlands "by me" or "at my house" (πὰρ ἔμοι, 14).

Repeatedly, Sappho adopts an admonishing or a hortatory tone towards her addressee. Sometimes she expresses indignation, but she never pleads–unless she is addressing Aphrodite. Hardly any of the fragments suggest that her companions were extremely young; that is, preadolescent. The exceptions are her daughter Cleis, possibly, and Atthis in Fragment 49, where loving someone below the age of sexual attractiveness is worthy of comment, and by implication a little surprising. The word used for "loved," *ēramān*, does imply desire, or at least very warm feeling, and not merely affection, like *philein*.

Finally, we come to the question of whether Sappho's relationships were with young girls rather than mature women. Although scholars have argued vehemently about her sexuality, even when they disagree they find the same kind of erotic intensity in her poems. Wilamowitz the champion of her virtue and Devereux the psychoanalyst of lesbian neuroses have both been struck by this.[26] In the twenty-first century, readers have no problem with her lesbianism, but they would prefer that she was not involved in child abuse. Whether she was or was not a pederast–to use the male term–depends on how one defines one's terms. A 14-year-old is a child to us, but may have been a young adult to Sappho.[27] Again, we really don't know what erotic behavior Sappho's group engaged in–she is anything but specific–or whether it would amount to what we would consider sexual abuse.[28] We bring our own sexual mores to bear on a society that saw things very differently. Recently Holt Parker has mounted a lively attack on the modern assumption that heterosexuality and homosexuality are genetic.[29] But his earlier article, "Sappho Schoolmistress," which argues that the Lesbian poet was a member of a *hetairia* of women her own age, seems to me to be a product of modern attitudes too, in this case about hierarchical relationships and about pedophilia. What little evidence there is points to Sappho being a mature woman while the others in her group were not–although, except for the young Atthis, they were not prepubescent. I suggest that the eagerness with which modern scholars argue for an egalitarian, same-age relationship between Sappho and her friends has more to do with our modern revulsion to pedophilia than to any proof in the ancient sources.[30]

NOTES

1. I follow Campbell (1982a) for citations from the Sappho fragments, testimonia, and commentaries. Translations are my own.

2. Earlier generations of scholars often felt that Sappho should be "pure." The trend was set by Welcker (1816). Wilamowitz (1913) took up the torch. By the middle of the last century this attitude was on the way out; it was roundly rejected by Page (1955, pp. 19-33).

3. In the present paper I focus on the erotic relationships that may be reflected in Sappho's poetry. I consider more fully elsewhere the question of the group to which she belonged and whether it was a *hetairia* of friends or a *thiasos* involved in the performance of religious rites—or both. See "Sappho's Company of Friends," forthcoming in *Women's Networks in the Ancient World*, ed. Judith Fletcher (University of Toronto Press).

4. On the notion of genetic homosexuality or heterosexuality as a modern idea, see, for example, Most (1995): "the very notion that people are either homosexual or heterosexual is a modern invention" (p. 27); Parker (2001): "Our own particular system divides people into two major classes on the basis of whether they have sex with others of the same sex or not. . . . This is a surprisingly rare system anywhere in the world and a comparatively recent development in the West" (pp. 313-314).

5. Yatromanolakis (2001) suggests that the depictions of Sappho and another female figure on the Bochum vase of ca. 480 BCE may be our earliest evidence for Sappho as a pursuer of female companions (p. 168).

6. P. Oxy. 1800 fr. 1, in Testimonia 1 (Campbell, 1982a).

7. According to Athenaeus (13.599c), Chamaeleon says some people thought these lines were addressed to Sappho–a most unlikely identification for the girl in the fancy sandals. Sappho's reputation as a "woman-lover," widely referred to by Athenaeus' time (ca. 200 CE), might be what prompted people in Chamaeleon's era to make this connection.

8. Menander is quoted by Strabo in his *Geography* (10.2.9). See Testimonia 23 (Campbell, 1982a). Athenaeus refers to plays about Sappho by Antiphanes and Diphilus (Athenaeus 10.450e, 11.487a). See Testimonia 25, 26. Campbell also notes several other lost comedies which may have treated the Sappho-Phaon story.

9. Dover (1978) comments that female homosexuality seems to have been a taboo subject in Attic art, and infers that, in comparison with earlier Lesbos, "an important variation between regions and periods becomes apparent." He refers to "the growth of inhibition and sexual respectability in the fourth and third centuries BC[E]" (p. 182 and n. 33). Hubbard (2003) finds a "growing moral problematization of pederasty" in the late fifth to early fourth centuries, and notes that male authors from the Hellenistic through the Roman period are extremely hostile to female homoeroticism (pp. 15, 17, resp.). However, Rabinowitz (2002) traces in Attic art a widespread depiction of female homoeroticism, broadly defined as "those looks and touches that seem to point to intimacy" (p. 112).

10. See Testimonia 17 and 34.

11. *Homosexuality in Greece and Rome* (a sourcebook of extracts in translation). In his Introduction, Hubbard questions the view of "the active/passive polarity as fundamental to the significance of pederasty as a social institution," and of boys as "passive 'victims' of penetration . . . parallel to women, slaves, and foreigners" (p. 12).

12. The *agelai*, "bands," in which Cretan and Spartan boys were trained under the mentorship of older youths who might become their lovers are described by Ephorus (fourth century BCE, quoted in Strabo 10.4.16 and 20) and Plutarch (*Lycurgus* 16-17).

13. He states that "The educational asymmetry of the love relationship between adolescent and adult is fundamental for both genders" (1999, p. 100), and that Greek homosexuality was always a *maître-élève* relationship (1977, Vol. 1, p. 439). Calame's theories, and the somewhat similar theories of Gentili about the function of women's groups (1976; 1988, pp. 72-89; and other publications), are adopted by Cantarella (1992) in her account of female homosexuality (pp. 78-88). Zaidman (1992) also relies on Calame (pp. 346-349).

14. The word τείρει has an established association with the power of love. Calame gives a long list of examples (1977, Vol. 2, p. 89, n. 2). See also Page (1951): "There is no doubt that . . . [the papyrus] has τείρει (not τηρει) ... I do not understand it, unless Ἀγησιχόρα με τείρει is equivalent to ἔρως Ἀγησιχόρας με τείρει" (p. 91). Calame (1983) notes that most editors print τηρεῖ ("takes care of," "preserves") (pp. 339-340). Campbell's (1982b) "τείρει makes no sense" (p. 209) takes no account of the erotic potential.

15. See Stehle (1997, pp. 93, 272-273, resp.); also Ingalls (2000, pp. 10-11).

16. For example, Blundell (1995, pp. 87-89); Greene (1996a, p. 235 n. 7; 1996b, p. 4; 1999, p. 14; 2002, p. 89); Rabinowitz (2002, p. 17); Skinner (1993, p. 133); Stehle (1997, pp. 270, 278); Williamson (1995, p. 123); Wilson (1996, pp. 121, 200). However, Page duBois (1995), who describes herself as "a Marxist historicist feminist classicist" explicitly takes issue with this position and believes that Sappho does indeed seek domination in love (pp. 147, 9, resp.).

17. Anne Carson has argued that the object of pursuit will be someone other than Sappho: her beloved will simply grow older and adopt the role of *erastēs*, the pursuer, instead of *erōmenos*, the pursued (Carson [Giacomelli], 1980, pp. 138-139).

18. The manuscripts are rather garbled at this point. See apparatus in Lobel-Page, Voigt.

19. "The isles of Greece, the isles of Greece / Where burning Sappho loved and sung" (line 2; title from line 1).

20. Burnett (1983) finds the line "wholly irreconcilable with the tranquil tone that the Sappho-lover uses in the anecdote" (p. 293). Lardinois (2001) attributes it to Sappho. He also thinks the mention of "soft beds is more likely to refer to taking a nap than to sexual gratification" (p. 86 and n. 51).

21. Wilson (1996) raises the possibility that "the erotic emotion expressed within Sappho's songs/circle had pluralistic dimensions" (p. 117).

22. Page attributes the poem to Sappho, Voigt to Alcaeus (Fr. 303A).

23. In the preceding line of this couplet, Eros is "limb-loosening," λυσιμέλης, like desire in Alcman 3.61, mentioned above.

24. Hallett (1979) believes "Sappho should not be read merely as a confessional poet" (p. 150); Wilson (1996) doubts that her representation of homoerotic relationships should be taken biographically (p. 83). Stehle (1997) argues that Sappho's supposedly personal poems take advantage of writing to create "a fictional 'I'" (p. 310).

25. On Sappho's use of this word, see Hallett (1982).

26. Wilamowitz (1913) uses emphatic language to describe her love poetry: "Die erotische Poesie der Sappho," "der Inhalt von Sapphos leidenshaftlicher, sehnsüchtiger Begierde" (pp. 74, 47, resp.). See also Devereux (1970).

27. Foxhall (1998) notes that in early Greece girls were married shortly after puberty, at 12 to 14, and became fully adult when their babies started to arrive, at 15 or 16 (p. 125). In Xenophon's *Oeconomicus* 7.5, the bride has not yet reached 15. In the youthful Demosthenes' orations against Aphobus, marriageable age for Demosthenes' sister is 15; see Demosthenes 27.4 and 29.43.

28. Compare Rabinowitz (2002): "I wonder whether Greek women might not have enjoyed ... a seamless continuum between homosocial and homosexual bonds" (p. 162 n. 95).

29 See note 4, above.

30. Compare Hallett's (1979) comment that past efforts to discredit belief in Sappho's physical homoeroticism were inspired by "revulsion at female homosexuality" (p. 451).

REFERENCES

Blundell, Sue. (1995). *Women in Ancient Greece.* Cambridge, MA: Harvard UP.

Burnett, Anne Pippin. (1979). Desire and Memory. *Classical Philology, 74,* 16-27.

_____. (1983). *Three Archaic Poets: Archilochus, Alcaeus, Sappho.* Cambridge, MA: Harvard UP.

Calame, Claude. (1977). *Les choeurs de jeunes filles en Grèce archaïque* (2 vols.). Rome: Ateneo.

_____. (1983). *Alcman.* Rome: Ateneo.

_____. (1996). Sappho's Group: An Initiation into Womanhood. In Greene (Ed.), *Reading Sappho* (pp. 113-124).

_____. (1997). *Choruses of Young Women in Ancient Greece.* (D. Collins and J. Orion, Trans.). Lanham, MD: Rowman and Littlefield. From *Choeurs de jeunes filles,* with updated bibliography.

_____. (1999). *The Poetics of Eros in Ancient Greece.* (J. Lloyd, Trans.). Princeton: Princeton UP. From *I Greci e l'eros: Simboli, pratiche e luoghi* (Rome: Laterza, 1992).

Campbell, David A. (Ed. and Trans.). (1982a). *Greek Lyric: Volume I. Sappho and Alcaeus.* Loeb. Cambridge, MA: Harvard UP.

_____. (1982b). *Greek Lyric Poetry* (2nd ed.). Bristol: Bristol Classical Press.

Cantarella, Eva. (1992). *Bisexuality in the Ancient World.* New Haven: Yale UP.

Carson, Anne. 1980. The Justice of Aphrodite in Sappho Fr. 1. *Transactions of the American Philological Association, 110,* 135-142. (Published under the name Anne Giacomelli)

Devereux, George. (1970). The Nature of Sappho's Seizure in fr. 31 LP as Evidence of Her Inversion. *The Classical Quarterly, 20,* 17-31.

Dover, Kenneth. (1978). *Greek Homosexuality.* London: Duckworth.

duBois, Page. (1995). *Sappho is Burning.* Chicago: U of Chicago P.

Foxhall, Lin. (1998). Pandora Unbound: A Feminist Critique of Foucault's *History of Sexuality.* In David H.J. Larmour, Paul Allen Miller, and Charles Platter (Eds.), *Rethinking Sexuality: Foucault and Classical Antiquity* (pp. 122-137). Princeton: Princeton UP.

Gentili, Bruno. (1976). Il Partenio di Alcmane e l'amore omoerotico femminile nei tiasi spartani. *Quaderni urbinati di cultura classica, 22,* 59-67.

_____. (1988). *Poetry and Its Public in Ancient Greece.* (A. T. Cole, Trans.). Baltimore: Johns Hopkins UP. From *Poesia e pubblico nella Grecia antica* (Rome: Laterza, 1985).

Giacomelli, Anne. See Carson.

Greene, Ellen. (1996a). Apostrophe and Women's Erotics in the Poetry of Sappho. In Greene (Ed.), *Reading Sappho: Contemporary Approaches* (pp. 233-247). Berkeley: U of California P. Repr. with modifications from *Transactions of the American Philological Association, 124* (1994), 41-56.

_____. (1996b). Sappho, Foucault, and Women's Erotics. *Arethusa, 29,* 1-14.

_____. (1999). Refiguring the Feminine Voice: Catullus Translating Sappho. *Arethusa, 32,* 1-18.

_____. (2002). Subjects, Objects, and Erotic Symmetry in Sappho's Fragments. In Rabinowitz and Auanger (Eds.), *Among Women: From the Homosocial to the Homoerotic in the Ancient World* (pp. 82-105). Austin: U of Texas P.

Hallett, Judith P. (1979). Sappho and Her Social Context: Sense and Sensuality. *Signs, 4,* 447-64.

_____. Beloved Cleis. (1982). *Quaderni urbinati di cultura classica, 10,* 21-31.

Halperin, David M. (1990). *One Hundred Years of Homosexuality and Other Essays on Greek Love.* New York: Routledge.

Hubbard, Thomas K. (Ed.). (2003). *Homosexuality in Greece and Rome: A Sourcebook of Basic Documents.* Berkeley: U of California P.

Ingalls, Wayne. (2000). Ritual Performance as Training for Daughters in Archaic Greece. *Phoenix, 54,* 1-20.

Lardinois, André. (1994). Subject and Circumstance in Sappho's Poetry. *Transactions of the American Philological Association, 124,* 57-84.

_____. (2001). Keening Sappho: Female Speech Genres in Sappho's Poetry. In André Lardinois and Laura McClure (Eds.), *Making Silence Speak* (pp. 75-92). Princeton: Princeton UP.

Lobel, Edgar, and Page, Denys (Eds.). (1955). *Poetarum Lesbiorum Fragmenta.* Oxford: Clarendon, 1955.

Most, Glenn W. (1995). Reflecting Sappho. *Bulletin of the Institute for Classical Studies, 40,* 15-38.

Page, Denys. (1951). *Alcman: The Partheneion.* Oxford: Clarendon.

_____. (1955). *Sappho and Alcaeus.* Oxford: Clarendon.

Parker, Holt N. (1993). Sappho Schoolmistress. *Transactions of the American Philological Association, 123,* 309-351.

_____. (2001). The Myth of the Heterosexual: Anthropology and Sexuality for Classicists. *Arethusa, 34,* 313-362.

Rabinowitz, Nancy Sorkin. (2002). Excavating Women's Homoeroticism in Ancient Greece: The Evidence from Attic Vase Painting. In Rabinowitz and Lisa Auanger (Eds.), *Among Women: From the Homosocial to the Homoerotic in the Ancient World* (pp. 105-166). Austin: U of Texas P.

Skinner, Marilyn B. (1993). Woman and Language in Archaic Greece, or, Why is Sappho a Woman. In Nancy Sorkin Rabinowitz and Amy Richlin (Eds.), *Feminist Theory and the Classics* (pp. 125-144). New York: Routledge.

Stehle, Eva. (1997). *Performance and Gender in Ancient Greece.* Princeton: Princeton UP.

Voigt, Eva-Maria (Ed.). (1971). *Sappho et Alcaeus: Fragmenta.* Amsterdam: Polak & Van Gennep.

Welcker, Friedrich Gottlieb. (1816). Sappho von einem herrschenden Vorurteil befreyt. In *Kleine Schriften, zweyter Theil* (pp. 86-144). Bonn: Weber, 1845.

Wilamowitz-Moellendorff, Ulrich von. (1913). *Sappho und Simonides: Untersuchungen über griechische Lyriker.* Berlin: Weidmann.

Williamson, Margaret. (1995). *Sappho's Immortal Daughters.* Cambridge, MA: Harvard UP.

Wilson, Lyn Hatherly. (1996). *Sappho's Sweetbitter Songs.* London: Routledge.

Yatromanolakis, Dimitrios. (2001). Visualizing Poetry: An Early Representation. *Classical Philology, 96,* 159-168.

Zaidman, Louise Bruit. (1992). Pandora's Daughters and Rituals in Grecian Cities. In Pauline Schmitt Pantel (Ed.), *From Ancient Goddesses to Christian Saints: Volume I. A History of Women in the West* (5 vols., A. Goldhammer, Trans.) (pp. 338-376 and 522-523). Cambridge, MA: Belknap Press of Harvard UP.

Some Myths and Anomalies
in the Study of Roman Sexuality

James L. Butrica, PhD

Memorial University

SUMMARY. This paper seeks to dispel several myths prevalent in the scholarship on Roman sexuality: that a freed slave was still obligated to serve his former master's sexual demands (I.A.), that the *cinaedus* cannot be the same as the modern male homosexual because the *cinaedus* was thought capable of performing cunnilinctus (I.B.), that *exoleti* were male prostitutes (I.C.), that the Romans were implacably hostile to lesbianism and that they "constructed" the lesbian as a phallic monstrosity (II.).

It also draws attention to some neglected, unfamiliar, or misinterpreted evidence–anomalous on the current understanding of Roman sexuality, where women, boys, and lower-class men are supposed to have equal standing as potential passive sexual partners for adult men–for adult men whose sexual partners are exclusively male, and either active or passive: *exoleti* as active partners (I.C.), a *puer delicatus* who is prized for a masculine appearance rather than a feminine one (I.D.),

---

James L. Butrica is Professor of Classics at Memorial University, St. John's, Newfoundland, Canada. Correspondence may be addressed: Department of Classics, Memorial University, St. John's, NL, A1C 5S7, Canada (E-mail: jbutrica@mun.ca).

[Haworth co-indexing entry note]: "Some Myths and Anomalies in the Study of Roman Sexuality." Butrica, James L. Co-published simultaneously in *Journal of Homosexuality* (Harrington Park Press, an imprint of The Haworth Press, Inc.) Vol. 49, No. 3/4, 2005, pp. 209-269; and: *Same-Sex Desire and Love in Greco-Roman Antiquity and in the Classical Tradition of the West* (ed: Beert C. Verstraete, and Vernon Provencal) Harrington Park Press, an imprint of The Haworth Press, Inc., 2005, pp. 209-269. Single or multiple copies of this article are available for a fee from The Haworth Document Delivery Service [1-800-HAWORTH, 9:00 a.m. - 5:00 p.m. (EST). E-mail address: docdelivery@haworthpress.com].

doi:10.1300/J082v49n03_08

and the Warren Cup, which glorifies a world of exclusively male-male sexuality (I.E.). *[Article copies available for a fee from The Haworth Document Delivery Service: 1-800-HAWORTH. E-mail address: <docdelivery@haworthpress. com> Website: <http://www.HaworthPress.com> © 2005 by The Haworth Press, Inc. All rights reserved.]*

KEYWORDS. Rome, Roman Empire, homosexuality, slavery, lesbianism, pedophilia, the Warren Cup

I. SEX BETWEEN MALES

A. Quintus Haterius and the Freedman's "Duty"

The first myth that will be addressed arises from the world of Roman slavery: that a male slave, even after the granting of his freedom ("manumission"), still had a "duty" to acquiesce to his former master's sexual advances. This proves to be only a rhetorician's unlucky flight of fancy, though it is universally cited as truth; see, for example, Dalla (1987, p. 48) (on homosexuality and the law); Fabre (1981, p. 213, n. 414) (on Roman freedmen); and Cantarella (1988), Williams (1999), and Hubbard (2003) (all on Roman homosexuality). For an example of its influence, compare the recent statement of Fredrick (2002a) to the effect that "freedmen clearly remain penetrable, subject to sexual advances and even physical assault by their former owners" (p. 242).

At issue is a statement made by the Augustan orator Quintus Haterius. He was defending a client who was a *libertus*, or freedman (a slave who had been manumitted), and was being attacked in court by the advocate for the other side for having been the *concubinus* (lit. "bedmate") of his former owner (*patronus*). According to Seneca the Elder (*Controversiae* 4.10), Haterius said that *impudicitia*–literally "shamelessness," "immodesty," but here evidently used as a euphemism for being an object of buggery–was a *crimen* in a freeborn man ("reproach" or "crime"), a *necessitas* in a slave ("necessity"), and an *officium* in a freedman ("obligation," but always translated "duty" in discussions of this passage). Hence the "rule" that a freedman, who certainly owed his *patronus* various forms of respect or service, also had a "duty" to accede to his sexual demands.

In a discussion of the "Indigenous characteristics of Roman homosexuality," Cantarella (1988) apparently assumes that this statement was uncontroversial and reveals the existence of a genuine "duty" (p. 131):

> *Scrive Seneca, nelle Controversie, che un liberto . . . , criticato per avere una relazione con il suo ex padrone, fu cosí difeso dal suo avvocato: La passività sessuale . . . per un uomo libero è un crimine, per lo schiavo una necessità, per un liberto un dovere. Neppure se era stato liberato, dunque, il liberto poteva sottrarsi al «servizio sessuale»: pur non essendo piú costretto a farlo, era tuttavia moralmente tenuto a lasciarsi sottomettere dall'ex padrone.*

> (Seneca writes in the *Controversiae* that a freedman . . . , criticized for having a relationship with his former master, was thus defended by his lawyer: Sexual passivity . . . is a crime for a free man, a necessity for the slave, a duty for a freedman. Not even if he had been freed, then, could the freedman escape 'sexual service': though no longer constrained to do it, he was still morally bound to let himself be subjugated by his ex-master.)

Williams (1999) first cites the passage when discussing the sexual roles of slaves (p. 31):

> The Augustan orator Haterius, defending a client in court, used as a mainstay of his defense the apparently axiomatic principle that the loss of one's sexual integrity (*impudicitia*), while a matter of 'reproach' for the freeborn and a matter of 'duty' for freedmen, is a matter of 'necessity' for slaves.

Again compliance is a matter of "duty"; but the reader can easily be forgiven for wondering exactly what the charge against this client could have been if admitting *impudicitia* provided the "mainstay" of a defense against it.

The likelihood that this was an "apparently axiomatic principle" seems to be weakened when Williams returns to Haterius on page 100, in a similar context but with more detail from Seneca:

> The Augustan orator Haterius, defending a freedman who was said to have been his patron's concubine, was able to argue that a freedman's duty to his patron might well include sexual services. . . . Haterius' use of *officium* in this sense became infamous: people

jokingly used the noun to refer to sexual services. . . . Both
Haterius' argument and the jokes it inspired all derive from the
generally unchallenged assumption that a Roman man's sexual
dominion over his slaves of both sexes might legitimately continue even after he freed them.

Again no charge is mentioned, unless "was said to have been" is supposed to represent it. This time Haterius' statement leads to the formulation of a "generally unchallenged assumption" (cf. also "was able to
argue," which implies some sort of agreement in his audience), but this
seems to be undermined by the "jokes" to which it led, and by note 21 on
the same page, which offers a further puzzling bit from the Senecan
context by asserting that "Seneca . . . cites Haterius' formulation as an
example of his unfortunate tendency to come up with expressions that
were liable to ridicule." How does the enunciation of an "axiomatic
principle" become an expression "liable to ridicule"? How can an expression "liable to ridicule" represent an "axiomatic principle"?

Most recently, Hubbard (2003, p. 389) presents part of the Senecan
passage as document 9.3, introduced with, "The following is used to illustrate how easily a brilliant and epigrammatic locution can be made to
sound ridiculous," but that is not what Seneca says. The full context is
lacking, and what is offered begins with a potentially misleading translation: "When Haterius was defending a freedman accused of being his
patron's male concubine. . . ." This is certainly wrong in its rendering of
the Latin tenses (*obiciebatur*, *fuisset*), which imply that the freedman
was no longer a *concubinus* at the time of the court case; and it is also
wrong if "accused" is supposed to represent the content of the charge on
which the freedman was tried–to be or to have been a *concubinus* was at
worst an embarrassment, never a crime. *Concubinus* may not even have
been a category recognized in Roman law, unlike its feminine equivalent *concubina*, given that the *Digest* is full of comment on the latter but
says nothing at all about the former.

This discussion will pursue three neglected lines of inquiry: what legal sources recognize as being owed by a *libertus* to a *patronus*;
Haterius' reputation, and the specific aspect of his style that Seneca illustrated by citing this remark; and other examples of the sexual use of
officium.

As to the first, it seems unlikely that *officium* was ever used formally
of a specific obligation owed by a *libertus* to his *patronus*, and extremely unlikely that such obligations included sexual acquiescence.
Though we lack the texts of the laws (if any) that regulated such obliga-

tions, we can form a fair impression of Roman legal traditions in this area from the *Digest*. The three sections most immediately relevant are the last two of Book 37, namely 14, *De iure patronatus* ("On the law of patronage") and 15, *De obsequiis parentibus et patronis praestandis* ("On the respect to be shown to parents and *patroni*"), and the first of Book 38, *De operis libertorum* ("On the works of freedmen"). As these Latin titles suggest, a freedman was expected to provide two things to his *patronus* (besides a general, nonspecific *honos* or "respect"; cf. 38.2.1), namely *obsequium* and *operae*. At no point does either of these words have a sexual reference, and at no point are sexual services mentioned. *Obsequium* is little discussed apart from 37.15, probably because it was essentially a matter of showing respect and therefore did not entail financial transactions subject to Roman law (cf. Ulpian, quoted at 37.15.7.9 as saying that "To a freedman and to a son the person of a father and of a *patronus* ought to seem honourable and sacred"). While it also barred the freedman from certain kinds of legal action against his *patronus*, *obsequium* would largely have been a matter of performing any attendance required by the Roman institution of *clientela* (this would have been much the same for a freedman as for a free client of the same financial standing). Much more attention is devoted to the *operae*, no doubt because financial transactions could be involved. While it was possible for a freedman and his *patronus* to agree that no work would be required, an expectation of *operae* seems to have been more common, generally day-labour of a sort that the freedman had performed while still a slave; a freedman might arrange to make cash payments instead, and the *operae* due to a *patronus* could actually be inherited by his heirs. (For these obligations and for *operae* in general, see Fabre (1981, pp. 317-30).) Two passages (38.1.6; 38.1.9.1–the latter is corrupt, but there is no significant doubt about the meaning) distinguish two categories of *operae*: *fabriles* ("of a workman") and *officiales* ("pertaining to duty/obligation"). These *operae* are never called *officia*, though performing them is of course an obligation (cf. 12.6.26.12).

The likelihood that sexual services were recognized as a normal part of the freedman's obligations to his *patronus* is diminished significantly by two more passages that concern what could properly be demanded of him. It appears from 38.1.7 that a freedman might swear an oath regarding the provision of *operae*, and Ulpian (who is quoted there) suggests that the oath should specify "whatever kinds of *operae* are imposed honourably, legally, and licitly" (*probe iure licito*). For a free Roman citizen (as the *libertus* was upon manumission), being buggered is not something that could be imposed honourably (*probe*)–or legally, for that matter, if the Lex Scantinia applied to other than freeborn citizens. (The Lex Scantinia is an obscure law dating to the Roman Republic which somehow regulated sexual relations between free men; our evidence suggests that it was seldom invoked, except to harass political opponents, until the only serious prosecutions, under Domitian at the end of the 1st century CE: for some necessarily inconclusive discussions, see Cantarella (1988, pp. 141-52), Williams (1999, pp. 119-24). Legal opinion regarded the *libertus* as a free man; in the *Institutiones* of Gaius, for example, citizens are divided into free and slave, with the former further divided into those freed and those born free (1.9-10).) At 38.1.38 Callistratus is quoted to the effect that the *operae* that are understood to be imposed are those that can be performed "without disgrace" and without mortal danger (*hae demum impositae operae intelleguntur quae sine turpitudine praestari possunt et sine periculo uitae*); thus a freedman cannot be required to fight as a gladiator, nor a freedwoman to work as a prostitute (cf. also 37.14.7.1, showing that such opinions can be traced back as far as Tiberius and are not an innovation under the Severan emperors, as suggested by Dalla (1987, p. 48)). Again, submission to buggery would not be "without disgrace" in a Roman citizen. One imagines that a *patronus* and *libertus* who had enjoyed a sexual relationship before manumission might work out an arrangement to continue, but there is not a trace of evidence in the legal tradition to suggest that one could be required by the *patronus* or that there existed a "duty" to submit. (For the possible role of homosexuality in relations between *patronus* and freedman, see Fabre (1981, pp. 258-61), and for a probably fictitious case of a man who makes his freedman and, it is implied, former lover his sole heir, see Juvenal, *Satire* 2.58-9, "It's notorious why Hister filled his testament with his freedman alone.")

We have a revealing converse situation in the story of how bond-slavery is supposed to have been banned. Originally, a free Roman citizen could settle debts by becoming a bond-slave of his creditor; but according to both Livy (8.28) and Valerius Maximus (6.1.9), the institution was eliminated when a man who had bound himself by debt to another was subjected to the sexual advances of his "owner" and even whipped for his refusal to provide what could be demanded from a slave. (Livy identifies debtor and owner as Gaius Publilius and Lucius Papirius, Valerius as Titus Veturius and Publius Plotius; for the episode cf. Fantham (1991, p. 278).) This shows clearly that a citizen who became a slave under these circumstances was thought to retain the right (and no doubt the responsibility as well) to resist demands for the sexual services that could be required in a slave. One would anticipate, then, that a slave, on becoming a citizen, would be expected to acquire and to maintain the inviolable status of the citizen, regardless of any former status as a *concubinus*, and perhaps even more so, if he wished to avoid scandal, precisely because of that background. Indeed, his worthiness to be a citizen might be questioned by some because of his status as a penetrated male–we can see from Dionysius of Halicarnassus, *Roman Antiquities* 4.24.4, for example, that some objected to slaves buying their freedom with money earned "from prostitution and any other disgraceful means," and one can easily imagine a *concubinus* freed in recognition of past sexual services being assimilated to such a category.

Next we turn to Haterius himself, and what Seneca was trying to convey about him; this requires that we put him into two contexts, the historical and the literary.

By combining notices in the historian Tacitus (who puts his death in the year that we call 26 CE) and Jerome (who reports from Eusebius that he was nearly ninety at the time) we can put Haterius' birth in the range 64-62 BCE; for a part of 5 BCE he served as one of Rome's two chief magistrates, having been appointed a *consul suffectus* ("substitute consul") by Augustus. His reputation was well established in his own day but (as Tacitus noted) did not last long beyond it. Seneca the Younger (nephew of Seneca the Elder) discusses him briefly at *Epistulae morales* 40.10. The text is unfortunately corrupt, but Seneca was clearly contrasting two very different orators, Publius Vinicius, who plucked his words one by one as if dictating rather than talking, and Haterius, whose style he characterizes as *cursus*, or "running"; Seneca says that he wants a "sane man" to have nothing to do with Haterius' manner, for he "never hesitated, never left off, would begin only once, would stop only once." That impetuous, unhesitant forward rush was noticed by the emperor Augustus, who is quoted approvingly by Seneca the Elder as saying that *Haterius noster sufflaminandus est*, "Our friend Haterius needs to have a brake applied." In his obituary notice at *Annals* 4.61, Tacitus says that Haterius *impetu magis quam cura uigebat*, that is, excelled in his forward drive–*impetus* is here a synonym of *cursus*–rather than any careful attention to detail, and sums up his distinctive characteristic as *canorum illud et profluens*, "that sonorousness and volubility," where *profluens* (lit. "flowing forth") again suggests his sheer momentum. Seneca the Elder, quoting him at *Controversiae* 1.6.12, likewise refers to "the usual *cursus* of his oratory" (*quo solebat cursu orationis*). At *Suasoriae* 3.7, Seneca relates an anecdote in which Haterius is one of several orators described by Gallio as *plena deo*, "full of the god" (but with a feminine form of the adjective "full," generally taken as an allusion to Virgil's description of the inspired Sybil of Cumae in Book 6 of his *Aeneid*, though Virgil does not use the actual phrase). Thus, even without the specific reference in Seneca the Elder that is being discussed here, an image emerges of an orator easily carried away and lacking a sense of just when to stop.

While Seneca was as happy to recall Haterius' faults as those of any other orator (and the statement about the former *concubinus* is quoted as an example of a fault), he clearly did not regard Haterius as a figure to be despised. The comment about *officium* is preserved in the *Controversiae*, a sort of history of Roman declamation based on Seneca's own recollections. Declamation was a form of rhetorical exercise that involved arguing on either or even both sides of a case, usually one not from the actual world of the Roman legal system but rather involving an artificial "law" (though sometimes resembling one known to have existed) and an often convoluted series of events, the better to encourage virtuosity in argumentation. Each book of the *Controversiae* that survives complete begins with a preface concentrating on one or two famous declaimers, then continues with examples of how they and many others active in Seneca's youth exercised this art; the *Suasoriae* presents the same orators in a different kind of rhetorical exercise, where the object was to urge or dissuade some celebrated person regarding a particular course of action. Seneca's general respect for Haterius is apparent in the fact that, in these two works combined, he quotes his "spin" on a given point on more than a dozen occasions and with multiple examples; but general respect does not preclude criticism of indisputable faults, most obviously that notorious *cursus*.

The preface to *Controversiae* 4 presents Haterius matched with Asinius Pollio like a pair of gladiators. Seneca deals with Pollio first, then effects his transition by contrasting their reactions to the death of a son (Pollio was declaiming within three days of the decease, while Haterius could not bear to recall it even in old age), and then notes that Haterius allowed spectators at his extemporizations while Pollio did not. Now Seneca begins his one extended treatment of Haterius as an orator, largely an enumeration of weaknesses. First of all, he was the only Roman known to Seneca able to equal the Greeks in facility in extemporization, though his speed of delivery was so great as to be a fault (obviously this is the *cursus* and *impetus* noted by others; Seneca says here that he did not so much *currere* ["run"] as *decurrere* ["run downward"]), and he was so good at saying the same thing again and again in different words that he needed a freedman to tell him when to dwell, when to move on, when to begin his epilogue; because of his *impetus*, there was a lack of clear logical division in his speeches; and not even his *cursus* could hide (i.e., keep people from noticing) the fact–significant for the Haterius anecdote–that he used words that had been employed by Cicero but were currently being avoided because they had acquired a shade of indecency in their connotations. After the anecdote at issue here, he concludes with a few final words of admiration, but not before offering another example of unintended indecency that became an object of jokes (*at . . . inter pueriles condiscipulorum sinus lasciua manu obscena iussisti*, "but amid the boyish laps of your fellow-pupils you gave obscene commands with naughty hand"). (For a recent discussion of Seneca's representation of Haterius' oratory see Gunderson (2003, pp. 97-101, 234-6).)

Now the controversial statement, as introduced by Seneca, who has just mentioned Haterius' propensity (no doubt connected with his age) for "off-colour" vocabulary:

> *Hoc exempto nemo erat scholasticis nec aptior nec similior, sed dum nihil uult nisi culte, nisi splendide dicere, saepe incidebat in ea quae derisum effugere non possent. Memini illum, cum libertinum reum defenderet, cui obiciebatur quod patroni concubinus fuisset, dixisse: impudicitia in ingenuo crimen est, in seruo necessitas, in liberto officium. Res in iocos abiit: 'non facis mihi officium' et 'multum ille huic in officiis uersatur.' Ex eo impudici et obsceni aliquamdiu officiosi uocitati sunt.*

With the exception of this [i.e., his choice of inappropriate vocabulary], no one was either fitter for the schoolmen or more like them, but in his wish to speak only elegantly, only impressively, he would often fall into the sort of thing that could not escape mockery. I recall that, when he was defending a freedman who was being criticized for having been his patron's *concubinus*, he said: "Immodesty is a reproach in the freeborn, a necessity in the slave, an obligation in the freedman." This became a source of jokes: "You're not performing your obligation to me," and "He's spending a lot of time with his obligations to him." For a while, immodest and obscene persons were frequently called "obliging" as a result. (4.10)

Before dealing with the comment per se, let us first clarify the circumstances of the court case insofar as possible. Seneca does not state the charge brought against Haterius' client; his status as *concubinus* was only something cast up at him, no doubt repeatedly (to judge by the tense of *obiciebatur*), as a reproach against his character–defamation through innuendo was of course a common strategy in the Roman legal world for increasing the likelihood of an accusation. As to the circumstances of the concubinage, the tense of *fuisset* ("he had been") implies that Haterius' client was no longer a *concubinus* at the time of the case; this might well be because the *patronus* had died (he is virtually certain to have been the older partner). While Haterius' client had perhaps been exclusively the adult lover of his *patronus* (for *concubinus* in the sense of "(adult) male lover," whether of a man or of a woman, see Martial 6.22.1, 6.39.13; Quintilian 1.2.8; [Quintilian] *Declamationes maiores* 3.6), it seems more natural to suppose that the client had been the kind of *concubinus* mentioned most prominently in Catullus 61, the wedding song for Junia and Manlius, where the term is used repeatedly in reference to a slave-boy who was in some sense the lover of his master (123, 125, 128, 130, 133). Though Catullus implies that such relationships ended upon the master's marriage (cf. esp. 61.123 *desertum domini audiens / concubinus amorem*, "the *concubinus*, hearing that his master's love has been abandoned"), it may be that an unusual continuation of such a relationship was being used to discredit Haterius' client. Against this stands the observation that it would be illogical to say that "immodesty" was an obligation in a freedman if the client was not a freedman when the "immodesty" occurred–an incongruity perhaps not entirely impossible in someone who *impetu magis quam cura uigebat*, as Tacitus said. All the same, the likeliest suggestion is perhaps that, while a sexual relationship of this kind had begun while the client was still a boy, it had continued into his adulthood and after his manumission. Certainly there are other cases of such relationships; for one, see [anon.] *Bellum Hispaniense* 4.33, where the rebel Scapula is assisted in his suicide by a *libertus* who had been his *concubinus*.

However the client had been a *concubinus*, Haterius naturally wanted to counteract the bad image being crafted by the advocate for the other side. Presumably the facts of the relationship were too well known for denial (and may not have been a source of shame to the participants); hence, for the sake of his client's reputation and even more for the success of his case, he needed to take something that was being presented as negative and turn it around into something positive, and the mockery resulted from the way he put this strategy into effect while also trying to create a striking effect, in his usual manner. His comment was not "made to sound ridiculous"; it was inherently ridiculous, an accident caused by his striving for effect, no doubt abetted by his tendency to run on unchecked–we must not forget, after all, that Haterius was improvising here, not composing in advance. In this case, his desire to speak "only elegantly, only impressively" expressed itself in the creation of a tricolon, a highly favoured figure involving three parallel clauses. The availability of three social categories–slave, freedperson, and freeborn citizen–provided an enticing opportunity for the effect, but each needed a corresponding category of sexual relation; and while two readily suggested themselves–"necessity" in the slave, who cannot refuse the commands of master or mistress, and "reproach" in the free man, for whom sexual penetration by another is a disgrace (or even a matter of criminal prosecution, if the Lex Scantinia applied)–there seems to have been no explicit Roman tradition regarding the status of an ex-slave. To complete his tricolon, and to rescue his client's character, Haterius–all the while thinking "on his feet" and speaking with his customary rush–had to come up with something that didn't exist, not just a way to distinguish a freedman's sexual status from a free man's, but a formulation of the circumstances under which one free male might be penetrated honourably by another.

As we know from Seneca, the result struck contemporary Romans as ridiculous. The reason, however, probably has nothing to do with the simple application of the exalted and dignified concept of *officium*–think of Cicero's celebrated essay *De officiis*–to sex per se, since it is not unique to Haterius, though it does tend to occur in "light" contexts where at least an element of conscious humour is likely. (See, in general, Adams (1982, pp. 163-4).) The earliest extant occurrence is the only other application to the passive experience of anal intercourse: in Plautus' comedy *Cistellaria* (written during the first half of the 2nd century BCE) a slave comments that he "must do the slave-boy's duty" and bend over (657; here, of course, *officium* really does mean "duty," since the slave can only obey). *Officium* is used of a wife's supposed "duty" to have sex with her husband at Ovid, *Ars Amatoria* 2.687f., and at Ovid, *Amores* 1.10.46 it seems to be a matter of a woman's compliance with her lover. In three passages (Ovid, *Amores* 3.7.24; Propertius 2.24.24; Petronius, *Satyricon* 140) it is unquestionably used of the sexual act, but always in reference to active penetration (of a woman in Ovid and Propertius, of a man in Petronius) rather than acquiescence in penetration; hence we should probably not see any of these passages as reflecting the jokes that arose from Haterius' formulation (even though Haterius' reputation was still alive in Petronius' day [Petronius and Seneca the Younger both died under Nero], and even though we cannot exclude absolutely the influence of Haterius on Propertius and Ovid, since he was already in his 30s when they began to write). Here the idea is again "service," but specifically the poet's sexual "servicing" of his mistress. There is also an evidently euphemistic medical use attested in Theodorus Priscianus, *Euporista* 2.11 (34), where *uirile officium* means "male sexual functioning" (cf. also *usus uenerii officium* earlier in the same section).

Presumably, therefore, what made Haterius' use of *officium* so funny was not its simple association with sex but the specific sense that he attached to it as a sexual term. As noted earlier, it is generally translated "duty" in this anecdote, but we have already seen that the *Digest*, when discussing the obligations of *libertus* toward *patronus*, uses *officium* in a non-specific way of the duty of the *libertus* to perform *operae* but not of those specific duties. In addition, it would have been rhetorically ineffective here to use *officium* with the sense "duty" since that would be essentially a synonym of *necessitas*, leaving no distinction between the "duty" of a freedman and the "necessity" that had bound him while still a slave. For all these reasons, it seems more likely that *officium* here is not a *binding* obligation but a *voluntary* one, in effect a "courtesy" or "favour," hence my own choice of "obligation" in the translation above, which can convey a comparable ambiguity–compare *A Latin Dictionary* [*L&S*], s.v., introduction, "that which one does for another, *a service*, whether of free will or of (external or moral) necessity, I. A voluntary service, a kindness, favor, courtesy"; *The Oxford Latin Dictionary* [*OLD*], s.v. 1 "A helpful or beneficial act done to someone in fulfillment of an obligation, a service, friendly office, or sim." In other words, Haterius suggested that his client had been the sexual partner of his *patronus* not because, as his ex-slave, he had an absolute and compelling duty to do so–a duty for which no evidence exists, a duty which the *Digest* suggests could not have been demanded, a duty which would hardly have seemed ridiculous for Haterius to mention if it did exist–but because he regarded it as a favour or courtesy, to be done no doubt in recognition of the kindness shown in his manumission, thus making the "bad thing" a "good thing." According to Haterius, even though his client was no longer a slave and therefore no longer lacking in free choice, even though he was now free and was courting disgrace thereby, he had complied with the sexual advances of his *patronus*, not because he was some dirty *concubinus* or *cinaedus*: it was because he was a decent chap and this was the decent thing to do for the one to whom he owed his freedom. Thus the undignified disgrace of being a penetrated male received a thoroughly honourable dressing–or would have done, if people had been able to stifle their laughter.

Once the Haterius anecdote has been understood in its full rhetorical context, it becomes clear that the "axiomatic principle" with regard to freedmen that it supposedly attests never existed. The unique statement of it is quoted in a context which shows that it was only a case of "foot-in-mouth" from a man known for aiming high and missing, often in a way that proved suggestive. In this respect too the *libertus* was a citizen, entitled (and expected) to behave accordingly.

B. The Cinaedus and Cunnilinctus

It used to be commonplace to equate the Roman *cinaedus* with the modern male homosexual, but the identification is stoutly rejected by constructionist scholars, who like to present Roman sexuality not as something comprehensible to any modern Neapolitan or Sicilian–as it was for Housman in his "*Praefanda*"–but as an utterly alien landscape. Their ultimate proof–"the testing ground for whether *cinaedus* matches up with our concept of homosexual" (Parker, 1997, p. 52)–is another myth in the study of male same-sex relations, the rather exotic idea that the *cinaedus* was thought capable of performing cunnilinctus.

Williams (1999), who is as determined as Parker to dissociate the *cinaedus* from the homosexual, bases his own claim upon inconclusive or false evidence (pp. 109-203). For example, he builds (*inter alia*) upon the common misconception that *fellare* is somehow the same as *irrumari*, as if *irrumare* simply expressed fellatio from the point of view of the fellated (in fact they designate two different applications of the same body parts, one in which the man whose penis is involved is the active participant [*irrumare*], one in which he is the passive participant [*fellare*]; in the modern world, both might well occur during the same sexual encounter, but they could have been distinguished more carefully by the Romans, given the vital importance of penetration to their construction of sexuality). More specifically, he notes that "a variety of sources attribute to certain men a predilection both for cunnilinctus and for fellatio" (p. 200)–but in fact they do not, nor are the men that Williams adduces as examples even labeled *cinaedi*. Certainly the evidence is not well grounded in Roman society; Commodus is the only "real" person mentioned, the others being figures in epigrams. I will deal with the alleged evidence from Ausonius when discussing Parker (1997), since Williams relies more on Martial. In 11.45, a certain Cantharus is evidently anxious not to be seen by anyone at the brothel, whether he has sex with a boy or with a girl; Williams' claim that he performs oral sex on the prostitutes he hires (and is ashamed of performing oral sex on people of both sexes) is only an assumption–why should we not suppose that the prostitutes perform oral sex on him? Williams' "star" witness appears to be Martial's Zoilus, identified as a fellator in 3.82 and 11.30 and as a cunnilingus in 6.91 and 11.85, but (as will be shown in more detail in Essay II) Martial's targets are not real people, only literary constructs, and poems that use the same name only rarely concern the same person. In fact, Martial uses the name Zoilus in 13 other epigrams as well, and there is no reason to identify any one holder of this name with any other; Zoilus, like nearly everyone else in Martial, is simply whoever and whatever the poet needs him to be in a given context.

As to Parker (1997), his argument depends to a significant extent upon accepting the reality of the "teratogenic grid" that he constructs, but this reductivist Procrustean bed has no reality beyond his own imagination. Like any system that privileges penetration, it quickly fails when applied to oral sex, which was difficult for the Romans to conceptualize because in fellatio, at least, the penetrated partner is the active one and indeed penetrates himself with another man's penis. (It is also striking that the grid does not accommodate the term *tribas*, for which see Essay II.) One might be willing to concede that it has some validity if the results that it predicts theoretically–such as a *cinaedus* who performs oral sex on both men and women–could be shown to have been recognized in reality, but it fails this vital test. However vigorously Parker asserts that "Men who perform fellatio are expected to perform cunnilingus as well" (p. 52), he simply has no evidence. He claims that "the (orally) passive male is indifferent to the gender of the person who violates him" and seems to pretend that Ausonius, *Epigram* 78 proves his case, but his account of that poem, like many of his references to Latin literature, is more hysterical exaggeration than accurate summary: "raging oral lust" drives a fellator "to the perverted extremity of cunnilingus with his own wife" according to Parker, but according to Ausonius, "Castor, when he wanted to lick the members of men's middles and was unable to have a crowd at home, discovered how to waste no groin as fellator: he started to lick his wife's member"–a formulation, by the way, that clearly implies (through "discovered") that this situation is a novelty, not an everyday reality. In any case, I believe that cunnilinctus has nothing to do with this epigram; there is very little evidence for *membrum* in reference to the clitoris, and the poem is not very witty if this is what Ausonius means (note especially that *suae*, "his own

[wife]," must be part of the epigrammatic point, since it is saved for the last word as if to surprise or shock). Instead, the *membrum* that Castor begins to lick when he has no men available for fellatio is likely to be an artificial phallus that his wife uses for penetrative sex with other women (for the strap-on dildo see Essay II), and thus the real "joke" of the epigram is that Castor, the husband who fellates, has a wife who fucks. As to his other evidence, I have no idea at all what Parker is trying to convey when he says that in 11.61 Martial "attacks a man so passive that his mouth becomes a cunt for a cunt"; the poem is actually about a well-endowed man who normally inserts his tongue into women's vaginas in preference to intercourse but has gotten it infected, thus creating an opportunity for women at last to have vaginal intercourse with his substantial member instead of this odd form of oral sex.

If the Romans really had conceived the *cinaedus* as capable of performing oral sex on women, the idea would surely surface somewhere in the many references we have to *cinaedi*, and the only evidence to support the notion is the alleged implications of an imaginary grid. Of course the term is applied to men that we would not call homosexuals, such as Julius Caesar, but that is because it could be used abusively as well as literally (though never as a clinical diagnosis), not unlike English "faggot" (cf. the Dire Straits lyric about the "faggots on the MTV" who get "money for nothing and their chicks for free"–a pointless advantage for someone who is literally a "faggot").

C. The Exoleti

A particularly damaging myth in the study of male-male sexual relations is the now widespread belief that *exoleti* were male prostitutes, and more specifically "over-age male hustlers," as it is rendered in Hubbard (2003) in a passage of Cicero. The reality is that they were adult sexual partners of adult males, and the by-product of Roman pedophilia–survivors of childhood sexual abuse, in modern terms.

The elite Roman household could be a sexually charged place for male children, both free and slave, and not just because of the barracks-like conditions in which very young slaves can be presumed to have lived along with older ones and perhaps even adults, comparable to an orphanage or a private-school dormitory. In particular, a select few of these slaves, chosen for their looks and for their personality, went about the house naked apart from some jewelry, amusing owners and guests with their childish and sometimes forward chatter; such a boy was a *(puer) delicatus* or *deliciae*. In connection with the marriage of

Livia to the future Augustus, Cassius Dio (48.44) mentions "one of the prattling boys, such as the women keep about them for their amusement, naked as a rule" (trans. E. Cary), who made a "fresh" remark to Livia. Suetonius tells us that Augustus liked to play at children's games with small boys that he had "collected" as being "loveable for beauty and prattling," especially Moors and Syrians (*Augustus* 83), while Plutarch's biography of Marc Antony mentions "one of the boys the Romans call *delicia*" owned by Augustus, named Sarmentus (*Antony* 59). When Marc Antony himself bought a pair of alleged twins, "outstanding in beauty," who proved not to be twins in fact, they were no doubt intended for precisely such display (Pliny, *Natural History* 7.56). Dio also refers to "one of the naked prattling boys" (using the same adjective as at 48.44) in connection with Domitian (67.15.3). Still later, Herodian (1.17.3) mentions "a quite young child from the naked ones adorned with gold and expensive gems in which extravagant Romans always take joy," a favourite of the emperor Commodus, who called him Philocommodus ("Commodus-lover"). (For *deliciae* in general see especially Pomeroy (1992).) The terms *deliciae* and *delicati* associate such boys with the world of Roman luxury. The former (source of the English "delicious") suggests something that exists purely for pleasure, without practical use, the element of luxury residing presumably in the fact that the owner can afford to divert slaves from their proper function as workers to become "useless" instruments of pleasure and nothing else. The latter has more explicit connotations of refined taste and luxury; applied to adults, it conveys a meaning similar to the Greek *truphōntes* (translated "extravagant" in the passage of Herodian above), with a hint at least of decadence, though its application to the boys rather than to their owners is striking.

It appears from Catullus' wedding song for Junia and Manlius (61) that a Roman groom could at least be teased by being told that marriage would end his relationship with a boy *concubinus* (see Essay I.A), though it is not clear whether or to what extent the *deliciae* can be equated with these *concubini*; there need not have been an exact correspondence, but the nudity of the former seems actually designed to invite erotic attentions. (One wonders whether the function of this bachelor-*concubinus* relationship was perhaps to prepare the young Roman for exercising authority as a *paterfamilias* by assigning him at the earliest possible age a subordinate for whom he was responsible; modern parents might buy a pet.) In any case, such boys need to be distinguished from the category of the *pueri meritorii* (lit. "wage-earning boys"), who were apparently prostituted openly and earned fees for their owners. (Valerius Maximus 6.1.6 mentions one such boy, Atilius Philiscus, who became an excessively strict father and killed his own daughter over an extramarital liaison.)

But what happened when such slave-boys reached puberty? Pure pedophilia, after all, involves an inherent obsolescence, as the beloved matures beyond the possibility of sexual attractiveness. One can imagine a variety of scenarios, ranging from the reward of freedom and some hope of dignity, to a continuing relationship, to simple, heartless discarding. The evidence, such as it is, suggests that all of these scenarios did indeed occur. Some boys became freedmen, and even of these some continued to have sexual relations with their masters (Haterius' client being an example, of course); but many, it seems, were relegated to the status of human wallpaper. Unfortunately, the last may have been the most common, with the boys remaining as handsome liveried servants on conspicuous display. Though they have outgrown their status as *delicati* and therefore, in theory at least, their sexual attractiveness as well, yet some of them evidently continue to be sexual partners of men. It appears from Servius' commentary on Virgil (in the note on *Aeneid* 3.119) that such men were called *pulchri* in early Latin ("pretties"), but far more familiar is the later *exoleti*.

Establishing this as the true meaning of *exoletus* depends upon studying both its etymology and its usage.

In origin, the word is a participle of the verb *exolesco*, whose basic meaning is "to grow up, become adult" (*OLD*, s.v. 1), and in early Latin it could be a simple synonym of *adultus* ("grown up"); *uirgo exoleta*, "a grown up maiden," is quoted by the grammarian Priscian from a lost play of Plautus. But the prefix *ex-* (suggesting "out of") leads to a more common secondary sense of passing from currency ("to fade away, die out," s.v. 2b; "to fall out of use, lose effect, be forgotten," s.v. 3), and this is often applied to words, customs, or laws. Because of the prefix, therefore, the word ought to mean something like "outgrown" rather than simply "adult" when referring to persons. (Williams (1999, p. 81) is in any case wrong to translate it "adults" when discussing Suetonius' statement that Galba preferred "the very hard and *exoleti*.") The other occurrences of *exoletus* in Plautus (*Curculio* 473; *Poenulus* 17) involve forms of the phrase *scortum exoletum*, which may mean "adult whore" or "outgrown whore," that is, too old to work profitably.

Etymology, then, gives us the sense "outgrown," and since the *exoletus* is regularly mentioned in passages with sexual implications, he is likely to be a grown up *delicatus*, "obsolete" because no longer attractive, at least to a pedophile. Pomeroy (1992) is a rare exception among recent scholars in knowing this: "Favourites retained past that age [sc. up to 18] would appear to be retained as adult sexual partners and would receive the disapproving label *exoleti*" (p. 47, n. 10). Close to this is the definition offered in *L&S*, though Victorian euphemism threatens to submerge it ("an abandoned youth of ripe age"). Other scholars have not always given due weight to the element of "outgrowing." Clarke (2003, p. 112), on no evidence at all, defines *exoleti* as men with large penises. Cantarella (1988, p. 222) equates the *exoletus* with the *cinaedus* and the *pathicus* as simply an adult "passive homosexual." It is true that the earliest occurrence of the noun (in a fragment of Laberius, an author of mimes) contains the phrase *exoleto . . . patienti* ("to/for an *exoletus* who 'receives'"), but this does not mean that this is all that the *exoletus* did sexually, and (more importantly) it does not account for the fact that Roman writers consistently defame men by associating them with *exoleti*, not with *pathici* or *cinaedi*. This is already in evidence in Cicero's speech *Pro Milone*, where Clodius' reputation is blackened through association with what Cicero calls his usual retinue of *scorta*, *exoleti*, and *lupae* ("whores, *exoleti*, and harlots," 55), and it continues through the imperial biographies of Suetonius to those of the *Historia Augusta*. The *OLD* has a separate entry for *exoletus* as a noun and defines it as "a male prostitute," but that sense is unlikely or outright impossible in all of the passages it cites (which represent only a portion of those in which the word occurs).

Unfortunately, the definition "male prostitute" has achieved new currency thanks to its adoption in modified form by Williams (1999), who asserts that *exoletus* "denoted a male prostitute past the age of adolescence, who might well be called upon to play the insertive role in penetrative acts with his male clients, but who might just as well also play the receptive role. His distinctive feature was not his sexual specialty, but rather his age, although sometimes even that was not a definitive characteristic, as the word seems in some contexts to refer to a male prostitute of any age" (p. 84). This seems contrary to common sense; one expects prostitutes generally to be younger, not older, all the more so if there really was a stigma regarding mature same-sex partners for men. In any case, Williams' own definition is not based upon a full survey of the evidence, and he seems to have no difficulty taking the word to mean simply "adult" when he discusses Galba.

My own investigation (see also Butrica, 2002, pp. 510-512) begins with the only place where *exoleti* do seem unambiguously to be male prostitutes, the collection of later imperial biographies known as the

Historia Augusta–a work widely recognized to be of questionable value as history. *Exoleti* are mentioned ten times in all here, but only in the three biographies that are attributed in the textual tradition to the single author Aelius Lampridius. Even here there is one passage where the word seems to mean simply "sexual partner," the implausibly exaggerated reference in the life of Commodus (5.4) to his 300 female and 300 male concubines. Unless the meaning of *exoletus* had changed drastically since the 1st and 2nd centuries CE, this is easily unmasked as an invention by the nonsensical claims that Commodus collected *puberes exoleti*, and did so "equally from the common people and the nobility." First, since *puber* itself means "that is grown up, of ripe age, adult" (*L&S*, s.v.), *puberes exoleti* is senseless and/or redundant whether it means "outgrown (*or* adult) adults" or "adult *exoleti*." Moreover, since (as we will see), *exoleti* are generally slaves, Commodus could not have collected them from among the citizen body unless what is meant is that he forced people of all social classes to hand over their suitably attractive male slaves.

All in all, the passage looks like defamatory invention. The other references to *exoleti* are found in the lives of Elagabalus and his successor Alexander Severus, where their function is unquestionably to characterize. The vicious Elagabalus adores *exoleti*: he likes contact with them at dinners (12.4); he addresses them as he might an army (26.4); he establishes a one-year *canon*–perhaps a sort of allowance–for them (27.7); he has a train of 600 vehicles to bear them along with the rest of his retinue (31.6). On the other hand, the virtuous Alexander loathes them: he bars revenues from them from the "sacred" treasury, using them to build places of public entertainment (24.3); he considers banning them, but relents lest the vice go private (24.4); he expels them, and drowns a few for good measure (34.4); he is so chaste that he never touches one (39.2).

One might well be forgiven for thinking on the basis of these two biographies that *exoleti* were indeed prostitutes of some sort: the biography of Elagabalus makes them parallel with *meretrices* by having the emperor address them after the female prostitutes, "in the garb of the boys who are prostituted" (26.4), says that the *canon* they received also went to pimps and prostitutes (27.7), and further says that the emperor's extensive train also included "pimps, bawds, prostitutes" (31.6), while in the biography of Alexander Severus the revenues rejected from the "sacred" treasury include those from "pimps and prostitutes" as well (24.3). And yet one must again wonder whether the author of these biographies really understood the term. One clue that he did not is the notion that Alexander relented from "forbidding" *exoleti* because "he feared that by prohibiting a public shame he might turn it to private desires, since people in the grip of insanity demand the illicit all the more when it is prohibited"; unless Roman society had changed drastically in the previous 200 years, the use of *exoleti* was always a private affair between owner and slave. The reference to "singing *exoleti*" in the same biography as a form of entertainment on a par with the exhibition of dwarfs (34.2) is also odd; but I would not exclude it as completely unlikely since until the nineteenth century the Sistine Chapel Choir could have been described as "singing *exoleti*" in the sense of "singing eunuchs" (see below for this meaning of *exoletus*). Early Christian writers seem to share a perception that *exoleti* were somehow "bad" without knowing quite what they were beyond an awareness that same-sex attraction was involved. Arnobius, for example, uses the term three times in his *Aduersus nationes*, once implausibly identifying Phidias' lover Pantarces as an *exoletus* (6.13) and even claiming that some pagan gods were *exoleti* (5.31). Prudentius (*Peristephanon* 10.233) makes Ganymede an *exoletus* brought to Jupiter by his "swift, armour-bearing pimp," namely the eagle–an error that (on the interpretation of *exoletus* offered here) would strike a Roman of the 1st century CE as ludicrous. Alternatively, these passages might attest to a later broadening of the sense of *exoletus* into a synonym of *cinaedus* or *pathicus*, a broadening perhaps reflected in Aelius Lampridius as well.

Pending more reliable evidence that an extensive sex-trade featuring *exoleti* really did arise in the later Roman Empire and that the sense of the word changed accordingly, we are probably safe in assuming that the references in all three of Lampridius' biographies are based on those in the earlier imperial biographies of Suetonius (2nd century CE). This work associates Tiberius with "herds" of "girls and *exoleti*" in the alleged sexual excesses of his retreat on Capri (*Tiberius* 43.1), has Caligula somehow involve *exoleti* with his sisters sexually (*Caligula* 24.3: the text has been questioned), has Galba (who is attacked for effeminacy in Juvenal, *Satire* 2) attracted to two types of men, the *praeduri* ("very hard," i.e., muscular) and *exoleti* (*Galba* 22.1), and surrounds Titus with "herds" of *exoleti* and eunuchs (*Titus* 7.1). In fact, it seems likely that the claim that Alexander banished the *exoleti* and drowned a few is modeled directly on Suetonius' claim that Caligula considered doing the same to the *spintriae*, men (see Suetonius, *Tiberius* 43.1) who entertained by performing group sex: compare *Caligula* 16.1, "He removed from the City the prodigiously lustful *spintriae*, after barely being prevailed upon not to drown them in the deep." In all of these passages, the *exoleti* are mentioned as potential sexual partners of men, linked with other males in the cases of Galba and Titus, with women in the case of Tiberius; but we must not do as Williams does when discussing Galba and assume that either combination is "normal" in Roman terms, since there is no reason for Suetonius to go out of his way to indicate that someone's sexual activity is perfectly predictable. Certainly there are other passages where a pairing of *exoleti* and women as sexual partners is meant to have shock value within a negative characterization; compare Seneca, *Epistulae morales* 114.25, where a man "thrashes about with a whole crowd of *exoleti* and women," and Tacitus, *Annals* 16.19, where the will-like document drawn up by Petronius denouncing Nero—which some have sought to identify with the *Satyricon* attributed to Petronius—contains the names "of his *exoleti* and women." But nowhere in these early imperial sources is there a hint that *exoleti* or the women paired with them were prostitutes, or received compensation for their services. Damning by association with *exoleti* and prostitutes (and perhaps even the notion that *exoleti* were prostitutes) may only be a rhetorical escalation of what we find in Suetonius, but it may also have been assisted, if not in fact suggested, by the reference in Cicero's widely read *Pro Milone*. (Tacitus, *Annals* 15.37 refers to a debauched banquet aboard ship in which the rowers were *exoleti* arranged according to their age and sexual talents, *scientia libidinum* [lit. "knowledge of lusts"]; this latter, of course, need not mean that they were prostitutes.)

These and other references to *exoleti* in the literature of the early Empire tend to be generic and uninformative, but there is hardly a passage where the sense "male prostitute" can be imagined to be appropriate. In fact, there are some where *exoleti* seem not to be sexual partners at all, or at least are not mentioned in that function. In oriental contexts, for example, the *exoleti* at the court of the Assyrian king Sardanapallus were surely not male prostitutes (Ampelius, *Liber memorialis* 11.4), nor was the *exoletus* Nicomachus, loved by Dymnus (Curtius Rufus, *History of Alexander the Great* 6.7), nor were the *exoleti* at the court of Nicomedes (Suetonius, *Julius Caesar* 49.2), nor were those with whom a certain Pacuvius surrounded himself when living the Syrian lifestyle (Seneca the Younger, *Epistulae morales* 12.8). Given the oriental contexts, and the knowledge that Roman *exoleti* might be castrated (see below), we are probably safe in assuming that in these passages the word means "eunuch." Astonishingly, neither *L&S* nor the *OLD* nor the *Thesaurus Linguae Latinae* [*TLL*] acknowledges this sense, though it has been known to various translators.

This means, of course, that *exoleti* might also be eunuchs in some of the passages in early Imperial literature that are not set in the East, and this is a possibility for both sexual and nonsexual contexts, since eunuchs were sometimes sexual partners, of men or of women: perhaps the *exoletus* that hands guests their toothpicks at Martial 3.28.8 is a eunuch, or the ones by whom Seneca the Younger would rather not be massaged (*Epistulae morales* 66.54), or the ones that he says wealthy Romans maintained in "herds" arranged by nationality and hair-type (*Epistulae morales* 95.24), or the ones whose livery he claimed caused such pointless concern to their owners (*On the brevity of life* 12.5).

There cannot, of course, be a simple equating of *exoletus* and eunuch, if only because Suetonius explicitly pairs *exoleti* and *spadones* ("eunuchs") in his life of Titus. The clearest evidence for both the original meaning of *exoletus* and its transformation into "eunuch" comes from the mouth of the Augustan declaimer Titus Labienus as quoted at Seneca the Elder, *Controversiae* 10.4.17. The particular declamation discussed had a more bizarre theme than usual: a man who collected exposed infants, then enhanced their value as objects of sympathy and recipients of alms by deliberately maiming and crippling them as they grew, was charged with harming the state (no such law seems to have existed, of course). Labienus was one of the few declaimers who chose to speak for the defense, and trivialized this treatment of mere beggars by another beggar by contrasting it with the way in which "leading citizens wield their riches against nature: they have herds of castrated men, they amputate their *exoleti* so that they are suitable for a longer sufferance of indecency; and because they are ashamed of being men, they are determined that there should be as few of *them* as possible." Williams (1999, p. 84) naturally includes this passage in his discussion of *exoleti*, but refers to it in an inaccurate and misleading fashion, writing that "Seneca the Elder imagines decadent men castrating their *exoleti*" and that the castration is "an unambiguous way of saying that [they] will be used as the penetrated partners in phallic acts": that is the implication, of course, though it must not be allowed to overshadow the literal truth of the castration, and it is of course Labienus, not Seneca, whose words are involved, in reference to a social reality, not a fantasy, carried out not by "decadent" men but by prominent citizens (*principes*). Obviously the castration explains why *exoletus* can mean eunuch. Since this would normally be inflicted no later than puberty, the victims are still children at the time; the power that someone has to castrate them implies that they are slaves; and the "longer sufferance of indecency" implies that they have been objects of sexual penetration since childhood, and will continue to be beyond puberty. In other words, this passage shows, in agreement with the evidence from etymology, that *exoleti* are grown-up *delicati*. Eventually the castration of slave-boys was banned by Domitian, to spite his eunuch-loving brother Titus, according to Dio (67.2.3, though too late to save the manhood of his own *delicatus* Earinus), but it had to be reinforced under his successor Nerva and again by Hadrian, along with broader prohibitions against the creation of eunuchs (*Digest* 48.4.48).

As we have seen, most references to *exoleti* are generic ("herds" are mentioned repeatedly) and serve to characterize negatively someone who associates with them. While we know the names of several *delicati* (Augustus' Sarmentus, Domitian's Earinus, and a few others), there is but a single named *exoletus* in the whole of Roman history: Julius Caesar once put Rufio, an *exoletus* who was the son of a freedman of his, in charge of some troops at Alexandria (Suetonius, *Julius Caesar* 77.1; whether he was castrated or not, he was presumably born while his father was still a slave, and one suspects that Suetonius mentions the incident only because of the [unmentioned] resentment that it stirred among the "men"). We do, however, know of another, anonymous *exoletus* who perhaps played a significant role in the life (and death) of a powerful Roman citizen. Tacitus *Annals* 14.42 reports that Pedanius Secundus, while serving as City Prefect (a sort of Chief Magistrate for Rome itself), was murdered by one of his slaves, either because he had agreed on a price to sell the slave his freedom but reneged, or because the slave was "fired by love of an *exoletus*" and could not bear that his master was his rival for that love. The presence of a jealousy this extreme implies that relationships with *exoleti* could be not merely sexual but "romantic" as well, no less than those involving women or boys.

D. Philetos, the Manly Delicatus

The scholarly attention recently devoted to Roman male sexuality has not been extended to male-male pedophilia. Williams (1999) deals with the subject unsystematically in Chapters 1 and 2 but makes no attempt to exploit what is perhaps the most interesting source, the poetry of Statius (end of the 1st century CE), specifically the *Silvae*, where we find four poems dealing with "beloved boys": 2.1 (on the death of Glaucias, the *puer delicatus* of Atedius Melior, an event also commemorated in two epigrams of Martial), 2.6 (on the death of Philetos, the *delicatus* of Flavius Ursus), 3.4 (on the dedication of a lock of hair by Earinus, the beloved eunuch of Domitian), and 5.5 (on the death of

Statius' own boy). Despite the wealth of evidence available in 2.1 above all to illustrate the everyday relationship of adult male and boy-favourite, or at least the public face that it liked to wear, Williams does little more than acknowledge the existence of 2.1 and 3.4, ignoring the rest (Hubbard's sourcebook includes part of 2.6, but without noting its unique features).

The neglect of the anomalous 2.6 is especially unfortunate: on the current understanding of ancient same-sex attraction and relationships, this poem should simply not exist. While there is no evidence for a particularly close relationship between Statius and Ursus (as there is for Statius and Atedius), we are still entitled to understand the poem as "custom made" for the recipient and reflecting, to some extent, the realities of the relationship–all the more so when we see significant differences from the other poems on similar losses (note too that Statius claims to have witnessed the relationship, 2.6.30, "I have seen and still see . . ."). It is not a myth of modern scholarship that boys were generally regarded as essentially feminine partners of adult men; thus what makes *Silvae* 2.6 anomalous is the emphasis on this boy's *masculine* qualities. This theme is so strong and so thoroughgoing that it cannot simply reflect the fact that Philetos, who died at 14, was more mature physically than the younger boys commemorated in 2.1 and 5.5.

Now, some aspects of the poem are certainly shared with the other consolations. As elsewhere, Statius has the intensity of the adult partner's grief surpass that of the boy's blood relatives (82-5; Philetos' parents–presumably deceased–would not have mourned as extravagantly as Ursus did, and Ursus outdid even Philetos' brother, who was present; the theme of the "alternative family" is not a modern invention). In 2.1, Statius described a friendship between Atedius and Glaucias, though one in which the boy was clearly the lesser partner, more a source of amusement and diversion than a steady friend whose counsel could be relied upon. In 2.6, on the other hand, the relationship is closer to one between equals, though still a matter of the master dictating the mood (52-3): rather than snatching masticated food from his master's mouth, as Glaucias did, Philetos "often used to correct his willing master, and aided him with his effort (*studium*) and his deep counsels" (50-2), so that the slave (according to Statius) was a better friend than Pylades was to Orestes, and the friendship also surpassed "Attic fidelity" (generally seen as a reference to the Athenian hero Theseus rescuing Pirithous from the Underworld, but in this context perhaps referring instead to Harmodius and Aristogeiton, whose relationship was involved in the overthrowing of tyranny at Athens and prepared the way for democracy; they are cited as a model for same-sex couples at least as early as the middle of the 4th century BCE in Aeschines' speech *Against Timarchus*). Any illusion of real equality, however, is dispelled by the last mythological comparison, between Philetos and Odysseus' faithful swineherd Eumaeus–a slave (50).

The claim of Philetos' emotional maturity (cf. 47-8 "mature beyond his age") also has a parallel in 2.1. So does the claim of modesty; but the emphasis on physical maturity and outright manliness is unique. Despite his age (72-3), he had a beard, though not yet a heavy one (44); he surpassed both boys and men in beauty, inferior only to his master (33-4; this was perhaps a conventional compliment, since we find it in 3.4 as well, applied to Earinus and Domitian); he did not have the "feminine charm" and "soft beauty" of a castrated boy (38) but showed a "fierce and manly grace" (*torua et uirilis / gratia*, 40-1), with a gaze that was not wanton, his eyes "enticing with a severe flame" (41-2). When Statius (inevitably) turns to mythological examples for illustration, he does not use the pederastic cases cited in 2.1 like Hyacinthus and Hylas but rather young adult males, especially warriors and athletes: Theseus, Paris, Achilles, Troilus, Parthenopaeus (one of the Seven against Thebes), Spartan youths and first-time Olympic competitors.

The physical and sexual side of such relationships appears to have caused some unease to the participants, and it is difficult to judge therefore how important a role it played. Pomeroy (1992) minimizes it, and Statius does as well, except in the case of Earinus and Domitian, where the sexual attraction is mentioned prominently and the relationship is even called "marriage"; elsewhere he is at pains to mention the "modesty" of the boy or the "holy" love of the adult. In fact, given that Domitian may have been enforcing the Lex Scantinia at this time, the fact that the boys in both 2.1 and 5.5 had long since been freed may be a virtual advertisement that the relationships were not sexual in nature, all the more so when the boy was adopted and thus became the son of his former owner. On the other hand, such idealism (which might well represent a conscious "civilizing" of the institution of the *puer delicatus*) could not be expected universally, and we are surely right in assuming that sexual relations did occur in some situations, and that, when they did occur, it was most often a matter of the owner using the slave for anal intercourse.

The situation becomes more complex, however, when the *delicatus* becomes an *exoletus*. It has already been observed that the child is essentially a "feminine" partner. When a Roman aristocrat has a *delicatus* castrated "for a longer sufferance of indecency" (in Labienus' words), he can be presumed to be trying (whatever the psychological reason) to extend the "feminine" period of the boy's sexual life and to continue using him as a "feminine" partner. (The Roman obsession with feminine-looking male slaves appears also in the references to *glabri*, or "smooths," who appear to have been hairless attendants; see Seneca the Younger, *Epistulae morales* 47.7 and *On the brevity of life* 12.5, and especially Catullus 61.137-9, "You are said, anointed groom, to have difficulty keeping away from your *glabri*, but keep away from them.") But, as the case of Philetos shows, not all *delicati* were castrated, even before Domitian banned the practice (though the prohibition was in place by the time Statius wrote 3.4, it must have been recent: both Glaucias in 2.1 and Philetos in 2.6 presumably died at about the same time, but Glaucias was castrated–and *younger* than Philetos at the time of his decease). No doubt simple human feeling explains many cases (both Seneca the Younger and Pliny the Younger attest to sympathy with slaves), but it is worth raising the possibility that some men, like Ursus (whose name, whether ironically or appropriately, means "Bear"), did not castrate their *delicati* precisely because they wanted a masculine-looking partner to penetrate. Nor did Ursus, unlike Atedius and Statius himself, free his *delicatus*; this can seem ungenerous by comparison, unless his motive is connected with the continuation of a sexual relationship–to avoid possible prosecution under the Lex Scantinia over a sexual liaison with a free Roman male?

While we cannot, of course, predict how Philetos' life would have developed into adulthood, we should at least consider the possibility that he was destined to become a partner who would be "masculine" not only in appearance but in performance as well. Although Philetos was obviously "special" to Ursus and was no doubt exempt from the daily labour that would be expected of an ordinary slave, and though the term *exoletus* does not appear in Seneca's famous plea for humane treatment of slaves in *Epistulae morales* 47, Philetos' destiny might have been to become a partner like the slave described there who is "a boy in the dining room but a man in the bedroom": his garb is feminine, and his body is plucked smooth, but he has evidently been left uncastrated precisely so that he could be "a man in the bedroom" (some eunuchs, of course, could achieve erections, but Seneca hints at nothing more drastically feminizing than plucking, which even adult heterosexual men were doing in his time; presumably Philetos would have been left unplucked to preserve his masculine appeal). There is other evidence too for both slaves and *exoleti* as sexual penetrators of adult men, and I do not see how it can be asserted unquestioningly that, when Seneca, Tacitus, or

Suetonius lists a man's sexual partners as both *exoleti* and women, he means that the man penetrated both groups rather than using each group in a different way. Moreover, we surely need an explanation of why, if *exoleti*, *cinaedi*, and *pathici* were all categories of passive sexual partner, Romans slandered so consistently by association with the first, but not with the second and third; and perhaps the explanation is that *exoleti* could be *active* partners of the men who associated with them. (Thus the men who are connected with both *exoleti* and women might be full bisexuals in the modern sense of men who will perform sexual acts of any kind with both male and female partners, as opposed to the others–more "classical" in their behaviour–who perform only insertive acts with other men.)

Best known perhaps is the fictitious case of Trimalchio in Petronius' *Satyricon*, who boasts of having serviced both master and mistress while he was his master's *delicatus* (75). If Caligula did indeed "prostitute" his sisters to his *exoleti*, they might have been thought capable of sex with women, but Caligula's capricious sense of humour must be reckoned with. Galba's attraction to *praeduri* (muscular men who would presumably play the "active" role) could well imply that he interacted with *exoleti* (his other sexual "preference") in the very same way. In Martial 12.91 a woman named Magulla shares both a bed and an *exoletus* with her husband. I suppose that it is at least remotely possible that both Magulla and her husband penetrate the *exoletus*, though Magulla would have to use a dildo for this, and we would expect Martial to mention one if it was relevant; hence we should see the *exoletus* as the "masculine" partner of both husband and wife. If nothing else, allusions to *exoleti* penetrating women serve to remind us that, in antiquity as in the present, a boy who was used sexually by adult men did not inevitably grow up as a "homosexual" (cf. the case of Atilius Philiscus, mentioned earlier, who was both a boy prostitute and a severe father). No doubt this was the "real" specialty of the *exoletus*: while the *delicatus* was too young to have a fully formed sexual identity or a fully autonomous will and performed essentially under compulsion, the *exoletus*, having reached adulthood, was beyond such compulsion, and had a sexual identity compatible with sexual activity with other same-sex adults.

How precisely this evidence illuminates the world of the *delicatus/exoletus* is unclear. Perhaps there were adults who could love a single person from boyhood through puberty into adulthood (with sexual roles perhaps changing accordingly), or ones who sought out potentially masculine boys to "groom" as eventual partners to penetrate them; perhaps we could even distinguish two distinct groups among Roman pedophiles, what we might term the "heterosexual" pedophiles, who use boys as "feminine" partners exclusively (one might compare the child-molesting but happily married hockey coach or choirmaster of today), and the "homosexual" pedophiles, who have perhaps used boys as "feminine" partners when children but enjoy their services as "masculine" partners when they grow up. We might even imagine that each of these groups could be claimed to show a characteristic "orientation." We ought at least to wonder whether there were men who had sex only with *exoleti* and never with *delicati*, and whether Ursus was such a man, grooming a masculine partner for himself, whether as penetrated or as penetrator.

It may be possible to speculate further about relations between men and *delicati* or *exoleti* using models based on modern studies of pedophiles and their targets, especially in orphanages and other "barracks" situations, but the poor state of our documentation means that firm conclusions will always be elusive and perhaps beyond even the possibility of confirmation. For example, it seems impossible in our current state of knowledge to say how same-sex relationships were affected by the difference of ethnicity that would almost inevitably exist between master and *delicatus* or *exoletus*, or whether the Lex Scantinia interfered with the granting of freedom to the slaves in such "couples" on the grounds that sexual relations with them would become illegal. In any case, Philetos the manly *delicatus* may be one piece of evidence for a world of sexuality without women; another is offered in the next essay.

E. The Warren Cup

This object has been interpreted by Clarke (2003) as an anomaly on the grounds that it "breaks the rules" of Roman sexuality by depicting relations between two adult men who are social equals. I will argue that the real anomaly (on the current understanding of Roman sexuality) is the total exclusion of women, yet another sign of a homosexual male "subculture" at Rome.

For the Warren Cup, a masterpiece of erotic art (purchased by the British Museum at a price of £1.8 million), see Clarke (1998, pp. 61-72), with plates 1-2 and figures 16-22, and Clarke (2003, pp. 78-91), with figures 52-3, 56, 60-1, where some details are more readily visible than in Clarke (1998). A fine silver goblet, hampered artistically only by some weaknesses in perspective, it shows on one side (Side B) a young man wearing a wreath who is penetrating a boy; the way the boy's childish attributes are displayed as if on a platter–undeveloped body, no hair even in the pubic region, immature and unerect penis–can leave no doubt that this was made to please a pedophile. On the other side (Side A), a young man is using a strap to lower himself onto the penis of a bearded man wearing a wreath who lies on a couch, while a boy peers in from a side door. The depictions steer a nice course between "soft" and "hard core." Engorged genitalia are not displayed, but neither are they entirely concealed; instead, the artist has discreetly indicated the testicles of the man who is penetrating the boy on Side B and the base of the penis of the bearded man on Side A (with perhaps signs of pubic hair and even the scrotum as well; see fig. 60 in Clarke (2003)). This avoids the pornographic immodesty of flagrant display, but does not deny the viewer the erotic *frisson* of assuring himself that penetration is indeed occurring.

Clarke interprets the two men making love on Side A as adults of equal status (hence the defiance of Roman norms), but this is unlikely. On each side, the penetrator is wearing a wreath–and is the only one wearing a wreath. The wreath shows that its wearer is "partying": whether at another's home or (more likely) at his own, he is enjoying himself, and everyone else is secondary to his celebration of a *symposium* or *convivium*. Other evidence that the scene is sympotic comes from the musical instruments that are included, on Side A a cithara (lyre), on Side B a double aulos (a woodwind employing a reed). If the younger man on Side A were meant to be seen as the social equal of the bearded man under him, and as a fellow "partier," then he too would surely be wearing a wreath.

Side B, with the penetration of the boy, is a perfectly ordinary pederastic scene, whether we interpret it as a young bachelor with his *concubinus* or a young adult with his *delicatus*. Side A depicts sex between two adult men. If the wreath is indeed the clue that they are not to be seen as equals, and the one wearing a wreath is a free citizen, then his adult partner is surely an *exoletus*, a slave of his own household who has been his sexual partner, if only occasionally, since childhood. (With all due diffidence, however, I would make the further suggestion that the adult/boy couple on Side B and the adult/adult couple on Side A are the same two persons at different stages of their lives, with the cup as a whole meant to document the boy's progression from *delicatus* to *exoletus*, perhaps even made as a gift for him, or to commemorate the couple.)

There is one other figure on Side A, the boy at the door. The blurb to figure 61 in Clarke (2003) asks, "Who is the young boy? A voyeur? The man's next partner? A stand-in for the viewer?" Surely he is all of the above. Least important is his role as stand-in; in fact, for reasons that will soon become clear, I think that we are intended to be reading *his* thoughts, not projecting our own upon him. And of course he is not simply waiting to replace the *exoletus* in the bed, at least not immediately or even in the near future. Nor is he even a *delicatus*, since he is dressed, not nude, and dressed quite plainly in a simple tunic; but he is surely a slave, since a freeborn boy would probably wear a *toga praetexta* with a purple stripe. But this slave boy is obviously curious about what those two men in the bed are doing, and that curiosity surely marks him out as a likely candidate for "promotion" to *delicatus*. (Here modern studies of how pedophiles choose their targets might be illuminating.) His presence elevates the Warren Cup from mere erotica to a potentially moving piece of art, for what he sees as he peers through the door is nothing less than the goal of his own future life-course from slave to *delicatus* to *exoletus*, fraught with whatever hopes or fears the viewer will imagine. Thus Side A suggests the entire cycle of male same-sex relations in Rome from boy to man, and the cup as a whole, with a *delicatus* on one side and an *exoletus* on the other, is a comprehensive representation of a sexual culture in which women are simply not an option. Though possibly controversial to traditional moralists, nothing depicted here is risky, so long as the penetrated males are both slaves. For the kind of "revolutionary" sex between equal adults that Clarke (2003) sees here, we must turn to Juvenal's *Satire* 2 and to Martial, and to the "marriages" they depict: further evidence for a sexual world without women.

II. SEX BETWEEN WOMEN

Modern scholarship on Roman lesbians is dominated by two myths: that Roman men viewed them with an implacable hostility, and that they "constructed" them as biological freaks who used a "monstrously enlarged" clitoris to penetrate other women–and even men. In fact the evidence, such as it is, actually implies a near total indifference to the phenomenon except as a source of humour.

The evidence adduced for lesbianism and its criticism amounts to little more than a remark by a declaimer, a fable of Phaedrus, some epigrams of Martial, some lines in Juvenal, and scattered passages in writers on subjects like medicine, astrology, or dream-interpretation (these last being primarily Greek or Greek-derived). Yet despite this virtual silence–contrast the much more substantial evidence for same-sex relations between males–we are told throughout the scholarship of the last three decades that Roman men seriously disapproved of lesbianism. According to Cantarella (1988, p. 214), for example, the "scarce but explicit evidence" shows beyond a doubt that it was viewed as "the worst of female depravities" because it challenged not only the Roman male's view of himself as the exclusive giver of sexual pleasure but also the most basic foundations of Rome's male-dominated culture. More generally, Hubbard (2003) writes that "Male authors from the Hellenistic . . . through the Roman periods . . . for the most part take an extremely hostile view of female homoeroticism as the worst perversion of natural order" (p. 17). He also asserts that "virtually all references to lesbianism are deeply hostile and couched in terms of women taking on men's roles, often using some instrument of penetration (either of other women or, even more extraordinarily, of men)" (p. 385). The notion of women "penetrating" women has been a problem ever since a foundation-text of the modern constructionist approach to ancient sexuality, Winkler's *The Constraints of Desire*, observed that "Sexual relations between women can only be articulated here in the significant terms of the system, penetrator versus penetrated, not as what we would call lesbianism" (Winkler, 1990, p. 39). More recent scholars have produced variations on the theme that same-sex relations between women were misunderstood by the Romans and do not represent "lesbianism" in any sense in which we use the term. For example, Hallett (1997) argues that Roman men represented lesbianism "as abnormal and unreal, involving the use and possession of male sexual apparatus" (p. 257) and even sexual relations with males, but further argues that they actually denied its existence in contemporary reality, "constructing" lesbianism "as . . . a Greek practice . . . distanced from present-day Roman behavior" and the lesbian as a Greek (i.e., foreign) monstrosity. As to that sexual apparatus, Cantarella (1988) already endorses implicitly the view that lesbians used their clitorises for penetration, while for Parker (1997) the Romans "construct[ed] the *tribas*," a woman endowed with a monstrously enlarged clitoris who, in addition to penetrating women and men alike, might rub her vulva against another woman's vulva in a "parody of intercourse."

In fact, there is little that we do or can know about how the Romans regarded lesbians or about how any lesbians in the Roman Empire lived their lives; while we can identify many men who loved, or at least had sex with, other men, there is not a single historical woman whom we can identify with certainty as a sexual partner of other women. When Cantarella (1988) writes so spiritedly about the negative opinions supposedly held by Roman men, she does not have a single footnote to show where, for example, a Roman man expressed the view that women could not find sexual pleasure without a penis (see also Clarke, 2002, p. 169, who comments of a painting in the Suburban Baths of Pompeii that "it revealed the very male notion that women need to be penetrated by a phallus to feel sexual pleasure"). On the contrary, there is evidence that men were indeed aware of other avenues to pleasure. Ovid recommends that men masturbate women as a form of foreplay, claiming that Hector pleased Andromache this way, and Achilles Briseis (*Ars Amatoria* 2.707-16). Martial 7.67 (discussed below) refers to a woman who performs cunnilinctus. Perhaps most importantly of all, the word normally used of a woman who has sexual relations with other women–the Greek feminine adjective *tribas*, naturalized as a Latin noun ("tribad" in English)–comes from a verb meaning "to rub" and therefore presumably identifies (mutual) masturbation as their "standard" form of sexual expression; etymologically, at least, a lesbian in antiquity is primarily a "frictionist" rather than "phallic."

As to Roman revulsion, "disgust" at lesbians and lesbianism did not prevent the Roman male poet Catullus from translating a poem by the most notorious lesbian of antiquity, Sappho, and casting himself in the Sapphic role. When Roman writers address women's alleged sexual excesses, lesbianism is not mentioned at all. As to "the worst of female depravities," Pliny the Elder, *Natural History* 10.172 singles out abortion as women's great sexual crime, while condemning men for inventing all forms of "unnatural" perversion. (This dichotomy is not to be pressed too closely, of course; I would argue from it neither that Pliny regarded lesbianism as an invention of men nor that he thought it "natural.") When Seneca the Younger, in a passage quoted later, describes the masculinization of Roman women, the culmination of his charge is not lesbianism but the sexual penetration of men. When laws are passed or other actions taken to limit the sexual freedom of women–Augustus' *Lex Iulia de adulteriis coercendis* of 19/18 BCE; later prosecutions under the emperors Tiberius and Domitian–it is heterosexuals who are affected, not lesbians. Even if we can assume that the use of common language in the *Digest* does not exclude women as committers of adultery (and the importance put upon determining whether the lover is "in" the woman as a criterion for justifiable homicide suggests that women were not usually thought of as committing adultery with other women), the only apparent reference anywhere to a woman committing adultery with another woman is nothing more than a paradoxical jest in Martial 1.90 (see below). When Juvenal writes a satire on women, its 695 lines contain at most a single passing reference to lesbians (some have claimed one in the word *equitant* ["they ride"] in 311, but the passage is obscure and the interpretation uncertain), and when he describes a religious ritual attended only by women that degenerates into a depraved orgy, the climax is not lesbianism but the introduction of low-class men and even animals (327-34).

Though she claims that lesbianism was regarded as "criminal," Cantarella has to admit that not a single law addressed it (see also Dalla, 1987, pp. 215-21). Her claim that a married woman who had relations with another woman committed adultery (p. 214) seems inherently unlikely, given that nothing of the kind is recorded in the *Digest*, for example, or mentioned in connection with Augustus' law criminalizing adultery, or with the later repressions; and it turns out to be based on the punchline to Martial 1.90, where *adulterium* is used humorously in reference to a woman who penetrates other women with a dildo as a "virtual" man. The explanation for this neglect under Roman law is surely not far to seek: lesbianism cannot lead to unwanted pregnancy and therefore need not be prohibited by an authority whose principal goal is to preserve the integrity and indeed to maintain the existence of certain social classes. To judge by Roman law, heterosexual women represented an infinitely greater threat than lesbians.

Even in the days of the early Empire, when women's sexuality generated considerable anxiety and discussion (such as when Vistilia had herself enrolled as a prostitute in order to escape prosecution under the law against adultery), lesbianism is never mentioned as a problem. One could argue that, because their historical literature especially is largely male-centered, the Romans had little occasion to mention women at all, much less lesbians; yet many women are in fact mentioned in Imperial literature, and quite often in contexts of criticism, though not a single one in a nonfiction source can be identified as a lesbian. As we have seen, no laws regulated lesbianism. Martial wrote hundreds of poems mocking the sexual foibles of heterosexuals and of homosexual men but only three (or perhaps four) concerning lesbians; Juvenal wrote a satire on homosexual men and one on heterosexual women but none on homosexual women. Surely there is a contradiction here: a society supposedly feels revulsed to its very core by lesbianism but does nothing and says virtually nothing about it. In some special pleading, Cantarella suggests that "pagan morality, being the morality of a world of men, held that, all things being considered, female homosexuality was not important enough to merit a serious discussion": but then the scarcity of prohibitions and condemnations is only the more striking in view of all the words she has just devoted to describing the rigid control that lesbianism supposedly challenged.

For Roman condemnation of lesbianism as unnatural, Cantarella and others turn to the story of Iphis and Ianthe in Ovid, *Metamorphoses* 9.666-797, one of his many myths of transformation (it is most certainly not an historical anecdote). The following is a summary:

> Ligdus, a poor but honest man, tells his pregnant wife Telethusa on his departure that she should raise their new child if it is a boy but expose (i.e., abandon) it if it is a girl. Isis, along with a host of other Egyptian deities, appears to Telethusa in a dream and tells her reassuringly to raise whatever child she bears. The child, of course, proves to be a girl, but Telethusa resourcefully raises her as a boy under the name Iphis, which is not marked as to gender (various aspects of the language in Iphis' later monologue show clearly, however, that Iphis is aware that "he" is really female). Iphis is described as androgynous in appearance (711-12, *facies, quam siue puellae / siue dares puero, fuerat formosus uterque*, "whether you gave the looks to a girl or to a boy, either one would have been beautiful"), and is betrothed on reaching the age of thirteen to the equally androgynous Ianthe (718, *par forma*, "an equal form/beauty"). Each is strongly attracted to the other; but, while Ianthe is troubled only by the natural expectation that a young girl might feel over her impending marriage, Iphis is deeply upset by the attraction she feels to another girl, and repeatedly defers the marriage until it can be deferred no longer. An extended monologue follows (726-63): if only she had been afflicted with some *naturale malum* ("natural trouble," 730) instead of a sexual desire completely unknown to her or indeed to anyone (*cognita nulli*, 727); in nature, cow does not pursue cow (731); her love is *furiosior* ("more full of madness," 737) than that of Pasiphae for the bull, and even Daedalus (the famous craftsman who built the wooden cow in which Pasiphae was mounted by the bull) could not "repair" either of them (742-4). All turns out well, however, when Iphis prays for the aid of Isis and is transformed into a boy.

One can hardly take this as a significant cultural statement about views of lesbianism in Roman society. The story is set in the world of legend, not contemporary Rome, and it is hardly a straightforward case of lesbian attraction: an androgynous youth–a girl raised as a boy, no less–is attracted to a *par forma* who resembles herself (no one seems to have suggested that Iphis' socialization as a boy plays a role in the attraction, or that what appeals to her in Ianthe is the recognition of her own suppressed female identity). The implication that lesbianism is not a "natural trouble" is not an authorial comment; it is simply one element in a monologue that attempts to reflect, within the formal framework of a sophisticated rhetorical argument, the pastoral innocence of an inexperienced and deeply troubled child. If Iphis thinks that her attraction to Ianthe is not a "natural trouble," this does not reflect Roman social or legal traditions; it is the observation of a young girl who, having been raised as a boy, now finds herself on the verge of marriage to another girl who happens to think that she really is a boy and toward whom she is feeling an attraction that is completely outside her experience of life growing up in rural isolation with no "worldly" knowledge, one who has never known of same-sex mating among humans, much less cows, horses, sheep, deer, birds or any creature (731-4). (Iphis' observations have a remarkable parallel in Longus' somewhat later novel of sexual awakening in a pastoral setting, *Daphnis and Chloe*, where the innocent Daphnis, approached by a pederastic sot named Gnatho who tries to "mount" him, roughly shakes him off after reflecting that he has never seen he-goats with he-goats, rams with rams, or roosters with roosters (4.12). This surely supports the suggestion that we are dealing with a *topos* of rustic innocence rather than societal condemnation.) Rather than a blanket condemnation of lesbians and lesbianism on Ovid's part, Iphis' comment is a sympathetic touch drawn from the observation of daily life that will strike a chord with anyone familiar with the difficulties faced by people growing up as homosexuals in isolated rural communities without visible role models or guides to help them understand their experience. Moreover, given the change of sex to which everything leads, any connection with contemporary reality that Ovid had in mind is likely to have been not with lesbianism but with hermaphroditism (hermaphrodites were becoming fashionable in the early Empire, according to Pliny, *Natural History* 7.36) or, even more likely, the cases of sexual "transformation" that occurred occasionally around the Roman world (some from a slightly later period are collected by Pliny in the same passage; every one is, like Iphis' metamorphosis, a change from female to male). I would also suggest, not entirely frivolously, that if the Romans really did construct the lesbian as a creature bent on the phallic penetration of other women, then transformation into an actual man and acquisition of a real male organ ought to be their ultimate fantasy.

Some scholars have found a voice of condemnation in Phaedrus, *Fables* 4.16, a fanciful myth of the origins of homosexuals:

> The other man asked him [sc. Aesop] what reasoning had produced tribads and soft men. The old man explained: "That too was Prometheus, creator of the people of clay who shatter on their first run-in with fortune. After spending all day fashioning separately those parts of nature that modesty hides with clothing so that he could later fit them to their respective bodies, he was suddenly invited to dinner by Liber [the Roman god of wine]. When he returned home late, on staggering foot and with his veins flooded by much nectar, with his heart half-asleep and in drunken error he applied the maiden's part to the masculine sort and masculine parts to women; so lust now avails itself of an erroneous joy."

Phaedrus too is hardly a straightforward guide to Roman attitudes, but I would argue that his gently humorous account of where homosexuals come from is evidence of a fair degree of tolerance and acceptance in his environment. His poetry–a collection of fables in the tradition of Aesop–is fanciful in nature, and clearly humorous; Hallett herself, who begins her article on Roman lesbianism with this passage, calls this "a collection of stories [Phaedrus] himself acknowledged as purely make-believe" (Hallett, 1997, p. 256). As Hallett also notes, the fable has surely been influenced (if not in fact inspired) by the equally fantastic and equally humorous speech about the origins of heterosexuals and homosexuals that Plato has Aristophanes make at *Symposium* 189c-193d: humans were originally round, with double limbs and genitals, and came in three varieties, male, female, and androgyne; then they attacked the gods and were sliced in two, and each half now forever seeks after its missing complement. Whether influenced by Aristophanes or not, this is obviously an equally humorous myth of origins, since what it implies–that lesbians have a penis and gay men a vagina–does not correspond with observable physical reality. (It is appropriate here to recall that, as we can tell from Martial, many Romans kept their eyes wide open in the public baths.) Phaedrus' fable is simply a whimsical invention to account for the fact that some men want to be penetrated by sexual partners instead of penetrating, while some women want to penetrate instead of being penetrated: obviously Prometheus must have been drunk and a little distracted and put the wrong genitalia on a few of his creations.

The final line, with the phrase *prauo . . . gaudio*, is no doubt responsible for the impression of disapproval; but while this is usually translated as something like "perverted pleasure(s)" (Hallett; Hubbard), *prauus* is not a synonym of its English descendant "depraved," and the meaning and tone are better reflected in my own version "an erroneous joy." The precise combination *gaudium prauum* occurs in only one other place in extant Latin literature, at Livy 40.14.2, where it refers to nothing more base than a possibly immodest joy over success in a military competition. *Prauus* is simply not a term of strong disapproval, not when the likes of *nefastus, nefandus, impius, execrabilis,* and *detestabilis* are available ("wicked," "unspeakable," "criminal," "execrable," "despicable"), and it is really much closer to "mistaken" or "wrong-headed." The *OLD* classifies the Phaedrus passage under definition 2, "Deviating from the ideal . . . corrupt, debased," though 2b might in fact be more appropriate, "(in weakened sense) wrong-headed, misguided, perverse." The results of Prometheus' drunken accident experience a "misguided" or erroneous joy simply because they bear the "wrong" genitalia through which to experience it; the epithet is a comment on *his* error, not a moral judgment against its result. Nor does the passage support Hallett's contention that the Romans "constructed" lesbians as Greek; Prometheus is certainly a figure of Greek mythology, but the Romans had long ago adopted and even naturalized a good deal of that mythology, including the story of Prometheus as humankind's creator, for which they had no figure of their own. In any case, the fact that Prometheus' invitation to dinner comes not from the Greek Dionysus but from the Roman Liber shows a conflation of Greek and Roman elements that is perfectly normal for Roman Imperial culture. What *is* interesting and possibly significant about the passage in Phaedrus is that it implies a perception that distinct sexual preferences exist and can be determined by a person's biological "nature": in other words, it may attest to the perception of an actual sexual orientation (writers on astrology imply much the same, with the orientation determined at birth by the stars).

Cantarella (1988) does not cite Phaedrus, but she does discuss the passage of Juvenal and the poems of Martial that deal with lesbians, and (like everyone else from Sullivan (1979) on) she claims the presence there of a moral judgment that, as we will see, is simply illusory. In search of condemnation, she also extends her range of sources beyond the Roman to the Greek world, adducing a passage from the *Amores* of pseudo-Lucian (28) which contains exactly the sort of denunciation she would obviously like to find in a Roman source. (In studying later antiquity it is to some extent legitimate to combine Greek and Roman sources, since one could argue that the culture of the Roman Empire from about the 1st century BCE on is a largely undifferentiated Greco-Roman culture.) In this case, however, Cantarella might profitably have noted that the remarks against lesbians here occur within a debate between an exclusive lover of women and an exclusive lover of boys and constitute a highly polemical argument against pederasty, not a comment on lesbianism per se (if men are to love boys, then why shouldn't women use phallic devices to penetrate other women, especially if it is indeed better for a woman to act like a man than a man like a woman?).

She also says that in a passage in another work of Greek literature, Artemidorus' book on dream interpretation, "sexual relations between women, unlike those between men, are classified as 'against nature'" (p. 217), but this is a misleading oversimplification (see her fuller discussion, pp. 260-2). This passage also forms the focus of the opening chapter of Winkler (1990), and both scholars seem to have different misunderstandings of what Artemidorus means by "against nature." Cantarella does not define which "nature" she thinks is violated: perhaps human nature, perhaps some universal law that governs all living creatures. Winkler has an appendix discussing the use of the key term *physis* ("nature") in the sense of "genitalia," but that is not how he understands it in this passage, and he has set his discussion within the context of the familiar debate on the roles of *nomos* ("law," "custom") and *physis* ("nature") in human society that began among the Sophists of the 5th century BCE. Artemidorus does not in fact rely upon this contrast; his initial classification of sexual acts in dreams is threefold, those "in accordance with nature and law and character" (or possibly "habit"), those "against law" ("against custom" is also possible; Winkler prefers the still weaker "unconventional"), and those "against nature" (1.78). As Winkler notes, this last section contains "an apparently heterogeneous assortment of acts: necrophilia, sex with a god, sex with an animal, self-penetration and self-fellatio" as well as "a woman penetrating a woman," but he overintellectualizes Artemidorus' thought in finding the common element to be that "unnatural acts do not involve any representation of human social hierarchy" (Winkler, 1990, p. 38). It is much more likely that Artemidorus means *physis* in its most basic sense, as an abstract noun derived from the verb *phyō* ("to grow") and therefore meaning "the way something grows," that is, its *physical* nature. It is simply the physical lack of an organ of penetration that makes penetration by a woman a form of sex against *her* nature, while penetration by a man is never against *his* nature, whatever the object. It is striking to see Winkler neglect the vital distinction between penetrative and non-penetrative sexuality and assume that *all* sex between women is intended here; Artemidorus nowhere discusses cunnilinctus between women explicitly, but presumably it belongs where cunnilinctus performed by a man belongs, among dreams involving sex "against law/custom/convention" because of the conventional distaste for oral sex. It is also striking to see him commit a logical error that has recurred regularly in the study of sex between women, the failure even to consider the possibility that some women really did use dildos as part of their sexual expression. Perhaps he accepted the feminist orthodoxy that all references to sexual devices in antiquity represent male fantasy rather than reality, perhaps he simply knew nothing about sexuality between women; but whatever the reason, instead of noting that Artemidorus might refer to a dream involving sex of that kind, he arbitrarily relegates the possibility of a dildo to the worlds of fantasy and fiction (making an inaccurate reference to Lucian, *Dialogues of the Courtesans* 5 in a note on p. 40) and declares that "Sexual relations between women are here classed as 'unnatural' because 'nature' assumes that what are significant in sexual activity are (i) men, (ii) penises that penetrate, and (iii) the articulation thereby of relative statuses through relations of dominance" (Winkler, 1990, p. 39)–another overintellectualization. The other acts are just as much against physical nature as penetrative sex by a woman: self-buggering is an utter impossibility (except with a dildo), while self-fellatio is beyond the reach of most men; sex with gods, goddesses and animals violates one's physical nature as a distinct "species," and necrophilia certainly works against the physical nature of the corpse.

Cantarella also adduces a quotation from the late medical writer Caelius Aurelianus (*Tardae passiones* 4.8.132-3, translating the Greek author Soranus); his claim that female homosexuals, like male, suffer from a mental illness seems to be purely a medical opinion, and he does not express the moral outrage that we are assured the Romans felt toward lesbianism–not to mention that both the text of the passage and its interpretation are highly controversial. Cantarella (1988) ends her survey of the pagan Roman evidence with the statement that "The inexorably negative judgment on female homosexuality is therefore constant, and becomes more frequent with Christianity" (p. 217), but since she has not established that such a judgment ever existed in pagan Rome, it would be more accurate to say that condemnation *begins* with Christianity.

It is time now to turn to those three poems of Martial that refer to women who have other women as (or at least among) their sexual partners.

We will begin with the two in which the word *tribas* appears. The briefer is 7.70:

> Philaenis, the tribad of the tribads themselves, you are correct to call "girlfriend" the woman you fuck.

"Fuck" introduces us to the central problem in these poems and their representation of the Roman tribad, her seemingly male sexuality. The Latin verb *futuere* is the standard term for male-female vaginal intercourse, and so Philaenis is marked as mannish not only by her assumption of the traditional male role of insertor but also by the verb *futuis* itself. *Amica* ("girlfriend") also marks her as a man, since it is essential to Martial's point that this word is a standard term for a man's female lover. Looking only at this passage, one might begin to understand how theories arose about lesbian sexual expression as a parody of male-female intercourse, or even about the "monstrously enlarged clitoris," inasmuch as no apparatus is mentioned.

But modern discussions of Roman sexuality, which often have to exploit the poems of Martial for evidence, make some fundamental errors in dealing with him. For one thing, an assumption has somehow taken hold to the effect that Martial was a moralist and a scathing critic of contemporary sexual and social mores. Sullivan (1979) is cited often, but his argument for Martial as a loather of lesbians is simply so arbitrary that one suspects that the interpretation is driven not by logic but by Sullivan's own discomfort with the subject matter. Without citing a single piece of evidence in support, he suggests that the obscene poems in general were written "almost as fillers," because "Martial . . . was not necessarily, *in my critical opinion* [italics added], a natural writer of amusing or interesting obscene verse, hence the frequent grossness and reliance on sexual explicitness" (p. 289; note the apparent assumption that "grossness" and "explicitness" are not a natural component of "amusing or *interesting* [italics added] obscene verse"). (Scholars would do better to heed Anderson (1970), whose Martial is more genial and tolerant.) In fact, the view that Martial was a seething moralist can be held only by someone who has misread the prose preface to Book 1, where two important points are made. (Sullivan does seem to misunderstand it, though I cannot make out exactly how, since I do not see how Martial's reference to the anecdote about Cato recalled there could be regarded as having been made "disparagingly.") First, Martial does not attack real persons (*salua infimarum quoque personarum reuerentia*, "with no damage to the dignity even of the lowest persons"); thus ridicule, if present at all (and it is certainly present in his epigrams in the "skoptic" tradition), is directed against types, mere constructs of contemporary expectations, not "real" individuals. Second, Martial admits an element of prurience in his work when he declines to make excuses for the "lascivious truth of [his] words," namely his obscene language:

> *Lasciuam uerborum ueritatem, id est epigrammaton linguam, excusarem si meum esset exemplum: sic scribit Catullus, sic Marsus, sic Pedo, sic Gaetulicus, sic quicumque perlegitur. siquis tamen tam ambitiose tristis est ut apud illum in nulla pagina latine loqui fas sit, potest epistula uel potius titulo contentus esse. Epigrammata illis scribuntur qui solent spectare Florales. Non intret Cato theatrum meum aut, si intrauerit, spectet. Videor mihi meo iure facturus si epistulam uersibus clusero:*
>
> > *Nosses iocosae dulce cum sacrum Florae*
> > *festosque lusus et licentiam uolgi,*
> > *cur in theatrum, Cato seuere, uenisti?*
> > *an ideo tantum ueneras ut exires?*

I would excuse the wanton truth of my words–that is to say, the language of epigrams–if the example were my own: this is how Catullus writes, and Marsus, and Pedo, and Gaetulicus, and everyone who gets read through to the end. But if someone is so ostentatiously grim that, in his mind, it is wrong to speak Latin on any page, he can be content with the dedicatory letter or perhaps the heading. Epigrams are written for those in the habit of attending the (Ludi) Florales. Let a Cato not enter my theatre, or not look if he does. I think that I will exercise my legitimate right if I conclude this letter with the verses,

> Since you knew the sweet ritual of playful Flora
> and the festive sport and the crowd's license,
> why did you come into the theatre, strict Cato?
> Had you come only so that you could leave?

The Ludi Florales (games held in honour of the goddess Flora over the end of April and beginning of May) involved not only the performance of indecent mimes but also a display of prostitutes who were stripped naked in full view of the crowd. The anecdote to which Martial refers is reported by Valerius Maximus (2.10.8): once during the games Cato's presence made the audience "blush" to demand the stripping of the prostitutes; when this was pointed out to him, he left the theatre, to the crowd's applause, so as not to interfere with their enjoyment. Thus Martial does not defend the sexual language of his epigrams–obviously connected to their sexual content–on the grounds that he is castigating vice and at times must perforce call a spade a spade; he defends it on the grounds that his audience enjoys a prurient thrill. We cannot therefore simply assume the presence of a moralistic stance or of moral criticism unless the language of criticism is obviously present; in its absence, we are safer in assuming that Martial's poems about lesbian sex are meant to titillate the curious than to denounce the vicious.

Martial is an epigrammatist, and his chief goal is to amuse through the pointed manipulation of words and ideas in poems of small compass, not to voice a personal disgust or contempt. Nothing in 7.70 condemns Philaenis unless we assume that the term *tribas* itself, or the claim that a woman "fucks," is inherently hostile; *cinaedus* can certainly be a conscious insult, but we cannot make the same assumption about the far less well attested *tribas*. Surely Martial is simply playing on the paradoxical concept of a woman who "fucks" like a man, and on the sense of *amica*. While this is used as a normal term for any female friend (*OLD*, s.v. 1), it is far more frequently attested of a man's "girlfriend" or mistress (*OLD*, s.v. 2). Any woman can have an *amica* in the first sense, Martial suggests, but the mannish Philaenis is spot-on when she uses it in the second sense of the women that she "fucks," because it apes men's use of the word and therefore (like her "fucking") shows how manly she is–and why she is "the tribads' tribad."

A slightly earlier poem in the same collection, 7.67, also concerns a woman named Philaenis. Even though all of Martial's "targets" are fictitious, and even though he mentions other women named Philaenis who are certainly not meant to be seen as the same as the Philaenis of 7.70 (unpleasant to kiss, 2.33 and 10.22; one-eyed, 4.65 and 12.22; recently deceased, 9.29; see also Appendix B for 9.40 and 9.62), the proximity of 7.67 and 7.70 encourages us to think that these women are to be regarded as one, thereby permitting us to combine the two in a single composite "portrait."

The Philaenis of 7.67 also likes insertive sex with women, among others:

> The tribad Philaenis buggers slaveboys and, fiercer than [her] husband's tension, whacks eleven girls a day. She also draws up her robe and plays with the hand-ball and goes blonde from the dust, and she easily twirls weights that pathics find heavy; and muddied by the crumbling earth of the wrestling-ground, she is beaten by the lash of her oiled trainer, and she doesn't eat or even lie down to dinner before throwing up six pints of unwatered wine, and she follows the routine of repeating these after she's eaten sixteen coloephia. When she's being sexual after all this, she doesn't perform fellatio–this she thinks insufficiently manly–but just devours the middles of girls. Philaenis, may the gods grant you sanity, if you deem it manly to lick a cunt!

The essentially humorous nature of the poem ought to be clear from the conclusion, where Martial cannot possibly be diagnosing Philaenis' state of mind as a form of madness.

Previous scholars seem to have missed that Philaenis is probably married. Every translation I have seen (except Clarke, 2002, p. 169) renders *mariti* in *tentigine . . . mariti* in line 2 as "a husband's lust" (or "hard-on"). But a husband's erections will be no more "cruel" or "fierce" than any other man's, nor is *maritus* ever just a synonym of *uir* ("man"), and it would be perfectly idiomatic for *sui* to be understood here ("her own [husband's]"). A married tribad should arouse no more surprise among Rome's marriages of convenience than a married *cinaedus*, and the husband might be for the most part nothing more than a legal "beard," as it were, serving as *tutor*, or "guardian," for legal and financial transactions if the woman was unwilling to break with tradition by dispensing with one. The existence of a husband could also give more meaning to the statement that, when sexually active, Philaenis does not fellate. It seems surprising to have Martial mention this as though he imagined that his readers could think it a real possibility for a lesbian, or at least for one as "butch" as this one, but it would presumably be less surprising if there is a husband. (On the other hand, it is possible that Martial raises the possibility of fellatio for no reason other than the contrast with cunnilinctus and manhood that he needs for his punchline.)

In any case, Philaenis is again represented as if aspiring to manhood, though as someone who apes manliness rather than one who actually achieves it; note that the weights she lifts effortlessly are heavy for "pathics" (*drauci* in the Latin) rather than for "men." The presence of boys (presumably slaves) among her sexual targets makes her mannish. In fact, she is made more mannish than her husband through the obviously humorous exaggeration that she penetrates more slaves every day than he does–a parody of stereotypical male sexual promiscuity. (In most interpretations she has an unspecified number of boys and 11 girls, but perhaps we should understand 11 of each, with *undenos*, the adjective meaning "11 [each]," to be supplied retrospectively with *pueros* in 1 out of *undenas* [*puellas*] in 3.) Out of the poem's 17 lines, nine describe her athletic regimen, which again is so exaggerated as to appear parodistic (the coloephia–more correctly spelled colyphia in editions of Juvenal, who also mentions them–are cuts of pork, and even her drinking and vomiting are part of it); this is another area where she is very probably more "manly" than her husband. Hallett (1997, p. 262) adduces the Greek terms here among her evidence for lesbians being "constructed" as Greek, but no discussion of Roman athletics could avoid such words, since the vocabulary of athletic training, indeed the very institution, was Greek in origin.

Again we find no moral disapproval unless we simply assume its presence: Martial's report of Philaenis' activities is exaggerated, in order to make a point, but it is not morally coloured. Instead, he is playing again with Roman concepts of masculine and feminine. When Philaenis' thoughts turn to sex after a vigorous training session and a hearty meal (fit for a gladiator in training), she performs cunnilinctus, not fellatio. The reason (*her* reason, according to Martial, who has, after all, created her) is that fellatio is not manly–as indeed it could never be, whoever performed it–while cunnilinctus, as something that a man *can* do for a woman, is (by implication) sufficiently manly for a woman who shows so much manliness in her training. But cunnilinctus was not considered manly at all, being seen as disgraceful and even as a sort of last resort when one's real "manhood" had failed (cf. Mart. 3.81; 4.43; 7.95; 11.47, 61; 12.59, 85). Hence the "stinger" lies in Martial "correcting" the lesbian's impression that, by performing cunnilinctus, she is again acting like a man: cunnilinctus isn't manly at all. If there *is* a target of criticism (or at least ridicule) here, it is the *real* Roman males who perform cunnilinctus, not Philaenis. (An alternative explanation is that Martial's point is that Philaenis should be "fucking" women if she wants to be manly.)

As to exactly how Philaenis penetrates her slaves and "girlfriends," we must turn to Martial 1.90; this poem does not use *tribas* but obviously refers to a woman who interacts sexually with other women. Hallett (1997, p. 260) has expressed some suspicion regarding the absence of the word *tribas*, and many find criticism in the words *monstrum* and *prodigiosus* that are applied to that sexual interaction. Both features, however, are part of the riddling "mystery" that Martial crafts in this epigram; the avoidance of *tribas* mirrors his own alleged failure to suspect that Bassa is a lesbian and allows him to spring his "surprise" revelation, when the much more shocking term *fututor* ("fucker") shows that we are dealing with a woman who enters another woman as if she were a man:

> I never saw you with men, Bassa, and there was never a rumour that you had a lover, and you were always surrounded by an attendant crowd of your own sex, and men never approached; and so, I confess, I thought you were a Lucretia.* But what an outrage, Bassa: you were a fucker! You have the nerve to pit two cunts against each other, and your odd sexuality fakes a man. You've devised a prodigy worthy of the Theban riddle, crafting adultery where there is no man.

> *Lucretia, whose rape and subsequent suicide supposedly precipitated the end of the monarchy at Rome ca. 500 BCE, was frequently cited as a paradigm of virtuous chastity.

As in 7.70, the sex that Bassa has with other women is characterized through a derivative of *futuere*, this time the noun *fututor*. (It is striking that Martial uses this masculine noun when a feminine equivalent, *fututrix*, existed, used twice by Martial himself, though only as an adjective, modifying a hand and a tongue respectively.) Again there is wit, not outrage, when Martial says that Bassa has "feigned a man," that is, she uses a dildo, and surely a strap-on dildo, which will allow her to bring the two *cunni* together as Martial implies (see Clarke, 2002, pp. 166-168, with fig. 5.8, for a probable representation of precisely this activity). Though invoked to support the theory of the "monstrously enlarged clitoris," this poem actually seems to contradict it inasmuch as Martial says that Bassa has herself "devised" the means of penetrating other women, not that she was born with it.

The secondary literature on this poem seems unanimous that (to quote Sullivan, 1979, p. 293 *exempli gratia*) "Martial displays strong animosity against tribadism or lesbianism in any form." This is a fundamental misinterpretation that takes no account of the poem's literary nature and misreads both its language and its "culture." For one thing, the poem is not really "about" Bassa at all but about Martial as a failed diviner who rectifies his error. He had seen something remarkable, a woman who could never be found in the company of other than women (no doubt a man who owned only male slaves would attract some attention as well), and he thought–or so he pretends, for the sake of the poem–that he had solved the riddle with the hypothesis that Bassa was a woman of extraordinary chastity, shunning men to avoid even the slightest hint of scandal. But now (and Martial of course does not need to tell us how he acquired the knowledge to correct his error) he has the real solution: Bassa associates only with women because she is one of those women who "fuck" other women. The language that has been thought to express condemnation–*monstrum* and *prodigiosus*–is generated by this literary structure. Martial had been unable to solve Bassa's mystery because it was "worthy of the Theban riddle," that is, at least as difficult to solve as the riddle of the Sphinx (*not* the Sphinx herself, as in some interpretations); but now (by implication) he has outdone even Oedipus in the solving of riddles, because he has solved one comparable to the most famous riddle in history, the one that only Oedipus succeeded in solving. In the context of interpreting oddities, it is only natural that Martial uses words like *monstrum* and *prodigium* and their derivatives, since these terms from Roman augury (in the broad sense of all interpretation of omens and signs) designate freaks of nature, such as two-headed chickens or showers of frogs or blood, which were recorded and interpreted by a professional priesthood as messages from the gods for decoding and expiation. (Cf. *OLD*, s.v. *monstrum* 1, "An unnatural thing or event regarded as an omen, a portent, prodigy, sign"; s.v. *prodigium* 1, "An unnatural event or manifestation portending a disaster, etc., prodigy.") Modern scholars are perhaps influenced excessively by the derivatives of these Latin words found in their own native languages (especially English "monstrous"), but it cannot be emphasized too strongly that the words themselves comport no moral connotations whatsoever. A *monstrum* or *prodigium* was not "accursed" in any sense or morally "wrong"; it was only an unusual phenomenon that needed to be understood, whether for good or for ill, and expiated as appropriate. In addition, both words had long since ceased to have an exclusively religious meaning and were regularly used in much weakened senses, always–like the archaic Roman religious views from which they derive–without a moral dimension. In its later sense, *prodigiosus*–the word applied to Bassa's lovemaking–is much closer to "strange," "odd," or "remarkable," and other things described as *prodigiosus* in

Latin literature include, for example, mythical wonders like Cerberus or Circe's palace but more quotidian ones too like a mule giving birth, people who criticize Cicero, certain solar phenomena, a litter of a single pup or all of a single sex, Druidic rituals, and the price of *cinnamomum*. Martial is having fun, and perhaps titillating his readers, with the idea of artificial manhood, presenting it as Bassa's little secret, and teasing the reader, not only by presenting the whole as a riddle to be solved but also by merely suggesting the means by which she makes love, and using the sexually charged word *fututor*. The poem is a case of mystification clarified, not a condemnation of lesbian relations. The phrase *prodigiosa Venus* need be no stronger than "remarkable lovemaking" (i.e., because the strap-on dildo creates the unaccustomed phenomenon of a woman who can "fuck" like a man); and it most certainly does not mean "monstrous clitoris," not only because there is no evidence for *Venus* in the sense of "clitoris." Williams (1999, p. 329, n. 30 wants this meaning but has no solid evidence for it; I suppose that it is at least possible, since *Venus* = penis at Lucretius 4.1269).

One can find occasional acknowledgements in the literature that lesbians sometimes used or at least might have used dildos (Williams (1999, p. 329, n. 30), for example), but (unaccountably, in my opinion) modern scholars have somehow found it easier and more plausible to imagine a prodigiously enlarged clitoris that can penetrate a vagina or even an anus than a strap-on dildo. Yet it is the use of such dildos, not of an enlarged clitoris, that is alleged in pseudo-Lucian, *Amores* 28, and it is a dildo, not an enlarged clitoris, that a Roman declaimer anticipated when describing the emotions of a man who found his wife in bed with another woman in yet another passage from the Roman declamatory tradition (for this tradition in general see I.A). Seneca the Elder, *Controversiae* 1.2.23, on the general subject of handling indecent material, discusses a Greek named Hybreas who declaimed in Latin but slipped into Greek for his indecencies. The particular *controversia* under discussion is called "The prostitute priestess." The applicable law (which, as often, resembles Roman practice, in this case with regard to the Vestal Virgins, without corresponding exactly to any known law) is that a priestess must be herself chaste and pure and from parents who are the same. The case concerns a woman who seeks a priesthood despite her past, which casts multiple doubts upon any claim to purity: kidnapped by pirates, she was bought by a pimp, then killed a soldier who tried to rape her after refusing to pay her alms. (The Latin term used here, *stips*, could also refer to a fee.) Obviously there was much scope here for indecent innuendo. After reporting the various divisions and *colores* used by the declaimers against the girl, Seneca makes the point that "one needs to speak against [her] passionately, not meanly or obscenely," then passes into a more extended discussion of indecency. Subsequently, as an example of the fault of speaking "meanly or obscenely," he quotes Scaurus, who associated this fault with Greek declaimers ("who gave themselves every license"), and who related the anecdote under discussion. Hybreas was apparently pleading a different *controversia* (unattested elsewhere, so that we know neither the applicable "law" nor the precise charge against the husband [murder or some variation seems likely] nor who was having him prosecuted): a man caught two tribads in bed, one of them his wife, and killed them both. When "[Hybreas] began to describe the emotion of the husband, in whom a disgraceful examination should not have been required" (i.e., he should not have been in the position of having to examine the genitalia of his wife's lover), he spoke in the person of the husband, saying (in Greek), "I first considered whether the man was inborn or stitched on." ("Man" may be used here as a euphemism for penis, though this is not attested elsewhere as far as I know.) Thus the thought that Hybreas puts into the head of the man who discovers his wife in bed under another woman is not "I checked for the monstrously enlarged clitoris" but "I wanted to see whether the 'man' was natural or artificial."

(Immediately after this, Seneca cites a comparable remark of another Greek orator in the same *controversia* involving the two tribads, apparently speaking against the husband, though his words have perhaps been affected by textual corruption: "[in Latin] They would not have allowed adulterers to be killed this way; [in Greek] if I had caught a faux-male adulterer." [The Greek word translated here as "faux-male" is a unique compound adjective that occurs nowhere else.] The second part may be fragmentary, or an example of aposiopesis, where the speaker breaks off before fully expressing a thought, leaving it to be inferred. Such a gesture might seem inherently euphemistic here, and Seneca begins the next anecdote by reporting something said "no less obscenely," but the evidence can be reconciled on the supposition that what was suppressed was the speaker's asseveration that, under such circumstances, he would have *raped* the "faux-male" adulterer.)

Women even used dildos on (presumably heterosexual) male partners as well, to judge by a passage that has been mistakenly brought into the discussion of Roman lesbians as further evidence that they were thought to use their enlarged clitorises for the penetration even (it is alleged) of men's fundaments. The general theme of the relevant passage in Seneca the Younger, *Epistulae morales* 95.21 is that Roman women have completely desexed themselves in their conduct through "masculine" lifestyle choices like heavy drinking and wrestling–just like Philaenis–and now suffer from "male" diseases such as gout and baldness that formerly, according to Hippocrates at least, did not afflict them–a statement that should at least sound possible in a world where women's adoption of the formerly male habit of smoking has made lung cancer as much their enemy as breast cancer:

> But in lust they do not yield even to men. Though born to receive (*pati*)–may the gods and goddesses damn them!–they have contrived a kind of immodesty so perverse that they mount men. Is it any wonder then that the greatest of physicians and the man most knowledgeable about nature is caught in a lie when so many women are gouty and bald? They lost the benefit of their sex through their vices, and were condemned to manly ailments because they had shucked off their womanhood.

This was naturally a difficult passage at a time when women's sexuality, let alone the use of dildos, was either unknown territory because of innocence or denied outright as a delusion of the male ego. It is astonishing now to read *The Constraints of Desire* and to see that the possibility that some women actually penetrated each other with dildos is never even considered as an explanation of why Artemidorus discusses dreams involving penetration of one woman by another. When teaching a course recently on Roman sexuality, I was bringing the students gradually through a painstaking examination of the Roman sources for lesbianism and of the modern scholarly literature when the only self-identified gay student in the class interrupted, a little impatiently I thought, and asked "Couldn't they just have been using strap-ons?" What had been difficult for scholars of an older generation and a different background could not have been simpler for him. The practice mentioned here by Seneca is simply a contemporary sexual and social reality: anal penetration of heterosexual men by female partners, with fingers or with dildos or other devices, is by now relatively well documented in popular culture and sexual literature.

In addition to the claims that the Romans expressed revulsion at lesbianism, scholars also propound the notion that lesbians used their enlarged clitorises for penetration (even of men's anuses, as we have seen). The most systematic attempt at proving this theory, and undoubtedly the most extreme statements about lesbians and how the Romans saw them, can be found in Parker (1997) in the section "The Abnormal

Female" (pp. 58-9). All sexually active women were supposedly lumped together as somehow monstrous in Parker's "teratogenic grid": he asserts, for example, that even Sempronia and Clodia, whose sexual partners were men, were seen as "phallic" women, "monster[s] who violate boundaries"–even though Sallust's final judgment on the former is that "there was much wit and much charm in her." Obviously his claim that tribads were thought to rub their vulvas together misinterprets Martial 1.90.7. His assertion that "[these] women have to perform a parody of intercourse. Even when women become active, a woman is still the passive object of fucking" is based upon three alleged "facts": that we have but a single reference to cunnilinctus (probably not statistically significant given that we have so few references to lesbianism as a whole and given the nature of those references; but see now Clarke (2002, p. 174) for visual evidence of the practice); a denial of the practice in Juvenal 2–a problematic passage discussed in Appendix A; and the allegation that we have no reference to mutual masturbation, though, as I have already suggested, that is very probably the whole point of the term *tribas* itself.

There is a fundamental, unexpressed, and erroneous assumption at work in the logic applied by Parker and many others in the study of Roman lesbianism, similar to what happens in the study of imitation in Latin poetry: arguments are advanced as though the extant evidence were not merely all that survives but all that there ever was or could have been. In this case, the content of these few epigrams is assumed somehow to represent the totality of what not just Martial but all Roman males knew, thought, or suspected about lesbians–rather than simply what struck Martial as meat for a humorous epigram. There is no justification for such assumptions, or for the related assumption that, when Martial is depicting a lesbian in a poem, he is somehow "constructing the lesbian" as a concept rather than simply using some of the perceptions circulating in his society to construct "a" lesbian or two (or even relying on personal acquaintance). This should be all the more obvious when Martial's two lesbians are so different. Bassa is not an athlete, Philaenis is: which is constructed as "the lesbian"? Bassa is not said to perform cunnilinctus, Philaenis is: which is constructed as "the lesbian"? Bassa has sex with women, Philaenis with women, boys, and girls: which is constructed as "the lesbian"? Bassa is not married, Philaenis is: which is constructed as "the lesbian"? "Fucking" women is the only thing they share: is that the whole of "the lesbian"? Must a woman "fuck" another woman to partake of "the lesbian"?

Hallett (1997), though endorsing the theory of the enlarged clitoris, makes a shrewd observation that overturns the notion that the *tribas* was constructed as a figure that only penetrates (as it does the related and equally mistaken notion that a tribad was always an extremely masculine lesbian or "bull dyke"). Referring to the passage in Seneca the Elder concerning the advocate Hybreas, she notes that, when the plural form *tribades* is used in reference to the two women found in bed together (presumably one atop the other), no distinction is made between the "top" and the "bottom": both penetrator and penetrated are subsumed under the same term (p. 269). Philaenis' passive partners are just as much tribads as she is. (This observation has implications for the study of the term *cinaedus* as well, and challenges the purely constructionist approach to Roman sexuality, or at the very least to women's sexuality.)

When he goes on to argue that the "monstrous sexuality" of these active women, whether lesbian or straight, "has a physical incarnation," namely a "monstrous clitoris," Parker simply plays fast and loose with the evidence, none of which supports his claim. He does offer the parenthesis "*landicosa, CIL [Corpus Inscriptionum Latinarum]* 4.10004; *Priapea* 12.14; compare the implications of Phaedrus 4.16.13": but *landicosa* is only an adjective derived from the noun *landica* (an extremely obscene term for the clitoris), and while it might suggest abundance (cf. English "chesty," "busty"), nothing about it implies the monstrous; *Priapea* 12.14 simply mentions the shaggy private parts of an elderly woman in a clearly humorous context (her clitoris, gaping vulva, and shaggy pubic hair resemble the nose, mouth, and beard of the philosopher Epicurus yawning!); and the fable of Phaedrus–besides being by nature a humorous *jeu d'esprit*–says nothing about abnormal size and obviously uses the genitalia symbolically in any case. To prove that "[t]heir sex is masculinized," he asserts that "Juvenal's Messalina [in *Satire* 6] has a uterine hard-on," but she simply has a sore vulva from repeated intercourse. That "Fulvia has a monstrous clitoris" is supported by reference to one of the *glandes Perusinae*, or "Perugian acorns" (cf. Hallett, 1977, p. 152); these are lumps of lead inscribed with obscene and insulting messages that the forces of Octavian (the future Augustus) and those of Fulvia and her brother-in-law Lucius Antonius fired at each other during the siege of Perugia in 41 BCE. This one (= *CIL* 11.6721.5) simply says FULVIAE/[L]ANDICAM/PETO, that is, "I'm headed for Fulvia's clitoris" (with a sketch of a thunderbolt!). Parker's final ominous reference to the Greek medical authorities of late antiquity who describe the clitoridectomy (or rather, "nymphotomy") as an operation "to correct a phallic clitoris"–as if there was a danger that Roman men might force such an operation on a woman showing lesbian tenden-cies–is not necessarily relevant to Roman attitudes of five or six centu-ries earlier (we certainly do not hear of women having these operations), and in any case medical authorities do not connect the oper-ation with suppressing sexual desire for other women. (See Aëtius, *Iatrica* 16.115; Paulus, *Epitome* 6.70.)

Thus, with no lesbians identified in historical works, the direct evi-dence for lesbians in Roman society is limited to the denial of cunnilinctus in Juvenal (discussed in Appendix A) and the poems of Martial featuring Bassa and Philaenis, who are not real persons but fic-tional characters. Martial truly does "construct" his lesbians, and a strict approach to the evidence requires that we keep an open mind about whether lesbians exist outside these constructs.

Bassa in 1.90 is a woman who evidently shuns all association with men, even among her subordinates (presumably both personal and pro-fessional associates); every "duty" connected with her (*officium*, 3) is performed by a woman. Martial "outs" her secret: she "fucks" women, and does so by using what must be a strap-on dildo that allows her to feign the actions of a phallic male.

Philaenis (7.67, 70) is the more detailed "portrait." Unlike Bassa, she appears to be married, and fellatio is something that she can consciously reject. Everything about her suggests a pursuit of masculinity, and per-haps a self-identification as a man: she penetrates both slave-boys and slave-girls, as a man would do, but outdoes her husband in sexual appe-tite by having more of them per day than he does; she trains vigorously as an athlete, running, wrestling, lifting weights, and rigorously follows an athletic regimen in both food and drink; she interacts sexually with other (adult) women by performing cunnilinctus on them because she thinks it's what "men" do. While she may use a dildo when having sex with boys, there is no mention of her using one with women, but the ref-erence in 7.70 to her "fucking" women seems to presuppose it.

Thus these two women, despite sharing a desire for contact with other women, are in fact differentiated, and neither is the phallic mon-strosity claimed by modern scholars as constituting the Roman con-struction of "the lesbian," nor is either of them even remotely as "butch" as Megilla in Lucian, *Dialogues of the Courtesans* 5, who (in addition to mannish sex with other women) shaves her head, shows off "his" wife, and calls herself by the male name "Megillos," suggesting perhaps a case of gender dysphoria as much as lesbianism.

Of course Martial's "construction" of these figures must be based on something familiar to his readers, a recognizable "type" in other words, preferably based upon life rather than upon literature: otherwise the humour would be wasted or even impossible. But the precise relationship that exists between Martial's representation and the contemporary reality is impossible to state securely. For one thing, Martial's poems have links with Greek literary tradition that might initially seem to support Hallett's contention about the denial of lesbians in Rome. The language of his poem on Bassa and her artificial phallus has a striking point of similarity with a phrase used to denounce the artificial phallus in pseudo-Lucian, *Amores* 28, *ainigma terastion* ("portentous riddle"), where *ainigma* is obviously reflected by *aenigma* in Martial's Latin, and the adjective *terastion* is an exact equivalent of Latin *prodigiosus*. The literary connection of Philaenis is even clearer: there was a real Greek woman of that name who lived in the 4th century BCE and either was slandered falsely as having written a work on sex or really did write works on sexual positions, and in either case was explicitly associated with lesbianism (in fact, she is mentioned by name in the denunciation of lesbian penetrative sex at *Amores* 28). But this conflict between Roman reality and Greek literary tradition is an old problem in the study of Latin literature, and it is now widely recognized that Latin literature really fuses the two rather than privileging one of them. Here, whether or not the language of Martial's riddle has been borrowed, the woman to whom it is applied is set firmly in modern Roman reality by her Roman name Bassa. Even if the historical Philaenis ultimately suggested the use of the name in connection with a lesbian, she too is set in contemporary Rome by the fact that she speaks Latin. But without "real" lesbians in the historical record, and especially without the voices of lesbians, we face a dilemma; we may feel that we have good reason to believe that such women existed in the Roman world, and we may even feel that some of them are likely to have used dildos, even if there is nothing that could be called proof, but it will never be possible to understand what their use meant sexually or emotionally to these women—or even to be absolutely certain that they existed.

Thus the final judgment on the Roman lesbian must be that she really does lie beyond the range of our knowledge in ways that the male homosexual does not (and not simply because she is a woman; we are in a similar position with respect to the sexual life of the Roman soldier). The silence that surrounds such women implies indifference to their existence and activity, even if we take into account the male-centeredness of Roman literature, which complains a good deal about the conduct of women but not about them loving or making love to each other. Tribad, the standard term for them, implies an awareness of mutual masturbation, and our sources sometimes associate them with the use of a dildo; this does not mean that any actual Roman lesbians used a dildo, or that Roman men knew only of lesbians who used a dildo–it simply means that the use of a dildo by a woman was sufficiently paradoxical and amusing to be the subject of the epigrams that make up so much of our evidence. That general invisibility, however, becomes a source of information in its own right, since it suggests that the Roman men who wrote the literature that survives simply didn't notice lesbians among them under normal circumstances, or didn't care to remark on them, just as Roman lawmakers made no effort to criminalize even adulterous sex (as we would define it) between women.

It is quite possible that there are lesbians to be found elsewhere in the literature and the physical culture of the Roman world, but the sources will never allow us to be certain. For example, there are two more Philaenis poems in Martial that might refer to the same woman as 7.67 and 70 or at least to a lesbian (Appendix B). Brooten (1996) presents what she regards as a portrait of a lesbian couple, later recut as a heterosexual pair, but this identification has been disputed. One of the most remarkable things about political life at Pompeii is the fact that, in a town where women presumably had no vote and could not run for office, we find women endorsing male candidates: someone, it seems, thought their opinions worth soliciting and advertising for consideration. (For a discussion of women and electioneering at Pompeii see Savunen (1995).) Sometimes female names turn up on their own, and these are likely to be prominent businesswomen. Those whose names appear in combination with men's names are presumably married to those men, but may still be prominent businesswomen, and even business partners of their husbands. But what are we to make of a case where an endorsement joins two women? In *CIL* 4.3678, Statia and Petronia endorse Marcus Casellius and Lucius Alfucius for the office of aedile. Are they a business partnership? Are they a personal partnership as well?

REFERENCES

Corpus Inscriptionum Latinarum. (1869-98). Berlin.
A Latin Dictionary. (1879). C. T. Lewis and C. Short, Eds. Oxford.
The Oxford Latin Dictionary. (1982). P. G. W. Glare, Ed. Oxford.
Thesaurus Linguae Latinae. (1900-). Leipzig.
Adams, S. N. (1982). *The Latin Sexual Vocabulary.* Baltimore: Johns Hopkins UP.

Anderson, W. S. (1970). *Lascivia* vs. *ira*: Martial and Juvenal. *California Studies in Classical Antiquity*, 5, 1-34.

Braund, S. H. (1995). A woman's voice–Laronia's role in Juvenal *Satire* 2. In Hawley and Levick (1995), pp. 207-219.

———, (Ed.). (1996). *Juvenal*. Satires, *Book I*. Cambridge: Cambridge UP.

Brooten, B. J. (1996). *Love between Women: Early Christian Responses to Female Homoeroticism*. Chicago: U of Chicago P.

Butrica, J. L. (2002). Clodius the *Pulcher* in Catullus and Cicero. *Classical Quarterly*, 52, 507-516.

Cantarella, E. (1988). *Secondo natura: La bisessualità nel mondo antico*. Rome: Editori riuniti.

Clarke, J. R. (1998). *Looking at Lovemaking*. Berkeley: U California P.

———. (2002). Look who's laughing at sex: Men and women viewers in the *apodyterium* of the Suburban Baths at Pompeii. In Fredrick (2002), pp. 149-181.

———. (2003). *Roman Sex*. New York: Harry N. Abrams.

Courtney, E. (1980). *A Commentary on the Satires of Juvenal*. London: Athlone Press.

Dalla, D. (1987). «Ubi Venus mutatur» *Omosessualità e diritto nel mondo romano*. Milan: A. Giuffrè.

Doty, R. L., Orndorff, M. M., Leyden, J., and Kligman, A. (1978). Communication of gender from human axillary odors: Relationship to perceived intensity and hedonicity. *Behavioral Biology*, 23, 373-380.

Fabre, G. (1981). *LIBERTUS. Recherches sur les rapports patron-affranchi à la fin de la Republique Romaine*. Collection de l'École Française de Rome 50. Rome.

Fantham, E. (1991). *Stuprum*: Public attitudes and penalties for sexual offences in republican Rome. *Échos du Monde Classique/Classical Views*, 35(3), 267-291.

Fay, I. W. (1919). *The Chemistry of the Coal-Tar Dyes*, New York: D. Van Nostrand.

Font i Furnols, M., Gispert, M., Diestre, A. and Oliver, M. A. (2003). Acceptability of boar meat by consumers depending on their age, gender, culinary habits, and sensitivity and appreciation of androstenone odour. *Meat Science*, 64, 433-440.

Fredrick, D. (Ed.). (2002). *The Roman Gaze: Vision, Power, and the Body*. Baltimore/London: Johns Hopkins UP.

———. (2002a). Mapping penetrability in late republican and early imperial Rome. In Fredrick (2002), pp. 236-264.

Gunderson, Erik. (2003). *Declamation, Paternity, and Roman Identity: Authority and the Rhetorical Self*. Cambridge: Cambridge UP.

Hallett, J. (1977). *Perusinae glandes* and the changing image of Augustus. *American Journal of Ancient History*, 2, 151-171.

———. (1997). Female homoeroticism and the denial of Roman reality in Latin literature. In Hallet and Skinner (1997), pp. 255-273.

Hallett, J. and Skinner, M. (Eds.). (1997). *Roman Sexualities*. Princeton: Princeton UP.

Hawley, R. and Levick, B. (1995). *Women in Antiquity: New Assessments*. London/New York: Routledge.

Hubbard, T. K. (2003). *Homosexuality in Greece and Rome: A Sourcebook of Basic Documents*. Berkeley/Los Angeles/London: U of California P.

Kaitz, M., Good, A., Korem, A. M., and Eidelman A. I. (1987). Mothers' recognition of their newborns by olfactory cues. *Developmental Psychobiology*, 20, 587-591.

Lord, T. and Kasprzak, M. (1989). Identification of self through olfaction. *Perceptual and Motor Skills*, *69*, 219-224.

Parker, H. (1997). The teratogenic grid. In Hallett and Skinner (1997), pp. 47-65.

Porter, R. H. and Moore, J. D. (1981). Human kin recognition by olfactory cues. *Physiology and Behavior*, *27*, 493-495.

Porter, R. H., Makin, J. W., Davis, L. B., and Christensen, K. M. (1992). Breast-fed infants respond to olfactory cues from their own mother and unfamiliar lactating females. *Infant Behavior and Development*, *15*, 85-93.

Pomeroy, A. (1992). Trimalchio as *deliciae*. *Phoenix*, *46*, 45-53.

Pratt, L. S. (1947). *The Chemistry and Physics of Organic Pigments*. New York: J. Wiley.

Richlin, A. (1983). *The Garden of Priapus: Sexuality and Aggression in Roman Humor*. New Haven/London: Yale UP.

Savunen, L. (1995). Women and elections in Pompeii. In Hawley and Levick (1995), pp. 194-206.

Sullivan, J. P. (1979). Martial's sexual attitudes. *Philologus*, *123*, 288-302.

Weisfeld, G. E., Czilli, T., Phillips, K. A., Gall, J. A. and Lichtman, C. M. (2003). "Possible olfaction-based mechanisms in human kin recognition and inbreeding avoidance," *Journal of Experimental Child Psychology*, *85*, 279-295.

Williams, C. A. (1999). *Roman Homosexuality: Ideologies of Masculinity in Classical Antiquity*. Oxford: Oxford UP.

Winkler, J. J. (1990). *The Constraints of Desire: The Anthropology of Sex and Gender in Ancient Greece*. New York/London: Routledge.

APPENDIX A
Laronia in Juvenal, Satire 2.36-65

Though there is no reason to offer here a comprehensive interpretation of this speech or of the poem as a whole (easily our most important source for male homosexuality in the Roman Empire), something must be said about it and about the denial of cunnilinctus that Juvenal puts into the mouth of "Laronia." There is no indication that she is to be read as a tribad. More likely she represents an adulteress who faces or has faced prosecution for adultery under the Lex Julia; that is why she is responding to a homosexual man who is demanding prosecutions under that law, and why she spitefully suggests that homosexual men should be punished instead, for their violations of the Lex Scantinia. This enactment seems to have been applied seriously only under Domitian, which is precisely when *Satire 2* is set (Domitian's niece Julia is mentioned in line 32). It is unclear, however, precisely how Laronia's appeal is supposed to reflect that historical reality: are the prosecutions already occurring—or are we to imagine them as somehow resulting from Laronia's criticism? In any case, the memory of these prosecutions was undoubtedly still fresh when Juvenal was writing.

The poem thus far has concerned hypocrisy among men, exemplified by those who teach philosophy and virtue and have a masculine appearance but seek to be penetrated sexually by other men, in contrast to the "honesty" of those who are openly effeminate (I am irresistibly reminded of Homer Simpson saying to Marge in *The Simpsons*, episode #4F11 (1997), that the character voiced by film director John Waters should have "the good taste to mince around" and that "I like my beer cold, my TV loud, and my homosexuals fuh-laming."):

> Laronia couldn't stand one of those fierce men shouting so often "Where are you sleeping now, Lex Julia?," and she [said], smiling, "What a fortunate age, that has *you* to oppose to its mores! Rome shall have modesty now–a third Cato has tumbled down from the sky! But yet where do you buy these balsams that blow from your hairy neck? Don't be embarrassed to point out the owner of the shop! But if laws and statutes are being stirred up, the Scantinia should be cited before all the rest. First look to and examine the men, who do more: but their number protects them, and their phalanxes joined boss to boss–great is the harmony among the soft. In our sex there will be no example so detestable. Media doesn't lick Cluvia, nor Flora Catulla: Hispo undergoes young men, and is pale from both diseases. We don't plead cases, do we, or know the civil statutes, or stir your forum with any noise? Few women wrestle, few eat colyphia–you card wool, you carry back the finished wool in baskets, you turn the spindle, pregnant with slender thread, better than Penelope, more smoothly than Arachne, like a drab mistress sitting on her wooden block [i.e., for punishment]. It's notorious why Hister filled his will with his freedman alone, why in life he gave much to a girl: rich will be the woman who sleeps third in a great bed! You, be a bride and shut your mouth: secrets bestow gems! After this, will a severe sentence be passed against *us*? Censure forgives the crows, harasses the doves."
>
> As they heard her intoning the obvious truth, the Sons of the Stoics scattered: for what untruths [had] Laronia [told]?

The fact that Juvenal seems to vouch for the truth of Laronia's denunciation and the fact that it agrees to some extent with the observations of his own *persona* earlier in the poem have induced a kind of torpor in commentators, who largely take the passage without a hint of irony; yet it is exactly such an absolute statement as "For what had Laronia said that wasn't true?" that should induce us to look for lies, or at least shades of truth, especially in a poem about hypocrisy. Though Braund (1995; 1996) accepts the contradictions between what Laronia says about women and what Juvenal says in *Satire* 6, arguing that neither exactly reflects contemporary reality, others, such as Courtney (1980), take seriously the observation that Laronia's claims are contradicted not only by Juvenal himself in another satire but by independent sources: her denial that women are involved in the law courts is in conflict with historical evidence for the late Republic (when Maesia and Gaia Afrania both pleaded) and with Juvenal 6.242-5, and her denial that women train athletically is in conflict again with Juvenal (6.246-66, and 419-33 on the athletic regimen), with Seneca the Younger (*Epistulae morales* 95.21, quoted above), and of course with Martial 7.67. Moreover, her claim that men have taken over such traditional chores of virtuous women as spinning and weaving–which receives no confirmation anywhere and seems to be another invention (criticism of male effeminacy during this period is so widespread and so detailed that this would surely be mentioned somewhere if it occurred to any extent)–should leave us wondering exactly what it is that "virtuous" women like Laronia were doing instead of those traditional chores proper to their station and virtue. (It is, by the way, fascinating to find the Greek Stoic philosopher Musonius Rufus, whose life ended not long after Domitian's reign, including in a discussion of women's education the imaginary objection, "Do you think that men ought to learn spinning like women and that women ought to practise gymnastics like men?" [fr. 4]. He was willing to consider that men might take up lighter, "women"'s chores, but for reasons of health, of course, not effeminacy!) Laronia, then, should be seen as a self-interested liar, minimizing or simply denying the irregularities of women's conduct while suggesting that they (read "she") should not receive such close scrutiny from legal authorities because there are others more in need of restraint.

Moreover, she should surely be seen as a hypocrite too, yet another example of someone who preaches virtue, practices vice; she pretends to support old-fashioned virtues, at least when she is attacking homosexual men, but she has contempt for those values. This, I think, is the point of her reference (which has puzzled commentators) to the "drab mistress"–in her mind, women's traditional spinning and weaving is really only good enough to be done by slaves, and as punishment at that (this can again be paralleled from historical sources; for example, Augustus liked to have Livia appear in public in clothing that he claimed she made herself, to set an example for others, and Columella indicates that the practice was extinct in his own time). All in all, then, when Laronia claims that Roman women do not perform cunnilinctus, we should expect another self-interested fib; after all, Martial (who is a little earlier than Juvenal) does indeed depict a woman who performs cunnilinctus in 7.67. Scholars since Anderson (1970) have been arguing for a close intertextual relationship between Laronia's speech and Martial 7.67. I do not think that one exists or needs to be supposed: each poet simply reflects a shared world. But I do think that Martial's depictions of Bassa and Philaenis are relevant to understanding Laronia's denial of cunnilinctus, for they enable us to formulate what Juvenal surely expected would be the response of the Roman reader: "Yes, of course they don't perform cunnilinctus: they're strapping on dildos and fucking like men!" Ironically, the denial of cunnilinctus here just might be our strongest evidence for the reality of lesbianism in the Roman Empire.

APPENDIX B
Philaenis in Martial 9.40 and 9.62

In 9.40, the husband of a woman named Philaenis is sailing from Alexandria to Rome, and she has made a vow: if he arrives safely, she will fellate him. The implication seems to be that this is something she did not normally do. A Philaenis who ordinarily refuses to perform fellatio inevitably recalls the Philaenis of 7.67, and one wonders whether she is to be seen as the same person.

The identification does not seem impossible, but the great distance separating 9.40 from 7.67 does not seem to favour it (purely heterosexual women have been known to find fellatio unpleasant); or perhaps the historical associations of the name Philaenis led Martial to use it of women with lesbian tendencies on various occasions without intending the women to be seen as the same. On the other hand, 9.40 is in much closer proximity to 9.62, which refers to a Philaenis who also might be intended as a lesbian. This Philaenis likes to wear expensive cloth of Tyrian purple, not to display her wealth but because she enjoys the smell. (For what it is worth, I note that two epigrams in the *Greek Anthology*, 6.206 [Antipater of Sidon] and 6.207 [Archias], list dedications to Aphrodite by various marriageable women, including a Philaenis whose offering is her *purple* hairnet.)

An aroma in purple cloth is not remarked upon elsewhere, but there is likely to have been a "fishy" odour because of the origin of the dye, and there are two ways in which odours in purple cloth might be thought pleasurable to a lesbian.

My own suggestion is that Philaenis likes purple cloth because a lingering odour of shellfish surrounds her with the aroma of women's private parts. On the other hand, Mr. Alfred M. Kriman of the University of Notre Dame has suggested to me in personal communication that the methods of preparing purple cloth, especially for women, resulted in the presence of the hormone adrostenone in the cloth. While it seems unlikely that any Roman would understand why a certain kind of cloth appealed to a certain kind of woman for the latter reason, it is possible that the effect was more widely noticed in everyday life and simply not mentioned in our literary sources. Mr. Kriman has provided the following account, relevant to both views of why Philaenis liked purple, of how odours were retained or even created in the processing of the molluscs that yielded Tyrian purple dye:

> Humans have a fairly good sense of smell and can detect at the level of a part in 10^{12} to a part in 10^6. Women generally have better ability to smell, but almost everyone can improve by habituation. Studies show that a majority of people are able to distinguish their own smell from others' (Lord and Kasprzak, 1989) that mothers and their newborns can recognize each other by smell (Kaitz, Good, Korem, & Eidelman, 1987; Por-

ter, Makin, Davis and Christensen, 1992), that siblings can do the same (Porter and Moore, 1981), and that some people can distinguish adults' sex by odor (Doty, Orndorff, Leyden, & Kligman, 1978). For a review and some recent data, see (Weisfeld, Czilli, Phillips, Gall, & Lichtman, 2003). Mate choice in humans (today) is demonstrably correlated with odor, and the perceived pleasantness or unpleasantness to women of various odors is affected by hormones (i.e., is correlated with the phase of the menstrual cycle or with contraceptive pill use).

The colorant, the active ingredient, in Tyrian purple dye is dibromoindigotin and a number of related compounds. These are extremely fast and probably not significant as odorants. However, dyes and mordants can trap and bind other substances to the dyed textile. At the molecular level, this is due to their direct chemical reaction with proteins and other chemicals. Also, at the larger, microscopic level, dyes can form dendritic or star-like clumps that would trap bits of tissue (Pratt, 1947, pp. 287-296).

There are two obvious sources of odorants in purple-dyed cloth. One is rotten flesh from the shellfish. There are indications that this was recognized as a problem: early dyeing operations apparently used only the gland; later large-scale operations used the whole animal, but Pliny reports some effort to separate off non-dye ingredients, and that may have been partly to minimize the odor problem. Regardless of the precise odor of the freshly dyed material, one odor note that seems likely to have been important in dyed-and-washed cloth is that of rotten fish: bits of tissue trapped by the dye would continue to rot, and in the process small amines are released, which are universally described as smelling like rotten fish.

Mollusc flesh would be a source of long-term odors in *any* Tyrian-purple-dyed textile from the Roman period, when dye was extracted from whole whelks. Urine is a second source of odor, which would be relevant primarily for linen (and also cotton). Vegetable fibers do not take dye as readily as wool, and therefore require a mordant. As described by Pliny, the mordanting process used urine. This was evidently needed because stale urine is a weak ammonia solution; alum and other salts are reacted with ammonia for use as mordants (Fay, 1919, pp. 400-416).

Although whole (or stale) urine is not perceived as pleasant, there are components in it that some do find pleasant. After washes with, at most, the weak detergents available at the time, these components might well have been the dominant odorants. Two kinds of chemicals in urine that have received substantial research attention seem to be likely candidates.

One odorant is androstenone and related steroids. Androstenone is a boar pheromone, and in high concentration it generally indicates a sexually mature male; it has been found within different human body fluids. Men and women have statistically different reactions to the odor, and some women (and men) find it pleasant (Font i Furnols, Gispert, Diestre, & Oliver, 2003).

The other odorant is a set of compounds associated with the major histocompatibility complex (MHC). The principal known factor determining whether a person's odor is perceived as pleasant by another person is the degree of similarity between their MHC's. (This appears to be adaptive as an element of sexual selection. One hypothetical mechanism for which there is some evidence is that offspring of heterozygous MHC would have a broader range of immunities. MHC plays a central role in immune-system self-other recognition.) MHC genes exhibit great variability, so the main effect of the odor preference may be thought of as aversive: people specifically find unpleasant the MHC-related odor of potential mates genetically close to themselves. Although the experiment does not appear to have been done, it seems likely that a mix of odors from many unrelated individuals (like the urine source for dye mordanting) would be perceived as pleasant overall.

Representations of the *Cinaedus* in Roman Art: Evidence of "Gay" Subculture?

John R. Clarke, PhD

University of Texas at Austin

SUMMARY. Whereas analysis of ancient Roman texts reveals signs of a possible homosexual subculture, their interpretation is difficult. This article analyzes the content and context of visual representations of male-male intercourse, including wall paintings at Pompeii, a silver cup, and an engraved agate gemstone. Whether presenting negative stereotypes (Tavern of Salvius, Pompeii; Suburban Baths, Pompeii), or positive ones (Warren Cup, British Museum; Leiden gemstone), these

---

John R. Clarke is Annie Laurie Howard Regents Professor of Fine Arts at the University of Texas at Austin. He teaches the history of Roman art and culture, and is the author of five books, including *Roman Sex, 100 BC-AD 250* (Abrams, 2003), *Art in the Lives of Ordinary Romans: Visual Representation and Non-elite Viewers in Italy, 100 BC-AD 315* (Berkeley, 2003), and *Looking at Lovemaking: Constructions of Sexuality in Roman Art, 100 BC-AD 250* (Berkeley, 2003). He has written many articles on ancient wall painting and mosaics as well as essays on contemporary art and art criticism. He is recipient of the Guggenheim Fellowship and the National Endowment for the Humanities Fellowship for University Teachers. Correspondence may be addressed: Department of Art & Art History, 1 University Station D1300, University of Texas, Austin, TX 78712-0337.

[Haworth co-indexing entry note]: "Representations of the *Cinaedus* in Roman Art: Evidence of 'Gay' Subculture?" Clarke, John R. Co-published simultaneously in *Journal of Homosexuality* (Harrington Park Press, an imprint of The Haworth Press, Inc.) Vol. 49, No. 3/4, 2005, pp. 271-298; and: *Same-Sex Desire and Love in Greco-Roman Antiquity and in the Classical Tradition of the West* (ed: Beert C. Verstraete, and Vernon Provencal) Harrington Park Press, an imprint of The Haworth Press, Inc., 2005, pp. 271-298. Single or multiple copies of this article are available for a fee from The Haworth Document Delivery Service [1-800-HAWORTH, 9:00 a.m. - 5:00 p.m. (EST). E-mail address: docdelivery@haworthpress.com].

271

representations reveal the presence of well-developed social attitudes toward the practice of male-male sex and the practitioners themselves. *[Article copies available for a fee from The Haworth Document Delivery Service: 1-800-HAWORTH. E-mail address: <docdelivery@haworthpress.com> Website: <http://www.HaworthPress.com> © 2005 by The Haworth Press, Inc. All rights reserved.]*

KEYWORDS. Homosexuality and art, homosexuality and ancient, subculture and gay, subculture and homosexual, *Cinaedus*, Pompeii and art, Warren Cup

The search for what Amy Richlin calls "the materiality of the *cinaedus*" in ancient Roman culture has led scholars to comb classical literature for signs of his existence. *Cinaedus* is one of the most common words used by Romans to denote an adult male who liked to be penetrated by other males (Richlin, 1993, p. 531). In an ongoing polemic about the reality of the *cinaedus*, the scholarship roughly divides into two camps. There are those who, like Richlin, believe that the classical texts point to an actual homosexual subculture in ancient Rome. Others, following the strict "cultural constructionist" model first set forth by Michel Foucault, deny the possibility of a substratum of Roman society consisting of self-identified homosexuals; they maintain that there was nothing comparable to modern gay subcultures (Halperin, 1990, pp. 6-9).

The problem with textual analysis, as all scholars are quick to admit, is that elite men or men working for elites wrote all the texts. In these texts we fail to hear the voices of the other 98% of Roman society: non-elite men (including the freeborn poor, slaves, former slaves, and foreigners) and women of all classes (with the possible exception of Sulpicia, who–even so–sounds like an elite man when she writes poetry). The *cinaedus*, like non-elites and women, is conspicuous by his silence (Richlin, 1993, p. 524).

The one major class of nonliterary texts, the graffiti, ought to help flesh out attitudes toward the *cinaedus* and male-male sex–at least among the non-elite–but most often they are defamatory. We have to read them, as it were, backwards. If someone writes "Cosmus Equitias's [slave] is a big faggot and a cocksucker with his legs spread apart," does it mean that ordinary people believed that men who liked to suck cock also like to be penetrated anally? Or does it mean that the combination of the two activities was a nastier insult than just saying that Cosmus Equitia's slave was a *cinaedus* (*Corpus Inscriptionum Latinarum* [*CIL*] 4.1825, trans. Richlin, 1993, p. 549). Both literary and nonliterary texts that refer to male-male sex–or even those that deride men who rejected Roman stereotypical male behavior–require a lot of interpretation. In the end these texts are inconclusive. They can't tell us whether there was a gay subculture.

Visual representation, on the other hand, not only cuts across class boundaries–it offers us new information about non-elite perception of the *cinaedus*. Visual art from the period 100 BC-AD 250 both parallels the textual sources and–my angle here–overturns them. In other words, although we usually find visual artists representing elite standards for male-male sexual behavior, we also find them gleefully overturning those standards. What is more, when the visual art with sexual representations can be studied in its original architectural context, we can speculate with some degree of certainty about the social class of the patron who paid for the art and the viewers who looked at it.

How to be sure we are not "reading in" our own acculturation with regard to gay men when we're analyzing ancient Roman images? This was the charge leveled against John Boswell's pioneering book, *Christianity, Social Tolerance, and Homosexuality* (1980). While developing my own book on non-elite viewers in Roman Italy, I came up with a set of rules designed to keep my focus as objective as possible (Clarke, 2003b, pp. 7-13). With every image I asked: Who paid for it? Who made it? Who looked at it? Under what circumstances did the viewer look at it? What else did it look like?

Each of these questions addressed an aspect of the production and consumption of paintings, mosaics, sculptures, ceramics–especially those found in their original architectural contexts. Eventually, I was able to chart the variables that confront the investigator when she asks these questions (Figure 1).

Particularly important for this essay are the problems of determining the gender role of both maker and consumer, as well as where else the viewer might have seen the representation. For my first image, I will argue that the viewer likely saw the *cinaedus* on the street–and, more specifically, in popular bars.

THE POWERLESS CINAEDUS *IN THE TAVERN OF SALVIUS*

The humble Tavern of Salvius at Pompeii, destroyed in the eruption of Vesuvius in AD 79, came to light in excavations of 1876 (Figure 2;

FIGURE 1. A model for the reception of visual art in Rome.

A MODEL FOR THE RECEPTION OF VISUAL ART IN ANCIENT ROME

MAKING OF IMAGE

Who Is Patron?

Patron's Social Status
  elite
  non-elite
    freeborn
    freedman
    slave
    foreigner

Patron's Gender Role

Patron's Motivations:
  advertisement of goods/services
  commemoration
  entertainment
  mediation--to resolve community tensions
  appeasing gods/propitiation
  competition/one-upsmanship
  announcement of status/wealth
  apotropaic/admonition
  civic benefaction

Patron's Understanding of Image
  knows/does not know model or referent

Literate/illiterate

Patron's Occupation/Profession

TRANSMISSION OF IMAGES

Who Is Artist?

Training and Ability

Has Models:
  understands models
  does not understand models

Has no models:
  invents from observation
  invents through pastiche

Literate/illiterate

Viewer Address

Location of Image
  street
  temple
  dining room
  tomb
  house
  tavern
  latrine
  in moving procession

Viewing Context--seen while:
  working
  walking
  standing
  praying
  dining
  shopping
  mourning
  visiting
  defecating

Size and Scale of Image:
  close viewing
  distant viewing

Viewing Context:
  seen with what other images?

Cost and Medium of Image

Writing/no writing on Image

Who Is Viewer?

Viewer's Social Status
  Elite
  Non-elite
    freeborn
    freedman
    slave
    foreigner

Viewer's Gender Role

Viewer's Understanding of Image
  Knows/does not know model or referent
  Believes/does not believe image is a god or goddess

Past experience: saw image in
  temple
  forum
  theater
  coin
  house
  pattern book
  procession/triumph

Literate/illiterate

Viewer's Occupation/Profession

FIGURE 2. Pompeii, Tavern of Salvius (VI, 14, 36), view. With permission from the Ministero per i Beni e le Attività Culturali, Soprintendenza Archeologica di Pompeii. Reproduction prohibited. Photo Michael Larvey.

Clarke, 2003b, p. 161, n. 11). Noting the precarious state of preservation of the painted frieze that decorated the north wall of the main room, the excavator had it cut from the wall and removed to the Naples Museum (Figure 3). The frieze covered repairs made to the tavern's walls after the earthquake of AD 62, so it dated between AD 62 and 79. Four scenes, each about 50 cm square, follow each other from left to right to make a frieze 2.05 m long. The painting seems to have been the only decoration in this room, where ordinary people ate, drank, gambled, and perhaps dallied sexually with the male and female slaves who served them.

In the first scene, a man kisses a woman, and the caption declares: *nolo cum Myrtale.* . . . Although the final word, probably an infinitive, will keep us in eternal suspense, the rest of the phrase is clear: "I don't want to___with Myrtalis." Since Myrtalis is a woman's name, it seems

FIGURE 3. Tavern of Salvius, north wall, frieze. Naples Archaeological Museum, inv. 11482. With permission from the Ministero per i Beni e le Attività Culturali, Soprintendenza per le provincie di Napoli e Caserta. Reproduction prohibited. Photo Michael Larvey.

that the man is saying that he doesn't want to "go with" or "date" Myrtalis any more. In the second scene–the focus of my argument–two effeminate-looking men vie with each other to be served the jug of wine that a large woman server carries. Scenes three and four form a two-frame narrative where two men get into trouble over gambling. In scene three they are playing dice. The man on the left holds the dice-cup in his right hand. The artist has him saying, "I won" (*exsi*). His companion asserts: "It's not three; it's two" (*non / tria duas / est*). This disagreement turns ugly in the following scene, where the two men, now standing, come to blows. The man on the left grabs the right shoulder of his dice-partner, who in turn raises his right hand in a fist. They exchange insults. The man on the left says, "You no-name. It was three for me. I was the winner" (*noxsi / a me / tria / eco / fui*). The other responds, "Look here, cocksucker. I was the winner" (*orte fellator / eco fui*). The innkeeper wants none of this. He tells them, "Go outside and fight it out" (*itis / foras / rixsatis*).

I have dealt with all four scenes in detail elsewhere, pointing out how they got viewers to laugh by showing reversals: of love, of luck at the gambling table. What might be a tragedy for the lovers or the gamblers in the pictures is comedy for the tavern-goers who looked at their misfortunes (Clarke, 2003b, pp. 161-70). But here I would like to focus on scene two, for I believe that the two effeminate men in this scene are *cinaedi*. If so, this scene might tell us what ordinary Romans thought *cinaedi* looked like and how they expected them to act. Since the other scenes present stereotypes for the Roman viewers to laugh at (the star-crossed lovers; the hot-headed gamblers), what visual signs might identify the two men as *cinaedi*?

The artist presents them as men already in their cups competing for the wine that the female server carries (Figure 4). The men are seated in three-quarters view, hands outstretched, both demanding the jug of wine and the winecup that she holds. The figure on the left says *hoc* or "Here!" while his companion counters *non / mia est* or "No! It's mine!"[1] The server, feigning indifference, says, "Whoever wants it, take it" (*qui vol / sumat*)–but then with a somewhat ominous change of heart she offers the wine to someone else: "Oceanus, come and drink" (*Oceane / veni bibe*).

One scholar proposes that this man is none other than a famous Pompeian gladiator named Oceanus (Todd, 1939, p. 6). Even if the man she is addressing is not *that* Oceanus, the name itself must have carried a cachet in local circles. Martial uses the name four times for a person who performs the dual functions of usher and bouncer in the theater (Martial,

FIGURE 4. Tavern of Salvius, second scene. Naples Archaeological Museum, inv. 11482. With permission from the Ministero per i Beni e le Attività Culturali, Soprintendenza per le provincie di Napoli e Caserta. Reproduction prohibited. Photo Michael Larvey.

3.95.10; 5.23.4; 5.27.4; 6.9.2). A second, more likely, interpretation is that the serving woman is directly addressing one of the drinkers as Oceanus with the sense of "Okay, big boy, come and get it." Closer examination of the physical types of the two men, their hairstyles, and their body language support this second interpretation: that the barmaid is mocking and challenging their masculinity–she sees them as *cinaedi*. The man at the left, although he has a masculine face with large features, is wearing an anomalous hairstyle for the period (AD 60-79). His long hair is parted in the middle, with a thick gathering (or bun!) over his right ear. His burgundy robe, shaded in black, gathers around the seat of the four-legged, backless stool. He draws his left leg behind the right to cross it at the calf. It is clear that his pose was important to the artist, since he repainted the entire upper half of this figure. His drinking companion turns his long, oval face in three-quarters view; although his features are similarly masculine, his hair frames his face, perhaps gathered in a bun as well. This man's blue-green robe falls down to bunch at the seat of the stool, where it turns to shades of black. He crosses his feet in the same way that his fellow drinker does, as he makes a sweeping gesture with his outstretched arm to dramatize his plea for more wine.

The artist took pains to differentiate the barmaid both from the two men in the scene and from the woman in scene one. Her scale, facial features, and pose contrast so greatly with those of the men that she looks like the work of a different artist. She is much larger in stature than the men, and wears a singularly stern expression, her face in profile as she holds a wine jug in her left hand and a wineglass in the other. (Paint losses reveal guidelines in red pigment under the jug.) The artist represented her detachment from her customers spatially: she stands to the right, her feet nearly touching the bottom framing edge of the picture so that she appears to be closer to the viewer's space than the two men.

The serving woman's large size, stern expression, and her response to the men all stress her power over them. "Whoever wants it, take it" is the set-up line, expressing her lack of interest in the rival claims for her attention. But her second line, nastier than the first, reveals a change of mind. She becomes the quintessential female wiseguy, moving from annoyed indifference to challenging the annoying customers. Either she calls on Oceanus, the beefiest character in the bar, to settle the dispute (perhaps violently) or she mocks their virility by calling them by the name Oceanus. Not only do the men–probably drunk–make a spectacle of themselves by vying to be the first served, they both fail in their attempts–a mark of their impotence as men. They can't even control a barmaid.

The drinking men also look much weaker in both facial features, hairstyles, and gestures than the men who appear in the other three frames of the painting. The man kissing the woman in scene one is clean-shaven, and has a square jaw and short-cropped hair; his pose is straightforward and sexually direct: he leans into the woman with his whole body. The men arguing over dice in scene three and then coming to fisticuffs and being thrown out of the bar in scene four are also quite different from the drinkers of scene two. Their heads are smaller in relation to their bodies, and both are bearded, with closely cropped hair. In both body and head type they conform to an ideal of masculine beauty common to high-art mythological paintings produced at Pompeii and elsewhere in this period: thin, muscular but wiry, actively posed

(Clarke, 2003b, fig. 76). Like the kissing man in scene one, their faces and bodies are fiercely expressive.

The drinkers, by contrast, are beardless, rotund of body, and sitting. I believe that the ancient viewer recognized in them the stereotype of the passive male or *cinaedus*. Why else did the artist take such pains to make them as different as possible from the other six images of men in the frieze? They wear long dresses instead of short tunics; they have big heads and are clean shaven; they sit in passive rather than active poses, crossing their ankles; their hair is long and elaborately done up. Richlin demonstrates how texts characterize the appearance and mannerisms of the *cinaedus:* as men in drag or as men who wear the toga in a deviant fashion (Richlin, 1993, pp. 541-46). Here our drinkers play femmes compared to the butch men in the other scenes. Perhaps even more important, why did the artist make them powerless in their confrontation with a mere barmaid?

As countless studies of ancient Roman literature and culture have shown, the *cinaedus* constituted a preposterous inversion of the Roman rule that adult freeborn men penetrated but were never penetrated. Here they are trying to do the impossible: act like real men. And they fail. The comic effect depended on the viewer picking up the visual clues that suggested that they were *cinaedi*. Not only did the elite Romans consider *cinaedi* to be sexual monsters, they could also bear the same status of infamy that prostitutes, actors, and gladiators suffered (Richlin, 1993, pp. 554-71).

If the artist deliberately used these visual conventions to call up the *cinaedus* stereotype for his viewers, it was to make them laugh. In order for this to work, the viewers must have considered themselves "normal." For male viewers, whatever they thought about being the passive recipient of a penis, they (unlike the two men in the painting) conformed to norms of dress, hairstyle, gesture, and behavior that ancient Romans associated with proper, active, penetrator-males: the "straight male stereotype."

To test how elements of this stereotype might still have power in certain sectors of our contemporary Euro-American culture, I offer this loose translation of the scenario pictured in the Tavern of Salvius. What I've had to do is emphasize how out of place the two effeminate men are, and how their effeminate behavior annoys a masculine-identified female server (I've made her a lesbian):

> Two flaming queens wearing fluffy sweaters walk into a straight biker bar and order Pink Ladies. The server, a huge bull dyke,

gaffaws and tells them that it's only draft beer here. They arrange themselves in a corner table and order one, two, three pitchers, drinking them down like "real men." They get really drunk. When it's time for another pitcher, they start arguing. They both call the server and yell, "Another pitcher, Miss!" She's had about enough of these guys, so when they start to bicker about who gets the pitcher first, she first says, "Look *girls*, whoever's man enough come and get it." But then she has a better idea. She turns to Biff, the beefiest biker in the bar, and says, "Hey Biff, I gotta free pitcher for you."

What's interesting about this exercise is that there is one element that I can't elicit or match in my translation. Alongside the straight male stereotype–in fact, an important component of the straight male stereotype–was the expectation that Roman males might all have had homosexual experiences in their formative years between puberty and marriage. Non-elites, in particular slaves and former slaves, were the usual passive partners of freeborn elite men (Williams, 1999, pp. 18-9, 30-8, 49-51, 77-81, 226, 245-6). A large percentage of the male viewers in the Tavern of Salvius–slaves, former slaves, and foreigners–had experienced being penetrated anally and had also been penetrated orally; that is, they had fellated males. But their experience had not continued into adulthood, nor had it translated into the kind of dress and behavior that they saw in the scene of the two *cinaedi* and the barmaid. Otherwise they would not have found the image funny. As "real" men, they identified with the men depicted in the other three scenes who got into trouble over love (of women), dice, and fistfights.

Real-life *cinaedi* might have found the image funny as well, simply because the artist was so good at characterizing them. The little vignette is not necessarily offensive, since it is really about a battle of wills over the trivial matter of being served. And since this is a small neighborhood bar, we shouldn't leave out the possibility that the two *cinaedi* in the picture are portraits of "regulars" who always dressed up to come to this bar, got drunk, and started getting huffy over the service.

There is also a possible woman viewer in the tavern; she could either have been a customer or a tavern servant. Both men and women, mostly slaves, served customers in such taverns, and often their owners prostituted them to customers for a modest price (Riggsby, 1995, pp. 423-27). A woman working in the Tavern of Salvius could have found the scene of the barmaid standing up to the *cinaedi* both funny and empowering, especially if she could read the caption. The woman server turns the tables on two insistent, obnoxious, and effeminate men with a mild threat of potential violence. Her refusal to serve the demanding *cinaedi*–along with her ability to invoke Oceanus as a backup–gives her power that she is not supposed to have.

THE EROTIC CINAEDUS IN THE SUBURBAN BATHS

The *cinaedus* appears in relation to "straight" men and woman in another clear context at Pompeii–but this time he's having sex with them! Unlike the paintings from the Tavern of Salvius, where hairstyle, clothes, and gesture constitute the stereotypical markers showing how *cinaedi* are different from "normal" men, in the eight paintings from the Suburban Baths, where the protagonists are naked and in bed, it is their sexual activity that marks them. Like the "comic strip" in the Tavern of Salvius, the little sexual vignettes in the Suburban Baths were put there to make the customers laugh–but for a very different reason. They were supposed to protect the viewers from the Evil Eye.

If we step back and look at the decoration of the whole space, it turns out that it is a witty commentary on its function as a dressing room (Figure 5). The room had two decorative systems: one for the front part of the room and another for the area in back where the bathers undressed. Simple motifs on a black ground, with a white upper zone, decorated the front area. A tall thin panel divides the wall at midpoint, signaling a change in the decorative scheme from black to yellow. What is more, in the white upper zone of this back area the artist depicted a deep shelf in perspective that supports sixteen numbered boxes.

The sixteen boxes are two-dimensional representations of the real containers for bathers' clothing that once rested on wooden shelves directly below (Figure 6). Although none of the boxes survived intact, since they were of wood, the excavator, Luciana Jacobelli, did find the little metal *X* straps that served as reinforcing. The artist represented these reinforcing straps at the front and along the sides of each box (Jacobelli, 1995, pp. 61-64).

What was the purpose of the numerals? On the right wall they run right to left, from I to VIII, and on the back wall from IX to XVI. (Unfortunately, only eight of the pictures survived, the ones corresponding to the numbers I through VIII on the right wall.) By representing the boxes with numbers the artist also numbered the real containers below, where each bather deposited her or his things. As if the numbers were not sufficient, he added an unforgettable "label" atop each box: a sex

FIGURE 5. Pompeii, Suburban Baths, apodyterium 7, south and east walls. With permission from the Ministero per i Beni e le Attività Culturali, Soprintendenza Archeologica di Pompeii. Reproduction prohibited. Photo Michael Larvey.

picture! Even if a bather forgot the number of the box, he or she was not likely to forget the picture.

But the sex pictures were more than just locker labels. The Romans believed that someone who envied your beauty could emit particles from his or her Evil Eye that would enter you, harm you, and possibly kill you. A person undressing at the bath was particularly susceptible to the Evil Eye of someone who envied his or her beauty. To protect his customers, the owner of the Suburban Baths commissioned a painter to make pictures of taboo sex to make everyone laugh, since the Romans believed that laughter banished the Evil Eye.

Now imagine this scenario. You enter the dressing room of the Suburban Baths. The decoration of the anteroom is completely neutral and wallpaper-like. You proceed to the rear of the room, where you see the shelves and take down a numbered box. You've undressed, placed your clothes in the box, and just as you reach up to place the box under its

FIGURE 6. Suburban Baths, digital reconstruction with figures. With permission from the Ministero per i Beni e le Attività Culturali, Soprintendenza Archeologica di Pompeii. Reproduction prohibited. Reconstruction Kirby Conn.

number you see the perspective of the painted box leading to the sex-picture. Not an ordinary sex-picture, but an outrageous one. You laugh, and you've just dispelled the Evil Eye of the envious man or woman who's been eyeing your beautiful body. Safe!

As far-fetched as this explanation might sound to us moderns, it fits the ancient Roman mentality perfectly (Clarke, 2003a, pp. 121-23). It also explains several peculiarities of the erotic paintings in the dressing room of the Suburban Baths. For one thing, they are quite small and very high up on the wall. To photograph them, we needed scaffolding, ladders, and bright lights. Such aids were not available to the ancient bather, who had to crane his neck and take some time in this dark room to make out the imagery. All of this craning and squinting must have added to the comedy and general mirth. (Of course, with repeated visits the comic intensity would have faded. Perhaps that's why the owner later had them covered up.) A first-time bather must have made quite a spectacle of him- or herself–nude and on tiptoe–trying to decipher the goings-on depicted on the wall high above.

Unlike the romantic, ideal images of both male-female and male-male sexual intercourse that we find in houses or on fine silver and cameo glass vessels, these paintings portrayed taboo acts: fellatio, cunnilingus, sex between women and group sex highlighting the *cinaedus*. The Suburban Baths paintings catalogued the sex acts that a proper Roman was never supposed to do (or at least not admit doing). In the Suburban Baths, only two of the eight vignettes show what we might consider "straight" or "proper" sex between a male-female couple. The other six break the rules.

THE CINAEDUS *IN THE MIDDLE*

Our first *cinaedus* appears in scene VI–and he is the middle man in a sexual threesome. The man kneeling at the left is penetrating him anally, while the *cinaedus* in turn penetrates the woman crouching on the bed, her face in the pillow and her buttocks raised (Figure 7). The image is unique. The most standard component is the woman's pose–called the "lioness" by fourth-century BC Greeks, and used by Roman artists when they wanted to show the uninhibited woman (Stewart, 1996, p. 148; Clarke, 1998, pp. 230).

But it's not the woman's position so much as who's doing what to whom that a Roman viewer would consider outrageous–and therefore funny. After all, the woman is being penetrated by a man who has lost his phallic status by being penetrated by another man: he is a *cinaedus*. To drive this point home, the artist has depicted the man in the middle as an adult man, not a boy. He's the same size as the man who penetrates him, and–to emphasize that he likes being penetrated–the artist has him reaching back to grasp his penetrator's hand. This man, a bit more muscular, turns to the viewer as if to say: "Look at me/us–see what we're doing!" His gaze is the only link to the viewer, since the other two are fully engaged in their pursuit of pleasure.

If we look at standard representations of male-male sex, both in elite and non-elite art, the singularity of our man-in-the-middle strikes home. Mold-made terra-cotta vessels produced in Arretium (modern-day Arezzo) between 30 BC and AD 30 repeat a composition that sums up in visual terms the standard Roman mentality of the period: the Roman male can be bisexual with impunity, as long as he is the person inserting his penis into a woman or a boy–socially and conceptually inferiors.

A "bisexual" Arretine bowl, now in Boston, alternates a scene of a woman squatting down on a man's penis with a scene of a man entering

FIGURE 7. Suburban Baths, scene VI. With permission from the Ministero per i Beni e le Attività Culturali, Soprintendenza Archeologica di Pompeii. Reproduction prohibited. Photo Michael Larvey.

a boy's anus (Figure 8). The man-boy scene is as tender as the male-female scene is explicit and raw. It's a romantic encounter between a man and a boy on a bed. The man looks into the boy's eyes as he prepares to enter his anus. The man grips the boy's right thigh and plants his knee behind the boy's right knee. The boy grasps the man's arm just below the elbow. Is he resisting the man's entry, or is he pulling him in? This

FIGURE 8. Arretine Bowl Fragment, Museum of Fine Arts, Boston, inv. 13.109. Gift of E. P. Warren. Photograph copyright 2004 Museum of Fine Arts, Boston.

same composition (the same one used in man-girl scenes, but with the removal of female breasts and the addition of flaccid penis and testicles), gets repeated on a variety of vessels–and not just the mass-produced Arretine meant for buyers of slender means and exported throughout the Empire.

It is a composition that also shows up on costly, unique objects. It appears on the Ortiz perfume bottle, produced in the ultra-expensive cut cameo glass technique, where, predictably, it counterpoints a representation of a man penetrating a girl (Clarke, 2003a, pp. 84-87). On side B of the Warren Cup, a silver vessel dating to the first three decades of the first century AD, the artist tried an elegant variation on the composition: he turns the couple's heads away from each other (Figure 9). Rather than gazing at his partner, the man looks to the viewer's left, his head slightly lowered. The boy, in turn, leans on his flexed right elbow as he props himself up on the pillow and gazes up into space. Despite all this elegant twisting and posing, the act of sex is quite explicit: the artist has represented one of the man's testicles directly behind the boy's, indicating that he is already inside him.

What all these images–spanning the range from the mass-produced and cheap to the unique and expensive–have in common is the Roman stereotype of boy-love: romantic, with the full-grown man penetrating the boy, who is feminized, much smaller than the man, and sexually unexcited (if the tiny flaccid penis is any gauge). Given this context in the visual record, we can imagine the surprise–and the mirth–that the representation of a full-grown man being penetrated by another adult male must have provoked.

THE PENETRATED CINAEDUS
WITH WOMAN-TO-WOMAN CUNNILINGUS

In the adjacent scene VII, the artist ups the ante by adding to the mix two acts of oral sex: a woman performs cunnilingus on a woman who is fellating a man–a *cinaedus* at that (Figure 10). It is a sexual foursome. The man on the left of the bed looks out at the viewer and raises his right arm while he penetrates the man kneeling in front of him. The man being penetrated leans forward as a woman, kneeling on her left knee but with her right leg raised in the air, crouches on her elbows to fellate him. A second woman, kneeling on the floor, performs cunnilingus on her. (Remains of a green garland from the later painting campaign cover the back of the woman performing fellatio and the knees of the woman performing cunnilingus.) The Romans constructed strong taboos around the acts of cunnilingus and fellatio, principally because they believed it made the mouth of the individual who performed these acts impure. They saw acts of oral sex as defiling society (Clarke, 1998, pp. 220-225; 2003a, pp. 118-20).

FIGURE 9. Warren Cup, side B, London, British Museum. London, The British Museum, inv. 36683 G&R. Copyright The British Museum.

But since our focus is on the *cinaedus*, we must ask why the woman found him so attractive that she would debase herself, and risk social stigma, by fellating him. It turns out that Romans believed that the passive male homosexual was particularly attractive to women. Hence his danger to the social order, for he could entrap women in sexual acts,

FIGURE 10. Suburban Baths, scene VII. With permission from the Ministero per i Beni e le Attività Culturali, Soprintendenza Archeologica di Pompeii. Reproduction prohibited. Photo Michael Larvey.

such as adultery or performing oral sex, that would spoil their reputations (Edwards, 1993, pp. 83-84). In scene VII, the women illustrate double oral debasement, as it were, one by licking a woman's genitals, the other by sucking a man's penis. And he is not the stereotypical Roman male who appears in all other representations of a woman performing fellatio. He is a *cinaedus*–a man being penetrated by another man.

Although to modern eyes–accustomed, perhaps, to seeing such scenes enacted in bisexual pornography–scene VII looks like serious, hard-driving, no-holds barred sex, to the Roman viewer, the image is so filled with taboo-breaking that he or she could only properly laugh at it. Whatever private pleasures a Roman woman may have enjoyed in bed, she would never admit to performing fellatio or cunnilingus. As for our *cinaedus*, this image only reinforces the notion that he is a sexual freak, able to get a woman to fellate him while getting a "proper" phallic Roman man to penetrate him anally. The artist encoded the superior status of the phallic penetrator by raising his right arm–a standard gesture for the victorious general.

WHEN THE CINAEDUS ISN'T A JOKE: RECIPROCAL LOVE BETWEEN ADULT MEN

As I have shown elsewhere, the dressing-room decoration constructs its humor by representing various kinds of sexual transgression–both homosexual and heterosexual. The images of *cinaedi* in the Suburban Baths were funny to the ancient Roman viewer because they overturned the stereotype of "proper" male-male sex–sex between unequal male partners, with an adult man penetrating a pubescent boy. Were there alternatives to the stereotype of man-boy penetration that were not meant to be funny, but that expressed serious, romantic love between men? Did artists ever show two full-grown men mutually excited by having sex with each other?

If we turn to Side A of the Warren Cup, we encounter a unique image that approaches man-to-man–as opposed to man-to-boy–sex (Figure 11). Here the artist has framed the sex scene with a lyre on the left and a doorway to the right. The young man on top, who is clean-shaven, holds onto the strap so he can raise and lower himself onto the penis of the man beneath him. Flowing drapery conceals the arm that holds the strap but parts to reveal this man's right hip and buttocks, where we see his partner's penis entering his anus. The man beneath him has a close-cropped, curly beard and wears a laurel wreath tied with a ribbon at the back of his head.

The couple is not alone. To the right a boy opens one of the battens of the door–either to peer in or to glance back while quietly exiting. He has close-cropped curly hair and wears a simple tunic. Both the boy and the door are quite small in relation to the couple on the bed.

An ancient viewer who drank from this cup would have noticed that the young man on the top is about the same size as the man on the bottom. He's fully developed–not really a boy–so that he's more or less an

FIGURE 11. Warren Cup, Side A. London, The British Museum, inv. 36683 G&R. Copyright The British Museum.

equal of the man who penetrates him (Clarke, 1998, pp. 86-87; against which Pollini, 1999, p. 29). The only sign distinguishing him from his partner is the fact that he has no beard–a long-standing convention for denoting the penetrated youth. If the Roman viewer saw the two men as equals, the image breaks the Roman rule that the partners in male-male sex be unequal in both age and social status. Seen from the Roman point of view, the image of two nearly equal sex partners on one side of the Warren Cup is a good example of an artist breaking the rules. Nothing in the body size, facial type, or hairstyles (aside from the "active" lover's beard and laurel wreath) differentiates the two men. If we did not know the Roman legal writings against two males of the same age and class having sex, we would be inclined to read this image as modern gay sex: reciprocal sex between adult men.

Why did the artist break the rules? One scholar, Cornelius Vermeule, proposed that the Warren Cup was showing two princes of Augustus' family caught in the act (Vermeule, 1963). In his interpretation the cup is political satire. The only problem is that the scene on the other side of the cup, as we've learned, is quite standard: an adult man and a boy sex-slave. Furthermore, elite men did not wear beards at this time in history.

I believe that the person who commissioned the artist of the Warren Cup was interested in recording not what the law prescribed but what real men–elite or not–actually did. Someone with enough money to have a silver cup custom-made could order up any image he wanted. I think this someone was an elite man, who as an adult identified with the sexual pleasure of both penetrating and being penetrated. Although he didn't have a word for what he felt (as the Romans had no words corresponding to our modern concept of "gay" or "lesbian"), he enjoyed looking at this scene of equal, reciprocal, male-to-male sex.

If it is true that on the Warren Cup the artist was tweaking the stereotype to approach reciprocity, with the Leiden gemstone the artist did much more than make the penetrated, beardless youth more mature than usual (Figure 12). He dispensed entirely with all aspects of the stereotype.

Aside from famous old-master paintings, cut gems were the most expensive kind of art you could buy in Roman times. In the Royal Coin Cabinet in Leiden is a large agate gemstone ($3.1 \times 2.15 \times 0.4$ cm) that pairs an unusually sexy image of two men copulating with a tender poem addressed to one of them (Clarke, 1998, pp. 38-42). The poem, written in late Hellenistic Greek, says:

> Leopard–drink,
> Live in luxury,
> Embrace!
> You must die, for time is short.
> May you live life to the full,
> O Greek!

FIGURE 12. Agate Gemstone with Greek Inscription. Leiden, Royal Coin Cabinet, inv. 1948.

The poem combines a command to enjoy wine, luxury, and sex with a *memento mori*–a common notion in Greek and Latin poetry. One must seize the day (*carpe diem*), take life's pleasures when they offer themselves, for soon both pleasures and life itself will be gone. "Leopard" was most likely the special love-name of one of the men pictured on the gem. Since the poem is addressed to Leopard, it's likely that the gem was a love-gift for him (against this interpretation, see Butrica, 2004).

Important for our investigation of visual representations of the *cinaedus* is the fact that the image is much more transgressive than side A of the Warren Cup. Both partners are clearly adult men–not a man and a boy. And–unique among scenes of anal penetration–the man being penetrated (the "bottom") has a huge erection.

The artist devised the couple's unusual pose so that the viewer could see the erect penis of the man being penetrated. He had to raise the torso of the man on the bottom to leave a clear area where penis and testicles stand out in profile. The artist also used foreshortening to make the right side of the man on the bottom larger than that of the man on the top, so that the viewer could read relative body size as spatial depth. The next layer in, represented by the penetrator's torso and right leg, looks as though it is farther back in space. The penetrator's left leg, represented by the tip of his knee next to his partner's erect penis, is also the smallest and therefore farthest back in space.

The resultant image shows sex between physical and sexual equals. What is more, the artist has emphasized both the tenderness in the couple's mutual gaze and–quite exceptionally–the sexual excitement of the man being penetrated. And he is a man, not a boy, for the artist makes him no smaller nor any less endowed than the man who penetrates him.

If the Leiden gemstone is unique, I doubt that the sentiment it expresses was unique in the Roman world of the first century BC. It gives us insight into the sexual mentality of the individual who commissioned it and gave it to "Leopard." Of course, "Leopard" could be either the man on the top or the one on the bottom. Either way, the image insists on showing *reciprocal* sex between two men–an image that went counter to usual artistic and literary conventions of the time. Visual artists–like the poets–always equated romantic male-male love with representations of an adult male penetrating a flaccid boy, not an erect adult. It's only in invective literature, written to insult a man by calling him a *cinaedus*, that we find sex between adult men. This, of course, is the tack taken by the humorous images of *cinaedi* in the Suburban Baths.

The image on the Leiden Gemstone, like that on Side A of the Warren Cup, seems to be a case of an artist creating an explicit and extraordinary (if not to say transgressive) image of male-to-male sex. I like to imagine both men looking at the gem, taking turns holding it in their hands and reading the poem. The gem–even more than the Warren Cup–prompts the person contemplating it to imagine the pleasure that both men are experiencing, the pleasure invoked by the Greek word PERILAMBANE ("Embrace!"). The artist has captured the couple's mutual excitement at the moment of penetration as they embrace and gaze into each other's eyes. This, at least for the owner and viewers, was one important way to "live life to the full."

CONCLUSION

Visual representations like the ones we've looked at can arise only in a culture that knows what visual signs attach to non-stereotypical male sexual behavior. Put another way, the Roman people between 100 BC and AD 100 thought they knew what *cinaedi* did in bed and how they dressed and behaved in public (in taverns, on the street, in the forum). And they had a good idea of what they looked like when they did these things. There were stereotypes, both conceptual and–as we have seen–visual, that represented gay men and their behavior.

Now, stereotypes in texts and/or images do not a social reality make. They can only–especially considering the distance in time and place between us and the ancient Romans–*hint* at gay subculture. If–to take an extreme example–all the "gay" material to survive from contemporary Euro-American culture were one tape of *Will and Grace*, the researcher working in 2304 could only make some wild guesses about the social realities surrounding men who wanted to have sex with men. Where would social and legal issues, such as gay bashing, anti-sodomy laws, religious exclusion, gay marriage, adoption of children, differences in social class, and so on, come into our sociologist's picture, if at all? We must approach the scant visual evidence from ancient Rome with caution.

Even so, the images I have presented here emerge from contexts that are highly differentiated in terms of class, content, and audience. They span the range from parodic paintings in a tavern and a bath, to romantic representations on mass-produced terracotta vessels, to high-art productions in silver, cameo glass, and gemstones. Each type of visual representation had a different audience, from drinkers and bathers to elite viewers–and even one object, the Leiden gemstone, meant for the lovers' eyes only. They reveal both stereotypes of the *cinaedus* to be laughed at by "normal" Romans as well as images that upset the stereotype of the *cinaedus* in favor of something much more like our contemporary ideal of reciprocal sex between adult males. For me, they reveal as well the social understanding of same-sex identification, desire, and sexual gratification and–more important–a society that recognized certain public behaviors as "not-straight." In other words, the visual record complements the hints in the literature and indicates the existence of gay subcultures in ancient Rome.

NOTE

1. Anthony Corbeill points out (personal communication) that the *mia est* could suggest a sexual advance with the feminine adjective: "*She* is mine," with the barmaid responding with appropriate ambiguity.

REFERENCES

Boswell, J. (1980). *Christianity, Social Tolerance, and Homosexuality: Gay People in Western Europe From the Beginning of the Christian Era to the Fourteenth Century*. Chicago: U of Chicago P.

Butrica, J. L. (2004). Review *Roman Sex, 100 BC-AD 250*, by J. R. Clarke. *Bryn Mawr Classical Review*. Retrieved August 10, 2004, from http://ccat.sas.upenn.edu/bmcr/2004/2004-01-03.html

Clarke, J. R. (1998). *Looking at Lovemaking: Constructions of Sexuality in Roman Art, 100 BC-AD 250*. Berkeley: U of California P.

_____. (2003a). *Roman Sex, 100 BC-AD 250*. New York: Abrams.

_____. (2003b). *Art in the Lives of Ordinary Romans: Visual Representation and Non-elite Romans in Italy, 100 BC-AD 315*. Berkeley: U of California P.

Edwards, C. (1993). *The Politics of Immorality in Ancient Rome*. New York: Cambridge UP.

Halperin, D. (1990). *One Hundred Years of Homosexuality*. New York: Routledge.

Jacobelli, L. (1995). *Le pitture erotiche delle Terme Suburbane di Pompei*. Rome: L'Erma di Bretschneider.

Pollini, J. (1999). The Warren Cup: Homoerotic Love and Symposial Rhetoric in Silver. *The Art Bulletin 81*(1), 21-52.

Richlin, A. (1993). Not Before Homosexuality: the Materiality of the *Cinaedus* and the Roman Law Against Love Between Men. *Journal of the History of Sexuality, 3*(4), 523-73.

Riggsby. A. (1995). Lenocinium: Scope and Consequences. *Zeitschrift der Savigny-Stiftung für Rechtsgeschichte: Romanistische Abteilung 112*, 423-427.

Stewart, A. F. (1996). Reflections. In N. Kampen (Ed.), *Pornography and Representation in Ancient Art* (pp. 136-54). New York: Cambridge UP.

Todd, F.A. (1939). Three Pompeian Wall-inscriptions, and Petronius. *Classical Review 53*(1), 5-9.

Vermeule, C. (1963). Augustan and Julio-Claudian Court Silver. *Antike Kunst, 6*(1), 33-46.

Williams, C. (1999). *Roman Homosexuality: Ideologies of Masculinity in Classical Antiquity*. New York: Oxford UP.

The Originality
of Tibullus' Marathus Elegies

Beert C. Verstraete, PhD

Acadia University

SUMMARY. As far we can judge from the extant literature, Tibullus' three Marathus elegies are among the most sophisticated poetry of male same-sex desire and love composed in the ancient Greco-Roman world. These poems belong to a long and well-established tradition of male homo-

---

Beert C. Verstraete is Professor of Classics in the Department of History & Classics at Acadia University in Wolfville, Nova Scotia. He obtained his doctorate in Classics at the University of Toronto. He has contributed as a translator and annotator to the *Collected Work of Erasmus* and the *Index Emblematicus* published by the University of Toronto Press, is co-author, with Arnold Lelis and William Percy, of *The Age of Marriage in Ancient Rome*, and has published many articles on Roman literature, the Classical tradition in Western literature, and homosexuality in the Greco-Roman world. Correspondence may be addressed: Department of History and Classics, Acadia University, Wolfville, Nova Scotia, B4P 2R6, Canada (E-mail: beert.verstraete@ acadiau.ca).

Author note: This article is based on papers presented at the 2003 annual conferences of the Classical Association of Canada and the Atlantic Classical Association. Except where noted otherwise, translations are my own. I have used J. P. Postgate's edition (second edition) of the text of the *Corpus Tibullianum* in the Oxford Classical Texts series, writing, however, the consonantal "u" as "v." Excellent translations of all three Marathus elegies may be found in Thomas K. Hubbard (Ed.), *Homosexuality in Greece and Rome: A Sourcebook of Basic Documents* (Berkeley: U of California P., 2003), pp. 353-361.

[Haworth co-indexing entry note]: "The Originality of Tibullus' Marathus Elegies." Verstraete, Beert C. Co-published simultaneously in *Journal of Homosexuality* (Harrington Park Press, an imprint of The Haworth Press, Inc.) Vol. 49, No. 3/4, 2005, pp. 299-313; and: *Same-Sex Desire and Love in Greco-Roman Antiquity and in the Classical Tradition of the West* (ed: Beert C. Verstraete, and Vernon Provencal) Harrington Park Press, an imprint of The Haworth Press, Inc., 2005, pp. 299-313. Single or multiple copies of this article are available for a fee from The Haworth Document Delivery Service [1-800-HAWORTH, 9:00 a.m. - 5:00 p.m. (EST). E-mail address: docdelivery@haworthpress.com].

Available online at http://www.haworthpress.com/web/JH
© 2005 by The Haworth Press, Inc. All rights reserved.

doi:10.1300/J082v49n03_10

erotic poetry that goes back to the Greeks of the Archaic Age and was given new impetus centuries later in Roman literature. In this tradition, Tibullus' Marathus elegies stand out for their qualities of irony, dramatic engagement, and psychological finesse. *[Article copies available for a fee from The Haworth Document Delivery Service: 1-800-HAWORTH. E-mail address: <docdelivery@haworthpress.com> Website: <http://www.HaworthPress.com> © 2005 by The Haworth Press, Inc. All rights reserved.]*

KEYWORDS. Greek and Roman literature, male homoerotic poetry, Tibullus, Marathus elegies

It is useful at the beginning of this paper to underline the representational and psychological limitations of nearly all love poetry, both ancient and modern. In its essence, no matter how modulated by stances of objectivity, detachment, and irony, love poetry is thoroughly subjective, or to put it very simply: it is about the lover rather than the beloved. This is as true of classical Greek and Roman as it is of Western literature, in both of which, to quote from the American poet-critic, Edward Hirsch, in his engaging discussion of love poetry (ch. 5, "White Heat" of his *How to Read a Poem and Fall in Love with Poetry*), we witness "[t]he scandal of poetry: the words of praise coming alive in your mouth, in your body, the euphoria of flight" (p. 93). It is thus the person of the lover (or, as we might say more cautiously, the *persona*, the mimetic-confessional mask assumed, so to speak, by the poet) that is inscribed in the poetry, and the beloved can be glimpsed only dimly, if at all, through the subjectivity of the lover's lens.

In classical love poetry, literary artifices of dialogic communication between the lover and the beloved that also let the beloved Other reveal himself or herself are seldom utilized. A good example of such utilization is the amoebic *Idyll* 27 of Theocritus (which may not be by Theocritus), which presents an actual verbal exchange between a lover and his beloved, and there are also elements of dialogic interaction in Tibullus 1.8 (to be examined later), Ovid, *Amores* 3.7 and Propertius 1.3, 2.29b and 3.6 (in the last poem the dialogue being mediated by a messenger-servant), while, differently and uniquely, Propertius 4.7 in its entirety is a monologue spoken by the ghost of the poet-lover's deceased mistress, Cynthia. Thus, for any in-depth, richly individualized portrayal of the beloved Other which is not altogether enmeshed in the confessional *persona* assumed by himself or herself, the author must turn to other literary genres: in modern literature, this will be the short story, novella, novel and, of course, drama, to which we should add for Greco-Roman literature the epic and the epyllion.

Working within the conventions of theme and motif in Hellenistic and Roman literature, in particular those of comedy, pastoral, lyric, elegy, and epigram, Tibullus makes his female beloveds, Delia in Book 1 and Nemesis in the second Book, conform largely to the literary characteristics and stereotypes of the exploitative courtesan or courtesan-like woman; these have been admirably discussed by Sharon James in her 2001 article, "The Economics of the Roman Elegy: Voluntary Poverty, The *Recusatio*, and the Greedy Girl." I am not going to argue that Tibullus' Marathus, as he is portrayed in the first book, is more realistically individualized than Delia and Nemesis. Indeed, as becomes evident from a close reading of the two elegies in which he figures most prominently, 1.8 and 1.9, Marathus, even as a semi-fictional *persona*, remains something of a mystery, a bundle of contradictions perhaps, both as a social and as a psychological type. A substantial personal identity remains as elusive for him as it does for the two mistresses.

My principal objective is to explore how Tibullus takes the portrayal of male same-sex desire and of the poet-lover's relationship with his male beloved beyond what had been achieved in this regard in earlier extant Greek erotic poetry, and among the Romans, by Catullus in his Juventius poems, and, to a lesser degree, by Vergil in the second of his *Eclogues*. My paper will conclude with a brief reflection on the course taken in Roman literature, both poetry and prose, that depicted these subjects after Tibullus.

In the surviving Greek literature of the late Archaic and early Classical periods, there are some fine poems of the subjective-confessional type that celebrate the erotic allure of youthful male beauty and vividly describe the sexual longing that grips the lover, while other poems reprove the beloved for his noncompliance, fickleness or greed for material gain. I can give only a brief sampling. Ibycus fragment 286, which is usually given a homoerotic reading and deserves praise for its exquisite use of image and symbol, focuses solely on the intensity of the lover's passion, metaphorically represented as "the north wind of Thrace, [which] violently shakes my heart from its foundations." The picture of emotional devastation contrasts sharply with the tranquil beauty evoked by the garden image with which the poem opens–an image which is surprising in its heterosexually colored intimation of the gentle maturation of young girls into womanhood, as it speaks of "the maidens' inviolate garden, [where] the vine shoots blossom and swell to fullness under the shady sprays of the vine." Maurice Bowra's reading and appreciation (1967, pp. 257-264) of these and other fragments of Ibycus' homoerotic poetry remain unsurpassed.

Equally exquisite is Pindar fragment 123, which expresses the lover's entrancement by the "bright rays flashing from Theoxenus' eyes," and captures, through the image of the melting wax of the "holy bees," the as-it-were flesh-liquefying intensity of the lover's feelings as "he gazes at the fresh-limbed youth of boys." (See Hubbard, 2003, p. 48, for the complete translation; also highly recommended is his major 2002 article, "Pindar, Theoxenus, and the Homoerotic Eye.") Lovely as they are, though, both these poems are focused entirely and narrowly on the experience of the lover's arousal by the beauty of youth and additionally, in Ibycus, on the mental anguish that may accompany *eros*. In numerous poems, Theognis expands this purely inward focus into a dialectic of reproach with a fickle or unfaithful beloved, as, for instance, in Theognis 1263-66:

> Boy, you paid back a bad exchange for kindness.
> No thanks from you for favors.
> You've never given me pleasure. And though I've often
> Been kind to you, I never won your respect. (Translation in Hubbard, 2003, p. 42)

Among the Hellenistic poets who centuries later revitalized the literary representation of male homoerotic experience, we should note first of all Callimachus, a few of whose *Iambi* may have provided Tibullus with literary inspiration for the Marathus elegies–a subject to which I'll return later. But the finest homoerotic subjective poetry of this period and perhaps of all of extant ancient Greek literature is undoubtedly found in Theocritus' *Idylls*. The Twelfth *Idyll*, as Anna Rist (1978) observes in the introduction to her translation of this poem, may be a relatively early composition and suffer from flaws in literary technique such as "a certain crudity," as she puts it (p. 109), in its transitions. Even so, Rist aptly characterizes the poem as a *"dramatic representation* of the author 'surprised by joy'" (p. 110). In his recent study of the classical tradition in the homoerotic poetry of the Renaissance, *Homoerotic Space: The Poetics of Loss in Renaissance Literature*, Stephen Guy-Bray (2002) places his detailed appreciation of this poem right at the end of his book (pp. 220-224). The opening words of *Idyll* 12 point to the intergenerational nature of the relationship (something that Guy-Bray seems to have overlooked): "Have you come, dear youth?"

asks the long-waiting lover. However, Theocritus stresses not only the mutuality of the lover and his beloved, as opposed to the psychological asymmetry inherent in the more typical pederastic model of male same-sex love, but also the hope that, to quote Guy-Bray, "the love between these men will find expression even across the barriers of time and language" (p. 222). Although some critics have detected irony and even satire at the expense of the poem's speaker (mostly strongly Giangrande, more subtly Kelly and Nethercut), a depth of feeling and commitment is touched upon in this *Idyll* which is hardly matched in any other of the subjective-confessional homoerotic poetry of Greco-Roman antiquity.

Among the Roman poets, Catullus is Tibullus' most important precursor in the writing of homoerotic personal poetry. While Catullus' Juventius poems must be considered, on the whole, fine but still basically slight compositions, Catullus 99, the longest of the Juventius pieces, offers an unusual emotional complexity in its depiction of the hurt feelings of the poet-lover, who has been punished for stealing a kiss from Juventius by the young man's distaste for the act. In a recent article, David Konstan (2002) has given a detailed and subtle exposition of how Catullus has injected a large measure of role-reversal and psychological surprise into the familiar motif of 'boy rejects a man's erotic advances':

> The poem, which is quite remarkable in the context of Roman pederastic literature, makes the reader aware of the extent to which such scenes of seduction depend on a particular construction of roles and performances. . . . In wiping away the kiss, and in accepting rather than giving kisses in the first place, Juventius appears both as a spoiled but callow child and as an actor who assumes mastery in the situation by a canny manipulation on his part. (p. 367)

Vergil depicts the male homoerotic relationship most powerfully in the story of Nisus and Euryalus in books five and nine of the *Aeneid*, but the closest he comes to exploring it at length in the subjective-confessional lyric or elegiac mode is in the second *Eclogue*, which, except for the gender of the love-object, takes its principal literary inspiration from Theocritus' eleventh *Idyll*. As Erasmus (trans. 1978, pp. 683-687) already observed almost 500 years ago, the pathos and humor of this piece stem not so much from the frustration of the lover's desire as from his naive inability to perceive, until the very end, that the fundamental incompatibility in social milieu, status, and taste between himself and his beloved Alexis makes a reciprocal relationship impossible. For Erasmus, the same-sex nature of Corydon's passion is irrelevant to this important psychological lesson imparted by the poem, and therefore he contends that it is pedagogically appropriate for school-age children. Alexis himself, though, remains only the faintest of presences and is not made to play the manipulative power games that characterize Juventius in Catullus 99 and Marathus in Tibullus in 1.8 and 1.9.

We may safely speak of three Marathus elegies in Book 1 of Tibullus (1.4, 1.8, and 1.9), although Marathus is not explicitly named in 1.9, and in 1.4 the poet-lover's actual affair with the young man is not revealed until the second last distich. While connected by common motifs such as the presence of a rival and the material greed of the beloved, these poems are also strikingly different from one another. Hellenistic prototypes have been proposed for 1.4 and 1.9 by Christopher M. Dawson in a 1945 article. Francis Cairns in his 1979 study, *Tibullus: A Hellenistic Poet at Rome*, finds these elegies, like the rest of Tibullus, are thoroughly Hellenistic in their use of technique and their deployment of themes and motifs; on the other hand, however, also with respect to the Marathus elegies, his judgment is that "[c]ertainly Tibullus is consistently original in his combinations and modifications of the standard *topoi* which he inherited from the Hellenistic world" (p. 23). Other critics, too, have perceived Tibullus' originality. Although, like Cairns, he places the Marathus elegies firmly within the tradition of Greek and Roman pederasty poetry, P. Murgatroyd, in his 1977 article (as well as in his 1980 commentary on the first Book of Tibullus' elegies), shows a keen appreciation of their unique qualities of polish, humor, and ingenuity. There is also much insight in this regard in M. J. McGann's lengthy 1983 article in *Anustieg und Niedergang der Römis*che Welt and in Robert Maltby's recent edition of and commentary on Tibullus. Finally, approaching Tibullus from a somewhat different literary-critical perspective, in her 1998 study of Book 1 entitled *Powerplay in Tibullus: Reading Elegies Book One*, Parshia Lee-Stecum applies to the three Marathus poems, too, her detailed analyses, loosely informed by a Foucauldian hermeneutic framework, of the inevitable power games played by lovers. I hope to add further nuance to what these scholars have said, so that Tibullus' originality as an elegiac love poet working in the homoerotic mode may stand out in bold relief. 1.8 will be discussed last, as it is, in my judgment, the most accomplished psychologically and dramatically of the Marathus poems, and it will therefore also receive my most detailed attention.

Of the three Marathus elegies, 1.4 is perhaps the most humorous and ironic. Dawson may well be right in seeing the ninth of Callimachus' *Iambi* as Tibullus' prototype. Only its *diegesis* (summary) has survived:

> The lover of a handsome youth called Philetadas saw the ithyphallic statue of a Hermes in a small palaestra, and asked if his condition was not due to Philetadas. But the Hermes answered that he was of Tyrrhenian descent, and that he was ithyphallic because of a mystic story. On the other hand (he said) his questioner loved Philetadas with evil intent. (Callimachus; Trypanis, 1958, p. 136)

As far as we can judge from this summary, only the fiction of a dialogue with a talking statue of Priapus connects Tibullus 1.4 with its possible Callimachean model. Tibullus' originality lies in making his Priapus the bearer and proclaimer of an audacious *erotodidaxis* that enunciates numerous commonplace sentiments and pieces of advice related to the lover's experience in his wooing of the boy (all of these unfailingly noted in great detail by Kirby Flower Smith, pp. 265-287, in his still most serviceable 1913 edition and commentary). Thus the young must hurry to make the most of their all too transient physical beauty; such is the warning from Priapus to the beloved boy:

> *at si tardus eris errabis. transiet aetas*
> *quam cito! non segnis stat remeatque dies.*
> *quam cito purpureos deperdit terra colores,*
> *quam cito purpureos populus alta comas.* (Tibullus, 1.4.27-30)
> If you delay, you'll be going the wrong way. How swift time flies! The coming and going of days do not come in a stand-still sluggishness. How swiftly the earth loses her radiant colors, how swiftly the lofty poplar sheds its lovely foliage!

The lover must render his beloved boy faithful, unquestioning service and follow him wherever he goes:

> *tu, puero quodcumque tuo temptare libebit,*
> *cedas: obsequio plurima vincet amor.*
> *neu comes ire neges, quamvis via longa paretur*
> *et Canis arenti torreat arva siti.* (Tibullus, 1.4.39-42)
> You, whatever your boy wants to try out, must give it to him. Love that takes on faithful service triumphs over all. Don't hold back in accompanying him, no matter how long the journey lying ahead,

and even if the Dog-Star should scorch the land with drought and thirst.

By virtue of their incongruous, hyperbolic application, these truisms become imbued with an unmistakable irony, the irony being finally sealed by the poet-lover's confession, in the last two distichs, of his own inability as a would-be *magister amoris* to apply Priapus' advice successfully to his stormy relationship with Marathus.

> *eheu quam Marathus lento me torquet amore!*
> *deficient artes, deficient doli.*
> *parce, puer, quaeso, ne turpis fibula fiam,*
> *cum mea redebunt vana magisteria.* (Tibullus, 1.4.81-84)
> Ah how Marathus racks me with my passion's slow torture. All my clever tricks and arts–they are useless, useless! I beg you, my boy, have mercy, or I'll be laughed to scorn, a storybook case of futile teaching.

Dawson sees the third of Callimachus' *Iambi* as the most direct Hellenistic prototype of 1.9. The Callimachean text is unfortunately incomplete and fragmented, and despite Dawson's and other critics' partial reconstruction of it, it is safest to go, once more, with the poem's *diegesis*, which, after quoting the first line, reads (in translation):

> Callimachus criticizes the period as valuing wealth more than virtue, and he accepts the preceding period (as superior), in which the opposite view prevailed. He also criticizes a certain Euthydemus for exploiting his youth and beauty for profit, after being introduced to a wealthy man by his mother. (Callimachus; Trypanis, 1958, pp. 114-116)

However, more important than the possible Callimachean prototype, Tibullus 1.9 belongs, as noted by Maltby (2002), "to a well-recognized type, announcing the end of an affair . . . the *renuntiatio amoris*" (p. 323; see Maltby here for numerous parallels in Greek and Roman love poetry and for the observations of other scholars). Marathus is reproached for his greed and utter lack of taste and self-respect in taking up with an elderly, wealthy lover. Pointing back to 1.8, the Tibullan *persona* also reminds Marathus of his services as go-between for him and his girlfriend (lines 41-46). However, the originality of Tibullus' poem lies most of all in the prolonged invective and satire, worthy of a Catullus, Martial, or Juvenal, heaped upon Marathus' new lover, who is directly addressed for twenty-two lines (lines 53-74). He is ridiculed for being deceived and cuckolded by his sexually promiscuous wife–matching her equally rapacious sister in this respect (a piquant added detail, lines 59-60)–who turns to young lovers to satisfy her lust, while telling her old, unappetizing husband she is too tired for sex. The woman's orgiastic adultery and her outrageous deception of her legitimate spouse are vividly evoked–just to give a sample of six lines:

> *illam saepe ferunt convivia ducere baccho,*
> *dum rota Luceferi provocet orta diem:*
> *illa nulla queat melius consumere noctem*
> *aut operum varias disposuisse vices.*
> *at tua perdidicit : nec tu, stultissme, sentis,*
> *cum tibi non solita corpus ab arte movet.* (Tibullus 1.9.61-66)

It's said she often carries on her orgiastic rites until the Morning Star's rise summons a new day. No one can make better use of the night than she or better display her vast repertory of love-making tricks. Your wife has acquired a full expertise, and you, idiot, don't even know it when she wriggles her body in a novel way unfamiliar to you.

The dysfunctional relationship of old husband and young wife is the mirror image of the equally dysfunctional relationship between the youthful, handsome Marathus and his elderly, physically repulsive lover, which is sustained only by the latter's wealth. Satiric intensity and imagination infuse the poet-lover's anger over being betrayed by his beloved, but even so never eliminate the ironic, self-deprecating touch, which is struck most tellingly in the final three distichs (lines 79-84), where the poet-lover warns Marathus he will find another *puer* who will hold him bound fast (*vinctum*, line 79)–one will appreciate the irony of this!–so that, with mock-heroic gesture, he will be able to dedicate to Venus his metaphorical *aurea palma* (line 82), the golden palm of a lover's victory, accompanied by the dedicatory words as recorded in the final distich (lines 83-4): *Hanc tibi fallaci resolutus amore Tibullus / Dedicat et grata sis, dea, mente rogat*: " Released from the bonds of his treacherous love, Tibullus dedicates this to you, O goddess, praying that you will be gracious to him."

1.8 is, in my judgment, the masterpiece of the Marathus elegies, unfolding a psychodrama worthy of the pages of Marcel Proust's *Remembrance of Things Past*, if I may venture a comparison with 20th century literature. In his 1973 commentary on Tibullus, Michael Putnam rightly speaks rightly here of the poet's "mastery of human psychology, juggling three possible relationships" (p. 127). Very distant parallels can be seen in Propertius 1.9 and 1.10, where the poet-lover offers advice to male friends, in 1.9 to someone, formerly skeptical of any erotic entanglements, who is just beginning to taste the agonies and ecstasies of real *amor* and in 1.10, to a young man caught up in the euphoria of an affair that is going well. Other such parallels in Greek and Roman love poetry are provided by Maltby (2002, p. 302). One may also be reminded somewhat of the role played by the slaves Palaestrio and Pseudolus in Plautus' *Miles Gloriosus* and *Pseudolus*; the success of Pleusicles and Calidorus in finally winning, after the most formidable obstacles, their beloved girls is entirely owed to the cunning and stratagems of their slaves. However, Tibullus' elegy's elaborate scenario of the infatuated poet-lover trying to facilitate a heterosexual liaison for his *puer* is unique in extant Greek and Roman literature. Nowhere else in the Marathus or even in the Delia and Nemesis elegies is the poet-lover's *persona* developed with equal psychological complexity: he is selfless almost to the point of being self-abasing in what must seem to the reader, on first thought, an incomprehensible eagerness to provide Marathus with the pleasure of a successful romance with a woman, yet at the same time showing a spirit of firmness and self-confidence as to the rightness of his admonitions to Marathus and Pholoe, so that we come to realize that what motivates the poet-lover is not servile infatuation but a half-smiling empathy with Marathus and his incipient heterosexual interests–the Tibullan *persona* is, after all, bisexual. Equally important, for the one and only time in Tibullus Marathus is allowed twelve lines (lines 55-66) to speak in his own words, uttering his lament of spurned love to the cold-hearted Phoeloe.

Following earlier critics, Maltby (2002) rightly observes that "[t]he form of the poem is that of a dramatic monologue in which all three characters are imagined to be present together. T. has the pair of lovers before him and addresses each in turn . . ." (p. 302). He notes that "[s]uch triangular confrontation-scenes are a feature of New Comedy and mime" (p. 302) and thus plausibly suggests that "the present poem could in part have been inspired by them" (p. 302). Interestingly, there is no parallel for such a compactly structured dialogic configuration in other Roman love elegies, not even in any of the numerous elegies of Propertius and Ovid which feature multiple addressees.

With other critics, Lee-Stecum rightly observes the poet-lover's ironic assumption once more of the role of *magister amoris*, as in 1.4, but I question her assertion that, because his aim of persuading Pholoe is not successful, and because his very act of intervening on Marathus' behalf still shows him to be in the young man's power, ". . . the irony which emerges from the transformation of Marathus into a lover in the mould of the poet himself is prevented from reflecting favourably on the poet's position . . ." (Lee-Stecum, 1998, p. 245). Lee-Stecum's pervasive Foucault-inspired concern with power-driven interactions and relationships leads her, I believe, to miss out on much of the sheer erotic *jouissance* of 1.8. The poet-lover's own infatuation with Marathus adds a unique psychological edge to his exhortations to Pholoe that she ought surely to prefer the young man's physical beauty and desirability to any gift of gold and should therefore extract the utmost pleasure from their lovemaking.

> *munera ne poscas: det munera canus amator,*
> *ut foveat molli frigida membra sinu.*
> *carior est auro iuvenis, cui levia fulgent*
> *ora nec amplexus aspera barba terit.*
> *huic tu candentes umero suppone lacertos,*
> *et regum magna despiciantur opes.*
> *at Venus inveniet puero concumbere furtim,*
> *dum timet et teneros conserit usque sinus,*
> *et dare anhelanti pugnantibus umida linguis*
> *oscula et collo figere dente notas.* (Tibullus, 1.8.29-38)
>
> Don't ask the boy for gifts. Gift-giving is for the grey-haired lover, so that he may warm his cold limbs in a soft embrace. A young man is more precious than gold–his face is smooth and radiant and no raspy beard of his will scratch your kisses. So slide your gleaming arms beneath his shoulder and let kingly wealth be of no account. Yes, Venus will know how to lie down in secret with the still timorous boy, joining him to herself in a sweet, tight union, and, as tongues collide, planting moist kisses on the panting boy and leaving her bite-marks on his neck.

Notice how in lines 35-38 the identity of Pholoe is merged with that of Venus. There is more of a pleasurable empathy, unmarred by any jealousy, with Pholoe here–as she is hopefully imagined to be following his advice–than real self-abasement on the part of the part of the poet-lover. For all the ironic undercutting of himself, the Tibullan *persona* displays a greater sense of self-confidence and even superiority than in the two other Marathus poems.

A new nuance is also added to the personality of Marathus: from the other two elegies, we have seen him as both fickle and greedy, a thoroughly spoiled and willful young man perhaps a privileged slave and *puer delicatus* ("pleasure-boy") in a wealthy household since the name Marathus, a pseudonym of course, appears to be servile,[1] although, as with the elegiac mistresses, no firm picture is provided of his social status and background. His unrequited love for Pholoe (also a Greek pseudonym, typical of the Roman elegiac mistresses) serves as a fit punishment for his faithlessness to the poet-lover, as the latter pointedly reminds him in lines 71-76, but it also shows an appealing youthful vulnerability.

The dramatic and dialogic technique of 1.8 is masterful, highlighted especially by the skilful successive maneuvering of Marathus and Pholoe as the poet-lover's addressees and the assigning to Marathus of a lover's monologue-lament directed to Pholoe and, of course, overheard by the poet-lover. Here Tibullus 1.8 is unique in Greek and Roman pederastic poetry in that it allows the *puer delicatus* to speak in his own words as the boy is made to assume the role of the *exclusus amator* ("the shut-out lover" who is refused admittance by his mistress to see her)–a role otherwise reserved for the adult persona of the elegiac poet-lover, whether he be Tibullus, Propertius, or Ovid, in Augustan literature. After Marathus finishes his monologue in line 66, the poem's final movement as played out by the remaining six couplets is managed with admirable dispatch and economy: first a couplet addressed to Marathus telling him to stop his futile lamenting: Pholoe will not be moved (literally "broken"), "*non frangitur illa*" (line 67), and his tearstained face makes a sorry sight, *et tua iam fletu lumina fessa tument* (line 68), "your eyes are now swollen and weary with weeping"; next a distich addressed to Pholoe warning that she will incur the displeasure of the gods for her obstinacy; then three couplets in which the poet-lover dwells on Marathus' plight as a fitting punishment for his past callousness towards him; and then finally, a parting shot of warning at Pholoe: *at te poena manet, ni desinis esse superba. / quam cupies votis hunc revocare diem* (lines 77-8): "But punishment awaits you unless you stop being so haughty–how often you will want to make this day return."

Both Cairns (1979, p. 147) and Lee-Stecum (1998, pp. 227-245), followed by Maltby (2002, p. 302), call attention to a particularly striking aspect of dramatic technique in 1.8, namely that of gradual or delayed revelation of information, the 'facts' being reported in such a way that, for a while, the reader may be even misled; Lee-Stecum (1998), in fact, finds this technique so pervasive that the elegy becomes characterized by a constant emergence of "[n]ew ambiguities or competing possibilities" (p. 245). Thus it is not apparent until line 23, as noted by both Cairns (1979, p. 179) and Lee-Stecum (1998, p. 233 n.15)–and even then it may not be clear to some readers–that the person addressed and described as primping and preening himself in lines 9-14 is a male, and not a woman. The woman (*illa*, "she") briefly introduced in line 15 as affecting, in contrast, the natural look is Pholoe, but she is not directly addressed as yet, let alone named, and is dwelt upon for only one couplet. Then the poet-lover turns back to the person addressed earlier in lines 9-14 and for the next five distichs asks him if he has been bewitched, but corrects himself by saying that natural beauty needs no assistance from sorcery and that any harmful, bewitching power resides in the act of lovemaking. In line 27 he finally addresses the woman at greater length and continues to do so until line 54, telling her right away to stop being so difficult with the boy: *nec tu difficilis puero tamen esse memento* (line 27). Marathus still is not named, but the poem's scenario has now become much clearer, and the reader is not surprised when in line 49 the poet-lover finally tells Pholoe (who herself is not named explicitly until line 69), *neu Marathum torque: puero quae gloria victo est?* "But don't go on torturing Marathus: what glory is there in a conquest won over a boy?" Even more than in the other two Marathus poems, the reader is led through a nimbly executed succession of shifts and surprises in dialogical targeting and emotive playfulness, a poetic achievement which, in my judgment, makes 1.8 the equal of the most accomplished erotic–heterosexual, of course–elegies of Propertius and Ovid.

The unusual length Tibullus chose for nearly all his elegies–which are, on average, much longer than those of Propertius (with the exception of Book 4) and Ovid–was undoubtedly an important factor enabling him to compose a homoerotic love poetry that was dramatically more intricate and psychologically more complex and nuanced than that of his predecessors in extant Greek and Roman literature; Murgatroyd (1977, p. 117) nicely sums up these qualities in one word, "subtlety." Regrettably, the example set by Tibullus was not emulated by later Roman poets of male same-sex love such as Horace (*Odes, Odes* 4.1, with its deeply and unusually emotional ending, being perhaps the only exception) or Martial (*Epigrams*); maybe the elegiac and lyric forms had been stretched as far as they could. Edward Hirsch (1999) has made an observation on the narrative and dramatic potential of lyric poetry that is quite pertinent to the direction Roman love elegy might have taken after Tibullus, Propertius, and Ovid:

One might say that the individual lyric moves in the direction of the short story by introducing more and more narrative action into the poem. It moves in the direction of the one-act play and the short story by taking a glimpse at psychological prose and introducing more than one speaking character into a setting. (p. 125)

In fact, a leap from love poetry to prose fiction centered on love (both heterosexual and homosexual) was made in Greco-Roman antiquity. Even if we leave aside the Greek prose romances, Petronius' *Satyricon* amply demonstrates how nicely extended prose fiction, with its great possibilities of narrative momentum, of psychologically acute portrayal of character, and not to forget, of irony and satire, could accommodate lively stories of male same-sex desire and love.

NOTE

1. As is suggested by the name of Augustus' recorder, the freedman Julius Marathus (Suetonius, *Divi Augusti Vita*, 79.2 and 94.3). For more details, see Maltby (2002, pp. 45-46), who also discusses the possible etymologies of the name; he concludes "that no single interpretation is entirely satisfactory" (p. 46), but finds the derivation from the Greek verb *marainomai* "to die down" (of flames)–when the heat of the flames, in fact, reach their greatest intensity–the most plausible. Section D, "Philetos, the manly *delicatus*," of Jim Butrica's paper in this collection offers an excellent discussion of *pueri delicati* in the light of Statius' eulogy in *Silvae* 2.6 of a rather anomalous pederastic relationship.

REFERENCES

Bowra, C. M. (1967). *Greek Lyric Poetry*. (2nd ed.). Oxford: Clarendon Press.

Cairns, Francis. (1979). *Tibullus: A Hellenistic Poet at Rome*. Cambridge: Cambridge UP.

Callimachus. (1958). *Aetia-Iambi* etc. (C.A. Trypanis, Ed. and Trans.). Loeb Classical Library. London: William Heinemann/Cambridge, MA: Harvard UP.

Dawson, Christopher M. (1945). An Alexandrian Prototype of Marathus? *American Journal of Philology*, 67, 1-15.

Erasmus, Desiderius. (1978). *On the Method of Study*. (Annotated by B. McGregor, Trans.). *Collected Works of Erasmus*, 24. Toronto: U of Toronto P.

Giangrande, G. (1971). Theocritus' Twelfth and Fourteenth Idylls: A Study in Hellenistic Irony. *Quaderni urbinati di cultura classica*, 12, 95-112.

Guy-Bray, Stephen. (2002). *Homoerotic Space: The Poetics of Loss in Renaissance Literature*. Toronto: U of Toronto P.

Hirsch, Edward. (1999). *How to Read a Poem and Fall in Love with Poetry*. San Diego/New York/London: Harcourt.

Hubbard, Thomas K. (2002). Pindar, Theoxenus, and the Homoerotic Eye. *Arethusa*, *35*, 255-296.

_____. (Ed.) (2003) *Homosexuality in Greece and Rome: A Sourcebook of Basic Documents*. Berkeley: U of California P.

James, Sharon L. (2001) The Economics of Roman Elegy: Voluntary Poverty, The *Recusatio*, and the Greedy Girl. *American Journal of Philology, 122*, 223-253.

Kelly, S. T. (1979-1980). On the Twelfth Idyll of Theocritus. *Helios, 7*, 55-61.

Konstan, David. (2002). Enacting Erōs. In Martha Nussbaum and Juha Sihvola (Eds.), *The Sleep of Reason: Erotic Experience and Sexual Ethics in Ancient Greece and Rome* (pp. 354-373). Chicago and London: U of Chicago P.

Lee-Stecum, Parshia. (1998). *Powerplay in Tibullus: Reading Elegies Book One*. Cambridge: Cambridge UP.

McGann, M.J. (1983). The Marathus Elegies of Tibullus. *Anustieg und Niedergang der Römische Welt, 2*(30.3), 176-1799.

Murgatroyd, P. (1977). Tibullus and the Puer Delicatus. *Acta Classica, 20*, 105-119.

Nethercut, William R. (1984). The Interpretation of Theocritus 12.1-9. *Helios, 11*, 109-115.

Theocritus. (1978). *The Poems of Theocritus*. (A. Rist, Trans.). Chapel Hill: U of North Carolina P.

Tibullus. (1913). *The Elegies of Albius Tibullus*. (K. F. Smith, Trans.). New York: American Book Company. (Reprinted by Wissenschaftliche Buchgesellschaft, Darmstadt, 1964).

_____. (1915). *Tibulli Aliorumque Carminum Libri Tres*. (J.P. Postgate, Ed.). (2nd ed.). Oxford: Clarendon Press.

_____. (1973). *Tibullus: A Commentary*. (M. C. J. Putnam, Ed.). Norman: U of Oklahoma P.

_____. (1980). *Tibullus I, a Commentary*. (P. Murgatroyd, Ed.). Pietermaritzburg: Natal UP.

_____. 2002). *Tibullus: Elegies. Text, Introduction and Commentary*. (R. Maltby, Ed.). Cambridge: Francis Cairns.

On Kissing and Sighing: Renaissance Homoerotic Love from Ficino's *De Amore* and *Sopra Lo Amore* to Cesare Trevisani's *L'impresa* (1569)

Armando Maggi, PhD

University of Chicago

SUMMARY. This essay investigates the homoerotic connotations present in the so-called *treatises on love*, a popular philosophical and literary genre of the Italian Renaissance. The referential text of this sixteenth-century genre is Marsilio Ficino's *De amore* (1484), a deeply in-

Armando Maggi is Associate Professor at the University of Chicago in the Department of Romance Languages and Literatures, and the Committee on History of Culture. His scholarship includes works on Renaissance and baroque literature, mysticism, and philosophy with some fifty essays on rare or virtually unknown Neoplatonic treatises on love, Michelangelo's poetry, books of emblems, the philosophy of Giordano Bruno, and the writings of the Capuchin mystic Veronica Giuliani. His latest book is *Satan's Rhetoric, A Study of Renaissance Demonology* (University of Chicago Press, 2001). A new book, *Beings Against Nature*, on the concept of 'familiar spirits' in sixteenth- and seventeenth-century culture, is near completion. Correspondence may be addressed: Department of Romance Languages and Literatures, University of Chicago, 1050 East 59th Street, Chicago, IL 60637.

[Haworth co-indexing entry note]: "On Kissing and Sighing: Renaissance Homoerotic Love from Ficino's *De Amore* and *Sopra Lo Amore* to Cesare Trevisani's *L'impresa* (1569)." Maggi, Armando. Co-published simultaneously in *Journal of Homosexuality* (Harrington Park Press, an imprint of The Haworth Press, Inc.) Vol. 49, No. 3/4, 2005, pp. 315-339; and: *Same-Sex Desire and Love in Greco-Roman Antiquity and in the Classical Tradition of the West* (ed: Beert C. Verstraete, and Vernon Provencal) Harrington Park Press, an imprint of The Haworth Press, Inc., 2005, pp. 315-339. Single or multiple copies of this article are available for a fee from The Haworth Document Delivery Service [1-800-HAWORTH, 9:00 a.m. - 5:00 p.m. (EST). E-mail address: docdelivery@haworthpress.com].

novative interpretation of Plato's *Symposium*. Focusing on the initial section of Ficino's text, Maggi highlights some important structural differences between the *De amore* and the *Symposium*. Moreover, by comparing Ficino's Latin text with his own subsequent Italian translation (*Sopra lo amore*, 1544), Maggi examines how Ficino interprets some key terms such as "appearance" and "splendor." The second part of the essay studies Cesare Trevisani's *L'impresa* (1569), a later treatise on love with an explicit homoerotic foundation. *[Article copies available for a fee from The Haworth Document Delivery Service: 1-800-HAWORTH. E-mail address: <docdelivery@haworthpress.com> Website: <http://www.HaworthPress.com> © 2005 by The Haworth Press, Inc. All rights reserved.]*

KEYWORDS. Italian Renaissance literature, treatises on love, homoerotic love, Plato, Symposium, Neoplatonism, Ficino, Marsilio, Trevisani, Cesare

The most popular philosophical and literary genre of sixteenth-century Italy is the so-called *filosofia d'amore* (philosophy of love), more commonly known as *trattati d'amore* (treatises on love), a series of innumerable and diverse texts that question, censor, and expand Marsilio Ficino's commentary on Plato's *Symposium*. Although he had already completed it in 1469, Ficino published his seminal work in Latin in 1484 with the title *De amore*. His Italian translation by the title *Sopra lo amore* came out much later in 1544, many years after his death in 1499.[1] Ficino's *De amore* was the great bestseller of early modern Europe. Although the *trattati d'amore* were primarily an Italian phenomenon that flourished and died out at the end of the sixteenth century, Ficino's philosophical views, in particular his interpretation of the *Symposium*, molded and dominated European culture.

It is unquestionable that in Ficino's *De amore*, and thus in all its subsequent followers, the concepts of homoeroticism and homosexuality play a pivotal, albeit always controversial, role even when, especially after the second half of the century, their presence becomes hardly detectable due to the changing cultural and religious environment. In the Italian Renaissance, to write about love inevitably means to comment on Ficino's commentary of Plato's main treatise on love. In both referential texts (*De amore* and *Symposium*), love is depicted as an event that takes place between a male lover and a male beloved. This essential aspect of Renaissance philosophy of love still awaits a comprehensive analysis. What does it mean to posit same-sex desire as the most authentic manifestation of love? Do these sixteenth-century texts still have something to teach us about desire and knowledge? Or should we continue to address them as archeological artifacts expressing a system of beliefs foreign to us? After a brief introduction based on Ficino's *De amore*, the source of this philosophical genre, my essay will focus on Cesare Trevisani's *L'impresa* (Genoa, 1569), a virtually unknown treatise that blends in love philosophy and theories on Renaissance emblems. In *L'impresa*, Trevisani comments on an emblematic picture that he has created to manifest his devotion to his beloved prince of Piombino.

First of all, let us try to synthesize the main themes of the *trattati d'amore*. Does love have any sense? And what is the possible relationship between knowledge (the sense) expressed by love and the corporeal senses? This is the crux of this philosophical genre. Is sensual love against the possible sense or knowledge of love? What does it mean to be lovers without making love? Furthermore, how do friendship and love relate to each other? The Renaissance *trattati d'amore* found in Ficino's *De amore* an ambiguous, at times contradictory and thus extremely fertile source and model. The extinction of this prolific genre was due to two main reasons. First, its being blocked on a fixed set of assumptions (primarily its almost uniform insistence on the dichotomy between love and sexual intercourse) prevented it from evolving.[2] Second, at the end of the century, the progressive imposition of the Catholic Reformation turned these treatises into uninteresting manuals for young men in search of the right bridegroom.[3]

This introductory and brief reference to the *De amore* exclusively intends to foreground my subsequent reading of Trevisani's *L'impresa*. Ficino posits his retrieval and interpretation of Plato's love dialogue as a historic, groundbreaking, and far-reaching enterprise. More than updating Plato's thought, Ficino intends his commentary as the restoration of Plato's supreme and now forgotten insight on the love experience. To stress his closeness to the referential text, Ficino tries to reproduce a similar rhetorical form. Like the platonic dialogue, Ficino's *De amore* initially presents itself as the transcription of a past conversation. We will see that Cesare Trevisani's *L'impresa*, the main object of my essay, faithfully follows a similar structure. If in the *Symposium* the character Apollodorus tells Glaucon what he heard from a third friend, Aristodemus, about a past dialogue among friends on the topic of love, so does Ficino report what was said at a banquet organized on a unspecified November 7th to celebrate the alleged date of Plato's birthday and death.[4] *De amore* opens with the following solemn evocation of Plato, the "father of philosophers":

> Plato, the father of philosophers, died at the age of eighty-one, on November 7, which was his birthday, reclining at a banquet, after the feast had been cleared away. This banquet, in which both the birthday and the anniversary of Plato are equally contained, all of the ancient Platonists down to the times of Plotinus and Porphyry used to celebrate every year. But after Porphyry these solemn feasts were neglected for twelve hundred years. At last, in our own times, the famous Lorenzo de' Medici wish[ed] to renew the Platonic banquet. (*Commentary*, 1.1.35)

It is fundamental to understand that the newly restored Platonic banquet coincides with a new reading and interpretation of the *Symposium*. Ficino contends that the highest insight of the "father of philosophers" concerns the love experience. The Florentine philosopher also relates that, at the end of the banquet in the memory of Plato, the rhetorician Bernardo Nuzzi, one of Ficino's teachers, was asked to read the entire *Symposium*, whose seven sections were later to be analyzed by seven different participants, although Giovanni Cavalcanti ended up commenting on the first three. Let us remember that, in the *Symposium*, the discussion on love also takes place at the end of a meal. If Plato's philosophy finds its ultimate expression in the problem of love, Ficino's *De amore* is both memorial (a banquet in memory of the Platonic banquet) and recreation of a 'sacred' conversation on love. In fact, similar to a Eucharistic banquet, Ficino's *De amore* is at once remembrance and reactivation or appropriation. This second aspect in fact ends up prevailing in Ficino's commentary. Starting from the second chapter, the fictional dialogue disappears from the *De amore* and its overall relationship with the *Symposium* becomes more and more problematic.[5]

I would like to stress two essential points before we proceed. First, for Ficino, the highest point of Plato's philosophical discourse coincides with his view of love. Love is the quintessential expression of human longing for the divine. Second, love as the core of Platonic philosophy revolves around homoerotic desire.[6] These are two crucial tenets of Ficino's appropriation of Plato's most important dialogue on love.

I will focus on the first section of the *De amore*, the interpretation of Phaedrus' speech, the first of the *Symposium*. Ficino underscores the supremacy of homoerotic desire at the very beginning of his commen-

tary. As Michael Allen has convincingly proved, Ficino posits a fundamental identification between Giovanni Cavalcanti, who is in charge of
commenting on the first three speeches in the *Symposium*, and
Phaedrus, the protagonist of the other Platonic dialogue on love and a
central figure of Ficino's *De amore* (Allen, 1980). Cavalcanti is
Ficino's "sweet" (*suavissime*) friend, as the Florentine philosopher
writes in a dedicatory epistle to Cavalcanti in an earlier version of his
treatise (Ficino, 2003, p. 3). Ficino loves Cavalcanti as Plato and Socrates loved Phaedrus.[7] At the beginning of his commentary, Cavalcanti reminds his audience that Phaedrus was the object of Socrates' passionate
love, as Plato recounts in the *Phaedrus*:

> Phaedrus, whose appearance Socrates admired so much that one
> day, on the banks of the Ilissus River, Socrates was so excited by
> the beauty of Phaedrus that he became carried away, and recited
> the divine mysteries, though he had previously claimed that he was
> ignorant of all things. (*Commentary* 1.2.36)

In these initial lines Cavalcanti, Ficino's Phaedrus, synthesizes the
sense of his interpretation. First, he stresses that the opening discourse
in the *Symposium* is delivered by a man whose beauty triggered a great
admiration in Socrates. For Ficino, a fundamental connection or reflection exists in the *Symposium* between the first (Phaedrus') and last (Socrates') speech on love. Let us remember that *Phaedrus*, the other great
Platonic dialogue on love, is in fact a conversation between Phaedrus
and Socrates, and was commonly believed to be Plato's very first dialogue (Allen, 1980, pp. 132-133; Diogenes Laertius, 3.5, 31, 38).[8] In the
Phaedrus, Socrates starts his analysis of love by reminding Phaedrus of
love's divine nature (242d).[9] In the *Symposium*, Phaedrus, the first
speaker of the entire dialogue, opens his speech by echoing Socrates'
view of love from the *Phaedrus*. For the Phaedrus of the *Symposium*,
love is a "great god" that still has no song of praise composed in his
honor (*Symposium* 177b).

Second, the connection between the two male speakers is based on
homoerotic love. Ficino insists that in the *Phaedrus* Socrates had
gleaned some profound insight about the divine (his reciting the divine
mysteries) because he had been overwhelmed by the "beauty" of
Phaedrus.[10] The physical "appearance" of his interlocutor had initiated
a process of understanding. In his commentary on the *Phaedrus*, Ficino
insists that the main difference between the *Phaedrus* and the *Symposium* is that "the *Symposium* treats of love principally and of beauty as a

consequence; but the *Phaedrus* talks about love for beauty's sake" (Allen, 1980a, p. 72). Being a "young" text, *Phaedrus* understandably focuses on the appearance of love, of physical, visible beauty.

It is interesting to note that, in the modern English translation of Ficino's *De amore*, the term "appearance" seems to depend on Ficino's Italian translation rather than on the original Latin. In the *De amore*, Ficino in fact speaks of *indolem* (the natural qualities, the talents, the overall attitude) of Phaedrus, whereas in his Italian translation the Florentine philosopher uses the word "apparenza" (Ficino, 1544, p. 6).[11] In the Italian version, Ficino intensifies, or better yet, clarifies the strict connection between Phaedrus' demeanor and his physical beauty. If Phaedrus is a central figure in Ficino's view of the *Symposium*, the Florentine philosopher's own translation underscores that the centrality of Phaedrus derives from his physical presence. As a consequence, if we keep in mind that for Ficino the *Phaedrus* was Plato's first dialogue, we could infer that the homoerotic bond between Socrates and Phaedrus could be seen as the very foundation of Platonic thought. Moreover, we must also consider that Cavalcanti, who for Ficino represents Phaedrus, comments on the first three speeches of the *Symposium*, thus taking up a considerable portion of the entire *De amore*.

But what is beauty? In the above quotation, what the modern English translation renders as "beauty" in Ficino's original Latin and subsequent Italian version is in fact *splendor* ("splendore" in *Commentaire*, 1.2.7).[12] What is the connection between beauty and splendor? To understand this crucial point, we must briefly move to later sections of the *De amore*. In the second part of his commentary, Ficino explains that "[l]ove is the desire of enjoying beauty. But beauty is a certain splendor attracting the human soul to it" (*Commentary*, 2.9.58). In a later passage from book 5, chapter 7, commenting on Agathon's speech in the *Symposium*, Ficino explains further: "The poet Agathon . . . clothes this god in human form, and paints him as attractive, like men: *Young, tender, flexible or agile, well-proportioned and glowing*" (Ficino, 1985, pp. 95, 104 n. 31; cf. Ficino, 2002, p. 109). Love is "glowing" (*nitidus*) because it is similar to a "resplendent," beautiful surface. Ficino translates as "glowing" the expression "khróas dè kállos" (*Symposium* 196a). The word "khróas" indicates the superficial appearance of a thing, its skin. A "beautiful appearance" could be another acceptable translation. In a later passage of the *De amore*, Ficino adds that love is *nitidus* (glowing) because it "shines of pleasant colors" (*suavi colorum speciem refulgentem*, *Commentary*, 5.7; cf. Ficino, 1544, p. 110: "di suave spezie di colori rilucente").

Love is thus an appearance, a vision arising from a body that we perceive as beautiful. Beautiful is the "resplendent" skin of the person we love. We see that a certain glow emanates from the body we find attractive. But we are also aware that the luminosity of our beloved's body in fact shines within us. In Platonic terms, the two essential poles of the love experience are the exteriority of a beautiful man's body and his shining image residing in his male lover's mind. Love is thus a personal, private experience that concerns the lover more than the beloved.[13] The beautiful image of our beloved glowing inside of us is a visual reminder of our natural propensity toward what is harmonious, beautiful, and thus also good. According to Ficino, this is the ultimate goal of every philosophical pursuit. If to be human means to seek knowledge, the desire inspired by physical beauty signifies our inexhaustible longing for the ultimate good, that is, God.

Still in his commentary on Phaedrus' speech, Cavalcanti contends that "the desire for coitus (that is, for copulation) and love are shown to be not only not the same emotions but opposite" (*Commentary*, 1.4.41). Love exists as pure desire, a yearning for the divine that cannot and must not be satisfied through sexual intercourse, which Ficino sees as an intemperate and thus "ugly" act. Ficino's concept of love is at once a joyous perception, because in our love for a beautiful friend we see a reflection of divine love as the real essence of the world, and the persistent intellectual and emotional awareness of a void residing within us.[14] For the desire for the ultimate beautiful can never be fulfilled in the created world. Sex is a misleading substitute, for it pretends to fill the sense of the unquenchable absence brought to the surface of intellectual understanding by the glowing image of our beloved's body. Let us remember that in the *Symposium* Diotima defines Eros as the "son of Resource and Poverty" and is "shoeless and homeless" (*Symposium* 203c-d).[15]

We could say that Ficino radicalizes Plato's view of the conflictive relationship between physical desire and intellectual or even religious insight. However, throughout his commentary, Ficino maintains that the most natural (and thus potentially either enlightening or damning) desire is homoerotic. In the seventh and final section of the *De amore*, speaking of physical, "vulgar" love, he justifies the superiority of homoerotic attraction with these words:

> Perhaps someone will ask, by whom especially, and in what way, lovers are ensnared, and how they are freed. Women, of course, catch men easily, and even more easily women who display a certain masculine character. Men catch men still more easily, since

they are more like men than women are, and they have blood and spirit which is clearer, warmer, and thinner, which is the basis of erotic entrapment. (*Commentary*, 7.9.165)

This quotation comes from the final speech of the *De amore* and implicitly refers to the concluding part of the *Symposium* (216d-219e) in which Alcibiades recounts how he had tried to seduce Socrates. As I have explained, Ficino makes no direct allusion to this controversial part of the Platonic dialogue and inserts a laudatory chapter on Socrates as "true lover" (*Commentary*, 7.2.155-58). However, most of the seventh and final speech of the *De amore* is taken up by a lengthy discussion of physical or "vulgar" love, which is dominated by homoerotic desire. In the above passage, the essential question is: Why are men naturally drawn toward other men more than toward women? It is because in another man's beautiful form the lover recognizes something at once foreign and familiar. I have already stressed that Ficino intends love as private, inner occurrence. We could say that desire is a form of recognition. Through another man, I see myself "clearer." Men, Ficino states borrowing from a contemporary medical position, have a warmer and clearer blood. Men's blood is "clearer" as their lovable skin is more luminous and glowing. To love women is "of course" natural, but to love men is even more natural.

It is within this analysis of "vulgar" love that Ficino inserts a new and final reference to Phaedrus, the object of Socrates' love according to the homonymous dialogue. In the final section of the *De amore*, Ficino brings up the *Phaedrus* again. This time, Ficino evokes the love feelings between Phaedrus and Lysias, the famous orator Phaedrus had spoken with right before meeting Socrates (*Phaedrus* 227a). According to Ficino's recreation of the encounter that takes place before the opening of the *Phaedrus*, Lysias, who "was seized by love" of Phaedrus, "gapes at the face of Phaedrus. Phaedrus aims into the eyes of Lysias sparks of his own eyes, and along with those sparks transmits also a spirit" (*Commentary*, 7.4.161). This exchange of "spirits," the physical particles that the body emanates through the eyes according to contemporary medicine, lies behind their mutual attraction.[16] "O, my heart, Phaedrus, dearest viscera," Ficino makes Lysias say to Phaedrus. "O, my spirit, my blood, Lysias," Phaedrus replies. According to this passage, which is usually ignored by modern critics, Lysias indeed had a "vulgar" relationship with Phaedrus. According to Ficino, Lysias was the lover and Phaedrus was his beloved. Thus, Lysias' desire was stronger than Phaedrus'. Let us remember that the *Phaedrus* opens with Phaedrus reporting what he had learned about love from Lysias. Lysias had however depicted a negative view of love, seen primarily as a destructive physical passion, what Socrates had later defined as blasphemous because disrespectful of a deity.[17] In the *De amore*, Phaedrus thus embodies two opposite manifestations of love. If in the introductory scene Giovanni Cavalcanti, the new incarnation of Phaedrus for Ficino, speaks of the luminous presence of Phaedrus, the object of Plato's and Socrates' love, in the final part of the Italian treatise he somehow alludes to Alcibiades' physical passion for Socrates.

The innumerable sixteenth-century commentaries on Ficino's commentary on the *Symposium* had to deal with Ficino's ambiguous depiction of male friendship based on homoerotic desire. Although Ficino explicitly defines what we now call "homosexuality" as "vulgar" and establishes a series of textual echoes between homosexual desire and erroneous interpretations of the love experience, he also contends that "men catch other men still more easily." Male homosexuality is paradoxically the most "vulgar" and the most natural form of physical attraction. The Renaissance *trattati d'amore* either silenced this central aspect of Ficino's Neoplatonism or interpreted it as a metaphor for intellectual friendship.[18]

However, the boundaries between sodomy and Neoplatonism were very thin. In Francesco Sansovino's well-known dialogue by the title *Ragionamento d'amore* (Reasoning on Love, 1545), the character Panfilo suggests that the young Silio avoid the Neoplatonics because their behavior is questionable. Panfilo, an older and wise man, defines the "Platonics" as follows:

> The Platonics [are those who] contemplate the most perfect beauty, which they believe can only be male. Through this [the contemplation of male beauty] they ascend to divine beauty. But let us leave them alone, because their actions are suspicious. (Sansovino, 1912, p. 165)

The most direct and ferocious attack against the "Platonics" is in Tullia d'Aragona's famous *Dialogue on the Infinity of Love*, a treatise that openly deprecates homosexual practice as it is depicted in the *Symposium*. Addressing the philosopher Benedetto Varchi, Tullia states:

> I consider that those men who entertain a lascivious love for youths are not following the dictates of nature, so they fully deserve the punishments that canon and divine law have imposed on

them. . . . I can scarcely believe that people who practice such an ugly, wicked and hideous vice . . . are real human beings. (D'Aragona, 1997, p. 95)

Varchi replies that their discussion is "treading on a very difficult ground," although he sternly supports the metaphorical and virtuous interpretation of Platonic love toward young men (D'Aragona, 1997, p. 97).

It is worth mentioning one more example. In the complex and detailed *De la magia d'amore* (On the Magic of Love), which was first published in 1590 and can be thus considered as the final summa of this literary and philosophical genre, Guido Casoni makes numerous references to the *Symposium* and to the *De amore*. However, he presents two opposite interpretations of Plato as lover. Casoni first states that Socrates and Plato were "divine" lovers because they ascended from the physical beauty of their male friends to the "contemplation of God" (Casoni, 2003, p. 78). However, in a later chapter on how astrology can affect love, Casoni writes: "Plato, who was attacked because he naturally inclined too much toward dishonest loves, affirmed that wisdom can overcome the influences of the stars" (Casoni, 2003, p. 105).

The crux of the Renaissance appropriation of the Platonic view of love thus revolves around the blurry distinction between the natural or even the "most natural" desire toward the beautiful body of a friend and the insistence on the love experience as the joyous but distant contemplation of a "luminous" body as reminder of the divine presence existing in the created world. If Neoplatonic love, as I explained in an earlier section of this essay, is a desire that arises as a sudden recognition, a mirroring that moves from the image of the male beloved to his male lover, wouldn't it be natural to conclude that homosexual desire identifies with the most truthful experience of love? If we attempt to translate this Renaissance philosophical view into our modern stance on the nature of love and sex, we could say that Ficino and his followers hold that a perfect love between two men is nonsexual in the sense that it maintains an erotic, and never physically fulfilled, foundation. A Neoplatonic male friendship is undoubtedly homoerotic since it arises from the desire for a beautiful body, and is superior both to a mere acquaintanceship and whatever form of sexual involvement because the homo-Eros creates an unbridgeable opening, a distant mirroring that triggers the above process of inner recognition.[19] Love between two men, according to the Ficianian view, is not conceivable as sex. For Ficino, Eros and sex express two different experiences.

Male homoerotic friendship is a bond that has no equal. The recognition that takes place between the lover and his beloved is a unique occurrence and is the highest expression of the human condition, its yearning for divine love, which is echoed and evoked in the male erotic friendship. In the little known comedy *Erofilomachia overo il duello d'amore e d'amicitia* (Erofilomachia, or the Duel Between Love and Friendship) by Sforza Oddi (1540-1611), I find the most succinct and poetic synthesis of the above concept of homoerotic recognition. While in Florence, the Genovese Alfonso runs into his friend Leandro, who had disappeared from Genoa all of a sudden five years before. Leandro had followed a girl whose family had moved to Florence because her father didn't approve of Leandro's interest in his daughter. After having been enslaved by pirates while sailing from Genoa to Pisa, Leandro, disguised as a poor servant, now works at the house of his beloved girl, who still has not recognized him. On the contrary, Alfonso, who hadn't seen him for five years, spotted Leandro immediately even if now he now hides behind a long beard. Alfonso reminds his friend Leandro that he had always loved him for his "politeness and grace," for his "youthful presence" (Oddi, 1582, 2r and 3v). Alfonso's love for Leandro has not waned. Alfonso also reminds his friend that they used to converse on the mystery of love. "You know," Alfonso says to Leandro, "that love makes what is invisible to others more visible than the bright sun to two lovers?" (Oddi, 1582, 5r). If this girl thought of you, Alfonso continues, she would fall in love with you even if she doesn't recognize you. For when love arises between two human beings, it stays in them forever. Some believe that this is due to some "conformity of blood" between the two lovers (Oddi, 1582, 5v).

Alfonso, and not the girl, is Leandro's truthful and faithful lover. Love lives within Alfonso as a constant memory of the visible "bright sun" shining forth from the young Leandro. Alfonso's recognition of Leandro on the streets of Florence is his encounter with the persistent memory of Leandro's luminosity, his existing in Alfonso as a bright and unforgettable sun. Alfonso embodies the perfect Neoplatonic lover because his love is generous and expects no sexual fulfillment. Love is perception and not practice. Love is an inner vision of light given as gift by the beloved to the lover who cherishes it as an inextinguishable fire.

Love as recognition, longing, and inner vision are the essential themes of Cesare Trevisani's *L'impresa*, a complex, multilayered, and puzzling treatise that, like the *Symposium* and the *De amore*, presents itself as the narration of a previous discussion on the nature of love. However, *L'impresa* is more than just an additional rewriting of the two pillars of Renaissance Platonism. This treatise is at once *trattato d'amore* and exegesis of an actual emblematic picture that the author has created to express his dedication to his beloved Alessandro D'Aragona, prince of Piombino. *L'impresa* is a difficult, convoluted, and structurally imperfect piece of sixteenth-century literature.

Before we proceed, I think a brief outline of the story would help us understand the plot better. *L'impresa* is narrated by Luigi Malatesta who, after residing in Spain for eight years, on his way to Naples had stopped at Genoa for some days. In a bookstore he had come across a small book, which was in fact Cesare Trevisani's "ingenious and mysterious *Impresa*" (Trevisani, 1569, p. 4). After reading this intriguing but challenging little book, Luigi decides to meet the author to ask him to explain some obscure points of his treatise. Luigi learns that at the moment Cesare is at the palace of the prince of Piombino, Alessandro D'Aragona (p. 5). Luigi meets the author, the prince, and a group of other male friends who had gathered at the prince's house. Since it is getting late, Cesare suggests that Luigi come back the following morning so that they have more time to discuss his book in depth (p. 14). When the group gathers again, the prince proposes that Luigi, since his doubts and questions have led to this meeting, read Cesare's book out loud and stop whenever he or other members of their group feel like raising questions (p. 21). *L'impresa* is thus a book that posits a previous, nonexistent book, which is the basis for an in-depth communal discussion of an actual love emblem. Luigi reads in the first person the hypothetical booklet he had found in the Genovese store. The author of the book, the prince, and the other friends cut in to comment on each passage read by the friend Luigi.

What is the meaning of this tortuous narrative structure? First of all, in the tradition of the *Symposium* and the *De amore*, *L'impresa* is the fictional transcription of a past dialogue in which a group of male friends debated the significance of the love experience. However, to understand the structure of *L'impresa*, we must also clarify the nature of the relationship between Luigi Malatesta, the author Cesare Trevisani, and the prince Alessandro. As my analysis will explain in detail, Luigi, the narrator and the official reader of the text at the prince's house, and Cesare, the author of *L'impresa*, share a passionate friendship and a passionate love for the prince Alessandro d'Aragona. We have seen that Luigi had developed a great desire to meet Cesare Trevisani after reading his mysterious and inspiring *L'impresa*. But Cesare had developed a very similar desire for the prince after hearing about Alessandro's indomitable courage and noble appearance. Dying to meet him, Cesare had traveled to Genoa, but unfortunately had got there when the prince had already left for Spain. During a night of melancholy, Cesare composed an emblematic image to express his feelings for the absent prince. The treatise *L'impresa* thus revolves around an original melancholy, due to the absence of the author's beloved. What Luigi reads out loud in the gathering described in *L'impresa* is Cesare's longing for the prince Alessandro d'Aragona. Cesare's emblematic image in fact traces the circularity of desire and its expression, for it originates from Cesare, is heard, seen, and narrated by Luigi, but is directed at the prince Alessandro.

But what is an *impresa*? Renaissance treatises on emblematic expression usually distinguish between an emblem, which depicts a universal and easily interpretable image (for instance, the insignia of a noble family or the symbol of a city), and an *impresa*, the representation of a personal state of mind. Emblems and *imprese* have similar characteristics, namely, an image composed of a limited number of figures plus a brief motto. However, unlike an emblem, an *impresa* is directed at a specific addressee, even when its meaning can be decoded and shared among all its viewers.[20] An *impresa* endeavors to communicate a personal feeling for a particular person. As we will see in a moment, Trevisani's *impresa* in fact could be seen as a hybrid, because Trevisani's devotion for the prince is also the "shield" (the official symbol) of his identity. In other words, Cesare wishes every viewer to understand that his love for Alessandro is the ultimate meaning of his existence. Cesare's *impresa* represents a shield divided into four sections. These four parts correspond to four different forms of love symbolized by four distinct animals (eagle, lion, mermaid, and dragon) united to each other through a circular chain. The motto in Greek means: «Oh Eros, cause of every thing and toward which every thing moves» (Figure 1).

As I explained in a previous paragraph, the "Eros" mentioned in this motto does not regard Cesare and the prince only. *L'impresa* is a *trattato d'amore* that tries to show how the "erotic" (or better yet, the "homoerotic" according to Florentine Platonism) is a dynamic and circular experience shared by those who are united by the bond of friendship (consider the chain binding the four animals of Cesare's *impresa*). In the dedicatory epistle to Alessandro D'Aragona, Luigi Malatesta reminds the prince that "those who are similar naturally love each other" (Trevisani, 1569, no number). To clarify this concept typical of Renaissance Neoplatonism, Luigi refers to the myth of Narcissus:

[It is like when] a young man, who goes to a fountain to drink . . . , recognizes his own image in the fountain and is compelled by an occult force to contemplate it with great attention, and at times he even dips his young arm into the water hoping to touch that image. (Trevisani, 1569, no number)

As I reiterated throughout the first part of this essay, Neoplatonic male friendship is a form of self-recognition. I also explained that, unlike our

FIGURE 1

modern perception of love, Renaissance Platonic love is essentially a joyous contemplation. The other (the friend I love) is a luminous presence (his "splendor") in which I see myself and through whom I have a glimpse of the divine. I love my friend who is a mirror of my image and a visual echo of a third presence, the divinity. "Recognition" and "to contemplate" are the two key words of the above passage as well.

In the epistle, Luigi adds that he has (implicitly) mentioned the Narcissus myth because, since his first visits to the prince's house, he couldn't help but notice "how wisely you reasoned, how pensively you kept silence, and how gracefully you moved." As a consequence, he realized that his soul had been "invaded by a new and mysterious longing" (Trevisani, 1569, no number).[21] Continuing his praises of Alessandro, Luigi states that his preceptors have taught the prince how "to show the hidden virtues and beauty of your soul through your body." Like one of the animals depicted in Trevisani's *impresa*, Luigi has become "freely chained" to the prince and, like "the young man at the fountain," he constantly tries to reach Alessandro, the luminous image of himself (Trevisani, 1569, no number).

We could thus say that, although he had met the prince only because of his desire to meet Cesare Trevisani, Luigi had also developed a strong desire for the prince, the object of Cesare's desire, while reading *L'impresa* out loud in the presence of the prince, Cesare Trevisani, and a group of other male friends. If Cesare expresses his love for the prince by composing a treatise based on an *impresa*, Luigi expresses a similar feeling by reading the transcription of Cesare's love for the same prince Alessandro.

In the following introduction, Luigi recounts how he came across Trevisani's original (and in reality nonexistent) book. Since I have already summarized this part of the story, I will limit myself to highlighting a few details. After reading Trevisani's book two or three times with "utmost happiness," Luigi decided to meet the author to ask him to clarify some difficult points of his work and consequently "to remain his amorous brother" (p. 4-5). Before meeting him, Luigi received a description of this mysterious author by one of the prince's servants who happened to walk by the bookstore where Luigi was inquiring about Cesare. According to this servant, Cesare is a rather strange, quaint young guy. He is "twenty-three years old," "has a quick and funny way of speaking," and "wears a leather hat with a medallion of diverse colors and inside the image of a lion entangled in a thin golden chain" (p. 5-6). We have seen that the lion is one of the four animals present in Cesare's *impresa* for the prince Alessandro. When he finally meets Cesare and

Alessandro, Luigi will immediately spot Cesare because of his strange hat (p. 6).

As I have already mentioned, the prince suggests that Luigi read out loud Cesare's book and that each friend gathered at his house interrupt him when he has questions or doubts.[22] From a structural standpoint, the pages of Cesare's (hypothetical) book work as quotations within Luigi's transcribed reading and other friends' remarks, which are printed in italics to distinguish them from Cesare's referential text. In the first passage from the original *L'impresa*, which resembles a dedicatory epistle to prince Alessandro, Cesare introduces his emblematic image by saying that he had always felt a strong attraction toward "brave swords" (p. 22). Having heard about Alessandro's "glorious enterprises," Cesare "had fallen for" Alessandro.[23] Arriving in Genoa, he was told that the prince had left for Spain. Cesare devised his *impresa* one night in bed while waiting for the prince's return. Asked to explain how he could come up with such a complex image lying in bed in the dark, Cesare replies that he has always received crucial insights at night, because night is the moment when the mind opens itself to contemplation (p. 26).[24]

What was the object of Cesare's night contemplation? In the second passage from his book, we understand that his *impresa*, born during a night of solitude, revolves around love. "The universal texture of this *impresa*," Luigi states reading from Cesare's book, "only shows love and nothing but love to those who contemplate it" (p. 43). Furthermore, the author explains that the *impresa* has the form of a shield because the Trevisanis have no family emblem to represent their history and values (p. 42). Cesare's *impresa* is thus both personal expression (his love for the prince) and universal statement, an emblem depicting the essential value determining Cesare's existence.

Analyzing the four figures present in his *impresa*, Cesare contends that whereas "in the *Symposium* Plato (if I remember correctly) divides love into six stages and in the *Asolani* the illustrious [Pietro] Bembo only distinguishes between human and divine love, I decided to refute both opinions and divided love into four principal kinds" (p. 62).[25] For Trevisani, love is "either desire for wealth, or desire for beauty, or desire for virtue and spiritual valor, or desire for glory and fame" (p. 62-63). The four animals in the picture represent these four aspirations. If the dragon, "who presides over the treasures of the earth," embodies the first kind, the mermaid, "who is the most beautiful monster," corresponds to the second (p. 63). The lion, whose strength and bravery overcomes every other animal, is the third form of love. Finally, the eagle, "who flies higher than any other bird," symbolizes the fourth and final form of love. Explaining further, Cesare contends that "love is either totally bestial" (the dragon), or "or totally divine" (the eagle), or "part bestial and part human" (mermaid), or "part human and part divine" (lion). If the human-bestial desire loves a person's beauty without "considering the Creator," the human-divine desire sees in human beautiful forms a reflection of universal beauty. This kind of lover may move from being a lion to being an eagle. In a later section of the treatise, Cesare acknowledges that Ficino's *De amore* had influenced his four-stage love theory (p. 76). Summarizing Ficino, Cesare reminds his audience that God is the supreme good and the divine ray that penetrates everything is "called beauty. This ray then enters the angelic mind, later 'the soul of everything' (the so-called *anima mundi*) and every soul, and finally brute matter" (cf. *Commentary*, 1.3.37-40). Cesare's four stages of love echo Ficino's four degrees of being, from the divinity to mere materiality.

After this clear explanation of Cesare's emblematic picture, Luigi's reading is interrupted again. How does Cesare see the role of kissing in the love experience?[26] This is a crucial point of Trevisani's puzzling book also because, as I stressed at the beginning of this essay, one of the main problems of Florentine Neoplatonism is the relationship between love and physical contact. According to Trevisani, there are four kinds of kisses: "holy kiss, civil kiss, amorous kiss, and lascivious kiss" (p. 71). The first kind is the kiss one gives "in sign of peace or to sacred things." The second is the kiss is for kings, emperors, and in general for noble personages. The third sort of kiss "is the kiss that friends exchange in the name of their honest love and that real lovers give to their women." The fourth and last type is the kiss that "because of a lustful and lascivious love" people "give to men or women." Trevisani also adds that he "could specify which parts of the body are kissed" and debate whether "it is true that, as many believe, we should kiss our friends only on the forehead or on the mouth."

I have already insisted that one of the main interests of *L'impresa* lies in its incongruities, in its baffling, allusive, and unresolved issues. The problem of physical versus merely spiritual love had been directly tackled by Flaminio Nobili's *Trattato d'amore* (Treatise on Love, 1567), published only a couple of years before *L'impresa*. Unlike any previous book on this subject, Nobili's short but honest and straightforward work, which exerted a remarkable influence on Torquato Tasso's treatise on love, had dared to address the unavoidable issue of sexuality and reproduction. By "human love" (amore umano), the young Nobili meant a form of love that responds to human beings' natural sexual drive without indulging in any intemperate and excessive act.[27] For Nobili, "human love" is different from "bestial" and "divine" love because it naturally blends in physical expression and spiritual nourishment.

Trevisani's book offers no real and new insight on the relationship between love and physicality. This strange text seems to be working at two different levels. On the one hand, like most sixteenth-century writers on the subject of love, Trevisani does not dare to challenge the basic assumptions of Ficino's view. To write a *trattato d'amore* first and foremost means to show a solid familiarity and general agreement with Ficino's *De amore*. The possible originality of a *trattato d'amore* usually lies in its narrative frame, in its rhetorical construction, not in the ideas it expresses. In this regard, Trevisani's *L'impresa* stands out for its discordances, its contradictions, which seem to focus on homoerotic desire. It is indeed the undercurrent presence of homoeroticism that undermines the otherwise solid and traditional foundation of this peculiar book.

A friend present at the discussion disagrees with Cesare about his kiss theory. He thinks that "only beautiful women should be kissed on the mouth, and that the [male] friends and other people [should be kissed] on the forehead, and never on the hand, because hands are for other offices, no less important than kisses" (p. 91; the friend in question is Facondo). This remark, which made all the other friends laugh out loud, might be some sort of sexual innuendo. However, what matters is that, by stressing that his other friends laughed, Cesare intends to highlight his unusual theory according to which there is no distinction between a kiss to a beloved woman and to a beloved male friend. A kiss on the mouth, in Cesare's view, is the expression of a virtuous love. It is also interesting to note that, for Cesare, a "bestial," lascivious kiss can be given either to a man or to a woman.

The contrast between sexual ambiguity versus a canonical rewriting of Ficino's view of love becomes apparent again when Cesare is asked to explain three points of a lengthy and unoriginal *canzone* that he had recited during the intermission following his analysis of his kiss theory (pp. 78-82). Why does Cesare write that love, which proceeds from what is beautiful and good, is neither beautiful nor good (p. 83)? This first question offers the author the opportunity to show off his good knowledge of Florentine Platonism, in this case what Socrates learns from Diotima in the *Symposium*. Arguing with Agathon, Trevisani writes, Socrates states that love lies between wisdom and ignorance, between the divine and the merely human (p. 84). This in-between condition reveals love's demonic, neither human nor divine, condition. Cesare concludes his answer with a reference to the *Phaedrus*. In Cesare's words, Socrates believes that human beings are ruled by two "ideas" (p. 86).[28] One is "the desire for pleasures," which leads men toward "sensual actions." The other spurs us toward "celestial operations."

Right after repeating the above basic and trite tenets of Florentine Platonism, Cesare addresses two much more interesting questions. Why did his poem mention the seer Tiresias and why did it stress the role of sighing in the love experience? Tiresias is the quintessential embodiment of sexual ambiguity. Cesare narrates that Tiresias once saw two serpents intertwined in a sexual act. "After observing carefully which one was the female one," Cesare adds, Tiresias killed her, and immediately after he turned into a woman (p. 87). Years later, returning to the same mountain where he had witnessed the sex act between the two snakes, he now saw the other, male serpent, and killed him. This time, Tiresias resumed his original male identity. When Jupiter and Juno debated whether men or women received more pleasure from sex, the king of the gods asked Tiresias to give them his opinion since he had embodied both roles. Tiresias, Cesare stresses, "almost regretted having reacquired his male nature" because for seven years "he had felt sweetness below and softness above" (p. 89: il dolce di sotto e il morbido di sopra). This graphic and ironic reference to sexual intercourse viewed from a female perspective unquestionably clashes with the aseptic and abstract tone of most treatises on love. It is important to note that here Cesare at once makes an explicit allusion to carnal pleasure and relates it to a human being who originally was a man but enjoyed being a woman. The story of the sexually ambiguous Tiresias, which could be an indirect reference to Aristophanes' theory on the hermaphrodite in the *Symposium*, is the sole direct allusion to sex in the entire *L'impresa* (cf. *Symposium* 189c-191d).

The most interesting aspect of the final section of *L'impresa* still concerns the problem of kissing. Trevisani seems to perceive the act of kissing as the unique connector between physical drive and spiritual love. But again the emphasis of the author's interpretation falls on the physical, sexual side of the "honest" kiss. To understand the nature of kissing, Cesare explains to his friends, we must analyze the role played by sighing (p. 90). In the second speech of his *De amore*, Ficino had dedicated a brief reference to the connection between sighing and rejoicing: "They [two lovers] sigh because they are losing themselves, because they are destroying themselves. . . . They rejoice because they are transferring themselves into something better" (*Commentary*, 2.6.52). Ficino makes no allusion to the act of sighing while kissing. For Ficino, a sigh is primarily the expression of an inner longing.

In *L'impresa*, on the other hand, Cesare stresses that, when we kiss someone on the mouth, we give away our breath or spirits ("spirito") but receive breath from the other's mouth. Sighs can have three different causes: physical or mental tiredness, physical or mental pain, and love (Trevisani, 1569, p. 91). We sigh to expel the excessive warmth suddenly created in our body and to inhale some fresh air (p. 92). All real sighs, Cesare adds, "are warm and ardent, as poets have always stated" (p. 94). Real sighs are thus always related to love. Cesare mentions four kinds of sighs: simple sigh, double sigh, triple sigh, and mortal sigh. Human beings usually emit a simple sigh without knowing exactly why they have sighed, probably because of some thought they are not aware of. Warmer is a double sigh, but even warmer and more "passionate" (focoso) is a triple sigh made of three joined breaths, which is typical of lovers, due to the "sweetness" and "ardor" they feel inside (p. 95). The final form of sigh is obviously a sign of physical death.

I have translated the Italian "spirito" as "breath." However, the reader should be aware that, although in this context this term does refer to the air exhaled through the lover's mouth, "spirito" also alludes to the thin physical particles that depart from the beloved's body and enter the lover through the eyes. Ficino dedicates seminal pages to the "spirits" in the *De amore*. "If love arises from the beauty of the body and takes its form in the beauty of the soul," Cesare adds, it is justifiable that two lovers kiss on the mouth and exchange their spirits (p. 120). This kind of "honest" love "is usually between a man and a woman." Given that two lovers long for the impossible blending of their souls, when they kiss on the mouth, "with the warm quality of their mouth they exhale [spirano] an extremely sweet breath [respiro]" (p. 121).

The sexual undertone of Cesare's discourse on kissing and sighing can't be missed, in particular his allusion to the "triple sigh." I would like to reiterate that, in my view, the main interest of *L'impresa* in fact lies in its failures. First, this book is unable to make sense of the opposition between the abstract and simply unrealistic vision of spiritual love according to Florentine Platonism that equals love with contemplation, and human sexual drive. *L'impresa* approaches this issue through fleeting and bawdy allusions. The author seems to believe that kissing may work as the modest, pious, and restrained point of connection between body and soul. As Cesare repeats throughout the second part of

L'impresa, kissing is more than a symbolic act. When they kiss on the mouth, two lovers exchange their spirits, which could be seen as a simile for what in our much more explicit and obscene culture we call "fluid exchange." However, Trevisani also makes clear that this "spirit exchange" (which is at once spiritual and physical, since the spirits have a physical nature) can take place between a man and a woman or between two male friends. For it is licit for two male friends to kiss on the mouth.

L'impresa ends with a pause. Luigi, the official narrator of this communal discussion based on Cesare's emblematic picture for the prince Alessandro, writes that "tomorrow" the group of friends will gather again to continue their conversation (p. 135). But Trevisani never added a second part to his treatise. The issues of sexuality versus true love and the undefined distinction between erotic male friendship and heterosexual love could lead to no clear solution. In this failed text we can in fact recognize the failure of an entire cultural project. As I stressed at the beginning of this essay, Renaissance Neoplatonism died way before the imposition of Catholic Reformation because it rested on fixed and abstract foundations.

However, it is also unquestionable that the *trattati d'amore*, inspired by Ficino's seminal commentary on the *Symposium*, offer some enduring insights on the nature of love, homo and heterosexual alike. As *L'impresa* itself confirms, love knows no sexual distinction, for it arises from a deeply spiritual yearning. The *trattati d'amore* reminds us that love is a learning experience that regards first the soul (whatever we mean by "soul") and subsequently the body. If our culture insists on the importance of responding to the natural drives of the body, sixteenth-century Platonism focuses on the natural drives of the soul. But the *trattati d'amore* also recognize that it is from the body that love, the highest expression of human nature, arises and develops. The body of our beloved is a luminous presence. It seems to me that in the concept of "splendor" of the body Renaissance Platonism reminds us of the unfathomable nature of love and of the profound respect the body deserves and that our culture, including gay culture, all too often denies.

NOTES

1. Compare Sears Jayne in his introduction to Ficino (1985, pp. 1-32). On this genre, see Lorenzetti (1917); Eugenio Garin (1966, pp. 581-615). I offer a brief and updated analysis of this genre in the introduction to Casoni (2003, pp. 9-22).

2. An important exception to this rule is Leo Hebreo's *Dialoghi d'amore* (first edition 1535) in which marital love is placed at the center of the love experience. Leo Hebreo believes that men's sexual drive is much stronger than beasts' but men know

how to dominate it through reason. Men also have a stricter bond with their women (Hebreo, 1929, p. 64).

3. See, for instance, Melchiorre Zoppio's *Psafone* (1590) and the discourse *Ragionamento d'amore* that Lorenzo Giacomino de' Tebalducci Malespini delivered at the Florentine Academy. Zoppio's virtually unknown text, of very little value from a philosophical standpoint, is interesting because practically ignores most of the issues of the Ficinian concept of love. Malespini's discourse is of particular relevance because it openly attacks Ficino and Florentine Neoplatonism. Malespini holds that the *Symposium* treats love in an ironic way. Plato's myths are a bunch of ridiculous stories. Malespini suggests that young men take frequent cold showers and practice a lot of sport to avoid the temptations of love. See my analyses in Maggi (1997, pp. 23-34; 1997a, pp. 1-21).

4. Ficino mentions that an actual banquet took place in 1468 (*Opera Omnia*, 782).

5. For instance, the seventh discourse of the *Symposium*, the most controversial section of the Platonic dialogue in which Alcibiades narrates his failed attempts to seduce Socrates, is absent from the *De amore* and is replaced with a praise of Socrates as teacher. Moreover, whereas the sixth part of the *De amore* is a close reading of the *Symposium*, the second and seventh sections never refer to the Platonic dialogue.

6. Strauss (2001) holds that the *Symposium* is "a criticism of pederasty and not a praise of it" (p. 50). He defines pederasty as a "deviation from the natural." In the concept of pederasty, Strauss seems to include also homosexuality and bisexuality (p. 51). Strauss's insightful but also at times dated analysis of this Platonic dialogue ends with an important remark: "Plato's dialogues are truly imitation of what we call reality. The enigma of reality is limited by the Platonic dialogue. . . . Plato imitates [the riddle of reality] by writing many dialogues, each giving some articulation of a part" (p. 286). I believe that in the *Symposium* Plato does not "limit" the riddle of love but rather presents it in its unfathomable and contradictory complexity.

7. In Diogenes Laertius (3.29), Ficino finds the reference to Plato's and Socrates' alleged love for Phaedrus.

8. Ficino reiterates this idea at the very beginning of his *Phaedrus* commentary: "In his radiance, Plato gave birth to his first child [the *Phaedrus*], and it was itself almost entirely poetical and radiant" (Allen, 1981a, p. 72).

9. But it is important to remember that Socrates had previously followed Phaedrus in the wrongful assumption that love was a negative event. Socrates' second discourse was meant to correct the blasphemous words that Phaedrus and subsequently Socrates had uttered against the god love (*Phaedrus* 242c-d).

10. Compare *Phaedrus* 234d and 242a-b. Ficino modifies the actual Platonic text. Socrates doesn't mention Phaedrus' physical appearance as the source of his ecstasy, but rather his powerful rhetoric. However, later Plato does state the connection between divine vision and physical beauty (*Phaedrus* 250d-251a).

11. Compare Barbarasa (1544), who translates "indolem" as "aspetto" (2r).

12. Sorboli's virtually unknown work (1592) offers a good analysis of the concept of "splendor." See section three ("Terza Consideratione d'amore"), in particular 39v-41r and 42v-43r. Sorboli first mentions the trite idea that beauty is a splendor that arises from a well-proportioned figure. Later he associates the concept of perfect proportion to the sun's circumference, a metaphor of divine perfection. See the entry "indoles" in Forcellini (1940, p. 807).

13. Concluding his speech, Phaedrus stresses that the "lover, filled as he is with a god, surpasses his favorite in divinity" (*Symposium*, 180b, 107).

14. On joy as a crucial component of Ficino's view of love, see Saitta (1954, p. 193-238). Speaking of the "erotic coloring" of Ficino's numerous letters to his friends (thirty-six directed at Cavalcanti), Kristeller writes: "The expression of Ficino's cult of love and friendship may sometimes approach the ridiculous and may frequently offend our taste" (1943, p. 282). However, he adds, it corresponds to the "essence" of his philosophical system (p. 285).

15. On Diotima's view of Eros, see Strauss (2001, p. 192-194).

16. See *Commentary*, 6.6.115: "the spirit . . . is a certain very thin and clear vapor produced by the heat of the heart from the thinnest part of the blood."

17. It is interesting to note, though, that in his commentary on the *Phaedrus*, Ficino stresses that "Socrates and Lysias have openly censored the first [kind of love, the intemperate one]" (Allen, 1980a, p. 140). In this passage, Ficino posits three sorts of love: "intemperate, temperate, and divine."

18. In the first book of his *Dialoghi d'amore*, referring to Aristotle, Leo Hebreo states that "who is in a truthful friendship has a double life because it is shared by two persons." The ultimate goal of this virtuous union is wisdom (Hebreo, 1929, pp. 29-30).

19. Among the numerous studies on Florentine Platonic homoerotism, see Rocke (1996, esp. pp. 197-209); Dall'Orto (1989); Canosa (1991); and Gilman (1987).

20. The best and most comprehensive analysis of this subject is Tasso (1612). Tasso's book is the summa of sixteenth-century debate on emblematic expression. He dissects and discusses a vast number of emblem books published in Renaissance Italy.

21. The word for "longing" is "vaghezza." This term typical of Italian Renaissance poetry, which is firmly rooted in Petrarch, indicates a vague yearning resulting from the beloved's beauty.

22. The names of the other participants are Lorenzo Gorini, Tomaso Onofri, Ermolao Strozzi, Alipio Castaneo, and Facondo Corso. These young men, Trevisani writes, "are all extremely virtuous, gentle, and well-mannered."

23. If the noun "vaghezza" indicates a vague but persistent yearning (see note 23), the verb "invaghirsi di" has an unquestionable amorous connotation.

24. After this first interruption, the text presents a second puzzling insert taken from Cesare's hypothetical previous book. This part (pp. 35-39) presents a new unspecified narrator who recounts his casual encounter with Cesare. This character tells us that, while visiting Genoa, he had run into Cesare, an old friend of his. They had embraced and kissed repeatedly (p. 37). Later, Cesare had taken this anonymous friend to his house where he had shown him the *impresa* he had created for Alessandro.

25. Trevisani states that his four-stage vision comes from Giles of Rome's theory of the four grades of fruition (p. 65). Trevisani doesn't offer any specific detail. He probably refers to Giles of Rome's reading of Guido Cavalcanti's famous *canzone* "Donna me priega" (Romano, 1602, esp. pp. 19-20). Giles first compares light to love, which follows a similar generation. Speaking of how, by reflecting a sun ray, a mirror produces fire, Giles distinguishes four elements: the sun, the ray, "the splendor that arises from the enlightened mirror," and the thing that receives this splendor and turns into fire. This process, Giles writes commenting on Cavalcanti's verses, is similar to the love experience, which also includes four components. Similar to the sun, first comes the thing that is seen. Then, he mentions the image of the thing itself. This image enters the lover's soul and comes to reside in the part of the soul called memory. From this image arises "a spiritual form," which is like a "splendor." It is this splendor that gives birth to love. As far as the six stages of love in the *Symposium*, Cesare refers to Diotima's discourse to Socrates (201d-212a).

The allusion to Bembo's seminal *Asolani* probably refers to the third part of the book. The *Asolani* is a fundamental text of the Italian Renaissance not because of its philosophical content, but rather for the extensive influence it exerted on sixteenth-century poetry, not only in Italian. First published in 1505, the *Asolani* describes a dialogue divided into three days in the garden of the queen of Cyprus at Asolo. In the first part, the young Perottino defends a totally negative view of love, seen as the cause of infinite sorrows. In the second part, the young Gismondo, image of the happy lover, presents the opposite thesis. In the third section, Lavinello reports the dialogue he had with an old hermit, who stresses the difference between the desires directed at the worldly goods and human longing for the divine.

In a later part of his book, Trevisani repeats the same references to the *Symposium* and Bembo's *Asolani* (pp. 101-02). He adds Pico della Mirandola's *Commento a una canzone del Benivieni* (first edition 1519), another essential text of the Florentine Platonic concept of love (pp. 101-02). According to Trevisani, Pico believes that love is divided into six and seven stages (p. 102). Trevisani refers to the last section of Pico's *Commento* called "Commento particulare." Pico describes the six levels of human enlightenment that proceed from physical beauty toward the divine. The difference between the sixth and the seventh stage is that the mind stops at the sixth level, whereas the seventh corresponds to the "first Father, source of beauty" (primo Padre, fonte della bellezza (1942, p. 569)).

26. See Trevisani 1569, p. 65.

27. See Nobili (1895, 26v-27r). Nobili insists that nature has instilled such a strong physical desire in a man's body for a woman's beautiful body because reproduction ("il partorire") is part of our human condition. A man wishes to please his (female) beloved also in order to enjoy her physical beauty.

28. On the soul's two wings, see *Phaedrus* 246a-b.

REFERENCES

Allen, Michael. (1980). Cosmogony and love: the role of Phaedrus in Ficino's *Symposium* Commentary. *The Journal of Medieval and Renaissance Studies, 10*(2), 131-153.

_____. (Ed.). (1980a). *Marsilio Ficino and the Phaedran Charioteer.* Berkeley: U of California P.

Barbarasa, Ercole. (Tr.). (1544). *Il comento di Marsilio Ficino sopra il Convito di Platone.* Rome: Priscianese.

Canosa, Romano. (1991). *Storia di una grande paura: la sodomia a Firenze e a Venezia nel Quattrocento.* Milan: Feltrinelli.

Casoni, Guido. (2003). *Della magia d'amore.* (Armando Maggi, Ed.). Palermo: Sellerio.

D'Aragona, Tullia. (1997). *Dialogue on the Infinity of Love.* (R. Russell and B.Merry, Trans.). Chicago: U of Chicago P.

Dall'Orto, Giovanni. (1989). 'Socratic Love' as a Disguise for Same-Sex Love in the Italian Renaissance. In Kent Gerard and Gert Hekma (Eds.). *The Pursuit of Sodomy: Male Homosexuality in Renaissance and Enlightenment Europe* (pp. 33-65). New York: Harrington Park.

della Mirandola, Pico. (1942). *De hominis dignitate. Heptaplus. De ente et uno, e scritti vari.* (Eugenio Garin, Ed.). Florence: Vallecchi.

Ficin, Marsile. (2002). *Commentaire sur Le Banquet de Platon.* (P. Laurens, Ed.). Paris: Belles Lettres.

Ficino, Marsilio. (1544). *Sopra lo amore.* Florence: Neri Dortelata.

_____. (1959). *Opera Omnia.* (Facsimile) (2 vols.). Turin: Bottega d'Erasmo.

_____. (1985). *Commentary on Plato's Symposium on Love.* (S. Jayne, Trans.). Woodstock, Connecticut: Spring Publications.

Forcellini. (1940). *Lexicon totius latinitatis: Volume II.* Patavii: Typis Seminarii.

Garin, Eugenio. (1966). La filosofia dell'amore. Sincretismo platonico-aristotelico. In *Storia della filosofia italiana,* Vol. 2 (pp. 581-615). Turin: Einaudi.

Gilman, Sander L. (1987). Leonardo Sees Him-Self: Reading Leonardo's First Representation of Human Sexuality. *Social Research, 54*(1), 149-171.

Hebreo, Leo. (1929). *Dialoghi d'amore.* Ed. Santino Caramella. Bari: Laterza.

Kristeller, Oskar. (1943). *The Philosophy of Marsilio Ficino.* (V. Conant, Trans.). New York: Columbia UP.

Lorenzetti, Paolo. (1917). *La bellezza e l'amore nei trattati del Cinquecento.* Rome: Polla.

Maggi, Armando. (1997, Spring). Sensual Love and Ficinian Tradition in *Psafone* by Melchiorre Zoppio. *Quaderni d'italianistica, 28,* 23-34.

_____. (1997a). Critica del Neoplatonismo Fiorentino nell'inedito *Ragionamento d'amore* di Lorenzo Giacomino de' Tebalducci Malespini. *Giornale italiano di filologia, 49*(2), 209-28.

Nobili, Flaminio. (1895). *Il trattato dell'Amore Humano con le postille autografe di Torquato Tasso.* (Pier Desiderio Pasolini, Ed.). Rome: Loescher.

Oddi, Sforza. (1582). *Erofilomachia, over il duello d'amore e d'amicitia.* Venice: Sessa.

Plato. (1996). *Symposium.* (W. R. M. Lamb, Trans.). Cambridge, MA: Harvard UP.

Romano, Egidio Colonna. (1602). *Espositione sopra la canzone d'amore di Guido Cavalcanti.* Siena: Marchetti.

Rocke, Michael. (1996). *Forbidden Friendship. Homosexuality and Male Culture in Renaissance Florence.* New York: Oxford UP.

Saitta, Giuseppe. (1954). *Marsilio Ficino e la Filosofia dell'Umanesimo.* (3rd ed.). Bologna: Fiammenghi & Nanni.

Sansovino, Francesco. (1912). Ragionamento d'amore. In Giuseppe Zonta (Ed.), *Trattati d'amore del Cinquecento.* Bari: Laterza.

Sorboli, Girolamo. (1592). *Ritratto d'amore.* Venice: Polo.

Strauss, Leo. (2001). *On Plato's Symposium.* Chicago: U of Chicago P. Transcripts of a seminar offered by the author at the University of Chicago, 1959.

Tasso, Ercole. (1612). *Della realtà e perfezione delle imprese.* Bergamo.

Trevisani, Cesare. (1569). *L'impresa.* Genoa: Bellone.

Light in Hellas:
How German Classical Philology
Engendered Gay Scholarship

Wayne R. Dynes, PhD

SUMMARY. Beginning in the latter part of the eighteenth century, German classical philology acquired a hegemonic status that made it the envy of scholars in other nations. Among the tasks embraced by this great endeavor was the study of what is known of same-sex behavior in ancient Greece. Remarkably, the German philologists chose to present their findings straightfor-

---

Wayne R. Dynes is Professor of art history at Hunter College, City University of New York. Among his books are *Homolexis* (New York, 1985) and *Homosexuality: A Research Guide* (New York, 1987). He was editor-in-chief of the two-volume *Encyclopedia of Homosexuality* (New York, 1990), the first work of its kind. Professor Dynes is currently completing two books: *Homolexica* (a sequel to *Homolexis*) and *Myths and Fabrications Concerning Same-Sex Behavior*. Correspondence may be addressed: 90 Morningside Drive, Apt. 2K, New York, NY 10027.

Author note: This article reflects thinking and discussions extending over a number of years. This complicated history precludes a full roster of thanks. I would like, nonetheless, to acknowledge the following: my professors at the Institute of Fine Arts of New York University, who were exemplary products of the German university system; the late Warren Johansson, an incomparable preceptor in the field of homosexual history and philology; Manfred Herzer, whose precise studies of German gay history have been essential; and William A. Percy, to whom I am indebted for many insights in the realm of historiography.

[Haworth co-indexing entry note]: "Light in Hellas: How German Classical Philology Engendered Gay Scholarship." Dynes, Wayne R. Co-published simultaneously in *Journal of Homosexuality* (Harrington Park Press, an imprint of The Haworth Press, Inc.) Vol. 49, No. 3/4, 2005, pp. 341-356; and: *Same-Sex Desire and Love in Greco-Roman Antiquity and in the Classical Tradition of the West* (ed: Beert C. Verstraete, and Vernon Provencal) Harrington Park Press, an imprint of The Haworth Press, Inc., 2005, pp. 341-356. Single or multiple copies of this article are available for a fee from The Haworth Document Delivery Service [1-800-HAWORTH, 9:00 a.m. - 5:00 p.m. (EST). E-mail address: docdelivery@haworthpress.com].

Available online at http://www.haworthpress.com/web/JH
doi:10.1300/J082v49n03_12

wardly in modern German, accessible to every educated reader. The deposit of this inquiry is the basis of our contemporary knowledge of ancient Greek homosexuality. Moreover, by providing models of homosexual behavior that were more positive than those prevalent in Europe at the time, the research fostered the emergence of the German Gay Movement in 1897. *[Article copies available for a fee from The Haworth Document Delivery Service: 1-800-HAWORTH. E-mail address: <docdelivery@haworthpress.com> Website: <http://www.HaworthPress.com>* © 2005 by The Haworth Press, Inc. All rights reserved.]

KEYWORDS. Germany, classical studies, Greek literature, homosexual emancipation movement

The ascent of German classical scholarship to dominance in Europe during the latter part of the 18th century and the early years of the 19th was a remarkable achievement (Sandys, 1903-08; Briggs and Calder, 1990). Gradually, other countries in Europe acknowledged this supremacy. Significantly, the new nation of the United States, seeking to cloak itself in the legitimacy of a classical mantle, dispatched fledgling scholars to Germany as the only country where one could receive a solid foundation in philology.

For this ascendancy, several causal factors stand out. The first is the German self-image as a *Denker- und Dichter* nation, a country of thinkers and creative figures, more than of politicians and generals. This emphasis reflected the comparative weakness of the country at the time. Not successful politically or militarily, Germans must excel in the realm of *Bildung* or culture. The weakness stemmed from the partition of Germany into a series of princely states. Yet there was a silver lining, for disunion promoted intellectual competition, as universities in various principalities vied for prominence one with another. This pluralism was very different from the pyramidal hierarchy of universities in France and England, where one or two universities lorded it over all the others. As in other Western European countries classical studies formed the backbone of German higher education. Here things were the same, only different. For Germany, battered by religious conflict and foreign invasions, had come to internalize a bruising sense of cultural inferiority. For this Germans sought to compensate by a passionate attachment to classical Greece (Butler, 1935). Unlike the French and Italians, they neglected ancient Rome. Moreover, at this time they showed little interest in Egypt and the Near East, a situation that was to change in the 1840s as the effects of archeological finds in those regions trickled in. Yet during the crucial era of the later 18th and early 19th century, ancient Greece enjoyed a uniquely privileged position among German scholars and intellectuals.

The delay of the emergence of a major tradition of literature in the vernacular created a vacuum that helped to confirm the centrality of classical studies. And when the vernacular tradition did emerge, as it did with a bang with Goethe, Schiller, and Hölderlin, it flourished in tandem with classical studies, which paradoxically gained even more by the close association. The moderns did not replace the ancients, but made common cause with them. Contrast England, where such realist writers as Defoe and Richardson owed little to classical precedent.

Alongside classical philology and German literature, a third humanistic field throve during this period: the discipline of historiography, which underwent a fundamental reorientation. Stemming from the Renaissance, the older model of exemplary history was patently judgmental, seeking to distinguish figures and eras worthy of emulation from those that deserved to be shunned. Separating the wheat from the chaff, the historian functioned as a kind of value-connoisseur, picking winners and losers. The new German trend, termed *Historismus* or historicism, would have none of this (Jaeger & Rüsen, 1991). For all eras are equally worthy of our sympathy. The historian must examine each dispassionately and fairly. The new approach generated interest in neglected eras, such as the Hellenistic age and the Migrations period of the early middle ages. Yet classical Greek culture retained its special status. German commitment to that ideal had been too deep for the Hellenes to be toppled from their pedestal, to be relegated to the more humble status of one civilization among many. Yet by the same token, in the growing climate of cool objectivity nourished by historicism, the way lay open to examine aspects of the Greek legacy that had been obscured, such as the subjection of women and male-male love.

Compared with these three developments–classical philology, German literature, and historicism–homosexual scholarship was something of a stepchild. At the earliest it did not begin until the 1830s. Bereft of university support, its only practitioners were for a long time obscure independent scholars, such as the autodidact Heinrich Hössli and the maverick classicist Karl Heinrich Ulrichs (Lauritsen & Thorstad, 1974; Kennedy, 1987).

In a nutshell this article supports the following thesis. The first and last of the four forms of German achievement just noted are organically related, by means of specific links between the first stream–the classical–and the last–the homosexual.

At the outset it is necessary to address the social ecology out of which these developments grew. How did German scholars create a kind of "invisible university" in which the general public could ponder what was known about ancient Greek and Roman homosexuality? To this end contributions were couched in the German vernacular promoting general access, instead of the Latin formerly preferred–not least for the filter function the classical language afforded. The protocols of the earlier international Latin culture ensured that no "unsuitable" persons could access the discussion. To illustrate that ethos, the following analysis includes one transitional work, by Johann Matthias Gesner, which still observes the Latin-only convention. This text has its own intrinsic interest. Yet it was the ensuing vernacular discussion that provided the basis for the rise of gay scholarship in Germany. All in all, this development was sui generis in modern culture; there are no counterparts among the other learned nations of Europe.

It is to the scholarly drudges, if you will–professors and classical philologists for the most part–that we may turn. Archetypes of respectability, most enjoyed, at least in the eyes of the public, impeccable heterosexual credentials. With rare exceptions they could not be suspected of promoting a "homosexual agenda." This perception of detachment lent credibility to their findings. By approaching homosexuality in terms of predecessors who lived many centuries before, they gained distance, and accordingly the discussion became less threatening. When the focus became more directly contemporary, as with F. W. B. von Ramdohr, prudence suggested that it was best to write in highly veiled language.

The year 1767 saw the posthumous publication of Johann Matthias Gesner's landmark tract on ancient homosexuality. Born in 1691, the son of a pastor in eastern Germany, Gesner served as professor of poetry and eloquence at the University of Göttingen from 1734 until his death twenty-seven years later. In his day he ranked as an expert on the grammar and etymology of the Latin Language.

Gesner's little book bore the provocative title "Socrates sanctus paederasta." In part to ensure limited circulation, but also in keeping with standard practice for international scholarship in his day, the text appeared in Latin, embedding quotations in Greek from the original sources. After three centuries of accumulation embodying the labor of many classically trained humanists, the published repertoire of these sources was almost as extensive in Gesner's time as it is now. What mattered was the selection and interpretation of the surviving original texts. Nor was this resource lacking. Under the cloak of decency provided by the Latin philology, earlier generations had produced a considerable though scattered body of commentary on classical same-sex behavior. This body of writing, produced by such figures as Marsilio Ficino, Lilio Gregorio Giraldi, and Jean Bouhier de Versalieux, is little known today.[1] Gesner, however, was acquainted with it. He stands, then, at the end of a tradition of erudition rather than at the beginning.

Gesner's essay takes the form of a defense of Socrates' sexual continence and purity. The assumption that classical antiquity knew two types of paiderasteia governs the whole account. There was the sexually active form, familiar to us today, in which an adult practiced sexual relations with a youth. This must be condemned. However, Gesner believes (not entirely without support from the sources) that there was a second type, which was chaste ("honesta"). Just as today we hear that there is bad cholesterol and good cholesterol, Gesner distinguishes between bad paiderasteia and good paiderasteia. Socrates, the centerpiece of Gesner's investigation, practiced, he held, only the good type. He was a sanctus paederasta, understanding "sanctus" in the sense of "blameless."

With some overlap, Gesner's arguments fall into two main categories: those pertaining to Socrates himself and those reflecting the larger realities of the ancient Greek ethos as understood by the writer. The enumeration of the first category begins with an argument from silence: the various accusers of Socrates, at his trial and later, do not mention sexual abuse of boys as one of his crimes. (Of course, that could be because they did not regard such behavior as a crime, but, as we shall see, Gesner's approach excludes that possibility.) Then the German writer examined the Platonic dialogues for evidence of Socrates's conduct. Thus, the famous episode in the *Symposium*, where Socrates declined the youthful Alcibiades's sexual invitation, reveals Socrates' devotion to continence. Finally, Gesner presents and rejects some physiognomic theories purporting to derive a bad character from the philosopher's notoriously unprepossessing appearance.

The broader category of arguments also makes use of Plato. Gesner invokes the myth of the two horses from the Phaedrus, implying that Socrates would always follow the good horse on its upward path. He also cites Plato's preference for male couples who do not yield to sexual temptation, a special status symbolized by the metaphor of their growing wings. Then there are the two passages in Plato's last work, the *Laws*, that condemn male-male (and female-female) activity in unequivocal terms. Although Socrates does not appear in that dialogue, this does not matter, as the argument is now moving on a more general plane. Unlike many modern scholars, however, Gesner believes that Plato's ideas (and those of Socrates) faithfully mirror those of Greek society as a whole. So it is all grist for the mill. The last item figuring in the general category is one that many have thought to be the clincher, but which in fact is highly contested. This is the supposed citation of an earlier law against homosexual behavior in a speech by the orator Aeschines.

Given the emblematic role that Socrates played in the educational establishment of 18th century Germany, it is hard to see how, in his new *Apology for Socrates*, Johann Matthias Gesner could have reached any other conclusion. As the very model of the exemplary classical personality Socrates must be blameless. Embedded in his text, though, is a more subversive message. Some ancient Greeks did not restrict themselves to *sancta paiderasteia*, the chaste form, but sought sexual fulfillment in dalliance with their younger partners. Ensuing decades were to see a franker acknowledgment of this option. Moreover, this discussion took the form of a series of essays couched in the German vernacular, so that the issue was no longer confined to a narrow circle of erudite scholars.

As this account has begun in Göttingen and will for a time continue there, it is worth asking what the basis for its exceptionalism was (Marino, 1975). For that university had special characteristics fostering what was, for the time, a remarkably unfettered view of ancient sexuality. The university was founded in 1737 by the elector George Augustus of Hanover, better known as king George II of England. As a result of George I's assumption of the English throne in 1714, Hanover and England had been united in personal union, a connection lasting until 1837, when the two were separated owing to the fact that the Salic law forbade queen Victoria from succeeding to the throne of Hanover. During its great period the university harbored an extraordinary corps of luminaries, including the philologist Christian Gottlob Heyne, who succeeded Gesner as professor of poetry and eloquence; the historians G. C. Gatterer and L. T. Spittler; and the statistician Gottfried Achenwall. Foreigners flocked to this unusual center of learning with its fine library. Göttingen's special standing reflected its standing in the first golden age of German universities while, at the same time, under relatively liberal English patronage, it stood somewhat apart from them.

Christoph Meiners (1747-1810) served as professor of philosophy at the University of Göttingen from 1775 until his death. Outwardly

Meiners's life was uneventful. He married the daughter of a professor, and virtually his sole recreation was travel. He was one of the first enthusiasts for climbing in the Alps. A Freemason, he was a strong believer in spreading knowledge outside of narrow academic circles, in popularizing in short.

Delving deeply into the riches of the university library, Meiners produced a torrent of books and publications over a period of thirty-five years. His interests encompassed psychology, esthetics, the history of philosophy, and the history of religion. He published a four-volume *History of Women* (1788-1800). Although as early as the fourteenth century Giovanni Boccaccio (in his *De claris mulieribus*) had initiated an elitist tradition of extolling famous women, Meiners may have been the first to attempt a full-scale history of women from a general standpoint, heralding later accounts.

A volume of miscellaneous writings contains his essay on the "male love of the Greeks," intended as a prologue to a more complete account of the differences between that leading people of antiquity and the advanced modern nations. (That work appeared in the same year.) Meiners begins by differentiating the ancient Greek concept of love from the modern one. The idealism and the emotional intensity modern men invest in the opposite sex was deployed by ancient Greek men towards their own sex. Hence the expression "Männerliebe," which Meiners was probably the first to popularize in this context. The main reason for this difference between ancients and moderns is the seclusion of women, and their consequent exclusion from education. Because of this separation Greek men did not regard women as their equals.

Not surprisingly, Meiners expatiated at length on the pure form of male-male love. Although he does not cite Gesner, his encomium clearly stands alongside his Göttingen predecessor's concept of "blameless pederasty." In fact Meiners avoids the term pederasty altogether. He departs from his predecessor in one important respect, which Meiners believes as being necessary to provide a historical analysis of his subject. He believes that there were three stages. The first belongs to the heroic age of Greek society, in which male comradeship, as between Achilles and Patroclus, Orestes and Pylades, was necessary as a bulwark in turbulent times. He compares these relationships with similar ones found in medieval Europe (the chivalric link between the knight and his squire) and the contemporary Americas.

The institution of the gymnasium dominated the second stage. The beauty of the youthful male bodies on display there gave male love an added esthetic dimension. Still it remained pure. Only in the third stage did the phenomenon deteriorate into carnal indulgence, something unknown to Socrates and Plato. Meiners regards this decline as part of an overall pattern of decadence.

Meiners' view had two essential components: the diversion of ideal love towards males as a consequence of the seclusion of women; and a three-part sequence, from heroic rigor to mature classicism, followed by decadence.

The next figure, Friedrich Wilhelm Basilius von Ramdohr (1757?-1822), also attended the University of Göttingen, where he studied law and esthetics. A lawyer and diplomat, Ramdohr was passionately interested in art. This affinity was sealed by his 1784 sojourn in Rome, where he imbibed the esthetic approach so eloquently championed by Johann Joachim Winkelmann (who had died in 1768).

Ramdohr's diffuse magnum opus, *Venus Urania* (1798), addressed the topic of love understood as passionate friendship. He was writing at a time when friendship—one need only think of the case of Goethe and Schiller—was exalted in Germany. Yet Ramdohr identified a neglected component, for he believed that such same-sex friendships were erotically charged. There can be no true friendship without a core of sexual feeling. Sometimes regarded as heralding the work of Sigmund Freud, the insights of Ramdohr find a closer parallel in the novels of the Englishman D. H. Lawrence, who presents several deeply felt portrayals of passionate friendship among men.

Like Lawrence, Ramdohr seems to have had such feelings himself. But boundaries must be imposed, for when, as among the ancient Greeks, this component becomes overt, love vanishes, leaving only lust. Accordingly he gives with one hand what he takes away with another. Sexual feelings, he insists, are powerfully felt when two persons of the same sex are friends: they experience love. Yet when the partners attempt to advance to physical expression, love goes out the window. Accordingly, Ramdohr's endorsement of homoeroticism is restricted solely to what we would call the platonic form (Dirks, 1990, pp. 379-92).

Friedrich Gottfried Welcker (1784-1868) returns us, though briefly, to Göttingen, for it was there that he published his groundbreaking essay on Sappho. Shortly thereafter, in 1819 he was called to the new university at Bonn. Deeply impressed by his stay in Rome during 1806-07, Welcker strove to integrate philology with the study of classical art.

Several writers in contemporary France and Italy sought to short-circuit the question of Sappho's relations with women by emphasizing the concluding phase of her career (at least as reported by Ovid), her supposed tragic heterosexual affair with Phaon (De Jean, 1989). By contrast, during the opening years of the century several German authors, notably the literary critic Friedrich Schlegel, had frankly characterized the Greek poet as an early practitioner of same-sex relations with women. Differing from the custom in other Western European languages, where the term tribadism was preferred, these writers freely used the word "lesbisch" to refer to her presumed sexual orientation.

Yet Welcker, writing in 1816, would have none of this, rising instead to his self-appointed task of rescuing the poet from the taint of "a current prejudice." For Sappho, or so he strenuously argued, did not engage in physical love with members of her own sex.

Welcker shared the exaltation of the noble, chaste form of Greek pederasty defended by Gesner and Meiners, even adding new arguments. In this light one might expect that he would view Sappho as the exponent of an ideal love corresponding to that represented by Socrates and Plato. Not so. Welcker doubted that idealized male love of the Greeks had a feminine counterpart, for women were incapable of such high-minded detachment from sensuality. Barred from status as the patron of a higher form of love, Sappho assumed a more modest place as the exemplary director of a girl's finishing school. Later Welcker's illustrious pupil Ulrich von Wilamowitz-Moellendorf (1913) aggressively championed this reductive view, which remained dominant throughout Western Europe for a century after Welcker wrote.

William M. Calder III, probably the most careful modern analyst of Welcker's book, holds that "[I]ts methodology makes it the first scientific study of Sappho" (Calder, 1986). The German philologist assembled and critically reviewed the surviving sources with a thoroughness that had not been attempted before. Why then did he reach a conclusion that, since the work of Denys Page in the middle of the twentieth century, has finally been uniformly rejected? Few now would doubt that Sappho's love for her pupils sometimes assumed a physical expression. Perhaps the answer to this conundrum lies in the sobering fact that all research, no matter how carefully conducted, always risks becoming infected with the prejudices of the era. For Welcker's Sappho these seem to have been a paradoxical mixture of misogyny and the pedestal theory of women, a combination common enough during the nineteenth century–and after. The misogyny emerges in the philologist's denial of the existence of a female counterpart to "noble, blameless pederasty." The pedestal aspect dictated Welcker's unwillingness to assent to the possibility that Sappho engaged in sexual relations of the "baser" sort. The result is a bland Sappho, almost a cipher. Yet this seemed to be

350 SAME-SEX DESIRE AND LOVE IN GRECO-ROMAN ANTIQUITY

what the era required, and it must be conceded that Welcker, like a good lawyer, created a dense network of seemingly plausible, fact-based arguments. These served to assure admirers that the poet was eminently respectable. Exceptionally well crafted, his little book for long stood the test of time–but finally yielded to a better understanding.

The following years saw both advance and consolidation. Karl Otfried Müller (1797-1840) conceived the idea of a multivolume history of Greece based on the distinctive characteristics of the various subgroups. The masterwork of this series is his two-volume work on the Dorians, of which the first edition appeared in 1824. Although pederasty played but a modest part in this work, it launched the idea–to be explored in much more detail by Erich Bethe in 1907–that Greek pederasty had a particular Dorian stamp. Preoccupation with the Dorians long remained of particular concern in Germany, for of all the branches of the ancient Greeks the Dorians were believed to have the greatest affinity with modern Germans.

Friedrich Jacobs (1764-1833) spent much of his uneventful life in his native city of Gotha, where he was a teacher and museum director. His main philological work was his edition and commentary on the *Greek Anthology*, which contains much homoerotic material. In an 1829 essay on the education and morals of the Greeks he attempted a form of damage control. The physical expression of male love was, he held, not central to the ethos of the ancient Greeks. Instead, it is the reflection of the mad extravagance of a few wild individuals. This essay remained little known.

Quite different was the case of the popularizing work of Wilhelm Adolf Becker (1796-1846), professor of classics at the University of Leipzig. In his early studies of poetry Becker realized that the texts could not be understood without marshalling the findings of archeology and what can be gleaned of the private life of the ancients. It was to illuminate private life that he composed his highly successful *Charikles*, first published in 1840, and subsequently revised and enlarged by other hands. This contains a chapter frankly discussing the facts of Greek homoerotic behavior, which he describes as "etwas sehr gewöhnlich"–quite common.

Moritz Hermann Eduard Meier (1796-1855), the son of a Jewish merchant, became an honored professor of classics at the venerable University of Halle. In 1837 he published a lengthy encyclopedia article on "Päderastie." For the first time, this article attempted to sum up the facts of what came to be called "Greek love" in a comprehensive and relatively nonjudgmental manner. Significantly, almost a hundred years later the French scholar L. R. Pogey-Castries (pseudonym of Georges Herelle) saw fit to translate this article, attaching his own ideas to it as commentary.

The appearance of Meier's balanced synthesis in 1837 marked the end of a major phase. This phase began in 1775 when Meiners took the bold step of sharing scholarly inquiries about ancient Greek sex love with the general public. Meier's work coincided with a new development–the appearance of gay scholarship–something he did not anticipate, and may not have welcomed.

The world of learning owes this transformation to an unlikely figure, Swiss milliner Heinrich Hössli (1784-1864). Fascinated by a legal case that had occurred in his youth, Hössli resolved to learn all he could about the history of homosexuality (Meier, 2001). He quickly realized that there were two main areas of historical deposit where this could be found: classical antiquity and the Islamic middle ages. Hössli's two volumes drew extensively on this material. Although he knew no Islamic language, his two-volume work *Eros* quotes liberally from translations of homoerotic poetry of this type. In this way, Hössli, benefiting from his outsider status as an independent scholar, discovered the value of cross-cultural study.

As far as we know, Hössli's magnum opus was never reviewed, and copies of the original edition are rare today. However, they made their way to a select few. One of these was Karl Heinrich Ulrichs (1825-1895), who published a series of twelve booklets in defense of gay rights from 1864 to 1869. Although classical learning serves more as a series of examples rather than functioning as the main focus, Ulrichs was thoroughly trained in a gymnasium and the Universities of Göttingen and Berlin. With this background he was able to combine the professional standards of the classicists with the personal convictions and passion of Hössli. Scholarship and the call for gay emancipation flowed together.

Once the potential of this fusion became clear, the new approach served as the basis for the material assembled by the circle of Magnus Hirschfeld (1868-1935), especially in their remarkable scholarly periodical *Jahrbuch für sexuelle Zwischenstufen* (1899-1923). A distinguished physician of Jewish origin, Hirschfeld devoted an almost superhuman dedication and energy to his twin causes of homosexual emancipation and gay scholarship. His monumental *Die Homosexualität des Mannes and des Weibes* (1914) remains the longest printed book ever published by a single author on the subject. While the monograph is deliberately as inclusive as possible, two areas that figure prominently are classical studies (encompassing history, biography, literature, and lexicography) and sexology. It is generally acknowledged that the creator of the discipline of sexology was the German psychiatrist Richard von Krafft-Ebing (1840-1902; Oosterhuis, 2000). Beginning with Krafft-Ebing's landmark *Psychopathologia sexualis* (1886) this field took its place in the array of "German sciences," being practiced most brilliantly in Hirschfeld's base of Berlin.

The culminating figure in this remarkable roster of German scholars in the field of ancient Greek homosexuality is Paul Brandt (1875-1929), better known under his pseudonym of Hans Licht. He received a solid classical education, composing a doctoral dissertation on the challenging topic of Pindar's grammar. Brandt adopted his pseudonym of Licht in order to shield himself from possible consequences. Despite this precaution, a colleague at the Leipzig Gymnasium denounced him, and Brandt was forced to transfer to another institution in a remote mountain location. For this reason, much of his work was created under heroic circumstances, away from research libraries.

In a series of periodical contributions Brandt-Licht worked methodically through the main branches of classical literature as it pertained to homosexuality. These were then synthesized in his great work of 1926-28, still often consulted in the English translation. Although the book is in principle about all sexual life in ancient Greece, there is a strong emphasis on the records of same-sex behavior.

Brandt-Licht's death in 1929 coincided with the beginning of the world Depression, shortly followed by the ascendancy of Adolf Hitler in January 1933. This sequence of events put an end to the major age of German research on ancient same-sex behavior. After 1945 German gay scholarship revived slowly, for the most part observing other priorities. Although one laments the relative loss of classical sexual scholarship–what might have been–in a sense this research had served its purpose, allowing the calmness of distance to prevail over sometimes overheated contemporary concerns.

CONCLUSION

1. The rise of the new and thorough exploration of the evidence concerning ancient Greek homoeroticism coincided with the emergence of the major phase of German literary culture. For the first time, many felt, German was taking its place alongside French and English as a supple language capable of expressing

fine distinctions and nuances of feeling, while at the same time observing artistic principles of composition, vocabulary, and prosody. A new middle-class public arose to respond to this literature.

2. Paradoxically, this noble vernacularization was accompanied by an intensification of interest in classical philology, the study of the hallowed ancient languages of Latin and Greek, together with the emergence of archeology, which added objects of material culture to the well-known literary testimonia.

3. Archeology, though, reveals a dog that didn't bark. Some authors, who would seem obvious candidates, yield surprisingly little. Johann Joachim Winckelmann, for example, would be expected, based on his own sensibility and experiences, to discuss the link between Greek art and pederasty. His usual strategy, however, was artfully to evade any overt exploration of the link. For his part, Goethe's aperçus on homosexuality, including ancient Greek aspects, have long been known, but in the end do not amount to much.

4. A contrast with Britain is instructive. During the 18th century the leading British classicists equaled their German colleagues; it was only in the following century that they fell behind. There is another interesting difference. In their translations from the Greek the English habitually practiced two types of expurgation: outright omission (with or without asterisks) and bowdlerization, in which the offending passages were altered (Dover, 1988). In one English rendering of Plato, the word for "lover" was changed to "mistress," conveying the bizarre notion that ancient Greek armies consisted of both men and women. German translators and commentators, though not always perfectly candid, were much more honest and conscientious. During the 19th century a curious division arose. In England one could write pretty much as one pleased about politics, but frank writing about sex was taboo. In Germany it was the opposite. For this reason Karl Marx took refuge in England, while the later English sexologist Henry Havelock Ellis was obliged for many years to accept the fact that his pioneering book on homosexuality was available in German translation but not in the English original. This legacy of anglophone prudery has only recently dissipated.

5. The rise of the German gay-rights movement constituted a later and initially separate stream, eventually uniting with the first. In Central Europe the persistence of sodomy laws functioned as the

irritant that kept thoughtful individuals delving and questioning. Contrast France. Some advance was made here, but it is significant that L. R. de Pogey-Castries found after almost 100 years that it was still worthwhile to translate Meier. The French were just catching up.

6. What was the personal stake of these scholars? Hössli, Ulrichs, Licht–and possibly Ramdohr and Welcker before them–were homosexual. The others seem to have been heterosexual, though one cannot be absolutely sure. Still, there is the likelihood that the interest of some of these figures, despite the limitations that time has inevitably disclosed, was motivated solely by the ideal of the dispassionate pursuit of truth. The final product, codified by Magnus Hirschfeld's great work of 1914, was a consensus in which gay and straight could agree.

NOTE

1. I owe my knowledge of this material to the generosity of Giovanni Dall'Orto, the Dean of Gay Studies in Italy.

REFERENCES

Primary Sources

Becker, Wilhelm Adolph. (1840). *Charikles oder Bilder altgriechischer Sitte* (2 vols.). Leipzig: Fleixher.

Bethe, Erich (1907). Die dorische Knabenliebe: Ihre Ethik und ihre Idee. *Rheinisches Museum für Philologie, 62,* 438-475.

Brandt, Paul. (1925-28). *Sittengeschichte Griechenlands* (3 vols.). Berlin & Dresden: Aretz. (Published under the name Hans Licht). [English translation: (1932). *Sexual Life in Ancient Greece.* London: Routledge & Kegan Paul.]

Gesner, Johann Matthias (1767). *Socrates sanctus paederasta.* Utrecht: Van Schoonhoven.

Hirschfeld, Magnus. (1896). *Sappho und Sokrates.* Leipzig: Spohr. (Published under the name Theodor Ramien).

_____. (1914). *Die Homosexualität des Mannes und des Weibes.* Berlin: Marcus. [English version: (2000). *The Homosexuality of Men and Women.* (Michael A. Lombardi-Nash, Trans.). Buffalo: Prometheus.]

Hössli, Heinrich. (1836-38). *Eros: Die Männerliebe der Griechen: Ihre Beziehung zur Geschichte, Erziehung, Literatur und Gesetzgebung aller Zeiten* (2 vols.). Glarus: Author.

Jacobs, Friedrich (1829). Männerliebe. In *Vermischte Schriften* (Vol. 3, pp. 212-255). Leipzig: Dyk.

Licht, Hans. See Brandt, Paul.

Meier, Moritz Hermann Eduard. (1837). Päderastie. In *Allgemeine Enzyklopädie der Wissenschaften und Künste*, *3*(9), 149-190.

Meiners, Christoph. (1775). Betrachtungen über die Männerliebe der Griechen, nebst einem Auszug aus dem Gastmahle des Plato. In *Vermischte philosophische Schriften*. Leipzig: Weygand.

Müller, Karl Otfried. (1824). *Die Dorier* (2 vols.). Breslau: Max.

Ramdohr, Friedrich Wilhelm Basilius von. (1798). *Venus Urania: Über die Natur der Liebe, über ihre Veredlung und Verschönerung*. Leipzig: Göschen.

Ramien, Theodor. See Hirschfeld, Magnus.

Ulrichs, Karl Heinrich. (1975). *Forschungen über das Rätsel der mannmännlichen Liebe*. New York: Arno Press. Repr. as a series of twelve pamphlets from originals published 1864-1880. [English version: (1994). *The Riddle of "Man-manly" Love*. (Michael A. Lombardi-Nash, Trans.). Buffalo: Prometheus].

Welcker, Friedrich Gottlieb. (1816). *Sappho von einem herrschenden Vorurtheile befreit*. Göttingen: Vandenhoeck und Rupprecht.

Wilamowitz-Moellendorf, Ulrich von. (1913). *Sappho und Simonides*. Berlin: Weidmann.

Secondary Sources

Briggs, W. W. & Calder, W. M. (Eds.). (1990). *Classical Scholarship: A Biographical Encyclopedia*. New York: Garland.

Butler, E. M. (1935). *The Tyranny of Greece over Germany*. Cambridge: Cambridge UP.

Calder, W. M., III. (1986). F. G. Welcker's *Sapphobild* and Its Reception in Wilamowitz. In W. M. Calder, III, A. Köhnken, W. Kullmann, & G. Pflug, (Eds.), *Friedrich Gottlieb Welcker: Werk und Wirkung* (pp. 131-156). Stuttgart: Franz Steiner.

DeJean, J. (1989). Sex and Philology: Sappho and the Rise of German Nationalism. *Representations*, *27*, 148-171.

Derks, P. (1990). *Die Schande der heiligen Päderastie: Homosexualität und Öffentlichkeit in der deutschen Literatur 1750-1850*. Berlin: Verlag Rosa Winkel.

Dover, K. (1988). Expurgation of Greek Literature. In K. Dover, *The Greeks and Their Legacy: Collected Papers* (Vol. 2, pp. 270-291). Oxford: Basil Blackwell.

Herzer, M. (1982). *Bibliographie der Homosexualität*. Berlin: Verlag Rosa Winkel.

———. (2001). *Magnus Hirschfeld: Leben und Werk eines Jüdischen, schwulen and sozialistischen Sexologen* (2nd ed.). Berlin: Männerschrift.

Jaeger, F., & Rüsen, J. (1992). *Geschichte des Historismus*. Munich: C. H. Beck.

Karsch-Haack, F. (1908). *Der Putzmacher von Glarus: Heinrich Hössli, ein Vorkämpfer der Männerliebe*. Leipzig: Max Spohr.

Kennedy, H. (1987). *Ulrichs: Life and Work of Karl Heinrich Ulrichs, Pioneer of the Modern Gay Movement*. Boston: Alyson.

Kuzniar, A. A. (Ed). (1996). *Outing Goethe & His Age*. Stanford: Stanford UP.

Lauritsen, J. & Thorstad, D. (1974). *The Early Homosexual Rights Movement (1864-1935)*. New York: Times Change Press.

Marino, L. (1975). *I maestri della Germania: Göttingen 1770-1820*. Turin: Einaudi.

Meier, P. (2001). *Mord, Philosophie und die Liebe der Männer: Franz Desgouttes und Heinrich Hössli: Eine Parallelbiographie.* Zurich and Munich: Pendo Verlag.

Oosterhuis, H. (2000). *Stepchild of Nature: Krafft-Ebing, Psychiatry and the Making of Sexual Identity.* Chicago: U of Chicago P.

Sandys, J. E. (1903-08). *A History of Classical Scholarship* (3 vols.). Cambridge: Cambridge UP.

Hellenism and Homoeroticism
in Shelley and His Circle

John Lauritsen

Independent Scholar

SUMMARY. This paper discusses two leading English Romantic poets–Percy Bysshe Shelley and George Gordon, Lord Byron–and three of their friends, who lived close together in Italy during the first half of 1822. Despite the censorious efforts of family, friends and biographers, ample evidence survives to establish the importance of male love in their lives and works. They were ardent hellenists, whose reference point for male love was the homoerotic ethos of Ancient Greece. *[Article copies available for a fee from The Haworth Document Delivery Service: 1-800-HAWORTH. E-mail address: <docdelivery@haworthpress.com> Website: <http://www.HaworthPress. com> © 2005 by The Haworth Press, Inc. All rights reserved.]*

KEYWORDS. Shelley, Byron, Romantics, Plato, poetry, homoeroticism, hellenism

---

John Lauritsen's books include *A Freethinker's Primer of Male Love* (1998), *The AIDS War* (1993), (editor) Plato: *The Banquet*, translated by Percy Bysshe Shelley (2001), and (co-author) *The Early Homosexual Rights Movement (1864-1935)* (1974/ 1995). Correspondence may be addressed: <john_lauritsen@post.harvard.edu>.

[Haworth co-indexing entry note]: "Hellenism and Homoeroticism in Shelley and His Circle." Lauritsen, John. Co-published simultaneously in *Journal of Homosexuality* (Harrington Park Press, an imprint of The Haworth Press, Inc.) Vol. 49, No. 3/4, 2005, pp. 357-376; and: *Same-Sex Desire and Love in Greco-Roman Antiquity and in the Classical Tradition of the West* (ed: Beert C. Verstraete, and Vernon Provencal) Harrington Park Press, an imprint of The Haworth Press, Inc., 2005, pp. 357-376. Single or multiple copies of this article are available for a fee from The Haworth Document Delivery Service [1-800-HAWORTH, 9:00 a.m. - 5:00 p.m. (EST). E-mail address: docdelivery@haworthpress.com].

Available online at http://www.haworthpress.com/web/JH
© 2005 by The Haworth Press, Inc. All rights reserved.
doi:10.1300/J082v49n03_13

He who beholds the skies of Italy
Sees ancient Rome reflected, sees beyond,
Into more glorious Hellas, nurse of Gods
And godlike men.

–Walter Savage Landor, "Shelley"

Male love occupied a place of honor in Ancient Greece, and was at least accepted in Rome and the rest of pagan Europe. This changed radically in the 4th century AD, when Christianity became the state religion of the Roman Empire, bringing with it the Judaic taboo on sex between males (*Holiness Code of Leviticus*, ca. 500 BC). From this time forward, for well over a millennium, men suffered dishonor, imprisonment, torture and death . . . for loving each other. Male love became a sin and a crime: sodomy, which was *peccatum illud horribile inter Christianos non nominandum* (the sin so horrible it must not be named among Christians; Lauritsen, 1998).

With the Renaissance, homoerotic themes begin to appear in the works of Ariosto, Beccadelli, Marlowe, Michelangelo, Poliziano, and Shakespeare. The emancipation of male love came on the historical agenda in the 18th century, as the Enlightenment brought a secular viewpoint to questions of morality and extended free enquiry to the *peccatum mutum* (the mute or silent sin). In 1791 the French Constituent Assembly introduced legislation which left homosexual acts unpunished (a reform more than two centuries ahead of the United States), and in 1810 the *Code Napoléon* declared that private consensual acts between adults were not subject to punishment in countries under Napoleonic jurisdiction (Lauritsen, 1998).

Histories of the early homosexual rights movement usually begin with the writings of Heinrich Hössli (1836) and Carl Heinrich Ulrichs (1864), although underground gay scholarship undoubtedly existed much earlier. This article and my next book will examine two great English Romantic poets, Percy Bysshe Shelley and George Gordon, Lord Byron (hereafter Byron), and their circle of friends in Italy: Thomas Medwin, Edward John Trelawny, and Edward Ellerker Williams. My theses are that male love was present in their lives and works, that these men had what may be considered gay consciousness, and that their ardent hellenism comprehended Ancient Greece as a spiritual homeland for male love.

Before going into their story, a few words about terminology: I shall occasionally use *gay* as being in some contexts the least awkward and even least anachronistic word, defining a gay man as one who acknowledges homoerotic desire in himself. (*Homosexual* is unacceptable for linguistic as well as philosophical reasons.) Although all the men in the Shelley-Byron circle had wives and children, they were nevertheless gay (if we understand that the term includes both the bisexual and the exclusively gay categories). Rictor Norton (1997) has demonstrated that by Byron's time, the words *gay* and *lesbian* were already used and understood in their current, homoerotic sense.

I'll also use *camp*, a word that has been discussed often, but seldom well. I define camp as the unique sense of humor–and style and sensibility–of gay men. Camp combines elements of theatricality, irony and hyperbole. At the heart of camp is a mockery of the situation in which we find ourselves–our predicament as gay men in a malevolent culture–and so camp includes a mockery of sex-roles, a mockery of taboos and conventions, a mockery of danger, a mockery of condemnation.

The term *male love*, whose linguistic heritage goes back to classical antiquity, is understood as comprising sex, love and friendship.

The lives of the men in the Shelley-Byron circle have been purged and falsified by their friends, family and biographers, who attempted to destroy every trace of homoeroticism, as well as to fabricate spurious signs of heterosexuality. It is therefore important to recognize and reject two fallacies: (1) assuming that the evidence we now have (letters, manuscripts, etc.) is *all* there was, and (2) assuming that surviving evidence is *representative* of what there was.

In the case of Shelley, the waters have been muddied by a campaign of disinformation waged by his widow, Mary, and his son's wife, Lady Jane Shelley–a campaign described as "the fraudulent and mistaken efforts to turn the romantic, pagan Shelley, as Hogg, Peacock, and Trelawny knew him in the flesh, into a Victorian angel suitable for enshrinement among the gods of respectability and convention" (Smith, 1945). These two women suppressed and bowdlerized Shelley's writings, destroyed pages from diaries, and defamed the character of Shelley's first wife, Harriet. The destruction of evidence, and the manufacture of lies, has been so extensive that "no definitive biography of Shelley can now be written" (Smith, 1945).

Not only Shelley's life received this treatment. Byron's memoirs, on which he had lovingly worked for years, were burned after his death. Trelawny's letters also were burned. The final two volumes of Thomas Jefferson Hogg's *Life of Shelley* disappeared, through the treachery of Lady Shelley (Seymour, 2000). The men in the Shelley-Byron circle who survived long enough to challenge the "Shelley legend"–Medwin and Trelawny (as well as Shelley's friends in England, Hogg and Thomas Love Peacock)–were attacked for having done so, and to this day are treated unfairly by most Shelley and Byron biographers (Peacock, 1858-1860; Holmes, 1974; Smith, 1945; Massingham, 1930; Lovell, 1962; Scott, 1951; MacCarthy, 2002).

The discerning biographer must take seriously those expressions of homoeroticism that did slip by the censors. Sometimes these expressions were remarkably direct, but more often they were in the form of coded language or hints intended only for the initiated: the "*sunetoï*" or "esoteric few" or "discerning few"–as Shelley referred to his intended readers. In his 1925 study on Shelley, Edward Carpenter makes this crucial point:

> Since the whole weight of herd-suggestion actively fosters and encourages the expression of all feelings of love towards the opposite sex and actively represses any patently homosexual expression, one clear indication of the latter is worth more as evidence than a dozen conventional signs of the former. (p. 86)

During the entire lifetime of Shelley and Byron, males in England, including adolescent boys, were hanged for having sex with each other. Therefore, when we encounter male love in their writings, even expressed obscurely or in hints, we should realize that this took courage. Even *camp*, or perhaps especially camp, was a form of defiance.

There is more than enough material on this topic for a large book. The present essay, with limited space, can tell only part of the story, and must do so in broad strokes. It will be structured as follows: the formation of the Shelley-Byron circle; descriptions of the individual men, with particular attention to Shelley; hellenism; and the aftermath of the circle.

As told by Edward John Trelawny (1858), the story begins in Geneva, late 1819 or early 1820: Trelawny, an ex-sailor, meets Edward Ellerker Williams and Thomas Medwin, lieutenants on half-pay returned from India. Trelawny and Williams are in their late twenties, and Medwin a few years older. At the "pretty villa" where they are living, Medwin often turns conversations to his cousin, Percy Bysshe Shelley, who is living in Italy. From Medwin's descriptions of the "inspired boy, his virtues and his sufferings," Trelawny and Williams develop a longing to meet him. Without saying so directly, Trelawny manages to convey the impression that three gay men are discussing another gay man.

A letter from Shelley in 1820 urges Medwin to join him in Italy, "the Paradise of exiles, the retreat of Pariahs"; and Medwin does so. The two cousins, reunited after an absence of many years, collaborate intensely in writing poetry, translating Greek and German, and studying Arabic. Before long they are joined by Williams, together with his common-law wife, Jane–and later by Trelawny. The far more famous poet, Lord Byron, has moved his residence to be near Shelley. And so, at the beginning of 1822 the circle of men living close together in Italy comprises Shelley, Byron, Medwin, Williams and Trelawny. What brought them together, and what did they have in common? Biographers have shied away from asking these and other pertinent questions.

Both Shelley and Byron considered themselves to be in exile. Shelley in particular was homesick, and bitter that he was unable to return to England. Why did they choose Italy? One very good reason might be the disparity between Italian and English sexual legislation: in England sex between males remained punishable by death until 1861, but in Italy it was legal, thanks to the *Code Napoléon*. In addition, gay men have traditionally gone to Italy for the boys: famous from time immemorial for their beauty, their amiability, and their discretion.

PERCY BYSSHE SHELLEY

Percy Bysshe Shelley was born in 1792 to a rich squire in Sussex. In appearance he was tall, slender, good-looking, feminine, and youthful.

In 1925 the gay pioneer Edward Carpenter observed that Shelley's relations with women were unhappy, transitory or "up in the air"–whereas he "certainly attracted the devotion of his men friends . . . and was capable of warm and faithful attachment to them." Carpenter comments that "while the love-interest occupies such a large part of the general field of Shelley's poetry, it occurs almost always in a very diffused and abstract form." The many female characters in his poetry seem peculiarly epicene and sexless. I would go even further. Although Shelley was a feminist, and seemed to require sisterly female companionship; although he was married twice, and fathered several children; there is little evidence that he was erotically attracted to women. Both of his marriages were unhappy; both came about through the initiative of the women.

In early October of 1814 Shelley wrote to his friend, Thomas Jefferson Hogg:

> I saw the full extent of the calamity which my rash and heartless union with Harriet . . . had produced. I felt as if a dead & living body had been linked together in loathsome & horrible communion.

This refers to Shelley's wife of three years, Harriet: an intelligent, well-bred, loving, beautiful young woman, who was only 19 years of age at the time. It is hard not to interpret Shelley's effusion as abhorrence of female sexuality in general–and indeed, the sentiment is that of a gay man trapped in a heterosexual marriage.

In the summer of 1814 Shelley left Harriet and fled to the Continent with Mary Godwin and her stepsister, Jane (later Claire) Clairmont. Mainstream Shelley biographers have assumed that Shelley was so overwhelmed with love for Mary that he impetuously eloped with her. But if so, why on earth did he take along her stepsister Jane for the trip? An alternative explanation is that Mary, raised in a most radical household, had led Shelley to believe that she (and presumably also Jane) would be sympathetic to and understanding of his homoerotic desires. Mary's own lesbianism manifested itself after the death of Shelley (Seymour, 2000).

Harriet Shelley committed suicide in late 1816, two years after Shelley abandoned her. Despite Shelley's principled opposition to marriage, and his desire to respect the memory of Harriet, he was then coerced into marriage with Mary Godwin, who threatened suicide (St. Clair, 1989). Shelley's marriage to Mary, a cold and querulous woman, was not happy; for the last two years he slept on the sofa and spent as little time as possible in her company.

If Shelley had one great love in his life, it was Thomas Jefferson Hogg, who was expelled from Oxford with him when they were both 18, over a pamphlet they had written together, *The Necessity of Atheism*. They lived together in London briefly, until they were separated by their families. Nowhere in Shelley's correspondence does one find such passion as in his letters to Hogg:

> You have chosen me, and we are inseparable. . . . Are you not he whom I love . . . ? . . . If I thought we were to be long parted, I should be wretchedly miserable–half mad! . . . Will you come; will you share my fortunes, enter into my schemes, love me as I love you, be inseparable, as once I fondly hoped we were? . . . Oh! how I have loved you! I was even ashamed to tell you how! . . . Why did I leave you? I have never doubted you–you, the brother

of my soul, the object of my vivid interest; the theme of my impassioned panegyric. (Hogg, 1858, pp. 206-209, 230-232; Holmes, 1974, pp. 91-93)

As a prank Shelley and Hogg published some poems, which they had intentionally made ridiculous. The handsomely produced book, entitled *Posthumous Fragments of Margaret Nicholson: Being Poems found Amongst the Papers of that Noted Female Who Attempted the Life of the King in 1786*, was published under the pseudonym of John Fitzvictor. (The real Peg Nicholson, a washerwoman who had attempted to assassinate King George III with a carving knife, was still alive and residing in Bedlam.) In Hogg's (1858) account he states, tongue-in-cheek:

I have one copy, if not more, somewhere or other, but not at hand. There were some verses, I remember, with a good deal about sucking in them; to these I objected, as unsuitable to the gravity of a university, but Shelley declared they would be the most impressive of all. (p. 161)

Presumably this refers to the following stanza, from "FRAGMENT: Supposed to be an Epithalamium of Francis Ravaillac and Charlotte Cordé":

SOFT, my dearest angel stay,
Oh! you suck my soul away;
Suck on, suck on, I glow, I glow!
Tides of maddening passion roll,
And streams of rapture drown my soul.
Now give me one more billing kiss,
Let your lips now repeat the bliss,
Endless kisses steal my breath,
No life can equal such a death. (lines 82-90)

Death in line 90 is a metaphor for orgasm, and the rhythmic urgency of line 84 clearly conveys the act of *fellatio*. Though ostensibly heterosexual, the stanza indicates that the two Oxford freshmen were not unfamiliar with cocksucking.

According to Timothy Webb (1976), "Shelley was a translator of extraordinary range and versatility, whose acquaintance with European literature makes most English poets between Dryden and Eliot look provincial" (p. 2). He had a penchant for translating works with homoerotic content, including elegies of Bion and Moschus and epigrams of Plato. Here is his translation of the Plato epigram, *Kissing Agathon*:

> Kissing Agathon, together
> With the kiss, my spirit was
> Upon my lips and there I kept it–
> For the poor thing had come thither
> As if it were departing.

Shelley was not naive. He knew quite well that in 19th century Christendom two males could not kiss each other in an amorous context. And so, "Kissing Agathon" was reluctantly changed to "Kissing Helena" in the third revision (Webb, 1976).

In another epigram Plato expresses love and mourning for the boy Aster, whose name means "star" in Greek. Shelley renders it as follows:

> To Aster
>
> Thou wert the morning star among the living,
>   Ere thy fair light had fled–
> Now, having died, thou art as Hesperus, giving
>   New splendour to the dead.

Here he bowdlerized only the title, changing the masculine name Aster to the feminine name Stella.

During the summer of 1818, when he was 26 years old, Shelley translated Plato's Dialogue on Love, *The Banquet* (or *Symposium*). Judged as a work of literature in its own right, it is by far the best translation in the English language (Plato, Ed. 2001).

Shelley had lived with the dialogue for many years. While still a schoolboy at Eton, he was introduced to it by his mentor, Dr. James Lind ("that divine old man"), about whom he always spoke with reverence. Why did Dr. Lind introduce Shelley to this particular dialogue? Perhaps it was to inform his teenaged protégé, by means of the *Symposium*, that male love is a part of human nature, which had been highly esteemed by the Greeks. The significance of Dr. Lind's tutelage can be gauged through comparison with an event that occurred several decades later. In the 1850s, another English schoolboy, John Addington Symonds, read the *Symposium* for the first time. Alone in his room at Harrow, he experienced the great epiphany of his life:

Harrow vanished into unreality. I had touched solid ground. I had obtained the sanction of the love which had been ruling me from childhood. Here was the poetry, the philosophy of my own enthusiasm for male beauty, expressed with all the magic of unrivalled style. And, what was more, I now became aware that the Greek race–the actual historical Greeks of antiquity–treated this love seriously, invested it with moral charm, endowed it with sublimity. (Symonds, 1984, p. 99)

Realizing that a stumbling block for readers would be the fact that male love lies at the heart of the dialogue, Shelley wrote an introductory essay, *A Discourse on the Manners of the Antient Greeks Relative to the Subject of Love*. It is only the second in English (after an unpublished 1785 essay by Jeremy Bentham) to address male-to-male sexuality (Crompton, 1985).

The first part of Shelley's essay is an eloquent expression of hellenism. It begins:

The period which intervened between the birth of Pericles and the death of Aristotle, is undoubtedly, whether considered in itself or with reference to the effects which it has produced upon the subsequent destinies of civilised man, the most memorable in the history of the world.

For several pages, he describes the Greek miracle, in the realms of art, poetry, drama, philosophy, and science (Plato, Ed. 2001).

Unfortunately, when Shelley comes to his main topic, he flinches: he maintains untenably that the degraded status of women in Ancient Greece caused the males to turn to each other for sex, and he almost hysterically denies that "disgusting" acts or acts associated with "pain and horror" could have been practised by the Greeks. These references are obviously to anal intercourse: either he was afraid that it would hurt, or he knew from a bad experience that it did. Hinting at his own preference, Shelley, after alluding to the wet dreams of puberty, conceives of orgasms as "the almost involuntary consequences of a state of abandonment in the society of a person of surpassing attractions"–which suggests *frottage*, full-body contact, the *Princeton Rub* (Plato, Ed. 2001).

At any rate, Shelley doubted that he could publish either translation or essay in the foreseeable future, though he showed them to his friends. In 1822, just short of his 30th birthday, he was drowned in a boating accident. The translation was not published until 1841, and then in a bowdlerized form. His widow Mary mutilated the text to bring it into conformity with Victorian standards of decency. She changed "men" to "human beings" and "love" to "friendship"; she truncated the Alcibiades episode. Her travesty was the only version the world would know for almost a century, until essay and translation were finally published in their entirety in 1931 (Ingpen, 1931; Notopoulos, 1949).

In the fall of 1818 Shelley visited Byron in Venice, renewing their friendship after a hiatus of two years. Delighted with each other's company, they talked nonstop, from three in the afternoon until five the next morning. For days the two of them talked, dined, rode horseback, and travelled in gondolas together. Out of these experiences came *Julian and Maddalo*, a highly autobiographical and problematic work. There are three main characters in the poem: Julian, Maddalo, and the Maniac. Julian is Shelley, and Count Maddalo is Lord Byron, but who or what is the Maniac? In his introduction to the poem, Shelley writes:

> Of the Maniac I can give no information. He seems, by his own account, to have been disappointed in love. He was evidently a very cultivated and amiable person when in his right senses. *His story, told at length, might be like many other stories of the same kind.* (Italics added)

This is a very great, underappreciated, and misinterpreted poem. Its deeper meaning can best be appreciated by knowledgeable gay men (the "discerning few"), who can apprehend the coded references, and who can respond to the poem from their own experience. For them it is a beautiful and moving expression of alienation and undeserved suffering. A heterosexual red herring involving a "lady" is thrown in, but the references to her serve no purpose other than mystification; Shelley himself slyly indicates that the "lady" should not be taken seriously.

At home in Count Maddalo's palazzo in the evening, Maddalo and Julian decide to camp a bit less and have a serious talk about something they find difficult to discuss:

> Our talk grew somewhat serious, as may be
> As mocks itself, because it cannot scorn
> The thoughts it would extinguish:–'twas forlorn,
> Yet pleasing, such as once, so poets tell,
> The devils held within the dales of Hell. . . .

Julian and Maddalo discuss religion and philosophy until late in the night, and the next day they sail to "the island where the madhouse stands" to visit the Maniac, who is known to Maddalo. They listen to his long soliloquy, in which the references to male love, to the *unnameable sin* (what Lord Alfred Douglas would later term "the love that dare not speak its name") are clear and unmistakable. The Maniac speaks of having to "wear this mask of falsehood even to those/Who are most dear." He is bound to silence: "And not to speak my grief–O, not to dare/To give a human voice to my despair." He refers to "deeds too dreadful for a name." In the following passage, the Maniac touches on *the love that is friendship*:

> O Thou, my spirit's mate
> Who, for thou art compassionate and wise,
> Wouldst pity me from thy most gentle eyes
> If this sad writing thou shouldst ever see–
> My secret groans must be unheard by thee,
> Thou wouldst weep tears bitter as blood to know
> Thy lost friend's incommunicable woe.

He associates his form of love with the dungeon, shame, and the scaffold:

> Heap on me soon, O grave, thy welcome dust!
> Till then the dungeon may demand its prey,
> And Poverty and Shame may meet and say–
> Halting beside me on the public way–
> "That love-devoted youth is ours–let's sit
> Beside him–he may live some six months yet."
> Or the red scaffold, as our country bends,
> May ask some willing victim. . . .

Shame, which Shelley has capitalized, is a gay code word which surfaced towards the end of the 19th century, most famously in the poems of Lord Alfred Douglas, "Two Loves" and "In Praise of Shame" (McKenna, 2003). The "red scaffold" and "our country" can only refer to England, where men and boys were still being hanged for making love to each other. What the Maniac personifies, then, is the suffering of gay men, who are unjustly despised and persecuted.

The last love of Shelley's life, his inseparable companion for the last one-and-a-half years of their lives, was the handsome and sensitive Edward Ellerker Williams, the same age as himself. Their relationship is charmingly depicted in *The Boat on the Serchio*, in which "Melchior" and "Lionel" represent Shelley and Williams, and the boat symbolizes their relationship (Medwin, 1847/1913). The playful banter of the two friends, as they prepare for a boating excursion, could be that of a male couple sailing in Provincetown in the summer. It is perhaps the happiest poem that Shelley ever wrote.

Lionel and Melchior are obviously very fond of and at ease with each other. One line hints that they share a common bed, and in the final stanza Shelley communicates to the "discerning few" that their relationship is sexual. The "death which lovers love" can only mean *orgasm*, which not coincidentally rhymes with the terminal words in lines 3, 5, and 7. This may be the grandest portrayal of orgasm in literature:

> The Serchio, twisting forth
> Between the marble barriers which it clove
>   At Ripafratta, leads through the dread chasm
> The wave that died the death which lovers love,
>   Living in what it sought; as if this spasm
> Had not yet passed, the toppling mountains cling,
>   But the clear stream in full enthusiasm
> Pours itself on the plain. . . .

In 1822 Shelley and Williams died in a boating accident, together with "a smart sailor lad" named Charles Vivian (Trelawny, 1858). Shortly before this Shelley had written an epitaph expressing his desire to be united with Williams, both in life and after death:

> They were two friends, whose life was undivided.
> So let them mingle. Sweetly they had glided
> Under the grave. Let not their dust be parted,
> For their two hearts in life were single-hearted. (Medwin, 1847/1913)

The late poem *Epipsychidion* is particularly interesting for some additional lines, which were found and printed in 1903. Never intended for publication, they indicate that disguised male love is a theme of the poem, and that heterosexual red herrings (akin to "Helena" and "Stella") have been employed. In a letter to his publisher, Charles Ollier, Shelley insisted the poem be published in strict anonymity, in an edition of only 100 copies: "It is to be published simply for the esoteric few." In the passages below, "friend" and "mistress" are counterparts, meaning male and female lovers respectively. Note Shelley's reference to Shakespeare's sonnets, and his contempt for the "dull intelligence" of those readers who are not among his *sunetoi*:

> Here, my dear friend, is a new book for you
> I have already dedicated two
> To other friends, one female and one male,–
> What you are, is a thing that I must veil;
> What can this be to those who praise or rail?
> I never was attached to that great sect
> Whose doctrine is that each one should select
> Out of the world a mistress or a friend,
> And all the rest, though fair and wise, commend
> To cold oblivion. . . .
>
> If any should be curious to discover
> Whether to you I am a friend or lover,
> Let them read Shakespeare's sonnets, taking thence
> A whetstone for their dull intelligence. . . .

BYRON

Biographers and critics, with very few exceptions, have refused to acknowledge homoeroticism in the life and work of Shelley. This is not the case with Byron, whose sexual proclivities were known in gay circles at least as early as 1821 (Hirschfeld, 1914). A recently published biography by Fiona MacCarthy (2002), the best to date, treats Byron's sexuality candidly and sympathetically. In her Introduction MacCarthy makes two important points: "Our understanding of Byron's bisexuality, an open secret within his own close circle, throws important light on the pattern of his life." Yes, indeed, it is necessary to acknowledge Byron's homoeroticism in order to understand his life and his work; and yes, of course, those in Byron's circle knew that he was gay.

Byron was a bundle of contradictions. A wealthy peer of the Realm, his early childhood was spent in poverty. Shy, pale and effeminate, short and with a strong tendency to become fat, crippled with a foot deformity, he nevertheless became the reigning male sex symbol of the 19th century. To this day the Byronic hero is the archetype of the swaggering male adventurer, with his sardonic and defiant virility. Byron had an abundance of character defects–he could be mean and petty to even his best friends–but he also had charm and a gift for empathy, which gained lasting devotion from those close to him.

Byron had what may be called "gay consciousness": he had gay friends from Cambridge, with whom he corresponded using private code words derived from Greek myth and Roman literature (for example, *hyacinths*, referring to the myth of Apollo and his love for the beautiful youth, Hyacinthus; Crompton, 1985).

Byron was an adept at camp. Accused of carrying off a girl from a convent, he wrote, in an 1819 letter to Richard Belgrave Hoppner: "I should like to know *who* has been carried off–except poor dear *me*–I have been more ravished myself than anybody since the Trojan war." Fiona MacCarthy (2002) comments: "Here is Byron as progenitor of a high camp English manner of expression that extends to Oscar Wilde, Ronald Firbank, Noël Coward" (p. xiii).

Byron strongly preferred all-male company. From 1816 in Switzerland: "the evenings at Diodati were masculine ones. Shelley came alone, but Byron pacified the ladies by calling occasionally at Shelley's cottage" (Marchand, 1970, p. 249). By 1821, when Byron and the Shelley circle were living in Pisa, there were no longer even token visits to Shelley's residence. Instead, Shelley, Medwin, Williams, and Trelawny visited Byron's palazzo on an almost daily basis for pistol shooting, billiards and conversation. In December Byron began giving weekly stag parties for his small circle of friends, with fine food and wine; often he and his guests "talked over their wine until two or three in the morning." The ladies were never invited (Marchand, 1970; Medwin, 1966).

Byron's biographers have strained mightily to heterosexualize his life, for example, by overemphasizing his boyhood crush on Mary Chaworth, a girl several years older than he. The time has come to reevaluate this and other relationships, such as his famous affair with Countess Teresa Guiccioli.

The young Countess Teresa, or "La Guiccioli" as Byron and his friends affectionately called her, left her husband–the "evil" Count Guiccioli, a man 40 years older than herself–for Byron. Though their affair is always assumed to be sexual, it may not have been. In her old age Teresa commented on Byron's biographers:

> In all their writings they have romanticized my person, and converted into love and passion a sentiment which no one has the right to see in any other light than that of a warm and enthusiastic friendship. (Origo, 1949, p. 463)

Perhaps she was telling the truth. There are subtle indications in her reminiscences of Byron, that she knew he loved other males, and accepted this (Guiccioli, 1868). Perhaps she was one of those women who are especially attracted to gay men: Teresa was fond of Byron's friends, and they were fond of her. Teresa neither lived in Byron's palazzo in Pisa nor entered it; when he wished to see her, he went to her residence (Marchand, 1970).

Biographers tend to neglect Teresa's handsome younger brother, Count Pietro Gamba, who was Byron's constant companion for the last four years of his life. On 29 July 1820, Byron wrote Teresa: "I like your little brother very much." Within two months Pietro had become "Pierino" to Byron, and closer to him than Teresa (Origo, 1949). When Byron departed for Greece in 1823, to fight for Greek independence, he took Pietro with him, but left Teresa behind. A sobbing Pietro was at Byron's bedside when he died in 1824, aged 36. He accompanied Byron's remains back to England, where he wrote an account of the poet's last year. Then Pietro returned to Greece, where he died in 1827, only about 24 years of age (Marchand, 1970; Gamba, 1825; Origo, 1949; MacCarthy, 2002).

Byron's greatest poem, the very long *Don Juan*, is a unique mixture of satire, irony, whimsy, insouciance, and other qualities not easily defined. The poem is *camp*, and as such can be appreciated best by gay men, who know the conventions, rhythms, and language of camp. *Double entendres* abound. Throughout are hints and sly references to male love, for example (referring to Virgil's Second Ecologue, where the shepherd Corydon expresses his love for his master's darling, Alexis): "But Virgil's songs are pure, except that horrid one / Beginning with 'Formosum Pastor Corydon'" (*Don Juan*, Canto I: XLII).

What critics fail to grasp is that *Don Juan* is, on one level, a pederastic poem. The eponymous hero, Don Juan, is a teenaged boy, who is the object of erotic desire. He is pursued, but does not pursue. Always others (usually and ostensibly female) take the initiative. The male narrator is clearly in love with him, which is pure narcissism: since *Don Juan* is partly autobiographical, representing Byron as a boy, the love between narrator and hero is self-love; and to compound the matter, Don Juan is in love with himself: "He, on the other hand, if not in love, / Fell into that no less imperious passion, / Self-love. . . ." (Canto IX: LXVIII).

After Byron's death, his memoirs were burned by his publisher and literary executor. Testimony concerning the memoirs, from those who claimed to have read them, is so extremely contradictory that we can only speculate as to their contents. In my opinion it is entirely possible that they dealt with male love, and included a plea for its emancipation.

MEDWIN AND TRELAWNY

Both Medwin and Trelawny deserve, and in my book will receive, at least a chapter apiece. In brief, Medwin's life was a mess: he was disinherited by his father, and lived the last half of his life in near poverty. Nevertheless, he was a good and prolific writer, a fine classical scholar. His pioneering translations of Aeschylus, *Agamemnon* in particular, have great dramatic power and beauty of language. Medwin wrote the first biographies of both Byron (1824) and Shelley (1843), discreetly hinting the homoerotic tastes of his subjects. He died in 1869, at the age of 81 (Lovell, 1962).

Trelawny wrote two masterpieces of 19th century English literature: his partly autobiographical novel, *Adventures of a Younger Son* (1831), in which male love is expressed with passion and candor, and his *Recollections of Shelley and Byron* (1858), in which he says directly that Shelley and Williams loved each other, and that he loved both of them. When he met and fell in love with Shelley, Trelawny was tall, dark, handsome, and athletic. He kept his looks for the rest of his life. A man who saw him strip for a swim, when he was in his eighties, said he still had a fine, muscular physique. He died in 1881, at the age of 89. His ashes are buried next to Shelley's in the Protestant Cemetery in Rome (Massingham, 1930).

HOGG AND PEACOCK

Although they were outside the Italian Shelley-Byron circle, a few words should be said about Shelley's two best English friends. Thomas Jefferson Hogg was born into a wealthy professional family in 1792. He matriculated at Oxford in 1810, where he soon became Shelley's bosom friend. Though their personalities were complementary, they shared a contempt for superstition and conventional opinion. Hogg's reminiscences of Shelley, written 36 years after his death, are a loving tribute, and include numerous hints as to male love–for example, a decidedly campy episode where a French duke expresses to Hogg his admiration for the "truly charming physiognomy" of the young Shelley, and recommends: "Eau de Luce should be frequently rubbed on his chest by a soft, warm hand" (Hogg, 1858, p. 499).

Thomas Love Peacock was born in 1785. During Shelley's lifetime, Peacock was a good friend; a mentor, especially in Greek literature; and his literary agent. After Shelley's death, Peacock was the executor of his will. Peacock was a close friend of the philosophers John Stuart Mill and Jeremy Bentham. It is interesting that his friends included both the first English writer (Bentham) and the second (Shelley) to discuss sex between males. Peacock is an excellent poet in his own right, judging from his long poem, *Rhododaphne*, and one of the best satirists in the English language. A passage on "Uranian Love" from *Crochet Castle* is not only a marvelous specimen of high camp, but a vigorous assault on sexual prudery. (Later in the 19th century *Uranian* became a favored code word of gay men in England [d'Arch Smith, 1970].)

Good friends of each other, Hogg and Peacock were excellent classical scholars. When Trelawny returned to England, he became friends with both of them. It is significant that Greek references were used for coded communication on gay topics, not only by Byron and his friends (Crompton, 1985), but also by Shelley and his friends. In a letter from Hogg to Shelley of 21 May 1820, we note the phrase, *noctes atticae* ("Attic nights"):

> Peacock has lately married, and in my opinion very judiciously; notwithstanding his *various* occupations, we sometimes find time for *noctes atticae*, or long walks. [original emphasis] (Shelley, Ed. 1964)

This is almost certainly related to the phrase, *the Attic Mode*, which Jeremy Bentham and his friends secretly used to refer to male love (Crompton, 2003). Peacock was a personal friend of Bentham, and Hogg was an intimate and lifelong friend of a Bentham protégé and bachelor, Walter Coulson (Scott, 1951). In addition, Hogg and Peacock may have used *Athenian* as a gay code word (Scott, 1943).

In their correspondence Hogg and Shelley used the words *philautia* and *philautian*, both in Greek characters and transliterated, as code words for something (Hogg, 1858, pp. 224, 241). Etymologically, *philautian* can mean both self-lover and lover of his own kind; it is a synonym of sorts for *homophile*, the preferred word of the gay movement from 1950 to 1969. In addition, *philautia* probably relates to John Lyly's novel, *Euphues, the Anatomy of Wit* (1579), which portrays the romantic male friendship of Euphues and Philautus.

HELLENISM OF THE CIRCLE

All of the men in the Shelley-Byron circle were ardent hellenists. In addition to the translations, essay, and covert language already discussed, Shelley's hellenism was expressed in many of his poems, most notably *Hellas*. The preface to *Hellas* contains the familiar passage:

> We are all Greeks. Our laws, our literature, our religion, our arts have their roots in Greece. But for Greece–Rome, the instructor, the conqueror, or the metropolis of our ancestors, would have spread no illumination with her arms, and we might still have been savages and idolaters; or, what is worse, might have arrived at such a stagnant and miserable state of social institution as China and Japan possess.

Hellenism also pervades Byron's poetry, most memorably in the paean to Ancient Greece in Canto II of *Childe Harold's Pilgrimage*, which contains the famous line: "Where'er we tread 'tis haunted, holy ground." Byron spent the last year of his life attempting to aid the Greeks in their fight for independence. He did what he could, though his grisly death in Greece, at the age of 36, came not from combat, but from a combination of excessive dieting, alcoholism, laxatives and medical treatment, which consisted of bleedings (MacCarthy, 2002). Trelawny also fought, and was seriously wounded, in the Greek war.

AFTERMATH

The Shelley-Byron circle in Italy lasted for only half a year, before it was blown apart by the deaths of Shelley and Williams, the departure of Byron and Trelawny to fight for Greek independence, and the death of Byron.

Male love was an important part of their lives and work. They had a serious concern for justice. In the many hours they spent together, they surely must have discussed male love and its emancipation. Could the circle have been a gay think-tank? If so, they would have been forerunners of Heinrich Hössli, Karl Heinrich Ulrichs, John Addington Symonds, Sir Richard Burton, Edward Carpenter, the *Gemeinschaft der Eigenen*, the Scientific Humanitarian Committee, and the homophile and gay liberation movements of the 20th century.

No doubt much was lost, through the destruction of letters, manuscripts, and so forth. But some of their efforts may have gone into a Uranian underground, to surface later in the works of others. I now believe that the Shelley-Byron circle, directly or indirectly, was behind *Don Leon*, the first published work in English to argue for abolishing sodomy laws (*Don Leon*, 1934). At any rate, it is now time, as the 21st century begins, to cast off the blinders of theological prejudice and academic correctness; it is time to read the surviving work of these men boldly, to allow their muffled voices finally to be heard.

REFERENCES

Don Leon: A Poem by Lord Byron . . . and Leon to Annabella: An epistle from Lord Byron to Lady Byron. (ca. 1934). London: The Fortune Press. [Probably written in the 1830s, first known publication 1866.]

Byron, George Gordon, Lord. (1970). *Poetical Works*. (F. Page, Ed.). Oxford & New York: Oxford UP.

Carpenter, Edward and Barnefield, George. (1925). *The Psychology of the Poet Shelley*. London: George Allen & Unwin.

Crompton, Louis. (1985). *Byron and Greek Love: Homophobia in 19th Century England*. Berkeley: U of California P.

_____. (2003). *Homosexuality & Civilization*. Cambridge, MA and London: The Belknap Press of Harvard University.

d'Arch Smith, Timothy. (1970). *Love in Earnest: Some Notes on the Lives and Writings of English 'Uranian' Poets from 1889 to 1930*. London: Routledge & Kegan Paul.

Gamba, Count Peter (Pietro). (1825). *A Narrative of Lord Byron's Last Journey to Greece*. London: John Murray.

Guiccioli, Countess Teresa. (1868). *My Recollections of Lord Byron and Those of Eye-Witnesses of his Life*. (H. E. H. Jerningham, Trans.). Philadelphia: J.B. Lippincott, & Co. and London: Richard Bentley.

Hirschfeld, Magnus. (1914). *Die Homosexualität des Mannes und des Weibes*. Berlin and New York: Walter de Gruyter. Repr. 1984.

Hogg, Thomas Jefferson. (1858). *The Life of Percy Bysshe Shelley*. London: George Routledge & Sons and New York: E.P. Dutton. Originally published London 1858. Repr. 1906 with Introduction by Edward Dowden.

Holmes, Richard. (1974). *Shelley: The Pursuit*. New York: E.P. Dutton & Co.

Ingpen, Roger (Ed.). (1931). *Plato's Banquet, Translated from the Greek . . . Printed for private circulation MCMXXXI, One Hundred copies Only*. Plaistow, London: The Curwen Press.

Lauritsen, John. (1998). *A Freethinker's Primer of Male Love*. Provincetown, MA: Pagan Press.

Lovell, Ernest J., Jr. (1962). *Captain Medwin: Friend of Byron and Shelley*. Austin, Texas: U of Texas P.

MacCarthy, Fiona. (2002). *Byron: Life and Legend*. London: John Murray and New York: Farrar, Straus and Giroux.

Marchand, Leslie A. (1970). *Byron: A Portrait*. New York: Alfred A. Knopf.

Massingham, H. J. (1930). *The Friend of Shelley: A Memoir of Edward John Trelawny*. New York: Appleton and Co.

McKenna, Neil. (2003). *The Secret Life of Oscar Wilde*. London: Century.

Medwin, Thomas. (1966). *Conversations of Lord Byron—Revised with a New Preface by the Author*. (E. J. Lovell, Jr., Ed.). Princeton, New Jersey: Princeton UP. Originally published 1824.

_____. (1913). *The Life of Percy Bysshe Shelley*. (H. B. Forman, Ed.). London: Humphrey Milford. [Expanded edition of original work published in 1847]

Norton, Rictor. (1997). *The Myth of the Modern Homosexual*, London & Washington: Cassell.

Notopoulos, James A. (1949). *The Platonism of Shelley*. Durham, North Carolina: Duke UP.

Origo, Iris. (1949). *The Last Attachment: The Story of Byron and Teresa Guiccioli*. New York: Charles Scribner's Sons.

Peacock, Thomas Love. (1858-1860). *Memoirs of Percy Bysshe Shelley*. New York: New York UP. First published in *Fraser's Magazine*, June 1858 and January 1860. Repr. 1970 in Howard Mills (Ed.) *Thomas Love Peacock: Memoirs of Shelley and other Essays and Reviews*.

Plato. (2001). *The Banquet*. (P. B. Shelley, Trans., J. Lauritsen, Ed., Foreword). Provincetown, MA: Pagan Press.

Scott, Walter Sidney (Ed.). (1943). *The Athenians: Being Correspondence Between Thomas Jefferson Hogg and his Friends Thomas Love Peacock, Leigh Hunt, Percy Bysshe Shelley and Others*. London: Golden Cockerel Press.

Scott, Winifred. (1951). *Jefferson Hogg: Shelley's Biographer*. London: Jonathan Cape.

Seymour, Miranda. (2000). *Mary Shelley*. London: John Murray.

Shelley, Percy Bysshe. (1964). *The Letters of Percy Bysshe Shelley*. (F. L. Jones, Ed.). Oxford: Clarendon Press.

_____. (1970). *Poetical Works, edited by Thomas Hutchinson; a new edition, corrected by G.M. Matthews*. London: Oxford UP.

Smith, Robert Metcalf. (1945). *The Shelley Legend*. New York: Charles Scribner's Sons.

St. Clair, William. (1989). *The Godwins and the Shelleys: The biography of a family*. New York: Wm. Norton.

Symonds, John Addington. (1878). *Shelley*. London. [1887 edition repr. 1968, New York: AMS Press]

_____. (1984). *The Memoirs of John Addington Symonds: The Secret Homosexual Life of a Leading Nineteenth-Century Man of Letters*. (P. Grosskurth, Ed.). New York: Random House.

Trelawny, Edward John. (1831). *Adventures of a Younger Son*. London: H. Colburn and R. Bentley. Repr. 1890, E. Garnett, Ed. and Introduction, London: T. Fisher Unwin.

_____. (1858). *Recollections of Shelley and Byron*. London: Moxon. Repr. 2000 with Introduction by David Crane, New York: Carroll & Graf, 2000.

Webb, Timothy. (1976). *The violet in the crucible: Shelley and translation*. Oxford: Clarendon Press.

The Greek Mirror:
The Uranians and Their Use of Greece

D. H. Mader, BA, MDiv

University of Amsterdam

SUMMARY. The Uranians comprised a loosely knit group of British and American homosexual poets writing between approximately 1880 and 1930, sharing a number of basic cultural and literary assumptions derived on one hand from Walter Pater, and on the other from Walt Whitman. Although they used Oriental, Christian and other motifs, one of the major elements many shared was a use of various allusions and themes from ancient Greece, including paganism, male companionship or intimate friendship (which was not defined in terms of sameness), and

The Rev. D. H. Mader is an assistant pastor at the Pauluskerk, a city-center parish in Rotterdam, The Netherlands, where his duties include advising the church's sexuality committee. He is also a translator and independent scholar, having published in the *Journal of Homosexuality* and several editions of *Gay: een cultureel jaarboek voor mannen* and other journals, contributed to the first edition of the *Encyclopedia of Homosexuality*, provided introductions for reprints and translations such as *Men and Boys: An Anthology* (1978) and the first English edition of *Alcibiades the Schoolboy* (2000), and been photo reviewer for the German gay magazine *Euros*. He is currently a PhD candidate at the University of Amsterdam, working on a thesis on five Christian boy-love poets of the late 19th and early 20th centuries (G. E. Woodberry, Willard Wattles, W. A. Percy, E. E. Bradford and Willem de Merode). Correspondence may be addressed: Waterloostraat 155, 3062 TM Rotterdam, The Netherlands.

[Haworth co-indexing entry note]: "The Greek Mirror: The Uranians and Their Use of Greece." Mader, D. H. Co-published simultaneously in *Journal of Homosexuality* (Harrington Park Press, an imprint of The Haworth Press, Inc.) Vol. 49, No. 3/4, 2005, pp. 377-420; and: *Same-Sex Desire and Love in Greco-Roman Antiquity and in the Classical Tradition of the West* (ed: Beert C. Verstraete, and Vernon Provencal) Harrington Park Press, an imprint of The Haworth Press, Inc., 2005, pp. 377-420. Single or multiple copies of this article are available for a fee from The Haworth Document Delivery Service [1-800-HAWORTH, 9:00 a.m. - 5:00 p.m. (EST). E-mail address: docdelivery@haworthpress.com].

democracy and a natural aristocracy of virtue, which they applied to the concerns of their own society and era. The model of male relationships which they advocated (and in at least some cases practiced) was almost uniformly asymmetrical, either by age or class, or both. In addition to their poetry, various theoretical writings by members of the group are also involved in the discussion, and this article argues that these historical/literary allusions and themes should not be understood as means of evasion which allowed them to write of tabooed subjects safely, but as part of a consciously adopted artistic/cultural strategy for homosexual emancipation. It also suggests that their arguments should be reexamined as a corrective to the present egalitarian model of homosexuality. *[Article copies available for a fee from The Haworth Document Delivery Service: 1-800-HAWORTH. E-mail address: <docdelivery@haworthpress.com> Website: <http://www.HaworthPress.com> © 2005 by The Haworth Press, Inc. All rights reserved.]*

KEYWORDS. Poetry, homosexual, Uranians, Calamites, homosexuality, 19th century, homosexuality, 20th century (pre-1940), literary use of Greece, asymmetrical relationships, boy-love

With the assertive self-confidence that marked so many spheres of Victorian life, in 1901 the Oxford classicist (and Uranian poet) J. H. Hallard wrote in the introduction to the second edition of his translations of Theocritus, "It may be said without cavil that no age has better understood both the spirit and letter of Greek literature than our own" (Hallard, 1894, p. viii). He could not have been more right–or more wrong. Indeed, with the advances in archeology, and the scientific study of philology being applied to vastly more manuscripts than had been examined before, there was a firmer basis for understanding Greek life and literature than previous ages had had. Yet it is also undeniable that every age at the very least looks at history and literature through its own spectacles, perhaps seeing some things clearly that others did not see before, while equally failing to see other things, blinded to them by their presuppositions, failing even to ask questions which would discover them. In this contribution I will take that visual metaphor a step further, and suggest that what the particular group of British and American homosexual poets and literary figures in the late 19th and early 20th century saw in the Greeks was a reflection of themselves, of their own concerns, their own ideals, their own answers to their own questions.

This is not to say that what they saw there was false–there were certain objective outlines they perceived in the mirror which they filled in with their own image–but the question of whether their vision of ancient Greece accorded with the historical Greek situation (whatever that may have been) is something which ultimately falls outside the scope of this study.

URANIANS, CALAMITES AND OTHERS . . .

The existence of a group of poets writing in English on homosexual themes between roughly 1880 and 1930, who are the focus of our investigation here, was first noted in print and discussed by Walter Breen ("J. Z. Eglinton") in his pioneering study *Greek Love*, where he terms them "The Calamites: a Victorian Paidophilic Poetaster Clique" (Eglinton, 1964, pp. 375-405).[1] The group he discusses is specifically British, and includes A. E. Housman, John Addington Symonds, E. C. Lefroy, E. E. Bradford, Lord Alfred Douglas, Richard Middleton and Edmund John; he has already dealt with 19th century Americans such as Bayard Taylor, Thoreau and Whitman in a previous section.

Six years later the British bibliographer, reviewer and antiquarian book dealer Timothy d'Arch Smith first used the term "Uranians" for this literary movement, in his book-length 1970 study *Love in Earnest: Some Notes on the Lives and Writings of English 'Uranian' Poets from 1889 to 1930* (D'Arch Smith, 1970). As his use of quotation marks around the word indicates, it was not a designation the poets he discusses had used for themselves, although it was in use in that period as a designation for homosexuals in general, originally coined by Karl Heinrich Ulrichs, later being picked up by Marc Andre Raffalovich, E. I. Prime-Stevenson ("Xavier Mayne"), John Addington Symonds and Havelock Ellis–two of whom, Raffalovich and Symonds (as a "precursor"), figure in D'Arch Smith's study. The circumstances under which D'Arch Smith's book came to be written, however, make his delimitation of the group problematic. As a book dealer, D'Arch Smith had access to a collection of books by these poets, which became the basis both for his study and for the book catalog which forms a handlist of the Uranians, the Michael deHartington Booksellers catalog 3, *English Homosexual Poetry of the Nineteenth & Twentieth Centuries* (1972). This collection in turn had included (and been based on?) a previous sale catalog of a similar, but wider collection, *A Catalogue of Selected Books from the Private Library of a Student of Boyhood, Youth and Comrade-*

ship (1924), which includes not only a first section on poetry, but additional sections on "Belles-Lettres, Essays and Biography" and fiction. D'Arch Smith suggests this catalog may have represented the sale of the library of one of the Uranians themselves; he proposes two candidates, John Gambril Nicholson or Charles Kains Jackson (D'Arch Smith, 1970, p. 153). There was in fact a central core within this group, its existence established by their correspondence with one another, and also by their participation in the British Society for the Study of Sex Psychology (D'Arch Smith, 1970, pp. 137-138; 2001; 2004). But at the same time, the wider composition of the group as he discovered it was based on the critical judgements and knowledge (however broad that appears to have been) of one or more previous collectors. This meant that a number of poets (particularly World War I poets) who must somehow have caught the attention of the collector whose library it represented were included in the *Catalogue*, but whom D'Arch Smith admits appear, on the basis of their work and what is known of their lives, to have no connections or shared interests with the others. At the same time D'Arch Smith was forced to add a pair of appendices, one to cover two post-1924 poets (D'Arch Smith, 1970, p. 161 n. 102) and another on a figure who could not be ignored but did not appear in the *Catalogue*, Ralph Chubb (D'Arch Smith, 1970, pp. 219-232).[2] Inevitably, research since indicates that there were other poets who should have been included but who slipped through the net.

One of the most problematic areas was the relation to America. At least one Anglophile American plays a major role in D'Arch Smith's Uranian circle, the art dealer Edward Perry Warren, who wrote poetry and Uranian theory under the pseudonym Arthur Lyon Raile.[3] Both the *Catalogue* and D'Arch Smith also mention an American book which came out the same year as the *Catalogue*, the anonymous *Men and Boys: An Anthology* (Slocum, 1924/1978).[4] D'Arch Smith observes that it "still remains the best collection of Uranian poetry" (D'Arch Smith, 1970, p. 187), which perhaps should have alerted everyone that there were close ties between those who had produced it and the English Uranians.[5] Several of the British Uranians are given separate sections in the anthology under their own names, and yet others appear in the "Various Present-day Poets" section, along with poems by a larger number of Americans working with similar themes (Slocum, 1924/ 1978, pp. xxii-xxv). However, when my research, published as an introduction to the 1978 reprint, revealed this previously anonymous volume to have been edited principally[6] by an American chemist, Edward Mark Slocum, while he was working on his doctorate at Columbia University, his life remained shadowy enough that the full extent of his connections with the British Uranians was not yet clear. At the time, his only known letter was to the Uranian collector, the Rev. A. R. T. Winckley, found along with Winckley's copy of *Men and Boys* in the British Museum (D'Arch Smith, 1970, p. 146); since then some of his correspondence with the more central Uranian figure Leonard Green has turned up,[7] and D'Arch Smith, in an article on the poet Edmund John, suggests that Slocum may also have been in touch with Norman Douglas,[8] whom he proposes is the source for the biographical information in the introduction to John's poems in *Men and Boys* (D'Arch Smith, 1998, pp. 28-29), though why he should suppose this rather than what seems to me a more obvious connection, a direct correspondence between Slocum and John, is not made clear. At any rate, there now appears to have been considerably more contact between the Uranians and their American counterparts, at least through Slocum, than was realized twenty-five years ago.

In the light of what was known in 1978, in my introduction to the reprint of *Men and Boys* I made a distinction between the British and American circles, then believing the American poets to be an almost totally independent development. At that time, as a way of distinguishing them from their British compatriots I borrowed Breen's original term "Calamites" as a designation for the Uranians' American contemporaries, as its reference to the "Calamus" poems in Whitman's *Leaves of Grass* seemed appropriate for Americans, and to express my belief that Whitman–who, although an influence on the Uranians through Symonds and Edward Carpenter, was only indirectly so–was certainly more of a direct influence on his countrymen. Here too, however, there were problems in defining the group, the result of approaching them through an anthology representing the taste and knowledge of its editor. It rapidly appeared that some of the poets included were there as the result of editing which misrepresented their poems–the most egregious example being the inclusion of Louis Untermeyer (Slocum, 1924/1978, p. xxvii)–while others who clearly should have been present, such as George E. Woodberry, the only other American poet aside from Whitman discussed in Prime-Stevenson's *Intersexes* (Mayne, 1908/1975, p. 382), are inexplicably absent. Nonetheless, *Men and Boys* provides us with the names and access to the work of nearly 30 American counterparts to the British Uranians.

The names of still further American poets were added as a result of the valuable inventory conducted by Stephen W. Foster (Foster, 1982), who focused on American poets not included in *Men and Boys*. Valuable additions though these are, Foster's list is also limited as a result of what appears to have been his methodology, which at least on occasion seems to have come down to combing poetry collections for poems with Greek references. This means that work on homosexual themes which did not contain such–normally mythological–references might be missed, a prime example involving the work of James Lattimore McLane, where Foster does pick up his poem on Hyacinthus, while missing an impassioned sonnet cycle for McLane's dead lover, Charles MacVeagh Jr., the younger brother of the famous Lincoln MacVeagh, American diplomat and principal of the Dial Press, which began in the same volume with "Hyacinthus" and was concluded the following year in his next volume (McLane, 1920; 1921). Several further names which were similarly missed have also been added as a result of continued research through the 1980s and 1990s, perhaps most important among them that of Wilbur Underwood, an American diplomat who published five volumes of his homosexual verse in England, and so successfully covered his tracks that, despite his working for the State Department, during his lifetime the Library of Congress catalogued him as a British author![9]

A figure like Underwood, an American publishing with Elkin Mathews, the publisher of choice for many of the British Uranians, plus the revelations about the close connections E. M. Slocum maintained with several in the central circle of British Uranians, now force us to discard the distinction between "Calamites" and "Uranians" based on nationality. While some of the Americans were, as might be expected, more directly influenced by Whitman, as the work of Edward Carpenter and others demonstrates Whitman was not without influence in England; on the other hand many of the Americans still worked in traditional verse forms indistinguishable from most of the British Uranians. Aside from their homoerotic sentiments, one important theoretical quality is also shared by both the British and American groups–one which may prove problematic for many readers today–namely an acceptance of both age-structured and egalitarian erotic relationships between males as being of equal worth and value. This will necessarily become an issue as we examine their use of Greece. In recognition of all the connections and likenesses, perhaps it is best at this time to simply term the whole group "Uranians." Even at its best, on neither side of the ocean did the group contain any figures of signal importance to the development of modern poetry; on the other hand, the names of a number of 'minor major' and 'major minor' authors whose work continues to appear in anthologies and collections are to be found among their ranks.

One final point should be noted, namely that the Uranians' use of the Greek heritage in speaking about homosexuality was not limited to their poetry. Many of the poets also wrote theoretical treatises–J. A. Symonds's *Problem of Greek Ethics* (Symonds, 1901), George Ives's *Graeco-Roman View of Youth* (Ives, 1926), E. P. Warren's massive *Defence of Uranian Love* (as "A. L. Raile," Warren, 1928-30), and tangentially, in its handling of the theme of "paganism," G. E. Woodberry's *Relation of Pallas Athene to Athens* (Woodberry, 1877)–and there were several figures close to or in the Uranian movement who confined themselves entirely to prose–the homosexual socialist William Paine, who proposed age-structured relationships as a path to social reform (Paine, 1920), Kenneth Ingram (regarding Ingram: D'Arch Smith, 1970, p. 141; 2001, pp. 3-4) and Leonard Green, though many of the essays of the latter might be regarded as prose poems. Thus it will also be necessary to examine some of these prose texts here also.

FORMAL ALLUSIONS

Before beginning with an examination of the Uranians' use of the Greeks, we must note that there were other periods or peoples to which they also appealed. Indeed, among the precursors of the Uranians the Orient was almost a more common reference; one can think of Bayard Taylor's blatantly outspoken "To a Persian Boy" (Taylor, 1855, p. 125), which surely would not have passed muster in anything other than oriental dress.[10] The Middle Ages also enjoyed some popularity, with the term 'chivalry' often being used, and stories of knights and their pages. The use of the medieval would seem particularly frequent among Roman Catholic authors–one can think of Frederick Rolfe's various medieval romances, or the narrative poems by the American Uranian William Alexander Percy, "In April Once" and "Enzio's Kingdom" (Percy, 1920; 1924), as well as shorter pieces such as his "Page's Road Song" (Percy, 1915, p. 24), which also, in a somewhat "improved" form, shows up in *Men and Boys* (Slocum, 1924/ 1978, p. 81).[11] It would appear that with some level of deliberation they sought to both exploit the authority of the Gothic–the last era when Europe's moral, intellectual and political life was unified–with which the Roman Catholic Church clothed itself in that era, with its neo-Gothic architecture and ritual, while at the same time subverting it. There were also Christian references, both from the Old Testament–Jonathan and David in J. A. Symonds's "Meeting of David and Jonathan"

(Symonds, 1878, pp. 151-158), E. E. Bradford's sonnet "Passing the Love of Women" (Bradford, 1908, p. 11–which curiously enough does not appear in his volume which bears that title!) and George Sylvester Viereck's two poems "Ballad of King David" and "2. Samuel, I. 26" (Viereck, 1912, pp. 22-24, 44)–and the New–Jesus and John, in Willard Wattles's startling "John" ("I see the lanterns gleaming. Kiss me, John." (Wattles, 1918, pp. 104-105))–Christian art, as in G. L. Raymond's "On Raphael's Angels" ("I wonder not that artist's hands, / Inspired by themes of joy, / Presuming forms of angel-bands, / Are moved to paint the boy." (Raymond, 1870, pp. 157-158)), or Christian boy-saints such as Hugh of Lincoln (Bradford, 1980, p. 107; Rolfe, 1974, pp. 38-39) or William of Norwich (Rolfe, 1974, p. 50). Still, it was Greek allusions that predominated.

At the same time, we must also briefly note that there was a similar use of the Greeks in the visual arts, particularly photography. The Greek allusions in the photography of Baron Wilhelm von Gloeden (and his competitors Wilhelm Plüschow and Vincenzo Galdi) are too well known to need further commentary; those in the work of the American photographer F. Holland Day are much more complex and interesting, and we will return to them later. Suffice it to say here that an analysis such as we are doing here for poetry could equally be performed with these visual materials.

At the first level, the Uranians made formal use of the Greeks by translating or paraphrasing Greek (and Greco-Roman) texts which suited their purposes. Theocritus was twice subject to this–there is not only the Hallard translation with which we began (Hallard, 1894), but also the *Echoes from Theocritus* by E. C. Lefroy (Lefroy, 1885)–and further isolated translations from Theocritus can be found scattered elsewhere in Uranian collections, such as the pair by verses translated by H. C. Beeching and J.W. Mackail which appear in both of the collective volumes they did with J. B. B. Nichols, *Love in Idleness* (Beeching, 1883, pp. 173, 174) and *Love's Looking Glass* (Beeching, 1891, pp. 72, 73), though neither of these have quite the Uranian interest displayed elsewhere in the volumes. On the other side of the Atlantic, E. C. Stedman, who engaged in a three-way relationship with fellow poets Bayard Taylor and Richard Henry Stoddard,[12] also produced Theocritus adaptations–specifically, of "Hylas" (Stedman, 1869, pp. 186-192). Philostratus, the Greek poet of the Roman Imperial period, is similarly adapted in English by Percy Osborn in his *Rose Leaves from Philostratus* (Osborn, 1901)–the source from which the Philostratus in *Men and Boys* was taken (Slocum, 1924/1978, p. 15).

However, in comparison with these, there was almost an industry at translating the Twelfth Book of the Greek Anthology in its entirety, or Strato or Meleager as individual authors. At least four translations were done: the ill-fated collaboration between Frederick Rolfe/Baron Corvo and Sholto Douglas, which did not make it into print until 1937, and is, to cite D'Arch Smith's judgement of it, "almost unintelligibly put down" (D'Arch Smith, 1970, pp. 183-185; a longer account is found in Symons, 1934, pp. 146-153); a verse translation by two army officers, Sydney McIlree Lomer and Lionel Oswald Charlton (Lomer, 1914);[13] another verse translation of Meleager by F. A. Wright, who was normally more at home with heterosexual material (Wright, 1924); and lastly Shane Leslie's prose translation, published by Fortune Press in 1932 (Leslie, 1932), only to be ordered destroyed under the Obscene Publications Act with a number of other Fortune Press titles in 1934 (Craig, 1963, pp. 90-91). As had been the case for Theocritus, there are frequent translations of individual verses from the Twelfth Book to be found throughout the Uranians' work: at the one end, in 1885, J. A. Symonds contributed a translation of Strato's famous "Garland Weaver" (XII:8) to an anthology of poetry on roses, coyly altering the sex of the weaver (D'Arch Smith, 1970, p. 133), while at the other end the Rev. S. E. Cottam gives us his straightforward version in 1930, along with four others (Cottam, 1930, pp. 138-142), and five more appear in his posthumous collection of verse (Cottam, 1960, pp. 82-86).[14]

A next step in the formal use of the Greeks is their retelling of various Greek myths of gods and heroes involving male bonding, or the stories of historical figures. To begin at the top, so to speak, with Zeus, there are expectably references to Zeus and Ganymede. Both Cottam in "Ganymede on Mount Ida" (Cottam, 1960, p. 66) and Bradford tell the story in a rather upbeat manner, the latter characterizing Ganymede as "More dear to Jove than any other friend" and "Jove's eternal friend" (Bradford, 1913, pp. 70-79); Roden Noel, in his retelling, is rather more aware of the Greek's ambivalence about being loved of the gods, and emphasizes Ganymede's loss of worldly companionship (Noel, 1902, pp. 74-75).[15] Rather more attention is given to the loves of Apollo, particularly Hyacinthus. Once again both Cottam and Bradford weigh in (Cottam, 1960, p. 70; Bradford, 1913, pp. 91-102); among American authors Hyacinthus is the subject of three poems (Allen, 1919, pp. 11-12; McLane, 1920, pp. 57-58 and a rather purple–and extremely rare–version published by an otherwise unknown author, Phillip Steffens, *Hyacinthus, A Love-Myth* (Foster, 1982, p. 17). The later Virgilian account of Apollo and Iapis is retold rather more chastely by another American (Cranch, 1875, pp. 173-182). Apollo appears individually in Brian Hill's exquisite "Meeting at Millow" (Hill, 1959, pp. 8-9), and Hyacinthus appears individually in a poem by F. O. Call, a British-born Uranian living in Canada, in "White Hyacinth" (Call, 1944, p. 2), where Hyacinthus is resurrected in modern life as the poet's contemporary lover. One final relation involving an Olympian, that between Ares and Alectryon, is retold by an American (Stedman, 1869a, pp. 95-105).

At the level of demi-gods and heroes we find probably the most used pair of lovers, Hercules and Hylas. On the British side, the "Song of Hylas" appears in *Love in Idleness* (Beeching, 1883, pp. 59-61), and two other poets, E. E. Bradford and Cecil Roberts, provide retellings of the story (Bradford, 1913, pp. 80-90; Roberts, 1914, pp. 21-29). Roden Noel, in his "Waternymph and the Boy," gives us a tragic recasting of the story as a 'Black Forest' legend, in which the poet assumes the viewpoint of the nymph (Noel, 1902, pp. 126-128). On the other side of the Atlantic, the myth is first utilized by Bayard Taylor (Taylor, 1883, pp. 72-75)[16] and then, into the 20th century, by the justifiably obscure James B. Kenyon and the rather better known Hervey Allen (Kenyon, 1920, pp. 27-29; Allen, 1921, pp. 18-24; regarding Allen's homosexuality, see Sears & Allen, 2000, pp. 123-126). In his "Song of Friends," a poem dedicated to the theme of friendship, John Erskine, a pupil of G. E. Woodberry at Columbia and once prominent professor at the same University and novelist, uses the story as his central example (Erskine, 1907, pp. 31-34). If Bradford and Erskine tend to celebrate the friendship, Roberts and Allen, writing against the background of losses of comrades in the First World War, use the story to mourn the loss of a beloved. Hercules and Iolaus, curiously, do not rate any poetic treatments, although this relationship is memorialized in the title of Edward Carpenter's pioneering anthology of friendship (Carpenter, 1902). Another semi-divine pair celebrated for their relationship are Hesperus and Hymenæus (Symonds, 1880, pp. 51-56; Symonds, 1902, p. 27; see Sergent, 1986, pp. 109-110 for background). Symonds, always assiduous at uncovering such themes, found two other individual heroes to celebrate: Philippus (Symonds, 1878, pp. 33-36, 252) and Diocles, the hero at whose tomb outside Thebes *erastai* and *eromenoi* swore to be faithful to one another (Symonds, 1880, pp. 60-61; Sergent, 1986, pp. 167-173 for the background). Curiously, the devotion of the famous pair Achilles and Patroclus seems to merit far less attention, with only Cottam's "Achilles on the Trojan Plain" (Cottam, 1960, p. 67). Finally, the tragic mythical figure who spurned friendship, Narcissus, receives moderate attention, from the British clergymen Cottam in "Narcissus by a pool in Attica" (Cottam, 1960, p. 69) and Bradford (Bradford, 1913, pp. 50-51), and from the American judge Walter Malone in one of his few forays into mythology (Malone, 1919, pp. 277-296). In a spirit diametrically opposed to their praise of his beauty, he is also taken up by the American Carl MacIntyre in a cycle of poems mocking classical themes (MacIntyre, 1936, p. 36).

Moving into human pairs, we have celebrations by Cottam of Plato and Aster in his "Aster in the Grove of the Academy" and of Plato and Agathon in "Agathon in the Grove of the Academy" (Cottam, 1960, pp. 71-72), both based on poetic fragments attributed to Plato. Another historic pair of lovers to be celebrated by Symonds are Aristodemus and Callicrates (Symonds, 1878, pp. 92-102). But by far the most attention goes out to the Hellenic romance of Hadrian and Antinous. Again, the story is approached in a variety of ways. Cottam, as a Christian clergyman, emphasizes the almost 'Christian' virtue of Antinous's self-sacrifice in his "Antinoüs on the Nile off Aneinoe," writing, "Mistaken? Yes, but what a sacrifice!" and providing the poem with a footnote: "Antinoüs was within an ace of becoming the god of the modern world. We may say it was only the divinity of Christ which prevented this" (Cottam, 1960, p. 68). Others emphasize Hadrian's loss, casting their poems as his reflections: E. E. Bradford's "Hadrian's Soliloquy," again, as befits a poem by a clergyman, seeks to put the story somewhat in a Christian perspective: "Their Christ . . . taught that love was more than sacrifice" (Bradford, 1916, pp. 12-14); Fernando Pessoa, writing in English, is much more pagan, with its stunning first line, "The rain outside was cold in Hadrian's soul" (Pessoa, 1991), as is Hervey Allen's 'new legend' "Hadrian at Tivoli" (Allen, 1929, pp. 75-80): "Æsculapius himself could not cure my soul's disease!" J. A. Symonds's long "The Lotos-Garland of Antinous" is a straightforward retelling of the story (Symonds, 1878, pp. 121-134), as is Charles Kains Jackson's sonnet "Antinous" (Reade, 1970, p. 247). Alan Seeger's sonnet "Antinous" focuses on the boy before his meeting with Hadrian (Seeger, 1917, p. 85), although he also evokes the story in his longer poem "The Deserted Garden": "That gentle face, forever beautiful, forever sad" (Seeger, 1917, p. 19); the early-dead American Hugh McCulloch focuses on Antinous as he is preparing to sacrifice himself for his lover: "The fair face . . . that tells us without need of speech or breath / the joy of life, the wondrous peace of death" (McCulloch, 1902, pp. 53-58). For a decadent Montague Summers it is the extravagance and excess of the story that fascinates (Summers, 1995, pp. 33-39), while in the sonnet cycle which closes Robert Hillyer's *Five Books of Youth* it is precisely Hadrian's extravagance in "invoking the worship of the crowd" that is unfavorably compared with the poet's own private devotion to his lover (Hillyer, 1920, p. 110).

It is interesting that D'Arch Smith, when conducting a similar survey of classical themes in his *Love in Earnest*, chooses to do so under the title "The Ways of Evasion" (D'Arch Smith, 1970, pp. 180-187). It is his argument that the Uranian poets adopted all these allusions–not merely Greek, but also Oriental and Christian–as a means for smuggling their sentiments into the public domain without shocking readers, while at the same time addressing the initiated. To use the classics gave them a justification for saying things about which they would otherwise not have dared speak. However, it is not merely when one notes the complexity of concepts which these poets were expressing through some of these themes–the relationship of Heracles and Hylas and that of Hadrian and Antinous prime among them–that one begins to doubt that these were just sly ways of being able to talk about the beauty of boys.

Having begun my own research in that period in which D'Arch Smith wrote, I remember the atmosphere well; we were still convinced that homosexuality was the "love that dared not speak its name" in the Victorian era, whereas, after decades of rediscovering the various social and literary discourses that had been going on, and of which the Uranians were only one strand (cf. Gifford, 1995 for a not wholly satisfying summary and exposition of these discourses), and research into the various urban subcultures and their expressions (Chauncey, 1994; Shand-Tucci, 1995; and Robb, 2003 being perhaps the best examples), we have now come to realize it was precisely the love that would not shut up. (Around 1970-75 we were also quite busy congratulating ourselves on being so much braver and more open than our predecessors, who we thought had hidden and practiced ways of evasion.) Although in 1970 D'Arch Smith was at pains to dismiss any consideration of the Uranians as a movement (D'Arch Smith, 1970, p. 196)–and I would agree that one must not overstate their degree of organization–thirty years on I propose that we must reevaluate the Uranians' use of these allusions, not as a means of evasion but precisely as a very conscious and deliberate strategy for a sexual cultural politics through art, a valorization of homosexuality–in this case, their Uranian vision–on one hand by connecting it with the classics, which still enjoyed greater social and cultural authority than they do today, and on the other by means of esthetic arguments in poetic expression, the thought being that if some subject can produce a work of beauty, it must have a moral validity.

Thus it is not only a wider understanding of the currents that were at work in homosexuality, and at work in defining it, but also our understanding of the processes of art which allows us to see this. Since the 1970s, thanks especially to feminist, gay and queer art–and in particular to analysis of the intentions behind the work of figures such as Robert Mapplethorpe (Danto, 1995) at valorizing sexual dissidence in art–we now have the tools to read that process in the past. Once we can begin to see F. Holland Day as the Mapplethorpe of his era–not so large a step–we can perhaps also begin to see J. A. Symonds as akin to Mapplethorpe, outrageous as that comparison might initially sound. Indeed, the idea of an artistic strategy for valorizing homosexuality would particularly suit a personality such as Symonds, who, after all, in addition to his poetry and scholarship–often harnessed to his sexual interests–also wrote tracts "addressed especially to medical psychiatrists and jurists" and participated in the medical discourse in his collaboration with Havelock Ellis. I will acknowledge that this degree of consciousness was possibly not present in every Uranian who took up his pen to produce a handful of poems, but suspect it certainly was in the more vocal and prolific, such as E. E. Bradford (when someone publishes twelve books of poetry on the same controversial topic over a period of better than 20 years, one really must suppose a propagandizing purpose!), or others like George Ives and E. P. Warren who were also writing theoretical texts, or in more combative personalities like George Sylvester Viereck and Willard Wattles in America–and with the last of these, one touches on the circle which produced the *Men and Boys* anthology, and their reasons for producing it. Far from a means of evasion, allusions to the Greeks were a tool for valorization in a strategy for social acceptance.

Surveying the allusions, one sees that they are largely to asymmetrical relationships, either clearly age-structured, or between a god and a mortal, or a warrior/hero and his protégé ("Heroes and Their Pals," as Halperin famously put it), or various combinations of these. In light of the "ideal standards of reciprocity, equality and gender identity imposed by the crypto-normative force of the homosexual category" (Halperin, 2002, p. 136), such relationships today are regarded as inherently morally culpable, paternalistic and patronizing at best, exploitative or even 'abuse' at the worst; to hold up such relationships as an ideal is accordingly viewed either as self-justification on the part of the "superordinate" party, or hypocrisy. Yet this inequality is part of the objective outline that Uranians saw in their Greek mirror; the Greek relationships were asymmetrical, and the Uranians saw themselves in this outline and filled in their own features. Indeed, we find this asymmetrical model being accepted and advocated not only by those who explicitly idealized age-structured relationships, but also by those like Symonds and Roden Noel, whose personal interests were in age-consistent relationships (albeit relationships which crossed class lines). Were they all merely protecting their privilege? Did they fail to see or appreciate the significance of the social and power inequalities that were going on in the Greek allusions (and perhaps their own relationships)? Was this, on the part of figures like Symonds, simply cynical appropriation or reinterpretation of a culturally authoritative Greek ideal, as a strategy to gain acceptance for their own egalitarian relationships? Or was it indeed a valorization of the asymmetrical, the unequal as such, for a purpose and on the basis of values and ideals we no longer recognize, or to which we are no longer sympathetic?

Even in their day the asymmetrical model, at least with regard to age, was certainly not the only one available. We find the same acceptance of a cultural view of homosexuality, with a similar acceptance of asymmetrical relationships, on the part of Von Kupffer, Friedlander, Brand and the *Der Eigene* circle in Germany, where it stood opposed to Hirschfeld and his circle, whose medical and biological theories strongly implied reciprocity–if you are of a third sex, you will want to have relations with somebody like yourself, not with a boy–and who were already busily proposing age of consent laws which would criminalize relations which transgressed age equality, as a trade-off for legalizing their own relations (Oosterhuis, 1991, particularly the General Introduction). The Uranians fit well with this *Der Eigene* circle, with its emphasis on the arts, friendship, male bonding, pedagogical Eros–and asymmetrical relationships. Yet Brand and his circle were marked by a certain elitism, which we will discover that the Uranians lacked. In that lies the final key to the Uranians' handling of the Greek heritage as they perceived it.

REFLECTIONS IN A GREEK MIRROR

The first of the general themes which the Uranians saw reflected in the Greeks was what may be called 'paganism.' For them this had little or nothing to do with Greek religion as such, in contrast to Christianity; several of the leading Uranian voices were clergymen, and many others continued to identify with certain Christian values. Rather, it was a matter of a general approach to life, one which several of the Uranians indeed sought to reconcile with Christianity by redefining Christ as the ideal comrade, an ethical teacher and guide who also taught the essential life-affirming truths they found in this paganism, or, in contrast, by emphasizing the principle of suffering for truth (or even *as* truth) which they saw embodied in both, and equating the slain Socrates and Christ as twin lights. Others sought to hold the two, though irreconcilable, in creative tension. To the extent that the Uranians' paganism was in opposition to Christianity, it was to bourgeois, evangelical Christianity–with particular emphasis on the bourgeois; it swept in various elements of opposition to middle class, industrialized, mass society as well. Perhaps the first and best exponent of what it meant for them was Walter Pater, in his famous "Conclusion" to the first (1873) edition of his *The Renaissance*: "To burn always with this hard, gem-like flame, to maintain this ecstasy, is success in life" (Pater, 1919, p. 197). It involved a reorientation to this world, to its truths which emerge in analysis, to its beauty, to art, to experience, to the senses, to friendship and human values, and away from habit ("our failure is to form habits"), from dogmas and stereotypes, from convention, from a slavery to a hereafter to be gained by the practice of conventional morality, every bit as much as from slavery to material palliatives. It was this vitality and immediacy, something which had been present at the beginning of our culture, which the Uranians, looking through the lenses of Pater, Winckelmann and the Renaissance, saw reflected in the Greek mirror.[17] Or to use a different metaphor, from Alan Seeger, this was the "Deserted Garden" to which they sought return–and in which, among other things, stands "the dear Bithynian shepherd lad" (Seeger, 1917, p. 19). In the same year Brian Hill was writing that his Arcady ("I hate this modern world of strife. . . . My heart is back in Arcady, my soul is far away, far away in Arcady . . .") is peopled by "the shepherd in his coat of wool, the goatherd on the hill . . . the careless boys at play beside the merry chattering rill . . . the little fauns with cloven hoofs . . ." (Hill, 1917, p. 9).

There were some, even within the Uranians themselves, who had their doubts about this paganism, and particularly its effect on morals. The Rev. E. C. Lefroy, who could write to a friend, "I have an inborn admiration for beauty of form and figure . . . in most football teams I can find one Antinous, sometimes two or three . . . ," could also, in his 1877 address on "Muscular Christianity," write against what he termed "Pater–paganism and Symonds–sophistry." "What Mr. Symonds and Mr. Pater, and their followers, advise us to do may be summed up in a single sentence, 'Act according to the promptings of nature, and you cannot go wrong.'. . . In the present case, what is meant by the term 'nature'? Is it

Anglo-Byzantine . . . for the worst passions and most carnal inclinations
of humanity? I fear there is too much reason to dread an affirmative answer" (cited in Symonds, 1893, pp. 91-92). Lefroy opposes this with
both "Hellenism properly so-called" (Lefroy's own words) and "the
Christian faith as a divinely appointed way of surmounting the corruption and imperfection of nature" (Symonds's summary of the other half
of Lefroy's argument) (Symonds, 1893, pp. 92-93). Symonds's own response–"I need not discuss the question of how far Lefroy was just to either Mr. Pater or myself, as regards our doctrine *and our practice*
[italics added]" (Symonds, 1893, p. 94)–nonetheless makes it clear that
he regards accusations against the former as unfounded as the accusations against the latter are uncomfortable. He (and as we will see, other
Uranians such as Woodberry and Warren) regard the appeal to ideals in
their 'paganism' as providing an adequate ethical framework for it.[18] At
any rate, we must note that Lefroy's critique, involving a veiled reference to homosexuality as an immoral practice, is *not* the same as
modern objections to the Uranians' advocacy of asymmetrical relations
as 'non-reciprocal' and exploitative.

In America one of the first to fall under the influence of Pater's vision
was a brilliant Harvard student, George Edward Woodberry, who
would go on to become a distinguished and highly popular professor of
literature at Columbia, and, as we saw, be the only other American homosexual poet other than Whitman who Prime-Stevenson esteemed
worth mentioning in his *Intersexes*. In 1877, the year Pater published
the second edition of his studies on the Renaissance without the controversial "Conclusion," and also the year of Lefroy's attack on Pater and
Symonds, Woodberry's oration as valedictorian of his class, *The Relation of Pallas Athene to Athens*, was cancelled by the University authorities on the grounds that it was too "pagan" (Erskine, 1930, p. 276), or,
as Woodberry himself put it in an introductory note to the 30 copies he
had privately printed for friends, "This Oration was not delivered upon
Commencement Day because the Committee on Commencement Parts
decided that certain passages in it, which the author declined to change,
were likely to shock the religious sensibilities of the audience" (Woodberry, 1877, p. 3).[19] Leaving aside the equivalence between homosexual
practice and 'paganism' attributed by its enemies, on the face of things
it is a bit hard to see what all the fuss was about, though one could imagine the opening lines falling on rocky ground in certain circles of American Evangelicals yet today, though no longer at Harvard: "It is hard to
realize to ourselves that religion did not enter the world with Christianity; that long before the Blessed Feet trod the weary way to the Mount of

Sacrifice, men had in their hearts a faith which set their souls on noble living and strengthened their arms for fearless action" (Woodberry, 1877, p. 5). He continues, "Christ, who is love, is the centre of our civilization. Pallas Athene, who is intelligence, was the centre of Greek civilization" (Woodberry, 1877, p. 8), and then traces how from her sprang all the blessings the civilization of Athens–"and that means the civilization of the world" (Woodberry, 1877, p. 5)–enjoyed: peace, prosperity in trade, athletics, philosophy, ethics, art in its greatest glories, summed up in the Parthenon and its sculpture. This was what Greece was to mean for him in his poetry; his "Agathon" is not an opportunity to praise a human relationship, but a dramatic poetic dialogue in which "the desire which in early youth is fed by mortal loveliness" learns to discover its eternal object, following the passage of Agathon, instructed by Diotima and with Eros, "desire of beauty," as his companion and guide, to find "the eternal element in which life has its ground and being" (from "The Argument" of "Agathon," Woodberry, 1903, p. 227; poem, pp. 229-278): in short, a poetic syllabus of Platonic idealism. The pursuit of such idealism, which had made Greece supreme, he hopes will reemerge to provide its blessings to our world: in his "Winged Eros of Tunis, recovered from the sea near Mahdia in 1904" Woodberry both praises the beauty of the statue, and expresses his hopes that in its return, this Eros will be a guide for us today, as he was for Agathon:

Beautiful bronze boy . . .
Thy loveliness disdained
   A rude barbarian fate;
No Christian touch profaned
   Thy form inviolate;
But plunged in ocean-peace
   The blue waves did thee cover;
A score of centuries
   Thou hadst the sea for lover.
Late thence emerging now
   Into the gray light wan,
Thou bringest the youthful brow
   The world's dawn rests upon.
Strange is the sight, forlorn
   The heart with the sense thereof,
Beautiful boy, reborn
   Of the waves for our worship and love. (Woodberry, 1914, pp. 29-30)

Yet we must not think of Woodberry as someone turning endlessly in the aether of idealist philosophy; his poetry is equally rooted in the sense impressions from which this passionate search for the spiritual springs. Those impressions are often of place–his "Taormina" deals not with the Sicilians who modeled for Von Gloeden, whom he clearly was not unaware of on his visits there, but with the impressions of its landscape and nature (Woodberry, 1903, pp. 10-12)–but frequently also of boys and boy-children. As the author of the only study of Woodberry's poetry puts it, his poems contain "a whole row of young Sicilians" (Ledoux, 1918, p. 21), and in a letter to Ledoux, Woodberry enthuses about "a boy of ten and Sicilian of the Sicilians to look at" (Woodberry, 1930, p. 63); for their presence in his poetry, one should see, for example, his "Flower of Etna" or "The Sicilian" (Woodberry, 1914, pp. 68-70 and 79, respectively). His own relationships also provide a starting point for his passionate search for the ideal; his first long poem, "The North Shore Watch," is an elegy to a deceased companion of his youth, but more heartfelt is his "Comrades," another elegy to young friends, but in particular one whom Woodberry had met when he was 22 and newly arrived to teach at the University of Nebraska, and the boy 17:

> Where is he now, the dark boy slender
>   Who taught me bare-back, stirrup and reins?
> I loved him, he loved me; my beautiful, tender
>   Tamer of horses on grass-gown plains . . .
> O love that passes the love of woman!
>   Who that hath felt it shall ever forget,
> When the breath of life with a throb turns human,
>   And a lad's heart to a lad's heart is set? (Woodberry, 1914, pp. 55-56)[20]

Much more could be said of Woodberry–much more deserves to be said of him, in his quality as both a poet and homosexual poet–but we must move on.

By the end of his life, battered by a somewhat mysterious departure from Columbia in 1904 at the height of his powers,[21] years of occasional lecturing and roaming in somewhat genteel poverty[22] in Europe and North Africa, Europe closing to him with the start of World War I and the loss in that conflict of friends, both among former students from Columbia and young Italians he had known, one can sense from his letters that Woodberry's idealism was becoming somewhat brittle. Another American who similarly celebrated the 'pagan' faced his conflict earlier and more directly. For all its brightness, the pagan flame had its shadows: concentration on experience in this world and the search for the impersonal eternal truths that lay behind them meant the loss of the sense of ultimate transcendence, hope and moral values provided by Christianity, hope for an afterlife, and the assurance of forgiveness in relation to a personal God. William Alexander Percy made precisely this conflict the crux of his poetry. For the most part–that is to say, in his verse play "In April Once" and the narrative poem "Enzio's Kingdom"–he set this conflict between the attractions of pagan ecstasy and transcendent faith in the times of Frederick II, Holy Roman Emperor and King of Sicily, whose illustrious court was the first light in the sky heralding the dawn of the Renaissance, as it saw the first reentry of Greek scholarship–and with it Hellenistic attitudes–into Europe as a result of Frederick's contacts with Arab lands where they had been preserved. Percy's evocation of this era was far from just decorative, a chance to write of knights and their young pages–though the final scene of "In April Once," with Guido, the darkly handsome Sicilian knight expiring in the arms of his faithful little page Felice, is surely one of the most affecting in all Uranian literature. The issue runs deeper here: whether paganism, for all its attractions, was indeed (to cite Woodberry's words) a "faith which set . . . souls on noble living and strengthened . . . arms for fearless action":

> *Guido* Stay here.
> I am beyond the laying on of hands.
> My deeds were not. My aspirations lacked
> Not beauty, but singleness of purpose.
> And I have lived.
> No priest can mend what's broken here.
> And for the rest . . .
> I shall miss the iris skies and wet, clear stars
> Of these our April evenings . . .
> And thee, Felice . . .
> *Felice (sobbing).* I am thy page. Ah, leave me not alone.
> *Guido.* Hush, hush! But yet, forget me never . . .
>   O littlest comrade of my heart. (Percy, 1920, pp. 56-57)

Yet with equal fervor Percy continued to sing of paganism. As it was for Woodberry, Taormina becomes a focus for this (Percy, 1915, pp. 45, 61). Percy also appropriates the Arcadian metaphor we also noted with Seeger and Hill, a garden sometimes not merely deserted, but lost with

the death of a "comrade" ("Arcady Lost," Percy, 1915, p. 44), sometimes still occupied by

> A stripling, brown and roughened by the sun.
> Limpid breezes,
> Running slim fingers through his burnt black hair,
> Have tousled it to elf-locks;
> Slender and straight,
> His thighs are hardened to the upward pull. ("An Arcadian Idyll,"
> Percy, 1924, p. 59)

Still another Uranian to succumb to the attraction of "paganism," and
without Percy's ambivalence, was Edward Perry Warren. Several major
collections of classical art–including that of the Metropolitan in New
York and Boston Museum of Fine Arts–are testaments to his devotion
to all things Greek. His particular contribution was to seek a praxis of
boy-love–or, as he termed it "Uranian Love"–which would satisfyingly
hold together both the ecstasy of worldly experience and the eternal ideals behind it, doing justice to both. That is his quest from the first words
of his *Defence of Uranian Love*: "If a theory of love is to satisfy man, its
feet must be planted on the earth and its head raised toward the sky; in
other words, it must include both his bodily and his spiritual nature. If it
is true only to the latter, it is insubstantial; if it is true only to his fleshly
instincts, it is condemned by his self-respect" (Warren, 1928-30, Vol. 1,
p. 1). The same defense is present in his poem "Body and Soul":

> An earth-born love? Yea, love, nor nobler birth
> could lift thee from the earth.
> As bedded flower that drinketh all the sun . . .
> so doth thy soul its body bring to me . . .
> a gift of Love's own giving;
> for all that makes thee real is added grace;
> loves not who loves the face
> all other parts forgetting or forgiving.
> . . . and now I know
> that what I dreamed is so:
>   that love can melt the body and soul in one . . . (Warren,
> 1913, pp. 59-60)

On this basis he can appeal to the boy,

Take thou my love of body and of soul;
whether thou hold it dear or hold it light,
thou hast a man to love thee true and whole. (Warren, 1913,
p. 126)

In turn, this is expressed in his theoretical text when he writes, "The
boy-lover approaches the monk, but does not meet him . . . unlike the
monk, he bears with him . . . the sensual together with the spiritual love.
He and his beloved are in training, *askésis*; but it is not the Christian 'as-
cetic' mortification. There is no function of the human being which is to
be atrophied, while both lover and beloved are to be directly in relation
with their proper ideal, the masculine. This seems to be the particular
advantage of such love, the advantage which renders it indeed a philosophical passion" (Warren, 1928-30, Vol. 1, p. 79). The properly masculine plays a key role: the Philosophical Eros, which is the norm for the
lovers, is "a manly spirit, as the Greeks conceived manliness, blended of
strength and gentleness" (Warren, 1928-30, Vol. 1, p. 107). In his
"Hymn to Love" Warren invokes this Eros:

With healing in thy wings re-arisen to bless
thou comest in Hellenic nakedness . . .
and I believe thee as a vision sent
to a mourner in perpetual banishment
from his own ruined hearth or home
in Greece or Rome.
I worship thee, and from thy mandate take
the conduct that will make me or unmake . . . (Warren, 1913,
p. 30)

But there is occasionally a more personal side which breaks through in
Warren's poetry, and it is perhaps well to end there, with his "When I
am old":

When I am old, come to me, child, and say:
"I have tried another way,
and sweet hath been the bed whereon I have lain.
I have left thee to love again;
but take my hand today
and hear–for I will say it–what to hear
is not less just than dear,
words that are not less coveted than earned:

pleasure indeed I have learned,
have given my heart sincere,
have better loved, and found a love that now
shame were to disavow,
but not more true and perfect in the end
than thine, O perfect friend,
nor holier than thou." (Warren, 1913, p. 100)

Before leaving this discussion of 'paganism' we should mention another Bostonian, whose name already arose earlier, F. Holland Day, like
Woodberry and Warren influenced by Pater (Crump, 1995, p. 12), and
who like W. A. Percy explored the conflicts between paganism and
Christianity in his art. His Grecian themes involving boys and youths,
both before, but particularly after the 1904 fire in his studio, are precise visual equivalents of our pagan literary themes here (Crump,
1995, pp. 30-32; Jussim, 1981, pp. 166-181; for examples of the former
see the illustrations on p. 168 and plate 7 in the portfolio, for examples
of the latter, pp. 43-59 in the portfolio). At the same time there is his
struggle with his "sacred subjects" in his crucifixion series (Crump,
1995, pp. 27-30; Jussim, 1981, pp. 120-135; illustrations to that chapter
and pp. 17-23 in the portfolio; see also Crump, 1994) and the implications of suffering for–and as–an ideal, which is not far removed from
what obsessed Percy in his medieval dramas, or poems such as his "Ballad of St. Sebastien" (Percy, 1920, pp. 101-103).

With the phrase "O perfect friend," we encounter a second of the
themes which the Uranians saw in their Greek mirror: the model of male
friendship, or its cognate comradeship. It is not totally unrelated to 'paganism,' for as we have seen, one of the experiences to be had within the
focus on this world was that of comradeship, and further this was a paganism which had a ethic of its own, even if this was not always congru-
ent with Christian morality. The elevated importance of friendship in
'paganism' is perhaps underscored by reflecting on William Johnson
Cory's magnificent and most perfectly pagan version of Callimachus'
"Heraclitus" ("They told me, Heraclitus, they told me you were dead . . ."
(Cory, 1905, p. 7)), where it is precisely the lack of any hope of afterlife
where friends may meet again that gives the loss its utter poignancy.

In emerging gay scholarship thirty years ago "friendship" was regarded as just one more evasion by which 19th century homosexuals
sought to hide their love–perhaps even from themselves. It is now being
taken with utter seriousness and carefully contradistinguished from "the
heroic warrior with his subordinate male pal or sidekick (who inevitably

dies), in addition to the patron-client model of male friendship"–all the better to establish it as "another tradition that emphasizes equality, mutuality, and reciprocity in love between men" (Halperin, 2002, p. 118), albeit at the cost of "the erotic realms of difference and hierarchy" (Halperin, 2002, p. 120). "Friendship . . . by contrast, is all about sameness: sameness of rank and status, sameness of sentiment, sameness of identity. It is this very emphasis on identity, similarity, and mutuality that distances the friendship tradition, in its original social and discursive context, from the world of sexual love" (Halperin, 2002, p. 121). Yet this "tradition" as Halperin finds it is precisely what the Uranians were *not* advocating when they spoke of friendship; they used the term precisely for asymmetrical relationships. Again, is their problem that they had failed to perform the proper analysis, à la modern gay theorists? Or did they have another agenda in mind?

The Greeks, with their endless list of asymmetrical male pairs, provided the Uranians with an arsenal of examples for expounding this ideal of friendship; indeed, it is a "hero and his pal," Hercules and Iolaus, which provides Carpenter with the title under which he marshals his "Anthology of Friendship" (Carpenter, 1902). To take a selection of the examples we enumerated above, in describing that most unequal of relationships (divine/human, adult/boy) Bradford terms Ganymede "Jove's eternal friend" (Bradford, 1913, p. 79); Erskine accepts Hercules and "Hylas the young" as the central image in his "Song of Friends" (Erskine, 1907, pp. 31-34); Hervey Allen says of the same pair, "So these two were friends forever" (Allen, 1921, p. 19); interestingly, of all our poets, however much they may emphasize love and sacrifice, McCulloch is the only one who speaks of Hadrian and Antinous in terms of friendship, using the phrase "free companionship" (McCulloch, 1902, p. 56). In a theoretical text, "Ideals of Love," Symonds exhaustively lists examples of what he interchangeably labels "Platonic love," "masculine love," "Greek love," "friendship" and "comradeship": Hercules and his young men, Theseus and Peirithous, Orestes and Pylades, Damon and Pythias, Cratinus and Aristodemus, Harmodius and Aristogeiton, Philolaus and Diocles, Chariton and Melanippus, Epaminondas and his comrades, Alexander and his comrades, Pindar and Sophocles, Pindar and Theoxenos, Pheidias and Pantarkes. Keeping in mind the attacks of Lefroy and others, he is at pains to emphasize that it was "neither an effeminate depravity nor a sensual vice." He recalls that in Dorian custom the lover was called the "inspirer" and the beloved the "hearer," and that "it was the man's duty to instruct the lad in manners, feats of arms, trials of strength and music," and reminds his readers that "the relation of the elder to the younger is still assumed to exist by Plato" (Symonds, 1893, pp. 61-67). In a similar inventory in his *Problem in Greek Ethics*, in the course of an argument which essentially comes down to saying that anything so common and basic in Greek civilization could *not* be a problem, Symonds adds still more pairs, particularly from mythology (Symonds, 1901, p. 10); at no time in either text does he suggest the relations are anything other than asymmetric. The pedagogical nature of this Eros returns in one last poetic citation, from Cecil Robert's "Strayed Hylas": ". . . Heracles loved the young boy, / he trained him to feats of endurance, he gave him the wealth of his lore . . ." (Roberts, 1914, p. 22).

At the same time, there is no question that for the Uranians this friendship also had an erotic dimension. The term friendship was used with, and understood in terms of, love. In his first collection of poems, Douglas Cole, later a British Labor Party economist, includes a sonnet "Friendship and Love":

> "Not lovers they, but friends," I heard one cry;
> Shall friends not love, and lovers not be friends? . . .
> For this I know, that we are friends indeed,
> And that I love thee, and thy love is mine;
> Wherefore this knowledge is affection's creed,
> That where two souls are met, as mine with thine,
> Each soul supplying all the other's need,
> Friendship and love their willing gifts combine. (Cole, 1910,
> p. 48)

This by no means excluded a physical expression, as in Fabian Woodley's *Crown of Friendship*:

> More fair than He, by Hercules beloved;
> Than Ganymede, or that fond foolish boy,
> Whose image mirrored in the water proved
> A passion hopeless and a barren joy–
> You stood before me that bright summer's morn
> Most fair and splendid of the sons of men,
> And all the grace and beauty that was Greece
> In you united and were born again!
> . . . I longed to hold you in my arms, to kiss
> The curve of your soft cheek; I dared not speak
> Lest from our hearts true unison might evolve

To discord that we never should resolve;
But when I thought "Must Friendship end in this?"
You suddenly raised your face–and claimed my kiss! (Woodley,
1921, pp. 34-36)

And, although the poet in question, Francis Saltus, is not to be ac-
counted among the Uranians, but a decadent, and his poem makes it
clear that the friendship in this case is not asymmetrical but between
equal adults, it is instructive to note that language of friendship between
males could get considerably more passionate than a kiss on the cheek:

Friend, fate ordains we part no more to meet . . .
You go to Cuba, draped in flower and palm . . .
While I, whose whole soul thirsts for bird and bloom . . .
Must dwell forever in the boreal gloom
Of grim Archangel's sun-defying snows.
. . . Strange thoughts of dread
Follow and fill me with persistent power;
I fear that I shall rest when I am dead
Where ice-winds moan and awful glaciers tower . . .
Ah! Then, when freed by death, sweet spirit divine,
Though you be shadow, mirage, fire or form,
Fly through chill space to seek the soul once mine,
And clasp and cling to me till I am warm! (Saltus, 1890, pp. 173-174)

This combination of comrades and lovers is found explicitly in the
poem "Comrades and Lovers, Rest Not," by the American Nelson
Antrim Crawford, a writer, editor, teacher and sometime publisher of
and author of introductions to collections by fellow Uranians. The reference in this case is not Greek, but a paean to Walt Whitman on the 100th
anniversary of his birth:

Oh, you genteel, conventional, uncourageous,
Bank presidents, suave, and your anaemic women,
Professional Y.M.C.A. secretaries and directors of boards of wel-
fare,
Holders of doctorates from Leipzig . . . Village newspaper men . . .
Reactionary government officials . . . Blustering Western politi-
cians . . .
when you unctuously celebrated his centenary . . .

Do you think that Walt Whitman the egoist, the unconventional, the liberal, the sincere, the frank, the healthy, the free, the light-hearted, the heroic,
The glad, the rough, the tender, the democrat, the American, the world-citizen, the friend of the worker,
Poet of the body, poet of the soul, poet of every dauntless rebel,
Would want to associate with you, or do you think you would want to associate with him?
And you, carpenters, farmers, deckhands, weavers, printers, bridge builders, pickers of cotton in the South and harvesters of wheat in the North,
Sheep herders, brakemen, brick masons, telephone operators, shop girls, wheel tappers, waiters, hired girls, workers in mines, mail carriers, whitewings, laborers skilled and unskilled,
Yes, and you lawyers, doctors, writers, engineers, manufacturers, shop-keepers,
All of you who are fair and honest and seekers of justice for all men,
Walt Whitman will return to lead you on the open road of honesty, frankness, democracy.
Comrades and lovers,
Rest not! (Crawford, 1923, pp. 68-71)

Two of the words in that militant poem are worth lifting out. The first, "frankness," I noted a quarter of a century ago was something of a marker for homosexual sentiments in what I then called Calamite poems; the second, "democracy," launches us on our third and final theme that the Uranians saw in their Greek mirror.

Evocations of manual laborers similar to the list found here would be expected in American poets influenced by Whitman and his "frankness," and one indeed finds them, for instance in Willard Wattles's "Challenge to Youth" ("You who are young and clean and sweetened by the sun, / Who have followed the binder afield until the blinding day is done. . . . / Who have slept 'neath the open sky and pillowed a dusty head / On shiny saddle leather, nor wished for a better bed" (Wattles, 1916, p. 111)), and one recalls it was a young "tamer of horses on the grass-grown plains" who was Woodberry's ideal comrade. Wattles, indeed, in his "But a Great Laugher," even manages to fit Jesus into their proletariat (and sub-proletariat) company:

They do me wrong who show me sad of face,
Slender and stooped, gentle, and meek, and mild . . .

I was youth's lover, swiftest of the race,
Gay friend of beggars, brother of the wild . . .
Shepherd and fisher, sailor, carpenter,
I strode the hills and followed the sun,
Knew arms and bosoms and slow steady eyes,
Felt each new April through my body stir . . . (Wattles, 1918, p. 3)

But to whom should we attribute these lines?

. . . [companionship] spreads
Tents on the open road, field, ocean, camp,
Where'er in brotherhood men lay their heads,
Soldier with soldier, tramp with casual tramp . . . (Symonds, 1882,
p. 16)

The very British John Addington Symonds! The connection of course is
Edward Carpenter, with his *Towards Democracy*, where in a short
poem entitled "A Sprig of Aristocracy" Wattles's field-laborer shakes
hands with his British compatriot:

Browned by the sun, with face elate and joyous,
Pitching hay all day in the wide and fragrant hayfields,
Frank and free . . . O splendid boy, with many more like thee,
England might from her unclean wallowing rise again and live.
(Carpenter, 1911, p. 308)

It was the concern of the Uranians to reconcile the ideal of democracy, which, as Woodberry reminded us in his *Pallas Athene*, was a heritage from the pagan world, and the concept of a natural aristocracy
among men, the Greek ideal of the *areté* which could be found in a man
of any station—and it was friendship, comradeship, masculine love, precisely with its asymmetrical structure and pedagogic features, which
provided the instrument for accomplishing this. The equality of virtue
or excellence which the two socially unequal partners shared would, in
the presence of the masculine, pedagogic Eros, provide the basis for a
democratizing solution that would raise the younger or socially subordinate partner to equality.

It is not surprising then that the ranks of the Uranians would supply a
list of teachers at every level, from William Johnson Cory at their start,
through the prolific John Gambril Nicholson, to Arnold W. Smith
(Smith, 1919) and the schoolmaster and war casualty T. P. Cameron

Wilson and his touching "Mathematical Master to his Dullest Pupil" ("I came to you and caught your eagle wings / and gloomed your soul with Algebra and things, / and cast a net of pale Geometry / Wherein your laughter struggled to be free . . ." (Wilson, 1920, p. 104)). Nor should we be surprised that their poems contain a catalogue of references to working boys of various professions; Nicholson's "Your City Cousins" provides a list in itself:

> I like the boy that earns his bread;
> The boy that holds my horse's head,
> The boy that tidies up the bar,
> The boy that hawks the *Globe* and *Star*.
> Smart-looking boys are in my line;
> The lad that gives my boots a shine,
> The lad that works the lift below,
> The lad that's lettered *G.P.O.* (Nicholson, 1911, p. 27)

Newspaper boys and bootblacks (the latter perhaps even more than the former, because they were in physical contact with the man) are particularly noticed. Bradford blends in the theme of natural aristocracy:

> A little Lord, in sweet disguise,
> Kneels down to black my boots . . .
> A Prince, in rugged raiment cries
> The names of evening papers;
> And several serve in humble wise
> As grocers' boys or drapers' (Bradford, 1918, p. 33)[23]

On the other side of the Atlantic, N. A. Crawford has a poem to a Greek lad in a shoe-shine parlor (Crawford, 1923, p. 55), and Walter Malone notes a Greek boy waiter:

> . . . As I look
> Upon his poor surroundings here to-night
> I mutter, "Evil days have come to thee
> And thine, O boy of Hellas!" But I muse
> Deeply upon him, and his fine young face
> Allures me more and more . . . (Malone, 1919, p. 106)

For one Uranian thinker, comradeship in the setting of the boys' club occupies a special role in this constellation. William Paine, a lecturer on social issues and one-time president of a Working Boy's Athletic Club, produced a whole treatise on the programmatic role of "love" (along with other elements like athletics) in discovering the natural excellence of working-class boys and youth, overcoming class antagonism, and bringing about what he, in the title of his book, termed *The New Aristocracy of Comradeship*–"a new aristocracy whose watchword is comradeship and whose archetype the friend" (Paine, 1920, p. 5). Once again, we must be clear that this friendship involves a sexual dimension: "Friendship is not something dissimilar from love. Friendship is one of the manifestations of love. . . . The regular channels through which love manifests itself are comradeship (spiritual love) and sexual passion (physical love). If these two channels are kept open, and free from all impedimenta and all impurities, spiritual love reacts upon physical love, and vice versa, to the advantage of both . . ." (Paine, 1920, p. 51). After some facile Marxist analysis, Paine proclaims that the object of this ideal of comradeship "is entirely to overthrow the existing form of society and build up a new society in its place" (Paine, 1920, p. 52). This will be accomplished by "the spiritualisation of the relationship of the man and the boy" (Paine, 1920, p. 63). Explaining what he means by this in a footnote, Paine calls upon the Greeks: "The idea of protective love is not peculiar to Christian ethics, in which it is softened down to a sentiment of pity of or tenderness for the young. It dates back to the earliest times, and is co-eval with the heroic consciousness of mankind. In its origin it was the instinct and practice of the warrior to ensure the preservation of his tribe. The warrior took a boy or youth with him into battle to teach him the use of arms, and, while he sought to set him an example of valour, shielded the youth from harm with his own life. In that way there grew up between the protected and protector a tie that was stronger even than the tie of a blood relationship, for it was constantly being reaffirmed in the presence of danger and death" (Paine, 1920, p. 167, note 3). The working-class boys' club is the seedbed for such heroics today. Paine hypothesizes that "every boy is born an aristocrat, by which I mean he is born to the pursuit of an ideal of character which modern conditions make it almost impossible for him to realise. . . . But all are born aristocrats. We have to keep them so" (Paine, 1920, p. 65). The working-class boy comes to this naturally: "Almost as soon as he can walk the London working-class boy feels that the hand of society is against him, and prepares to resist it by an instinctive loyalty to his brother. . . . He is saturated with this feeling. It is his religion. All he wants to make it immediately heroic is a leader, and if he fancies ever so little that you are the leader he is looking for, he will instantly tender his affections to you provocatively, that you may declare yourself for what you are, and start with him on the great adventure of friendship, which adventure is to destroy the old order of things and create a new order in its place" (Paine, 1920, p. 117). Paine then provides pages of examples from his own experiences in reaching 'hard cases' through his friendship, guiding them particularly through sports such as boxing and wrestling, and swimming. His ultimate proposal is that these young natural aristocrats should be brought in contact with middle-class and upper class boys, at camps in nature and athletic competitions between working-boys' clubs and public schools, so that the boys of the higher classes will be won over by the comradeship with them, and "we stop the middle-class boy from becoming pretentious, the lesser middle-class boy from becoming invertebrate, the aristocratic boy from becoming stiff-necked" (Paine, 1920, p. 66).

But we must equally recognize that those of the Uranians who were interested in age-consistent relationships express no less of an asymmetry in their lists of those who fascinate them. Horatio Brown, in his *Drift,* writes, among others, "To a Great-Western Broadgauge Engine and Its Stoker," "Drive on! . . . Blow back the curly, close-cropped hair. /Ah! Western lad, would I might be / a partner in that ecstasy" (Brown, 1900, p. 5), to a 23-year-old guardsman (Brown, 1900, p. 8) and, in a humorous description of a visit to a concert with friends, "Bored at a London Music," of a footman: "[I] heard the whole laborious din, / Piano, 'cello, violin; / And so, perhaps, they hardly guessed / I liked their footman, John, the best" (Brown, 1900, p. 105). Edward Carpenter also found enginemen attractive (Carpenter, 1911, pp. 140-141), and bricklayers as well: "The thick-thighed hot coarse-fleshed young bricklayer with the strap around his waist. . . . The bricklayer shall lay me: he shall tap me into place with the handle of his trowel; / And to him I will utter the word which with my lips I have not spoken" (Carpenter, 1911, pp. 69, 73). As we saw before, in his handling of the Greek allusions, Roden Noel exhibits greater depth in his work, in a posthumously published elegy to a "comrade," J. H., obviously of lower social rank:

> Comrade, my comrade, they are calling names
> Of epoch-making men about the town
> Who died but now; and these are nought to me,
> Who mourn my brother, lowly, poor, unknown,
> Died with them in thy manhood's flower; thee Death
> Took using all thy strength to wrest a friend
> From his cold clutch; but he would take you both.

No famous man hath ended better; God
Approveth, and thy comrade honours thee . . . (Noel, 1902, p. 487)

It remains to note that for a fair number of the Uranians whose biographies we do possess, neither their political commitment to a basic democratization of society, nor their involvement with asymmetrical relations was just a matter of words. Aside from a curious olio of documents which tells us far more about its compiler than its subject (Heath, 1998), we have very little personal information about Roden Noel, son of the Earl of Gainsborough and later Groom of the Privy Chamber to Queen Victoria, whose duties, Rupert Croft-Cooke remarks, "interfered with the habits he had already formed of association with service men and good-looking manual workers, associations which in that kindly undiscerning age gave him no worse than a reputation for socialism, in spite of his effeminate appearance" (Croft-Cooke, 1968, p. 123). Noel's second volume of poetry was tellingly entitled *The Red Flag*. In his introduction to a scarce selection of Noel's verse which he edited, the Uranian poet Percy Addleshaw refers to Noel's interest in "the toiling masses and above all in the children" as being one of "the chief concerns of his life" (reprinted in Heath, 1998, p. 60), and (in a line which has apparently disappeared into one the ellipses that stud Heath's reprint, but is quoted by Croft-Cooke) to how "he had long laboured among the children of the lower classes and bidden successfully for their love"–which Croft-Cooke somewhat venomously proceeds to assure us Addleshaw did not mean tongue-in-cheek (Croft-Cooke, 1968, p. 124), for it is clear from J. A. Symonds's papers that along with his political and humanitarian interests, and whatever lovers he may have had, Noel did engage in purely pecuniary relations with young guardsmen and other working class youth. Carpenter's socialism, and his lifelong relationship with George Merrill, whose background in the slums contrasted sharply with Carpenter's upper-middle class and Cambridge background, is too well known to require documentation here.

Among the Americans, Woodberry's letters during World War I reporting the exploits of his "Italian boys" (Woodberry, 1933, pp. 153, 171-172, 176, 179, 181, 197) and a touching later note, in the last months of his life, to a correspondent who would be passing through Taormina–

Try to find Pancrazio Sciacca, who is employed at a small pension there to meet trains, and may be useful to you, if you tell him you are my friend. I haven't seen him since he was twelve years old, or less, but he is a devoted friend of mine, and has a boy of four who is my namesake, Giorgio. He is also the boy of the 'Ho! The Springtime!' poem, and of the sonnet 'On the Italian Front, 1916'. I haven't seen him since he was twelve, and I suppose he is all grown up, but he wrote me letters all through the war, and ever since very frequently. He knows a little French, and is *divotissimo* to his old 'Signore' . . . (Woodberry, 1930, pp. 264-265; on the same individual, see also pp. 272-273)

–tell something of his long relationships with these boys who inspired his poems. F. Holland Day, whom we mentioned as a visual parallel to the Uranians, was noted for his charity work, including personal involvement as a tutor among the children of the Boston slums, and in particular for his discovery and encouragement of an immigrant boy from those slums, Kahlil Gibran, of whom he produced several stunning portraits (Jussim, 1981, pp. 114-117; Gibran, 1974, pp. 51-68). Another of Day's models was the Italian immigrant boy Nicola Giancola, who was a shoe-shine boy when discovered by Day, and became a successful commercial artist. A recent critic has noted that there appears to be "a more complicit understanding in these photographs between photographer and subject than in any others of Day's repertoire" (Roberts, 2000, p. 26), and another of the essayists in the collection edited by Roberts notes that Giancola's letters to Day "document the stormy relationship between an arrogant teenager maturing into adulthood and Day, a surrogate father figure. Giancola remained unstintingly grateful to him, long after participating in Day's photographic projects, and credited Day's mentoring for his own financial success and personal fulfillment as a landscape painter" (Curtis, 2000, p. 49; the texts of some of these, and a further discussion of their relationship, are to be found in Curtis 1998). Curtis wishes to insist the relation between Day and Giancola was not homoerotic; Jussim, who got the rest of the relationship wrong, as she did not have access to all the letters, is however likely right in her assessment that it "bordered on the homoerotic, even if it was never consummated" (Jussim, 1981, pp. 176-178). In addition to these philanthropic and sexually charged relationships with immigrant boys, Day is also noted for another liberal–even, given the times, radical–social stand, namely his racial views, as expressed in his several series of photographs of black models (Jussim, 1981, pp. 106-109; Crump, 1995, pp. 23-25, 137, note 86; see also Michaels, 1994); Crump underscores both the political rhetoric of Day's work, and the role of homoerotic desire in shaping this stance.[24]

Perhaps the most radical of all in his making the personal political was William Alexander Percy. Various of his humanitarian and, for his time and place, radical activities were known–his volunteer service with the Belgian Relief Commission before the American entry into World War I (Percy, 1941, pp. 156-168),[25] his stand against the Ku Klux Klan (Percy, 1941, pp. 225-241), organizing flood relief in the Mississippi delta after the 1927 floods (Percy, 1941, pp. 249-269), the profit-sharing plan under which he operated his Trail Lake plantation, which became a subject for study as an economic model (Percy, 1941, pp. 278-80). Although a discerning eye could detect a certain amount in the chapter of his autobiography which deals with his chauffeur Fode (Percy, 1941, pp. 285-297), it remained for his great-nephew to confirm that in addition to a white "boyfriend" whose deathbed he could not attend because of social censure, but whom he had buried in the Percy family plot (Percy 1997, p. 85; see also Percy, 1941, p. 346: were there others?), Percy had a series of interracial homosexual relationships with black teenagers, including Fode, who were taken on as employees, for whom he would provide education and, as they grew older, a start in business or a trade (Percy, 1997, pp. 80-82).

DISCUSSION

To summarize: the Uranians, in their use of specific Greek allusions and in elaborating general themes that concerned them which they saw reflected in the Greek heritage as they perceived it, developed three interrelated notions. The first was of 'paganism' which comprehended a critique of their own materialistic, industrializing, bourgeois Christian society, and in its place emphasized direct experience of nature and beauty, incorporating Platonic idealism with this. The second was a discovery of 'friendship' or 'comradeship' as a manner by which males could relate to one another, constructing these concepts on models from Greek mythology and historiography; this friendship was specifically conceived as asymmetrical. It was precisely this asymmetry which allowed the Uranians to develop the third of their concerns, a reconciliation of their notions of democracy and aristocracy, namely by idealizing and attempting to create democratizing male relationships in which, beginning with the excellence inherent in both partners and subjecting it to the operation of a pedagogical Eros, the younger or otherwise socially subordinate partner was to be lifted to equality. Their social vision was thus essentially progressive and humane, and at least in some cases we know they united the personal and the political.

In its own time this was critiqued by Lefroy and others as possibly leading to sexual dissipation–or more precisely, to homosexual practices. By 1970, the critique was no longer on the grounds of Christian morality, but psychology. D'Arch Smith, in drawing his study to a close, offers his critique of the Uranians. After proposing that "the Uranians' need to form alliances with working-class boys may well have arisen from an inferiority complex forbidding them to stand up to the rigours and responsibilities of a love affair with an intellectual equal," he then goes on to suggest, "At the same time such boys could indulge their lovers with a brief, exciting sexual encounter after which they could be shaken off if they became too demanding, without the lover's feeling too guilty about discarding persons whom he had once encouraged" (D'Arch Smith, 1970, pp. 191-192). It should be noted that while D'Arch Smith is writing here of age-discrepant relationships, all that he says could be applied–and was applied, in Croft-Cooke's strictures on Roden Noel–to relations between adults in which the asymmetry ran across class lines. Nonetheless, the critique is essentially psychological and individualized: "There is, of course, a natural physical and mental inferiority inherent in every paederastic relationship; apart from his receptiveness to adult influences which encourages the man to believe he may be of help, the boy's only strength lies in his sexual attraction. His natural homosexual phase may for a time allow the relationship to proceed on an equal footing, but unless he inherit some of the man's mental maturity the friendship is surely doomed to failure as the years go by" (D'Arch Smith, 1970, p. 192). "Unless"? Of course it was not D'Arch Smith's purpose to investigate the lives and relationships of his authors–little enough is known of them now, and still less was known in 1970–but one somehow has the feeling that even in the face of evidence of enduring relationships, or evidence of continued devotion by the younger or originally subordinate partner such as was presented here for Uranians such as Woodberry or Day, whose lives are better researched, this view would be little altered. Reports by the "superordinate" partner would represent self-deception or justification; testimony such as the letters of Nicola Giancola could be symptomatic of a failure on the part of the witness to recognize the damage done to them, or of their identification as a 'victim' with their 'abuser'; if all else fails, and the success of the relation has to be acknowledged, it is deemed statistically insignificant.[26] At least D'Arch Smith concedes that the Uranians probably meant well.

Thirty years have passed; not even the possibility of D'Arch Smith's "unless" and his concession is left. All erotic relationships between adults and minors are "abuse"; relations which cross class or racial lines are regarded as deeply suspect or rejected, socially if not by law, not because of the inequalities of the individuals involved, but because they are prisoners of social structures. A new paradigm, essentially political and not psychological, is in place, an ideal standard of equality, mutuality and reciprocity (Halperin, 2002, p. 118), which looks not to the dynamics of the relationship, but to the circumstances surrounding it. Halperin's critique of DeVries is exemplary here, and could apply just as well to the Uranians: "Again and again, DeVries insists that paederastic relations between classical Athenian men and boys were, to quote his favorite adjectives, 'warm,' 'loving,' 'affectionate,' and 'tender'; he emphasizes the 'closeness,' 'intimacy,' 'love,' 'affection,' 'warm feelings,' and even 'responsiveness' that could characterize such relations. In all of this he is surely right. But what exactly does it prove? What kind of objection is it to say, against the view that paederastic relations were asymmetrical, hierarchical, and generally non-reciprocal in their distribution of sexual pleasure, that men and boys really loved each other? . . . The point at issue here is not the emotional temperature of personal relationships but the social structuration of erotic life" (Halperin, 2002, p. 153). A social consensus has been reached that–no matter how much we may recognize that difference (and, as S&M at an extreme reminds us, that includes difference in power) is the basis of eroticism–too much difference is simply not acceptable. This has been the result of a century of sexual politics: the recognition that 'love' was no answer to the inequalities in relations between men and women, which only a (still not entirely complete) equalization of social and legal structures could cure. Once this idea that sexual and social relations must be between equals was widely enough accepted, it became a tool for the acceptance of socially 'reciprocal' homosexual relationships too, and at the same time for the reclassification of age-structured sexual or erotic relations from merely being 'immorality' to being exploitation and 'abuse.' Relations now must be 'democratic'–between equals–and not, as the Uranians argued, democratizing. When we look at *our* Greek mirror, we see *our* concern: abuse.[27]

What sort of argument, Halperin asks, is it to say that men and boys (or men of radically different social power and status) love each other? A very strong one, it seems to me. With the arguments of the Uranians in the background, let me be so bold as to turn Halperin's question around: what kind of objection is it to say, against the views of those who are themselves engaged in such concrete relationships that these relationships are loving, satisfying, potentially even empowering, that the social context is too asymmetrical and hierarchical, insufficiently reciprocal for our prevailing ideology? What sort of paternalization and patronization does *that* represent? Acknowledging that social structuration of erotic life has its importance–something the Uranians acknowledged too–why should that be privileged to the exclusion of the emotional temperature experienced by those who are after all the partic-ipants? Why should reciprocity be narrowed down to a question of so-cial power, and become a precondition rather than an outcome? Why 'democratic' rather than 'democratizing'? *Pace* Halperin, a relationship need not be equal to be mutual, and even, depending on how one defines the term, reciprocal. The Uranians and their art may have something to say to us yet.

NOTES

1. The first use of the term "Calamites" appears to have been by Algernon Swinburne, as the editor of *Men and Boys* correctly observes in his note introducing John Addington Symonds's poetry there (Slocum, 1924/1978, p. 42)–an indication of this editor's familiarity with the British scene. Swinburne intended it as a mocking characterization, meant to both refer to Whitman's title and to pun on the word "catamites." In a typical minority strategy of salvaging derogatory terms and using them as positive designations, Breen here reclaims it for this group. For an assessment of Breen's role in homosexual liberation and scholarship, see Mader (2002).

2. As well as D'Arch Smith's appendix on Chubb being reprinted (D'Arch Smith, 1991), Chubb has been the subject of several separate studies (Rahman, 1991 and Reid, 1970; see also Cave, 2001). A recent contribution in Dutch (Mader, 2003) attempts to give a more balanced view of Chubb.

3. The most accessible biographical information on Warren is presently to be found in Sox (1991).

4. Other than this *Anthology*, the only American book listed in the poetry section of the *Catalogue* is Wilbur D. Nesbit's *The Trail to Boyland and Other Poems* (India-napolis: Bobbs-Merrill, 1904), a production not dissimilar to James Whitcomb Riley's earlier *Armazindy* (Indianapolis: Bowen-Merrill, 1894) or Burges Johnson's later *Youngsters: Collected Poems of Childhood* (New York: Dutton, 1921).

5. The fact that one of the seven or eight copies then known to exist bore a prelimi-nary page–excised from the others–announcing it was produced by a group calling it-self the American Society for the Study of Sex Psychology should have been a further clue (Slocum, 1924/1978, p. xlv).

6. Circumstantial evidence would indicate his co-editor was Willard Wattles, a peripatetic professor of literature at that time teaching at Connecticut Agricultural Col-lege (now University of Connecticut) in Storrs, CT, whose poetry is also included in the "Present-day Poets" section (Slocum, 1975/1924, p. xliv).

7. Offered by the American book dealer Priapean Tomes in their Winter, 2001, catalog; present whereabouts unknown.

8. Another of the American Uranian poets was definitely acquainted with Norman Douglas; William Alexander Percy provides an introduction for the American edition of Douglas's *Birds and Beasts of the Greek Anthology* (New York: Cape, 1929), and accordingly is briefly mentioned by Douglas in his *Late Harvest* (London: Drummond, 1946), p. 26.

9. Still another author turned up by research is "Michael Strange," actually the pseudonym of the actress, poet, suffragette and socialist Blanche Marie Louise Oelrichs, whose later marriages included those to the actor John Barrymore (1920-1928) and to the noted lawyer Harrison Tweed (1929-1950). Writing in the male voice, she produced Uranian poems to adolescents, and effusions to Walt Whitman (Strange, 1919, pp. 149, 158). For the rest, this study will not concern itself with possible female Uranians.

10. The curious case of "Laurence Hope"–the pseudonym of Adela F. Nicolson, neé Cory, is instructive here. In her *Stars of the Desert* she published passionate poems to adolescent (and even younger) Arab and North African boys, such as her "Song of the Enfifa River" ("In Memory of Abdullah, drowned at 16 . . .") (Nicolson, 1913, pp. 9-11); evidently it was regarded as more acceptable to sing to boys as a man, at least with the cover of the East (and particularly if the boys were safely dead) than for a Victorian lady to express such erotic sentiments under any circumstances.

11. Outside our language area, it might be noted that the Dutch homophile poet Willem de Merode also exploits the image of the medieval master/page relationship in his "De Page" I and II (Merode, 1919, pp. 65, 66). For an analysis of "De Page II" see Mader (1998, pp. 86-88).

12. Stoddard dedicates his *Poems* to Taylor, "Who I admire as a poet and love as a man," and adds a further sonnet to Taylor ("let us join our hands/and knit our souls in Friendship's bands" (Stoddard, 1852, p. 121)), and has a further, more restrained sonnet for Taylor in his *Book of the East*, followed by another to Stedman, accompanying a copy of Shakespeare's *Sonnets* ("fancies like these, where love and friendship blend" (Stoddard, 1871, pp. 177, 178)), while Stedman in turn dedicates his *Blameless Prince* to Stoddard, and it contains a sonnet to Taylor (Stedman, 1869, p. 145). The poetic implications of this triangle are addressed in Martin (1979, pp. 97-109). It is interesting to note that later Stedman is closely linked in various editing projects with George Edward Woodberry.

13. D'Arch Smith silently corrects his information regarding the authorship of this book (D'Arch Smith, 1970, pp. 132-133) in D'Arch Smith, 1998 (pp. 27 and 30 n. 8), where he offers his evidence for adding Charlton–and notes that Lomer and Charlton were the older gentlemen who 'befriended' a young Noel Coward in his days as a boy actor.

14. This list could be extended beyond the Uranian period, with for instance Tom Meyer's *Uranian Roses* (Scarborough, Ont.: Catalyst, 1977), or Jim Eggeling's hip versions, including his own of the Garland Weaver (Leyland, 1977, pp. 64-65). Moving out of our era in another direction, it should also be noted that several Romans–especially Martial–were also favored for translation. Although his two collections of translations of Martial were not published until the 1970s (*Ganymede in Rome*, London: Palatine Press, 1971, and *An Eye for Ganymede*, London: Palatine Press, 1972), by virtue of his poems published just after World War I Brian Hill must be counted among the Uranians. Perhaps one must also mention Kenneth Hopkins's original "ver-

sions" of Martial (*The Dead Slave and other Poems of Martial*, Scarborough, Ont.: Catalyst, 1977); Hopkins can, at least, claim to have reinvented himself as a Uranian in his *To the Uranian Muse: A Cycle of Sonnets by Vincent Holmes* ([pseud.], Toronto: A-Z Chapbooks, 2000).

15. It remained for Eggeling to be thoroughly irreverent about the image in his "The Ganymede Equation" (Leyland, 1977, p. 66).

16. Taylor also manages to smuggle a reference to Hylas (as well as one to Ganymede) into one of his oriental poems, the "Nilotic Drinking-Song" (Taylor, 1855, pp. 92-94).

17. A curious sidelight can be gained here from an early 20th century study, J. F. C. Gutteling's 1920 doctoral thesis (written in English) at the University of Amsterdam, *Hellenic Influence on the English Poetry of the Nineteenth Century*. Although only one of the poets she deals with was active into the last quarter of the century (Swinburne), and she avoids any discussion of sexual issues, it is nonetheless of interest for revealing what an academic contemporary of the Uranians saw in the Greeks. She defines the "Hellenic spirit" under six heads—a sense of beauty; love of freedom; directness of apprehension that avoided sentiment and applied reason and common sense; humanism; sanity; and manysidedness (Gutteling, 1920, pp. 3-7), several of these recur here in various forms. In discussing Swinburne she also speaks of "the sensuous beauty of paganism" and "a joyful, sensuous paganism" that contrasted with what for him was the "Christian religion of pain," leading to his rejection of the latter (pp. 39-40).

18. Their view is confirmed in historical hindsight by Linda Dowling's assessment of the Uranians: "Uranian poetry was able to give voice to a counterdiscourse of spiritual procreancy underwritten by the authority of Oxford Hellenism to precisely the degree it was able to represent itself as superior to the blind urgencies of merely animal sexuality . . ." (Dowling, 1996, pp. 114-116). For the rest, her delineation of "Uranian poetry," being based on D'Arch Smith, is much narrower than that being used here; while her assertion applies to many of the British poets, and Americans such as Woodberry who appealed to the Greeks, it should be noted that another idealism than the Platonic—namely Whitman's ideal of democratic comradeship—performed the same function for other Uranians.

19. Further insight into the influence of Pater at Harvard, albeit in the following decade, and on F. Holland Day's being introduced to Pater's thought there, is to be found in Crump (1995, p. 12).

20. For those interested in the calculations, the key is to be found in Woodberry's essay "The Ride," in his *Heart of Man*, recording a philosophical conversation which he and a former student—obviously the same person referred to in "Comrades," having died between the time the essay in the 1890s and the poem circa 1910—engage in during a journey on one of Woodberry's returns to the mid-west; in introducing the incident Woodberry tells us there was five years' difference in their ages (Woodberry, 1899, pp. 268-269). Knowing Woodberry went to Nebraska in 1877, determining their ages is easy. It remains for John Erskine, a later student of Woodberry's, to put a name to this friend—Eugene Montgomery, to whom *Heart of Man* is dedicated (Erskine, 1948, p. 202). *Heart of Man* also contains an essay characteristically celebrating Taormina, once part of Magna Graecia, as a humble, enduring repository for the ideals of civilization. For the rest, note the allusion to II Samuel 1:26.

21. John Erskine attributes the departure from Columbia to power-plays in the faculty, and the departure to Europe to Woodberry's deep disappointment (Erskine, 1947, pp. 148-159, 242; 1948, pp. 104-105). It is not impossible this was merely a faculty

quarrel, but one is left wondering if there are not other reasons relating to his sexuality to account for such a radical removal from the scene.

22. See, for instance, his plaint to Harry Harkness Flagler in a 1906 letter from Sorrento, about "hearing the old wolf coming up to scratch at the door," and his longer and more melancholy complaint on the same theme in a 1910 letter from Naples to Merideth Nicholson (Woodberry, 1933, pp. 48, 81-82). Flagler, son of an American railroad tycoon and philanthropist, was possibly homosexual; regarding his links to E. I. Prime-Stevenson/Xavier Mayne, who dedicated one of his books to him, see Hafkamp (1988, p. 128).

23. The iconography of the working boy, as developed particularly by the British-born New York painter of street boys J. G. Brown, is discussed in Mader (1999). Further sources on Brown can be found there. The newsboy of course had his apotheosis in the work of Horatio Alger, whose dismissal as a clergyman for sexual relations with boys was well-hidden during his lifetime, and many years after (see Chapter 1 of Edwin P. Hoyt's *Horatio's Boys: The Life and Works of Horatio Alger, Jr.* (Radnor, PA: Chilton, 1974)).

24. It is interesting to note that one of the few other figures in American art in that period to also positively portray Afro-Americans was J. G. Brown (Mader, 1999).

25. The connection here is admittedly slim, but this is an opportunity to mention an interesting contribution to the debate about masculinity and homosexuality in America in the first decades of the 20th century which others have missed, Charles Hanson Towne's poem "Young Rupert": Rupert, the very picture of the pansy ("His hair was golden as a girl's, his cheeks were pink and white . . .") who responds to the call of duty ("But when they needed youngsters, those early days in France / Young Rupert packed his grip and went to drive an ambulance") leaving behind the he-men who laughed at him to their empty boasting in dingy bars (Towne, 1919, pp. 87-88).

26. The reception of James Gardiner's *A Class Apart: The Private Pictures of Montague Glover* (New York/London: Serpent's Tail, 1993) is informative in this regard: while widely proclaimed as proof of stable, long-lasting gay relationships, almost no reviewer noted–despite the clear allusion in the title–that this was the visual history of precisely the sort of cross-class relationship which is suspect, and the age difference at the time Glover and Hall met was totally consigned to silence.

27. To those who think this generalization is irresponsible: the Library of Congress catalogues Félix Buffière's *Eros adolescent. La pédérastie dans la Grèce antique* under "Child sexual abuse–Greece": http://catalog.loc.gov and perform a subject search under that heading!

REFERENCES

Allen, Hervey. (1921). *Wampum and Old Gold*. New Haven: Yale UP.
_____. (1929). *New Legends*. New York: Farrar & Rinehart.
Allen, William F. (1919). *Monographs*. Boston: Four Seas.
Beeching, H. C., Mackail, J. W., and Nichols, J. B. B. (1883). *Love in Idleness*. London: Kegan Paul.
_____. (1891). *Love's Looking Glass*. London: Percival.
Bradford, E. E. (1908). *Sonnets, Songs and Ballads*. London: Kegan Paul.
_____. (1913). *Passing the Love of Women and Other Poems*. London: Kegan Paul.

_____. (1916). *Lays of Love and Life*. London: Kegan Paul.

_____. (1918). *The New Chivalry*. London: Kegan Paul.

Breen, Walter. See Eglinton, J. Z.

Brown, Horatio. F. (1900). *Drift: Verses*. London: Richards.

Call, Frank Oliver. (1944). *Sonnets for Youth*. Toronto: Ryerson.

Carpenter, Edward (Ed.). (1902). *Ioläus: An Anthology of Friendship*. London: Sonnenschein.

_____. (1911). *Toward Democracy. Complete Edition in Four Parts*. London: Sonnenschein.

Cave, Roderick. (2001). Blake's Mantle: The Press of Ralph Chubb. In *Fine Printing and Private Presses: Selected Papers by Roderick Cave* (pp. 62-66). London: British Library.

Chauncey, George. (1994). *Gay New York: Gender, Urban Culture, and the Making of the Gay Male World, 1890-1940*. New York: Basic Books.

Cole, G. D. H. (1910). *Poems*. London: Scott.

Cory, William [Johnson]. (1905). *Ionica*. London: George Allen.

Cottam, S. E. (1930). *Cameos of Boyhood and Other Poems*. London: Stockwell.

_____. (1960). *Friends of My Fancy and Other Poems*. Eton: Shakespeare Head Press.

Craig, Alec. (1963). *Suppressed Books: A History of the Conception of Literary Obscenity*. Cleveland: World.

Cranch, Christopher Pearse. (1875). *The Bird and the Bell, with Other Poems*. Boston: Osgood.

Crawford, Nelson Antrim. (1923). *The Carrying of the Ghost*. Boston: Brimmer.

Croft-Cooke, Rupert. (1968). *Feasting With Panthers: A New Consideration of Some Late Victorian Writers*. New York: Holt, Rinehart & Winston.

Crump, James. (Winter, 1994). F. Holland Day: 'Sacred Subjects' and 'Greek Love.' *History of Photography*, *18*(4), 322-333.

Crump, James. (1995). *F. Holland Day: Suffering the Ideal*. Santa Fe: Twin Palms.

Curtis, Verna Posever. (1998). F. Holland Day and the Staging of Orpheus. In Patricia J. Fanning (Ed.), *New Perspectives on F. Holland Day: Selected Presentations from the Fred Holland Day In Context Symposium held at Stonehill College, North Easton, Massachusetts, April 19, 1997* (pp. 50-60). North Easton, MA: Stonehill College.

_____. (2000). Actors and Adolescents–The Idealised Eye of F. H. Day. In Pam Roberts (Ed.), *F. Holland Day* (pp. 39-52). Amsterdam/Zwolle: Van Gogh Museum/Waanders.

Danto, Arthur C. (1995). *Playing with the Edge: The Photographic Achievement of Robert Mapplethorpe*. Berkeley: U of California P.

D'Arch Smith, Timothy. (1970). *Love in Earnest: Some Notes on the Lives and Writings of English 'Uranian' Poets from 1889 to 1930*. London: Routledge.

_____. (1991). Ralph Nicholas Chubb: Prophet and Paederast. In *The Books of the Beast* (pp. 65-77). Oxford: Mandrake.

_____. (1998). Edmund John. In Mark Valentine, Roger Dobson, Ray Russell (Eds.), *AKLO: A Volume of the Fantastic* (pp. 22-29). Oxford: Tartarus/Caermaen.

_____. (2001). Introduction. In *The Quorum: A Magazine of Friendship* (pp. 1-15). North Pomfret, VT: Asphodel Editions/Elysium Press.

_____. (2004). Montague Summers, the Marquis de Sade & the Curious World of the British Society for the Study of Sex Psychology. *Strange Attractor, 1,* 207-218.

de Merode, Willem. (1919). *De overgave.* Baarn: Bosch.

Dowling, Linda. (1996). *Hellenism and Homosexuality in Victorian Oxford.* Ithaca: Cornell UP.

Eglinton, J. Z. (1964). *Greek Love.* New York: O. Layton.

Erskine, John. (1907). *Actæon and Other Poems.* New York: Lane.

_____. (May, 1930). George Edward Woodberry, 1855-1930: An Appreciation. *The New York Public Library, 34*(5), 275-279.

_____. (1947). *The Memory of Certain Persons.* Philadelphia: Lippincott.

_____. (1948). *My Life as a Teacher.* Philadelphia: Lippincott.

Foster, Stephen W. (1982). Beauty's Purple Flame: Some Minor American Gay Poets, 1786-1936. *Cabirion and Gay Books Bulletin,* 7, 15-18. Reprinted in Wayne R. Dynes and Stephen Donaldson, *Studies in Homosexuality,* Vol. VIII, *Homosexual Themes in Literary Studies* (pp. 141-144), New York: Garland, 1992.

Gibran, Jean and Kahlil. (1974). *Kahlil Gibran: His Life and World.* Boston: New York Graphic Society.

Gifford, James. (1995). *Dayneford's Library: American Homosexual Writing, 1900-1913.* Amherst: U of Massachusetts P.

Gutteling, J. F. C. (1920). *Hellenic Influence on the English Poetry of the Nineteenth Century.* Doctoral dissertation, University of Amsterdam.

Hafkamp, Hans. (1988). De geheime identiteit van een Amerikaan in Europa: Xavier Mayne (1868-1942). In Hans Hafkamp and Maurice van Lieshout (Eds.), *Pijlen van naamloze liefde, pioniers van de homo-emancipatie* (pp. 127-132). Amsterdam: SUA.

Hallard, James Henry. (1901). *The Idylls of Theocritus, translated into English Verse.* London: Rivingtons.

Halperin, David M. (2002). *How To Do the History of Homosexuality.* Chicago: U of Chicago P.

Heath, Desmond. (1998). *Roden Noel (1843-1894): A Wide Angle.* London: DB Books.

Hill, Brain. (1917). *Youth's Heritage.* London: McDonald.

_____. (1959). *Eight Poems.* London: [Privately printed].

Hillyer, Robert. (1920). *Five Books of Youth.* New York: Brentano's.

Ives, George. (1926). *The Græco-Roman View of Youth.* London: Cayme.

Jussim, Estelle. (1981). *Slave to Beauty: The Eccentric Life and Controversial Career of F. Holland Day.* Boston: Godine.

Kenyon, James B. (1920). *The Harvest Home.* New York: White.

Ledoux, Louis V. (1918). *The Poetry of George Edward Woodberry: A Critical Study.* New York: Dodd Mead.

Lefroy, Edward Cracroft. (1885). *Echoes from Theocritus.* London: Stock.

Leslie, Shane. (1932). *Strato's Boyish Muse, now first translated wholly into English.* London: Fortune.

Leyland, Winston, (Ed.). (1977). *Orgasms of Light.* San Francisco: Gay Sunshine.

Lomer, Sydney. (1914). *The Greek Anthology: Epigrams from Anthologia Palatina XII, Translated into English Verse*. London?: [privately printed]. (Published under the name Sydney Oswald)

McCulloch, Hugh. (1902). *Written in Florence*. London: Dent.

MacIntyre, Carl F. (1936). *Poems*. New York: Macmillan.

McLane, James L. (1920). *Spindrift*. Boston: Four Seas.

_____. (1921). *Shafts of Song*. Baltimore: Norman, Remington.

Mader, Donald. (1998). Religie en intergenerationele relaties: acht verkennende aantekeningen. In Hans Visser (Ed.), *De andere kant van de medaille* (pp. 81-98). Rotterdam: KSA. [The section on De Merode also appears in English as: A Christian BL Poet: Willem de Merode. *Paraklesis*, *3*(1) (Winter, 2002), 1, 4-5.]

_____. (Winter, 1999). J. G. Brown's Boys. *Gayme*, *4*(1), 32-7.

_____. (2002). Walter H. Breen (J. Z. Eglinton) 1928-1993. In Vern L. Bullough (Ed.), *Before Stonewall* (pp. 312-321). New York: Harrington Park.

_____. (2003). Ralph Nicholas Chubb: Dichter, drukker, pacifist, propheet. In *Gay 2004: Cultureel jaarboek voor mannen* (pp. 342-353). Amsterdam: Vassallucci.

Malone, Walter. (1919). *Selected Poems*. Louisville, KY: Morton.

Martin, Robert K. (1979). *The Homosexual Tradition in American Poetry*. Austin: U of Texas P.

Mayne, Xavier. (1908/1975). *The Intersexes: A History of Similisexualism as a Problem in Social Life*. New York: Arno.

Michaels, Barbara L. (Winter, 1994). New Light on F. Holland Day's Photographs of African Americans. *History of Photography*, *18*(4), 334-347.

Nicolson, Adela F. (1913). *Stars of the Desert*, by Laurence Hope [pseud.]. London: Heinemann.

Nicholson, John Gambril. (1911). *A Garland of Ladslove*. London: [Murray].

Noel, Roden. (1902). *Collected Poems*. London: Kegan Paul.

Oosterhuis, Harry. (1991). *Homosexuality and Male Bonding in Pre-Nazi Germany*. New York: Harrington Park.

Osborn, Percy. (1901). *Rose Leaves from Philostratus*. London: Unicorn.

Oswald, Sydney. See Lomer, Sydney.

Paine, William. (1920). *New Aristocracy of Comradeship*. London: Parsons.

Pater, Walter. (1919). *The Renaissance*. New York: Modern Library.

Percy, William Alexander. (1915). *Sappho in Levkas and Other Poems*. New Haven: Yale UP.

_____. (1920). *In April Once*. New Haven: Yale UP.

_____. (1924). *Enzio's Kingdom and Other Poems*. New Haven: Yale UP.

_____. (1941). *Lanterns on the Levee: Recollections of a Planter's Son*. New York: Knopf.

Percy, William Armstrong III. (1997). William Alexander Percy (1885-1942): His Homosexuality and Why It Matters. In John Howard (Ed.), *Carryin' On in the Lesbian and Gay South* (pp. 75-92). New York: NYUP.

Pessoa, Fernando. (1991). *Antinoüs*. N.p.: Fata Morgana.

Prime Stevenson, Edward Irenaeus. See Mayne, Xavier.

Rahman, Tariq. (1991). Ephebophilia and the Creation of a Spiritual Myth in the Works of Ralph Nicholas Chubb. In T. Sandfort, E. Brongersma & A. van Naerssen,

Male Intergenerational Intimacy (pp. 103-127). New York: Harrington Park. (Original work published 1990, *Journal of Homosexuality, 20*(1/2))

Raile, Arthur Lyon. See Warren, E. P.

Raymond, George Lansing. (1870). *Haydn and Other Poems*, by the author of "Life Below." New York: Hurd & Houghton.

Reade, Brian. (1970). *Sexual Heretics: Male Homosexuality in English Literature from 1850 to 1900*. London: Routledge & Kegan Paul.

Reid, Anthony. (1970). *Ralph Chubb, the Unknown*. N.p.: [the author].

Robb, Graham. (2003). *Strangers: Homosexual Love in the Nineteenth Century*. London: Picador.

Roberts, Cecil. (1914). *Through Eyes of Youth*. London: Clarke.

Roberts, Pam. (2000). Fred Holland Day (1864-1933). In Pam Roberts (Ed.), *F. Holland Day* (pp. 11-28). Amsterdam/Zwolle: Van Gogh Museum/Waanders.

Rolfe, Frederick. (1974). *Baron Corvo: Collected Poems*. London: Woolf.

Saltus, Francis S. (1890). *Shadows and Ideals: Poems*. Buffalo: Moulton.

Sears, James T., and Allen, Louise A. (2000). Museums, Friends, and Lovers in the New South: Laura's Web, 1909-1931. *Journal of Homosexuality, 40*(1), 105-144.

Seeger, Allan. (1917). *Poems*. New York: Scribner's.

Sergent, Bernard. (1986). *Homosexuality in Greek Myth*. Boston: Beacon.

Slocum, Edward Mark (Ed.). (1924/1978). *Men and Boys: An Anthology*. New York: [privately printed]; Repr. 1978, New York: Coltsfoot.

Shand-Tucci, Douglass. (1995). *Boston Bohemia, 1881-1900: Ralph Adams Cram: Life and Architecture*. Amherst: U of Massachusetts P.

Smith, Arnold W. (1919). *A Boy's Absence: Poems by a Schoolmaster*. London: Allen & Unwin.

Sox, David. (1991) *Bachelors of Art*. London: Fourth Estate.

Stedman, Edmund Clarence. (1869). *The Blameless Prince and other Poems*. Boston: Fields, Osgood.

_____. (1869a). *Alice of Monmouth . . . with Other Poems*. Boston: Fields, Osgood.

Stoddard, Richard Henry. (1852), *Poems*. Boston: Ticknor, Reed & Fields.

_____. (1871). *Book of the East*. Boston: Osgood.

Strange, Michael. (1919). *Poems*. New York: Brentano's.

Summers, Montague. (1995). *Antinous and Other Poems*. London: Cecil Woolf.

Symonds, John Addington. (1878). *Many Moods: A Volume of Verse*. London: Smith, Elder.

_____. (1880). *New and Old: A Volume of Verse*. London: Smith, Elder.

_____. (1882). *Animi Figura*. London: Smith, Elder.

_____. (1893). *In the Key of Blue and other Prose Essays*. London: Mathews & Lane.

_____. (1901). *A Problem in Greek Ethics, being an Inquiry into the Phenomenon of Sexual Inversion*. London: Smithers.

_____. (1902). *Fragilia Labilia*. Portland, ME: Mosher.

Symons, A.J.A. (1934). *The Quest for Corvo: An Experiment in Biography*. New York: Macmillan.

Taylor, Bayard. (1855). *Poems of the Orient*. Boston: Ticknor & Fields.

_____. (1883). *Poetical Works*. Household Ed. Boston: Houghton Mifflin.

Towne, Charles Hanson. (1919). *A World of Windows*. New York: Doran.

Viereck, George Sylvester. (1912). *The Candle and the Flame.* New York: Moffat, Yard.

Warren, Edward Perry. (1913). *The Wild Rose. A Volume of Poems.* London: Nutt. (Published under the name Arthur Lyon Raile)

_____. (1928-30). *The Defence of Uranian Love.* (3 vols.). London: Cayme. (Published under the name Arthur Lyon Raile)

Wattles, Willard. (Ed.). (1916). *Sunflowers: A Book of Kansas Poems.* Chicago: McClurg.

_____. (1918). *Lanterns in Gethsemane: Biblical and Mystical Poems.* New York: Dutton.

Wilson, T. P. Cameron. (1920). *Waste Paper Philosophy, to which has been added Magpies in Picardy and Other Poems.* New York: Doran.

Woodberry, Georgio Edvardo. (1877). *Relation of Pallas Athene to Athens. Oratio written for the Harvard Commencement, 1877.* [Privately printed, Abington, MA].

Woodberry, George Edward. (1899). *Heart of Man.* New York: Macmillan.

_____. (1903). *Poems.* New York: Macmillan.

_____. (1914). *The Flight and Other Poems.* New York: Macmillan.

_____. (1933). *Selected Letters.* New York: Houghton Mifflin.

Woodley, Fabian S. (1921). *A Crown of Friendship and Other Poems.* Taunton: Woodley, Williams and Dunsford.

Wright, F. A. (1924). *Complete Poems of Meleager of Gadara.* London: Birch.

Eros Underground:
Greece and Rome in Gay Print Culture, 1953-65

Amy Richlin, PhD

University of Southern California

Amy Richlin is Professor of Classics at the University of Southern California. She is the author of *The Garden of Priapus: Sexuality and Aggression in Roman Humor* (rev. ed. Oxford University Press, 1992), editor of *Pornography and Representation in Greece and Rome* (Oxford University Press, 1992), and co-editor of *Feminist Theory and the Classics* (Routledge, 1993). She is at work on a book on the love letters of the young Marcus Aurelius and his teacher, Cornelius Fronto, and has just completed a translation of the letters. Correspondence may be addressed: Department of Classics, THH 256, University of Southern California, Los Angeles, CA 90089-0352.

Author note: This essay forms part of a larger project on the letters of Marcus Aurelius and Cornelius Fronto; thanks to the American Council of Learned Societies for funding it, to Henry Abelove for starting me on the twentieth-century trail, to Laurel Brake for generous help with *The Artist and Journal of Home Culture*, to Mary Beard and Christopher Stray, Queen and God-Emperor of Victorian Classics, to Maria Wyke for her pop culture expertise, to Beert Verstraete for excessive patience, and to the late and sorely lamented Jonathan Walters for letting me raid his brain and library. Special thanks to all at the ONE National Gay & Lesbian Archives for their help and support, especially to Joseph Hawkins and Stuart Timmons for much time spent filling me in on the lived history of ONE, and to Ashlie Mildfelt for putting up with me at all hours. This essay is dedicated to the memory of Jim Kepner and W. Dorr Legg for their courage and unquenchable intellectual curiosity.

[Haworth co-indexing entry note]: "Eros Underground: Greece and Rome in Gay Print Culture, 1953-65." Richlin, Amy. Co-published simultaneously in *Journal of Homosexuality* (Harrington Park Press, an imprint of The Haworth Press, Inc.) Vol. 49, No. 3/4, 2005, pp. 421-461; and: *Same-Sex Desire and Love in Greco-Roman Antiquity and in the Classical Tradition of the West* (ed: Beert C. Verstraete, and Vernon Provencal) Harrington Park Press, an imprint of The Haworth Press, Inc., 2005, pp. 421-461. Single or multiple copies of this article are available for a fee from The Haworth Document Delivery Service [1-800-HAWORTH, 9:00 a.m. - 5:00 p.m. (EST). E-mail address: docdelivery@haworthpress.com].

SUMMARY. This essay surveys the building of intellectual community through print culture in the nascent gay movement in the United States and in Europe in the mid-twentieth century. Amateur historians, especially Jim Kepner and W. Dorr Legg of ONE, used Greece and Rome as models on which to base claims for gay rights. Ancient history figured in ONE's educational enterprises, including articles in the magazine *ONE*, the ONE Institute, and *Homophile Studies*. The magazine writers and their readership faced problems in the accessibility of knowledge, which the increasing circulation of the magazines corrected, to a degree. Biases surviving from the Victorian period caused the popular idea of ancient homophile culture to favor Greece over Rome, and made "Greek" a code word. Antiquity also played a large, though decreasing, role in formations of homoerotic fantasy during this period. *[Article copies available for a fee from The Haworth Document Delivery Service: 1-800-HAWORTH. E-mail address: <docdelivery@ haworthpress.com> Website: <http://www.HaworthPress.com> © 2005 by The Haworth Press, Inc. All rights reserved.]*

KEYWORDS. Print culture, gay movement, underground magazine, classical tradition, homosexuality and Greece, homosexuality and Rome, *ONE*, Mattachine, Jim Kepner, W. Dorr Legg, 1950s

The freedom of the press belongs to those who control the press.

–Big Bill Hayward

For those in search of a gay identity, from the Renaissance onward, Greek and Roman sexual practices have stood for freedom in same-sex love. The mid-twentieth century was a dark age for gay people. What of the sex/gender system of the ancient Mediterranean was known to ordinary people at this time, and what use did they make of their knowledge? Following the traces of antiquity through the underground publications of this period provides a lesson in the circulation and persistence of knowledge outside authorized precincts, and in the nature of what might be called "shadow scholarship." Print culture, as Laurel Brake has shown for the 1890s, built a community through shared knowledge. Greece and Rome were useful in the process, but in the end a community leery of elitism rejected an alibi it no longer needed.[1]

This essay will focus on *ONE*, the magazine published in Los Angeles by a small group of ardent activists from 1953 to 1969. (The group was smaller even than it looks; the board members often wrote under one or more pseudonyms as well as in their own names.) Two central members of the group, Jim Kepner and W. Dorr Legg, devoted their lives to writing, teaching, and documenting gay history, not only in *ONE* but in its spinoff educational institute and in a scholarly journal (*Homophile Studies*); the enormous collection Kepner amassed became the ONE National Gay & Lesbian Archives, now housed at the University of Southern California.[2] *ONE* makes an especially good symbol of the circulation of knowledge due to its most famous victory: the 1958 Supreme Court decision in *ONE*'s case against the Postmaster of Los Angeles (One Inc. v. Olesen), a major step forward in the fight to circulate printed matter about homosexual life through the US mail. It is useful to recall, in these days of Internet access, how much more difficult it once was to find forbidden knowledge.

ONE's battle marked a major advance. In Europe in the eighteenth and early nineteenth centuries, knowledge about antiquity was largely the property of the wealthy; higher education was for elite males (Payne Knight, Lord Byron), and classical books were both scarce and expensive–the leatherbound library. Even within the academy, the canonical curriculum would not have exposed young men to ancient sources dealing with the homoerotic, though this began to change when Benjamin Jowett introduced Plato's dialogues into the Oxford curriculum in the 1840s (Dowling, 1994). With the growth of the middle class, the number of young men trained in the Classics also grew, and knowledge of the homoerotic in antiquity no longer depended so much on access to aristocratic collections of erotica (Reade, 1970, pp. 7, 17). By the 1880s, a flourishing literary and artistic subculture was making full use of this material, as first chronicled by Timothy d'Arch Smith in *Love in Earnest* and Brian Reade in *Sexual Heretics* (both 1970). Though even the university curriculum was bowdlerized, the clothbound series of classical texts which began to be produced by Oxford University Press around 1900 put uncut editions of writers like Horace (1901) and Juvenal (1903) into the hands of undergraduates.[3] Moreover, the publishing industry sought to reach a large audience, maybe a mass audience, with series of translations of the Classics–for example, Bohn's Classical Library in the 1840s, the Loeb Classical Library from 1911.[4] And with the spread of free public libraries, especially in the 1900s thanks to Andrew Carnegie, it was at least possible for any literate person to find enough to gain a sense of the degree to which the foundations of Western culture incorporated the homoerotic. Yet despite the move from leatherbound to clothbound, this knowledge seems mostly to have slumbered on in the libraries, while the Classics made their way to gay subcultures of the twentieth century via underground rivers.

Private publication and small publishing houses did circulate historical overviews of ancient sexuality, notably those by Richard Burton (1885-86; see below), Hans Licht (1931), and Otto Kiefer (1934/1976); John J. Winkler's brief account of such works emphasizes their limited circulation and kinship with pornography, and, with the work of German pioneer activist Magnus Hirschfeld, the risks they ran (1990). Other writers accentuated the positive, as with Edward Carpenter's lists of exemplary gay people in history (1917), and, perhaps most influential of all, John Addington Symonds' *A Problem in Greek Ethics* (1883; see Norton, n.d.). These books reproduce a canon of knowledge that seems sometimes to derive from independent reading, but often just from a tradition. They show what was available for general consumption if a person could get hold of the book, but do not show how widely this information was circulated.

With *ONE*, we get a window into a new class of consumers of knowledge. The magazine periodically gave figures on circulation and information on where it was available for purchase, but it is especially the Letters column that suggests how knowledge spread and grew, changing from a halting and fearful expression to a sense of free speech.[5] And for this widespread community, antiquity had a range of meanings and uses that changed over time.

ONE was founded in postwar Los Angeles by a small group of activists, an offshoot of the newly formed Mattachine Society. Most of them had been or still were members of the Communist party; Kepner had been a columnist for *The Daily Worker*.[6] They called themselves "ONE" and began publication of *ONE* in 1953, taking the name from Carlyle: "a mystic bond of brotherhood makes all men one."[7] Alas, only temporarily: in 1954, there was a schism amongst the Mattachines and a conservative faction forced out the radical founders. The leadership of the group moved to San Francisco, where *Mattachine Review* began publication in 1955. Both ONE and the Mattachines made it a priority to publish a magazine, to be available both by subscription and on newsstands.

In doing so, they were following a model established by similar groups in Europe. From early on, *ONE* carried lists of these groups and their publications: a list from January 1954 (p. 26) gives full mailing addresses for groups in Switzerland, France, Italy, Denmark, Holland, and Germany; a list from *Mattachine Review* (March-April 1955, p. 38) adds groups in Norway, Sweden, and India (*International Journal of*

Sexology, published by "Dr. A. P. Phillay, O.B.E., M.B.B.S.," in Bombay). *ONE* also carried the occasional translated or reprinted article (the Swiss journal *Der Kreis/Le Cercle* was published trilingually, in German, French, and English; there was no comparable magazine in England or the Commonwealth). The European magazines carried photographs and sometimes lonely hearts columns, and the groups had a more exclusively social function than either *ONE* or the Mattachine Society, focusing on conventions and parties rather than on political reform. Their magazines were not available on newsstands, and *Der Kreis* carried no masthead.[8]

In 1955 the Daughters of Bilitis (DOB) was formed in San Francisco, and though *ONE* carried notices of the inception of the DOB publication, *The Ladder* (October-November 1956, p. 37), relations with the DOB were never as chummy as with *Der Kreis*, and *ONE* never reprinted a piece from *The Ladder*. *ONE* did include women on its editorial board from the outset, most notably the art director, Eve Elloree, and several editors–Ann Carll Reid, Sten Russell (Stella Rush), Alison Hunter; but the magazine focused mainly on men's issues, assuming that gay men were generic for all homosexual concerns.

ROLE MODELS

Jim Kepner, who was found as an infant wrapped in a Houston newspaper and left Texas for a life of activism in California, at his death in 1997 had a two-column obituary in the *New York Times* (Dunlap, 1997). The obituary quotes from a 1992 interview in which Kepner explained how he had been inspired in his youth by "mail-order tracts" on great homosexuals in history, including "all the old Greeks." This fascination with the past as a possible model for the future stayed with Kepner throughout his life and shaped both his writings and the archive he left behind. He was self-conscious about his preoccupation, and was ahead of his time in his ability to theorize what he was doing, as in a *ONE* essay (May 1957) titled "Do Homosexuals Hide Behind Great Men?" Arguing against a piece in the "right-wing socialist" *New Leader*, Kepner postulates that "it slanders [the] memory" of great men to hide their sexuality, and that "the child is morally nourished by heroic models." He fires off barrages of famous names, including "most of the Roman Caesars [. . .] among philosophers: Socrates, Plato [. . .] among poets almost every classical Roman or Greek, [. . .] David and Jonathan, Ruth and Naomi, Jesus and John, [. . .] Plato, Sappho, Michelangelo, Shakespeare, Milton, Whitman" (pp. 4-6).

His teaching notes show that he brought role models with him as exemplars into the classroom, starting from himself. He says he has been lecturing on "Gays in History" at ONE Institute from the spring of 1957 onward, "doing research one step ahead of the lecture"; he describes himself as a "self-educated 21 year gay activist and writer." For a class on "History Items to Cover," he gives "A line of emperors–Caesar, Augustus, Tiberius, Caligula, Nero, Hadrian, Marcus Aurelius, Galba, Heliogabalus"; on Achilles and Patroclus in the *Iliad*, his notes read,

> The heart and theme of the Iliad is the love of Achilles and Patroclus and the whole plot turns on this. *But*, some writers protest, there is no evidence the lovers had sex. To a het, this makes the big difference and scores of writers knock down a hx or Gay reading of many of these stories–

And here he instances Sappho.[9]

Kepner's was not the only perspective on the importance of history for gay consciousness. Alison Hunter, Women's Editor of *ONE* from February 1959, used historical examples in an editorial (March 1962, p. 4) arguing for a tie between gay culture and high civilization, steered by a gay elite. This tie between the Classics and class would prove to be a serious obstacle to the general use of ancient history within the movement.

Kepner's 1957 essay already problematizes the fact that among the most common manifestations of a consciousness of historical forerunners were canonical lists, often of pairs of lovers: David and Jonathan, Achilles and Patroclus, Alexander and Hephaistion, and Hadrian and Antinous. Occasionally the Sacred Band of Thebes shows up (the famous "army of lovers"), and a roster of Roman emperors, most often represented by Julius Caesar, whose putative youthful liaison with King Nicomedes of Bithynia was surprisingly well known.[10]

Lesbians and women's history never got equal time in *ONE* (a perennial source of self-critique and reader complaint), but female homoeroticism also had classical models, usually Sappho. The famous October 1954 issue that triggered the legal battle with the Postmaster included a piece called "Sappho Remembered" (pp. 12-15) that was repeatedly analyzed in court papers; except for a parting allusion to Sappho, the title was the only Greek thing about it, but that was meaningful enough, as will be seen. In December of the same year, *ONE* published a story called "The Gateway" (pp. 5-10), which begins with two lines of verse about "a passage-way through Lesbos' wall." The magazine *Der Neue Ring* carried a running feature called "Aphrodite" in which one stewardess wrote to another about her amorous experiences (see, e.g., the *Ring* column translated in *ONE*, May 1958, pp. 26-27). As in Kepner's list above, Ruth and Naomi are occasionally cited as exemplars of Lesbian love. In general, ancient names are connected with Lesbian contexts more as adornment than as part of an argument about a lost golden age; when a reader in 1964 refers to Lesbians as "the disciples of Sappho" (February, p. 31), it just sounds like a periphrasis.

Classical names were favored for groups, especially in Europe. The French magazine *Arcadie* appears on a list in *ONE* in February 1954 (p. 29) and thereafter; the word "Arcadian" had been used as a code word for male homoeroticism in the nineteenth century, for example by Symonds (Blanshard, 2000, p. 105). Other groups and/or magazines with classical names included the German *Hellas* (*ONE*, January 1954, p. 26), the Danish *Pan* (*ONE*, July 1954, p. 29), the vanished *Uranus* (*Weg zu Freundschaft*, May 1958, p. 149), the Danish group Ganymedes that was "disbanded" by the police (*ONE*, May 1958, pp. 18-20), and a hip French magazine, aimed at a younger audience than *Arcadie*, called *Juventus*, announced by *ONE* in August 1959 (p. 13). Its demise was recorded in a November 1960 article (pp. 27-29); it had lost its printer, due to the criminalization of homosexuality in France. Even in Japan, there was a magazine called *Adonis* (*ONE*, February 1960, p. 30, per a letter from Mr. L. in Tokyo); even in Orange County, a co-ed group called "Dionysus" (June 1962, p. 18).

A desire for role models also derived from–and inspired–material culture. By the early 1960s *ONE* had started running ads for a company that made marble medallions of Great Men, suitable for hanging on your wall: Homer, Socrates, Hippocrates, "Oscar Wilde, Byron, and Nijinsky done with particular appreciation for homophile tastes" (November 1962, p. 18). Mr. L. C. from Ardmore, Pennsylvania, writes in 1964 to say that he has seen "the Hermes of Praxiteles. . . . If possible every homosexual should see the statues in Athens as well as the architecture and then he will know there is no greater group of men in the whole world than the homosexual" (July, p. 30).

Historical examples were also called in to illustrate social phenomena in *ONE*: male/female confusion (February 1959, p. 5: "the same effeminate spirit among the Caesars"); nude sculpture (March 1961, p. 30, a letter from Edward Denison in __, Texas: the Greeks and Romans thought it should be "a part of the public scenery"); Halloween

(November 1958, p. 4: supposedly derived from the Bacchanalia by way of the Greek Dionysia); the life of Lawrence of Arabia (September 1958, p. 7: Asia Minor a site "sacred to the memory of the love of Achilles and Patroclus").

Despite frequent allusions to the Platonic dialogues, the topic of pederasty as such was avoided, and was not explicitly raised until the March 1958 issue (p. 30, a letter from Mr. A. in New York). September 1958 saw a theme issue, "For Love of a Boy," featuring the Lawrence of Arabia piece as the lead. Discussion on this taboo topic was evidently stimulated by the publication of *Lolita* that year (reviewed in *ONE*, October 1958, p. 31), and Mr. B. from New York wrote in to say that although he had often known male nymphets, a novel featuring one could not be published unless it were set in ancient Greece (January 1959, p. 31). *ONE*'s airing of the subject peaked with a keynote address on boy love at the 1958 Midwinter Institute by Dr. Mario Palmieri, paying tribute to Plato and "Greek civilization" (reported in the April 1959 issue, p. 16). The May 1959 issue followed up with a title story on the pedophilia question by "Didgeon"; it listed the age of consent in various ancient cultures (pp. 12-14).

But already in 1954 the opinion had been voiced in the Letters column that the use of Plato and "great artists, writers, and musicians of the past" as models was a cliché (January 1954, p. 23, signed "P.H.D."). A *ONE* article in May 1959, on great armies of the past that glorified "comradely love" (pp. 20-22), provoked a letter from Rudolf Burkhardt, English Editor of *Der Kreis*, objecting that "the Theban warriors [. . .] cannot have any counterpart in modern warfare" (September 1959, p. 30). The same argument appears in an essay on gays in the military by Robert Gregory in August 1960 (pp. 12-13). In 1963, a lead article by Randy Lloyd endorses gay marriage on the premise that "We are not living in the days of ancient Greece, our movement does not stem from those days, and it is not based on the homosexual ethics of those days" (June 1963, p. 10).

TEACHING THE COMMUNITY

Education was a main goal of ONE from the outset; Kepner took it as axiomatic that every gay person was looking for his or her identity and that there was no way of establishing a gay identity without learning, especially without learning history. In the account of the 1955 Midwinter Institute, ONE's Education Committee went first in the report of activities, stressing the "need for full fledged educational institution to study all aspects of homosexuality," with classes to start "this year" (January 1956, p. 4). Kepner put the case strongly in an editorial published in 1958 (September, p. 4):

> The homophile desperately needs to know his identity and his status. [. . .] Those who find this knowledge have a chance to find their place in the world. [. . .] Homophile education is a practical and urgent matter, for teenagers who are moving inexorably in this direction as well as for those long set in their ways. "Know thyself . . ." For the homophile, condemned otherwise by modern society as a lost soul, this has exceptional urgency.

Kepner shared this belief not only with Dorr Legg but with Sten Russell, one of the Lesbian members of the editorial board. In a 1960 editorial, Russell emphasized self-acceptance, and education as a means to that end (September, p. 5):

> [The] Education Division [. . .] brings to the homosexual the opportunity (for the first time that we know) to make a systematic attack on his vast ignorance of himself, his nature, his history. [. . .] [But we] will not be able to serve more than a few thousand at the outside [. . .] The responsibility falls back upon the homophile to educate and accept himself with whatever tools are available to him.

Although Legg was always self-consciously intellectual, both Kepner and Russell wrote out of a deep sense of the need for mass consciousness and wanted to reach everyone they could. Similarly, a 1961 editorial by Marcel Martin called for volunteers with knowledge of "every modern language; we need a really profound knowledge of Latin, Greek, Sanscrit and Hebrew–even Egyptian hieroglyphics" (May, p. 5). It was ONE's goal both to ransack the past and to reach a worldwide public. In contrast, the pamphlet *Mattachine Society Today* called for education, but in the context of "a personal behavior code which will be above criticism from anyone"–members were to "integrate" themselves into society–and disclaimers of Communism, including a pledge (1955, pp. 4-9). In the first issue of *Mattachine Review*, the Mattachines actually identified their three San Francisco chapters with the Greek letters Alpha, Beta, and Gamma, like a fraternity, noting that they met monthly "in 1 of the Bay Area's fine restaurants" (January-February 1955,

p. 17). A Mattachine speech reported in *ONE* in 1956 (January, inside front cover) said, "Our guiding principle was evolution, not revolution . . . we do not advocate a homosexual culture of community, and we believe none exists."

By February 1957 ONE's Education Division was advertising the ONE Institute, with courses, a library, and a Summer School (pp. 10, 11). The April editorial describes the Institute (1957, p. 4) as "especially interested in history," and for political reasons. Succeeding issues of the magazine carried plugs for education and the Institute, starting in May (pp. 7-9) with a trumpet blast from Dorr Legg, who berated *ONE* for "dullness" stemming from lack of education along with "our universities" for their "long refusal [. . .] to undertake such tasks." The Institute took shape as a set of night classes offered at ONE's offices. The courses were numbered and titled like college courses, and HS-211, "Homosexuality in History," was among those most frequently offered. The teachers included Jim Kepner, Dorr Legg, Thomas M. Merritt, and Don Slater, and were listed with titles: in February 1961, W. Dorr Legg is "Associate Professor," Don Slater only an "Instructor" (p. 16). This was probably Dorr Legg's idea; he certainly saw himself as the senior professor, though his only graduate degree was an M.L.D. in landscape architecture from the University of Michigan (September 1962, p. 31; in the opinion of Stuart Timmons, T. M. Merritt was USC faculty member Merrit Thompson, here listed as "Ph.D., Professor of Philosophy [Emeritus]"). By 1960 the Institute was well established, and the plug for it in the September issue called it "The Only School of Its Kind in the World" (back cover). Indeed it predated the arrival of Gender Studies in the college curriculum by a good twenty-five years.

ONE always had both a local and a far-flung readership, and the announcements of the Institute's offerings inspired periodic wistful responses in the Letters column. Miss T. in Salt Lake City wrote in 1957 asking whether they might not set up a correspondence course (June/July, p. 31). Mr. K. in Chicago wrote in 1958 to say "I envy those who can attend your classes in Los Angeles. [. . .] Come to Chicago" (December, p. 31). In August 1959, *ONE* announced a set of extension courses to be offered in Denver, taught by Jim Kepner, for a fee of $2.50 (back cover). In 1961, someone at *ONE* had the brilliant idea of printing a crossword puzzle in the magazine, enabling readers to generate for themselves language much more explicit than anything *ONE* was as yet printing ("Queerzzle," December, pp. 26-27); many of the clues postulate familiarity with the historical subjects taught at the ONE Institute, for example 37 Across, "Classic by Apuleius, THE GOLDEN___"; 20

Down, "Derivation of the word *tribade*." Distance learning seems to have become available at least by September 1964, when HS-100E was advertised on the back cover; the course inspired a letter from Mr. C. in White Plains, New York (December 1964, p. 30).

The history courses were joined by a literature course in October 1959 (back cover); another favorite was sociology, and the three courses represented the somewhat conflicting motives behind the desire for education and correspond with the range of work carried in the magazine. Though some evidently shared Kepner's passion for history, others just liked stories, and others again wanted to know about current gay issues–legal matters, updates on police actions and prosecutions both in the US and abroad, information on health, discussions of religion, marriage, family, money. Alfred Kinsey was an early supporter of the magazine, much loved, and the reach of the Kinsey Report inspired an interest in what was knowable about gay people in current everyday life. In January of 1961, Kepner, under his pseudonym of Lyn Pedersen, left the masthead for the first time, and in February of 1962 the Institute offered no history course (p. 14), though history returned the following September (back cover). Both Kepner and Legg had interests outside of history–Kepner wrote the popular "tangents" column, a collection of clippings, under the name "Dal McIntire," and Legg began doing research on sociology–and, as will be seen, past and present came to be considered mutually exclusive.

A lengthy set of Dorr Legg's notes and class outlines remains in the ONE files, along with a 1960 draft outline of a book he was writing, *Homosexuality in History: From the Dawn of Time to the Pandects of Julian* (this title is Dorr Legg all over). Tidily illustrating the relation between activism and scholarship, the draft is typed on the back of leftover copies of an ambitious letter sent out by ONE to a long list of famous authors to solicit work from them (see *ONE*, November 1953, pp. 12-13. Though the list included, for example, Truman Capote, Colette, Noel Coward, Christopher Isherwood, and Tennessee Williams, Norman Mailer was the only writer to oblige, which shows how far out *ONE* was).

Legg begins with an overview of theories of history, with reference to an article he had published in *Homophile Studies* in 1959. He devotes chapters six through nine to antiquity: the ancient Near East, the Greeks, the Jews, the Romans. A rarity even today, he gives equal time to all four cultures, and includes rigorous study questions and eclectic bibliographies; the chapter on Greece, for example, includes E. R. Dodds *The Greeks and the Irrational*, Hans Licht, Mary Renault *The Last of the Wine*, and John Addington Symonds *A Problem in Greek Ethics*, with Greek authors from Aeschylus to Xenophon. He is among very few people anywhere in the magazines to discuss the *kinaidos*, and makes his position clear: "we have him with us today in every city in America, a bit altered to be sure, but still as indigestible to our society as he was to that of Hellenistic Samos" (Legg, 1959, p. 97; cf. Richlin, 1993b). His book outline arrives at the level of any good introductory textbook now in use–the tone and amount of support are much like those of Sarah Pomeroy's *Goddesses, Whores, Wives, and Slaves* (1975); unfortunately the book predates by a generation the arrival of a market for books on gender for use in college courses, and it was never completed. Though other overviews did make it into print (Eglinton, 1964; Garde, 1964), Legg's book had an air of pedagogy, an earnest desire to teach, and a sober thoroughness that set it apart from other works. But Legg put his time into the Institute rather than into the textbook.[11]

ACCESSIBILITY OF KNOWLEDGE

A hundred years before gender studies, homosexual love got into print through the elsewhen (Classics, the Renaissance) and the elsewhere (the Rubaiyyat). The most spectacular work of Orientalist homoerotica was Richard Burton's translation of the *Arabian Nights* (1885-86), to which *The Sotadic Zone* was originally a "Terminal Essay." Here Burton discussed the work's homoerotic material and set it in the context of classical homoerotic literature, quoting from Greek and Latin sources and providing his own novel theory of the origins of pederasty (he claimed it existed in a particular geographical belt around the world, which he named after the Greek poet Sotades, famous for writing about *kinaidoi*). His footnotes suggest how much of his knowledge came from a familiarity not only with the unexpurgated classics but with European pornography going back to the early modern: this is expensive knowledge, leatherbound, not clothbound. It is thus somewhat ironic that it is Burton who most explicitly demonstrates the exclusivity of Latin and Greek, in a tirade incorporated in the "Terminal Essay" (1885-86, Vol. 10, pp. 253-54):

> In an age saturated with cant and hypocrisy, here and there a venal pen will mourn over the "Pornography" of The Nights [. . .] and will lament the "wanton dissemination (!) of ancient and filthy fiction." This self-constituted Censor morum [censor of morals]

reads Aristophanes and Plato, Horace and Virgil, perhaps even Martial and Petronius, because "veiled in the decent obscurity of a learned language;" he allows men Latine loqui [to speak Latin]; but he is scandalised at stumbling-blocks much less important in plain English.

"Veiled in the decent obscurity of a learned language" is the phrase Gibbon used to describe his own practice of printing in the original Latin or Greek illustrative material that he thought too racy. Before unexpurgated translations started becoming available, only those trained in the languages–which until the late nineteenth century meant middle- and upper-class men–could read the dirty parts. Translation itself thus becomes transgressive, and the erudite Burton, despite his casual slips into Latin, becomes a transgressor of class boundaries as well as sex norms.

The problem for the first generation of gay educators in the US was that they were, of necessity, largely self-taught: the academy treated with contempt both the openly gay and the study of homosexuality. Moreover, unlike Victorian self-educated pundits like Charles Kains Jackson and Gleeson White of *The Artist and Journal of Home Culture*, the *ONE* writers had no special interest in addressing elite circles.[12] Whereas the members of the European editorial boards would probably have had some classical education, less would have been available to the *ONE* board members, and Kepner's university experience consisted of coursework at Los Angeles City College from 1961 to 1963. The results make an interesting contrast with the European magazines, which mostly inhabit a dreamy, well-read Arcadia. The knowledge displayed in *ONE*, by comparison, is like a collection made by a purposeful scavenger–like Adrienne Rich's swimmer "diving into the wreck." There is not much sense of how the pieces fit together, or of the general histories of the times from which the pieces come, though both Kepner and Legg in their teaching worked toward a grand narrative. In the magazine, each new piece is triumphantly produced as proof and validation of existence–and we must bear in mind that the people in *ONE* were constantly under pressure to conceal their existence. Only rarely does it seem that history is being read for the sake of those in the past; here the past is clearly being used for the sake of the present.

Still, one or two people on the board and among the contributors to the magazine must have known some Latin. A quotation from Vergil's *Eclogues* 2 (about the love of the shepherd Corydon for the boy Alexis) appears in an article (October 1955, p. 4). The contributor of several pieces to the magazine wrote under the pen name "Arcades Ambo" (August 1960, p. 25; November 1961, p. 13)–more Vergil: *Arcades ambo*, "both Arcadians," describes Corydon and Daphnis in *Eclogues* 7 (line 4). The Juvenalian exclamation *quis custodiet ipsos custodes*, "Who will guard the guards themselves?" appears as a heading in Kepner's "tangents" column (October 1960, p. 20), and the tags *rus in urbe* ("a garden in the city") and *Ave atque vale* ("Hail and farewell") pop up in an essay (November 1960, p. 7) and the Letters column (April 1961, p. 29). Didgeon contributes *dura lex sed lex*, "a tough law, but the law," in an essay on pederasty and the law (May 1959, p. 47), and dedicates an essay on marriage "For Rudy–*si quaeris, circumspice*," "If you're looking for one, look around" (September 1960, p. 6; this is part of the inscription about Christopher Wren in St. Paul's Cathedral, "If you're looking for his tomb, look around"). A 1964 love poem is titled "Antisonnet: Thamyris to Hyacinth" (February, p. 19), suggesting an unusually complex level of classical reading: Hyacinthus was familiar as the boy loved by Apollo, but the blind poet Thamyris seems to be here due to his appearance in a sexually explicit poem by Ovid (*Amores* 3.7.62), which the Loeb edition prints in Latin.

But most of this is at the familiar-quotations level, and there is nothing to suggest that anyone on the board had a firsthand reading knowledge of ancient texts pertaining to the homoerotic. Indeed, the classical references throughout the magazines bespeak expertise at an amateur level, with garbled information not only in *ONE* but in the European magazines.[13] Even so, these scraps sometimes demonstrate the way in which learning can immediately be used for one-upmanship and elitism (as here). "Watch Your Language" (August-September 1956, p. 16) instructs readers to use English words for sex acts, rather than "ancient Greek and Latin words," but advocates what turns out to be a list of hifalutin Latinate terms: "irrumation," "cunnilinctus," "pedication." After all, the passing of historical information from the academy into journalism usually results in distortions, as in a game of "Telephone"; this is perhaps an inevitable by-product of the transmittal of knowledge. Classicists can only offer the end result of two thousand years of the same process.

On the other hand, there are hints throughout the magazines of a diffusion of knowledge about antiquity at a grassroots level. The playwright James Barr, a perennial hero of *ONE*, published an autobiographical essay in the first issue of *Mattachine Review* (January-February 1955, pp. 9-12) about returning to live in his small Kansas hometown as a known homosexual (p. 11):

[. . .] the most colorful indication of cordiality came from a seventy year old lady. She called me one afternoon, identified herself and asked bluntly, "What do you know about Plato?"

I told her very little, other than his famous Republic had been successfully paralleled with both Fascism and Communism, and that he had practiced the vilest literary deceit by putting his own views into the mouth of Socrates to give them added credence.

"Can you prove that," she asked.

"I think so, if Russell and H. G. Wells are good enough for you."

She said they were, and asked me if I would like to become a member of a Great Books discussion group she attended in a small city fifty miles away.

En route to the first meeting she tells him how she saw Oscar Wilde as a girl; the train came through town and there he was, "flowing cape, flowing hair and all." Barr's story has him passing a political and social test (he doesn't bring up the wrong sort of thing about Plato) and receiving a veiled endorsement in return.

The most direct historical service *ONE* provided to its readers was the reprinting of translations of classical texts. But even Kepner bowdlerized. A speech from Aristophanes' *Thesmophoriazusae* describing the effeminate playwright Agathon–not a widely known text–appeared in a piece by Kepner in 1953 (writing as Hieronymous K., May, pp. 15-17). He notes (p. 14): "Incidentally, this is edited and revised because of terms which are thought shocking now but were wholly acceptable then"; he wants to avoid "terms unsuitable to our times." The preeminence of Plato's *Symposium* is underscored by a series that ran in six issues in 1955, with excerpts from four speeches in the *Symposium*; an introductory essay by Robert Gregory in the February issue hopes that "this series . . . will encourage many of *ONE*'s readers to study and embrace the idealism with which Plato infused the actualities of homoerotic feeling" (p. 38).[14] A note in the March issue (p. 41) explains that "some minor liberties have been taken with the translator's text, so as to de-emphasize the age differential, and to bring the Greek conception into greater consistence with modern conditions"–as noted, pederasty would not be discussed in *ONE* until 1958; it was a dangerous subject for a movement seeking legitimacy–it still is–making the Greek model a mixed blessing, in need of airbrushing. Ironically, a later *ONE* contributor complained that "Even Plato's writ-

436   SAME-SEX DESIRE AND LOVE IN GRECO-ROMAN ANTIQUITY

ings have been 'cleaned up' by the filthy-minded in order that the truth of the Symposium be largely hidden" (July 1963, p. 7).[15] But all the truths of the *Symposium* were not equally convenient; real Greeks were not the point.

This was *ONE*'s most ambitious excursion into translation. J. P. Starr, described in the author notes as a "Professional Engineer" and "Historical Student" who had been working on a study of homosexuality through the ages for forty years, published two pairs of anecdotes from Greek and Roman history (October-November 1957, p. 17; January 1958, p. 25; neither gives source or translator). This led a reader the next month (February 1958, p. 29–a Mr. G. in New York, possibly Noel Garde, on whom more below) to complain that better material is available:

> Julius Caesar's yielding his young body to the King of Bythnia to get a Roman naval base (see Suetonius); the birth of democracy at Athens as a result of intrigues arising from the tyrant taking a youth from his lover (see almost any Greek classical history); The Sacred Band of Thebes, with Philip's beautiful epitaph (see Plutarch's Life of Pelopidas) over their mass death in battle . . .

He wants what he already knows, though he is unusual in citing primary sources. Know-it-all testiness like Mr. G.'s presumably contributed to an eventual reaction against history.

Meanwhile an eighteenth-century translation of one of Martial's few epigrams on Lesbians pops up in 1958 (February, p. 22), and a single Sappho poem makes a belated appearance in 1962 (November, p. 5)–translated from the French. It should be noted that there is very little translation from anything *but* classical texts in *ONE*–very little Asian material, nothing from Arabic or Persian (a Victorian favorite, now gone), and not much European material. An uncharacteristically high-art exception appears in a two-page spread in 1955, reproducing a photograph of a Renaissance bust of a young man with a comment on the facing page that draws on Plato's *Phaedrus*.[16] But the model of reception here is usually unmediated: the Greeks and us, the Romans and us, the Renaissance and us. There is a strong sense of exploration across broken connections.

Yet some contributors produced essays attesting to a level of scholarly reading. A 1954 piece in *Weg zu Freundschaft* analyzes the relationship between Gilgamesh and Enkidu, illustrated from the text (October, pp. 345-50). The *ONE* contributor who wrote as "Brother

Grundy" describes himself (in a comic poem titled "The Insomniad") as reading "Ovid, Lucretius, Plato's *Apology*," and pondering a life that joins "opposites as mad as sex/ In rolling spheres, like Aristophanes/ (Note: Similars were joined in some of these)" (August 1959, p. 19). This piece is incorporated in an obituary identifying him as a Canadian professor of philosophy. Less commonly, same-sex love in early Christianity swims into view: Mr. L. in San Francisco writes in to point out the frequency of cross-sex identity in Butler's *Lives of the Saints* (August 1960, p. 30); two priests contribute an article in the Christmas issue of 1960 (pp. 12-13) on a soldier and his *pais* in the New Testament, with the inevitable allusion to David and Jonathan.

Most intriguingly, the *ONE* Books section of March 1960 ran a piece about the Greek novel *Leucippe and Clitophon* by Noel I. Garde (pp. 22-25).[17] Garde discusses all available translations and assesses how each deals with explicitly sexual passages; most editions he cites were rare books (many "de luxe, subscribers editions") and would have been very expensive, but he leads with the humble Loeb translation, which, however, translated all the dirty parts into Latin.[18] This is the only place in *ONE* that shows awareness of the Loeb series, and a rare instance of a magazine explicitly recognizing a primary source available in translation and comparing translations to the original. The novel, which probably dates to the late second century CE (i.e., six hundred years after Plato, in the Roman empire) includes a debate on the relative virtues of sex with women and sex with boys; it is not among the texts most widely discussed in the nineteenth and early twentieth centuries. Garde includes in his essay his own version of part of the debate, "never before published in a complete and accurate translation"; his is based on previous translations into Latin "with reference to" the Greek.

Only a single response to Garde's essay was published, though a telling one (July 1960, p. 31). Mr. S. in Chicago writes in to say:

> I was interested in the account of the ancient Greek novel [. . .] for the character Menelaus put well into words my own feelings [. . .] Plato did likewise for me about love in his *Symposium* and *Phaedrus* many years ago when I was just turned eighteen. One Saturday while in the public library to do research for a term paper in Freshman English, I found the *Symposium*. Great was my surprise and joy when I for the first time saw an exact statement of my own feelings and views. This was several years before I knew that there was anyone else in the world who had the same thoughts and feelings toward the male sex that I did. [. . .] Yes, I would have

been very much at home with Charmides, Menelaus and Clitophon in their time.

This is one of the few voices in *ONE* attesting to the liberatory potential of the public library. It also brings us back to Plato in a single step. The letter goes on to reminisce about observing the cruising scene at Grant Park concerts, and we are again reminded that the ancient world for most people is not primarily of interest for its own sake.

In February 1963, Garde has fallen out with *ONE* over some rejected book reviews (Letters, p. 31), and the Board has clearly decided to avoid what it considers pedantry. Garde would later publish a book on the history of homosexuality in the West–*Jonathan to Gide: The Homosexual in History* (1964)–consisting mainly of short biographies of canonical forerunners. The bibliography includes Suetonius along with previous name lists like Magnus Hirschfeld's, as well as popular biographies. It was plugged in *ONE*'s booklist as "a superb biographical dictionary" (August 1964, p. 23), and received a highly positive review that September (pp. 26-27).

By contrast, Kepner's clippings file includes three major articles from the gay popular press of the 1980s: a piece on Amazons by Kennedy Smith from the *Washington Blade* (December 22, 1989, pp. 27-31); a piece by Paul D. Hardman from the *Voice* on the phallus (August 14, 1981, pp. 8-9); and another by the same author on Tiberius (*Voice*, April 9, 1982, pp. 8-9). Each of these pieces has a substantial bibliography and is supported by primary sources in translation, including the Loeb, Penguin, and Modern Library series. Hardman cites John Boswell (1980) in both pieces, and in the essay on the phallus ranges from Payne Knight's *Worship of Priapus* (1786) to an article in *American Journal of Archaeology*. In these essays the boundary between scholarship and journalism finally seems to be breaking down.

The book review sections of *ONE* and other magazines, though they cast a wide net, did bring historical work to the attention of readers, as occasionally did the Letters column as well.[19] The continuance in use of early shadow scholarship is notable.[20] A reader in Richmond, Virginia, reacting to the Aristophanes translation in the May 1953 issue of *ONE*, recommended Hans Licht's 1931 book on Greek sexuality (October 1953, p. 13): "I think it might give your [. . .] writer a better and truer picture of what the Greeks thought of it all." *ONE* carried Dorr Legg's positive review of a translation of Julius Rosenbaum's *The Plague of Lust*, originally written in 1893 (February 1959, p. 30). Despite its lurid and hostile tone, Legg appreciated "the value of his work in bringing together so many relatively obscure documents," and says students are lucky this work, "long available, if at all, only in a costly two-volume edition," is now generally available.

This review was critiqued in a letter signed by Noel I. Garde in the July 1959 issue (p. 30), pointing out that antiquity was no bed of roses for gay people:

> It is in connection with its quotes from the classics that this book has tremendous value, with respect to their English translation "by an Oxford M.A.," as the original Carrington edition (Paris, 1902) had it. For the reader patient enough to plow slowly through these footnotes, as perhaps your reviewer was not, there emerges in terms of the English translations of Greek and Latin generally-banned-as-obscene poems, dialogues and essays, a comprehensive picture of homosexuality in classical times, especially as viewed by non-homosexuals. And there's the shock: it's not the rosy, idealized picture so popular these days. Reading the epigrams of Martial, the diatribes of Lucian, the plays of Aristophanes in complete, straight unbowdlerized translation, it is soon clear that "public opinion" was very much the same in those days.

Here Garde anticipated scholarly arguments that are still battling an overly rosy view of ancient sex/gender systems (see Richlin, 1993b). Legg was one of the few who would have known what he meant. But Garde doesn't realize this, and can't resist one-upping him.

The *ONE* board pretty clearly had decided to aim its magazine at the rank and file and felt that scholarship was not appropriate for this audience. Just as it put out a separate publication, *ONE Confidential* ("fearless, hard-hitting," January 1956, p. 5), for an activist readership willing to risk receiving more explicit material, it endorsed the creation of a separate journal to be put out by the ONE Institute as a quarterly. *Homophile Studies* was announced in *ONE* in March 1958 (p. 28): "Designed for the serious student, its appeal will be scholarly, not 'popular.'" The nature of intellectual community promptly made itself known in a nasty review by Marc Daniel in *Arcadie* (November 1958), which *ONE* translated and reprinted in the February 1959 issue (pp. 23-24): the journal was not "what we in Europe expect of a 'learned periodical'"; the ambition of the Institute would make "the intellectual maturity of the United States strangely more advanced than that of our country. And may I be permitted to add that I will be very much surprised if that is so?" So

much for *fraternité*. Daniel had the grace to admit to the generosity of
ONE's move, calling the Board ("our Anglo-Saxon friends") "good
sports," in a grudgingly more favorable review of *Homophile Studies*,
translated and reprinted in *ONE* in May 1960 (pp. 5-11). Along with
plugs for *Arcadie* and a short history and overview of the European
magazines, he muses that the US shows an interest in sociology and
sexology not found at all in France, while the French have philosophy, which the US does not.[21] In the end, *Homophile Studies* outlived
ONE itself, publishing from 1958 through 1970 a mass of articles representing the beginning of every area of research in gay studies.

And, inspiringly, the magazines themselves include the first seed-
lings of a theory of the history of sexuality. The moralizing maxim that
pederasty caused the fall of (check one): [__Greece__Rome] spurred
contributors and correspondents to grapple with the relation between
sexual and political history.[22] T. M. Merritt produced a short grand narrative of gay history (*ONE*, February 1958, pp. 23-24); he had earlier
critiqued Greece and Rome as built on slavery (January 1958, p. 17-18).
Even in 1954 a reader in Los Angeles, without reference to Popper, had
dared to critique Plato as "out of key with our democratic heritage"
(July 1954, p. 26). Such a degree of political consciousness regarding
classical Greek sources is rare to this day, and shows that ONE's
socialist roots still influenced the magazine's content.

Jim Kepner published in an early issue of *Mattachine Review* an
essay on writing history for gay people (September-October 1955,
pp. 28-32):

> Only by understanding the past can we begin to liberate ourselves
> from its worst effects [. . .] Homosexual history is as yet unwrit-
> ten. [. . .] Who will write this history? Few professionals can risk
> touching the subject, much less handling it without bias. Perhaps
> the history that will emerge, being largely the work of amateurs,
> will suffer some of the telltale effects of scholastic shortcomings,
> yet this will not be the first field to be staked out by autonomous
> students, and in time, when the foundations have been laid, the
> professionals may be emboldened to apply the finishing touches.
> [. . .] Another block is the limited and unaccessible sources.
> Source materials are seldom available in ordinary libraries, nor are
> they so classified as to facilitate the search. [. . .] We have our sec-
> ondary sources, but slim ones [. . .] few of the general works are
> detailed or reliable. [. . .] to many homosexuals the sole value of
> historic study is the search for heroes. My own inclination is other-

wise. Our primary job is not to glorify or apologize for homosexuality, but to understand it and make it understood.

Marc Daniel makes the same point about sources in his first review of *Homophile Studies* (*ONE*, February 1959, p. 24): "it would have been much more helpful to have stressed the difficulty in homophile studies of an historical nature owing to the lack of good editions and adequate translations of ancient and of exotic texts." Yet all this time the Loeb series stood on the library shelves, and Budé had been publishing similar translations into French since the 1920s. What we see are historians confronting *all* history and *all* languages, confronted by walls of books with no maps yet drawn, and sensing that the translations are incomplete at just the crucial points (the Loeb Martial slipping improbably into Italian, not revised until 1968; the Loeb *Leucippe and Clitophon*, as seen above, translating Greek with Latin). These are not gentlemen of leisure; they have day jobs; as A. E. Smith remarked, "Symonds inherited money" (*ONE*, December 1964, p. 26). Kepner drove a cab.

Indeed, reactions to scholarship within *ONE* included a strain of anti-intellectualism–the 1950s, after all, spawned the term "egghead" (1952), and a conflict between scholarship and populism is perhaps axiomatic in this period. A set of cartoons in the October 1954 issue, showing customers in a gay bar as different animals, had a learned monkey in spectacles speaking on love in ancient Athens (p. 24). Responses to the *Symposium* series, pro and con, began in the June 1955 issue (pp. 19, 20):

> [female reader, Minneapolis] Congratulations on introducing the Classics, as illustrated by the extracts from Plato's SYMPOSIUM . . . While it is true that many of us, both homosexual and otherwise, have some acquaintance with the Greek and other philosophers, it does us much good to be reminded of them. For those whose reading has not taken them in this direction, your reprints will be a source of much intellectual and moral stimulation. It is quite refreshing to see the SYMPOSIUM presented without circumlocutions or apologies. [Note that she has not registered the notice that the piece has been bowdlerized.]

> [female reader, Lexington, Kentucky] First Whitman and now Plato and Socrates . . . ! I'm sick and tired of your "he was 'one' too" approach to the thinkers and artists of history. After all, does it really matter . . . ?

The February issue following the series carried a positive response from Mr. C. in Ann Arbor (1956, p. 29): "Applause to you for that!" The March issue carried a complaining letter from Mr. R. in Texas, explicitly linking the hinterlands, machismo, the working class, and antipathy to books (p. 28):

> I enjoy your magazine but I think it is too damn literary. Not all of us are as esthetic as you apparently think. For instance–what the hell do I care about Plato, Socrates, Walt Whitman, etc. How does reading about them help a gay guy to get along better in this day and age? [. . .] Highly literary efforts with too many dictionary words may be just what some of the big city, effeminate fags want, but simpler, more practical, down-to-earth articles fill the need of the country and small town boys and those of us of the laboring class with limited educations who work like, who look like, and who act like real, hairy chested He Men.

The same issue carried a rave from the educated and unusually well-read Mr. E. in Lexington, Virginia (pp. 29-30):

> I graduate from college in June [. . .] *Out of the Past* is a superb perspective to lend your readers; I hope future reprints will be of the same high quality as the Symposium. The classics, of course, form a monumental backlogue of material from Sappho's fragmentary love lyrics to Pindar's 8th Pythian Ode, Bion's 8th Idyll, Plutarch's Agesilaus, Virgil's 2nd Eclogue, Petronius' Satyricon. Should you desire a more philosophical plane there are salient parts of Plato's *Phaedrus* (used by Mann in *Death in Venice*) and *Lysis*, and Aristotle's more abstract speculations on friendship. [tour through European literature] Because it deals with the classical world, I should also mention what is perhaps the best work dealing with homosexuality since *Death in Venice*. Marguerite Yourcenar's *Hadrian's Memoirs*, a book even more remarkable considering that its author is a scholarly lady.

Mr. E. believes *ONE*'s main audience are "'reformable' heterosexuals," hence "we must look our Sunday best"–he worries that the quality of the fiction in *ONE* is too low. This letter in turn provoked a reaction in the June-July 1956 issue from Mr. P. in Minneapolis, defending *ONE*'s fiction (p. 45): "I have nothing against occasional reprints of selections from the classics, but these are, after all, available in any library, and what you are giving us is not." The protest "too literary" shows up again from Mr. N. in Detroit–"Let us live in the present"–though he does find the past "beneficial, helping me understand myself a little more" (August-September 1956, p. 44).

Even Dorr Legg, writing in an editorial as William Lambert, says, "There are readers who might perhaps favor the literary-coterie, charm-school, Continental approach," but *ONE* must march on; the cover of this issue shows two men with their arms around each other (January 1958, p. 5). Mr. M. in Riverside (September 1958, p. 30) suggests that subscriptions may be down because *ONE* is not practical enough: "Theoretical and historical aspects of the subjects are available to anyone with opportunity and intelligence to run an index in any good library." But that's not everyone: Mr. P. in Cedar Rapids writes in to say "I know absolutely nothing about homosexuality. There is precious little information on this subject at the local library, none at the college library" (March 1965, p. 31). It is instructive to compare these complaints with a review of Bernard Sergent's *Homosexuality in Greek Myth* from Kepner's clippings file (*Washington Blade*, April 17, 1987, pp. 13-14), protesting that it "reads like a doctoral dissertation. Only the most dedicated reader will be able to wade through it."

There were also testimonials from a grateful public. A female reader from Hamden, Connecticut, says she especially appreciates the nonfiction articles, since she "is not in a position to do research" (July 1954, p. 25). Mr. L. in Baltimore finds the "anti-intellectualism" in the Letters column worrisome (January 1956, p. 28). Mr. L. in Indianapolis responds enthusiastically to the two-page spread with the Renaissance bust and the *Phaedrus* reference, explaining how it fits in with his reading (February 1956, p. 28): "I attempted to paste the illustration inside Mary Renault's Charioteer, but the volume was too small, so I put it inside Hadrian, which I thought was next in spirit, so that I can preserve it where it belongs." Some readers literally shared their books: the issue of April 1955 lists donations to the ONE library (p. 29), including the "limited numbered edition" of Richard Burton's *The Sotadic Zone* that is still in the ONE Archives.

The lists of places to buy *ONE* begin in April 1954 (p. 30), with a roster of bookstores, addresses, and phone numbers in seven cities: Berkeley; Cleveland; Copenhagen; Gardiner, Maine; Los Angeles; San Francisco (City Lights); and New York (dial ORegon 3).[23] The May issue of that year discusses the magazine's mail circulation, saying it has risen from 146 in January 1953 to include subscribers in all forty-eight states and around the world, with 2704 in New York, 2536 in Los Angeles, and under a thousand in the rest of the world (p. 2). Mr. T. in Studio City (November 1960, p. 31) was "both pleased and appalled" to find that *ONE* was advertising on the radio–on a show on KBLA that featured "pop music and hill-billy songs." The editor asked him to name another show that would accept advertising from *ONE*, and suggested that this target audience was worth reaching. Paid subscriptions were always a problem for the magazine, and the Letters column often carried touching tributes from faithful readers who were sending in a few dollars every month to help the magazine keep going. (A report of the Mattachine Society convention of April 30, 1955, gave the *Review*'s circulation as 314 and the cash on hand as $9.23 [*Mattachine Review* May-June, end matter].) The December 1954 issue of *ONE* carried a geographical count of subscribers, showing them broken down by state and in twenty-three countries abroad, with most in Canada (p. 28); in July 1958 the editor notes a substantial subscriber base in Australia and New Zealand (p. 30). In September 1958 many letters discuss starting branches, and Mr. N. in Vancouver stresses "the dire need in this country" (p. 29). By January 1963, the newsstand listing showed *ONE* as available in twenty-one American cities (back cover), now including Long Beach, Sarasota, Atlanta, New Orleans, Baltimore, Detroit, Kansas City, Omaha, Toledo, Oklahoma City, Portland, Philadelphia, Dallas, Houston, and San Antonio, along with Denmark and Holland.

In turn, the European magazines repeatedly ran ads in *ONE*. Dal McIntire's "tangents" column carried excerpts from news stories from all over the world, evidently sent in by readers. A letter signed "Socrates" chronicles a Communist investigation at the University of Florida (September 1959, pp. 31-32); a letter from Mr. F. in Cape Town tells of finding a copy of *ONE* left behind in a hotel room drawer (October 1959, p. 29).

Buying *ONE* on a newsstand was a public act that took courage; Mr. L. in New York describes his newsstand man hiding a copy in a newspaper for him (January 1961, p. 32). Other readers occasionally wrote in to describe themselves as reading the magazine in public (for example the "defiant" Rev. G. J. T. in Los Angeles, July 1964, p. 30)–a big deal, because *ONE* carried on its cover the legible subtitle "The Magazine of Homosexuality," later "The Homosexual Viewpoint." This conscious decision on the part of the Board distinguishes *ONE* from the Victorian periodicals and from the previous and contemporary European magazines, which were not available on newsstands and never carried such an explicit label, though coded labels, often using the word "friend," were common. The label gave reading the magazine the potential to become a political action, and the newsstand lists and geographical distributions, as well as the Letters column, show how wide a reach the magazine came to have–bringing Plato with it. So often in the history of sexual subcultures it is impossible to know what is happening in the hinterlands; if a group is marginal in the cities, consider the situation for its members in villages, also constantly diminished in number by departures to the city; nor is the village Plato reading group often noticed in even the marginal city publications, so that without local archival work, luck, and the accident of local courage or tolerance, most local subcultures go unrecorded. The same of course is true for most people, period, but the historian aches for the small lost histories that would balance the remarkable with the widespread.[24]

All this enterprise must be seen in light of the then-current legal and political climate. The story of *ONE*'s battle against the Los Angeles Postmaster has been well told by Rodger Streitmatter (1995, pp. 31-36); the 1954 issue stopped by the Postmaster contains nothing today remotely classifiable as obscene. A letter from G. S. in Washington, D.C., tells of his experience in a previous American group, founded in 1925, which published a paper called *Friendship and Freedom*; a postal inspector tried to have the group "indicted for publishing an 'obscene paper' although of course, like your paper, no physical references were made" (July 1953, p. 22). The "tangents" column is full of accounts of police raids and witchhunts; even the coded Classics were not safe, with a "Beverly Hills bookseller feuding with Postoffice censors" over the sale of *Lysistrata* (May 1955, p. 4).

ONE's repeated mentions and lists of homophile groups at home and abroad chart their own history. A particularly close relationship with *Der Kreis* and its leader, Rolf, begins with a story on *Der Kreis* in 1955 (September, pp. 21-22). This is followed in August-September 1957 (pp. 4-7) by a "salute" to Rolf and *Der Kreis*, complete with cover photo, in which Rolf traces the magazine's history back to 1932; he stresses its avoidance of political activism, which was felt to be much too risky. In December 1958, the English Editor, here Rudolph Burkhardt, has visited Los Angeles and sends back a report on "Christmas in Zurich" (pp. 5-8), describing the annual party (they put on a play every year with an all-male cast; Jews are rarely heard from even in *ONE*, let alone *Der Kreis*). By 1961 *ONE* is reporting on the death of some European magazines and the restrictions on sale they faced–most circulated only through member subscriptions: "There is very little freedom in talking to oneself" (February, pp. 4-5).

The ancient past, then, as seen in *ONE* and its cousins, is both potentially liberatory and potentially exclusive, accessible and inaccessible, useful both as code and as model, but not for its own sake. Nor does this exhaust its meanings.

GREECE BUT NOT ROME

The reader of the magazines would have picked up a curiously one-sided picture of the ancient Mediterranean. A list of maxims on friendship in *Weg zu Freundschaft* quotes six ancient authors, five of them Greek (1970, *Heft* 228, p. 52; the sixth is Marcus Aurelius, who wrote in Greek). An excerpt in *Weg* from Horst Gasse's *Liebesdichtung der Griechen und Römer* quotes the book's praise of epigrams to boys, "vor allem in hellenistischer Zeit" (1965, 15.1, p. 16). A special Lesbian issue of *ONE* has a cover featuring line drawings of women in Greek dress (February 1954). A writer in April 1954 cites "the necessity for the individual . . . to assume his life in a naked direct sense, as the Ancient Greeks did" (p. 6). A writer in May 1954 echoes him (p. 20): "We are not yet near the freedom that permitted . . . an ancient Greek to proudly announce he had been chosen by another man"; he extols "the magic of Athens, that small city that created in a few generations a culture still dominant in every western nature" (p. 23). The same writer gives Athenian glory as the answer to "the sin of Sodom" (June 1954, p. 6). Big Brothers of America, the foster-fathers group, are said with amusement to be following the Platonic model (March 1956, p. 5). Writing on the 1907 Prince Eulenburg scandal, Jim Kepner uses the example of "the regimented Spartans" and "the cultured Athenians" to explain how gay romance could have flourished in Prussia (October-November 1956, p. 5); he turns to Greece again as a culture that made good use of "the talents possessed by homosexuals" (August-September 1957, p. 12). "These incredible Greeks" are credited with evolving the basis of "our modern scientific theory" of homosexuality (April 1957, p. 5). A piece on "The Older Homosexual" praises "the ancient Greek man-and-boy relationships" (June-July 1957, p. 6). A survey of censorship starts with Socrates (August 1958, p. 4). A reviewer paraphrases: homosexuality "is rarely taken in stride in the modern world as it was by the Greeks" (April 1961, p. 20). Indeed, in a passage of self-analysis, Marcel Martin observes that step one in any argument on behalf of homosexuality is to instance "the glorious example of the manly Greek warriors and athletes" (November 1961, p. 7). Dorr

Legg's history syllabus divides "homophilic literatures" into Non-Hellenic, Pre-Hellenic, Hellenic, Post-Hellenic, the Hellenic Revival (Renaissance), and Neo-Hellenism. Don Slater is unusual in listing "the Greeks, the Romans, and some Orientals" as models of high civilization (December 1957, p. 4).

The word "Greek" itself is used to mean "homoerotic," and not only in the familiar phrase "Greek love." A ONE Institute "Symposium" held at San Francisco and co-sponsored by the Daughters of Bilitis featured "The Glory that was Greece" and "The 'New Athens' in America" (October-November 1957, p. 21). A short story about a doomed Lesbian crush at a horrible dinner party puts the line "It seemed so Greek" into the heroine's mouth as a suspicious gaffe, recouped by her hostess's respect for culture (January 1958, p. 10). The "tangents" column reports a mailing case against three "beefcake" magazines, including *Grecian Guild Pictorial* (November 1960, p. 16). And the term "Greek gods" recurs to mean "unattainably handsome young men": in a letter from Mr. T. W. in Brooklyn (January 1960, p. 7–here contrasted with "the intellectual side of life"); in a letter from Mr. A. in Paterson, NJ (July 1960, p. 30); in a poem (October 1963, p. 25). As Maria Wyke has pointed out, a similar code prevailed in the physical-culture magazines and films of this period (Wyke, 1999, pp. 364-67): note the appearance of the short film "Days of Greek Gods" in 1954.[25]

The fact that Greece was not the only ancient Mediterranean culture often appears in a canonical narrative in which Greece is good and Rome is bad. Questions from the floor at the first national DOB convention show this idea in general circulation (reprinted in *ONE*, July 1960, p. 18):

> One person asked if, as Miss Lyon had suggested, Lesbianism had generally become acceptable in societies like the late Roman empire that were on the point of collapse. Someone else said that in contrast to the Romans, who admittedly degenerated from puritanism to licentiousness, the Greeks and Egyptians had both risen and fallen with free acceptance of male and female homosexuality. Dr. Reider observed that reports of the sexual proclivities of the ancients weren't always too reliable.

A review of *Eros: An Anthology of Male Friendship* says, "The sexual mores of the ancients are familiar enough to us. In this, as in so many things, it is the Greeks who represent an ideal, lost humanism–lost to us as well as to the Romans, whose more spurious sophistication seems closer to the temper of the present age" (*ONE*, September 1963, p. 22). The reviewer notes the uneasiness of the editors of the anthology with the "physical aspects" of same-sex love. Kepner's notes on Wainwright Churchill's 1971 *Homosexual Behavior Among Males* contrast the joyous, unfettered Greeks with the dour, priggish Romans, with their "basic distrust of the sexual instinct," also somehow incorporating "general moral decay, sheer voluptuousness [. . .] sadomasochism, exploitation of slaves [. . .] Such cruel and eccentric acts were virtually unknown among the Greeks [. . .] homosexuality [. . .] among the Romans suffered a marked decline in comparison with the Greek ideal." Paul D. Hardman in the *Voice* piece on the phallus (August 14, 1981, p. 8) starts with "[t]he easy-going Greeks" and fast-forwards to "[t]he destruction of the classic Greek ethos with the collapse of the Roman world." The London *Times* review of Anthony Birley's biography of Hadrian (Kepner clippings file) observes that "the Romans did not regard pederasty with the same tolerance, let alone enthusiasm, as sophisticated Greeks," and this has been marked with pen in the margin.

Though the "Greece good, Rome bad" dichotomy appears each time as just something everybody knows, this stereotype in fact goes back to the nineteenth century and has complicated roots in politics long gone. The adoption of the Roman Republic as a model by the designers of the French Revolution caused a reaction against Rome especially in England, while Winckelmann's exaltation of Greek art and the adoration of Greece within the Romantic movement had long-lasting effects.[26] Meanwhile, imperial Rome came to be adopted as a model for imperial England, though with some unease due to Roman persecutions of Christians and the martyrdoms in the arena. Thus Victorian culture came to be saturated with art and popular novels featuring cruel deaths, or narrow escapes, in the arena, in which early Christian purity was contrasted with Roman sensuality and brutality. That these works addressed a double audience of Christians and fans of sensuality and brutality, often difficult to distinguish, is by now well established (Prettejohn, 1999; Vance, 1997, pp. 204-13, 247-68). Thus it is not surprising that Burton in *The Sotadic Zone*, having quoted ancient sources from Sappho to the *Priapea*, remarks, "Pederastia had in Greece, I have shown, its noble and ideal side; Rome, however, borrowed her malpractices, like her religion and polity, from those ultra-material Etruscans and debauched with a brazen face . . . With increased luxury the evil grew" (p. 37).

J. Z. Eglinton's *Greek Love* (1964) shows the direct link between the Victorians and the 1960s. Eglinton's book is remarkable for the thoroughness of his reading, mostly in translation but sometimes in the original; his chapter on Greece covers Meleager, Strato, and Philostratus along with the usual canon, while his chapter on Rome covers Catullus, the *Priapea*, Virgil, Tibullus ("a neurotic friend of Horace," p. 284), Horace, Statius, Martial ("doubtless a case of interest to psychiatrists," p. 289), Suetonius, and Juvenal. This does not mean he liked what he read. The period of Strato and Philostratus (the high Roman empire) he dubs "this largely dreary period" (p. 266), "this frankly decadent period" (p. 274). The chapter on Rome leads with "The Romans were originally, and largely remained, a race of pragmatic and brutal peasants" (p. 276). And the chapter concludes with a long quotation from Symonds' *A Problem in Greek Ethics* (p. 294):

> Greece merged in Rome: but, though the Romans aped the arts and manners of the Greeks, they never truly caught the Hellenic spirit. Even Virgil only trod the court of the Gentiles of Greek culture. It was not, therefore, possible that any social custom so peculiar as paiderastia should flourish on Latin soil. Instead of Cleomenes and Epameinondas, we find at Rome Nero the bride of Sporus, and Commodus the public prostitute. Alkibiades is replaced by the Mark Antony of Cicero's *Philippic*. Corydon, with artificial notes, takes up the song of Ageanax. The melodies of Meleager are drowned in the harsh discords of Martial. Instead of love, lust was the deity of the boy-lover on the shores of the Tiber.

John Addington Symonds' *A Problem in Greek Ethics* was written in 1873, privately printed in 1883, but not widely available until 1896, and then still only from a small press. It must be among the most widely read underground documents ever written, and is available today on the Internet.[27] By maintaining this commonly held Victorian attitude, Symonds saw to it that few after him would bother to read Roman homoerotic texts; even one who did, like Eglinton, would know how he was supposed to read. The effects of Symonds' authoritative opinion are still felt today in the balance of scholarly work on Greek versus Roman homoeroticism. Roman homoerotic love poetry became almost invisible, as did the existence of a Roman sex/gender system in which pederasty was normative. Along with a popular tradition about the lives of some emperors, "Rome" is used in the magazines as shorthand for "brutal sensuality."[28]

Yet even the notional Greece of the magazines bore the seeds of its own end. In August 1963, *ONE* scandalized its readers by printing a set of line drawings that included one of a naked sailor sitting on what appeared to be a toilet. Amongst the horrified reactions printed in the Letters column was one from a representative of the Mattachine Society, who suggested (October 1963, p. 29):

> If your purpose in printing the drawing was to test the law, a sensuous Greek statue or a critically well-regarded painting or drawing of a male nude by an exceptional artist would have been much more appropriate. People get the impression from such a drawing, from some of the other art work, and from the stories in ONE that homosexuals are not the cultured persons and do not have the elevated culture which shines through such persons as John Addington Symonds, Edward Carpenter, Walt Whitman, and others like them.

The Mattachine letter shows the use of high art to defer or deny the physicality of same-sex love, much as Plato is appealed to for proof of its spiritual nature, and the letter's insistence on external validation attests to the internalized homophobia that is driving this bus. But the time was clearly passing when it was necessary to print a picture of a Greek statue in lieu of what the readers really wanted: a picture of a living person, available in the present.[29]

FANTASY

The implication of Greece and Rome in the fantasy life of the magazines' readers is amply attested. This is especially true in the European magazines, with their classicizing titles and their coded references to "friendship" (as in Plato and the Sacred Band). They also used photographs much more frequently than did the American magazines. *Weg zu Freundschaft* printed photographs inside the front cover of each issue, as well as in the body of the magazine, and sometimes the lead photographs showed classical sculpture rather than a live model (e.g., May 1954; 15.1 and 15.3, 1965). The use of classical art to legitimate discussion of ancient sexual behavior–and sneak in a peek–appears again in Kepner's clippings file in a two-part series in the magazine *Sex Behavior*. Good Greece is illustrated with photographs of art depicting wives, hetaerae, boys, and famous men who had boyfriends (1971, 1.3, pp. 61-67): "the Greeks revered the genitals as holy organs of generation, not objects of shame." Bad Rome is illustrated with photographs of eighteenth-century depictions of Roman orgies (1971, 1.4, pp. 82-87): "A certain crudeness, directness, and violence marked the sexuality of the Empire period."

Similar fantasies pervade the textual world of the magazines. We might usefully compare the richly allusive discourse of Victorian magazines like the *Artist and Journal of Home Culture* or *The Studio*, with their poems purportedly inspired by paintings seen in galleries, themselves inspired by classical texts and art, and their lists of suitable topics for paintings, inspired by classical texts, and their reviews and descriptions of illustrations and poems and paintings, sometimes going directly back to classical sources, sometimes mediated by Leonardo or Michelangelo (see Reade, 1970 for an anthology and d'Arch Smith, 1970 for a catalogue; note that in the *Artist and Journal* it's all buried in tiny type, without illustrations.) The twentieth-century world of allusion is by comparison impoverished, reduced to a handful of examples, and showing little consciousness of this earlier period of discourse that overlapped (barely) with its own (Edward Carpenter, for example, died in 1929; Jim Kepner was born around 1923). A fading memory of Oscar Wilde waving from a train platform, that's about it.[30] Yet nothing so starkly shows that we are here dealing with a readership separate from that of the *Artist and Journal*, never mind Wilde and his friends. After all, both *Love in Earnest* and *Sexual Heretics* were published in 1970, and the prefaces of both attest to the freshness of the tracks of the Uranian poets. There were doubtless people among the readers of *ONE* and its contemporaries who knew and understood that Victorian discourse, which now labored under the disadvantage of sounding quaint as well as dated, but the magazines are now not being written by such people, and they are written for an audience whose aesthetic options included "Rawhide" (1959-65) and Tomorrowland (1955). Classics just ain't the only game in town any more.

Yet in the European magazines it lasts a long time. *Der Kreis* in 1952 has a lot of classical material: a serial on "L'enlévement de Ganymède" that ran from February through April, with art; an essay giving an overview of homosexual history in the West from Greece onwards, in June (pp. 21-24); a collection of excerpts from Yourcenar's *Memoirs of Hadrian* translated into German, with a poem, comments, and a photograph of the Vatican Antinous, in July (pp. 9-15); a photo essay by Rolf, "Ganymed und der Adler," with pictures–a young man in shorts titled "Ganymed 1952," an 1890 oil painting, and an Art Deco bronze Ganymede in Zurich (September, pp. 14-17). *Weg zu Freundschaft* prints a Hölderlin poem on Socrates and Alcibiades (August 1954, p. 290). In 1965 *Weg* still finds antiquity stimulating, printing a short excerpt from

Rosen für Apoll, with a vision of young Athenians out for their morning ride, naked but for their little cloaks (15.1, p. 16); "Antinous 1965" (15.4, pp. 74-78); and an excerpt from the novel *Alexander* (*Heft* 176, p. 225). Alexander reappears in a two-page fantasy in which he and Hephaistion work out with the other tanned young men, who call them "Achill" and "Patroklos" (1969, *Heft* 215, pp. 7-8).

ONE liked fiction that updated classical stories, as in "The Laughter of Antinous" (January 1957, pp. 4-14), a drawing-room drama featuring characters named Domenica, Tony, and Adrian; it leads with a stanza on Antinous from a poem by Wilde. A special issue devoted to poetry (October-November 1957) begins with an editorial tracing same-sex love poetry "down through the ages," and quoting Sappho (p. 4); the issue included a poem to Sappho by Jody Shotwell in which the speaker becomes Sappho's lover (p. 12). A 1960 issue included two short poems, one identifying "Hellas" with maleness, and a comic one on eunuchs (August, pp. 16-17); the April 1962 issue ran a poem "Ganymede Revisited" (p. 11). In a Salingeresque story titled "The Spear of Cyparissus" (July 1964, pp. 27-29) a young Manhattanite tells a boy the story of one of Apollo's unlucky loves. The only full-flown fantasy really set in antiquity appears late, in August 1962 (pp. 11-14), in the story "Black Onyx and Golden Hued," a hot tale about a young blond Roman governor and the dark young barbarian prince he comes to love, set in "Laodacia." This piece forms part of *ONE*'s move toward printing more explicitly sexual material–Ann Bannon's "Beebo and Paula" ran in the April 1962 issue; though Martius Romanus and Prince Arius do no more than hold hands, they view one another's bodies in feverish detail.

The Victorian predilection for classical dress-up (see Beard, 2000, pp. 37-53) surfaces in Los Angeles at ONE's Midwinter banquets. The January 1958 issue of *ONE* carries a notice of the festivities, including "A Dramatic Portrayal" called "THE PATTERN OF SPARTA" (back cover); the performance is described in full in the March issue (pp. 7-8). It was a dramatic reading by "Miss Rachel Rosenthal, actress and dramatic coach" featuring a love scene between "King Kleomenes of Sparta and Panteus his lover"; at the end of this "delicately tasteful reading" Miss Rosenthal was presented with a bouquet of yellow roses: an early appearance by a now legendary performance artist. The 1959 banquet featured a variety show put on by the drama department of the Education Division, including readings from the Greek Anthology, Sappho, and Michelangelo: "Few of the women in attendance will ever forget Rachel Rosenthal as she read the Sappho poems in an astonishingly sheer costume" (April 1959, p. 16).

A similar respect for antiquity combined with its use as excuse shows up in the advertisements for classical paraphernalia that begin to appear in *ONE* around 1960. As well as the medallions discussed above, they marketed statuettes of Michelangelo's David (September 1960, p. 28) and of the "Sleeping Satyr," which came with a magnetic figleaf (December 1963, p. 15). As the magazine began to carry more sexually explicit stories and poems, it also carried ads for BUTCH, a company that sold bath oil as well as a personal massager that attached to the end of your vacuum cleaner. The BUTCH bath oil ads included the line, "The Greeks and Romans had pleasures like this" (November 1962, p. 23). An ad began appearing in 1964 headed "TO HOLLYWOOD FROM ROME: THE TOGA," offering "a beautiful blue and gold short gown" for "that stately roman look" (May, p. 30)–never mind the white, baggy folds of an actual toga. Art combined with fiction in a 1964 story, "Donatello's David," about a bookseller and a boy who buys a book with a photograph of the sculpture on its cover (September, pp. 13-15). And, spectacularly, art combined with life in the December 1964 issue, which featured an illustrated cover story on a gay male couple whose house and garden were lavishly decorated with "many marble and bronze busts and seductive ancient and Renaissance glorifications of the male figure" (pp. 7-11, front and back covers).

And *ONE* commodified more than art. Travel stories appeared sporadically, e.g., a letter from Mr. P. in Michigan recommending a trip to Naples, where one should go to the Vomero section to see "the glories that were once of Pompeii" (November 1960, p. 31). (Compare a writer for *Weg zu Freundschaft* who visits Rome in 1969 and muses, as he watches a man/boy couple kiss at a concert: "Rome is, after all, so tolerant, and that's how it's always been. Here, where the Caesars and gladiators, the catamites and youthful partners were at home–just like in Athens."[31] A rhapsodic list of cruising sites follows.)[32] Vicarious sex tourism is dramatically upstaged by the ONE "cruise" around Europe, culminating in a trip to Naples and Pompeii, to be led by William Lambert (= Dorr Legg). The announcements and ads begin in November 1960 (back cover), progress through a grand set of letters from the heads of European groups inviting the ONE group to visit (September 1961, pp. 30-31), and culminate in a fiasco when the travel agency falls through on the arrangements (October 1961, back cover); the November editorial (p. 4) delivers a warning to readers against the agency.

Moreover, the magazines refer the reader to a wider market of fantasies in the form of historical novels and biographies. Indeed, the *Weg zu Freundschaft* essay on Rome leads into an excerpt from Marguerite

Yourcenar's *Memoirs of Hadrian*, the most widely hailed novel of the period.[33] A critic in *Mattachine Review* seems to believe Hadrian was the actual author (November-December 1955, pp. 21-24). In comparison, *Weg* reprints a dismissive review of *Antinous, Geliebter!* which calls it a historical and fit only for amateurs (1967, *Heft* 200, pp. 227-28). Mary Renault is another favorite writer; a review of *The Charioteer* appears in *ONE* in June 1955 (p. 17: "do not be misled by the sex of the author"), and a notice of *The Last of the Wine* appears in the "Book Service" section (February 1957, p. 6), with a review, condensed from *Der Kreis*, printed later in the issue (pp. 33-34). (The Book Service provided a modest mail-order option for *ONE* readers, and promoted books the Board found worthwhile along with assorted packages of back issues of *ONE*.) A review of Renault's *The King Must Die* appears in August 1958 (p. 26), and the Book Service plugs it as "spiced with homosexual scenes" in the next issue (p. 25). By 1962 A. E. Smith is using Renault to demonstrate what a golden age Greece was in comparison with the present (June, p. 8).

Though the magazines deal only rarely with popular culture–movies, TV, rock and roll–they do take notice when antiquity hits the screen. An early look at the Dutch magazine *Vriendschap* notes that it carried a review of the movie *Julius Caesar* (*ONE*, April 1955, p. 33); in 1959, on the German film *The Third Sex*, the reviewer says that "[t]he highlight of the picture is unquestionably The Spirit of Ancient Greece: A fast wrestling match by two almost naked youths in sexy white satin trunks" (October, p. 19). Don Slater discussed the film on a radio panel (September, p. 25). The "tangents" column includes a description of a BBC broadcast on Greek sculpture, sent in by a reader (September 1960, p. 11), and provides a brief subversive take on it.

In the early 1960s things were opening up. In 1961 *ONE* prints a passage from John Barth's *The Sot-Weed Factor* about Plato, Greek sculpture, and male genitalia (July, p. 24). Gore Vidal's book on the emperor Julian is reviewed in 1964 (August, p. 20). In 1963, a review discusses *Family Favorites*, a novel about the Roman emperor Heliogabalus, whose androgynous persona had in 1888 inspired a painting by Alma-Tadema that provoked a series of strictures in the *Artist and Journal*.[34] Now the reviewer treats the emperor with indulgence, claims "the Rome of his time placed no stigma upon homosexuality," and praises the novel's "mature objectivity" (February, pp. 22-24). The issue of March 1963 includes a group review of three unexpurgated art books: Mulk Raj Anand, *Kama Kala*, and Jean Marcadé, *Roma Amor* and *Essay on Erotic Elements in Greek Art* (pp. 6-9). Here, though, the

Romans are back to their old brutal selves ("They were engaged in struggle, in conquest, in submission," p. 7), while the Greeks are still upholding "sensuality for its own sake" (p. 8). And a reader subsequently writes in to complain that the books reviewed are "priced too high for general interest" (July 1963, p. 24). Indeed a sense of ambivalence about classical fantasies goes back to a James Barr review of *Memoirs of Hadrian* in the *Mattachine Review* of 1955 (July-August, pp. 38-40): he complains that the magazine's readership needs to focus on now, not "the miasma of antiquity" (p. 40).

CONCLUSION

The use of Greece and Rome in the nascent gay movement posed a classic problem in vanguardism. Is it possible to use the master's tools to dismantle his house? Do we need them, and does teaching their use corrupt us? The dilemma oddly recapitulates a debate in sixth-century Christianity that led to the death of classical rhetoric–along with pederastic poetry–as the evangelical church rejected learned language for simple words everyone could understand (Riché, 1976, pp. 90-95). For *ONE* and its cousins, the past remains useful as long as talking about the present remains dangerous. But times change. *ONE*'s report brags of the Supreme Court victory, "Never before have homosexuals claimed their rights as citizens"; not even the Greeks "have managed to mean so much to so many" (February 1958, p. 17). In September 1960, Mr. T. in Miami sends money and comments, "It's a wonder a moment in history has come to pass that we even have something to give to" (p. 29). The sketch of the sailor in August 1963 marks a sense of real freedom, despite the shock to readers (Ann Carll Reid wrote in to say she was changing her will [December, p. 30]). In November 1963, a reader writes in about the "Negroes' Freedom March": "Perhaps the gay people can learn something from them" (p. 31). Five years to Stonewall.[35]

At this point shadow scholarship could have emerged into official knowledge, and indeed the first open discussions of ancient sex/gender systems begin when the children of the sixties finish graduate school (Henderson, 1975; Pomeroy, 1975; see Richlin, 1997). But there was a gap, filled by activism. Kepner hoped the foundation built by amateurs would be used by professionals someday; sadly, few professional classicists have even been aware of underground work–mainly Jonathan Walters and Jack Winkler. The world of scholarship in which Greeks and Romans matter for their own sakes lies as far as ever from the world of activism. Both worlds, though, are ones *ONE* worked for and helped to create, truly using print to build a culture. Faced with a problem in the circulation of knowledge via the luxury book trade, translation, and libraries, they sidestepped it using pulp magazines, newsstands, and the mails. As always, some loved history, and their work reminds us that "amateur" comes from *amator*, lover: they did it for love, and it shows. As I completed the reading for this essay, a photograph of Del Martin and Phyllis Lyon getting married in San Francisco topped the front page of the *Los Angeles Times* (Friday, February 13, 2004)–Del Martin, who hits the pages of *ONE* in 1961 as the leader of the Daughters of Bilitis.[36] It was good to see it in the papers.

NOTES

1. For Greece and Rome as an "alibi" for homophile publications, see Wyke (1999). "Alibi" in Latin literally means "elsewhere"; for the use of antiquity and the exotic as the "elsewhen" and "elsewhere," see Richlin (1993a), and below.

2. Materials read in their entirety for this study at the ONE National Gay & Lesbian Archives include: the print run of *ONE* from 1953 through March 1965; *Mattachine Review* for 1955; selected issues of *Weg zu Freundschaft* and *Der Kreis/Le Cercle*; various monographs; Jim Kepner's clippings file on ancient history; Jim Kepner's and Dorr Legg's teaching files for the history courses at the ONE Institute. *ONE* continued publication through 1969, but there was a schism in the spring of 1965, and production values dropped sharply by January 1964, along with interest in history. I have not been able to do justice to the work of Harry Hay and *Mattachine Review*; much remains to be done. For basic method and principles of historicizing print cultures, see Brake (2001). Materials here have been quoted as originally printed, without the use of "sic," which counters the aims of this essay; spellings of Greek and Roman names and words may also vary due to inconsistencies in modern conventions.

3. See Burn (1862); Mayor (1874); Stray (2000) on Oxford vs. Cambridge. On the history of pornography, see Kendrick (1988); DeJean (2002).

4. For a brief history of the Loeb Classical Library, with its rationale, see http://www.hup.harvard.edu/Loeb/history.html. Note there the excerpt from Virginia Woolf's 1917 review in the *Times Literary Supplement*, stressing how "the existence of the amateur was recognised by the publication of this Library, and to a great extent made respectable." A full translation of Roman satire became available in 1914 (Lewis Evans, *The Satires of Juvenal, Persius, Sulpicia, and Lucilius*. London: G. Bell and Sons).

5. Letters to the Editor in *ONE* always included place of origin. Before July 1955, they are signed with the letter "m" or "f"; starting with that issue, most letters are signed "Mr." or "Miss" with an initial.

6. On the history of the Mattachines, see D'Emilio (1983, pp. 84-85); Timmons (1990, pp. 144, 150-51) discusses founder Harry Hay and the group's roots in the Party and elsewhere. Kepner's biography at http://www.usc.edu/isd/archives/oneigla/bulletin/Profiles/Kepner/KepObit.html states that he was expelled from the Party when it became known he was gay.

7. For the story, see *ONE*, February 1955, p. 9, where the idea is attributed to "Guy Rousseau, a hard-working young negro member of the group"–a rare mention of race.

8. In March 1965 (p. 16) *ONE* noted the end of *Vriendschap*, then one of the oldest European magazines, and its replacement by *Dialoog*, which would be the first European magazine to be sold on newsstands.

9. Kepner's sources here are unidentified; the emperors from Caesar through Nero, plus Galba, would be most easily tied to same-sex love through Suetonius *Twelve Caesars*, while the lives of Hadrian and Heliogabalus are attested mainly in the less well known *Historia Augusta*. By 1974, the probable date of these notes, he might also have derived this list from secondary sources, for example Garde (1964). Connections between Marcus Aurelius and same-sex love seem to derive solely from his denials in the *Meditations*, rather than from his letters to his teacher Fronto, which are never mentioned in any of the magazines here surveyed. But Marcus is very rarely included in lists like these; elsewhere to my knowledge only at *The Gay and Lesbian Review*, March-April 2003, p. 8: "There have always been rumors about a number of ancient Roman rulers, starting with Julius Caesar and including Hadrian and the great Marcus Aurelius." He is not in Garde (1964) or in Kiefer (1934).

10. Ruth, Naomi, Plato, and Sappho, Kepner in *ONE* August-September 1957, p. 12; David and Ruth, *ONE* December 1960, p. 5, editorial by Lyn Pedersen (= Kepner); a poem about David and Jonathan, *ONE* December 1955, p. 27; David and Jonathan again, *ONE* September 1953, pp. 22-23, and again in March 1961, p. 31 (in a letter from Mr. F. in San Francisco); Achilles and Patroklos, Alexander and Hephaistion, *Weg zu Freundschaft* January 1954, pp. 5-6; comic poem citing Julius Caesar and "the Greeks," *ONE* March 1954, p. 20; "Gomorrah, Pompeii, Corinth, Tyre, / Rome, London . . . / Athens" in a comic poem by "Brother Grundy," an erudite contributor, *ONE* October 1954, p. 19; indirect reference to the Sacred Band of Thebes, *ONE* November 1953, p. 11; review of biography of Julius Caesar, *ONE* July 1955, p. 7; a book of verse biographies, *Uncommon Men*, reviewed *ONE* March 1964, p. 28. This sort of collecting persisted in later gay ephemera; Kepner's clippings file includes, from a series of cartoons in the *Washington Blade*, commemorations of Julius Caesar (July 12, 1985), Tiberius (November 11, 1983), Hadrian (July 8, 1988), and classicist Edith Hamilton (August 9, 1985). *ONE* even covered a flap over the naming of the Walt Whitman bridge across the Delaware River: the Holy Name Society campaigned against it as a "threat to decency," and *ONE* quoted a counter protest that if Walt Whitman was out, so was Michelangelo; Kepner threw in St. Augustine (March 1956, p. 7). This is all much in the spirit of Edward Carpenter's *Ioläus*, but he is rarely mentioned.

11. For a history of the Institute, see Legg et al. (1994, pp. 9-77); for some samples of the kinds of historical projects done there, Legg et al. (1994, pp. 80-116).

12. On Kains Jackson and Gleeson White, see Brake (2001, pp. 110-23); Reade (1970, pp. 40-47); d'Arch Smith (1970, pp. 17-18, 59-66).

13. Some examples: *Weg zu Freundschaft* identifies "Sagitta" as the Greek word for "arrow" (it's Latin; July 1958, p. 213, and see below on "Greece not Rome"). An essay in *ONE* in 1955 attributes to Magnus Hirschfeld the opinion that the Greek "Hetaerae" (courtesans) were actually male-to-female transsexuals (not so; March, p. 28, in the "Science" section). A *ONE* essay states that both homosexuality and incest were accepted by the Greeks (not incest, and not all forms of homosexuality; April 1960, p. 8). Compare an article in *Nightlife* (February 13, 1994, pp. 12-13, Kepner clippings file), which describes "Human Degradation in the Roman Slave Market," making up most of the details and exemplifying a long tradition of imagining Roman excesses.

458   SAME-SEX DESIRE AND LOVE IN GRECO-ROMAN ANTIQUITY

14. The Aristophanes translation is not attributed and the Plato translation says only "as translated by W. Hamilton"; this would be the Penguin edition of the *Symposium*, translated by Walter Hamilton and first published in 1951. The Aristophanes is copied, with alterations, from *Aristophanes: The Eleven Comedies* (New York: Liveright Publishing), possibly from the 1943 seventh edition, which was widely marketed. This book credits no translator, and itself has a colorful history: Liveright pirated it from a limited edition published in 1912 in London by the Athenian Society, and the first Liveright version (1928) was a deluxe edition, "published for subscribers only," with Art Deco illustrations by Jean de Bosschère. The Liveright translation was already somewhat bowdlerized: for example, line 142 literally says, "And where's your dick?" (*kai pou peos*?); Liveright renders this "Where's the sign of your manhood, pray?" Kepner changes this to "Where's your equipment, pray?" For a full literal translation of lines 134-43, see Richlin (1997, p. 31).

15. Compare translations of Pausanias's speech from the *Symposium* in *Der Kreis* for December 1952, into German (pp. 7-9) and French (pp. 45-48). *Mattachine Review* reacted to the *ONE* series with a piece in its Christmas issue on love both Christian and Greek (1955, pp. 20-21).

16. December, pp. 8-9; in Stuart Timmons' opinion, the work of Dorr Legg.

17. Garde seems to have sent the piece in over the transom; it ran here without a by-line, and the Letters section published his letter delightedly claiming credit and (characteristically) correcting several printers' errors, May 1960, p. 30.

18. For the history of bowdlerized translations of *Leucippe and Clitophon* going back to the sixteenth century, see Nakatani (2004).

19. Reviews: Bailey (1955), a forerunner of Boswell (1980), in *Mattachine Review*, November-December 1955, pp. 10-12, and by Jim Kepner in *ONE*, November 1955, pp. 19-21; Cory (1956), which included classic essays by Symonds, Burton, and Licht, in *ONE*, June-July 1956, p. 28; Flacelière (1962) in *ONE*, January 1963, pp. 25-26; Eglinton (1964), in *Weg zu Freundschaft* 1965, *Heft* 175, pp. 213-14.

20. The strength of this tradition now clarifies for me the attitude of Nick Tosches, reviewing *The Garden of Priapus* in the *Village Voice* in 1984: he took me to task for not using Burton (1885-86). Despite the best efforts of Jack Winkler, who was a reader of my dissertation, the world of Burton then made no contact with the world of Yale Classics.

21. Compare a later letter in which Daniel bristles at an article on the crackdown on homosexuality in French law, November 1964, p. 30. For *Arcadie*'s encounters with Michel Foucault, see Davidson (2001; 2004).

22. *ONE* April 1958, pp. 22-23, a reprint from the Toronto *Globe and Mail*; October 1958, p. 24, letter from Chicago; *Weg zu Freundschaft* 1965, 15.2, p. 37; compare *GCN*, October 1980, pp. 13-14, Kepner clippings file, "The Fall of Rome and Other Bullshit": "an old canard."

23. See further lists July 1954, p. 28, adding Minneapolis, Chicago, and Salt Lake City; November 1954, inside front cover, adding Mexico City, Washington, D.C., and San Jose.

24. Compare a *New Yorker* account of drag shows in Omaha (Singer, 2004), which walks a fine line between witnessing and patronizing: "The pageant . . . had 'such prestige that people know about it in Nashville, Kansas City, Iowa, Minnesota, all those places'" (p. 54); most of the former winners "had grown up in Omaha or found their way there after escaping from small towns on the prairie (Spearfish, South Dakota; Gering, Nebraska; Mead, Nebraska; Minot, North Dakota)" (p. 55).

25. *ONE*'s attitude towards nude photographs and muscle culture was ambivalent (see editorial, January 1961). For a discussion that dealt with "the ancient Greek ideal of physical perfection" in connection with muscle culture, see Ray Evans (January 1964, p. 6); Donald Webster Cory and John P. LeRoy (March 1964, p. 6).

26. See Turner (1989; 1993, pp. 231-61; 1999); Habinek (1998, pp. 15-33).

27. For histories of the text see d'Arch Smith (1970, p. 12); Norton n.d.; d'Arch Smith (1970, pp. 12-18), which provides an excellent view of the limits on the circulation of Symonds' work.

28. See Richlin (1992, pp. 32-56, 220-26; 1993b); Richlin forthcoming. This attitude was probably one of the main obstacles to a homophile reading of the letters of Marcus Aurelius and Cornelius Fronto.

29. Compare Wyke (1999, p. 367) tracing the same chronology for the disappearance of "classicizing circumventions for the homoerotic display of the male body."

30. The Wilde centenary in 1955 drew comment from both *Mattachine Review* and *ONE*, though largely borrowed from European magazines. A *ONE* contributor conscious of an Edwardian heritage is A. E. Smith: see his review of Carpenter's *My Days and Dreams* (July 1964, p. 23); and on Symonds, December 1964, pp. 25-26.

31. *Heft* 225, p. 244: "Vor mir ein Liebespaar . . . Er vielleicht fünfundfünfzig, rassig, gescheit, überlegen, der Freund anschmiegsam und hingebend, vielleicht zweiundzwanzig. [They kiss.] Rom ist ja so tolerant, und so war es schon immer. Hier, wo die Kaiser und Gladiatoren, wo die Lustknaben und jugendlichen Partner zu Hause waren-fast wie in Athen."

32. Compare the (pretty tame) adventures of Harry Otis in *ONE*, beginning in the June-July 1957 issue (pp. 15-16), when he encounters a *hijra*; in February 1958 (pp. 25-28) he meets a Sikh; in March 1958 (pp. 22-25) he writes a tale of a Nubian; in February 1959 (pp. 18-22) he goes to Lima. The tales were eventually collected in a volume marketed in *ONE* (May 1959, p. 25, *The Keval and Other Gay Adventures*).

33. Yourcenar was also reviewed in *ONE*, April 1955, pp. 28-29, with Eleanor Clark, *Rome and a Villa*.

34. See Prettejohn (1999); *The Artist and Journal of Home Culture*, August 1, 1888, p. 244, "a picture which we have all seen and probably condemned"; November 1, 1888, p. 335; February 1, 1890, p. 36.

35. For a brief overview of the years 1963-69, see D'Emilio and Freedman (1988, pp. 318-25).

36. *ONE*, March 1961, pp. 18-20: the DOB saw no necessity for a "Homosexual Bill of Rights"; see the DOB position paper in *ONE*, April 1961, pp. 9-10, referring readers to Martin's editorial in *The Ladder*.

REFERENCES

Bailey, Derrick Sherwin. (1955). *Homosexuality and the Western Christian Tradition*. London: Longmans, Green and Co.

Beard, Mary. (2000). *The Invention of Jane Harrison*. Cambridge, MA: Harvard UP.

Blanshard, Alastair. (2000). Hellenic fantasies: aesthetics and desire in John Addington Symonds' *A Problem in Greek Ethics*. *Dialogos*, 2, 99-122.

Boswell, John. (1980). *Christianity, Social Tolerance, and Homosexuality*. Chicago: U of Chicago P.

Brake, Laurel. (2001). *Print in Transition, 1850-1910: Studies in Media and Book History*. London: Palgrave.

Burn, R. (1862). On the course of reading for the classical tripos. In *The Student's Guide to the University of Cambridge* (pp. 103-139). Cambridge, UK: Deighton, Bell.

Burton, Richard. (1885-86). *Arabian Nights* (10 vols). Benares: Kama Shastra Society. (Privately printed, subscribers only.)

_____. (n. d.). *The Sotadic Zone*. New York: The Panurge Press. (Limited edition.)

Carpenter, Edward. (1917). *Ioläus: An Anthology of Friendship*. New York: Mitchell Kennerley.

Cory, Donald Webster (Ed.). (1956). *Homosexuality–A Cross Cultural Approach*. New York: Julian Press.

d'Arch Smith, Timothy. (1970). *Love in Earnest*. London: Routledge & Kegan Paul.

Davidson, James. (2001). Dover, Foucault and Greek homosexuality: penetration and the truth of sex. *Past and Present, 170*, 3-51.

_____. (2004, February). *Anti-Semitism and 'Greek homosexuality': Foucault and the Boasians*. Paper presented at the Literature Seminar of the Classics Faculty, University of Cambridge.

DeJean, Joan. (2002). *The Reinvention of Obscenity: Sex, Lies, and Tabloids in Early Modern France*. Chicago: U of Chicago P.

D'Emilio, John. (1983). *Sexual Politics, Sexual Communities*. Chicago: U of Chicago P.

D'Emilio, John, and Freedman, Estelle B. (1988). *Intimate Matters: A History of Sexuality in America*. New York: Harper & Row.

Dowling, Linda. (1994). *Hellenism and Homosexuality in Victorian Oxford*. Ithaca: Cornell UP.

Dunlap, David W. (1997, November 20). Jim Kepner, in 70's, is dead; historian of gay rights effort. *The New York Times*, C1.

Eglinton, J. Z. (1964). *Greek Love*. New York: Oliver Layton Press.

Flacelière, Robert. (1962). *Love in Ancient Greece*. (James Cleugh, Trans.). New York: Crown.

Garde, Noel I. (1964). *Jonathan to Gide: The Homosexual in History*. New York: Vantage Press.

Habinek, Thomas N. (1998). *The Politics of Latin Literature: Writing, Identity, and Empire in Ancient Rome*. Princeton: Princeton UP.

Henderson, Jeffrey. (1975). *The Maculate Muse*. New Haven: Yale UP.

Kendrick, Walter. (1988). *The Secret Museum*. New York: Viking Penguin.

Kiefer, Otto. (1934). *Sexual Life in Ancient Rome*. London: Abbey Library. Repr. 1976.

Legg, W. Dorr. (1959). Homosexuality in history: introductory chapter for a proposed textbook. *Homophile Studies, 6*, 93-98.

Legg, W. Dorr, Cameron, David G., and Williams, Walter. (Eds.). (1994). *Homophile Studies in Theory and Practice*. Los Angeles: One Institute Press; San Francisco: GLB Publishers.

Licht, Hans [pseud. of Paul Brandt]. (1931). *Sexual Life in Ancient Greece*. (J. H. Freese, Trans., Lawrence H. Dawson, Ed.). London: Routledge. Translation of (1925-28) *Sittengeschichte Griechenlands* (2 vols.). Dresden, Zurich: Paul Aretz.

Mayor, Joseph Bickersteth. (1874). *Guide to the Choice of Classical Books*. London: George Bell and Sons.

Meier, M. H. E., and de Pogey-Castries, L. R. (1952). *Histoire de l'amour Grec*. Paris: Guy Le Prat.

Nakatani, Saiichiro. (2004, April). *Self-censorship in early French and English translations of Achilles Tatius' Leucippe and Clitophon*. Paper presented at the meeting of the Classical Association, Leeds.

Norton, Rictor. (n.d.). The John Addington Symonds Pages. Retrieved from www.infopt.demon.co.uk/symfram1.htm.

Pomeroy, Sarah B. (1975). *Goddesses, Whores, Wives, and Slaves*. New York: Schocken.

Prettejohn, Elizabeth. (1999). 'The Monstrous Diversion of a Show of Gladiators': Simeon Solomon's *Habet!*. In Catharine Edwards (Ed.), *Roman Presences* (pp. 157-172). Cambridge: Cambridge UP.

Reade, Brian. (1970). *Sexual Heretics*. New York: Coward McCann.

Riché, Pierre. (1976). *Education and Culture in the Barbarian West, Sixth through Eighth Centuries*. (John J. Contreni, Trans.). Columbia, SC: U of South Carolina P.

Richlin, Amy. (1992). *The Garden of Priapus* (rev. ed.). New York: Oxford UP.

———. (1993a). The ethnographer's dilemma and the dream of a lost golden age. In Nancy Sorkin Rabinowitz and Amy Richlin (Eds.), *Feminism and the Classics* (pp. 272-303). New York: Routledge.

———. (1993b). Not before homosexuality: the materiality of the *cinaedus* and the Roman law against love between men. *Journal of the History of Sexuality*, *3*, 523-573.

———. (1997). Towards a history of body history. In Mark Golden and Peter Toohey (Eds.), *Inventing Ancient Culture* (pp. 16-35). London: Routledge.

———. (forthcoming). *Marcus + Fronto: Love Letters of a Roman Prince and His Teacher*.

Singer, Mark. (2004, March 22). Homecoming Queens. *The New Yorker*, 50-59.

Stray, Christopher. (2000). Curriculum and style in the collegiate university: Classics in nineteenth-century Oxbridge. *History of Universities*, *16*, 183-218.

Streitmatter, Rodger. (1995). *Unspeakable: The Rise of the Gay and Lesbian Press in America*. Boston: Faber and Faber.

Timmons, Stuart. (1990). *The Trouble with Harry Hay*. Boston: Alyson Publications.

Turner, Frank M. (1989). Why the Greeks and not the Romans in Victorian Britain? In G. W. Clarke (Ed.), *Rediscovering Hellenism: The Hellenic Inheritance and the English Imagination* (pp. 61-81). Cambridge: Cambridge UP.

———. (1993). *Contesting Cultural Authority: Essays in Victorian Intellectual Life*. Cambridge: Cambridge UP.

———. (1999). Christians and Pagans in Victorian Novels. In Catharine Edwards (Ed.), *Roman Presences* (pp. 173-187). Cambridge: Cambridge UP.

Vance, Norman. (1997). *The Victorians and Ancient Rome*. Oxford: Blackwell.

Winkler, John J. (1990). Methods of study: history of the field. In David M. Halperin, John J. Winkler, and Froma I. Zeitlin (Eds.), *Before Sexuality* (pp. 7-13). Princeton: Princeton UP.

Wyke, Maria. (1999). Herculean muscle! The classicizing rhetoric of bodybuilding. In James I. Porter (Ed.), *Constructions of the Classical Body* (pp. 355-379). Ann Arbor: U of Michigan P.

Table of Abbreviations

CIL *Corpus Inscriptionum Latinarum* (Berlin 1869-98)
L&S A Latin Dictionary, ed. C.T. Lewis and C. Short (Oxford 1879)
OLD The Oxford Latin Dictionary, ed. P.G.W. Glare (Oxford 1982)
TLL Thesaurus Linguae Latinae (Leipzig 1900-)

Journals

AC L'antiquité classique
AJA American Journal of Archaeology
BICS Bulletin of the Institute for Classical Studies
CA Classical Antiquity
CB The Classical Bulletin
CP Classical Philology
CQ The Classical Quarterly
CW Classical World
GRBS Greek, Roman, and Byzantine Studies
HSCP Harvard Studies in Classical Philology
ICS Illinois Classical Studies
JHS Journal of Hellenic Studies
MD Materiali e discussioni per l'analisi dei testi classici
MH Museum Helveticum
QUCC Quaderni urbinati di cultura classica
TAPA Transactions of the American Philological Association

Index of Names and Terms

Maltby, R.; *V*
Mann, C.; *S*
Männerliebe; *D*
Mapplethorpe, R.; *Md*
Marcadé, J.; *Rc*
Marcus Aurelius; *Rc*
Marcuse, H.; *In,*
Marlowe; *L*
Marrou, H. I.; *Pe, Hb*
Martial; *In, B, C, V, Md, Rc*
Martin, M.; *Rc*
Mathews, E.; *Md*
Mattachine Society, The; *Rc*
  Mattachine Review; *Rc*
  Mattachine Society Today; *Rc*
Maximus of Tyre; *K*
Mayne, X.; See Prime-Stevenson, E. I.
McCulloch, H.; *Md*
McGann, M. J.; *V*
McLane, J. L.; *Md*
Medwin, T.; *L*
Meier, M. H. E.; *D*
Meiners, C.; *D*
  History of Women; *D*
  popularization of term Männerliebe; *D*
Meleager; *Md, Rc*
Menander; *Pe, K*
meretrices; *B*
Merritt, T. M.; *Rc*
Meyer, T.; *Md*
Michelangelo; *Pr, L, Rc*
Middleton, R.; *Md*
Mill, J. S.; *L*
Milton; *Rc*
Monoson, S. S.; *Pe*
Moschus; *L*
Most, G. W.; *K*
Mullen, W.; *Hb*
Müller, K. O.; *D*
Murgatroyd, P.; *V*
Musonius Rufus; *B*

Nethercut, W. R.; *V*
Nichols, J. B. B.; *Md*

Nicholson, J. G.; *Md*
Nicholson, N.; *Hb*
Nicolson, A. F.; *Md*
Nobili, F.; *Mg*
Noel, R.; *Md*
nomos; Pr, *B*
Norton, R.; *L*
Nussbaum, M.; *Pe, Pr*
Nymphodorus; *K*

Oddi, S.; *Mg*
officium (in a sexual context); B
oikos/oikoi; Pr
Ollier, C.; *L*
ONE; *Rc*
  ONE Confidential; *Rc*
  ONE Institute; *Rc*
  ONE National Gay & Lesbian
    Archives; *Rc*
Osborn, P.; *Md*
Osborne, R.; *Pe*
Ovid; *Pe, Pr, K, B, V, Rc*

Page, D.; *K*
Paglia, C.; *Pr*
paideia; *Pe, S, Pr*
paiderastēs, paiderastia; *Pe, Pr*
paidika; *Pe*
paidotribes/paidotribai; *Hb*
Paine, W.; *Md*
pais; *Pr, Rc*
palaestra; *Hb*
Pan; *Rc*
Papyrus Oxyrhynchus; *K*
Parker, H. N.; *Pe, K, B*
Pater, W.; *Md*
paterfamilias; *B*
pathic; *Pr, B*
patronus; *B*
Patzer, H.; *In, Pe*
Paulus; *B*
Pausanias; *Hb, Hp*
Peacock, T. L.; *L*

Index Locorum

ACHILLES TATIUS
Leucippe and Clitophon
   2.35-38   *Pr*
AELIAN
Varia Historia
   3.12   *Hb*
   12.7   *Pe*
AELIUS ARISTIDES
In Defense of Oratory
   74   *Pe*
AESCHINES
Against Timarchus
   10-12   *Hb*
   12   *Hb*
   102   *Hb*
   138-39   *Hb*
AESCHYLUS
   fr. 228   *Pe*
   fr. 135-37 *TGrF*   *Hb*
ALCMAN
   1.77   *K*
   3.61-62   *K*
ALCAEUS
   fr. 303a   *K*
AMPELIUS
Liber memorialis 11.4   *B*
ANACREON
   358.8   *K*
ANTHOLOGIA PALATINA
   7.15   *Pe*
   9.506   *Pe*
   9.66   *Pe*
   12.39   *Pe*
APOLLODORUS
Bibliotheca
   3.5.5   *Hp*

ARCHILOCHUS
   fr. 25.1-4 W   *Hb*
ARISTOPHANES
Acharnenses
   515ff   *Pe*
Aves
   139-42   *Hb*
   283a   *Hb*
   284b   *Hb*
Ecclesiazusae
   920   *K*
   962-65   *Hb*
Nubes
   889-1104   *Pe*
   953f   *Pe*
   959f.   *Pe*
   973-76   *Hb*
   983-994   *Pe*
   1009-14   *Pe*
   1076-91   *Pe*
   1086ff.   *Pe*
Pax
   762-63   *Hb*
   894-905   *Hb*
Ranae
   1308   *K*
Vespae
   1023-28   *Hb*
   1346   *K*
ARISTOTLE
Athenaion Politeia
   28.2   *Hb*
   42.2-3   *Hb*
De generatione animalium
   4.3 767b8ff.   *Pe*
Ethica Nicomachea
   7.5.3-5   *Pe*

Odyssey		
10.276ff	*Pe*	
HORACE		
Episulae		
1.19.28	*K*	
Odes		
2.13.24-25	*K*	
HYGINUS		
Fabulae		
9	*Hp*	
HYMN TO APHRODITE		
1-6	*Pr*	
39	*Pr*	
45-46	*Pr*	
45-48	*Pr*	
49-52	*Pr*	
53	*Pr*	
54	*Pr*	
55	*Pr*	
56-57	*Pr*	
77	*Pr*	
84-91	*Pr*	
133	*Pr*	
149-51	*Pr*	
188-190	*Pr*	
194-95	*Pr*	
196-199	*Pr*	
200-206	*Pr*	
201	*Pr*	
202-6	*Pe*	
205	*Pr*	
244-46	*Pr*	
247-255	*Pr*	
IBYCUS		
fr. 286	*V*	
fr. 289	*Pe, Pr*	
Inscriptiones Graecae [IG]		
I². 77	*Pe*	
ISIDORUS		
Etymologiae		
6.3.3-5	*Pe*	
ISOCRATES		
On the Two-horse Chariot		
33	*S*	
JUSTIN		
9.6.4-8	*Pe*	

JUVENAL		
Satires		
2.36-65	*B*	
2.58-9	*B*	
6.246-66	*B*	
6.311	*B*	
6.327-34	*B*	
6.419-33	*B*	
LACTANTIUS		
Divinae institutiones 1.20	*S*	
LIBANIUS		
8.28	*B*	
40.14.2	*B*	
fr. 50b.2	*Hb*	
LONGUS		
Daphnis and Chloe		
4.12	*B*	
LUCIAN		
Asinus		
8-10	*Hb*	
Dialogi meretricii		
5	*B*	
LUCRETIUS		
De Rerum Natura		
4.1269	*B*	
MARTIAL		
preface to 1	*B*	
1.90	*B*	
2.33	*B*	
3.28.8	*B*	
3.82	*B*	
3.95.10	*C*	
4.65	*B*	
5.23.4	*C*	
5.27.4	*C*	
6.9.2	*C*	
6.91	*B*	
7.67	*B*	
7.70	*B*	
9.29	*B*	
9.40	*B*	
9.62	*B*	
10.22	*B*	
11.30	*B*	
11.45	*B*	

636ab	S
636b-d	Hb
636b1-4	Pr
636c7-d4	Pr
636d4-e7	Pr
764c-766c	Hb
813e	Hb
836b	Pe
836b4-c7	Pr
836c	Hp
837b6-d1	Pr
837d2-7	Pr

Lysis

204a-206a	Hb
206e-207b	Hb

Phaedrus

227a	Mg
228d	Pe
232e-233a	Pe
234d	Mg
237d-e	Pe
242a-b	Mg
242c-d	Mg
242d	Mg
246a-b	Mg
250d-251a	Mg
251	Pr
251c5-d1	Pr
255b7-c4	Pr
255c4-e4	Pr
256a7-b7	Pr
256a-e	Pe
257	Pr

Symposium

179e-180b	Pe
180a	Hb
180b	Mg
182a-c	Hb
182b1-b6	Hp
182c	Pe
182d2-4	Hp
184e	K
189c-191d	Mg
189c-193d	B
191e	K

196a	Mg
177b	Mg
201d-212a	Mg
203c-d	Mg
212c-223b	Pe
216a-219e	Hb
216d-219e	Mg

Respublica

5.451-457	Pr

PLAUTUS

Cistellaria

657	B

Curculio

473	B

Poenulus

17	B

PLINY THE ELDER

Naturalis historia

7.36	B
7.56	B
10.172	B
34	Pe
55	Pe
58	Pe
65	Pe

PLUTARCH

Alcibiades

4.5	Pe

Alexander

9	Hp

Amatorius

751f-752a	S
751f	Hb

Antonius

59	B

Lycurgus

14.2-15.1	S
16-17	Hp
17.1	Hb
18	Hp

Moralia

15	Hp
761b	Hp
761d	Hp

47	*B*
47.7	*B*
66.54	*B*
95.21	*B*
95.24	*B*
114.25	*B*

SEXTUS JULIUS AFRICANUS
List of Olympic Victors	*S*
Sylloge Inscriptionum	
Graecarum [SIG³]	
578	*Hb*

SIMONIDES
fr. 507 PMG	*Hb*

STATIUS
Silvae
2.1	*B*
2.6	*B, V*
3.4	*B*
5.5	*B*

STRABO
13.2.3	*Pe*
10.4.16	*K*
10.4.20	*K*

STRATO
Anthologia Palatina
12.206	*Hb*
12.222	*Hb*

SUETONIUS
Divus Augustus
79.2	*V*
83	*B*
94.3	*V*

Gaius Caligula
16.1	*B*
24.3	*B*

Galba
22.1	*B*

Divus Julius
49.2	*B*
77.1	*B*

Tiberius
43.1	*B*

Divus Titus
7.1	*B*

TACITUS
Annales

4.61	*B*
14.42	*B*
15.37	*B*
16.19	*B*

THEOCRITUS
Idylls
12	*V*
27	*V*

THEODORUS PRISCIANUS
Euporista
2.11.34	*B*

THEOGNIS
2.1259-62	*Pr*
2.1263-66	*V*
2.1282	*Pr*
2.1327-34	*Pe*
2.1335-36	*S,Pr,Hb*
2.1341-1345	*Pr*
2.1345-1348	*Pr*
2.1345-1350	*Pr*
2.1346	*Pr*

THEOPOMPUS
FGrH 115 F225	*Pe*

THUCYDIDES
1.5.1	*S*
1.6.2-6	*S*
1.6.5	*S*
1.13.5	*S*
1.20.2-3	*Pe*
1.45.3	*S*
2.15.5	*S*
2.43.1	*Pe*
3.104.3	*S*
3.104.6	*S*
6.54-59 ref	*Pe*
8.94.1	*S*

TIBULLUS
1.4	*V*
1.4.27-30	*V*
1.4.39-42	*V*
1.4.81-84	*V*
1.8	*V*
1.8.9-14	*V*
1.8.27	*V*
1.8.29-38	*V*

General Index

Oddi, Sforza, 325
Olympia, 23
   introduction of athletic nudity at,
     73-74
Olympian 10 (Pindar), 138
ONE (magazine), 11,422-456
   classical scholarship at, 432-446
   Der Kreis and, 445,451
   early history of, 422-425
   Education Committee of, 428-432
   emphasis on Greek culture and,
     446-450
   fantasy and, 450-455
   fiction in, 452-453
   postmasters and, 445
   purchasing, 443-445
   readership of, 430-431
   role models for, 425-428
   topic of pederasty and, 428
   types of stories in, 453-455
One Nation Gay & Lesbian Archives,
   423
Onesimus, 156-157
Oral sex, Romans and, 288-291
Osborn, Percy, 384

Page, Denys, 349
Paine, William, 383,404-406
Pan-Hellenic games, 23
Pater, Walter, 391,392
Patzer, 3
Peacock, Thomas Love, 373
Pedagogy, 167
   in Plato's *Phaedrus,* 115-120
Pederasty, 90-92. *See also* Athletic
     nudity; Athletic trainers;
     Homosexuality
   Aristotle and, 45
   athletic trainers and, 146,142
   beginnings of, 65-66
   in Crete, 21-22
   Greek perceptions of, 3-5,5-16
   influence of Plato on legacy of
     Greek, 8-9

   institutionalization of, 17-21,65
   nudity as evidence of, 72
   Pindar and, 138-146
   in Plato's *Laws,* 120-126
   in Plato's *Phaedrus,* 115-120
   rise of, in ancient Greece, 64-67
   time and, 107-115
   as topic, in *ONE* magazine, 428
Pedophilia, Roman perceptions of, 3-5
Peisistratus, 25-27
Percy, William Alexander, 1,2,3,10,
     88-89,174,383,398,409
Pericles, 31-33
Perry, Milman, 17
Phaedrus (Plato), 436
   pedagogy in, 115-120
   pederasty in, 115-120
Phidias, 32,42
Philetos, 231-236
Philip II of Macedonia, 43,179
Photography, use of Greek allusions
   in, 384
Pindar, 29-31,111-115,138-141
   on homosexuality in Boetia,
     180-182
   pederasty and, 138-146
Plato, 36-42,92
   influence of, legacy of Greek
     pederasty and, 8-9
   pederasty and pedagogy in *Laws,*
     120-126
   pederasty and pedagogy in
     Phaedrus, 115-120
Platonic love, 8-9
Plüchow, Wilhelm, 384
Plutarch, 177-179
Poetry, love, 300-312
Pogey-Castries, L. R. de, 354
Polyclitus, 32,42
Polycrates, 25-27
Popper, Karl, 11
Praxiteles, 42
Prime-Stevenson, E. I., 379,381,
   392

BOOK ORDER FORM!

Order a copy of this book with this form or online at:
http://www.haworthpress.com/store/product.asp?sku=5694

Same-Sex Desire and Love in Greco-Roman Antiquity and in the Classical Tradition of the West

___ in softbound at $49.95 ISBN-13: 978-1-56023-604-7 / ISBN-10: 1-56023-604-3.
___ in hardbound at $69.95 ISBN-13: 978-1-56023-603-0 / ISBN-10: 1-56023-603-5.

COST OF BOOKS _____

POSTAGE & HANDLING _____
US: $4.00 for first book & $1.50
for each additional book
Outside US: $5.00 for first book
& $2.00 for each additional book.

SUBTOTAL _____

In Canada: add 7% GST. _____

STATE TAX _____
CA, IL, IN, MN, NJ, NY, OH, PA & SD residents
please add appropriate local sales tax.

FINAL TOTAL _____
If paying in Canadian funds, convert
using the current exchange rate,
UNESCO coupons welcome.

❏ BILL ME LATER:
Bill-me option is good on US/Canada/
Mexico orders only; not good to jobbers,
wholesalers, or subscription agencies.

❏ **Signature** _____

❏ **Payment Enclosed: $** _____

❏ **PLEASE CHARGE TO MY CREDIT CARD:**

❏ Visa ❏ MasterCard ❏ AmEx ❏ Discover
❏ Diner's Club ❏ Eurocard ❏ JCB

Account # _____

Exp Date _____

Signature _____
(Prices in US dollars and subject to change without notice.)

PLEASE PRINT ALL INFORMATION OR ATTACH YOUR BUSINESS CARD		
Name		
Address		
City	State/Province	Zip/Postal Code
Country		
Tel		Fax
E-Mail		

May we use your e-mail address for confirmations and other types of information? ❏ Yes ❏ No We appreciate receiving
your e-mail address. Haworth would like to e-mail special discount offers to you, as a preferred customer.
We will never share, rent, or exchange your e-mail address. We regard such actions as an invasion of your privacy.

Order from your **local bookstore** or directly from
The Haworth Press, Inc. 10 Alice Street, Binghamton, New York 13904-1580 • USA
Call our toll-free number (1-800-429-6784) / Outside US/Canada: (607) 722-5857
Fax: 1-800-895-0582 / Outside US/Canada: (607) 771-0012
E-mail your order to us: orders@haworthpress.com

For orders outside US and Canada, you may wish to order through your local
sales representative, distributor, or bookseller.
For information, see http://haworthpress.com/distributors

(Discounts are available for individual orders in US and Canada only, not booksellers/distributors.)

Please photocopy this form for your personal use.
www.HaworthPress.com

BOF05